Barnet & Stubbs's

Practical Guide

to Writing

ROBERT KEATING 212-84-3946

Barnet & Stubbs's
Practical Guide to Writing

Third Edition
With Additional Readings

Sylvan Barnet
Tufts University

Marcia Stubbs
Wellesley College

Little, Brown and Company
Boston   Toronto

Acknowledgments

Maya Angelou, "Graduation" (editors' title), *I Know Why the Caged Bird
Sings*, pp. 142–156. Copyright © 1969 by Maya Angelou. Reprinted by permission
of Random House, Inc.

Anonymous, "Confessions of an Erstwhile Child," *The New Republic*, 15
June 1975. Reprinted by permission of *The New Republic*, © 1974 The New
Republic, Inc.

Isaac Asimov, "Imagination in Orbit," *The Writer*, March 1961, pp. 16–18,
36. Reprinted by permission of the author.

Associated Press, "Dodgers Keep Perfect Record in Knocking Out Southpaws," *Michigan Daily,* 29 September 1955, p. 3. Reprinted by permission of the
Associated Press.

James Baldwin, "Stranger in the Village," *Notes of a Native Son*, pp. 159–175.
Copyright © 1953, 1955 by James Baldwin. Reprinted by permission of Beacon
Press.

Jude Bell, "Everybody Hated *Seagull*," *The New York Times*, 19 September
1976. © 1976 by The New York Times Company. Reprinted by permission.

Eric Berne, "Can People Be Judged by Their Appearance?" *A Layman's
Guide to Psychiatry and Psychoanalysis*. Copyright 1947, 1957, 1968 by Eric Berne.
Reprinted by permission of Simon & Schuster, a Division of Gulf & Western
Corporation.

Wendell Berry, "Mayhem in the Industrial Paradise," *A Continuous Harmony*,
pp. 174–182. Copyright © 1972 by Wendell Berry. Reprinted by permission of
Harcourt Brace Jovanovich, Inc.

(*Continued on page 627*)

Preface

Where there is too much,
something is missing.

We have tried to keep this proverb in mind; we hope we have written a compact book rather than an undiscriminating one.

The book is designed for college courses in which students write essays, instructors read them, and students and instructors together discuss them. We hope we offer a practical guide to all three activities. The student, looking for information about choosing a topic, writing an analysis, constructing a paragraph, using a semicolon, can use the text as a guide to writing the week's essay. The instructor, after reading the essay, can suggest chapters or passages the student should consult in revising the essay or in writing the next one. Students and instructors together can discuss the exercises, the techniques used in the reprinted essays, the assumptions we make and the suggestions we offer.

Although we include discussions and examples of description and narration, we emphasize analysis, exposition, and argument because those are the chief activities, usually rolled into one, that we all engage in, both in school and later. When students write papers for a course, or professors write reports for a committee, or psychiatric social workers write case studies, most of what they write is exposition, a statement of what's what; usually they have come to see what's what by analyzing or dividing the subject into parts, and because they want to be believed, they construct as persuasive an argument as possible.

In addition to including many examples from the writing of our students, we have included some fifty short essays, as well as numerous paragraphs from books and essays, the work for the most part of first-rate contemporary writers. These essays appear in the chapters on Analysis, Definition, Exposition, Persuasion, Description, Narration, Defining Style, and Acquiring Fluency, and in Part 4, which consists of sixteen selections. There are also a sample book review, an explication, and a research paper. We include all of these readings both to illustrate ways of writing and to provide students with something to write about. Similarly, the suggested exercises often require the students to write about something outside of themselves. The usual Polonian advice, offered to Laertes — "This above all, to thine own self be true" — seems to us as useless to most people of college ages as it is to Laertes. As Erik Erikson has helped us to see, most young people are engaged in a "search for something and somebody to be true to." They experiment with roles in a search for "the rock-bottom of some truth."[1] Asked to write about how they spent last summer, they may feel a profound uneasiness; however necessary last summer was, they are not sure what it added up to, and though they probably would not spend the next summer in the same way, they are not yet distant enough from their experience to be articulate about it. Some of our exercises do present clear opportunities for introspection, and all of them in fact require it, but we think that much of students' writing should be directed outward, not solely a look into the heart but a look around — at people, at places, and especially at ideas.

We have tried therefore to balance the advice "Trust your feelings," "Ask yourself questions," with prescriptions: "Avoid clichés," "Keep your reader in mind." We have tried to increase the student's awareness that writing is both an exploration of self ("Choose a topic you can write about honestly") and a communication with others ("Revise for clarity").

Chapter 1 includes three essays by students, a brief article by Philip Roth, and some informal exercises. Instructors may find these passages useful for the first few class meetings. During the first week of the semester, we commonly suggest that students browse through the book from beginning to end, reading what interests them, skimming the rest, and generally familiarizing themselves with the book's contents and organization. But because

[1] *Identity: Youth and Crisis* (New York: W. W. Norton, 1968), pp. 235–36.

each chapter can stand by itself, the instructor can assign chapters for study in whatever seems a suitable order, probably interweaving chapters on writing, revising, and editing. Similarly, the student can consult whatever passages seem most relevant to writing, revising, or correcting a particular essay. After all, it has never been established that in a college course in English certain topics must be taught before others. Listen to Boswell describing a conversation, more than two hundred years ago, with Dr. Johnson:

> We talked of the education of children; and I asked him what he thought was best to teach them first. JOHNSON: "Sir, it is no matter what you teach them first, any more than what leg you shall put into your breeches first. Sir, you may stand disputing which is best to put in first, but in the meantime your breech is bare. Sir, while you are considering which of two things you should teach your child first, another boy has learnt them both."

A Note to the Third Edition

In preparing the third edition we have extensively revised and in some important ways reorganized our book. First, without altering our emphasis on analysis, exposition, and persuasion, we have expanded and improved our chapters on description and narration, and the exercises that follow them. Second, we have also expanded the chapter on exposition, in part by moving to it our discussion of writing summaries, which now includes a student's summary of an essay appended to the chapter. Third, we have made our instructions on how to correct fragments, comma splices, and run-on sentences more accessible by placing them up front in the chapter on punctuation. Fourth, we have added many exercises throughout, including some on punctuation and on using the library. Fifth, we have moved the entire section on editing — a brief, self-contained handbook — to the back of the book. With this change, the Glossary, to which we have made many additions, becomes the final chapter, and we hope we have thus made it easier for students to find and to use. Finally, we have once again found many opportunities to edit each other's prose.

In making these changes, and in countless other ways, we have increased, and gratefully acknowledge, our indebtedness to many colleagues, students, editors, and other friends. The reader will be the only judge of how well we have fulfilled our aims. If we have come near, we owe debts to Mary Adams, Dale Anderson, Edgar Alward, James Beaton, Kay Berenson, Barbara Jane Berk, Morton Berman, Gary Brienzo, Daniel V. Brislane, Pearl L. Brown, Peter Brunette, Carroll Burcham, William Burto, A. Butrym, Terry P. Caesar, Joan Carberg, Thomas Carnicelli, Sally Carson, Charles H. Christensen, John M. Clum, James Cobb, Phyllis Cole, William F. Coles, S. Cooney, Leah Creque, Mary Bryan H. Curd, Leopold Damrosch, Imogene De Smet, Aviva Diamond, Denise Ferguson, Cathy Fiore, Jan Fontein, C. Denny Freese, Yolette Garcia, Thomas J. Gasque, Walker Gibson, David Giele, James Gifford, David Goldfaden, Margaret Gooch, James Hauser, Thomas W. Herzing, Gervase Hittle, Owen Jenkins, Peter M. Johnson, Mary D. Jones, George Kearns, Joseph Keefe, Kathryn Keller, Timothy J. Kenslea, Nancy Kneeland, Molly Moore Kohler, Nancy Kolodny, Joseph Komidar, Richard L. Lane, Andrea La Sane, Jonathan Lawson, Helen M. Lewis, Peter Lindblom, Bernard McCabe, George Marcopoulos, Lynda Martin, Celeste A. Meister, Michael Meyer, Richard Milburn, Gerald Mimno, Nancy Mimno, Melodie Monahan, Joan Moon, Betty Morgan, Rose Moss, Stanley Moss, Margaret A. Murphy, Robert A. Myers, Thomas Newkirk, Richard D. Olson, John O'Neill, Donald Pattow, Russell O. Peterson, Elizabeth Philipps, Bill Pierce, Anna Post, Andrea Pozgay, Charles Quagliata, Martha Reid and her colleagues at William and Mary, Stephen Reid, Leo Rockas, Judity C. Root, Zelda Rouillard, Tina Samaha, Frances W. Sauers, Gerald Schiffhorst, William Scott, Patrick W. Shaw, James M. Siddens, Martha Simonsen, Edward Sims, Audrey Smith, Ann Steinmetz, Gail Stewart, April Stokes, Frances M. Stowe, Eugene Stubbs, Ann M. Tarbell, Kathy Valdespino, Renita Weems, Anita C. Wilson, Elizabeth Wood, Arthur P. Wooley, Haruo Yanagi, Margaret Zusky; and to all our students, from whose mistakes we hope to profit. It should be noted, too, that several passages in the book appeared earlier in slightly different form in Sylvan Barnet, *A Short Guide to Writing about Literature*.

Sylvan Barnet
Marcia Stubbs

Contents

PART FIVE
Editing   *537*

Barnet & Stubbs's
Practical Guide
to Writing

PART ONE
Writing

The Balloon of the Mind

Hands, do what you're bid:
Bring the balloon of the mind
That bellies and drags in the wind
Into its narrow shed.
— WILLIAM BUTLER YEATS

1

From Subject to Essay

STARTING

How to Write: Writing As a Physical Act

"One takes a piece of paper," William Carlos Williams wrote, "anything, the flat of a shingle, slate, cardboard and with anything handy to the purpose begins to put down the words after the desired expression in mind." Good advice, from a writer who produced novels, plays, articles, book reviews, an autobiography, a voluminous correspondence, and more than twenty-five books of poetry, while raising a family, enjoying a wide circle of friends, and practicing medicine in Rutherford, New Jersey. Not the last word on writing (we have approximately 85,000 of our own to add), but where we would like to begin: "One takes a piece of paper . . . and . . . begins to put down the words. . . ."

Writing is a physical act. It requires materials and energy. And like most physical acts, to be performed skillfully, to bring pleasure to both performer and audience, it requires practice. Talent helps. But few of us are born to become great writers, just as few of us are born to become great athletes. When Mark Spitz won seven gold medals in the 1972 Olympics, *Time* described him as having hands like "a pair of scoop-shovels . . . that can pull him cleanly through the water with scarcely a ripple," and noted his "curious ability to flex his lower legs slightly forward at the knees, which allows him to kick 6 to 12 inches deeper in the water than his opponents." Most of us are not born with the "curious ability" of the great writer or the great swimmer. But we can learn to write, as we can learn to swim, for all practical purposes, including pleasure.

In this book we offer some suggestions, definitions, rules, and examples to help you learn not simply to write, but to write well. We hope they will help you avoid some of the trials and errors — and the fear of drowning — of uninstructed practice. Our first suggestion is this: buy a notebook that you can carry with you (so you won't waste time looking for loose shingles) and write in it regularly. For suggestions about what to write, see "Keeping a Journal," pp. 424–26.

Why Write? Writing As a Mental Activity

Born writers often describe their need to write as a compulsion, an inner drive to put their feelings and ideas into words. Despite that compulsion, or because of it, they also regularly complain that writing is hard work: "hard labor for life" was Joseph Conrad's summary of his own career. For the rest of us, perhaps, writing is easier because it is not our vocation; we demand less than perfection from ourselves. But it's still hard work, and we accept the occasional sentence to hard labor only if we have made some commitment or anticipate some reward. In real life (as opposed to school) people are regularly committed by their jobs and other interests to communicating their ideas in writing. Scientists and social scientists, to secure contracts, must put their proposals in writing, and then must report, again in writing, the results of their work to their sponsors and colleagues. Citizens and parents write their petitions and grievances to lawmakers and school boards; through prepared talks and newsletters, volunteers reach the communities they serve. Even television and tape have not diminished the importance of the written word. In short, anyone who is engaged with ideas or who wants to influence the course of events finds it necessary to put what Dr. Williams called "the desired expression in mind" into words.

As students, you may or may not make the connection between the assignment you are given today and the need you will have several years hence to put your ideas in writing. The rewards

— getting the contract, serving your community — are probably a bit distant to motivate you to write five hundred words on a possibly irrelevant topic this week. There is, though, a closer reward. "To be learning something new," said Aristotle, "is ever the chief pleasure of mankind." We believe that. We also believe that writing is not simply a way to express ideas, but a way to acquire them. To quote Aristotle again, "What is expressed is impressed."

We emphasize ideas because we are making some assumptions about you: that you are an adult, that you're acquiring an education, either in school or on your own, and that the writing skill you need most help with is the expression of ideas in clear expository essays. Most of our book will concentrate on that skill. We begin, then, with some ideas about ideas.

Some Ideas about Ideas

Would-be writers have one of two complaints: either "I have the ideas but I don't know how to express them," or "I have nothing to say." They are really the same complaint, known to both professional writers and novices as "writer's block." But let's treat them, to begin with, as if they were indeed separate.

STARTING TO WRITE BY WRITING

If you have the ideas but don't know how to express them, sit down and start writing. It is a universal law that given two tasks, one of which is writing, a person will prefer the other task. You must actively resist the temptation to procrastinate. Resist the temptation to sharpen another pencil, to make yourself a cup of tea, to call your mother. Now is *not* the time to do your laundry or make your bed. Start writing. It doesn't matter where you begin, only that you do begin. Sit down and start putting one word after another. One of the writers of this book finds it useful to start writing notes on three-by-five-inch file cards, then to arrange the cards, and from that arrangement to jot down a sort of outline. Not a formal outline, with capital and lowercase letters and roman and arabic numerals, but simply a list of key phrases in some reasonable order. If that way of starting helps you, fine, do it. It doesn't help me, and I'm writing this chapter.

Let's assume you either have an outline or you don't. Again, start writing. As you write, forget any rules you may have learned. In particular forget anything you've heard about opening paragraphs. Forget there is a paper shortage. (The shortage of decent writers is more critical.) If, after writing a sentence, a paragraph, a half page, you find yourself going in the wrong direction (not just a direction you hadn't anticipated — that's probably a good one — but toward a dead end), throw the page away. Take another sheet and start again. After a few false starts, your ideas, if you really have some, will begin to take visible form, and it's much easier to improve ideas once you see them in front of you than it is to do the job in your head.

You may realize, as you near the end of a sentence, that you no longer believe it. Never mind. Be glad that your first idea led you to a better one, pick up the better one and keep going with it. By now, you don't need to throw pages away. Take a pencil and cross out the unwanted sentence if it distracts you. Don't erase it; that takes too much time, and you may make something of that sentence later on if you have a record of it. Again, keep going.

At some point you will begin to see where the words already on paper promise to lead you. That's the point at which I would make a rough outline (and my colleague would be revising his). Now you begin to see which ideas must be developed and which discarded, where ideas must be clarified by specific details and examples and where connections between ideas must be made. When you get these thoughts into notes on paper — and you must write them down or you'll forget them — you are close to having a first draft. We'll have more to say in a while about first drafts and how to pull them into shape. But for the moment, you can go ahead and make your bed and, if you like, climb into it. Meanwhile we have something to say to those who think they have nothing to say.

ASKING QUESTIONS AND ANSWERING THEM

If you think you have nothing to say about a particular topic, ask yourself questions and answer them. You can often get a start by asking these questions:

> Who are my readers? (You can usually assume that you are writing for your classmates.)
>
> What do they need to know?
>
> What do I want them to believe?

These questions will at least help you to recognize some of the things you must say. We'll talk more about your readers later, on pages 18–20, but for the moment let's look at an example of how to go about asking other questions and answering them. First, read the following article from *The New York Times*. We have numbered the paragraphs to facilitate reference to them.

The Newark Public Library
Philip Roth[1]

What will the readers of Newark do if the City Council goes 1 ahead with its money-saving plan to shut down the public library system on April 1? Will they loot the stacks as Newarkers looted furniture and appliance stores in the riot of 1967? Will police be called in to Mace down thieves racing off with the *Encyclopaedia Britannica*? Will scholars take up sniping positions at reference room windows and school children "seize" the main Washington Street building in order to complete their term papers? If the City Council locks up the books, will library card holders band together to "liberate" them?

I suppose one should hope not. Apparently there must be re- 2 spect for Law and Order, even where there is none for aspiration and curiosity and quiet pleasure, for language, learning, scholarship, intelligence, reason, wit, beauty, and knowledge.

When I was growing up in Newark in the forties we assumed 3 that the books in the public library belonged to the public. Since my family did not own many books, or have much money for a child to buy them, it was good to know that solely by virtue of my municipal citizenship I had access to any book I wanted from that grandly austere building downtown on Washington Street, or from the branch library I could walk to in my neighborhood. No less satisfy-

[1] In February 1969, after riots had already destroyed much of Newark's black slum neighborhoods, the Newark City Council voted to strike from the city budget the $2.8 million required to finance the Newark Museum and the Newark Public Library. Hundreds of Newark residents vehemently opposed this move, which would have shut down two exceptional civic institutions. In the face of the protest, the Council eventually rescinded their decision. This article appeared on the editorial page of *The New York Times*, March 1, 1969, about two weeks after the Council had announced the budget cutback [Roth's note].

ing was the idea of communal ownership, property held in common for the common good. Why I had to care for the books I borrowed, return them unscarred and on time, was because they weren't mine alone, they were everybody's. That idea had as much to do with civilizing me as any I was ever to come upon in the books themselves.

If the idea of a *public* library was civilizing so was the place, with 4 its comforting quiet, its tidy shelves, its knowledgeable, dutiful employees who weren't teachers. The library wasn't simply where one had to go to get the books, it was a kind of exacting haven to which a city youngster willingly went for his lesson in restraint and his training in self-control. And then there was the lesson in order, the enormous institution itself serving as instructor. What trust it inspired — in both oneself and in systems — first to decode the catalogue card, then to make it through the corridors and stairwells into the open stacks, and there to discover, exactly where it was supposed to be, the desired book. For a ten-year-old to find he actually can steer himself through tens of thousands of volumes to the very one he wants is not without its satisfactions. Nor did it count for nothing to carry a library card in one's pocket; to pay a fine if need be; to sit in a strange place, beyond the reach of parent and school, and read whatever one chose, in anonymity and peace; finally, to carry home across the city and even into bed at night a book with a local lineage of its own, a family-tree of Newark readers to which one's name had now been added.

In the forties, when Newark was mostly white and I was being 5 raised there, it was simply an unassailable fact of life that the books were "ours" and that the public library had much to teach us about the rules of civilized life, as well as civilized pleasures to offer. It is strange, to put it politely, that now when Newark is mostly black, the City Council (for fiscal reasons, we are told) has reached a decision that suggests that the books don't really belong to the public after all, and that the lessons and pleasures a library provides for the young are no longer essential to an education. In a city seething with social grievances there is, in fact, probably little that could be *more* essential to the development and sanity of the thoughtful and ambitious young than access to those libraries and books. For the moment the Newark City Council may, to be sure, have solved a fiscal problem; it is too bad, however, that they are unable to calculate the frustration, cynicism, and rage that such an insult must inevitably generate, or to imagine what shutting down the libraries may cost the community in the end.

Now answer the following questions.

1. a. What was the occasion for this article? (one sentence)
   b. Summarize Roth's response. (one sentence)
2. a. *How* does he support his position in paragraph 3? Describe his strategy. (one sentence)
   b. What are the two main reasons he gives in paragraph 3 in support of his position? (one or two sentences)
3. Explain what he means by "civilizing" in paragraphs 3 and 4. (two to four sentences)
4. In paragraph 5, what new reasons does he state or imply in support of his position? (two to four sentences)
5. Describe and explain his strategy in paragraph 1 and paragraph 2. (one short paragraph)
6. Optional: Evaluate Philip Roth's article.

If you were now to take your answers and revise them a bit, you'd have an essay something like the student's essay that follows.

On Philip Roth's "The Newark Public Library"

The City Council of Newark introduced a plan to shut down the public library system in order to save money. (1a) Philip Roth, in his article (*The New York Times,* March 1, 1969), argues that the closing of the libraries will be a costly mistake, and that the action will be an insult to the citizens of Newark. (1b)

He supports his position by telling how the library helped him when he was young. (2a) He says that the public library gave him a chance to use books that his family couldn't afford, but more important, the very idea of a public library, of the communal ownership of books, played a part in civilizing him. (2b) By civilizing Roth means socializing. The quiet and orderly fashion in which the library was arranged and run taught him restraint, and taught him to value solitude, privacy, and self-control. Looking for books was itself a lesson in order; he learned, for example, that he could find, through the card catalog, one book among the many thousands there. (3)

Roth suggests that since Newark has become predominantly black, the City Council's attitude toward the library's functions and importance has changed. He implies that the Council's plan is irresponsible and discriminatory. He points out that in a city with as many social problems as Newark's, the lessons and pleasures given to the young by the library are more, not less, essential to their education. He says that although the Council's move may solve an immediate fiscal problem, it will in the end create greater social problems because of the frustration and rage it will generate.(4)

He questions what the readers might do if the library is shut down. He hypothesizes that they might riot and loot the library, or that they might seize the library and liberate the books. His questions are, of course, ironic. By overdramatizing the possible reactions, he gains the interest of the reader, and he shows the senselessness of the Council's plan. Through sarcasm, he discloses a further irony: the City Council, whose members are the first to insist on respect for law and order, have no respect themselves for communal as opposed to private property, or for the civilized qualities law and order should foster and support: beauty, knowledge, pleasure, aspiration.(5)

Organizing Ideas

Notice that in the preceding exercise we arranged the questions so that the essay composed of answers to them would be clear and effectively organized. In the essay we chose as an example, the student's first paragraph provides the information a reader who has not read Roth's article will need. It briefly summarizes both the circumstances that provoked Roth's article and the gist of his argument. (It also tells where the article appeared.) The body of the student's essay explains and analyzes the means Roth employs to persuade his readers: first, his use of his own experience growing up in Newark; second, his analysis of Newark's current political and social climate; and finally, his use of irony. Although irony appears in several places in Roth's article, it is especially rich and interesting to analyze in his first two paragraphs. The student's essay, therefore, saves its comment on Roth's opening paragraphs for its concluding paragraph. The essay builds from the beginning to what is most interesting to think about. (But remember, we invented and arranged the questions!)

When, in looking for something to say, *you* ask *yourself* questions, some questions will come to mind at once. They'll pop into your head while you read or while you reflect about an experience, and you'll wisely write them down before you forget them. But if you get stuck, think of the four categories into which our specific questions on Roth's article fall, and see if these generate specific questions about your topic. Here are the four categories of questions and methods of answering them.

1.	What happened?	Summarize or narrate
2.	What does the happening mean? Or, what do the words mean?	Interpret or paraphrase
3.	What is it? How does it work? How does it yield meaning?	Define or analyze
4.	How good is it? What makes it good? Or, what makes it bad?	Evaluate

To generate ideas, then, if you have a topic but nothing to say about it, ask yourself questions and answer them. You may write your questions down in whatever order they occur to you, but when you write your essay rearrange your answers with your reader in mind. Your arrangement should be clear: it should make sense to someone who isn't inside your head. And it should be emphatic: it should build to a climax, ending with what you found to be the most interesting questions to answer.

Note that arranging answers to questions in clear and emphatic order is equivalent to arranging note cards, or to writing an outline after the shape of your ideas has become visible to you. So, whether you see your problem as having ideas but not knowing how to express them or as not having any ideas to express, the solution may be either to start writing or to ask yourself questions and answer them. Either way you'll end up with at least a first draft of an essay.

FOCUSING

What to Write About:
Subject, Topic, Thesis

If you're taking a course in composition you will probably receive assignments to write on something you are reading or on something out of your personal experience, which may include your experience of books. In other courses it's usually up to you to choose a *subject* from those covered in the course, to focus on a *topic* within the subject, and to narrow the topic by adopting a specific *thesis.* Any assignment requires you to narrow the subject so that you can treat it thoroughly in the allotted space and time. Therefore you write not on *Time* magazine, but on a comparison of *Time* and *Newsweek*, based on one or two issues of each, arguing for the superiority of one over the other; not on political primaries (a subject), but on a specific proposal to abolish them (a topic); not on penguins (a subject), but on the male penguin's role in hatching (a topic). A good general rule in finding a topic is to follow your inclinations: focus on something about the subject that interests you.

Suppose you're in a composition course and the class has been assigned to read the Book of Ruth in the Old Testament and to write an essay of 500–1000 words on it. If you start with a topic like "The Book of Ruth, A Charming Idyll" you're in trouble. The topic is much too vague. In writing about it you'll find yourself hopping around from one place in the book to another, and in desperation saying insincere things like "The Book of Ruth is probably one of the most charming idylls in all literature," when you haven't read all literature, have precious little idea of what *idyll* means, and couldn't define *charm* precisely if your life depended on it.

What to do? Focus on something that interested you about the book. (If you read the book with pencil in hand, taking some notes, underlining some passages, putting question marks at others, you'll have some good clues to start with.) The book is named after Ruth, but perhaps you find Naomi the more interesting character. If so, you might say: "Although the Book of Ruth is named after Ruth, I find the character of Naomi more interesting."

Stuck again? Ask yourself questions. Why do you find her more interesting? To answer that question, reread the book, focusing your attention on all the passages in which Naomi acts or speaks or is spoken of by others. Ruth's actions, you may find, are always clearly motivated by her love for and obedience to Naomi. But Naomi's actions are more complex, more puzzling. If you're puzzled, trust your feeling — *there is something puzzling there.* What motivated Naomi? Convert your question to "Naomi's Motivation" and you have a topic. If you explore Naomi's actions one by one you may conclude that "Although Naomi shows in many of her actions her concern for her daughter-in-law, her actions also reveal self-interest." Now you have a *thesis,* that is, a brief statement of your main point. It's a bit awkwardly worded, but you can work on a smoother, more natural expression later. Now you have other things to do: you must select, clarify, and arrange evidence to support your thesis.

"Naomi's Motivation" is a topic in literary criticism. If you have not been specifically assigned a literary analysis and if you would prefer not to do one, focus on something that interests you more and that you know something about. If your special interest is, for example, economics, or sociology, or law, your topic might be one of these:

> Economic Motivation in the Book of Ruth
> Attitudes toward Intermarriage in the Book of Ruth
> The Status of Women in the Book of Ruth

Any one of these topics can be managed in 500–1000 words. But remember, you were assigned to write on the Book of Ruth. Formulate a thesis and support it with evidence from that book. Suppress the impulse to put everything you know about economics or intermarriage or the-status-of-women-through-the-ages in between two thin slices, an opening sentence and a concluding sentence, on the Book of Ruth.

Or take another example. You're in a composition course and you're asked to write about something out of your own experience. You try to think of something interesting you've done, but you've led a most unremarkable life. Your classmates, all strangers, seem to know more than you do about almost everything. They've all been to Europe — well, most of them. All you did last summer was file cards and run errands in an office full of boring people.

Let's examine two essays, each written by a student during the first weeks of the semester in response to this assignment: Explain something clearly — a process, a concept, a place, an experience — that you know well but that others in the class may not know about or may understand less well than you. The first essay is on a boring job; the second, on an unremarkable incident.

A Lesson

As I look back at it, my first thought is that my job was a waste of time. It consisted of compiling information from the files of the Water and Assessor's Department in a form suitable for putting on the city's computer. Supposedly this would bring the water billing and property taxing to an efficient level. If the job sounds interesting, don't be deceived. After the first week of work, I seriously doubted that I would survive through the summer.

But I was able to salvage a lesson in the self-discipline of coping with people. Of course we all know how to succeed with friends, family, acquaintances, and employers. But try it in a situation where you have a distinct disadvantage, where you are the seller and they are the customers. And remember, the customer is always right.

By observing the situation, though I was not a participant, I learned that patience, kindness, and understanding can remove the difficulties you cross at the time.

Not a bad topic, really. One can learn something valuable from a boring, menial, frustrating job. Or if not, one can examine boredom (what exactly is it? is it the same as impatience? how does it come about? how does it feel?) and write about it without boring the reader. But this essay doesn't teach us anything about boredom. It doesn't allow us through concrete, specific details to feel with the writer that we too would have doubted we could survive the summer. Instead, it offers generalizations such as "compiling information from the files" and "form suitable for putting on the city's computer," which give us no sense of the tedium of daily transferring numbers from five hundred manila index cards to five hundred gray index cards. In fact, the essay gives us almost no sense of the job. The second paragraph ends "the customer is always right," but nothing in the essay suggests that the writer (whose work "consisted of compiling information from the files") had any contact with customers. We really don't know what she did. Nor does the essay present any evidence that the experience was redeemed by a lesson in "patience, kindness, and understanding."

As it turns out, there was no such lesson. In class discussion, the student frankly admitted that the job *was* a waste of time. She had, out of habit, tried to come up with some pious thought to please the instructor. The habit had short-circuited the connection between the student's feelings and the words she was writing. The class discussion led to some genuinely interesting questions. Why, for example, are we reluctant to admit that something we've done was a waste of time? "The job was a waste of time" would have been, for most of us, a more productive thesis than "I was able to salvage a lesson." What experiences lead to the conclusions: I must write what the instructor expects; the instructor expects a pious thought? (We'd like to hear from a student willing to explore that topic in 500–1000 words.)

The class discussion, as we said, revealed the student's real attitude toward her job. It provided a focus which then allowed us to formulate what would have been a more productive thesis for an essay. It's helpful to think of such discussions as dramatizations, or imitations, of the writer's solitary work in the early stages of writing, as she gropes for what she really has to say on a subject. For although it would be tidy if writers could simply, and in the following order, (1) choose a subject, (2) focus on a topic, (3) formulate a thesis, (4) write the essay, things don't often work out that way. More commonly, writers discover their topics and formulate their theses in the act of writing and revising, in asking questions and in answering them, in discarding the answers, or even the questions, and starting again.

The second student's essay, for example, though precisely focused, has no thesis sentence. Nor does it need one. (The title, however, might need explanation; the motto, "Live Free or Die," appears on New Hampshire's license plates.)

Live Free or Die

Idaho. Famous potatoes. The two identically yellow Volkswagens were parked on either side of the '57 multicolored pick-up truck like flies on a dead cat. The other one was from Wisconsin, America's dairyland. Kent stood with one foot on the battered running board and I waited, reading license plates and kicking the tire. I wanted to talk, but my mind was resting on each tiny thing in the parking lot, Kent's knees, and my feet.

Do you know what it's like to think about someone every second until you almost feel embarrassed about his control over you, then by chance you happen to mention that you love him even though that phrase has never meant a whole lot to you because you've never felt the same about any two people; after all that, do you know what it feels like to have him shake his head and say, "No, you don't love me, you're just fooling yourself"? It feels somewhat like a kick in the teeth. You're taken aback for a minute, considering. Then the pain comes; a sharp clear pain that makes you want to give up. You begin to wonder how often you kid yourself. Of course you deny his statement over and over trying to convince yourself that you really do love him, what ever the hell that means. But I didn't say it. I looked at my October hands still brown and thin from summer work in the sun. They were my hands, I recognized the rings.

I could see the two of us standing there by the truck, silent and tired. It was as though I'd been suspended slightly, or set aside from my life with the unappealing chance to look back and down on everything so far. We were told shadows are nothing, only eels breed in the Sargasso Sea, and History is real. We wrote everything down and have it still, crammed into notebooks that allow us to forget things. And what seeming innocence amid the plotting and twisting of the formed-in-the-air ideas, the humor, the grudges, the silence! Each time we began to slide away from their logic that turned the walls white and made the world as inaccessible as a glazed winter day, we were drawn back by their trust and our insecurity. And not one thing we learned, or were learning, or would ever learn was going to help me now, standing three feet from the only thing I cared about.

My head hurt. The kind of hurt that goes right through my head so for a split second I could feel the center of my mind. I took a step back. Kent didn't move, just stood with his hands deep in his pockets, filtered through me like a literary creation.

"See ya, Kent."

"See ya." My mind grabbed every word as I walked. Massachusetts. Massachusetts. Massachusetts. New Hampshire. "Live free or die."

THE GROUCHO MARX COMPLEX

Clearly — examining these essays should make it clear — there is no such thing as an uninteresting life, or moment in life. There are only uninteresting ways to talk about them. It's also clear that some people are more interested in introspection and in talking and writing about their personal experiences than others. The others may be suffering from the Groucho Marx Complex: as Groucho put it, "I don't want to belong to any club that would have me as a member." Students who freeze at the notion of writing about themselves often feel that everything they have done is so ordinary, no one else could possibly be interested in it; anything they know is so obvious, everyone else must know it already. If this is your problem, remember that no one else knows exactly what you know; no one else can know what it feels like to live inside your skin.

Remember too that writing from your own experience does not necessarily mean writing about private experience. We all have areas of experience we'd rather keep private, and have a right to remain private about. The important thing in writing about experience is, as Marianne Moore said, that "we must be as clear as our natural reticence allows us to be." Think, then, of experiences that you are willing to share and to be clear about. If, for example, you have just learned in a psychology course what "operant conditioning" means, define it for someone unfamiliar with the term. You might find yourself narrating an experience of your own to exemplify it; to be clear, you will have to provide an example. Or if an object in a local museum or craft exhibit or store interests you, ask yourself questions — why do I like it? — and you'll probably be able to turn an object into an experience. You'll also be turning an experience into an object — an essay — that will interest your readers.

Let's take an example of a writing assignment outside of a composition course. Suppose that in a course on Modern Revolutionary Movements you're assigned a term paper on any subject covered by the readings or lectures. A term paper is usually about three thousand words and requires research. You're interested in Mexican history, and after a preliminary search you decide to focus on the Revolution of 1910 or some events leading up to it. Depending on what is available in your library, you might narrow your topic to one of these:

Mexican Bandits — The First Twentieth-Century Revolutionaries

The Exploits of Joaquin Murieta and Tiburcio Vasquez — Romantic Legend and Fact

(See pages 270–71, on narrowing a topic in research.)

In short, it is not enough to have a subject (the Book of Ruth, a boring summer, revolutions); you must concentrate your vision on a topic, a significant part of the field, just as a landscape painter or photographer selects a portion of the landscape and then focuses on it. Your interests are your most trustworthy guides to which part of the landscape to focus on.

Once you think you know what your topic is, ask yourself questions. We have already suggested that perhaps the first questions are about your audience: Who are my readers? What do they need to know? What do I want them to believe? Whatever the audience and whatever the topic, some of the following questions probably will help you to clarify your ideas and feelings for your readers and yourself:

1. How can the crucial word be defined? (definition)
2. What are the parts of the thing I am talking about? (analysis)
3. How does it differ from similar things? (analysis: comparison)
4. How did it come about? (analysis: causation)
5. What was or is its function or purpose? (analysis: purpose)
6. What are or might be the consequences? (analysis: effects)
7. What is its significance? (evaluation)
8. What are its weaknesses and strengths? (evaluation)
9. How do I feel about it? (evaluation)

THE WRITER'S ROLE:
THE WRITER AS TEACHER

Sharing experiences. It will help you to focus on a manageable topic and to develop it thoroughly if you keep in mind that, although you are writing because of an assignment from a teacher, *when you write you are the teacher.* It's your job to clarify your responses to what you have read or otherwise experienced and to share them with another person who is not you and who has something to learn from you. Writing an essay, then, requires that you look not only outside of you and in front of you, but also within you. You not only explore the text or the topic you're writing about, you also explore your responses to it and make them accessible to others.

Imagining your readers. Who are these others for whom the writer writes? Mostly, they are imagined. We might suppose, for example, that Philip Roth in writing about the Newark Public Library (pages 7–8) had in mind the readers of *The New York Times*. But surely he did not think of each reader individually; that would have been impossible. At first, he probably did not think of them consciously at all. More likely, when he began to think about his article, he was doing something like talking to himself, asking himself questions (in the peculiar shorthand of reverie). Why did he feel so angry about the plan to close the library? Why did it strike him as a personal insult and a threat? He might then have thought of others, like himself, who had benefited from the library without ever before having given the specific benefits much conscious thought. Surely those others would understand, or *should* understand, why the council's plan was irresponsible, and why it ought to be opposed.

We're only guessing at Roth's mental processes, of course, but we think it a fair guess that, as his essay began to take shape, Roth had no individual readers in mind, but what might be called a generalized reader made up of the shared characteristics of many individual, unknown readers. This imagined reader, being in some ways like Roth, would be interested in what Roth had to say, but would not know exactly how Roth felt, and would not necessarily share his convictions. The imagined reader might not even know some of the facts that were so evident to Roth. Even a reader from Newark might not know, for example, that the Newark City Council planned to save money by shutting down the public library. To acquaint readers with the facts, Roth does not merely refer to the council's "plan"; rather, in his first sentence, he cues the reader in by referring to the council's "money-saving plan to shut down the public library system on April 1."

What we have just attempted to describe is the writer's normal situation. Writers write not for themselves but for partly imagined and generalized others. *Partly* imagined because the audience is usually in some ways already defined. Film reviewers write for an audience of moviegoers who have not yet seen the new film under review; medical social workers write for the hospital staff who will consult their reports, though they don't think of (or even know) each member of the staff individually. The writers of this book, because we talk to students daily and were once students ourselves, have a general sense of what the readers of this book already know about writing, and what they want to know or need to know more about.

One of the things we know is that *student writers are not in the writer's normal situation*. They face the problem of imagining their readers in a most perplexing form, and we therefore recommend that they face the problem consciously. Who is your reader? The obvious answer — the teacher who assigned you the essay — is, paradoxically, often the least helpful. To learn to write well, you'll have to force that fact out of your mind, pretend it isn't true, or you're likely to feel defeated from the beginning. Write instead for someone who understands your material less well than you. Remember: *when you write you are the teacher*. It's probably easier to assume the role of the teacher if you imagine your reader to be someone in your class, that is, someone intelligent and reasonably well informed who shares some of your interests but who does not happen to be you, and who therefore can't know your thoughts unless you organize them and explain them clearly and thoroughly.

We'll discuss some specific patterns of organization in later chapters, but if you remember that when you write you are teaching, you'll organize your essay so that it will be clear, and you'll present your ideas at a pace that sustains your reader's interest. It's not enough to present your ideas as they happened to occur to you; your reader should profit from the trials and errors of your early drafts, not labor through them.

CLARIFYING IDEAS

On page 6 we wrote "Now you begin to see . . . where ideas must be clarified by specific details and examples." You'll find more discussion of this point on pages 84–88 (about topic ideas) and pages 341–44 (on revising sentences). Here we consider two directions in which the mind of the essayist frequently moves as he expresses and clarifies his ideas.

There must, on the one hand, be ideas or, let us say, generalizations. (Example: "Except for human beings, animals rarely seek to do serious harm to members of their own species.") On the other hand, there must be specific details that support and enliven these generalizations. (Example: "When male rattlesnakes fight among themselves they strike with their heads but they do not bite, and when giraffes fight among themselves they butt but they do not use their hooves, as they do against other attackers.") In a moment we will discuss how to give the reader both generalizations and specific details, but first let us define some terms.

General and Specific Writing

A general word refers to a class or group; a specific (or particular) word refers to a member of the class or group. For example, *vehicle* is general compared with *automobile* or with *motorcycle*. But "general" and "specific" are relative. *Vehicle* is general when compared to *automobile,* but specific when compared to *machine,* for *machine* refers to a class or group that includes not only vehicles but clocks, typewriters, and dynamos. Similarly, although *automobile* is specific in comparison with *vehicle,* it is general in comparison with *Volkswagen* or *sportscar.* Since the aim of writing is to help a reader to see things your way, try to be as specific or as particular as is reasonable. We say "as is reasonable" because your job is not to describe everything in microscopic detail; it may, for example, be entirely reasonable to say "he smoked a pack of cigarettes a day," and not to specify the kind of cigarette. In fact, to specify the kind of cigarette might only get in the way — readers will wonder, why are we being told that he smoked Camels? Again, keep your reader in mind.

Most good writing offers a judicious mixture of the general and the specific. A page of highly general writing may seem to have nothing to get hold of; a page of nothing but specific details may seem a kleptomaniac's trunkful of bric-a-brac. To keep your reader's attention, try to enliven your generalizations with specific examples, and try to unify your details with occasional generalizations. Since students tend to write too generally rather than too specifically, it is good to keep in mind Nietzsche's assertion that the more general the truth you want to teach, the more you must "seduce the senses to accept it." Or, as the Zen saying puts it, "Better to see the face than to hear the name."

Suppose, for example, a writer offered us the following paragraph:

> Certain biological changes which occur as we grow older are apparent whenever you look at an old person. These age changes in the surface of the body are gradual, and vary according to diet, genetic factors, even climate. Like all other aspects of aging, it is not the biological changes themselves (because they are quite natural) but the subsequent changes in self-regard which have the most impact on the individual.

It makes sense, we get the gist of it, and it is even moderately interesting; but could we read many pages of such writing? We hear about "biological changes," but we do not see them in this paragraph.

Now look at what the author really wrote — the previous sentences, but also others rich with details. Notice how the details clarify and add interest to the generalizations. The words we omitted in the previous version we restore in italic.

> Certain biological changes which occur as we grow older are apparent whenever you look at an old person. *The hair becomes thin, brittle, dull, and gray. The skin becomes paler and may become blotchy; it takes on a parchmentlike texture and loses its elasticity. The loss of subcutaneous fat and elastic tissue leads to a wrinkled appearance. Sweat gland activity and oil secretion decrease and the skin may look dry and scaly.* These age changes in the surface of the body are gradual, and vary according to diet, genetic factors, even climate. Like all other aspects of aging, it is not the biological changes themselves (because they are, after all, quite natural) but the subsequent changes in self-regard which have the most impact on the individual. *Gray hair can be softening and becoming to a woman; and look quite distinguished on a man. Yet the individual may resent the change, and regard gray hair as the external sign of all the internal effects — slowness, muscular weakness, waning sexual powers.*
>
> —Sharon R. Curtin

The generalizations in the first version made all of the points — but how weakly, without the specific details that clarify and enliven them.

SOME PRELIMINARY REMARKS
ON REVISING

Picasso said that in painting a picture he advanced by a series of destructions. A story about a sculptor makes a similar point. When asked how he had made such a lifelike image of an elephant from a block of wood, the sculptor answered, "Well, I just knocked off everything that didn't look like elephant."

Revising is a major part of a writer's work, and we have therefore devoted to it a separate section of our book (Part II). There we show you, for the most part, what to cut away: the deadwood that clutters sentences and paragraphs, the empty words, the meaningless repetitions. Where we can, we also suggest what needs to be added (an advantage the writer has over the sculptor). Cutting away the deadwood allows you to see where your main points need to be clarified by examples or more details, where a transitional sentence or a new paragraph would make your argument clearer, or more emphatic, and more readable. In reorganizing paragraphs, in pruning deadwood out of sentences, even in such small changes as replacing a period with a semicolon, the writer shapes and clarifies his ideas and feelings for his reader. In a sense, the imagined reader becomes, like the class we described on pages 14–15, a collaborator in the revision, posing questions, demanding clarification. At the same time, the writer clarifies his ideas for himself. Successful revision is, after all, a re-vision, a new and clearer view.

AN OVERVIEW:
FROM SUBJECT TO ESSAY

We each must work out our own procedures and rituals (John C. Calhoun liked to plough his farm before writing); but the following suggestions may help. The rest of this book will give you more detailed advice.

1. *If a topic is assigned, write on it; if a topic is not assigned, turn a subject into a topic.* Get an early start. The day the assignment is given — or the next day — try to settle on a topic that excites or at

least interests you and that you can discuss sensibly in the assigned length. Unfortunately, almost none of us can in a few pages write anything of interest on a large subject. We simply cannot in five hundred words say anything readable (that is, true and interesting to others) on subjects as broad as music, sports, ourselves. Given such subjects, we have nothing to say, probably because we are desperately trying to remember what we have heard other people say. Trying to remember blocks our efforts to look hard and to think. To get going, we must narrow such subjects down to specific topics: from music to country music, from sports to commercialization of athletics, from ourselves to a term with a roommate.

2. *Get a focus.* Once you have turned a subject into a topic, you need to shape the topic by seeing it in a particular focus, by having a thesis, an attitude, a point: Country music is popular because . . . ; College athletes are exploited . . . ; How I came to know that I want a single room. Probably you won't find your exact focus or thesis immediately, but you will be able to jot down a few things, including some questions to yourself, that come to mind on the topic you have carved out of the broad subject. For example: Why is country music popular? What kind of people like it? Why are some performers more successful than others? If you ask yourself questions now, you'll probably be able to answer them a day or two later. It doesn't matter whether you make each jotting on a separate card or group them on a sheet of paper as a list or in a few roughly sketched paragraphs; the important thing is to write something, perhaps a few generalizations, perhaps a few striking details, perhaps some of each. You'll probably find that jotting an idea down leads to something else — something you probably would not have thought of if you hadn't jotted down the first thing. Few of us have good ideas about anything at the start, but as we put our ideas into words we find better ideas coming to mind.

3. *Turn your reveries into notes.* Put your jottings aside for a day or two (assuming you have a week to do the essay), but be prepared to add to them at any moment. Useful thoughts — not only general ideas, but details — may come to you while you are at lunch, while you read a newspaper or magazine, while your mind wanders in class. Write down these thoughts: do not assume that you will remember them when you come to draft your essay.

4. *Sort things out.* About two days before the essay is due, look over your jottings (you ought to have at least a dozen phrases by now) and sharpen your thesis, rejecting what is not relevant. Arrange the surviving half-dozen or so jottings into what looks like a reasonable sequence. Perhaps now is the time to give your essay a provisional title. A title will help you to keep your thesis in focus. Don't be afraid to be obvious. If you look back at some of the titles of sections in this book, you will see such things as "Why Write?," "Starting to Write by Writing," and "Clarifying Ideas." Such titles help the writer to keep to the point, while letting readers know what the topic will be. (Leave uninformative titles to the Marx Brothers: *Duck Soup, Horse Feathers.*) Sometimes word-play produces an attractive but still informative title, for example a student's "If You Have *Time,* Read *Newsweek.*" In any case, whether or not you choose a title at this point, you should now have a focus. Next, look again at your jottings and add what comes to mind. Keep asking yourself questions, and try to jot down the answers. Draw arrows to indicate the sequence you think the phrases should be in.

5. *Write.* Even if you are not sure that you have a thesis and an organization, start writing. Don't delay; you have some jottings, and you have a mind that, however casually, has already been thinking. Don't worry about writing an effective opening paragraph (your opening paragraph will almost surely have to be revised later anyway); just try to state and develop your argument, based on the phrases or sentences you have accumulated, adding all of the new details that flow to mind as you write. If you are stuck, ask yourself questions. Have I supported my assertions with examples? Will a comparison help to clarify the point? Write on one side of the page only, leave lots of space between the lines, and leave wide margins; later you'll fill these spaces in with additional details, additional generalizations, and revisions of sentences. Keep going until you have nothing left to say.

6. *Save what you can.* Immediately after writing the draft, or a few hours later, look it over to see how much you can salvage. Don't worry about getting the exact word here or there; just see whether or not you have a thesis, whether or not you keep the thesis in view, and whether or not the points flow reasonably. Delete irrelevant paragraphs, however interesting; shift paragraphs that are relevant but that should be somewhere else. You can do

this best by scissoring the sheets and gluing the pieces onto another paper in the right order. Don't assume that tomorrow you will be able to remember that the paragraph near the bottom of page 3 will go into the middle of page 2. Scissor and glue it now, so that when you next read the essay you will easily be able to tell whether in fact the paragraph does belong in the middle of page 2. Finally, settle on a title. Probably you can't do much more with your manuscript at this moment. Put it aside until tomorrow.

7. *Revise.* Reread your draft, first with an eye toward large matters. Revise your opening paragraph or write one to provide the reader with a focus; make sure each paragraph grows out of the previous one, and make sure you keep the thesis in view. Remember, when you write, you are the teacher. As you revise, try to imagine that you are the reader, and let this imagined reader tell you where you get off the point, where you are illogical, where you are in any way confusing. Next, after making the necessary large revisions, read the draft with an eye toward smaller matters: make sure that each sentence is clear and readable, and that the necessary details and generalizations are there. Cross out extra words; recast unclear sentences. Keep pushing the words, the sentences, the paragraphs into shape until they say what you want them to say from the title onward. (Perhaps this contest between writers and their words is part of what Muhammad Ali had in mind when he said, referring to his work on his autobiography, "Writing is fighting.") Correct anything that disturbs you — for instance, awkward repetitions that grate, inflated utterances that bore.

8. *Edit.* When your draft is as good as you can make it, take care of the mechanical matters: if you are unsure of the spelling of a word, check it in a dictionary; if you are unsure about a matter of punctuation, check it in this book. You will also find footnote form and manuscript form (for example, where to put the title, what margins to leave) in this book in the section on editing. And be sure to acknowledge the source not only of quotations but also of any ideas that you borrowed, even though you summarized or paraphrased them in your own words. (On plagiarism, see pages 546–48.

9. *Prepare the final copy.* Now write or type the final copy; if you are on schedule, you will be doing this a day before the essay is due. After writing or typing it, you will probably want to proof-

read it; there is no harm in doing so, but even if you do so now you will have to proofread it again later because at the moment you are too close to your essay. If you put the essay aside for a few hours and then reread it, you will be more likely to catch omitted words, transposed letters, inconsistent spelling of names, and so forth. Change these neatly (see pages 540–41.)

   10. *Hand the essay in on time.*

   In short, the whole business of moving from a subject to a finished essay on a focused topic adds up to Mrs. Beeton's famous recipe: "First catch your hare, then cook it."

EXERCISES

1. Summarize, analyze, and evaluate a current or recent editorial. Include a copy of the editorial with your essay, but write for a reader who does not have access to the editorial. Suggested length: 350 words.

2. The following passages are bloodless. Revise them into something with life:

   a. Women are not officially allowed to engage in contact sports, with a few exceptions. Probably this practice reflects our cultural principle of protecting women. But possibly, too, it reflects physical differences between men and women.

   b. What bothers students about nontraditional methods of grading is a concern about their chances of being accepted at the next level of education.

   c. The city has plenty of sights to offer, but greenery is rarely among them. Yet many people have a need for some contact with nature, and of the various ways of satisfying this need one of the cheapest and easiest is growing houseplants.

3. In reading the following passages note which sentences or phrases move toward the general, and which toward the specific.

   a. The really fascinating thing about baby talk is the universality of its linguistic form and content, as demonstrated by a comparison of the way it is spoken in six quite different languages: American English, Spanish, Syrian Arabic, Marathi of India, Gilyak of Siberia, and Comanche Indian of North America. The actual baby-talk vocabularies in the six languages are of course different; nevertheless, the words reveal surprising similarities in linguistic characteristics. All six languages simplify clusters of consonants (as English speakers do when they substitute *tummy* for *stomach*); they reduplicate syllables (*choo-choo*); they alter words in consistent ways to form diminutives (such as the *y* in *doggy*); they eliminate pronouns (*daddy wants* instead of *I want*); and most of the languages drop unstressed syllables (as when *good-bye* becomes *bye* or *bye-bye*). The existence of such similarities in widely different languages suggests that adults with no knowledge of one another's tongues have arrived at much the same linguistic formulas.

— Peter Farb

b. I never really liked the doctrine of Indulgences — the notion that you could say five Hail Marys and knock off a year in Purgatory.

— Mary McCarthy

c. A man is in general better pleased when he has a good dinner upon his table than when his wife talks Greek.

— Samuel Johnson

d. If you saw a bullet hit a bird, and he told you he wasn't shot, you might weep at his courtesy, but you would certainly doubt his word.

— Emily Dickinson

e. Actions speak louder than words.

f. What a country calls its vital economic interests are not the things which enable its citizens to live, but the things which enable it to make war. Gasoline is much more likely than wheat to be a cause of international conflict.

— Simone Weil

g. There is no such thing as a free lunch.

2
Analysis

All there is to writing is having ideas. To learn to
write is to learn to have ideas.

— ROBERT FROST

SORTING AND THINKING

Look at this drawing by Pieter Brueghel the Elder, entitled
"The Painter and the Connoisseur" (about 1565), and then read the
paragraph below.

The painter, standing in front of the connoisseur and given more than two-thirds of the space, dominates this picture. His hand holds the brush with which he creates, while the connoisseur's hand awkwardly fumbles for money in his purse. The connoisseur apparently is pleased with the picture he is looking at, for he is buying it, but his parted lips give him a stupid expression and his eyeglasses imply defective vision. In contrast, the painter looks away from the picture and fixes his eyes on the model (reality) or, more likely, on empty space, his determined expression suggesting that he possesses an imaginative vision beyond his painting and perhaps even beyond earthly reality.

This paragraph is a concise piece of analysis. It doesn't simply tell us that the picture shows two people close together; it separates the parts of the picture, pointing out that the two figures form a contrast. It explains why one figure gets much more space than the other, and says what the contrasting gestures and facial expressions imply. The writer of the caption has "read" the picture by seeing how the parts relate to the whole.

Most of the material that you read in courses, except in literature courses, is chiefly analytic: you read of the various causes of a revolution, of the effects of inflation, or of the relative importance of heredity and environment. Similarly, most of your writing in college will be chiefly analytic: you analyze the characters in a play, the causes and effects of poverty, the strengths and weaknesses of some proposed legislation.

But analysis (literally a separating into parts) is not only a kind of writing, it is a way of thinking, a way of arriving at conclusions (generalizations), or of discovering how conclusions were arrived at. It is, at its simplest, an adult version of sorting out cards with pictures of baseball players on them. Now, if you have identical items — for instance, one hundred bricks to unload from a truck — you can't sort them; you can only divide them for easier handling into groups of, say, ten, or into armloads. But if the items vary in some way you can sort them out. You can, for example, put socks into one drawer, underwear into another, trousers or dresses in a closet — all in an effort to make life a little more manageable. Similarly, you can sort books by size or by color or by topic or by author; you do this, again, in order to make them manageable, to

make easier the job of finding the right one later, and so, ultimately, to learn about what is in the book.

When you think seriously or when you talk about almost
anything, you also sort or classify. When you think about choosing
courses at school, you sort the courses by subject matter, or by
degree of difficulty ("Since I'm taking two hard courses, I ought to
look for an easy one"), or by the hour at which they are offered, or
by their merit as determined through the grapevine, or by the
degree to which they interest you. When you sort, you establish
categories by breaking down the curriculum into parts, and by then
putting into each category courses that significantly resemble each
other but that are not identical. We need categories or classifications; we simply cannot get through life treating every object
as unique. Almost everything has an almost infinite number of
characteristics and can therefore be placed in any number of
categories, but for certain purposes (and we must know our purposes) certain characteristics are significant. It is on these significant
characteristics that we fasten.

In sorting, the categories must be established on a single basis
of division: you cannot sort dogs into purebreds and small dogs, for
some dogs belong in both categories. You must sort them into
consistent, coordinate categories, let us say either by breeding or by
size. Of course you can first sort dogs into purebreds and mutts and
then sort each of those groups into two subordinate categories, dogs
under twelve inches at the shoulder and dogs twelve inches or more
at the shoulder. The categories, as we shall see in a few minutes,
will depend on your purpose. That the categories into which things
are sorted should be coordinate is, alas, a principle unknown to the
American Kennel Club, which divides dogs into six groups. The
first four seem reasonable enough: (1) sporting dogs (for example,
retrievers, pointers, spaniels), (2) hounds (bassets, beagles, whip-
pets), (3) working dogs (sheepdogs, St. Bernards, collies), (4) terriers (airedales, Irish terriers, Scottish terriers). Trouble begins with
the fifth classification, toy dogs (Maltese, Chihuahuas, toy poodles), for size has not been a criterion up to now. The sixth category
is desperate: nonsporting dogs (chow chow, poodle, dalmatian).
Nonsporting! What a category. Why not nonworking or non-
hound? And is a poodle really more like a chow chow than like

a toy poodle? [1] Still, the classifications are by now established, and every purebred must fit into one and only one, and thus every purebred can be measured against all of the dogs that in significant ways are thought to resemble it.

Thinking, if broadly defined, must include intuitions and even idle reveries, but most of what we normally mean by serious thinking is analysis, separating into parts and seeing how the parts relate to each other. For example, if we turn our minds to thinking about punishment for killers, we will distinguish at least between those killers whose actions are premeditated, and those killers whose actions are not. And in the first category we might distinguish between professional killers who carefully contrive a death, killers who are irrational except in their ability to contrive a death, and robbers who contrive a property crime and who kill only when they believe that killing is necessary in order to commit the robbery. One can hardly talk usefully about capital punishment or imprisonment without making some such analysis of killers. You have, then, taken killers and sorted or separated or classified them, not for the fun of inventing complications but for the sake of educating yourself and those persons with whom you discuss the topic. Unless your attitude is the mad Queen of Hearts's "Off with their heads," you will be satisfied with your conclusion only after you have tested it by dividing your topic into parts, each clearly distinguished from and then related to the others.

A second example: if you think about examinations, you may see that they can serve several purposes. Examinations may test knowledge, intelligence, or skill in taking examinations; or they may stimulate learning. Therefore, if you wish to discuss what constitutes a good examination, you must decide first what purpose an examination *should* serve. Possibly you will decide that in a particular course an examination should chiefly stimulate learning, but that it should also test the ability to reason. To arrive at a

---

[1] The American Kennel Club's categories, though, are better than those given in an old Chinese encyclopedia, whose fourteen classifications of dogs (according to Jorge Luis Borges) include "those belonging to the Emperor," "stuffed dogs," "free-running dogs," "those getting madly excited," "those that look like flies from the distance," and "others." Equally zany were the labels on the five cells in the jail at Beaufort, Texas, a few decades ago: White Male, White Female, Colored Male, Colored Female, and U.S. Marines.

reasonable conclusion, a conclusion worth sharing, and if need be, defending, you must first recognize and sort out the several possibilities.

Often too, the keenest analytic thinking considers not only what parts are in the whole, but what is *not* there — what is missing in relation to a larger context that we can imagine. For example, if we analyze the women in the best-known fairy tales, we will find that most are either sleeping beauties or wicked stepmothers. These categories are general: "sleeping beauties" includes all passive women valued only for their appearance, and "wicked stepmothers" includes Cinderella's cruel older sisters. (Fairy godmothers form another category, but they are not human beings.) Analysis helps us to discover the almost total absence of resourceful, productive women. A thoughtful essay might begin with a general statement to this effect and then support the statement with an analysis of "Cinderella," "Little Red Riding Hood," and "Hansel and Gretel."

Another analysis that forces us to call to mind what is not there is a Chicano saying, "There are only two kinds of Anglos who are interested in us — the sociologists and the police." And, for a third example, notice in the following paragraph, written during World War II, how George Orwell clarifies our understanding of one kind of military march, the goose-step, by calling our attention to how it differs from the march used by English soldiers. (Orwell might have contrasted the goose-step with the march used by American soldiers, but he was an Englishman writing for Englishmen.)

> One rapid but fairly sure guide to the social atmosphere of a country is the parade-step of its army. A military parade is really a kind of ritual dance, something like a ballet, expressing a certain philosophy of life. The goose-step, for instance, is one of the most horrible sights in the world, far more terrifying than a dive-bomber. It is simply an affirmation of naked power; contained in it, quite consciously and intentionally, is the vision of a boot crashing down on a face. Its ugliness is part of its essence, for what it is saying is "Yes, I *am* ugly, and you daren't laugh at me," like the bully who makes faces at his victim. Why is the goose-step not used in England? There are, heaven knows, plenty of army officers who would be only too glad to introduce some such thing. It is not used because

the people in the street would laugh. Beyond a certain point, military display is only possible in countries where the common people dare not laugh at the army. The Italians adopted the goose-step at about the time when Italy passed definitely under German control, and, as one would expect, they do it less well than the Germans. The Vichy government, if it survives, is bound to introduce a stiffer parade-ground discipline into what is left of the French army. In the British army the drill is rigid and complicated, full of memories of the eighteenth century, but without definite swagger; the march is merely a formalised walk. It belongs to a society which is ruled by the sword, no doubt, but a sword which must never be taken out of the scabbard.

When we begin to think analytically about a topic, whether it is the appropriate treatment of killers, or women in fairy tales, or a kind of military march, we don't instantly see what the parts are and how we can separate and discuss them. Only when we get into the topic do we begin to see the need for subtle distinctions. Remember, though, you can stimulate your ability to see distinctions (and thus to have ideas) by asking yourself questions:

1. To what group does it belong?
2. How do the parts work together?
3. What are its uses, purposes, functions?
4. What are its causes?
5. What are its consequences?

An essay chiefly devoted to answering such questions is an analytic essay, though of course you may think analytically in preparation for some other kind of writing too. For example, a finished essay may be primarily narrative — a story, true or false — but analytic thinking will help you to decide what episodes to include, whether to give the episodes consecutively or to begin at the end and then use a flashback, whether to quote dialogue or to report it indirectly. But in this chapter we are concerned chiefly with analytic thinking that finally manifests itself in an analytic essay — that is, in an essay chiefly devoted to showing the reader how the parts of a topic are related or how one part functions in relation to the whole.

It is useful to practice with familiar materials. Any subject that you are interested in and already know something about can be treated analytically. Let's say, for example, you are interested in blues. You have noticed that singers of blues often sing about traveling, recalling the lines

> When a woman takes the blues
> She tucks her head and cries
> But when a man catches the blues
> He catches a freight and rides

You wonder, among other things: Why all this talk of traveling? You decide you want to look into this question, so you search your memory of blues, play whatever records are available, perhaps read some anthologies that include blues, and generally try to sort things out: that is, try to set your thoughts in order. You find that blues often talk about traveling, but the travel is not all of the same kind, and you begin to analyze the blues that use this motif. You begin to jot down words or phrases:

> disappointed lover
> travel to a job
> from the South
> fantasy travel
> back to the South
> life is a trip
> ~~my first trip out of the state~~
> jail

You are making a scratch outline, for you are establishing categories, fiddling with them until they are as nearly coordinate as possible, and indicating the order in which you will discuss them. You rearrange them as you refine your thinking, because your essay will not record your thought processes as they occurred, with all the false steps; the finished essay will record your best thoughts in the order that you judge to be best for a reader. Then perhaps you find it useful to describe your categories a bit more fully:

1. travel as an escape from unhappy love
2. travel as an economic necessity when jobs are not available at home

3. travel as an escape from the South to the North
4. travel as an escape from the North back to the South
5. travel as sheer wishful thinking, an image of escape from the unhappiness of life
6. travel as an image of the hard job of living until death releases one, as in "It's a long old road, but I'm gonna find the end"
7. enforced travel to prison

You have now taken the theme of travel and separated it into various parts; you are educating yourself and you will educate your reader. Having made these or similar distinctions you can go on to say some interesting things about one or all of these superficially similar but essentially different motifs of travel. Perhaps you arrived at a generalization about them. You have had to divide the motif of travel into parts before you can answer the question you began with: "Why all this talk about traveling?" Perhaps your answer is that talking about travel is a way of talking about life.

Once you have established your categories and tentatively settled on the order in which you will treat them, your job is half done. You have arrived at a thesis, assembled evidence to persuade your reader to accept the thesis, and begun to organize your essay. Possibly your finished essay will make the following points, in the order given below, but with convincing detail (for example, quotations from some blues) to support them.

1. Singers of blues sing of traveling, but the travel is of various sorts.
2. Often it is because of economic, social, or even physical pressure (to get a job; to get to a more congenial environment in the urban North — or back to the rural South; to go to jail).
3. Most often, however, and perhaps in the most memorable songs, it is for another reason: it is an attempt to reduce the pain of some experiences, especially betrayed love, and the hearer senses that the attempt cannot succeed.
4. In such songs it is usually the men who travel, because they are more mobile than women (women are left to take care of the children), but whether it is the man who has deserted the woman, or the woman who has deserted the man, both are pathetic figures because even the deserter will be haunted by the memory of the beloved.

5. But all of these variations on the theme of travel overlap, and almost always there is a sense that the trip — whether to the North or South, to a job or to jail, to a man or to a woman or to nowhere in particular — is an image or metaphor for the trip through life, the long, painful road that everyone must walk.

ANALYSIS AND SUMMARY

Analysis should be clearly distinguished from summary, though of course, as the essay on Roth's article (pages 9–10) illustrates, an analysis usually includes some summary of information the reader needs. For example, when (in the second sentence) the writer says, "Roth, in his article . . . argues that the closing of the libraries will be a costly mistake, and that the action will be an insult to the citizens of Newark," she is summarizing Roth's essay; she is briefly reporting, without personal comment, what Roth said. But when she says, "Roth supports his position" and goes on to cite those of Roth's points that actually provide the support, she is analyzing; she is not reporting *what* he said but is calling attention to *how* he makes his points, *how* certain parts of the essay function. Similarly, when she says "By overdramatizing the possible reactions, Roth gains the interest of the reader," she is also analyzing, showing how an effect is achieved. Again, she is analyzing when she says "Through sarcasm, he discloses a further irony," but summarizing when she reports what this irony is: the City Council insists on law and order but it does not respect communal property.

Most of your writing about other writing will be chiefly analytical. You will not, in most essays, simply summarize X's report of what happened at the Little Bighorn, or Y's account of role-playing, or Z's arguments on the dangers of cloning. You will try to teach your readers *how* the writings of X, Y, and Z achieve their effects, or how well the writers have used evidence, or what evidence they have omitted, or what initial assumptions their arguments are based on. Similarly, when you write an essay on the function of school vacations, or on the purposes of the gasoline tax, you will be writing an analysis — provided that you don't lapse into a mere summary of the history of these topics or of what other writers have said about them.

COMPARING

Analysis frequently involves comparing; things are examined for their resemblances to and differences from other things. Strictly speaking, if one emphasizes the differences rather than the similarities, one is contrasting rather than comparing, but we need not preserve this distinction; we can call both processes "comparing."

An essay may be devoted entirely to a comparison, say of two kinds of tribal organization, but even an essay that is not devoted entirely to a comparison may include a paragraph or two of comparison, for example, to explain something familiar by comparing it to something unfamiliar. An essay on the heart may, for instance, include a paragraph comparing the heart to a pump. Let us spend a moment discussing how to organize a paragraph that makes a comparison.

The first part of a paragraph making a comparison may announce the topic, the next part may discuss one of the two items being compared, and the last part may discuss the other. Or the discussion of the two items may run throughout the entire paragraph, the writer perhaps devoting alternate sentences to each. Because almost all writing is designed to help the reader *see* what the writer has in mind, it may be especially useful here to illustrate this last structure with a discussion of visible distinctions. The following comparison of a Japanese statue of the Buddha with a Chinese statue of a bodhisattva (a slightly lower spiritual being, dedicated to saving humankind) shows how a comparison can run throughout a paragraph.

> The Buddha is recognizable by the cranial bump, representing a super mind. Because the Buddha is free from attachment to things of this world, he wears only a simple monk's robe and his head is unadorned, in contrast to the bodhisattva, whose rich garments and crown symbolize his power as a spiritual creature who still moves on this earth. Moreover, the Buddha is, or was, gilded, symbolizing his heavenly, sun-like nature, whereas the bodhisattva is more or less naturalistically colored. These differences, however, are immediately obvious and, in a sense, superficial. The distinction between the two kinds of spiritual beings, one awesome and one compassionate, is chiefly conveyed by the pose and the carving. The

Buddha sits erect and austere, in the lotus position (legs crossed, each foot with the sole upward on the opposite thigh), in full control of his body. The carved folds of his garment, equally severe, form a highly disciplined pattern. The more earthly bodhisattva wears naturalistically carved flowing garments, and sits in a languid, sensuous posture known as "royal ease," the head pensively tilted downward, one knee elevated, one leg hanging down. Both figures are spiritual but the Buddha is remote, constrained, and austere; the bodhisattva is accessible, relaxed, and compassionate.

Buddha (wood, 33 1/2"; Japanese, late tenth century).

Bodhisattva (wood, 56 1/2"; Chinese, twelfth century).

Next, let's think about a comparison that extends through two or three paragraphs. If one is comparing the indoor play and the sports of girls with those of boys, one can, for example, devote a paragraph to girls, and then a separate paragraph to boys. The paragraphs will probably be connected by beginning the second one with "Boys, on the other hand," or some such transitional expression. But one can also devote a paragraph to indoor play (girls and boys), and a separate paragraph to sports (again girls and boys). There is no rule, except that the organization and the point of the comparison be clear. Consider these paragraphs from an essay by Sheila Tobias on the fear of mathematics. The writer's thesis in the essay is that although this fear is more commonly found in females than in males, biology seems not to be the cause. After discussing some findings (for example, that girls compute better than boys in elementary school, and that many girls tend to lose interest in mathematics in junior high school) the writer turns her attention away from the schoolhouse. Notice that whether a paragraph is chiefly about boys or chiefly about girls, the writer keeps us in mind of the overall point: reasons why more females than males fear math.

> Not all the skills that are necessary for learning mathematics are learned in school. Measuring, computing, and manipulating objects that have dimensions and dynamic properties of their own are part of the everyday life of children. Children who miss out on these experiences may not be well primed for math in school.
>
> Feminists have complained for a long time that playing with dolls is one way of convincing impressionable little girls that they may only be mothers or housewives — or, as in the case of the Barbie doll, "pinup girls" — when they grow up. But doll-playing may have even more serious consequences for little girls than that. Do girls find out about gravity and distance and shapes and sizes playing with dolls? Probably not.
>
> A curious boy, if his parents are tolerant, will have taken apart a number of household and play objects by the time he is ten, and, if his parents are lucky, he may even have put them back together again. In all of this he is learning things that will be useful in physics and math. Taking parts out that have to go back in requires some examination of form. Building something that stays up or at least stays put for some time involves working with structure.
>
> Sports is another source of math-related concepts for children

which tends to favor boys. Getting to first base on a not very well hit grounder is a lesson in time, speed, and distance. Intercepting a football thrown through the air requires some rapid intuitive eye calculations based on the ball's direction, speed, and trajectory. Since physics is partly concerned with velocities, trajectories, and collisions of objects, much of the math taught to prepare a student for physics deals with relationships and formulas that can be used to express motion and acceleration.

The first paragraph offers a generalization about "children," that is, about boys and girls. The second paragraph discusses the play of girls with dolls, but discusses it in a context of its relevance, really irrelevance, to mathematics. The third paragraph discusses the household play of boys, again in the context of mathematics. The fourth paragraph discusses the outdoor sports of boys, but notice that girls are not forgotten, for its first sentence is "Sports is another source of math-related concepts for children which tend to favor boys." In short, even when there is a sort of seesaw structure, boys on one end and girls on the other, we never lose sight of the thesis that comprises both halves of the comparison.

ORGANIZING AN ESSAY DEVOTED TO A COMPARISON

Let us now talk about organizing a comparison or contrast that runs through an entire essay, say a comparison between two political campaigns, or between the characters in two novels. Probably your first thought, after making some jottings, will be to discuss one-half of the comparison and then to go on to the second half. We'll return to this useful method of organization in a moment, but here we want to point out that many instructors and textbooks condemn such an organization, arguing that the essay too often breaks into two parts and that the second part involves a good deal of repetition of categories set up in the first part. Let's say you are comparing the narrator of *Huckleberry Finn* with the narrator of *The Catcher in the Rye,* to show that despite superficial similarities, they are very different, and that the difference is partly the difference between the nineteenth century and the twentieth. An organization often recommended is something like this:

    1. first similarity (the narrator and his quest)
      a. Huck
      b. Holden
    2. second similarity (the corrupt world surrounding the narrator)
      a. society in *Huckleberry Finn*
      b. society in *The Catcher in the Rye*
    3. first difference (degree to which the narrator fulfills his quest and escapes from society)
      a. Huck's plan to "light out" to the frontier
      b. Holden's breakdown

And so on, for as many additional differences as seem relevant. Here is another way of organizing a comparison:

    1. first point: the narrator and his quest
      a. similarities between Huck and Holden
      b. differences between Huck and Holden
    2. second point: the corrupt world
      a. similarities between the worlds in *Huck* and *The Catcher*
      b. differences between the worlds in *Huck* and *The Catcher*
    3. third point: degree of success
      a. similarities between Huck and Holden
      b. differences between Huck and Holden

But a comparison need not employ either of these structures. There is even the danger that an essay employing either of them may not come into focus until the essayist stands back from his seven-layer cake and announces, in the concluding paragraph, that the odd layers taste better. In one's preparatory thinking one may want to make comparisons in pairs, but one must come to some conclusions about what these add up to before writing the final version. The final version should not duplicate the thought processes; rather, it should be organized so as to make the point clearly and effectively. The point of the essay is not to list pairs of similarities or differences, but to illuminate a topic by making thoughtful comparisons. Although in a long essay one cannot postpone until page 30 a discussion of the second half of the comparison, in an essay of, say, less than ten pages, nothing is wrong with setting forth half of the comparison and then, in light of what you've already said, discussing the second half. True, the essay will break into two unrelated parts if the second half makes no use of the first or fails to modify it; but the essay will hang together if the second half looks back to the first half and calls attention to differences that the new material reveals. Students ought to learn how to write an essay with interwoven comparisons, but they also ought to know that there is another, simpler and clearer, way to write a comparison.

The danger of splitting the essay into unrelated parts can be avoided if you remember that the point of a comparison is to call attention to the unique features of something by holding it up against something similar but significantly different. If the differences are great and apparent, a comparison is a waste of effort. ("Blueberries are different from elephants. Blueberries do not have trunks. And elephants do not grow on bushes.") Indeed, a comparison between essentially and evidently unlike things can only obscure, for by making the comparison the writer implies there are significant similarities, and the reader can only wonder why he does not see them. The essays that do break into two halves are essays that make uninstructive comparisons: the first half tells the reader five things about baseball, the second half tells the reader five unrelated things about football.

ARRIVING AT
AN ANALYTICAL THESIS

As we have suggested, the writer of an analytical essay arrives at the idea he will offer as a thesis by asking questions and answering them, by separating the topic into parts and by seeing how those parts relate. Or, we might say, analytic writing presupposes detective work: the writer looks over the evidence, finds some clues, pursues the trail from one place to the next, and makes the arrest. Elementary? Perhaps. Let's observe a famous detective at work.

The Science of Deduction
Arthur Conan Doyle

"I wonder what that fellow is looking for?" I asked, pointing to a stalwart, plainly dressed individual who was walking slowly down the other side of the street, looking anxiously at the numbers. He had a large blue envelope in his hand, and was evidently the bearer of a message.

"You mean the retired sergeant of Marines," said Sherlock Holmes.

"Brag and bounce!" thought I to myself. "He knows that I cannot verify his guess."

The thought had hardly passed through my mind when the man whom we were watching caught sight of the number on our door, and ran rapidly across the roadway. We heard a loud knock, a deep voice below, and heavy steps ascending the stair.

"For Mr. Sherlock Holmes," he said, stepping into the room and handing my friend the letter.

Here was an opportunity of taking the conceit out of him. He little thought of this when he made that random shot. "May I ask, my lad," I said, in the blandest voice, "what your trade may be?"

"Commissionaire, sir," he said, gruffly. "Uniform away for repairs."

"And you were?" I asked, with a slightly malicious glance at my companion.

"A sergeant, sir, Royal Marine Light Infantry, sir. No answer? Right, sir."

He clicked his heels together, raised his hand in salute, and was gone.

I confess that I was considerably startled by this fresh proof of the practical nature of my companion's theories. My respect for his powers of analysis increased wondrously. There still remained some lurking suspicion in my mind, however, that the whole thing was a prearranged episode, intended to dazzle me, though what earthly object he could have in taking me in was past my comprehension. When I looked at him, he had finished reading the note, and his eyes had assumed the vacant, lack-lustre expression which showed mental abstraction.

"How in the world did you deduce that?" I asked.

"Deduce what?" said he, petulantly.

"Why, that he was a retired sergeant of Marines."

"I have no time for trifles," he answered, brusquely; then with a smile, "Excuse my rudeness. You broke the thread of my thoughts; but perhaps it is as well. So you actually were not able to see that that man was a sergeant of Marines?"

"No, indeed."

"It was easier to know it than to explain why I know it. If you were asked to prove that two and two made four, you might find some difficulty, and yet you are quite sure of the fact. Even across the street I could see a great blue anchor tattooed on the back of the fellow's hand. That smacked of the sea. He had a military carriage, however, and regulation side whiskers. There we have the marine. He was a man with some amount of self-importance and a certain air of command. You must have observed the way in which he held his head and swung his cane. A steady, respectable, middle-aged man, too, on the face of him — all facts which led me to believe that he had been a sergeant."

"Wonderful!" I ejaculated.

"Commonplace," said Holmes, though I thought from his expression that he was pleased at my evident surprise and admiration.

— From *A Study in Scarlet*

EXPLAINING AN ANALYSIS: WRITER TO READER

Even when, as a writer, you have solved a problem, that is, focused on a topic and formulated a thesis, you are, as we have said before, not yet done. It is, alas, not enough simply to present the results of your analytical thinking to a reader who, like Dr. Watson, will surely want to know "How in the world did you deduce that?" And like Holmes, writers are often impatient; we long to say with him "I have no time for trifles." But the real reason for our impatience is, as Holmes is quick to acknowledge, that "It was easier to know it than to explain why I know it." But explaining why or how, presenting both the reasoning that led to a thesis and the evidence that supports the reasoning, is the writer's job.

In your preliminary detective work (that is, in reading, taking notes, musing, jotting down some thoughts, and writing rough drafts) some insights (perhaps including your thesis) may come swiftly, apparently spontaneously, and in random order. You may be unaware that you have been thinking analytically at all. In preparing your essay for your reader, however, you become aware, in part because you must become aware. To persuade *your* Dr. Watson that what you say is not "brag and bounce," to replace his natural suspicion with respect for your analysis (and for yourself), you must, we repeat, explain your reasoning in an orderly and interesting fashion and you must present your evidence.

In the hypothetical example on pages 34–37, we showed a writer of an essay musing over the frequency of the motif of travel in blues. Perhaps, we imagined, those musings were triggered by a few lines he happened to remember, or to hear. The writer then began to ask himself questions, to listen to some records, to jot down some notes. His thesis (represented by point three in the revised outline on page 36) might have been formulated only in a final draft of the essay. But it might easily have occurred to the writer much earlier. Perhaps the conclusion, that the themes of travel are a metaphor for the trip through life, came almost simultaneously with the writer's first musings. But no matter when or how he arrived at a conclusion interesting enough to offer as the thesis of an essay, he still had the job of explaining to his reader (and perhaps to himself) how he had arrived at it. He probably had to examine his own thought processes carefully — replaying them in slow motion to see each part separately. He would certainly have had to marshal some evidence from available books and records. And he would have had to arrange the parts of his analysis and the supporting evidence clearly and interestingly to demonstrate the accuracy of his conclusion to a reader who knew less about blues than he did.

To turn to a real example of an analytic essay, notice how Jeff Greenfield, on pages 54–56, solves and presents his case, one involving another famous detective. We will never know in what order the thoughts leading to his thesis came to him. But we can observe how Greenfield organized and supported his analysis. How can we do this? Elementary. By asking questions and answering them.

EXERCISES

1. Analyze the seating pattern in a cafeteria or other public room. Are groups, including groups of empty chairs, perceptible?
2. Look over the birthday cards in a store. What images of girls and women are presented? Are they stereotyped images of

passivity and domesticity? If such images predominate, what exceptions are there? Do the exceptions fall into categories? What images of boys and men are presented? Are they stereotyped images of vigor and authority? Again, if there are exceptions, do they form a pattern? (After you have studied the rack for a while, and jotted down some notes, you may find it useful to buy two or three cards, so that when you write your essay — of 500–1000 words — you will have some evidence at hand.)

3. Write an essay of 500–1000 words analyzing either why people have house plants or why people have pets.

4. Write an essay of not more than three paragraphs analyzing the functions of one of the following:

   credit-noncredit grading
   a minor character in a TV series
   the gasoline tax
   the death penalty
   the preface to this book
   the Twenty-fifth Amendment to the Constitution
   pay toilets
   monumental fountains near public buildings
   Mother's Day

5. An aunt has offered to buy you a subscription to *Time* or *Newsweek*. Compare in about 500 words the contents of the current issues and explain which magazine you prefer. (If neither magazine is of interest, try comparing *Sport* and *Sports Illustrated*, or *Cosmopolitan* and *Ms*.)

6a. Compare baseball with hockey or soccer as a sport suitable for television. Consider the visual appeals of the sports, the pace — including the degree to which the camera operator can predict the action and thus follow it with the camera, the opportunity for replays and for close-ups — and anything else you think relevant.

b. It is often said that television has had a bad effect on sports. If you believe this, write an essay of 500–1000 words setting forth these effects.

7. Compare the function of the setting in *The Tonight Show* with *Saturday Night Live*.

8. In a paragraph analyze the appeals of an advertisement. An advertisement for a book club may, for example, appeal both to snobbism and frugality; an advertisement for a cigarette may appeal to vanity, and perhaps also to reason, by giving statistics about the relatively low amount of tar.

9. Write a paragraph comparing a magazine advertisement of the 1970s with a counterpart of the 1950s. (You can easily find ads for cars and cigarettes in old copies of *Time* and *Newsweek* in your library.) How are the appeals similar and how are they different?

10. This photograph of Sitting Bull and Buffalo Bill was taken in

Sitting Bull and Buffalo Bill, 1886.

1886 by William McFarlane Notman. Reread the discussion of
Brueghel's drawing on pages 29–30, and then write two or
three paragraphs describing and analyzing this photograph,
paying special attention to the contrasting poses, expressions,
and costumes. (Reading brief biographical accounts of Buffalo
Bill [William Frederick Cody] and Sitting Bull will help you to
understand the photograph. Append a list of "Works Consulted" to your paper, and footnote where appropriate. See
pages 559–62 and 549–59.)

11. Reread the discussion of Brueghel's drawing on pages 29–30,
and of the comparison on pages 38–39, and then write a paragraph comparing the photograph of Picasso's son Paul with the
painting that Picasso made from it in 1923.

Photographer unknown. Picasso's Son Paul on a Donkey, *c. 1923.*
Photograph, Collection Pablo Picasso.

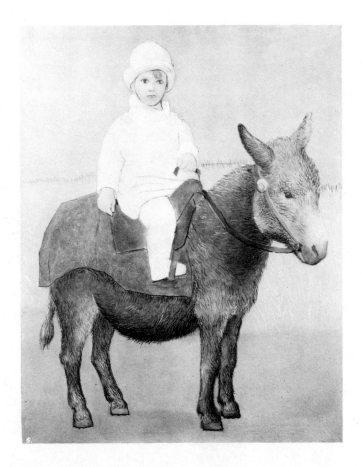

Pablo Picasso. Paul, Son of the Artist. *1923. Gouache, 40 × 32 inches.
Collection of Pablo Picasso, Grasse, France. Permission © S.P.A.D.E.M.,
Paris/V.A.G.A., New York*

12. Study the two drawings on pages 52 and 53, by Francisco
    Goya (1746–1828), entitled "El amor y la muerte" (Love and
    Death). They show a woman holding a dying lover, who has
    fought a duel for her. The first version, on the left, is a
    watercolor; the revised version, on the right, is in chalk. Write
    a brief essay, of one to three paragraphs, comparing the draw-
    ings.

13. Write up a newly discovered example of Sherlock Holmes's
    wonderful powers of analysis. Invent a character, and assign
    him or her a profession (the wilder the better). Show Holmes
    first making the correct deduction, and then explaining to an
    incredulous and admiring Watson the evidence for it.

ANALYSIS AT WORK

*Columbo Knows
the Butler Didn't Do It*
Jeff Greenfield

The popularity of *Columbo* is as intense as it is puzzling. Dinner parties are adjourned, trips to movies postponed, and telephone calls hastily concluded ("It's starting now, I gotta go." "Migod, it's 8:40, what did I miss?"), all for a detective show that tells us whodunit, howhedunit, and whyhedunit all before the first commercial.

Why? Peter Falk's characterization is part of the answer of course; he plays Lieutenant Columbo with sleepy-eyed, slow-footed, crazy-like-a-fox charm. But shtick — even first-class shtick — goes only so far. Nor is it especially fascinating to watch Columbo piece together clues that are often telegraphed far in advance. No, there is something else which gives *Columbo* a special appeal — something almost never seen on commercial television. That something is a strong, healthy dose of class antagonism. The one constant in *Columbo* is that, with every episode, a working-class hero brings to justice a member of America's social and economic elite.

The homicide files in Columbo's office must contain the highest per-capita income group of any criminals outside of antitrust law. We never see a robber shooting a grocery store owner out of panic or savagery; there are no barroom quarrels settled with a Saturday Night Special; no murderous shootouts between drug dealers or numbers runners. The killers in Columbo's world are art collectors, surgeons, high-priced lawyers, sports executives, a symphony conductor of Bernsteinian charisma — even a world chess champion. They are rich and white (if Columbo ever does track down a black killer, it will surely be a famous writer or singer or athlete or politician).

Columbo's villains are not simply rich; they are privileged. They live the lives that are for most of us hopeless daydreams: houses on top of mountains, with pools, servants, and sliding doors; parties with women in slinky dresses, and endless food and drink; plush, enclosed box seats at professional sports events; the envy and admiration of the Crowd. While we choose between Johnny Carson and *Invasion of the Body-Snatchers,* they are at screenings of movies the rest of us wait in line for on Third Avenue three months later.

Into the lives of these privileged rich stumbles Lieutenant Columbo — a dweller in another world. His suspects are Los Angeles paradigms: sleek, shiny, impeccably dressed, tanned by the omnipresent sun. Columbo, on the other hand, appears to have been plucked from Queens Boulevard by helicopter, and set down an instant later in Topanga Canyon. His hair is tousled, not styled and sprayed. His chin is pale and stubbled. He has even forgotten to take off his raincoat, a garment thoroughly out of place in Los Angeles eight months of the year. Columbo is also unabashedly stunned by and envious of the life style of his quarry.

"Geez, that is some car," he tells the symphony conductor. "Ya know, I'll bet that car costs more than I make in a year."

"Say, can I ask you something personal?" he says to a suspect wearing $50-dollar shoes. "Ya know where I can buy a pair of shoes like that for $8.95?"

"Boy, I bet this house musta cost — I dunno, hundred, what, hundred fifty thousand?"

His aristocratic adversaries tolerate Columbo at first because they misjudge him. They are amused by him, scornful of his manners, certain that while he possesses the legal authority to demand their cooperation, he has neither the grace nor wit to discover their misdeeds. Only at the end, in a last look of consternation before the final fadeout, do they comprehend that intelligence may indeed find a home in the Robert Hall set. All of them are done in, in some measure, by their contempt for Columbo's background, breeding, and income. Anyone who has worked the wrong side of the counter at Bergdorf's, or who has waited on tables in high-priced restaurants, must feel a wave of satisfaction. ("Yeah, baby, *that's* how dumb we working stiffs are!")

Further, Columbo knows about these people what the rest of us suspect: that they are on top not because they are smarter or work harder than we do, but because they are more amoral and devious. Time after time, the motive for murder in *Columbo* stems from the shakiness of the villain's own status in high society. The chess champion knows his challenger is his better; murder is his only chance to stay king. The surgeon fears that a cooperative research project will endanger his status; he must do in his chief to retain sole credit. The conductor owes his position to the status of his mother-in-law; he must silence his mistress lest she spill the beans and strip him of his wealth and position.

This is, perhaps, the most thorough-going satisfaction *Columbo* offers us: the assurance that those who dwell in marble and satin, those whose clothes, food, cars, and mates are the very best, *do not deserve it.* They are, instead, driven by fear and compulsion to murder. And they are done in by a man of street wit, who is afraid to fly, who can't stand the sight of blood, and who never uses force to take his prey. They are done in by Mosholu Parkway and P. S. 106, by Fordham U. and a balcony seat at Madison Square Garden, by a man who pulls down $11,800 a year and never ate an anchovy in his life.

It is delicious. I wait only for the ultimate episode: Columbo knocks on the door of 1600 Pennsylvania Avenue one day. "Gee, Mr. President, I really hate to bother you again, but there's *just one thing.* . . ."

QUESTIONS

1. What is Greenfield's thesis? Where does he state it?
2. Describe what Greenfield is doing in his first paragraph; in his second paragraph.
3. Beginning with the third paragraph, Greenfield looks first at the characterization of the hero and villains, then at the underlying conflict, and finally at the implicit meaning of the conflict. Why does he present the parts of his analysis in this order?

The Appeal of Children's Games
Iona and Peter Opie

Play is unrestricted, games have rules. Play may merely be the enactment of a dream, but in each game there is a contest. Yet it will be noticed that when children play a game in the street they are often extraordinarily naïve or, according to viewpoint, highly civilized. They seldom need an umpire, they rarely trouble to keep scores, little significance is attached to who wins or loses, they do not require the stimulus of prizes, it does not seem to worry them if a game is not finished. Indeed children like games in which there is a sizeable element of luck, so that individual abilities cannot be directly compared. They like games which restart almost automatically, so that everybody is given a new chance. They like games which move in stages, in which each stage, the choosing of leaders, the picking-up of sides, the determining of which side shall start, are almost games in themselves. In fact children's games often seem laborious to adults who, if invited to join in, may find themselves becoming impatient, and wanting to speed them up. Adults do not always see, when subjected to lengthy preliminaries, that many of the games, particularly those of young children, are more akin to ceremonies than competitions. In these games children gain the reassurance that comes with repetition, and the feeling of fellowship that comes from doing the same as everyone else. Children may choose a particular game merely because of some petty dialogue which precedes the chase:

> "Sheep, sheep, come home."
> "We're afraid."
> "What of?"
> "The wolf."
> "Wolf has gone to Devonshire
> Won't be here for seven years,
> Sheep, sheep, come home."

As Spencer remarked, it is not only the amount of physical exercise that is taken that gives recreation, "an agreeable mental excitement has a highly invigorating influence." Thus children's "interest" in a game may well be the incident in it that least appeals to the adult: the opportunity it affords to thump a player on the back, as in "Strokey Back," to behave stupidly and be applauded for the stupidity, as in "Johnny Green," to say aloud the color of someone's panties, as in "Farmer, Farmer, may we cross your Golden River?" And in a number of games, for instance "Chinese Puzzle," there may be little purpose other than the ridiculousness of the experiment itself:

> Someone as to be on. The one who is on as to turn round while the others hold hands and make a round circul. Then you get in a muddle, one persun could clime over your arms or under your legs or anything ales that you could make a muddle, then when they have finished they say "Chinese Puzzle we are all in a muddle," then the persun turns round and goes up to them and gets them out of the muddle without breaking their hands, and then the persun who was on choose someone ales, and then it goes on like that. It is fun to play Chinese Puzzle.

Here, indeed, is a British game where little attempt is made to establish the superiority of one player over another. In fact the function of such a game is largely social. Just as the shy man reveals himself by his formalities, so does the child disclose his unsureness of his place in the world by welcoming games with set procedures, in which his relationships with his fellows are clearly established. In games a child can exert himself without having to explain himself, he can be a good player without having to think whether he is a popular person, he can find himself being a useful partner to someone of whom he is ordinarily afraid. He can be confident, too, in particular games, that it is his place to issue commands, to inflict pain, to steal people's possessions, to pretend to be dead, to hurl a ball actually at someone, to pounce on someone, or to kiss someone he has caught. In ordinary life either he never knows these experiences or, by attempting them, makes himself an outcast.

It appears to us that when a child plays a game he creates a situation which is under his control, and yet it is one of which he does not know the outcome. In the confines of a game there can be all the excitement and uncertainty of an adventure, yet the young player can comprehend the whole, can recognise his place in the scheme, and, in contrast to the confusion of real life, can tell what is right action. He can, too, extend his environment, or feel that he is doing so, and gain knowledge of sensations beyond ordinary experience. When children are small, writes Bertrand Russell, "it is biologically natural that they should, in imagination, live through the life of remote savage ancestors." As long as the action of the game is of a child's own making he is ready, even anxious, to sample the perils of which this world has such plentiful supply. In the security of a game he makes acquaintance with insecurity, he is able to rationalise absurdities, reconcile himself to not getting his own way, "assimilate reality" (Piaget), act heroically without being in danger. The thrill of a chase is accentuated by viewing the chaser not as a boy in short trousers, but as a bull. It is not a classmate's back he rides upon but a knight's fine charger. It is not a party of other boys his side skirmishes with but Indians, Robbers, "Men from Mars." And, always provided that the environment is of his own choosing, he — or she — is even prepared to meet the "things that happen in the dark," playing games that would seem strange amusement if it was thought they were being taken literally: "Murder in the Dark," "Ghosties in the Garret," "Moonlight, Starlight, Bogey won't come out To-night." And yet, within the context of the game, these alarms *are* taken literally.

QUESTIONS

1. The first two sentences might be thought of as answering the question "What distinguishes games from play?" or "How do play and games contrast?" Try to formulate a question answered by the next two sentences. List some other questions answered in the paragraph. What comparisons other than that between play and games appear in this paragraph?

2. Why do the Opies devote more space to examples of children's

games in the first half of their discussion than in the second?
3. Suppose that instead of quoting a child's explanation of "Chinese Puzzle" the Opies had written their own. What would be gained or lost?
4. Think of some of the activities you enjoyed as a child. Which would the Opies classify as play and which as games? Why?
5. How would you distinguish games and play from sports?
6. If there are games you enjoyed as a child and still enjoy, list them and analyze their appeal to you then and now.

On Various Kinds of Thinking

James Harvey Robinson

We do not think enough about thinking, and much of our confusion is the result of current illusions in regard to it. Let us forget for the moment any impressions we may have derived from the philosophers, and see what seems to happen in ourselves. The first thing that we notice is that our thought moves with such incredible rapidity that it is almost impossible to arrest any specimen of it long enough to have a look at it. When we are offered a penny for our thoughts we always find we have recently had so many things in mind that we can easily make a selection which will not compromise us too nakedly. On inspection we shall find that even if we are not downright ashamed of a great part of our spontaneous thinking it is far too intimate, personal, ignoble or trivial to permit us to reveal more than a small part of it. I believe this must be true of everyone. We do not, of course, know what goes on in other people's heads. They tell us very little and we tell them very little. The spigot of speech, rarely fully opened, could never emit more than driblets of the ever renewed hogshead of thought — *noch grösser wie's Heidelberger Fass*.[2] We find it hard to believe that other people's thoughts are as silly as our own, but they probably are.

We all appear to ourselves to be thinking all the time during our waking hours, and most of us are aware that we go on thinking while we are asleep, even more foolishly than when awake. When uninterrupted by some practical issue we are engaged in what is now known as a reverie. This is our spontaneous and favorite kind of

[2] Editors' note: German, meaning "even bigger than the vat at Heidelberg."

thinking. We allow our ideas to take their own course and this course is determined by our hopes and fears, our spontaneous desires, their fulfillment or frustration; by our likes and dislikes, our loves and hates and resentments. There is nothing else anything like so interesting to ourselves as ourselves. All thought that is not more or less laboriously controlled and directed will inevitably circle about the beloved ego. It is amusing and pathetic to observe this tendency in ourselves and in others. We learn politely and generously to overlook this truth, but if we dare to think of it, it blazes forth like the noontide sun.

The reverie or "free association of ideas" has of late become the subject of scientific research. While investigators are not yet agreed on the results, or at least on the proper interpretation to be given to them, there can be no doubt that our reveries form the chief index to our fundamental character. They are a reflection of our nature as modified by often hidden and forgotten experiences. We need not go into the matter further here, for it is only necessary to observe that the reverie is at all times a potent and in many cases an omnipotent rival to every other kind of thinking. It doubtless influences all our speculations in its persistent tendency to self-magnification and self-justification, which are its chief preoccupations, but it is the last thing to make directly or indirectly for honest increase of knowledge. Philosophers usually talk as if such thinking did not exist or were in some way negligible. This is what makes their speculations so unreal and often worthless.

The reverie, as any of us can see for himself, is frequently broken and interrupted by the necessity of a second kind of thinking. We have to make practical decisions. Shall we write a letter or no? Shall we take the subway or a bus? Shall we have dinner at seven or half past? Shall we buy U.S. Rubber or a Liberty Bond? Decisions are easily distinguishable from the free flow of the reverie. Sometimes they demand a good deal of careful pondering and the recollection of pertinent facts; often, however, they are made impulsively. They are a more difficult and laborious thing than the reverie, and we resent having to "make up our mind" when we are tired, or absorbed in a congenial reverie. Weighing a decision, it should be noted, does not necessarily add anything to our knowledge, although we may, of course, seek further information before making it.

A third kind of thinking is stimulated when anyone questions our beliefs and opinions. We sometimes find ourselves changing our minds without any resistance or heavy emotion, but if we are told that we are wrong we resent the imputation and harden our hearts.

We are incredibly heedless in the formation of our beliefs, but find ourselves filled with an illicit passion for them when anyone proposes to rob us of their companionship. It is obviously not the ideas themselves that are dear to us, but our self-esteem, which is threatened. We are by nature stubbornly pledged to defend our own from attack, whether it be our person, our family, our property, or our opinion. A United States Senator once remarked to a friend of mine that God Almighty could not make him change his mind on our Latin-American policy. We may surrender, but rarely confess ourselves vanquished. In the intellectual world at least peace is without victory.

Few of us take the pains to study the origin of our cherished convictions; indeed, we have a natural repugnance to so doing. We like to continue to believe what we have been accustomed to accept as true, and the resentment aroused when doubt is cast upon any of our assumptions leads us to seek every manner of excuse for clinging to them. *The result is that most of our so-called reasoning consists in finding arguments for going on believing as we already do.*

I remember years ago attending a public dinner to which the Governor of the state was bidden. The chairman explained that His Excellency could not be present for certain "good" reasons; what the "real" reasons were the presiding officer said he would leave us to conjecture. This distinction between "good" and "real" reasons is one of the most clarifying and essential in the whole realm of thought. We can readily give what seem to us "good" reasons for being a Catholic or a Mason, a Republican or a Democrat, an adherent or opponent of the League of Nations. But the "real" reasons are usually on quite a different plane. Of course the importance of this distinction is popularly, if somewhat obscurely, recognized. The Baptist missionary is ready enough to see the Buddhist is not such because his doctrines would bear careful inspection, but because he happened to be born in a Buddhist family in Tokyo. But it would be treason to his faith to acknowledge that his own partiality for certain doctrines is due to the fact that his mother was a member of the First Baptist church of Oak Ridge. A savage can give all sorts of reasons for his belief that it is dangerous to step on a man's shadow, and a newspaper editor can advance plenty of arguments against the Bolsheviki. But neither of them may realize why he happens to be defending his particular opinion.

The "real" reasons for our beliefs are concealed from ourselves as well as from others. As we grow up we simply adopt the ideas presented to us in regard to such matters as religion, family relations, property, business, our country, and the state. We unconsciously absorb them from our environment. They are persistently whispered in our ear by the group in which we happen to live. Moreover, as Mr. Trotter has pointed out, these judgments, being the product of suggestion and not of reasoning, have the quality of perfect obviousness, so that to question them

> . . . is to the believer to carry skepticism to an insane degree, and will be met by contempt, disapproval, or condemnation, according to the nature of the belief in question. When, therefore, we find ourselves entertaining an opinion about the basis of which there is a quality of feeling which tells us that to inquire into it would be absurd, obviously unnecessary, unprofitable, undesirable, bad form, or wicked, we may know that that opinion is a nonrational one, and probably, therefore, founded upon inadequate evidence.

Opinions, on the other hand, which are the result of experience or of honest reasoning do not have this quality of "primary certitude." I remember when as a youth I heard a group of businessmen discussing the question of the immortality of the soul, I was outraged by the sentiment of doubt expressed by one of the party. As I look back now I see that I had at the time no interest in the matter, and certainly no least argument to urge in favor of the belief in which I had been reared. But neither my personal indifference to the issue, nor the fact that I had previously given it no attention, served to prevent an angry resentment when I heard *my* ideas questioned.

This spontaneous and loyal support of our preconceptions — this process of finding "good" reasons to justify our routine beliefs — is known to modern psychologists as "rationalizing" — clearly only a new name for a very ancient thing. Our "good" reasons ordinarily have no value in promoting honest enlightenment, because, no matter how solemnly they may be marshaled, they are at bottom the result of personal preference or prejudice, and not of an honest desire to seek or accept new knowledge.

In our reveries we are frequently engaged in self-justification, for we cannot bear to think ourselves wrong, and yet have constant illustrations of our weaknesses and mistakes. So we spend much time finding fault with circumstances and the conduct of others, and shifting on to them with great ingenuity the onus of our own failures and disappointments. *Rationalizing is the self-exculpation which occurs when we feel ourselves, or our group, accused of misapprehension or error.*

The little word *my* is the most important one in all human affairs, and properly to reckon with it is the beginning of wisdom. It has the same force whether it is *my* dinner, *my* dog, and *my* house, or *my* faith, *my* country, and *my* God. We not only resent the imputation that our watch is wrong, or our car shabby, but that our conception of the canals of Mars, the pronunciation of "Epictetus," the medicinal value of salicin, or thè date of Sargon I, are subject to revision.

Philosophers, scholars, and men of science exhibit a common sensitiveness in all decisions in which their *amour propre* is involved. Thousands of argumentative works have been written to vent a grudge. However stately their reasoning, it may be nothing but rationalizing, stimulated by the most commonplace of all motives. A history of philosophy and theology could be written in terms of grouches, wounded pride, and aversions, and it would be far more instructive than the usual treatments of these themes. Sometimes, under Providence, the lowly impulse of resentment leads to great achievements. Milton wrote his treatise on divorce as a result of his troubles with his seventeen-year-old wife, and when he was accused of being the leading spirit in a new sect, the Divorcers, he wrote his noble *Areopagitica* to prove his right to say what he thought fit, and incidentally to establish the advantage of a free press in the promotion of Truth.

All mankind, high and low, thinks in all the ways which have been described. The reverie goes on all the time not only in the mind of the mill hand and the Broadway flapper, but equally in weighty judges and godly bishops. It has gone on in all the philosophers, scientists, poets, and theologians that have ever lived. Aristotle's most abstruse speculations were doubtless tempered by highly irrelevant reflections. He is reported to have had very thin legs and small eyes, for which he doubtless had to find excuses, and he was wont to indulge in very conspicuous dress and rings and was accustomed to arrange his hair carefully. Diogenes the Cynic exhibited the impudence of a touchy soul. His tub was his distinction.[3] Tennyson in beginning his "Maud" could not forget his chagrin over losing his patrimony years before as the result of an unhappy investment in the Patent Decorative Carving Company. These facts are not recalled here as a gratuitous disparagement of the truly great, but to insure a full realization of the tremendous competition which all really exacting thought has to face, even in the minds of the most highly endowed mortals.

And now the astonishing and perturbing suspicion emerges that perhaps almost all that had passed for social science, political

---

[3] Editors' note: Diogenes (412–323 B.C.), a Greek philosopher, scorned the usual comforts, and is said to have lived in a tub.

economy, politics, and ethics in the past may be brushed aside by future generations as mainly rationalizing. John Dewey has already reached this conclusion in regard to philosophy. Veblen and other writers have revealed the various unperceived presuppositions of the traditional political economy, and now comes an Italian sociologist, Vilfredo Pareto, who, in his huge treatise on general sociology, devotes hundreds of pages to substantiating a similar thesis affecting all the social sciences. This conclusion may be ranked by students of a hundred years hence as one of the several great discoveries of our age. It is by no means fully worked out, and it is so opposed to nature that it will be very slowly accepted by the great mass of those who consider themselves thoughtful. As a historical student I am personally fully reconciled to this newer view. Indeed, it seems to me inevitable that just as the various sciences of nature were, before the opening of the seventeenth century, largely masses of rationalizations to suit the religious sentiments of the period, so the social sciences have continued even to our own day to be rationalizations of uncritically accepted beliefs and customs. *It will become apparent as we proceed that the fact that an idea is ancient and that it has been widely received is no argument in its favor, but should immediately suggest the necessity of carefully testing it as a probable instance of rationalization.*

This brings us to another kind of thought which can fairly easily be distinguished from the three kinds described above. It has not the usual qualities of the reverie, for it does not hover about our personal complacencies and humiliations. It is not made up of the homely decisions forced upon us by everyday needs, when we review our little stock of existing information, consult our conventional preferences and obligations, and make a choice of action. It is not the defense of our own cherished beliefs and prejudices just because they are our own — mere plausible excuses for remaining of the same mind. On the contrary, it is that peculiar species of thought which leads us to *change* our mind.

It is this kind of thought that has raised man from his pristine, subsavage ignorance and squalor to the degree of knowledge and comfort which he now possesses. On his capacity to continue and greatly extend this kind of thinking depends his chance of groping his way out of the plight in which the most highly civilized peoples of the world now find themselves. In the past this type of thinking has been called Reason. But so many misapprehensions have grown up around the word that some of us have become very suspicious of it. I suggest, therefore, that we substitute a recent name and speak of "creative thought" rather than of Reason. *For this kind of meditation begets knowledge, and knowledge is really creative inasmuch as it makes things look different from what they seemed before and may indeed work for their reconstruction.*

In certain moods some of us realize that we are observing things or making reflections with a seeming disregard of our personal preoccupations. We are not preening or defending ourselves; we are not faced by the necessity of any practical decision, nor are we apologizing for believing this or that. We are just wondering and looking and mayhap seeing what we never perceived before.

Curiosity is as clear and definite as any of our urges. We wonder what is in a sealed telegram or in a letter in which someone else is absorbed, or what is being said in the telephone booth or in low conversation. This inquisitiveness is vastly stimulated by jealousy, suspicion, or any hint that we ourselves are directly or indirectly involved. But there appears to be a fair amount of personal interest in other people's affairs even when they do not concern us except as a mystery to be unraveled or a tale to be told. The reports of a divorce suit will have "news value" for many weeks. They constitute a story, like a novel or play or moving picture. This is not an example of pure curiosity, however, since we readily identify ourselves with others, and their joys and despair then become our own.

We also take note of, or "observe," as Sherlock Holmes says, things which have nothing to do with our personal interests and make no personal appeal either direct or by way of sympathy. This is what Veblen so well calls "idle curiosity." And it is usually idle enough. Some of us when we face the line of people opposite us in a subway train impulsively consider them in detail and engage in rapid inferences and form theories in regard to them. On entering a room there are those who will perceive at a glance the degree of precious-ness of the rugs, the character of the pictures, and the personality revealed by the books. But there are many, it would seem, who are so absorbed in their personal reverie or in some definite purpose that they have no bright-eyed energy for idle curiosity. The tendency to miscellaneous observation we come by honestly enough, for we note it in many of our animal relatives.

Veblen, however, uses the term "idle curiosity" somewhat ironically, as is his wont. It is idle only to those who fail to realize that it may be a very rare and indispensable thing from which almost all distinguished human achievement proceeds, since it may lead to systematic examination and seeking for things hitherto undiscov-ered. For research is but diligent search which enjoys the high flavor of primitive hunting. Occasionally and fitfully idle curiosity thus leads to creative thought, which alters and broadens our own views and aspirations and may in turn, under highly favorable circumstances, affect the views and lives of others, even for generations to follow. An example or two will make this unique human process clear.

Galileo was a thoughtful youth and doubtless carried on a rich and varied reverie. He had artistic ability and might have turned out to be a musician or painter. When he had dwelt among the monks at Valambrosa he had been tempted to lead the life of a religious. As a boy he busied himself with toy machines and he inherited a fondness for mathematics. All these facts are of record. We may safely assume also that, along with many other subjects of contemplation, the Pisan maidens found a vivid place in his thoughts.

One day when seventeen years old, he wandered into the cathedral of his native town. In the midst of his reverie he looked up at lamps hanging by long chains from the high ceiling of the church. Then something very difficult to explain occurred. He found himself no longer thinking of the building, worshipers, or the services; of his artistic or religious interests; of his reluctance to become a physician as his father wished. He forgot the question of a career and even the *graziosissime donne*.[4] As he watched the swinging lamps he was suddenly wondering if mayhap their oscillations, whether long or short, did not occupy the same time. Then he tested this hypothesis by counting his pulse, for that was the only timepiece he had with him.

This observation, however remarkable in itself, was not enough to produce a really creative thought. Others may have noticed the same thing and yet nothing came of it. Most of our observations have no assignable results. Galileo may have seen that the warts on a peasant's face formed a perfect isosceles triangle, or he may have noticed with boyish glee that just as the officiating priest was uttering the solemn words, *ecce agnus Dei*,[5] a fly lit on the end of his nose. To be really creative, ideas have to be worked up and then "put over," so that they become a part of man's social heritage. The highly accurate pendulum clock was one of the later results of Galileo's discovery. He himself was led to reconsider and successfully to refute the old notions of falling bodies. It remained for Newton to prove that the moon was falling, and presumably all the heavenly bodies. This quite upset all the consecrated views of

[4] Editors' note: Italian, meaning "most lovely girls."
[5] Editors' note: Latin, meaning "behold the Lamb of God."

the heavens as managed by angelic engineers. The universality of the laws of gravitation stimulated the attempt to seek other and equally important natural laws and cast grave doubts on the miracles in which mankind had hitherto believed. In short, those who dared to include in their thought the discoveries of Galileo and his successors found themselves in a new earth surrounded by new heavens.

On the twenty-eighth of October, 1831, two hundred and fifty years after Galileo had noticed the isochronous vibrations of the lamps, creative thought and its currency had so far increased that Faraday was wondering what would happen if he mounted a disk of copper between the poles of a horseshoe magnet. As the disk revolved an electric current was produced. This would doubtless have seemed the idlest kind of an experiment to the stanch businessmen of the time, who, it happened, were just then denouncing the child-labor bills in their anxiety to avail themselves to the full of the results of earlier idle curiosity. But should the dynamos and motors which have come into being as the outcome of Faraday's experiment be stopped this evening, the businessman of today, agitated over labor troubles, might, as he trudged home past lines of "dead" cars, through dark streets to an unlighted house, engage in a little creative thought of his own and perceive that he and his laborers would have no modern factories and mines to quarrel about had it not been for the strange practical effects of the idle curiosity of scientists, inventors, and engineers.

The examples of creative intelligence given above belong to the realm of modern scientific achievement, which furnishes the most striking instances of the effects of scrupulous, objective thinking. But there are, of course, other great realms in which the recording and embodiment of acute observation and insight have wrought themselves into the higher life of man. The great poets and dramatists and our modern storytellers have found themselves engaged in productive reveries, noting and artistically presenting their discoveries for the delight and instruction of those who have the ability to appreciate them.

The process by which a fresh and original poem or drama comes into being is doubtless analogous to that which originates and elaborates so-called scientific discoveries; but there is clearly a temperamental difference. The genesis and advance of painting, sculpture, and music offer still other problems. We really as yet know shockingly little about these matters, and indeed very few people have the least curiosity about them. Nevertheless, creative intelligence in its various forms and activities is what makes man. Were it not for its slow, painful, and constantly discouraged operations through the ages man would be no more than a species of primate living on seeds, fruit, roots, and uncooked flesh, and wandering naked through the woods and over the plains like a chimpanzee.

The origin and progress and future promotion of civilization are ill understood and misconceived. These should be made the chief theme of education, but much hard work is necessary before we can reconstruct our ideas of man and his capacities and free ourselves from innumerable persistent misapprehensions. There have been obstructionists in all times, not merely the lethargic masses, but the moralists, the rationalizing theologians, and most of the philosphers, all busily if unconsciously engaged in ratifying existing ignorance and mistakes and discouraging creative thought. Naturally, those who reassure us seem worthy of honor and respect. Equally naturally those who puzzle us with disturbing criticisms and invite us to change our ways are objects of suspicion and readily discredited. Our personal discontent does not ordinarily extend to any critical questioning of the general situation in which we find ourselves. In every age the prevailing conditions of civilization have appeared quite natural and inevitable to those who grew up in them. The cow asks no questions as to how it happens to have a dry stall and supply of hay. The kitten laps its warm milk from a china saucer, without knowing anything about porcelain; the dog nestles in the corner of a divan with no sense of obligation to the inventors of upholstery and the manufacturers of down pillows. So we humans accept our breakfasts, our trains and telephones and orchestras and movies, our national Constitution, our moral code and standards of manners, with the simplicity and innocence of a pet rabbit. We have absolutely inexhaustible capacities for appropriating what others do for us with no thought of a "thank you." We do not feel called upon to make any least contributions to the merry game ourselves. Indeed, we are usually quite unaware that a game is being played at all.

We have now examined the various classes of thinking which we can readily observe in ourselves and which we have plenty of reasons to believe go on, and always have been going on, in our fellow-men. We can sometimes get quite pure and sparkling examples of all four kinds, but commonly they are so confused and intermingled in our reverie as not to be readily distinguishable. The reverie is a reflection of our longings, exultations, and complacencies, our fears, suspicions, and disappointments. We are chiefly engaged in struggling to maintain our self-respect and in asserting that supremacy which we all crave and which seems to us our natural prerogative. It is not strange, but rather quite inevitable, that our beliefs about what is true and false, good and bad, right and wrong, should be mixed up with the reverie and be influenced by the same considerations which determine its character and course. We resent criticisms of views exactly as we do of anything else connected with ourselves. Our notions of life and its ideals seem to us to be *our own* and as such necessarily true and right, to be defended at all costs.

We very rarely consider, however, the process by which we gained our convictions. If we did so, we could hardly fail to see that there was usually little ground for our confidence in them. Here and there, in this department of knowledge or that, some one of us might make a fair claim to have taken some trouble to get correct ideas of, let us say, the situation in Russia, the sources of our food supply, the origin of the Constitution, the revision of the tariff, the policy of the Holy Roman Apostolic Church, modern business organization, trade unions, birth control, socialism, the League of Nations, the excess-profits tax, preparedness, advertising in its social bearings; but only a very exceptional person would be entitled to opinions on all of even these few matters. And yet most of us have opinions on all these, and on many other questions of equal importance, of which we may know even less. We feel compelled, as self-respecting persons, to take sides when they come up for discussion. We even surprise ourselves by our omniscience. Without taking thought we see in a flash that it is most righteous and expedient to discourage birth control by legislative enactment, or that one who decries intervention in Mexico is clearly wrong, or that big advertising is essential to big business and that big business is the pride of the land. As godlike beings why should we not rejoice in our omniscience?

It is clear, in any case, that our convictions on important matters are not the result of knowledge or critical thought, nor, it may be added, are they often dictated by supposed self-interest. Most of them are *pure prejudices* in the proper sense of that word. We do not form them ourselves. They are the whisperings of "the voice of the herd." We have in the last analysis no responsibility for them and need assume none. They are not really our own ideas, but those of others no more well informed or inspired than ourselves, who have got them in the same careless and humiliating manner as we. It should be our pride to revise our ideas and not to adhere to what passes for respectable opinion, for such opinion can frequently be shown to be not respectable at all. We should, in view of the considerations that have been mentioned, resent our supine credulity. As an English writer has remarked:

"If we feared the entertaining of an unverifiable opinion with the warmth with which we fear using the wrong implement at the dinner table, if the thought of holding a prejudice disgusted us as does a foul disease, then the dangers of man's suggestibility would be turned into advantages."

The purpose of this essay is to set forth briefly the way in which the notions of the herd have been accumulated. This seems to me the best, easiest, and least invidious educational device for cultivating a proper distrust for the older notions on which we still continue to rely.

The "real" reasons, which explain how it is we happen to hold a particular belief, are chiefly historical. Our most important opinions — those, for example, having to do with traditional, religious, and moral convictions, property rights, patriotism, national honor, the state, and indeed all the assumed foundations of society — are, as I have already suggested, rarely the result of reasoned consideration, but of unthinking absorption from the social environment in which we live. Consequently, they have about them a quality of "elemental certitude," and we especially resent doubt or criticism cast upon them. So long, however, as we revere the whisperings of the herd, we are obviously unable to examine them dispassionately and to consider to what extent they are suited to the novel conditions and social exigencies in which we find ourselves to-day.

The "real" reasons for our beliefs, by making clear their origins and history, can do much to dissipate this emotional blockade and rid us of our prejudices and preconceptions. Once this is done and we come critically to examine our traditional beliefs, we may well find some of them sustained by experience and honest reasoning, while others must be revised to meet new conditions and our more extended knowledge. But only after we have undertaken such a critical examination in the light of experience and modern knowledge, freed from any feeling of "primary certitude," can we claim that the "good" are also the "real" reasons for our opinions.

I do not flatter myself that this general show-up of man's thought through the ages will cure myself or others of carelessness in adopting ideas, or of unseemly heat in defending them just because we have adopted them. But if the considerations which I propose to recall are really incorporated into our thinking and are permitted to establish our general outlook on human affairs, they will do much to relieve the imaginary obligation we feel in regard to traditional sentiments and ideals. Few of us are capable of engaging in creative thought, but some of us can at least come to distinguish it from other and inferior kinds of thought and accord to it the esteem that it merits as the greatest treasure of the past and the only hope of the future.

QUESTIONS

1. In his first two paragraphs Robinson suggests that most of our thoughts are trivial and egoistic. What precautions does he take to gain our sympathy while making these unflattering assessments?
2. Do you agree with the italicized sentence on page 61? Can you offer any examples from your own behavior or from the behavior of others?
3. On page 61 Robinson makes a distinction between the "good" reasons for our beliefs and the "real" reasons. What does he mean by "real" reasons?
4. Make a list of a few beliefs you hold, and reflect on how you acquired each. Do you find any that you "unconsciously absorbed" from your environment? If so, try to identify the specific parts of your environment (for example, family, schools, television) that were the sources of your beliefs.
5. In the italicized sentence on page 64, Robinson suggests that ancient ideas are especially likely to be rationalizations. Has his discussion of rationalization reasonably led him (and us) to this position? How might it be argued that ancient, widely held ideas are *less* likely to be rationalizations than one person's new idea?
6. Explain what Robinson means by "game" in the last two sentences before the new paragraph beginning "We have now examined" on page 68. Is his use of the word surprising here?

Confessions of a News Addict
Stanley Milgram

Let me begin with a confession. I am a news addict. Upon awakening I flip on the *Today* show to learn what events transpired during the night. On the commuter train which takes me to work, I scour the *New York Times,* and find myself absorbed in tales of earthquakes, diplomacy, and economics. I read the newspaper as religiously as my grandparents read their prayerbooks. The sacramental character of the news extends into the evening. The length of my workday is determined precisely by my need to get home in time for Walter Cronkite. My children understand that my communion with Cronkite is something serious and cannot be interrupted for light and transient causes.

But what is it, precisely, that is happening when I and millions of others scour our newspapers, stare at the tube, and pore over the news magazines that surround us? Does it make sense? What is news, and why does it occupy a place of special significance for so many people?

Let us proceed from a simple definition: news is information about events that are going on outside immediate experience. In this sense, news has always been a part of the human situation. In its earliest form, it took the shape of an account brought by a traveler, or a member of the group who wandered further than the rest and found water, game, or signs of a nearby enemy. The utility of such information is self-evident. News is a social mechanism that extends our own eyes and ears to embrace an ever wider domain of events. A knowledge of remote events allows us to prepare for them and take whatever steps are needed to deal with them. This is the classic function of news.

News is the consciousness of society. It is the means whereby events in the body politic are brought into awareness. And it is curious that regimes which we call *repressive* tend to exhibit the same characteristic of repressed personalities: they are unable, or unwilling, to allow conflictive material into awareness. The disability stems from deep insecurities. The censoring of the repressed material does not eliminate it, but forces it to fester without anyone's rationally coming to grips with it.

Inevitably news comes to be controlled by the dominant political forces of a society. In a totalitarian regime the government attempts to create the image of a world, and of events, that reflects most favorably on those in power. The democratization of news, which goes hand in hand with the diffusion of political power among those governed, is a relatively recent development whose permanence cannot be assured. Democracies are far better able to cope with the reality of events than are totalitarian regimes. Such regimes promulgate a myth of their omnipotence, and are threatened even by events outside the control of the political process. Thus, typically, the Soviet press does not report air crashes, and even natural disasters such as earthquakes are suppressed, out of the notion — rooted in political insecurity — that the event in some manner reflects badly on the regime.

The question for any society is not whether there shall be news, but rather who shall have access to it. Every political system may be characterized by the proportion of information it has which is shared with the people and the proportion withheld. That is why the growth of secret news-gathering agencies, such as the C.I.A., is a troubling one for a democracy. It appears our government wants to keep some news to itself.

At a deeper historical level we can see that news in its present form is closely tied to the rise of economy, and specifically to the exploitative and risk elements of capitalism. For the nineteenth-century merchant, news meant reports of his ship, of resources to exploit, and the means of minimizing the risk element inherent in entrepreneurship by gaining as much information as possible before his competitors. News services, such as Reuters, developed to serve business and investment interests, who discovered that getting the news quickly was the first step to financial gain.

In a civilization in which all activities tend toward commercial expression — for example, our own — news becomes a product to manufacture and dispense to the consumer. Thus a large-scale industry for the production and consumption of news has evolved. We ingest it with the same insatiable appetite that moves us to purchase the manifold products of our commercial civilization.

News under such circumstances tends toward decadent use. It no longer serves first the classic function of giving us information on which to act, or even to help us construct a mental model of the larger world. It serves mainly as entertainment. The tales of earthquakes, political assassinations, and bitterly fought elections are the heady stuff of which drama or melodrama is made. Happily, we are able to indulge our taste for thriller, romance, or murder mystery under the guise of a patently respectable pursuit. All enlightened people are supposed to know what is going on in the world. If what is going on also happens to be thrilling and exciting, so much the better.

Another feature of the decadent use of news is its increasing ritualization. The information becomes subservient to the form in which it is delivered. News is broadcast every evening, whether or not there is vital information to be conveyed. Indeed, the problem for the news networks is to generate sufficient news to fill a given time period. The time period becomes the fundamental fact, the framework into which events must be fitted. As in any ritual, the form persists even when a meaningful content is missing.

Those groups whose survival and well-being are most affected by remote events will be most persistently attuned to them. For example, Israelis, who view the survival of their state as a day-to-day contingency, are among the most news-oriented people in the world. During periods of crisis, portable radios blare in buses and in the market place. Jews, in general, have felt the need to develop antennae for remote events because of a communal insecurity. Any event, no matter how remote — even a farcical *putsch* in Munich led by a paper hanger — may grow into a formidable threat. Thus, constant monitoring of events is strongly reinforced.

Although I am a news addict, my addiction is strongest for news that in many respects seems most remote from my own life and experience. International news receives top priority, followed by national domestic news, and finally — and of least interest — local news. I feel more concerned reading about a student strike in Paris than a murder in my own neighborhood. I am especially uninterested in those news programs that provide a constant litany of fires and local crimes as their standard fare. Yet there is a paradox in this. Surely a criminal loose in my city is of greater personal consequence than an election outcome in Uruguay. Indeed, I sometimes ask what difference it makes to the actual conduct of my life to know about a fracas in Zaire, or a train wreck in Sweden. The total inconsequences of the news for my life is most strikingly brought home when we return from a vacation of several weeks where we have been without any news. I normally scan the accumulated pile of newspapers, but cannot help noticing how little difference it all made to me. And least consequential of all were those remote international events that so rivet my attention in the normal course of the week.

Why this interest in things far away, with a lesser interest in events close at home? Perhaps it is essentially a romantic impulse in the projection of meaning into remote countries, places, and people. Such a romantic impulse stems from a dissatisfaction with the mundane reality of everyday life. The events and places described in the news are remote, and thus we can more readily fix our imaginative sentiments to them. Moreover, an interest in news reinforces the "cosmopolitan" attitude which characterizes modern life, a desire to focus not only on the immediate community, but on the larger world. It is thus the opposite of the "provincialism" which characterized an earlier rural existence.

Living in the modern world, I cannot help but be shaped by it, suckered by the influence and impact of our great institutions. The *New York Times, CBS,* and *Newsweek* have made me into a news addict. In daily life I have come to accept the supposition that if the *New York Times* places a story on the front page, it deserves my attention. I feel obligated to know what is going on. But sometimes, in quieter moments, another voice asks: If the news went away, would the world be any worse for it?

QUESTIONS

1. Why does Milgram describe himself as an addict? How seriously is he using the term? (Consider the connotations of "addict" compared with "reader," "consumer," and "fan.")
2. What reasons does Milgram give for being more interested in "things far away" than in those "close to home"? Do you find his reasons adequate? In answering this question reflect on the three or four items of news that have been of absorbing interest to you. What did those items have in common? Why did they interest you?

Education

E. B. White

I have an increasing admiration for the teacher in the country school where we have a third-grade scholar in attendance. She not only undertakes to instruct her charges in all the subjects of the first three grades, but she manages to function quietly and effectively as a guardian of their health, their clothes, their habits, their mothers, and their snowball engagements. She has been doing this sort of Augean task for twenty years, and is both kind and wise. She cooks for the children on the stove that heats the room, and she can cool their passions or warm their soup with equal competence. She conceives their costumes, cleans up their messes, and shares their confidences. My boy already regards his teacher as his great friend, and I think tells her a great deal more than he tells us.

The shift from city school to country school was something we worried about quietly all last summer. I have always rather favored public school over private school, if only because in public school you meet a greater variety of children. This bias of mine, I suspect, is partly an attempt to justify my own past (I never knew anything but public schools) and partly an involuntary defense against getting kicked in the shins by a young ceramist on his way to the kiln. My wife was unacquainted with public schools, never having been exposed (in her early life) to anything more public than the washroom of Miss Winsor's. Regardless of our backgrounds, we both knew that the change in schools was something that concerned not us but the scholar himself. We hoped it would work out all right. In New York our son went to a medium-priced private institution with semi-progressive ideas of education, and modern plumbing. He learned fast, kept well, and we were satisfied. It was an electric, colorful, regimented existence with moments of pleasurable pause and giddy incident. The day the Christmas angel fainted and had to be carried out by one of the Wise Men was educational in the highest sense of the term. Our scholar gave imitations of it around the house for weeks afterward, and I doubt if it ever goes completely out of his mind.

His days were rich in formal experience. Wearing overalls and an old sweater (the accepted uniform of the private seminary), he sallied forth at morn accompanied by a nurse or a parent and walked (or was pulled) two blocks to a corner where the school bus made a flag stop. This flashy vehicle was as punctual as death: seeing us waiting at the cold curb, it would sweep to a halt, open its mouth, suck the boy in, and spring away with an angry growl. It was a good deal like a train picking up a bag of mail. At school the scholar was worked on for six or seven hours by half a dozen teachers and a nurse, and was revived on orange juice in mid-morning. In a cinder court he played games supervised by an athletic instructor, and in a cafeteria he ate lunch worked out by a dietitian. He soon learned to read with gratifying facility and discernment and to make Indian weapons of a semi-deadly nature. Whenever one of his classmates fell low of a fever the news was put on the wires and there were breathless phone calls to physicians, discussing periods of incubation and allied magic.

In the country all one can say is that the situation is different, and somehow more casual. Dressed in corduroys, sweatshirt, and short rubber boots, and carrying a tin dinner-pail, our scholar departs at crack of dawn for the village school, two and a half miles down the road, next to the cemetery. When the road is open and the car will start, he makes the journey by motor, courtesy of his old man. When the snow is deep or the motor is dead or both, he makes it on the hoof. In the afternoons he walks or hitches all or part of the way home in fair weather, gets transported in foul. The schoolhouse is a two-room frame building, bungalow type, shingles stained a burnt brown with weather-resistant stain. It has a chemical toilet in the basement and two teachers above stairs. One takes the first three grades, the other the fourth, fifth, and sixth. They have little or no time for individual instruction, and no time at all for the esoteric. They teach what they know themselves, just as fast and as hard as they can manage. The pupils sit still at their desks in class, and do their milling around outdoors during recess.

There is no supervised play. They play cops and robbers (only they call it "Jail") and throw things at one another — snowballs in winter, rose hips in fall. It seems to satisfy them. They also construct darts, pinwheels, and "pick-up sticks" (jackstraws), and the school itself does a brisk trade in penny candy, which is for sale right in the classroom and which contains "surprises." The most highly prized surprise is a fake cigarette, made of cardboard, fiendishly lifelike.

The memory of how apprehensive we were at the beginning is still strong. The boy was nervous about the change too. The tension, on that first fair morning in September when we drove him to school, almost blew the windows out of the sedan. And when later we picked him up on the road, wandering along with his little blue lunch-pail, and got his laconic report "All right" in answer to our inquiry about how the day had gone, our relief was vast. Now, after almost a year of it, the only difference we can discover in the two school experiences is that in the country he sleeps better at night — and *that* probably is more the air than the education. When grilled on the subject of school-in-country *vs.* school-in-city, he replied that the chief difference is that the day seems to go so much quicker in the country. "Just like lightning," he reported.

QUESTIONS

1. Which school, city or country, does White prefer?
2. How do you know which school he prefers?
3. How does he persuade you to accept his evaluation?
4. What are some of the notable features of the essay's style? Cite a passage or two illustrating each.

3
Outlining

When you write an outline, you do pretty much what an artist does when he draws an outline: you give, without detail and shading, the general shape of your subject.

An outline is a kind of blueprint, a diagram showing the arrangement of the parts. It is, then, essentially an analysis of your essay, a classification of its parts. Not all writers use outlines, but those who use them report that an outline helps to make clear to them, before or while they labor through a first draft, what their thesis is, what the main points are, and what the subordinate points are. When the outline is drawn, they have a guide that will help them subordinate what is subordinate, and they can easily see if development from part to part is clear, consistent, and reasonable.

An outline drafted before you write, however, is necessarily tentative. Don't assume that once you have constructed an outline your plan is fixed. If, as you begin to write, previously neglected points come to mind, or if you see that in any way the outline is unsatisfactory, revise or scrap the outline. One other caution: an outline does not indicate connections. In your essay be sure to use transitions like "equally important," "less important but still worth mentioning," and "on the other hand" to make clear the relationships between your points.

SCRATCH OUTLINE

The simplest outline is a *scratch outline,* half a dozen phrases jotted down, revised, rearranged, listing the topics to be covered in the most effective and logical order. For an example, see the jottings on page 35. These phrases serve as milestones rather than as a road map. Most writers do at least this much.

PARAGRAPH OUTLINE

A *paragraph outline* is more developed: it states the thesis (usually in a sentence, but sometimes in a phrase) and then it gives the topic sentence (or a phrase summarizing the topic idea) of each paragraph. Thus, a paragraph outline of Jeff Greenfield's "Columbo Knows the Butler Didn't Do It" (pages 54–56) might begin like this:

> Thesis: *Columbo* is popular because it shows a privileged, undeserving elite brought down by a fellow like us.
> I. *Columbo* is popular.
> II. Its popularity is largely due to its hostility toward a social and economic elite.
> III. The killers are all rich and white.
> IV. Their lives are privileged.

And so on, one roman numeral for each remaining paragraph. A paragraph outline has its uses, especially for papers under, say, a thousand words; it can help you to write unified paragraphs, and it can help you to write a reasonably organized essay. But after you write your essay, check to see if your paragraphs really are developments of what you assert to be the topic sentences, and check to see if you have made the organization clear to the reader, chiefly by means of transitional words and phrases (see pages 94–96). If your essay departs from your outline, the departures should be improvements.

FORMAL OUTLINE

For longer papers, such as a research paper (usually at least eight pages of double-spaced typing), a more complicated outline is usually needed. As you can see from the outline preceding the sample research paper on pages 288–89, the *formal outline* shows relationships, distinguishing between major parts of the essay and subordinate parts. Major parts are indicated by capital roman numerals. These should clearly bear on the thesis. Chief divisions within a major part are indicated by capital letters. Subdivisions within these divisions are indicated by arabic numerals. Smaller subdivisions are indicated by lowercase letters. Still smaller subdivisions — although they are rarely needed, because they are apt to provide too much detail for an outline — are indicated by small roman numerals.

Notice that you cannot have a single subdivision. In the example that follows, part I is divided into parts A and B; it cannot have only a part A. Similarly, part B cannot be "divided" into 1 without there being a 2. If you have a single subdivision, eliminate it and work the material into the previous heading. Note also that some authorities require that an outline be consistent in using either sentences or phrases, not a mixture. (Look again at the outline on pages 288–89.) But when you are writing an outline for yourself, you need not worry about mixing phrases with sentences.

Here is a formal outline of Greenfield's "Columbo." Other versions are, of course, possible. In fact, in order to illustrate the form of divisions and subdivisions, we have written a much fuller outline than is usual for such a short essay.

Thesis: *Columbo* is popular because it shows the undeserving rich brought low by a member of the working class.
- I. Popularity of *Columbo*
  - A. What it is *not* due to
    1. Acting
    2. Clever detection of surprising criminal plot
  - B. What it is due to
    1. Hostility to privileged elite
    2. Columbo is poor and shoddy.
    3. The high are brought low.
       a. No black (minority) villains
       b. The villains live far above us.
- II. The hero
  - A. Physical appearance
    1. Dress
    2. Hair, beard
  - B. Manner

C. Success as an investigator
    1. Adversaries mistakenly treat him as negligible.
        a. They assume his lack of wealth indicates lack of intelligence.
        b. They learn too late.
    2. Columbo understands the elite.
        a. They are not superior mentally or in diligence.
        b. They are in a shaky position.
III. Our satisfaction with the program
    A. The villains do not deserve their privileges.
    B. Villains are undone by a man in the street.
    C. We look forward to an episode when Columbo visits the most privileged house.

There is, of course, no evidence that Greenfield wrote an outline before he wrote his essay. But he may have roughed out something along these lines, thereby providing himself with a ground plan or a roadmap. And while he looked at it he may have readjusted a few parts to give more emphasis here (changing a subdivision into a major division) or to establish a more reasonable connection there (say, reversing A and B in one of the parts). Even if you don't write from an outline, when you complete your final draft you ought to be able to outline it — you ought to be able to sketch its parts. If you have trouble outlining the draft, your reader will certainly have trouble following your ideas. Even a paragraph outline made from what you hope is your final draft may help to reveal disproportion or faulty organization that you can remedy before you write your final copy.

EXERCISES

1. Read the one-paragraph essay in Exercise 9, pages 113–115. Then write a scratch outline of it.
2. Write a paragraph outline of one of the following:
    a. "Indecent Exposure" (pages 153–55)
    b. "A Note on the Use of Computers in Research and Writing" (pages 304–6).

4
Paragraphs

PARAGRAPH FORM
AND SUBSTANCE

It is commonly said that a good paragraph has *unity* (it makes one point, or it indicates where one unit of a topic begins and ends); it has *organization* (the point or unit is developed according to some pattern); and it has *coherence* (the pattern of development, sentence by sentence, is clear to the reader). We will say these things too. Moreover, we will attempt to demonstrate that, generally speaking, they are true. Along the way we also hope to show you how to shape your ideas into effective paragraphs. But first we feel obliged to issue this warning: you can learn to write a unified, organized, coherent paragraph that no one in his right mind would choose to read. Here is an example, which we ask you to force yourself to read through. (It may remind you of many paragraphs you wrote in order to graduate from high school.)

Charles Darwin's great accomplishments in the field of natural science resulted from many factors. While innate qualities and characteristics played a large part in leading him to his discoveries, various environmental circumstances and events were decisive factors as well. Darwin, himself, considered his voyage on the *Beagle* the most decisive event of his life, precisely because this was to him an educational experience similar to if not more valuable than that of college, in that it determined his whole career and taught him of the world as well.

Notice that the paragraph is unified, organized, and coherent. It has a topic sentence (the first sentence). It uses transitional devices ("while," "as well," "Darwin," "himself") and, as is often helpful, it repeats key words. But notice also that it is wordy, vague, and inflated ("in the field of," "many factors," "qualities and characteristics," "circumstances and events," "precisely because," "educational experience," "similar to if not more valuable than"). It is, in short, thin and boring. Who but a hired sympathy (John Ciardi's definition of an English teacher) would read it? To whom does it teach what?

Consider, by contrast, these two paragraphs from the beginning of another essay on Darwin:

> Charles Darwin's youth was unmarked by signs of genius. Born in 1809 into the well-to-do Darwin and Wedgwood clans (his mother was a Wedgwood, and Darwin himself was to marry another), he led a secure and carefree childhood, happy with his family, indifferent to books, responsive to nature. The son and grandson of impressively successful physicians, he eventually tried medical training himself, but found the studies dull and surgery (before anesthesia) too ghastly even to watch. So, for want of anything better, he followed the advice of his awesome father (6'2", 336 pounds, domineering in temperament) and studied for the ministry, taking his B.A. at Christ's College, Cambridge, in 1831.
>
> Then a remarkable turn of events saved Darwin from a country parsonage. His science teacher at Cambridge, John Stevens Henslow, arranged for Darwin the invitation to be naturalist on H.M.S. *Beagle* during a long voyage of exploration. Despite his father's initial reluctance, Darwin got the position, and at the end of 1831 left England for a five-year voyage around the globe that turned out to be not only a crucial experience for Darwin himself, but a passage of consequence for the whole world.
>
> — Philip Appleman

Notice how full of life these paragraphs are, compared to the paragraph that begins by asserting that "Charles Darwin's great accomplishments in the field of natural science resulted from many factors." These far more interesting paragraphs are filled with specific details, facts and names that combine to convey ideas. We finish reading them with a sense of having learned something worth knowing, from someone fully engaged not only with the topic, but also with conveying it to someone else.

The one indispensable quality of a good paragraph, the quality that the first paragraph on Darwin lacks, is *substance*. A paragraph may define a term, describe a person or a place, make a comparison, tell an anecdote, summarize an opinion, draw a conclusion; it may do almost anything provided that it holds the reader's attention by telling him something he wants or needs to know, or is reminded of with pleasure.

But even a substantial paragraph, as we shall soon see, does not guarantee the reader's attention, because readers (like writers) are lazy and impatient. The important difference is that readers can afford to be. If they find that they must work too hard to understand you, if they are puzzled or confused by what you write, if they find that the difficulty in following your sentences is greater than the difficulty inherent in your material, if, in other words, the effort they must expend is greater than their reward, they can — and will — stop reading you. Because the art of writing is in large part the art of keeping your readers' goodwill while you teach them what you want them to learn, you should learn, among other things, how to write substantial paragraphs that are also unified, organized, and coherent. Now, experienced writers can usually tell — not so much while they are writing as while they are revising — what does or does not make a satisfactory unit, and their paragraphs do not always exactly follow the principles we are going to suggest. But we think that by following these principles, more or less as you might practice finger exercises in learning how to play the piano, you will develop a sense of paragraphing, or, to put it another way, a sense of how to develop an idea.

PARAGRAPH UNITY: TOPIC SENTENCES, TOPIC IDEAS

The idea developed in each paragraph often appears, briefly stated, as a topic sentence. Topic sentences are most useful, and are therefore especially common, in essays that offer arguments; they are much less common, because they are less useful, in narrative and descriptive essays.

A topic sentence often comes at the beginning of a paragraph, but it may come later, even at the end; it may even be dispensed with if the topic idea — the idea that unifies the sentences of the paragraph — is clear without an explicit statement. (You have just read the topic sentence of this paragraph. The rest of the paragraph will develop the threefold point that a topic sentence often begins a paragraph, often ends a paragraph, and often is omitted.) The topic sentence usually is the first sentence in the paragraph — or the second, following a transitional sentence — because writers usually want their readers to know from the start where the paragraph is going. And, because writers want to keep their readers' attention, an opening topic sentence should be as precise and as interesting as possible (*not* "People oppose school busing for several reasons," but "People offer many good reasons for opposing school busing, but seldom offer their real reasons"). Sometimes, though, you may not wish to forecast what is to come; you may prefer to put your topic sentence at the end of the paragraph, summarizing the points that earlier sentences have made, or drawing a generalization based on the earlier details. Even if you do not include a topic sentence anywhere in the paragraph, the paragraph should have a topic idea — an idea that holds the sentences together.

The following paragraph begins with a topic sentence.

> The Marx Brothers' three best films at Paramount — *Monkey Business* (1931), *Horse Feathers* (1932), and *Duck Soup* (1933) — all hurl comic mud at the gleaming marble pillars of the American temple. The target of *Monkey Business* is money and high society, the rich society snobs merely happen to be gangsters who made their money from bootlegging. The target of *Horse Feathers* is the university; knowledge and the pursuit of it are reduced to thievery, bribery, lechery, and foolishness. The target of *Duck Soup* is democracy and government itself; grandiose political ceremonies, governmental bodies, international diplomacy, the law courts, and war are reduced to the absurd. All three films also parody popular "serious" genres — gangster films, college films, and romantic-European-kingdom films. The implication of this spoofing is that the sanctified institution is as hollow and dead as the cinematic cliché; the breezy, chaotic, revolutionary activities of the comic anarchists give society's respectable calcifications a much-deserved comeuppance.
>
> — Gerald Mast

Everything that follows the first sentence develops or amplifies that sentence, first by commenting one by one on the three films named at the outset, then by speaking of the three films as a group, and then by offering a closely related generalization (the films spoof serious films) and a comment on the implications of this generalization. In short, the writer begins by stating or summarizing his idea, then offers specific evidence to support it, and then offers a related idea. The development is from the general to the particular and then again to the general.

Next, a paragraph with the topic sentence at the end. A paragraph that begins with the topic sentence offers the reader the satisfaction of receiving, as he moves through the paragraph, what was promised at the outset; a paragraph with the topic sentence at the end usually offers the reader the pleasure of mild suspense during most of the paragraph and finally, in the topic sentence, the clarification that the reader had half anticipated. When the topic sentence is at the end, the paragraph usually develops from the particular to the general.

> If we try to recall Boris Karloff's face as the monster in the film of *Frankenstein* (1931), most of us probably think of the seams holding the pieces together, and if we cannot recall other details we assume that the face evokes horror. But when we actually look at a picture of the face rather than recall a memory of it, we are perhaps chiefly impressed by the high, steep forehead (a feature often associated with intelligence), by the darkness surrounding the eyes (often associated with physical or spiritual weariness), and by the gaunt cheeks and the thin lips slightly turned down at the corners (associated with deprivation or restraint). The monster's face is of course in some ways shocking, but probably our chief impression as we look at it is that this is not the face of one who causes suffering but of one who himself is heroically undergoing suffering.

This structure, with the topic sentence at the end of the paragraph, can be especially effective in presenting an argument: the reader hears, considers, and accepts the evidence before the argument is explicitly stated, and if the evidence has been effectively presented the reader willingly accepts the conclusion.

Next, a paragraph without a topic sentence:

> A few years ago when you mentioned Walt Disney at a respectable party — or anyway this is how it was in California, where I was then — the standard response was a headshake and a groan. Intellectuals spoke of how he butchered the classics — from *Pinocchio* to *Winnie the Pooh,* how his wildlife pictures were sadistic and coy, how the World's Fair sculptures of hippopotamuses were a national if not

international disgrace. A few crazies disagreed, and since crazies are always the people to watch, it began to be admitted that the early Pluto movies had a considerable measure of *je ne sais quoi,* that the background animation in *Snow White* was "quite extraordinary," that *Fantasia* did indeed have *one* great sequence (then it became two; now everyone says three, though there's fierce disagreement on exactly which three).

— John Gardner

The topic here is, roughly, "Intellectuals used to scorn Disney, but recently they have been praising him." Such a sentence could easily begin the paragraph, but it is not necessary because even without it the reader has no difficulty following the discussion. The first two sentences talk about Disney's earlier reputation; then the sentence about the "crazies" introduces the contrary view and the rest of the paragraph illustrates the growing popularity of this contrary view. The paragraph develops its point so clearly and consistently (it is essentially a narrative, in chronological order) that the reader, unlike the reader of a complex analytic paragraph, does not need the help of a topic sentence either at the beginning, to prepare for what follows, or at the end, to pull the whole together.

Finally, we examine another paragraph without a topic sentence, this one from a descriptive essay; it does not have the obvious orderliness of the previous example, but it still hangs together.

I remember my mother's father, called Granddad, as a small silent man, a cabinetmaker and carpenter with a liking for strong drink. For a time I guess he was the town drunk, and my memories of him are as fogged by shame as his mind was by whiskey. When he was working — and he managed to support himself until his death — he was a different man. I remember watching him build a cabinet in our house; his hands were craftsman's hands, marked by his trade. The ends of two fingers were missing, lost in the first power saw brought to the county, when they built a bridge over the North Platte. The nails of the remaining fingers were ridged, horny, discolored, misshapen, not like fingernails but more like the claws of some very old and tough bird. The knuckles had been crushed and mauled until each had its own special shape and size. Every inch of skin was mapped by the building he had done. I can't remember his face and can't forget those'hands. When he touched wood those mutilated old hands would turn into something beautiful, as if pure love was flowing from his fingers into the wood.

— Sharon R. Curtin

A paragraph can make several points; but the points must be related and the nature of the relationship must be indicated so that there is, in effect, a single unifying point to the paragraph. In the example just quoted, we get details about the man's physical appearance and also details about his trade; these two motifs are united by the idea that although he was superficially unattractive, when his maimed hands went to work they became beautiful.

UNIFYING IDEAS INTO PARAGRAPHS

Although we emphasize unity in paragraphs, don't assume that every development or refinement or alteration of your thought requires a new paragraph. Such an assumption would lead to an essay consisting entirely of one-sentence paragraphs. A good paragraph may, for instance, both ask a question and answer it, or describe an effect and then explain the cause, or set forth details and then offer a generalization. Indeed, if the question or the effect or the details can be set forth in a sentence or two, and the answer or the cause or the generalization can be set forth in a sentence or two, the two halves of the topic should be pulled together into a single paragraph. It is only if the question (for example) is long and complex and the answer equally long or longer that you need two or more paragraphs — or, to put it more precisely, that your reader needs two or more paragraphs.

Let's consider three paragraphs from an essay on ballooning. In the essay from which the following paragraphs were taken, the writer has already explained that ballooning was born in late eighteenth-century France and that almost from its start there were two types of balloons, gas and hot air. Notice that in the paragraphs printed below the first is on gas, the second is chiefly on hot air (but it helpfully makes comparisons with gas), and the third is on the length of flights of both gas and hot-air balloons. In other words, each paragraph is about one thing — gas balloons, hot-air balloons, length of flight — but each paragraph also builds on what the reader has learned in the previous paragraphs. That the third paragraph is about the flights of gas *and* of hot-air balloons does not mean that it lacks unity; it is a unified discussion of flight lengths.

Gas balloons swim around in air like a sleeping fish in water, because they weigh about the same as the fluid they're in. A good, big, trans-Atlantic balloon will have 2,000 pounds of vehicle, including gas bag and pilot, taking up about 30 cubic feet (as big as a refrigerator), plus 300 pounds of a "nothing" stuff called helium, which fills 30,000 cubic feet (as big as three houses). Air to fill this 30,030 cubic feet would also weigh 2,300 pounds, so the balloon system averages the same as air, floating in it as part of the wind.

Hot-air balloons use the same size bag filled with hot air instead of helium, kept hot by a boot-sized blowtorch riding just over the pilot's head. Hot air is light, but not as light as helium, so you can't carry as much equipment in a hot-air balloon. You also can't fly as long or as far. Helium will carry a balloon for days (three and a half days is the record), until a lot of gas has leaked out. But a hot-air balloon cools down in minutes, like a house as soon as its heat source runs out of fuel; and today's best fuel (heat-for-weight), propane, lasts only several hours.

A good hot-air flight goes a hundred miles, yet the gas record is 1,897 miles, set by a German in 1914 with the junk (by today's standards) they had then. Unmanned scientific gas balloons have flown half a million miles, staying up more than a year. Japan bombed Oregon in World War II with balloons. Two hot-air balloonists, Tracy Barnes and Malcolm Forbes, have made what they called transcontinental flights, but each was the sum of dozens of end-to-end hops, trailed by pick-up trucks, like throwing a frisbee from Hollywood to Atlantic City.

— David Royce

Now contrast the unity of any of the previous three paragraphs on ballooning with the lack of focus in this paragraph from a book on athletic coaching.

Leadership qualities are a prerequisite for achievement in coaching. A leader is one who is respected for what he says and does, and who is admired by his team. The coach gains respect by giving respect, and by possessing knowledge and skills associated with the sport. There are many "successful" coaches who are domineering, forceful leaders, gaining power more through fear and even hate than through respect. These military-type men are primarily from the old school of thought, and many younger coaches are achieving their goals through more humanistic approaches.

Something is wrong here. The first half of the paragraph tells us that "a leader is one who is respected for what he says and does," but the second half of the paragraph contradicts that assertion, telling us that "many" leaders hold their position "more through fear and even hate than through respect." The trouble is *not* that the writer is talking about two kinds of leaders; a moment ago we saw that a writer can in one paragraph talk about two kinds of balloons. The trouble here is that we need a unifying idea if these two points are to be given in one paragraph. The idea might be this: "There are two kinds of leaders, those who are respected and those who are feared." This idea might be developed along these lines:

> Leadership qualities are a prerequisite for achievement in coaching, but these qualities can be of two radically different kinds. One kind of leader is respected and admired by his team for what he says and does. The coach gains respect by giving respect, and by possessing knowledge and skills associated with the sport. The other kind of coach is a domineering, forceful leader, gaining power more through fear than through respect. These military-type men are primarily from the old school of thought, whereas most of the younger coaches achieve their goals through the more humane approaches of the first type.

ORGANIZATION IN PARAGRAPHS

A paragraph needs more than a unified point; it needs a reasonable organization or sequence. After all, a box containing all of the materials for a model airplane has unity (all the parts of the plane are there), but not until the parts are joined in the proper relationships do we get a plane. In the following paragraph, a sentence is out of place.

> Leonardo da Vinci's "Mona Lisa" has attracted and puzzled viewers for almost five hundred years, and I don't suffer from the delusion that I can fully account for the spell the picture casts. Still, I think it is easy enough to account for at least part of the mystery. The most expressive features of a face are the mouth and the eyes, and we notice that Leonardo slightly blurred or shaded the corners of the mouth so that its exact expression cannot be characterized, or, if we characterize it, we change our mind when we look again. Lisa herself is something of a mystery, for history tells us nothing about her personality or about her relationship to Leonardo. The corners of her

Leonardo da Vinci: "Mona Lisa."

eyes, like the corners of her mouth, are slightly obscured, contributing to her elusive expression.

Which sentence is out of place in the paragraph you have just read? How might you work it into its proper place?

Exactly how the parts of a paragraph will fit together depends, of course, on what the paragraph is doing. If it is describing a place, it may move from a general view to the significant details — or from some immediately striking details to some less obvious but perhaps more important ones. It may move from near to far, or from far to near. Other paragraphs may move from cause to effect, or from effect back to cause, or from past to present. In the following paragraph, written by a student, we move chronologically — from waking at 7:00 A.M., to washing and combing, to readiness for the day's work, and then to a glance at the rest of the day that will undo the 7:00 A.M. cleanup.

> I can remember waking at seven to Ma's call. I'd bound out of bed because Ma just didn't allow people to be lazy. She'd grab me and we'd rush to the bathroom for the morning ritual. Bathing, toothbrushing, lotioning, all overseen by her watchful eyes. She didn't let anything go by. No missing behind the ears, no splashing around and pretending to bathe. I bathed and scrubbed and put that lotion on till my whole body was like butter on a warm pan. After inspection it was back to my room and the day's clothes were selected. A bit of tugging and I was dressed. Then she'd sit me down and pull out the big black comb. That comb would glide through my hair and then the braiding would begin. My head would jerk but I never yelled, never even whimpered. Finally I was ready. Ready to start the day and get dirty and spoil all of Ma's work. But she didn't care. She knew you couldn't keep a child from getting dirty but you could teach it to be respectable.

If a paragraph is classifying (dividing a subject into its parts) it may begin by enumerating the parts and go on to study each, perhaps in climactic order. Here is an example.

> The chief reasons people wear masks are these: to have fun, to protect themselves, to disguise themselves, and to achieve a new identity. At Halloween, children wear masks for fun; they may, of course, also think they are disguising themselves, but chiefly their motive is to experience the joy of saying "boo" to someone. Soldiers wore masks for protection, in ancient times against swords and battle-axes, in more recent times against poison gas. Bank robbers wear masks to disguise themselves, and though of course this disguise is a sort of protection, a robber's reason for wearing a mask is fairly distinct from a soldier's. All of these reasons so far are easily understood, but we may have more trouble grasping the reason that primitive people use masks in religious rituals. Some ritual masks seem merely to be attempts to frighten away evil spirits, and some seem merely to be disguises so that the evil spirits will not know who the wearer is. But most religous masks are worn with the idea

that the wearer achieves a new identity, a union with supernatural powers, and thus in effect the wearer becomes — really becomes, not merely pretends to be — a new person.

In short, among the common methods of organizing a paragraph are:

1. general to particular (topic sentence usually at the beginning)
2. particular to general (topic sentence usually at the end)
3. enumeration of parts or details or reasons (probably in climactic order)
4. question and answer
5. cause and effect
6. chronology

The only rule that can cover all paragraphs is this: the reader must never feel that he is stumbling as he follows the writer to the end of the paragraph. The reader should not have to go back and read the paragraph again to figure out what the writer had in mind. It is the

Vladimir Koziakin: "Spaghetti."

writer's job, not the reader's, to give the paragraph its unity and organization. A paragraph is not a maze; it should be organized so that the reader can glide through it in seconds, not minutes.

COHERENCE IN PARAGRAPHS

It is not enough to write unified and organized paragraphs; the unity and organization must be coherent, that is, sufficiently clear, so that the reader can unhesitatingly follow your train of thought. Coherence is achieved largely by means of transitions and repetition.

Transitions

Richard Wagner, commenting on his work as a composer of operas, once said "The art of composition is the art of transition," for his art moved from note to note, measure to measure, scene to scene. Because transitions establish connections between points, they contribute to coherence. Here are some of the most common transitional words and phrases.

1. amplification or likeness: *similarly, likewise, and, also, again, second, third, in addition, furthermore, moreover, finally*
2. emphasis: *chiefly, equally, indeed, even more important*
3. contrast or concession: *but, on the contrary, on the other hand, by contrast, of course, however, still, doubtless, no doubt, nevertheless, granted that, conversely, although, admittedly*
4. example: *for example, for instance, as an example, specifically, consider as an illustration, that is, such as, like*
5. consequence or cause and effect: *thus, so, then, it follows, as a result, therefore, hence*
6. restatement: *in short, that is, in effect, in other words*
7. place: *in the foreground, further back, in the distance*
8. time: *afterward, next, then, as soon as, later, until, when, finally, last, at last*
9. conclusion: *finally, therefore, thus, to sum up*

Make sure that each sentence in a paragraph is properly related to the preceding and the following sentences. Such obvious transitions or roadsigns as "moreover," "however," "but," "for example," "this tendency," "in the next chapter" are useful, but remember that (1) these transitions should not start every sentence (they can be buried: "Smith, moreover . . ."), and (2) explicit transitions need not appear at all in a sentence, so long as the argument proceeds clearly. The gist of a paragraph might run thus: "Speaking broadly, there were two comic traditions. . . . The first. . . . The second. . . . The chief difference between them. . . . But both traditions. . . ."

Consider the following paragraph:

> Folklorists are just beginning to look at Africa. A great quantity of folklore materials has been gathered from African countries in the past century and published by missionaries, travelers, administrators, linguists, and anthropologists incidentally to their main pursuits. No fieldworker has devoted himself exclusively or even largely to the recording and analysis of folklore materials, according to a committee of the African Studies Association reporting in 1966 on the state of research in the African arts. Yet Africa is the continent supreme for traditional cultures that nurture folklore. Why this neglect?
> — Richard M. Dorson

The reader gets the point, but the second sentence seems to contradict the first: the first sentence tells us that folklorists are just beginning to look at Africa, but the next tells us that lots of folklore has been collected. An "although" between these sentences would clarify the author's point, especially if the third sentence were hooked on to the second, thus:

> Folklorists are just beginning to look at Africa. Although a great quantity of folklore materials has been gathered from African countries in the past century by missionaries, travelers, administrators, linguists, and anthropologists incidentally to their main pursuits, no fieldworker has devoted himself . . .

But this revision gives us an uncomfortably long second sentence. Further revision would help. The real point of the original passage, though it is smothered, is that although many people have incidentally collected folklore materials in Africa, professional folklorists have not been active there. The contrast ought to be sharpened:

> Folklorists are just beginning to look at Africa. True, missionaries, travelers, administrators, linguists, and anthropologists have col-

lected a quantity of folklore materials incidentally to their main pur-
suits, but folklorists have lagged behind. No fieldworker . . .

In this revision the words that clarify are, of course, the small but
important words "true" and "but." The original paragraph is a
jigsaw puzzle, missing some tiny but necessary pieces.

Repetition

Coherence is achieved not only by means of transitional
words and phrases but also through the repetition of key words.
When you repeat words or phrases, or when you provide clear
substitutes (such as pronouns and demonstrative adjectives), you
are helping the reader to keep step with your developing thoughts.
Grammatical constructions too can be repeated, the repetitions or
parallels linking the sentences or ideas.

> The purpose of science is to describe the world in an orderly
> scheme or language which will help us to look ahead. We want to
> forecast what we can of the future behavior of the world; particularly
> we want to forecast how it would behave under several alternative
> actions of our own between which we are usually trying to choose.
> This is a very limited purpose. It has nothing whatever to do with
> bold generalizations about the universal workings of cause and ef-
> fect. It has nothing to do with cause and effect at all, or with any
> other special mechanism. Nothing in this purpose, which is to order
> the world as an aid to decision and action, implies that the order
> must be of one kind rather than another. The order is what we find
> to work, conveniently and instructively. It is not something we
> stipulate; it is not something we can dogmatize about. It is what we
> find; it is what we find useful.
>   — J. Bronowski

Notice the repetition of key words: "purpose," "orderly" ("order"), "world," "behavior" ("behave"), "actions" ("action"),
"cause and effect." Notice also the repeated constructions: "we
want to forecast," "it has nothing to do with," "it is not something
we," "it is what we find."

In the next example the repetitions are less emphatic, but
again they provide continuity.

Sir Kenneth Clark's *The Nude* is an important book; and, luck-ily, it is also most readable; but it is not a bedside book. Each sentence needs attention because each sentence is relevant to the whole, and the incorrigible skipper will sometimes find himself obliged to turn back several pages, chapters even, in order to pick up the thread of the argument. Does this sound stiff? The book is not stiff because it is delightfully written. Let the student have no fears; he is not going to be bored for a moment while he reads these 400 pages; he is going to be excited, amused, instructed, provoked, charmed, irritated and surprised.

Notice not only the exact repetitions ("each sentence," "stiff") but also the slight variations, such as "an important book," "not a bedside book"; "he is not going," "he is going," and the emphatic list of participles ("excited, amused, instructed," and so on) at the conclusion.

Here is one more example of a paragraph that unobtrusively uses repetition.

The main skill is to keep from getting lost. Since the roads are used only by local people who know them by sight nobody com-plains if the junctions aren't posted. And often they aren't. When they are it's usually a small sign hiding unobtrusively in the weeds and that's all. County-road-sign makers seldom tell you twice. If you miss that sign in the weeds that's *your* problem, not theirs. Moreover, you discover that the highway maps are often inaccurate about county roads. And from time to time you find your "county road" takes you onto a two-rutter and then a single rutter and then into a pasture and stops, or else it takes you into some farmer's backyard.

— Robert M. Pirsig

What repetitions do you note? (For additional comments on repeti-tion and variation as transitions, see pages 368–70.)

Transitions between Paragraphs

As you move from one paragraph to the next — from one step in the development of your thesis to the next — you probably can keep the reader with you if you make the first sentence of each new paragraph a transition, or perhaps a transition and a topic sentence. The first sentence of a paragraph that could follow the paragraph quoted a moment ago on Kenneth Clark's *The Nude* might run thus:

Among the chief delights of these 400 pages are the illustrations.

Clearly "Among the chief delights of these 400 pages" is a transition, picking up the reference to "400 pages" near the end of the previous paragraph, and the rest of the sentence introduces the topic — the illustrations — of the new paragraph. Only if your two paragraphs are extremely complex, and you believe the reader needs lots of help, will you need to devote an entire paragraph to a transition between two other paragraphs. Often a single transitional word or phrase (such as those listed on page 94) will suffice.

GROUPS OF PARAGRAPHS

Since a paragraph is, normally, a developed idea, and each developed idea has its place in explaining your thesis, as one paragraph follows the next the reader feels he is getting somewhere. Consider the neat ordering of ideas in the following four consecutive paragraphs. The paragraph preceding the first of these was chiefly concerned with describing several strategies whereby the Marx Brothers succeeded in making full-length talking films, in contrast to the short silent films of a decade earlier. In the first of the following paragraphs, "also" provides the requisite transition.

The Marx Brothers also overcame the problem of the talkies by revealing individual relationships to talk. Groucho talks so much, so rapidly, and so belligerently that talk becomes a kind of weapon. He shoots word bullets at his listeners, rendering them (and the audience) helpless, gasping for breath, trying to grab hold of some argument long enough to make sense of it. But before anyone can grab a verbal handle, Groucho has already moved on to some other topic and implication that seems to follow from his previous one — but doesn't. Groucho's ceaseless talk leads the listener in intellectual circles, swallowing us in a verbal maze, eventually depositing us back at the starting point without knowing where we have been or how we got there. Groucho's "logic" is really the manipulation of pun, homonym, and equivocation. He substitutes the quantity of sound and the illusion of rational connection for the theoretical purpose of talk — logical communication.

Chico's relationship to talk also substitutes sound for sense and the appearance of meaning for meaning. To Chico, "viaduct" sounds like "why a duck," "wire fence" like "why a fence," "shortcut" like "short cake," "sanity clause" like "Santa Claus," "dollars" like "Dallas," "taxes" like "Texas." He alone can puncture Groucho's verbal spirals by stopping the speeding train of words and forcing Groucho to respond to his own erroneous intrusions. Groucho cannot get away with his coy substitution of sound for sense when Chico makes different (but similar) sounds out of the key terms in Groucho's verbal web. Chico's absurd accent (this Italian burlesque would be considered very impolite by later standards) makes him hear Groucho's words as if he, the Italian who speaks pidgin English, were speaking them.

The substitution of sound for sense reaches its perfection in Harpo, who makes only sounds. Harpo substitutes whistling and beeps on his horn for talk. Ironically, he communicates in the films as well as anybody. He communicates especially well with Chico, who understands Harpo better than Groucho does. Chico continually interprets Harpo's noises for Groucho. The irony that a bumbling foreign speaker renders a mute clown's honks, beeps, and whistles into English so it can be understood by the supreme verbal gymnast plays a role in every Marx Brothers film.

Harpo also substitutes the language of the body for speech. In this system of communication, Harpo uses two powerful allies — props and mime. He gives the password ("swordfish") that admits him to a speakeasy by pulling a swordfish out of his pocket. He impersonates Maurice Chevalier by miming a Chevalier song to a phonograph record, produced out of his coat especially for the occasion. Or he orders a shot of Scotch in the speakeasy by snapping into a Highland fling. In these early talkies, talk became one of the comic subjects of the films as well as one of the primary comic devices. As in the early Chaplin sound films, the Marx Brothers made talk an ally simply by treating it so specially.

— Gerald Mast

A few observations on these paragraphs may be useful. Notice that the first sentence of the first paragraph is, in effect, an introduction to all four paragraphs; because it is too thin to stand by itself, this transition is acceptably attached as a preface to the first paragraph of what is really a unit of four paragraphs. Second, notice that the first paragraph is devoted to Groucho, the second to Chico, and the third and fourth to Harpo. We might think that symmetry requires that Harpo get only one paragraph, like his brothers, but the writer, feeling that each of Harpo's two languages — noises and gestures — is a major point and therefore worth a separate paragraph, rightly allows significance to overrule symmetry. Third, note the simple but adequate transitions at the beginnings of the paragraphs: "Chico's relationship to talk also . . . ," "The substitution of sound for sense reaches its perfection in Harpo," and "Harpo also substitutes the language of the body for speech." Although the repetition of "also" is a trifle mechanical, it serves to let the reader know where he will be going. Finally, notice that this unit discussing the three brothers is arranged climactically; it ends with Harpo, who is said to achieve "perfection" in the matter under discussion. And in this discussion of distorted language, the two paragraphs on Harpo similarly are arranged to form a climax: the second, not the first, gives us the ultimate distortion, language that is not even sound.

PARAGRAPH LENGTH

Of course hard-and-fast rules cannot be made about the lengths of paragraphs, but more often than not a good paragraph is between one hundred and two hundred words, consisting of more than one or two but fewer than eight or ten sentences. It is not a matter, however, of counting words or sentences; paragraphs are coherent blocks, substantial units of your essay, and the spaces between them are brief resting places allowing the reader to take in what you have said. One page of typing (approximately 250 words) is about as much as the reader can take before requiring a slight break. On the other hand, one page of typing with half a dozen paragraphs is probably faulty because the reader is too often interrupted with needless pauses and because the page has too few *developed* ideas: an assertion is made, and then another, and another. They are unconvincing because they are not supported with detail. To put it another way, a paragraph is a room in the house you are building. If your essay is some five hundred words long (about two double-spaced typewritten pages) you probably will not break it down into more than four or five rooms or paragraphs; if you break it down into a dozen paragraphs, the reader will feel he is touring a rabbit warren rather than a house.

THE USE AND ABUSE OF SHORT PARAGRAPHS

A short paragraph can be effective when it summarizes a highly detailed previous paragraph or group of paragraphs, or when it serves as a transition between two complicated paragraphs, but unless you are sure that the reader needs a break, avoid thin paragraphs. A paragraph that is nothing but a transition can usually be altered into a transitional phrase or clause or sentence that starts the next paragraph. But of course there are times when a short paragraph is exactly right. Notice the effect of the two-sentence paragraph between two longer paragraphs:

> After I returned to prison, I took a long look at myself and, for the first time in my life, admitted that I was wrong, that I had gone astray — astray not so much from the white man's law as from being human, civilized — for I could not approve the act of rape. Even though I had some insight into my own motivations, I did not feel justified. I lost my self-respect. My pride as a man dissolved and my whole fragile moral structure seemed to collapse, completely shattered.
>
> That is why I started to write. To save myself.
>
> I realized that no one could save me but myself. The prison authorities were both uninterested and unable to help me. I had to seek out the truth and unravel the snarled web of my motivations. I had to find out who I am and what I want to be, what type of man I should be, and what I could do to become the best of which I was capable. I understood that what had happened to me had also happened to countless other blacks and it would happen to many, many more.
>
> — Eldridge Cleaver

If the content of the second paragraph were less momentous, it would hardly merit a paragraph. Here the brevity helps to contribute to the enormous impact; those two simple sentences, set off by themselves, are meant to be equal in weight, so to speak, to the longer paragraphs that precede and follow. They are the hinge on which the door turns.

Now read the following horrible example, a newspaper account — chiefly in paragraphs of one sentence each — of an unfortunate happening.

Fish Eat Brazilian Fisherman
Reuters

MANAUS, BRAZIL — Man-eating piranha fish devoured fisherman Zeca Vicente when he tumbled into the water during a battle with 300 farmers for possession of an Amazon jungle lake.

Vicente, a leader of a group of 30 fishermen, was eaten alive in minutes by shoals of the ferocious fish lurking in Lake Januaca.

He died when the farmers — packed in an armada of small boats — attacked the fishermen with hunting rifles, knives, and bows and arrows after they refused to leave.

The farmers, who claimed the fishermen were depleting the lake's fish stocks, one of their main sources of food, boarded the fishing vessels and destroyed cold storage installations.

Last to give way was Vicente, who tried to cut down the farmers' leader with a knife. But farmers shot him and he fell wounded into the water, and into the jaws of the piranhas.

Fifteen persons have been charged with the attack which caused Vicente's death and the injury of several other fishermen.

Lake Januaca, about four hours from this Amazon River town by launch, is famous for its pirarucu and tucunare fish which are regarded as table delicacies.

Most marvelously wrong is the final paragraph, with its cool guidebook voice uttering as inappropriate a fact as is imaginable, but what concerns us at the moment is the writer's failure to build his sentences into paragraphs. Probably all six paragraphs (the seventh, final paragraph is irrelevant) can be effectively combined into one paragraph. Better, perhaps, the material can be divided into two paragraphs, one describing the event and another describing the cause or background. At the most, there is the stuff of three paragraphs, one on the background, one on the event itself, and one on the consequences (fifteen people are charged with the attack). Imagine how it could be reorganized into one paragraph, into two paragraphs, and into three. Which do you think would be most effective? Even the present final paragraph can be worked in; how?

If you spend a few minutes revising the newspaper account of the Brazilian fisherman's death, you will notice that sometimes you can make at least a small improvement merely by joining one paragraph to the next, such as the second to the third. But unsatisfactory short paragraphs usually cannot be repaired so simply; most are unsatisfactory not because sentences have been needlessly separated from each other, but because sentences with generalizations have not been supported by details. Consider these two consecutive paragraphs from a student's essay on Leonardo's "Mona Lisa."

> Leonardo's "Mona Lisa," painted about 1502, has caused many people to wonder about the lady's expression. Different viewers see different things.
>
> The explanation of the puzzle is chiefly in the mysterious expression that Leonardo conveys. The mouth and the eyes are especially important.

If you have read pages 90–91 you know that we have already made some use of Mona Lisa's mysterious expression, but here is another version, strengthening the two feeble paragraphs we have just quoted.

> Leonardo's "Mona Lisa," painted about 1502, has caused many people to wonder about the lady's expression. Doubtless she is remarkably life-like, but exactly what experience of life, what mood, does she reveal? Is she sad, or gently mocking, or uncertain or self-satisfied, or lost in daydreams? Why are we never satisfied when we try to name her emotion?
>
> Part of the uncertainty may of course be due to the subject as a whole: What can we make out of the combination of this smiling lady and that utterly unpopulated landscape? But surely a large part of the explanation lies in the way that Leonardo painted the face's two most expressive features, the eyes and the mouth. He slightly obscured the corners of these, so that we cannot precisely characterize them; and although on one viewing we may see them one way, on another viewing we may see them slightly differently. If today we think she looks detached, tomorrow we may think she looks slightly threatening.

This revision is not simply a padded version of the student's earlier paragraphs; it is a necessary clarification of them, for without the details the generalizations mean almost nothing to a reader.

INTRODUCTORY PARAGRAPHS

Beginning a long part of one of his long poems, Byron aptly wrote, "Nothing so difficult as a beginning." Woody Allen thinks so too. In an interview published in the December 1977 issue of *Media & Methods* he says that the toughest part of writing is "to go from nothing to the first draft." Almost all writers — professionals as well as amateurs — find that the first paragraphs in their drafts are false starts. Don't worry too much about the opening paragraphs of your draft; you'll almost surely want to revise your opening later anyway. (Surprisingly often your first paragraph may simply be deleted; your second, you find, is where your essay truly begins.) When writing a first draft you merely need something — almost anything may do — to break the ice. But in your finished paper, the opening cannot be mere throat-clearing. It should be interesting. "Webster says . . ." is not interesting. Nor is a paraphrase of your title, "Anarchism and the Marx Brothers": "This essay will study the anarchic acts of the Marx Brothers." There is no information about the topic here, at least none beyond what the title already gave, and there is no information about you either, that is, no sense of your response to the topic, such as might be present in, say, "The Marx Brothers are funny, but one often has the feeling that under the fun the violence has serious implications." But in your effort to find your voice and to say something interesting, don't yield to irrelevancy ("*Hamlet* is full of violence" is true, but scarcely relevant to the Marx Brothers) or to the grandiloquence that has wickedly but aptly been called Freshman Omniscience ("Ever since the beginning of time, man has been violent").

Your introductory paragraph will be at least moderately interesting if it gives information, and it will be pleasing if the information provides focus: that is, if it lets the reader know exactly what your topic is, and where you will be going. Remember, when you write, *you* are the teacher; it won't do to begin, "Orwell says he shot the elephant because. . . ." We need at least, "George

Orwell, in 'Shooting an Elephant,' says he shot the elephant because. . . ." Even better is, "In 'Shooting an Elephant,' George Orwell's uneasy reflections on his service as a policeman in Burma, Orwell suggests that he once shot an elephant because . . . but his final paragraph suggests that we must look for additional reasons."

Compare, for example, the opening sentences from three essays written by students on Anne Moody's *Coming of Age in Mississippi*. The book is the autobiography of a black woman, covering her early years with her sharecropper parents, her schooling, and finally her work in the civil rights movement.

> The environment that surrounds a person from an early age tends to be a major factor in determining their character.

This is what we call a *zonker* (see page 324), an all-purpose sentence that serves no specific purpose well. Notice also the faulty reference of the pronoun (the plural "their" refers to the singular "a person"), the weaseling of "tends to be a major factor," and the vagueness of "early age" and "environment" and "character." These all warn us that the writer will waste our time.

> It is unfortunate but true that racial or color prejudice shows itself early in the life of a child.

Less pretentious than the first example, but a tedious laboring of the obvious, and annoyingly preachy.

> Anne Moody's autobiography, *Coming of Age in Mississippi,* vividly illustrates how she discovered her black identity.

Surely this is the best of the three openings. Informative and focused, it identifies the book's theme and method, and it offers an evaluation. The essayist has been considerate of her readers: if we are interested in women's autobiographies, life in the South, or black identity we will read on. If we aren't, we are grateful to her for letting us off the bus at the first stop.

But of course you can provide interest and focus by other, more indirect means. Among them are:

1. a quotation
2. an anecdote or other short narrative
3. an interesting fact (a statistic, for instance, showing the reader that you know something about your topic)

4. a definition of an important term — but not merely one derived from a desk dictionary
5. a glance at the opposition (disposing of it)
6. a question — but an interesting one, such as "Why do we call some words obscene?"

Many excellent opening paragraphs do not use any of these devices, and you need not use any of them if they seem unnatural to you. But observe in your reading how widely and successfully these devices are used. Here is an example of the second device, an anecdote that makes an effective, indeed an unnerving, introduction to an essay on aging.

> There is an old American folk tale about a wooden bowl. It seems that Grandmother, with her trembling hands, was guilty of occasionally breaking a dish. Her daughter angrily gave her a wooden bowl, and told her that she must eat out of it from now on. The young granddaughter, observing this, asked her mother why Grandmother must eat from a wooden bowl when the rest of the family was given china plates. "Because she is old!" answered her mother. The child thought for a moment and then told her mother, "You must save the wooden bowl when Grandma dies." Her mother asked why, and the child replied, "For when you are old."
> — Sharon R. Curtin

The following opening paragraph also is in effect a short narrative, though the point is deliberately obscured — in order to build suspense — until the second paragraph.

> For a couple of days after the thing happened, I moved around Los Angeles with an oddly suspended feeling. It was as if I had not known the city before, and the faces on the street that were once merely blank were more personal in their blankness because I was watching them through different eyes, searching out the fugitive among them, or perhaps the victim, and having the feeling that there were lots of both.
>
> I had joined the brotherhood of the victim, a silent membership with high initiation fees. I got robbed and for a while I thought I was going to be killed.
> — Charles T. Powers

The third strategy, an interesting detail, shows the reader that you know something about your topic and that you are worth reading. We have already seen (page 83) a rather quiet example of this device, in a paragraph about Charles Darwin, which began

"Charles Darwin's youth was unmarked by signs of genius." Here is a more obvious example, from an essay on blue jeans:

> That blue jeans or denims are not found only in Texas is not surprising if we recall that jeans are named for Genoa (Gene), where the cloth was first made, and that denim is cloth *de Nimes,* that is, from Nimes, a city in France.

(These scraps of learning are to be had by spending thirty seconds with a dictionary.)

The fourth strategy, a definition, is fairly common in analytic essays; the essayist first clears the ground by specifying what his topic really is. Here is the beginning of an essay on primitive art.

> The term "primitive art" has come to be used with at least three distinct meanings. First and most legitimate is its use with reference to the early stages in the development of a particular art, as when one speaks of the Italian primitives. Second is its use to designate works of art executed by persons who have not had formal training in our own art techniques and aesthetic canons. Third is its application to the art works of all but a small group of societies which we have chosen to call civilized. The present discussion will deal only with the last.
>
> — Ralph Linton

The author reviews three meanings of the term, and focuses our attention on the relevant one by putting it last.

We leave it to you to find in your reading examples of the fifth and sixth strategies (a glance at the opposition, and an interesting question), but, lest a reader assume that an opening must be of one of these six kinds, we quote an opening that doesn't fit our list:

> Time and again I wanted to reach out and shake Peter Fonda and Dennis Hopper, the two motorcyclist heroes of *Easy Rider,* until they stopped their damned-fool pompous poeticizing on the subject of doing your own thing and being your own man. I dislike Fonda as an actor; he lacks humor, affects insufferable sensitivity and always seems to be fulfilling a solemn mission instead of playing a part. I didn't believe in these Honda hoboes as intuitive balladeers of the interstate highways, and I had no intention of accepting them as protagonists in a modern myth about the destruction of innocence. To my astonishment, then, the movie reached out and profoundly shook me. (Reprinted by permission; © 1970 The New Yorker Magazine, Inc.)
>
> — Joseph Morgenstern

Here Morgenstern deliberately misleads us in his first three sentences. When he reverses direction in the final sentence, he emphasizes the chief point he wants to make.

Such an opening paragraph is a variation on a surefire method: you cannot go wrong in suggesting your thesis in your opening paragraph, moving from a rather broad view to a narrower one. This kind of introductory paragraph can be conceived as a funnel, wide at the top and narrowing into what will be the body of the essay. A common version of this kind of paragraph offers some background and concludes with the subject at hand. It may, for example, briefly sketch the past that contrasts with the present. The following paragraph is from an essay on the pictorial effects in modern films.

> There are still people who remember when there were no talking pictures, when "movies" were simply moving pictures. In 1927 the first full-length sound film was made, and sound soon took over. Coffee cups rattled, rain pattered, and people talked and talked and talked. But film continues to be an essentially visual medium; films are not dramatic plays frozen on celluloid but are essentially moving *pictures*.

But bear in mind that although the first sentence of an introductory paragraph may be broader, more general than the last, it must nevertheless have substance. "Charles Darwin's great accomplishments in the field of natural science resulted from many factors" (look back at page 82) is so broad, so general, so lacking in substance, that it teaches us nothing either about Darwin or about the writer of the essay. If your opening sentence lacks substance, it will not matter what you say next. No one will bother to read more.

CONCLUDING PARAGRAPHS

Concluding paragraphs, like opening paragraphs, are especially difficult if only because they are so conspicuous. Fortunately, you are not always obliged to write one. Descriptive essays, for example, may end merely with a final paragraph, not with a paragraph that draws a conclusion. In an expository essay explaining a process or mechanism you may simply stop when you have finished. Just check to see that the last sentence is a good one, clear and vigorous, and stop. In such essays there is usually no need for a crescendo signaling your farewell to the reader. Persuasive essays are more likely to need concluding paragraphs, not merely final paragraphs. But even persuasive essays, if they are short enough, may end without a formal conclusion; if the last paragraph sets forth the last step of the argument, that may be conclusion enough.

Let's assume, however, that you do feel the need to write a concluding paragraph. With conclusions, as with introductions, try to say something interesting. It is not of the slightest interest to say "Thus we see . . ." and then echo your title and first paragraph. There is some justification for a summary at the end of a long paper because the reader may have half forgotten some of the ideas presented thirty pages earlier, but a paper that can easily be held in the mind needs something different. A good concluding paragraph does more than provide an echo of what the writer has already said. It rounds out the previous discussion, normally with a few sentences that summarize (without the obviousness of "We may now summarize"), but it also may draw an inference that has not previously been expressed. To draw such an inference is not to introduce a new idea — a concluding paragraph is hardly the place for a new idea — but is to see the previous material in a fresh perspective. A good concluding paragraph closes the issue while enriching it. For example, the essay on being assaulted and robbed (the opening paragraphs are quoted on page 106) ends with these two paragraphs:

> What do they take when they rob you? Maybe a thousand dollars' worth of stuff. A car. A jar of pennies and small change — the jar, which they would probably end up breaking, worth more than the change inside. A portable radio bought years before at an Army PX. Little things that it takes days to discover are missing.
> And what else? The ability to easily enter a darkened apartment or to freely open the door after going out. The worst loss is the sense of private space, whether it's in your head or your home, and you can never be certain it will not be invaded again.
>
> — Charles T. Powers

Powers moves from the theft of material objects to the psychological implications of the theft, that is, to a more profound kind of robbery. This is not a new topic because the idea is implicit throughout a discussion of assault and robbery and so it enlarges rather than abandons the topic. It is just that Powers is explicitly stating the idea for the first time.

We hesitate to offer a do-it-yourself kit for final paragraphs, but the following simple devices often work:

1. End with a quotation, especially a quotation that amplifies or varies a quotation used in the opening paragraph.
2. End with some idea or detail from the beginning of the essay and thus bring it full circle.
3. End with an allusion, say to a historical or mythological figure or event, putting your topic in a larger framework.
4. End with a glance at the reader — not with a demand that he mount the barricades, but with a suggestion that the next move is his.

If you adopt any of these devices, do so quietly; the aim is not to write a grand finale, but to complete or round out a discussion.

Here are two concluding paragraphs; notice how they wrap things up and at the same time open out by suggesting a larger frame of reference. The first example, from a student's essay on Anthony Burgess' *A Clockwork Orange,* includes quotations from the book and an allusion to a common expression.

> Both worlds, youthful anarchy and repressive government, are undesirable. For while "you can't run a country with every chelloveck comporting himself in Alex's manner of the night," there should never be a government with the power to "turn you into something other than a human being . . . with no power of choice any longer." What is frightening is that there is no apparent solution to this futuristic society's dilemma. In fact, with the friendly alliance of Alex and the Minister of the Interior at the end of the book come hints that society may soon enjoy the worst of both worlds.

The second is a concluding paragraph from a student's essay on *Black Elk Speaks,* the life story of an Oglala Sioux holy man. The paragraph includes quotations, and then goes on to suggest that the rest is up to the reader.

> "Truth comes into this world with two faces. One is sad with suffering and the other laughs; but it is the same face." The terrible tragedy of the Indian people can never fully be undone. Their "hoop

is broken, and there is no center anymore." But perhaps the rising circulation of Black Elk's story will inspire people to look more closely into person-to-person and person-to-nature relationships. Black Elk's message "was given to him for all men and it is true and it is beautiful," but it must be listened to, understood, and acted on.

All essayists will have to find their own ways of ending each essay; the four strategies we have suggested are common but they are not for you if you don't find them comfortable. And so, rather than ending this section with rules about how to end essays, we suggest how not to end them: don't merely summarize, don't say "in conclusion," don't introduce a totally new point, and don't apologize.

EXERCISES

1. Reread the paragraph on page 85, in which a topic sentence (about three films by the Marx Brothers) begins the paragraph. Then write a paragraph with a similar construction, clarifying the topic sentence with details. You might, for example, begin thus: "When facing a right-handed batter, a left-handed pitcher has a distinct advantage over a right-handed pitcher." Another possible beginning: "All three major television networks offer pretty much the same kinds of entertainment during prime time."
2. Reread the paragraph on page 86, discussing the face of Frankenstein's monster, and then write a paragraph on some other widely known face (Mick Jagger? Jane Fonda?), ending your paragraph with a topic sentence. The cover of a recent issue of *Time* or *Newsweek* may provide you with the face you need.
3. Many people strongly prefer dogs to cats — or the other way round. Write one paragraph in which you express your preference, supporting this preference by a detailed account of the traits of the two kinds of beasts. (If cats and dogs don't interest you, choose some other pair. For ideas about writing a comparison, see pages 38–44.)

4. The following paragraph is unified, but incoherent. How should it be reorganized?

> Abortion, the expulsion of a fetus which could not develop and function alone successfully, is an issue which has caused much discussion in the past decade. There exist mainly two opposing groups concerning this subject, but many people's opinions lie somewhere in the middle. Some believe that abortions should be legalized unconditionally throughout the United States, while others believe that abortions should be illegal in all cases.

5. The following paragraph is both unified and fairly well organized, but it is still lacking in coherence. What would you do to improve it?

> The cyclist must also master prerace tactics. Not only what to wear and what food to bring are important, but how to strip the bike of unnecessary weight. Cycling shoes are specially designed for bike racing. They have a metal sole that puts the energy directly to the pedal, thus efficiently using one's power. The food that one brings is important in a long-distance race. It must not only be useful in refueling the body, but it must be easily eaten while pedaling. Candy bars and fruit, such as bananas, satisfy both requirements. The bike must be stripped of all unnecessary weight, including saddlebags and reflectors. Some cyclists drill holes in parts of the frame, saddle post, and handlebars to lessen the weight of the bike.

6. On page 89 we printed a paragraph on athletic coaches and we also printed a more unified revision of the paragraph. But the revision (on page 90) is still weak, for it lacks supporting details. Revise the revision, giving it life.

7. Here is the opening paragraph of an essay (about 750 words) on the manufacture of paper in the fifteenth century, the days of the earliest printed books. On the whole it is very good, but the unity and the organization can be improved. Revise the paragraph.

> We take paper for granted, but old as it is it did not always exist. In fact, it was invented long after writing was invented, for the earliest writing is painted or scratched on cave walls, shells, rocks, and other natural objects. Paper was not even the first manufactured surface for writing; sheets made from papyrus, a reed-like plant, were produced about 2500 B.C., long before the invention of paper. Although the

Chinese may have invented paper as early as the time of Christ, the oldest surviving paper is from early fifth-century China. The Arabs learned the secret of paper-making from the Chinese in the eighth century, but the knowledge traveled slowly to Europe. The oldest European paper, made by the Moors in Spain, is of the twelfth century. Early European paper is of poor quality and so not until the quality improved, around the fourteenth century, did paper become widely used. Most writing was done on parchment, which is the skin of a sheep or goat, and vellum, which is the finer skin of a lamb, kid, or calf. Whatever the animal, the skin was washed, limed, unhaired, scraped, washed again, stretched, and rubbed with pumice until a surface suitable for writing was achieved. Until it was displaced by paper, in the fourteenth century, parchment was the chief writing surface in Europe.

8. Here is the concluding paragraph of a book review. Analyze and evaluate its effectiveness.

> Mr. Flexner's book is more than a political argument. He has written so vividly and involved us so deeply that there are moments when we yearn to lean over into the pages, pull Hamilton aside, and beg him to reconsider, to pity, to trust, to wait, or merely to shut up. Yet the book's effect is not melodramatic. It is tragic — a tragedy not of fate but of character, the spectacle of an immensely gifted man who tried to rule a nation and could not rule himself.
>
> — Naomi Bliven

9. Read the following brief essay (from *The New Yorker*) once through. Then read it again and decide where you would introduce paragraph breaks. For each of your paragraphs identify the topic sentence, or state in a sentence the topic idea.

> On the morning the bus and subway fares were raised to fifty cents, we happened to enter the West Side I.R.T. at 110th Street. From the street above, we heard the din of raised voices, and when we got down into the station we found ourself face to face with four or five young people shouting "No fare at this station!" and "Say no to the Rockefeller banks!" and "Don't pay the fare!" Two of the young people held the exit gates to the platform open while the others, without blocking the way to the token window or the turnstiles, pointed to the open gates. The activists, though they were only a foot or two away from the approaching passengers, bellowed their instructions at the top of their voices. We passed through a

turnstile and then, while we waited for a train, turned to observe the proceedings. The moment of decision came and passed swiftly for the people descending the stairs. It came as soon as they reached the bottom; most people walked right on to the platform, whether by the paying or the non-paying route, without breaking stride. About four out of five were accepting the invitation to a free ride. In most cases, it was not until people got through to the platform that their grim, set, closed-in subway expressions dissolved into expressions reflecting a reaction to this unexpected experience. Some of those who were taking a free ride looked exhilarated, or were laughing, but sometimes the laughter had a hollow ring to it, and often the laugher's eyes darted around the platform, as though he were looking for companionship in his gaiety. Others who had entered free seemed almost irritated to find themselves on the platform without having gone through the usual procedures. Some of those who had paid had embarrassed looks, and seemed, with deferential glances and smiles, to be apologizing to their fellow-riders. (The command "Don't pay!" was constantly booming in everyone's ears.) Others who had paid looked outraged by what was happening, and stalked away up the platform. We could discern no pattern in the types of those who paid and those who did not pay. Neither age nor race nor style of dress seemed to provide any clue to the choice that a person would make. One young black man loped through the exit gates, but a young black man just behind him paid. A silver-haired, professorial-looking man stopped, scrutinized the scene with a severe look, and then paid. Shortly afterward, three men in suits and carrying attaché cases sailed through without paying. One elderly man held back for a full two minutes, seeming to give the matter the most solemn thought, and then, holding his face in a rigid deadpan, made a beeline at a rapid clip through the open exit gates. Although there was no guessing from examining someone's appearance which choice he might make, we did notice that the numbers of those going in free seemed to increase considerably when the shouting was loudest. Whenever it abated slightly, the people coming down the stairs tended to surge on past the activists and pay the fare. The shouting, which seemed so repellent and so likely to harm the activists' cause, was turning out to be an effective tactic. Every morning, subway riders, held on course, perhaps, by the great inertia that is born of daily habit, had flowed through the turnstiles and onto the platform on their way to work. On this one morning, many were deflected to a new course — through the open exit gates — like a river that has been diverted into a new bed. For when the shouting reached a certain level of loudness more energy appeared to be required to decide to defy the activists and pay than to break the law and go in free, just as on most mornings more energy would have been required to open the exit gates on one's own than to pay. No one had really decided to break the law. On that morning, as on others, people had made no decision at all. (Reprinted by permission; © 1975 The New Yorker Magazine, Inc.)

5
Definition *READ*

Many things are not what they sound like: a seedless orange is (according to the citrus industry) an orange with five seeds or less; there is no lead in a lead pencil; plum pudding contains no plums; a two-by-four is one and five-eighths inches in thickness and three and three-eighths inches in width; peanuts are not nuts (they are vegetables, related to peas and beans); coffee beans are not beans (they are the pits of a fruit); minorities, according to the Department of Health, Education and Welfare, include only blacks, American Indians, Orientals, and the Spanish-surnamed. Asked to define a word, most of us want to take advantage of St. Augustine's ingenious evasion: "I know what it is when you don't ask me." Or we sound like Polonius talking about Hamlet (II.ii.92–94):

> Your noble son is mad.
> Mad call I it, for, to define true madness,
> What is't but to be nothing else but mad?

A dictionary can be a great help, of course; but don't begin an essay by saying "Webster says. . . ." Because the name Webster is no longer copyrighted, it appears on all sorts of dictionaries, bad as well as good.[1] Moreover, there is no staler opening.

---

[1] Of the five desk dictionaries that we recommend, two have "Webster" in the title: *Webster's New Collegiate Dictionary* and *Webster's New World Dictionary*. The other three recommended desk dictionaries are *The American College Dictionary, The American Heritage Dictionary of the English Language*, and *The Random House Dictionary of the English Language: College Edition*. If you didn't receive one of these five as a graduation present, you should buy one. You should also become acquainted, in the

DEFINITION BY ORIGIN

Sometimes we know the origin of the word, and the origin may be worth recounting for the light it sheds on the present meaning.

> **Low Rider**. A Los Angeles nickname for ghetto youth. Originally the term was coined to describe the youth who had lowered the bodies of their cars so that they rode low, close to the ground; also implied was the style of driving that these youngsters perfected. Sitting behind the steering wheel and slumped low down in the seat, all that could be seen of them was from their eyes up, which used to be the cool way of driving. When these youthful hipsters alighted from their vehicles, the term *low rider* stuck with them, evolving to the point where all black ghetto youth — but *never* the soft offspring of the black bourgeoisie — are referred to as low riders.
>
> — Eldridge Cleaver

Or we may know the foreign origins of an English word; *pornography*, for example, comes from Greek words meaning "writing of prostitutes." That's interesting enough and relevant enough to be useful. Or take *yoga*. If you are writing an essay on yoga, you may want to say something like this:

> The word "yoga" comes from a Sanskrit root meaning "to join," "to yoke," and indeed our words "join" and "yoke" both come from this same root. Yoga seeks to join or to yoke the individual's consciousness to its spiritual source.

A word's origins, or etymology (from the Greek, meaning "true word") may be found in any good dictionary. It may be interesting and relevant and therefore worth mentioning — but of course a word's present meaning may be far from its original meaning, or those of its origins. *Doctor*, for instance, is from a medieval Latin

---

library, with the great *New English Dictionary* (*NED*), issued in ten volumes, 1888–1928; reissued in twelve volumes with a supplement, in 1933, as the *Oxford English Dictionary* (*OED*). Although this dictionary of course does not include recent words, it is unrivaled in its citations of illustrative quotations indicating the meanings of a word over the centuries. Far less exhaustive, but useful, are three American unabridged dictionaries: *Webster's Third New International Dictionary*, *Funk and Wagnall's New Standard Dictionary of the English Language*, and *The Random House Dictionary of the English Language*.

word meaning "teacher." Although this etymology is relevant if
you are talking about the classroom skills of Ph.D.'s, it is probably
irrelevant (and therefore of no use to you or to your reader) if you
are talking about the word in its commonest sense today, "physician."

DEFINITION BY SYNONYM

Usually when we are trying to define a word we can come up
with at least a single word as a synonym; so we define *helix* by
saying "spiral," or *to civilize* by saying "to socialize." Definition
by synonym, however, doesn't go very far; it merely equates one
word with another. And often no close synonym exists. In any
case, definition by synonym is only a beginning.

STIPULATIVE DEFINITION

You may stipulate (contract for) a particular meaning of a
word, as we saw in the passage on primitive art (page 107),
where the writer briefly set forth three meanings of the word, and
then announced he would deal only with the third. Similarly, if for
instance you are writing about Catholics, you may stipulate that in
your essay the word refers to all who have been baptized into the
Catholic faith. Or you may stipulate that it refers only to those who
consider themselves practicing Catholics. As another example, take
the expression "third world people." This term has at least three
related but separate meanings:

1. a group of nations, especially in Africa and Asia, that are not
   aligned with either the Communist or the non-Communist
   blocs
2. the aggregate of underdeveloped nations of the world
3. the aggregate of minority groups within a larger predominant
   culture

In fact, a fourth meaning, a variation of the third, seems to be most
common in recent American writing: the aggregate of minority
groups *other than blacks and Orientals* within the United States.
Many discussions of third world people limit themselves to American Indians and to Spanish-speaking people, apparently considering

American blacks and Orientals as part of the larger predominant culture. Thus, in an essay you may announce what you mean by "third world": "In this essay, 'third world' refers not to A or B but to C."

It is entirely legitimate to stipulate or contract for a particular meaning. In fact, you often must stipulate a meaning, for although technical words have relatively stable meanings, many of the words that you will be defining — words such as *education* and *society* — have so many meanings that the reader won't know which you're using until you say so.

FORMAL DEFINITION

A formal definition is a kind of analysis. It normally takes a term (for instance, *professor*) and places it within a class or family ("a teacher") and then goes on to differentiate it from other members of the class ("in a college or university"). Such a definition is sometimes called *inclusive/exclusive* because it includes the word in a relevant category and then excludes other members of that category. Plato is said to have defined *man* as "a featherless biped," but a companion pointed out that this definition is not sufficiently exclusive: a plucked chicken fits the definition. Plato therefore amended it satisfactorily by adding "with flat toenails." Another example: in Hitchcock's *Stage Fright*, Marlene Dietrich suggests that "Detectives are merely policemen with smaller feet." If this definition is inaccurate, it is not so because of its structure. Notice, by the way, that a definition demands a parallel form — for example, a noun for a noun: "A *professor* is a *teacher* in a college or university." Avoid saying "A professor is when you teach . . ." or "Love is never having to say you're sorry."

What use can be made of a formal definition? Suppose you are writing about organic food. You may want to clear the ground by saying something like this:

> From a chemical point of view, all foods are organic, for they are compounds containing carbon. So-called organic foods do not differ from other foods in their chemical makeup, but they have been grown with the help only of fertilizers or pesticides of animal or vegetable origin rather than with the help of manufactured chemicals.

Or suppose you want to discuss sharks. A desk dictionary will give you something like this: "a cartilaginous (as opposed to bony) fish with a body tapering toward each end." Such a definition puts sharks within the family of a type of fish and then goes on to exclude other members of this family (which happens also to include rays) by calling attention to the distinctive shape of the shark's body. But if you are not writing a strictly formal definition you may want to talk not only about sharks as remote objects but about your sense of them, your response to them:

> Although the shark and the ray are closely related, being cartilaginous rather than bony fish, the two could scarcely be more different in appearance. The ray, a floppy pancake-like creature, is grotesque but not terrifying; the shark, its tapering body gliding through the water, is perhaps the most beautiful and at the same time the most terrifying sight the sea can offer.

In short, a formal definition can structure your definition even if you go beyond it.

LONGER DEFINITIONS

Most of the terms we try to define in college courses require lengthy definitions. If you are going to say anything of interest about machismo or obscenity or freedom or poverty or mother wit you will have to go far beyond a formal definition. If you are writing on a subject you care about, you may find that you will have to write at least several paragraphs until you get to the limits of the word. *Definition*, by the way, is from the Latin *de* "off" and *finis* "end, limit."

One way of getting toward the limits of the word is to spend some sentences, perhaps a paragraph, on a comparison or contrast. In the paragraph on sharks, half of one sentence compares sharks to rays, which are closely related to sharks but different. In a more extended definition of a less easily defined topic, more space might be devoted to establishing distinctions. For example, the writer of an essay on gallows humor (briefly defined as humor that domesticates a terrifying situation by making fun of it) might wish to compare it with black humor (not the humor of black people, but a brutal or sadistic humor). The superficial similarity of gallows humor to black humor might require the essayist to discuss black humor in order to make clear the special quality of gallows humor; but of course the discussion of black humor should be clearly subordinated to the main topic lest the essay lose focus.

The point of such a strategy is to help the reader see something clearly by holding it against something similar but significantly different. The following extended definition of a proverb follows such a strategy.

> A proverb is a concise didactic statement that is widely used in an unchanging form. Among the examples that come to mind are "Look before you leap," "A rolling stone gathers no moss," and "Red sky at night, sailors delight." These, and almost all other proverbs that one can think of, concisely and memorably summarize everyday experience. This everyday experience is usually a matter of conduct; even "Red sky at night, sailors' delight" — which seems purely descriptive — is followed by "Red sky at morning, sailors take warning." Most commonly, proverbs advise the hearer to avoid excess.
>
> We should distinguish proverbs from other concise utterances. Clichés such as "cool as a cucumber," "last but not least," and "a sight for sore eyes," though they may be called proverbial phrases, often do not offer advice implicitly or explicitly. More important, clichés are not complete sentences. He or she or they can be or are or were "cool as a cucumber"; but a proverb has an independent and unvarying form. Proverbs should be distinguished, too, from such conventional utterances as "Good morning," "Thank you," and "Please pass the salt." These are unvarying, but unlike proverbs they are not didactic.
>
> Closer to proverbs, superficially at least, are epigrams, such as Oscar Wilde's "A cynic is a man who knows the price of everything and the value of nothing." Most epigrams are obviously literary; they usually employ a clever contrast (antithesis) that is rare in proverbs. And most epigrams, unlike proverbs, are not really communal property: their authorship is known, and they are not used by ordinary people in ordinary speech. When used by someone other than the author, they are used by educated speakers or writers as conscious quotations. In contrast, the speaker of a proverb, though he knows that he did not invent it, rightly feels that it is part of his own wisdom.

Notice that this extended definition of proverbs begins by including the proverb within a class ("concise didactic statement") and then proceeds to exclude other members of the class by specifying that a proverb is "widely used in an unchanging form." The definition, then, is inclusive and exclusive; it includes the term to be defined within a class, and it excludes other members of the class. Notice too that examples are given throughout. If the examples were omitted, the paragraphs would be less lively and less clear. But of course, a definition cannot be a mere list of examples ("a proverb is a saying such as . . ."); generalizations as well as concrete illustrations are needed.

The definition of a proverb was just that; it was not a focused essay on proverbs. And it was not an attempt to woo the reader to be interested in proverbs or an attempt to persuade the reader that proverbs really have no wisdom to offer because they are often contradictory ("Look before you leap" contradicts "He who hesitates is lost," and "Birds of a feather flock together" contradicts "Opposites attract"). Rather, it was an attempt to make clear the meaning of a word. If more space had been available, especially if the word were a more elusive one, such as *democracy* or *personality* or *feminism*, the essay might have had the following structure:

1. statement of the need for a definition
2. survey of the usual definitions (calling attention to their inadequacy)
3. the writer's definition, set forth with illustrative examples, comparisons, and contrasts

Clearly the heart of such an essay is the third part.

Though some essays seek to do nothing more than to define a term, essays with other purposes often include paragraphs defining a word. Here, from a long essay on the recent fad for country music, are some paragraphs defining country music. Notice how this selection moves from a moderately jocose and obviously imprecise definition ("anything that Grandma can hum, whistle, or sing is country") to a list of the subjects of country music and then to a hypothetical example.

> What is the fuss all about? Glen George, manager of Kansas City's country radio KCKN, says: "Anything that Grandma can hum, whistle or sing is country." Its traditional message is one of despair, hope, loss, death, the land and, often with cloying sentimentality, love. Country lyrics have always been the cry of the common man. They can, and do give comfort to everyone from sharecrop-

pers and truck-stop waitresses to University of Texas Football Coach Darrell Royal, former Energy Czar John Love, Novelist Kurt Vonnegut, Jr. and Operatic Tenor Richard Tucker. Says Moon Mullins, program director of the all-country WINN in Louisville: "If you listen to our station long enough, one of our songs will tell your story."

Cynics like to say that whomever the story belongs to, it will probably deal with trucks, trains, prison, drinking (or moonshine), women misbehaving ("slippin' around" in the country vernacular) or death. The ideal country song might be about a guy who finally gets out of prison, hops a truck home, finds that his wife is slippin' around, gets drunk, and staggers to his doom in front of a high-balling freight.

The music itself, at least as purveyed by many of the superstars of Nashville and Bakersfield, has a vanilla sameness to it that often does not reflect the pain and sorrow of the words. The voices of the singers are often less charged with emotion than their blues and rock counterparts. Most male country stars have deep bass baritones that seem to say: this man sits tall in the saddle. Women stars tend to have bright, unstrained sopranos — or a Lynn Anderson kind of nasal chirpiness — that rule out not only women's lib but any other kind of defiance. In the past, country lyrics have been astonishingly repressive. Blind loyalty to husband, parents, even political leaders has been a common theme. When men have sung about women, the subject (always excepting long-suffering Mother) has often been the pain, not the pleasure.

Today, however, country is taking on a new sound, a new diversity and message as well. Partly that is due to the influence of rock, partly to the visible softening of the once strong accents of American regionalization. Says Kris Kristofferson, 37, the former Rhodes scholar who is now a leader of country's progressive wing: "There's really more honesty and less bullshit in today's music than ever before."

EXERCISES

1. Define blues or rock or soul or folk music in 250–500 words.
2. Write one paragraph defining one of the following terms: security blanket, twilight zone, holding pattern. Your paragraph should disclose the origin of the term (if you can't find it, make a reasonable guess) and some examples of current use distinct from its original meaning.

3. Write an opening paragraph for an essay in which you stipulate a meaning for *death*, excluding one or two other meanings. Don't write the essay, just the opening paragraph.

4. If you are fluent in a language other than English, or in a dialect other than Standard American, write a paragraph defining for native speakers of Standard American a word that stands for some concept. Examples: Spanish *machismo*, Yiddish *haimish* or *chutzpa*, Japanese *shibui*, German *Gemütlichkeit*, black English *bad* or *the dozens*.

5. Write an essay of approximately 500 words on the word *natural* as it is used to advertise products such as cereals, yogurt, cosmetics, and cigarettes. Your essay should stipulate a definition of natural, and should have a thesis. An example of a thesis: "Yogurt may be a wholesome food, but most commercial yogurts are not as 'natural' as we are led to believe."

6. Write an essay (about 500 words) explaining one of the following terms: disaster film, situation comedy, soap opera, junk food, underground newspaper, nostalgia, ethnic joke. Your essay will probably include a definition, reference to several examples, and perhaps an extended discussion of one example, explaining the reasons for its popularity, or arguing its merits or lack of merits. Your essay, then, will probably blend exposition with narration, description, and argument.

DEFINITION AT WORK

Mechanic's Feel
Robert M. Pirsig[2]

The mechanic's feel comes from a deep inner kinesthetic feeling for the elasticity of materials. Some materials, like ceramics, have very little, so that when you thread a porcelain fitting you're very

---

[2] Editors' note: This passage is not an independent essay. It is taken from Pirsig's *Zen and the Art of Motorcycle Maintenance* (New York: Bantam, 1975), pp. 317–18. In the previous paragraph Pirsig has mentioned kinesthesia, sensitive muscular response to things.

careful not to apply great pressures. Other materials, like steel, have tremendous elasticity, more than rubber, but in a range in which, unless you're working with large mechanical forces, the elasticity isn't apparent.

With nuts and bolts you're in the range of large mechanical forces and you should understand that within these ranges metals are elastic. When you take up a nut there's a point called "finger-tight" where there's contact but no takeup of elasticity. Then there's "snug," in which the easy surface elasticity is taken up. Then there's a range called "tight," in which all the elasticity is taken up. The force required to reach these three points is different for each size of nut and bolt, and different for lubricated bolts and for locknuts. The forces are different for steel and cast iron and brass and aluminum and plastics and ceramics. But a person with mechanic's feel knows when something's tight and stops. A person without it goes right on past and strips the threads or breaks the assembly.

A "mechanic's feel" implies not only an understanding for the elasticity of metal but for its softness. The insides of a motorcycle contain surfaces that are precise in some cases to as little as one ten-thousandth of an inch. If you drop them or get dirt on them or scratch them or bang them with a hammer they'll lose that precision. It's important to understand that the metal *behind* the surfaces can normally take great shock and stress but that the surfaces themselves cannot. When handling precision parts that are stuck or difficult to manipulate, a person with mechanic's feel will avoid damaging the surfaces and work with his tools on the nonprecision surfaces of the same part whenever possible. If he must work on the surfaces themselves, he'll always use softer surfaces to work them with. Brass hammers, plastic hammers, wood hammers, rubber hammers and lead hammers are all available for this work. Use them. Vise jaws can be fitted with plastic and copper and lead faces. Use these too. Handle precision parts gently. You'll never be sorry. If you have a tendency to bang things around, take more time and try to develop a little more respect for the accomplishment that a precision part represents.

QUESTIONS

1. Is Pirsig sufficiently specific?
2. What is the function of the first sentence in the third paragraph?

Sophistication   *R E A D*

Bergen Evans

Words are living, protean things. They grow, take roots, adapt to environmental changes like any plant or animal. Take *sophisticated*, for example. Originally it meant "wise." Then, through its association with the Sophists, it came to mean "over subtle," "marked by specious but fallacious reasoning," "able to make the worse appear the better reason."

While retaining this meaning, it acquired the additional, derivative sense of "adulterated." A tobacconist in Ben Jonson's "The Alchemist" is said to sell good tobacco: "he doesn't sophisticate it," they say, with other materials. Montaigne had the idea of adulteration in mind when he said that philosophy was nothing but "sophisticated poetry." And so did the eleventh edition of *The Encyclopaedia Britannica* when it said (1913) that ground rice was "one of the chief sophistications" of ginger powder.

From adulteration to corruption is a short step and the meaning of corruption ran side by side with that of adulteration. Coryat (1611) called dyed hair "sophisticated." Lear, going mad in the storm, starts to strip off his clothes because they are trappings of civilization and civilized man is "sophisticated." Judge Walter J. LaBuy of the Federal District Court in Chicago, in sentencing an enterprising young woman who was married to twelve sailors and drawing a dependent's allotment from each of them, told her, with stern disapproval, that she was "thoroughly sophisticated" (Chicago *Tribune*). Judge LaBuy may have been blending both meanings.

Up until about thirty years ago, the most common meaning conveyed by the word was of a particular kind of corruption, the corruption of idealism by worldly experience. And this is still given as its principal meaning in most dictionaries.

Then suddenly the attitude implicit in the word was reversed; it ceased to mean unpleasantly worldly-wise and came to mean admirably world-wise. Something — possibly depression-begotten cynicism, urbanization, army experience, the perfume ads, or the glamorous pornography of the picture magazines — had led the populace to revise its estimate of worldly wisdom. For the past fifteen years *sophistication* has been definitely a term of praise.

And even more. "Sophistication," writes Earl Wilson, "means the ability to do almost anything without feeling guilty." Blum's, the celebrated San Francisco candy manufacturers, on opening a branch store in New York, wooed their new clientele by advising them that their "old-fashioned, home-made-type candies" had been "sophisticated" by their master candy maker. Lloyd Shearer informs the readers of *Parade* that a famous movie actress' husband "seemed sophisticatedly impervious to jealousy," losing his wife "graciously, understandingly and philosophically . . . to another man." It is no wonder that — gog-eyed with awe and envy — a sophomore English class at New Trier High School, in Winnetka, Ill., defined sophistication as "a grace acquired with maturity."

The beginnings of this reversal can be seen in the words of Duke Ellington's "Sophisticated Lady" (1933). The lady of the title has "grown wise." Disillusion is "deep in her eyes." She is "nonchalant . . . smoking, drinking . . . dining with some man in a restaurant." She misses "the love of long ago" but, plainly, has no intention of returning to its meager ecstasies. She has lost innocence but has acquired polish, and when she dines some man picks up the tab. In the minds of many rustic maidens this — one gathers from the change in *sophisticated*'s meaning — was to be preferred to dewy freshness that dined alone at home on leftovers or carried lunch in a paper bag. And by 1958 in John O'Hara's *From the Terrace, sophistication* had come to signify not corruption but almost the irreducible minimum of good manners.

Not content with such audacious change, about three years ago *sophisticated* went hog wild and started to mean "delicately responsive to electronic stimuli," "highly complex mechanically," "requiring skilled control," "extraordinarily sensitive in receiving, interpreting and transmitting signals." Or at least that is what one must guess it means in such statements as "Modern radar is vastly more sophisticated than quaint, old-fashioned radar" (*Time*); later "the IL-18 is aeronautically more sophisticated than the giant TU-114." "Pioneer V is exceedingly sophisticated" (Chicago *Sun-Times*) and "The Antikythera mechanism is far more sophisticated than any described in classical scientific texts" (*Scientific American*).

The connections between these and any previously established meanings of the word are not clear, but since they are definitely favorable, they must spring some way from the post-Ellington uses. My own guess would be this: the sophisticated are not unperceiving, insensitive clods; on the contrary, they are particularly aware of nuances, act on the merest hints, are moved by suasion and respond to subtle stimuli. They don't have to be shoved. They know their way around and move with ease in their allotted orbits.

1. At the end of his fifth paragraph, Evans (writing in 1961) says "For the past fifteen years sophistication has been definitely a term of praise." Where did he find his evidence?
2. More than fifteen years later, is *sophistication* still a term of praise? What is your evidence? What words currently might be considered antonyms for *sophisticated?*

All the World's a Stage

Joan Daremo

"Role-playing" is often fairly loosely used to mean something like engaging in hypocrisy; it seems to suggest insincerity. But the word need not have a pejorative meaning, and indeed as sociologists use it the word does not connote dishonesty.

The meaning of "role," as sociologists use it, is close to its common theatrical meaning. In the theater a role is a part played by an actor; a role — say, Hamlet — exists independently of any performer. The lines, and to some degree the interpretation of the lines, are prescribed. An actor may omit some lines, or speak some of them in a new way, but he cannot say and do whatever he wishes; he must say and do pretty much what the role calls for. Similarly, outside of the theater there are established roles; that is, there are socially expected patterns of behavior: we are fathers or mothers, sons or daughters; we are students, teachers, policewomen, bank presidents, or waiters, and we behave in appropriate ways. When a student visits the college's financial aid officer he expects to find an informed, courteous, and at least moderately sympathetic person. The role exists, independent of any individual who happens to be performing it. Now, of course Mrs. Dunn, the financial aid officer at Bayside University, may be uninformed and aggressive; if so, she performs the role badly, and the student feels that something is wrong. The student rightly expects other behavior.

But does a role require total subjugation of the performer's personality? When one performs a role successfully, is one being false to one's self? Three points should be made. First, most roles allow for some degree of interpretation: the financial aid officer may or may not display a sense of humor, may or may not seem bookish, may or may not seem reserved or motherly. Second, mature people, after a while in their roles, probably merge their personalities with their roles. Though at first the financial aid officer may have to suppress her personality in an effort to adopt the manner of a financial aid officer, after a while on the job the chief requirements of the role become (as we say) second nature. For example, techniques for putting students at ease that were at first consciously employed are now performed easily and willingly — naturally. The performer, that is, has become committed to the role and senses no conflict between the self and the role. Third, and perhaps most important, even though the performer of a role may sometimes sense a discrepancy between the role and what she considers to be her true personality, it does not follow that performing a role makes for insincerity. If, for instance, the financial aid officer says to a colleague after a student has left the office, "I felt like telling him off," it does not follow that her real "I" is someone who tells people off. "Why didn't you do it?" the colleague might ask. "Because I'm not that sort of person" is a fair and natural reply. Our true self need not be identified with our undisciplined impulses; it may properly be identified with our behavior, and our behavior is at least in part established by our awareness of how we ought to behave in a given situation — how, in short, we ought to play our role.

QUESTION

Daremo's definition of role-playing is implicit in the entire essay, rather than stated in any single sentence. Drawing only on this essay, define *role-playing* in a sentence or two.

Socialization

Lewis Coser

Socialization may be defined as the process by which an individual is fitted into the social framework and induced to play his assigned roles. The major agency in the process of socialization is usually the family, which inculcates in the growing child the basic disciplines necessary for social living. The family, then, is the main link between child and society; it leads the child to internalize social norms by creating in it the desire to live up to the expectations of significant others. The attitudes of significant others — typically the parents — towards the child mark his primary self-image and self-conception and fashion his moral orientation. As the child grows up and his field of social vision and social contact widens, other adults such as teachers, as well as peers, become significant others to him. Finally the perceived appraisals of many particular others are organized into a pattern, thus forming a "generalized other" or internalized "conscience."

The internalized constraints that prompt men to live up to society's rules and so to acquire uniquely human attributes become part of the individual in the process of socialization. Society imposes on the biological organism a series of restricting injunctions; but it must be understood at the same time that human potentialities can be realized only in and through society so that a certain amount of repression is the very condition of human growth. Man is human only to the extent that he is socialized and can participate in the specifically human achievement which we call culture. Yet, lest we subscribe to an over-socialized view of man, we must bear in mind that certain conflicts between cultural requirements and biological drives are also the distinctive mark of the human animal.

While in relatively undifferentiated societies the family usually is the only major agency of socialization, in modern societies more specialized agencies such as schools, voluntary associations, and churches assume a considerable burden in the socialization process. Moreover, when persons are being inducted into more specialized roles, there exist specialized agencies of socialization preparing the neophyte for the specialized tasks he is about to undertake. To the extent that persons necessarily change some of their roles as they move through the life cycle it may be said that the process of socialization is never completed — from infancy to death men must continually learn new roles into which they must be socialized.

QUESTIONS

1. Coser's writing is highly abstract. Explain his definition of socialization to someone else. First summarize it in your own words (in a sentence or two), and then clarify it by writing a case history: To write a case history, first invent a character based on someone you know well, and describe his or her socialization. Use examples — specific events and details — and other characters in his or her environment to clarify each point Coser makes in his first paragraph.

2. In the second paragraph, Coser says "certain conflicts between cultural requirements and biological drives are also the distinctive mark of the human animal." Again, explain what Coser means by providing an example or two of such a conflict.
3. If you have read Robinson's essay on pages 59–71, compare what Coser says in the first sentence of his third paragraph with what Robinson says about how we acquire ideas.

A Perfectly Beautiful Laundress
Joseph Hudnut

When I was very young — five years old, as I remember it — I heard my mother say that she had engaged a *perfectly beautiful laundress*, and being by endowment curious of feminine charm I hid behind the kitchen sink to have my first look at beauty.

My first look and my first disenchantment. The face of my mother's laundress was as yellow-red as the soap which she exercised upon my jumpers and my stockings and her figure was, like that of her tub, round, stable, and very wide.

My mother had spoken in a metaphor, inaccessible to my understanding. She had used the word beauty to signify not an attribute of the laundress but a quality of workmanship for which the laundress, irrespective of her appearance, had become an embodiment. That which was called beautiful was neither the laundress nor the objects of her laundering but the performance to which these were machine and medium, a performance made express and visible in the comforting crisp cleanliness of linens, pajamas, towels, and pillowcases. The work done was well done; the task and the process were perfectly mastered; the end was attained completely and without excess; and my mother, perceiving this unity of intention, method, and product, cast over all of these the aureole of beauty.

In my mind the basket of my mother's laundress, thus filled with the magical effects of the art of laundering, stands as type and symbol of all that universe of beauty which is identified with skill in making and doing: the beauty entangled with our delight and surprise and wonder at man's ingenuity and invention and with the release which a fragment of perfection brings into our imperfect world.

QUESTIONS

1. Think of instances when you might use the word beautiful. In any of them are you describing a "quality of workmanship" or a "performance"? How would you make clear to someone else what you found beautiful about it? Would Hudnut's definition — "the task and the process were perfectly mastered; the end was attained completely and without excess" — be applicable?

2. The job Hudnut describes is essentially handwork. Can you think of a machine whose performance can be described as beautiful? If so, explain.

The Reach of Imagination
Jacob Bronowski

> Before me floats an image, man or shade,
> Shade more than man, more image than a shade.
> — W. B. YEATS, *BYZANTIUM* (1930)

For three thousand years, poets have been enchanted and moved and perplexed by the power of their own imagination. In a short and summary essay I can hope at most to lift one small corner of that mystery; and yet it is a critical corner. I shall ask, What goes on in the mind when we imagine? You will hear from me that one answer to this question is fairly specific: which is to say, that we can describe the working of the imagination. And when we describe it as I shall do, it becomes plain that imagination is a specifically *human* gift. To imagine is the characteristic act, not of the poet's mind, or the painter's, or the scientist's, but of the mind of man.

My stress here on the word "human" implies that there is a clear difference in this between the actions of men and those of other animals. Let me then start with a classical experiment with animals and children which Walter Hunter thought out in Chicago about 1910. That was the time when scientists were agog with the success of Ivan Pavlov in forming and changing the reflex actions of dogs, which Pavlov had first announced in 1903. Pavlov had been given a Nobel prize the next year, in 1904, although in fairness I should say that the award did not cite his work on the conditioned reflex, but on the digestive glands.

Hunter duly trained some dogs and other animals on Pavlov's lines. They were taught that when a light came on over one of three tunnels out of their cage, that tunnel would be open; they could escape down it, and were rewarded with food if they did. But once he had fixed that conditioned reflex, Hunter added to it a deeper idea: he gave the mechanical experiment a new dimension, literally — the dimension of time. Now he no longer let the dog go to the lighted tunnel at once; instead, he put out the light, and then kept the dog waiting a little while before he let him go. In this way Hunter timed how long an animal can remember where it has last seen the signal light to its escape route.

The results were and are staggering. A dog or a rat forgets which one of three tunnels has been lit up within a matter of seconds — in Hunter's experiment, ten seconds at most. If you want such an animal to do much better than this, you must make the task much simpler: you must face it with only two tunnels to choose from. Even so, the best that Hunter could do was to have a dog remember for five minutes which one of two tunnels had been lit up.

I am not quoting these times as if they were exact and universal: they surely are not. Hunter's experiment, more than fifty years old now, had many faults of detail. For example, there were too few animals, they were oddly picked, and they did not all behave consistently. It may be unfair to test a dog for what it *saw*, when it commonly follows its nose rather than its eyes. It may be unfair to test any animal in the unnatural setting of a laboratory cage. And there are higher animals, such as chimpanzees and other primates, which certainly have longer memories than the animals that Hunter tried.

Yet when all these provisos have been made (and met, by more modern experiments), the facts are still startling and characteristic. An animal cannot recall a signal from the past for even a short fraction of the time that a man can — for even a short fraction of the time that a child can. Hunter made comparable tests with six-year-old children, and found, of course, that they were incomparably better than the best of his animals. There is a striking and basic difference between a man's ability to imagine something that he saw or experienced, and an animal's failure.

Animals make up for this by other and extraordinary gifts. The salmon and the carrier pigeon can find their way home as we cannot; they have, as it were, a practical memory that man cannot match. But their actions always depend on some form of habit: on instinct or on learning, which reproduce by rote a train of known responses.

They do not depend, as human memory does, on the recollection of absent things.

Where is it that the animal falls short? We get a clue to the answer, I think, when Hunter tells us how the animals in his experiment tried to fix their recollection. They most often pointed themselves at the light before it went out, as some gundogs point rigidly at the game they scent — and get the name "pointer" from the posture. The animal makes ready to act by building the signal into its action. There is a primitive imagery in its stance, it seems to me; it is as if the animal were trying to fix the light in its mind by fixing it in its body. And indeed, how else can a dog mark and (as it were) name one of three tunnels, when it has no such words as "left" and "right" and no such numbers as "one," "two," "three"? The directed gesture of attention and readiness is perhaps the only symbolic device that the dog commands to hold on to the past, and thereby to guide itself into the future.

I used the verb "to imagine" a moment ago, and now I have some ground for giving it a meaning. "To imagine" means to make images and to move them about inside one's head in new arrangements. When you and I recall the past, we imagine it in this direct and homely sense. The tool that puts the human mind ahead of the animal is imagery. For us, memory does not demand the preoccupation that it demands in animals, and it lasts immensely longer, because we fix it in images or other substitute symbols. With the same symbolic vocabulary we spell out the future — not one but many futures, which we weigh one against another.

I am using the word "image" in a wide meaning, which does not restrict it to the mind's eye as a visual organ. An image in my usage is what Charles Peirce called a "sign," without regard for its sensory quality. Peirce distinguished between different forms of signs, but there is no reason to make his distinction here, for the imagination works equally with them all, and that is why I call them all images.

Indeed, the most important images for human beings are simply words, which are abstract symbols. Animals do not have words, in our sense: there is no specific center for language in the brain of any animal, as there is in the human brain. In this respect at least, we know that the human imagination depends on a configuration in the brain that has only evolved in the last one or two million years. In the same period, evolution has greatly enlarged the front lobes in the human brain, which govern the sense of the past and the future; and it is a fair guess that they are probably the seat of our other images.

(Part of the evidence for this guess is that damage to the front lobes in primates reduces them to the state of Hunter's animals.) If the guess turns out to be right, we shall know why man has come to look like a highbrow or an egghead: because otherwise there would not be room in his head for his imagination.

The images play out for us events which are not present to our senses, and thereby guard the past and create the future — a future that does not yet exist, and may never come to exist in that form. By contrast, the lack of symbolic ideas, or their rudimentary poverty, cuts off an animal from the past and the future alike, and imprisons it in the present. Of all the distinctions between man and animal, the characteristic gift which makes us human is the power to work with symbolic images: the gift of imagination.

This is really a remarkable finding. When Philip Sidney in 1580 defended poets (and all unconventional thinkers) from the Puritan charge that they were liars, he said that a maker must imagine things that are not. Halfway between Sidney and us, William Blake said, "What is now proved was once only imagin'd." About the same time, in 1796, Samuel Taylor Coleridge for the first time distinguished between the passive fancy and the active imagination, "the living Power and prime Agent of all human Perception." Now we see that they were right, and precisely right: the human gift is the gift of imagination — and that is not just a literary phrase.

Nor is it just a literary gift; it is, I repeat, characteristically human. Almost everything that we do that is worth doing is done in the first place in the mind's eye. The richness of human life is that we have many lives; we live the events that do not happen (and some that cannot) as vividly as those that do; and if thereby we die a thousand deaths, that is the price we pay for living a thousand lives. (A cat, of course, has only nine.) Literature is alive to us because we live its images, but so is any play of the mind — so is chess: the lines of play that we foresee and try in our heads and dismiss are as much a part of the game as the moves that we make. John Keats said that the unheard melodies are sweeter, and all chess players sadly recall that the combinations that they planned and which never came to be played were the best.

I make this point to remind you, insistently, that imagination is the manipulation of images in one's head; and that the rational manipulation belongs to that, as well as the literary and artistic manipulation. When a child begins to play games with things that stand for other things, with chairs or chessmen, he enters the gateway to reason and imagination together. For the human reason discovers new relations between things not by deduction, but by that unpredictable blend of speculation and insight that scientists call induction, which — like other forms of imagination — cannot be formalized. We see it at work when Walter Hunter inquires into a child's memory, as much as when Blake and Coleridge do. Only a restless and original mind would have asked Hunter's questions and could have conceived his experiments, in a science that was dominated by Pavlov's reflex arcs and was heading toward the behaviorism of John Watson.

Let me find a spectacular example for you from history. What is the most famous experiment that you had described to you as a child? I will hazard that it is the experiment that Galileo is said to have made in Sidney's age, in Pisa about 1590, by dropping two unequal balls from the Leaning Tower. There, we say, is a man in the modern mold, a man after our own hearts: he insisted on questioning the authority of Aristotle and St. Thomas Aquinas, and seeing with his own eyes whether (as they said) the heavy ball would reach the ground before the light one. Seeing is believing.

Yet seeing is also imagining. Galileo did challenge the authority of Aristotle, and he did look hard at his mechanics. But the eye that Galileo used was the mind's eye. He did not drop balls from the Leaning Tower of Pisa — and if he had, he would have got a very doubtful answer.[3] Instead, Galileo made an imaginary experiment (or, as the Germans say, "thought experiment") in his head, which I will describe as he did years later in the book he wrote after the Holy Office silenced him, the *Discorsi . . . intorno a due nuove scienze,* which was smuggled out to be printed in The Netherlands in 1638.

Suppose, said Galileo, that you drop two unequal balls from the tower at the same time. And suppose that Aristotle is right — suppose that the heavy ball falls faster, so that it steadily gains on the light ball and hits the ground first. Very well. Now imagine the same experiment done again, with only one difference: this time the two unequal balls are joined by a string between them. The heavy ball will again move ahead, but now the light ball holds it back and acts as a drag or brake. So the light ball will be speeded up and the heavy ball will be slowed down; they must reach the ground to-

---

[3] So Vincenzo Renieri wrote to Galileo from Pisa as late as 1641, reporting on a recent test between a cannonball and a musketball. Galileo had made one of the characters in the *Discorsi* say that this test works well enough "provided both are dropped from a height of 200 cubits." This is twice as high as the Leaning Tower's 185 feet (1 cubit = 60 cm) [Bronowski's note].

gether because they are tied together, but they cannot reach the ground as quickly as the heavy ball alone. Yet the string between them has turned the two balls into a single mass which is heavier than either ball — and surely (according to Aristotle) this mass should therefore move faster than either ball? Galileo's imaginary experiment has uncovered a contradiction; he says trenchantly, "You see how, from your assumption that a heavier body falls more rapidly than a lighter one, I infer that a (still) heavier body falls more slowly." There is only one way out of the contradiction: the heavy ball and the light ball must fall at the same rate, so that they go on falling at the same rate when they are tied together.

This argument is not conclusive, for nature might be more subtle (when the two balls are joined) than Galileo has allowed. And yet it is something more important: it is suggestive, it is stimulating, it opens a new view — in a word, it is imaginative. It cannot be settled without an actual experiment, because nothing that we imagine can become knowledge until we have translated it into, and backed it by, real experience. The test of imagination is experience. But then, that is as true of literature and the arts as it is of science. In science, the imaginary experiment is tested by confronting it with physical experience; and in literature, the imaginative conception is tested by confronting it with human experience. The superficial speculation in science is dismissed because it is found to falsify nature; and the shallow work of art is discarded because it is found to be untrue to our own nature. So when Ella Wheeler Wilcox died in 1919, more people were reading her verses than Shakespeare's; yet in a few years her work was dead. It had been buried by its poverty of emotion and its trivialness of thought: which is to say that it had been proved to be as false to the nature of man as, say, Jean Baptiste Lamarck and Trofim Lysenko were false to the nature of inheritance. The strength of the imagination, its enriching power and excitement, lies in its interplay with reality — physical and emotional.

I doubt if there is much to choose here between science and the arts: the imagination is not much more free, and not much less free, in one than in the other. All great scientists have used their imagination freely, and let it ride them to outrageous conclusions without crying "Halt!" Albert Einstein fiddled with imaginary experiments from boyhood, and was wonderfully ignorant of the facts that they were supposed to bear on. When he wrote the first of his beautiful papers on the random movement of atoms, he did not know that the Brownian motion which it predicted could be seen in any laboratory. He was sixteen when he invented the paradox that he resolved ten years later, in 1905, in the theory of relativity, and it bulked much larger in his mind than the experiment of Albert Michelson and Edward Morley which had upset every other physicist since 1881. All his life Einstein loved to make up teasing puzzles like Galileo's, about falling lifts and the detection of gravity; and they carry the nub of the problems of general relativity on which he was working.

Indeed, it could not be otherwise. The power that man has over nature and himself, and that a dog lacks, lies in his command of imaginary experience. He alone has the symbols which fix the past and play with the future, possible and impossible. In the Renaissance, the symbolism of memory was thought to be mystical, and devices that were invented as mnemonics (by Giordano Bruno, for example, and by Robert Fludd) were interpreted as magic signs. The symbol is the tool which gives man his power, and it is the same tool whether the symbols are images or words, mathematical signs or mesons. And the symbols have a reach and a roundness that goes beyond their literal and practical meaning. They are the rich concepts under which the mind gathers many particulars into one name, and many instances into one general induction. When a man says "left" and "right," he is outdistancing the dog not only in looking for a light; he is setting in train all the shifts of meaning, the overtones and the ambiguities, between "gauche" and "adroit" and "dexterous," between "sinister" and the sense of right. When a man counts "one, two, three," he is not only doing mathematics; he is on the path to the mysticism of numbers in Pythagoras and Vitruvius and Kepler, to the Trinity and the signs of the zodiac.

I have described imagination as the ability to make images and to move them about inside one's head in new arrangements. This is the faculty that is specifically human, and it is the common root from which science and literature both spring and grow and flourish together. For they do flourish (and languish) together; the great ages of science are the great ages of all the arts, because in them powerful minds have taken fire from one another, breathless and higgledy-piggledy, without asking too nicely whether they ought to tie their imagination to falling balls or a haunted island. Galileo and Shakespeare, who were born in the same year, grew into greatness in the same age; when Galileo was looking through his telescope at the moon, Shakespeare was writing *The Tempest*; and all Europe was in ferment, from Johannes Kepler to Peter Paul Rubens, and from the first table of logarithms by John Napier to the Authorized Version of the Bible.

Let me end with a last and spirited example of the common inspiration of literature and science, because it is as much alive today as it was three hundred years ago. What I have in mind is man's ageless fantasy, to fly to the moon. I do not display this to you as a high scientific enterprise; on the contrary, I think we have more important discoveries to make here on earth than wait for us, beckoning, at the horned surface of the moon. Yet I cannot belittle the fascination which that ice-blue journey has had for the imagination of men, long before it drew us to our television screens to watch the tumbling of astronauts. Plutarch and Lucian, Ariosto and Ben Jonson wrote about it, before the days of Jules Verne and H. G. Wells and science fiction. The seventeenth century was heady with new dreams and fables about voyages to the moon. Kepler wrote one full of deep scientific ideas, which (alas) simply got his mother accused of witchcraft. In England, Francis Godwin wrote a wild and splendid work, *The Man in the Moone*, and the astronomer John Wilkins wrote a wild and learned one, *The Discovery of a New World*. They did not draw a line between science and fancy; for example, they all tried to guess just where in the journey the earth's gravity would stop. Only Kepler understood that gravity has no boundary, and put a law to it — which happened to be the wrong law.[4]

All this was a few years before Isaac Newton was born, and it was all in his head that day in 1666 when he sat in his mother's garden, a young man of twenty-three, and thought about the reach of gravity. This was how he came to conceive his brilliant image, that the moon is like a ball which has been thrown so hard that it falls exactly as fast as the horizon, all the way round the earth. The image will do for any satellite, and Newton modestly calculated how long therefore an astronaut would take to fall round the earth once. He made it ninety minutes, and we have all seen now that he was right; but Newton had no way to check that. Instead he went on to calculate how long in that case the distant moon would take to round the earth, if indeed it behaved like a thrown ball that falls in the earth's gravity, and if gravity obeyed a law of inverse squares. He found that the answer would be twenty-eight days.

[4] Kepler may have got the idea of a universal gravity from the neoplatonic thought that all things in nature must attract one another because they are infused with a share of God's universal love. If this is so, then this farfetched path of the imagination runs back through Nicholas of Cusa to the fifth-century imposter who called himself Dionysius the Areopagite. See Pierre Duhem, *Le Système du Monde*, IV-58, p. 364 [Bronowski's note].

In that telling figure, the imagination that day chimed with nature, and made a harmony. We shall hear an echo of that harmony on the day when we land on the moon, because it will be not a technical but an imaginative triumph, that reaches back to the beginning of modern science and literature both. All great acts of imagination are like this, in the arts and in science, and convince us because they fill out reality with a deeper sense of rightness. We start with the simplest vocabulary of images, with "left" and "right" and "one, two, three," and before we know how it happened the words and the numbers have conspired to make a match with nature: we catch in them the pattern of mind and matter as one.

QUESTIONS

1. Why does Bronowski, early in his essay, spend a page describing Hunter's experiment with dogs?
2. What are some of the devices that Bronowski uses in order to explain to us his concept of imagination?
3. What does Bronowski mean, in his final paragraph, when he says that landing on the moon is "not a technical but an imaginative triumph"?
4. Do the final three paragraphs merely clarify Bronowski's earlier definition or do they also add to the definition?
5. In a paragraph define *imagination* in accordance with Bronowski's essay.

6

Exposition

In our discussion of analytic writing (page 30), we said that most of the essays a student reads and writes are chiefly analytic; that is, by separating something into its parts the essayist draws conclusions and explains those conclusions.

But most writing can also be classified as exposition, persuasion (or argument), description, or narration. This does not mean, of course, that any given essay must belong exclusively to one of these four kinds of writing. More often than not a single essay combines at least two. For example, an expository essay on Zen Buddhism — an essay chiefly concerned with explaining what Zen is — may include a description of a Zen monastery, a narrative of the writer's visit to the monastery, and an argument (that is, a reasoned statement) for the relevance of Zen to us. If the essay is primarily exposition, the descriptive and narrative and argumentative parts will chiefly function to enliven and clarify the explanation of Zen. Similarly, an essay that is primarily an argument for the relevance of Zen to American life may have to sketch the tenets of the creed (exposition) and may tell an anecdote or recount the history of Zen (narration) in order to strengthen the argument.

For the sake of clarity, however, we will talk about relatively pure examples of these four kinds of writing as we take them up one by one in this and the next three chapters. To talk about them all at once would require the skill of Stephen Leacock's knight, who leaped on his horse and rode madly off in all directions.

In a college catalog, the information telling students how to apply or how to register or how to complete the requirements for a degree is exposition (from the Latin *exponere,* "to put forth"), a setting forth of information. It doesn't assume a disagreement, so it doesn't seek to persuade. Note, also, that those paragraphs in the catalog describing the lovely campus are not exposition but description — or, more exactly, description and persuasion combined, because they seek to persuade the reader to come to the campus. Exposition, too, may be permeated by persuasion, because writing that explains something usually at the same time seeks to persuade us that the topic is worth our attention. But exposition in its purest form seeks only to explain — to expose, we might say — what's what.

Here is a short piece, primarily expository. If typed, double-spaced, it would probably be a little more than one page.

In Search of the Elusive Pingo

Canadian scientists are preparing an expedition to the Beaufort Sea to study underwater ice formations that are blocking use of the Northwest Passage as a long-sought commercial route. The formations, called pingoes, are cones of antediluvian ice, coated with frozen muck, that stick up like fingers from the bottom of the sea to within 45 feet of the surface. They could rip the bottom of ships, such as supertankers, that ride deep in the water.

The pingoes are an obstacle to exploitation of oil resources and expansion of trade in the Arctic region that were expected to follow the successful pioneer voyage of the *S.S. Manhattan* through the ice-clogged Northwest Passage five years ago. One tanker ripped open could disrupt the ecological balance of much of the region.

The existence of the pingoes was not known until 1970 when scientists aboard the Canadian scientific ship *Hudson,* using special sonar equipment to plot the shape of the Beaufort Sea's basin, detected batches of them that the *Manhattan* was lucky to miss. Since then, oceanographers have charted about 200 pingoes, and there is no telling how many more there are.

Scientists at the United States Geological Survey and the Bedford Institute of Oceanography in Nova Scotia, where the *Hudson*'s expedition originated, have been exploring the origin of the pingoes and seeking in vain ways to neutralize them. Dynamiting has proved ineffective. So scientists from Bedford are going back this summer for another look.

You may not want to learn much more about pingoes, but we hope you found this brief account clear and interesting. You might ask yourself how the writer sustains your interest:

1. Is the title attractive?
2. What expression in the first paragraph is especially effective? Why?
3. Are the paragraphs given in a reasonable order?
4. Is the final paragraph a satisfactory ending?

By asking such questions and then answering them, you will discover some of the principles of good expository writing.

Exposition need not, of course, deal only with the remote or the impersonal. The following essay is chiefly an explanation of what makes a book good for reading aloud during the otherwise silent meals in an Anglican monastery. Notice how full of information it is. The first paragraph defines a good book and gives a detailed description of a specific example. In succeeding paragraphs, the writer, a monk of Saint Gregory's Abbey, continues to give specific titles of books, again with brief but detailed descriptions of many of them. He provides, too, some relevant facts about life in a monastery. Notice also that despite the abundant information in this short piece, the reader is not overwhelmed by the material. For one thing, the writer has organized it clearly. And throughout his exposition of the facts, his voice — lively, amusing, often shrewd — persuades us that his topic, though we have probably never given it a thought before, is interesting.

Everybody Hated Seagull
Jude Bell

===

The meals of the monks should not be without reading. — St. Benedict

The monks are currently listening to William Manchester's *The Glory and the Dream* during lunch and supper. The book is a good one for reading in the refectory. It is long enough, 1,300 pages, to give a feeling of continuity to our days and weeks; it is non-fiction, the sole explicit requirement for meal-time reading (although I can remember two times when the rule has been broken in the last three or four years); it is timely, being a history of the United States from 1932 to 1972; and it is easy to read and easy to listen to.

There are some meals when there is no reading — breakfasts, and lunch and supper on Sundays and important holy days. At Sunday lunch the monks listen to recorded music, most often chamber works, from the common room record players; supper on Sundays and holidays is an informal buffet in the common room. Great feasts are celebrated with a talking dinner in the refectory. Even so, during 10 or 12 short periods, the reader for the week can get through about 50 pages before someone else is "blessed in" on Sunday to take his place.

The present book is the longest we have read since I have been at the Abbey. The runner-up must be Antonia Fraser's *Mary Queen of Scots.* It lasted from early spring through summer, as I remember, and it remains one of my own favorite refectory books. Some of the brethren were wearied by its wealth of detail, however; and some passages, such as an account of what drawing and quartering involves, were not entirely suitable for meal-time reading. The only comparably unsuitable passage I can remember was one from Peter Matthiessen's *The Tree Where Man Was Born,* a book about Africa, describing the feeding habits of vultures. Some of the medical details in James Herriot's books, *All Things Bright and Beautiful* and *All Creatures Great and Small,* caused discomfort to the squeamish, but the light humor and easy style of the English veterinarian's memoirs made the books general favorites.

The exceptions that I remember to the rule banning fiction from the reading desk were Truman Capote's "A Christmas Memory," which we had as a holiday treat one year — it lasted only two or three days and was generally enjoyed — and *Jonathan Livingston Seagull,* a book which everyone cordially hated, and the reading of which established the rule against fiction more firmly.

We do read serious works sometimes. A recent success was William Johnston's *Silent Music,* a book on meditation, which circulated widely among the monks and guests after it had been read in the refectory. I liked Sister Penelope's *The Coming,* and checked it out of the library to read some passages which I had not fully caught. (There are frequently things that one misses because one is serving tables, washing dishes, or has to answer the telephone; but it is not very often that one bothers to look up what one missed.) Fr. Capon's books read well aloud; Bernard Haring's do not. Articles from monastic and other religious periodicals vary widely in their suitability for oral reading.

One of the first books I can remember hearing read at the Abbey, during a visit many years ago, was Rachel Carson's *At the Edge of the Sea*. Since I have been here to stay, we have had a few more books by naturalists, but Carson is hard to equal. Fr. Abbot remembers Loren Eiseley's books as among the most enjoyable ever read in the refectory; Br. Wilfrid would rank *The Last Wilderness* by Murray Morgan as his own all-time favorite. But the nature books that we have heard during the past three or four years have had a mixed reaction. One nature book, in a diary format, was actually abandoned about one-third of the way through by popular demand, an unusual unanimous rejection.

Br. Gabriel says that *Black Elk Speaks* is the book that he has liked most. Br. Andrew remembers vividly *The Hiding Place* by Corrie ten Boom, a story of adventures in the Dutch underground during World War II. Br. William liked Henry Miller's *Colossus of Maroussi* best of all. Fr. Anthony says *The Spirit of St. Louis* is the perfect refectory book. Br. Bernard is partial to history and remembers Archbishop Carrington's two-volume *The Early Christian Church* as being particularly good. Br. James prefers religious books, and wishes that we would have more of them. Fr. Leo takes a functional view of meal-time reading, saying that its main benefit to a religious community is keeping people from dawdling over their food so that the dish-washers and table-clearers can get to their work on schedule.

In introducing "Everybody Hated *Seagull*," we described it as clearly organized. *How* is it organized? (One way to answer the question is to reread it quickly, jotting down the topic idea of each paragraph.) We also characterized the writer's voice. In what passages are you most aware of the writer's voice? What do you make of the title? (It may interest you to know that *Jonathan Livingston Seagull*, by Richard Bach, was on best-seller lists for eighteen months in 1972–73 and sold 2,370,000 copies in hardcover alone. If you have read the book, or if you look at the brief reviews of it in *Book Review Digest* for 1972, you'll understand the particular irony in the book's having been cordially hated by all of the monks.)

EXPLAINING A PROCESS

Exposition is often used to explain how something works, or how to do something. The following brief example comes from a popular book by a physician.

How to Deal with the Crying
Leonard Cammer

If you are a soft, sentimental person you probably cannot stand to see your sick relative cry. It breaks you up. However, where tears serve as a necessary emotional outlet they can be encouraged. In a grief reaction especially, when the person has suffered a loss, crying comes easily and produces a healthy release for pent-up emotion. Momentarily, the tears wash away the depressed feelings.

However, when an exhausting bout of tearfulness continues on and on with extreme agitation, breast beating, and self-abuse, it is time for you to call a halt. Let me show you how to terminate almost any flood of tears by the correct use of a psychologic device.

First, sit directly in front of your relative and say, "Go on crying if you want to, but face me. Look into my eyes." It is a simple fact that no one can sustain crying while gazing straight into another's eyes. If the person does what you ask, his tears will stop. Not right away; he may continue to cry and avert his gaze. Take his hands in yours and again coax him to look at you. You may have to repeat the request several times, but at last he will turn and fix his eyes on you, almost hypnotically. The flow of tears then trickles to an end, and the person may begin to talk about the things that give him mental pain.

Every time you shorten such a spell of crying you stem the waste of energy and give the person a chance to preserve his or her stamina in fighting the depression.

Notice that in addition to describing a process, the essay begins by explaining the value of crying and ends by explaining the value of bringing crying to an end. Would the essay be equally good if the first paragraph came last? Notice, too, that although the essay is fairly impersonal, we do get some sense of a human being behind the words. Try, in a sentence or two, to characterize the author. (For more conspicuously personal expository essays, see the pieces by Pirsig, pages 124–25, and Kraemer, pages 153–55.) Cammer is explaining a process, not offering an argument, yet (like every other writer) he must somehow persuade his readers that he knows what he is talking about. How does he persuade us?

Here is another essay, this one a little longer, on a process.

How to Grow an Avocado

To grow an avocado tree indoors, begin with a ripe Florida avocado. (The varieties grown in California, Puerto Rico, and the West Indies can be used, but for some reason they often do not flourish.) The fruit is ripe if the stemmed end yields to the pressure of your thumb. Remove the pit and place it in warm water for about three hours (during the interval you may eat the fruit) and then gently rub off any remaining traces of the fruit and also as much of the paper-thin brown coating as comes easily off the pit. Dry the pit and set it aside for a moment.

Fill a glass almost to the top with warm water. (Remember, the avocado is a tropical tree; cold water harms it.) Next, notice where the base of the pit is (an avocado has a relatively flat base and a relatively tapered top) and insert four toothpicks to half of their length about one-third the way up from the base. If you look down on the avocado from the top, toothpicks are sticking out at what on a clock would be 12:00, 3:00, 6:00, and 9:00. Next, place the avocado in the glass; the base will be in about half an inch of water, but the toothpicks will prevent the pit — or seed, for that is what it is — from sinking to the bottom of the glass. Put the glass in a warm dark place, such as a kitchen closet.

A root may appear at the base within a week, but it is quite usual for nothing to happen for several weeks. Be patient; unless the water turns cloudy, which is a sign that the seed has rotted and must be tossed out, sooner or later the seed will germinate. During this waiting period, all you can do is keep the water at the proper level. (Reminder: make sure the added water is warm.) In time the root will appear at the base and some time later a pale green shoot will appear at the top. Possibly several shoots will appear, but one will establish itself as the main shoot; ignore the others, which may or may not survive. When the main shoot or stem is about eight inches tall, with a scissors cut off the top four inches so that the top growth will not outstrip the root development. Failure to cut the stem will result in a spindly plant with few leaves. By cutting, you force the stem to send out a new shoot which will grow slowly but which will hold its leaves longer.

When the glass is fairly full of roots (this may be about two weeks after cutting the stem, or as many as six weeks after you prepared the pit), it is time to take it out of the dark and to pot the plant. Use a clay pot about eight and a half inches in diameter. Cover the drainage hole with some pieces of broken pot, and fill the pot to about two-thirds of its height with a mixture of equal parts of good garden soil and sand, mixed with a teaspoon of bonemeal or a couple of tablespoons of dried manure for fertilizer. Remove the toothpicks from the seed, place it on the soil, and then add more of the mixture, until the seed is covered to half of its height. Pour the glass of water over the seed, and then pour an additional glassful of warm water over it. The soil will probably settle; if so, add enough soil to cover the lower half of the seed. Under the pot put a saucer with warm water, and place the saucer and pot in the sunniest place you have.

Water the plant with warm water when the soil appears dry, probably once a day, and be patient. When you cut the main stem you interrupted the plant's growth, and weeks may pass before another stem grows out of the first. But if you water it and give it light, and add plant food about once a month, you are doing all that you can. The main stem — really the trunk of a tree — will in time produce branches that will produce leaves. When leaves develop, you need do nothing except insert a dowel in the pot and loosely tie up any sagging branches. In time you may wish to prune at the top, in order to encourage the lower branches, so that your tree will be bushy rather than spindly. With luck, the tree will flourish; when it is about six feet tall, transplant it to a larger clay pot simply by smashing with a hammer the first pot and then by placing the tree with its ball of roots and earth in a pot prepared just as the first one was. Aside from daily watering (but don't fret if you sometimes miss a day) and occasional fertilizing and pruning, you need do nothing to your tree but enjoy it. But do not spoil your enjoyment by hoping for flowers or fruit; they will never appear.

A good expository essay tries to anticipate any questions the reader might have (how? who? what? why? when? where?). Reread the essay on growing an avocado and notice how the writer answers questions almost before the reader forms them. For example, in the first paragraph, the writer does not simply assert that a Florida avocado should be used; he answers our question, "why?" (we will have a greater chance for success).

ORGANIZING AN EXPOSITORY ESSAY

The organization of the preceding essay is simple but adequate: because it describes a *process* (from the Latin *pro* = "forward" and *cessus* = "movement, step") the essay begins at the beginning and takes the reader through a sequence of steps. This chronological organization is almost inevitable in describing a process, although it is possible to vary the beginning — you needn't begin with step one of the process. The commonest variation uses the opening paragraph to set forth the goal (here, it might be a description of a flourishing avocado, or a gently persuasive paragraph on the pleasures of growing things) — but the process itself would still be described chronologically.

Other patterns of organization common in expository essays are

1. movement from cause to effect, or from effect to cause (see, for example, Chuck Kraemer's "Indecent Exposure," pages 153–55)
2. comparison (see pages 38–44)
3. classification into subgroups (see pages 29–37)

WRITING SUMMARIES

Another common form of exposition is the summary, a compressed version of a piece of writing. It gives the gist of the original, stripped of details, examples, dialogue, or extensive quotations. A summary is usually said to be about one-fourth the length of the original. The rule is arbitrary, but useful; anything longer can probably be further condensed. But there are times when a shorter summary suits your purpose. In writing a letter to the editor, you may summarize the view you're opposing in a sentence or two; in reviewing a book, you may summarize its contents in one or two paragraphs.

In summaries of about one-fourth the length of the original, one usually follows the organization of the original. Sometimes, though, a reorganization allows for greater condensation or clarity. If, for example, the writer begins with an anecdote, or a setting forth of the evidence, and only states the essay's thesis in its conclusion, it may be economical to reverse the order: first a summary of the thesis, then a summary of the evidence. Summaries may also use the key terms and expressions of the original. But, since it should be clear from your work that you are summarizing someone else's, there is little need for quotation marks or such expressions as "she says," "she then goes on to prove," and so forth. Transitions, though, are still useful. Remember that a summary of someone else's writing is a sample of your own writing; it should be clear and coherent. Remember, too, that it's customary in writing summaries of literary works to use the present tense, though that rule too can be altered to suit your purpose.

The following example is a student's summary of Chuck Kraemer's "Indecent Exposure," an essay you'll find at the end of this chapter.

> Chuck Kraemer believes that sunbathing is "demented." Exposure to the sun's rays is harmful to the body: a day in the sun will upset the molecular structure of the skin's layers, destroy skin cells, and wound tissues; long-term exposure may promote skin cancer, wrinkling, spotting, freckling, yellowing, and coarsening of the skin. Today, suntans are believed to be a sign of health and social status, but this belief is only a "long-running fad." Before the nineteenth century, a pallid complexion was the sign of wealth and leisure; bronzed arms and faces belonged to the inferior working class.
>
> For those who insist on sunbathing, summer issues of almost any women's magazine offer instructions on tanning without burning; the best burn-preventing sun lotions are those that contain

para-aminobenzoic acid. Those who enjoy the outdoors, but are not concerned with skin color, should stay in the shade.

After you have read "Indecent Exposure," reread this summary of it. Did the student who wrote it follow Kraemer's organization? If not, what departures do you find? Are they justified? Did she present the key points of the original? Did she omit any material you feel ought to be included? Was her summary well written? These are the chief questions to keep in mind when you write summaries, either as parts of longer essays, or as exercises in reading and writing.

In most of your writing, a summary will appear as part of a longer essay in which your purpose might be to analyze an argument, or to compare two interpretations of a text or a problem, or to persuade. But in studying composition, in learning how to improve your own writing, practice in writing summaries alone is useful because it requires of you a more thorough understanding of someone else's writing than you would have had from merely reading it. In organizing a summary you are studying not only what the passage says but how the writer thinks. If his organization is clear, you learn by imitating it; if unclear, you learn by improving it. In condensing the material you get practice in the precise use of key terms, and of course, in writing concisely.

Finally, though a summary of someone else's thoughts must be faithful to those thoughts and will probably imitate or reflect the style of the original, a summary may also have a style of its own. Notice how in the newspaper article, "It's the Portly Penguin That Gets the Girl" (pages 155–57), chiefly a summary of a lecture, the journalist's own style and the lecturer's happily coexist.

EXERCISES

(Reminder: A good expository essay anticipates questions a reader may have about *how, who, what, why, when,* and *where.*)

1. In 300–500 words explain a process, for example, how to do one of the following: perform a card trick; tell a joke; apply to college; refinish a table; develop a photograph. (A reminder: as

pages 146–47 imply, readable expository essays not only let the reader understand something; they also let the reader hear a human voice. If you choose a topic you are strongly interested in, you will probably find that an interesting voice will emerge.)

2. Reread the essay on pingoes (pages 142–43), and then write an expository essay of similar length (about 250 words) on something that is likely to be unfamiliar to your classmates. Examples: a little-known group of musicians; a little-known kind of cooking; a natural phenomenon you have closely observed.

3. Choose a current editorial and summarize it in about one-fourth its number of words. Include a copy of the editorial with your summary.

4. Using the outline of "Columbo Knows the Butler Didn't Do It" (pages 80–81) and the essay itself (pages 54–56), write a summary of the essay, in about 250 words.

5. Attend a lecture in your community on a topic that interests you. Go prepared to take notes and, if possible, meet the speaker. Then write a two to three page summary of the lecture, including some of your sense of the speaker and perhaps of the occasion.

6. Write an expository essay objectively setting forth someone else's views on a topic or limited range of topics. Suggested length: 500 words. Your source for these views should be a published interview. If possible, submit a copy of the interview with your essay. Suggested sources: Dick Cavett and Christopher Porterfield, *Cavett* (New York: Harcourt Brace Jovanovich, 1974); *Rolling Stone Interviews* (New York: Paperback Library, 1971); Charles Thomas Samuels, *Encountering Directors* (New York: G. P. Putnam's Sons, 1972); *Writers at Work: The Paris Review Interviews,* ed. Malcolm Cowley (New York: Viking Press, 1958–1968); and the *Paris Review,* a quarterly publication, which usually includes an interview with an author. If you found Philip Roth's essay (pages 7–8) interesting, you may want to summarize an interview with Roth. He prints several of them in his *Reading Myself and Others* (New York: Farrar, Straus & Giroux, 1975).

EXPOSITION AT WORK

Indecent Exposure

Chuck Kraemer

I spotted my first one of the season on a warm day in mid-March, beside the Charles River near No. Harvard St., lying on his back with his shirt off, arms spread, palms up, chin high, letting the UV photons in the 3500–4000 angstrom range severely agitate the molecular structure of his keratin layer.

Actually, he was just sunbathing, but it was, biologically, a strange, masochistic bath indeed. Ultraviolet radiation was attacking his epidermis, sending its molecules into reactive states, producing dangerous reaction products. Deeper down, the dark pigment called melanin was being manufactured as a shield against the attack, but the process was slow, and if my sun worshipper was as unwary as most on this, his first exposure of the season, he probably killed off a few billion skin cells within fifteen minutes — long before his biological defenses could muster. It was truly a bloodbath — the blood being rushed through swollen vessels to the surface of the skin to begin repairing wounded tissue, producing the lobster-red color we call a sunburn.

The harmful effects of his worship were not as transient or superficial as this supplicant probably assumed, especially if he paid regular spring-through-September homage. The adverse vascular effects of a moderately severe burn may last for a year or more. Skin cancer is a distinct possibility. Twenty-three percent of all cancers in men and 13 percent in women are cancers of the skin, and of all those, 90 percent are sun-related. Most are cured, but often only by surgery.

Perhaps no less dire to the average narcissistic sunbather, the cosmetic toll can be very high. Prolonged exposure to the sun can cause long-lasting and permanent yellowing, wrinkling, spotting, freckling, and coarsening of the skin, such as that seen on the necks of sailors, farmers, and cowboys. It usually takes years, but it can start very early. Loss of skin elasticity has been found in solarphiles as young as 20 years — a condition interestingly omitted from the luscious body of the 20-year-old model in those Coppertone ads.

If only these war wounds were incurred for a just cause, maybe it would all make sense. But as far as I can see, sun worship is just plain demented — stranger than even its sister, star worship (astrology), which is bizarre enough but has no adverse physical effects, as far as I know. Getting a tan is, literally, self-abuse. As dermatologist John Knox of Baylor has said, "A suntan is a response to an injury." For anybody with an adequate diet, direct sunshine is medically useless at best, dangerous at worst.

Of course we justify our masochism on cosmetic grounds. Bronze is beautiful. Strident advertising by the suntan lotion companies, airlines, and Florida real estate outfits assures us of that, and fervently, by the peeling beachfuls, we believe. (One ad for a Bahamas vacation implores, "Get out of the kitchen and bake.")

But history shows that the tan body as a sign of health and status is only a rather long-running fad, rooted in ignorance and elitism. Before the nineteenth century a *pallid* complexion was considered fashionable and wholesome. The working classes toiled mostly outdoors, where they acquired the dark skins that marked them as socially inferior. The rich sensibly avoided the sun, preferring an iced tea in the shade, or a stroll in the filtered aura of an expensive parasol. Hence the poetic necks and bosoms "as white as alabaster," and upon them the consequently prominent blue veins — giving rise to the term "blue bloods."

Then came the Industrial Revolution, reversing the code of snobbery. Workers now spent their daylight hours in factories in coal-smoke-polluted cities, so sun became fashionable for those who could afford it. Sunshine was even seriously prescribed as a panacea for tuberculosis — a quaint over-reaction to the plague of tuberculosis and rickets among the vitamin-D-deficient working classes.

Today, the summer tan is less a status symbol than an imagined necessity. (The status-conscious must now graduate to the *year-round* tan, which implies sufficient wealth to vacation in the South Seas.) There may not be a mass leisure class yet, but the masses manage to cram plenty of leisure into their summer outings at the Cape or Nantucket or Nahant, where they bask 10,000 per acre for hours on end, sizzling away like Cornish hens in a pit at the Kiwanis Memorial Day barbecue.

I have no sympathy for these folks, but I am obliged — this being a practical column — to advise them how to protect themselves from the sun, even as they so indecently expose themselves to it. Truth to tell, my secret desire is that if they're all going to abuse themselves this way they should fry to a crisp and get washed out to sea like bits of burned bacon, but I'll set prejudice aside for the moment and grudgingly offer the following three tips:

(1). For the specific instructions on the absurdly complicated art of getting a tan without getting burned, see the May, June, or July issue of almost any women's magazine, where "Good Sense in the Sun" articles are a regular seasonal item. These are usually written by the in-house doc or a consulting dermatologist, and appear to be authoritative.

(2). For the dullards among us who enjoy the outdoors and don't want to burn, but don't give a squint about skin color either, the solution is simple: stay in the shade.

(3). The magazine pieces often go into greater detail on this, but, very briefly, the best sun lotions for preventing burns are those containing para-aminobenzoic acid, or PABA. Check the label — any product claiming to prevent sunburn must list the key ingredient.

See you at the beach. I'll be the one in long sleeves and work boots.

QUESTIONS

1. How is this essay organized?
2. Kraemer might have begun his essay thus: "I saw my first sunbather of the season. . . ." What does he gain by beginning the way he does? How does the technical language in the first paragraph contribute to the effect?
3. Drawing on the entire essay, in two or three sentences characterize the writer.

It's the Portly Penguin That Gets the Girl, French Biologist Claims

Anne Hebald Mandelbaum

The penguin is a feathered and flippered bird who looks as if he's on his way to a formal banquet. With his stiff, kneeless strut and natural dinner jacket, he moves like Charlie Chaplin in his heyday dressed like Cary Grant in his.

But beneath the surface of his tuxedo is a gallant bird indeed. Not only does he fast for 65 days at a time, sleep standing up, and forsake all others in a lifetime of monogamy, but the male penguin also guards, watches over, and even hatches the egg.

We owe much of our current knowledge of the life and loves of the king and emperor penguins to — *bien sûr* — a Frenchman. Twenty-eight-year-old Yvon Le Maho is a biophysiologist from Lyons who visited the University last week to discuss his discoveries and to praise the penguin. He had just returned from 14 months in Antarctica, where he went to measure, to photograph, to weigh, to take blood and urine samples of, to perform autopsies on — in short, to study the penguin.

Although his original intent had been to investigate the penguin's long fasts, Monsieur Le Maho was soon fascinated by the amatory aspect of the penguin. Copulating in April, the female produces the egg in May and then heads out to sea, leaving her mate behind to incubate the egg. The males huddle together, standing upright and protecting the 500-gram (or 1.1-pound) egg with their feet for 65 days. During this time, they neither eat nor stray: each steadfastly stands guard over his egg, protecting it from the temperatures which dip as low as −40 degrees and from the winds which whip the Antarctic wilds with gusts of 200 miles an hour.

For 65 days and 65 nights, the males patiently huddle over the eggs, never lying down, never letting up. Then, every year on July 14th — Bastille Day, the national holiday of France — the eggs hatch and thousands of penguin chicks are born, M. Le Maho told his amused and enthusiastic audience at the Biological Laboratories.

The very day the chicks are born — or, at the latest, the following day — the female penguins return to land from their two-and-a-half month fishing expedition. They clamber out of the water and toboggan along the snow-covered beaches toward the rookery and their mates. At this moment, the males begin to emit the penguin equivalent of wild, welcoming cheers — *"comme le cri de trompette,"* M. Le Maho later told the *Gazette* in an interview — "like the clarion call of the trumpet."

And, amid the clamorous thundering of 12,000 penguins, the female recognizes the individual cry of her mate. When she does, she begins to cry to him. The male then recognizes *her* song, lifts the newborn chick into his feathered arms, and makes a beeline for the female. Each singing, each crying, the males and females rush toward each other, slipping and sliding on the ice as they go, guided all the while by the single voice each instinctively knows.

The excitement soon wears thin for the male, however, who hasn't had a bite to eat in more than two months. He has done his duty and done it unflaggingly, but even penguins cannot live by duty alone. He must have food, and quickly.

Having presented his mate with their newborn, the male abruptly departs, heading out to sea in search of fish. The female, who has just returned from her sea-going sabbatical, has swallowed vast quantities of fish for herself and her chick. Much of what she has eaten she has not digested. Instead, this undigested food becomes penguin baby food. She regurgitates it, all soft and paplike, from her storage throat right into her chick's mouth. The chicks feed in this manner until December, when they first learn to find food on their own.

The penguins' reproductive life begins at age five, and the birds live about 25 years. Their fasting interests M. Le Maho because of its close similarities with fasting in human beings. And although many migratory birds also fast, their small size and indeed their flight make it almost impossible to study them closely. With the less-mobile and non-flying penguin, however, the scientist has a relatively accessible population to study. With no damage to the health of the penguin, M. Le Maho told the *Gazette,* a physiobiologist can extract blood from the flipper and sample the urine.

"All fasting problems are the same between man and the penguin," M. Le Maho said, "The penguin uses glucose in the brain, experiences ketosis as does man, and accomplishes gluconeogenesis, too." Ketosis is the build-up of partially burned fatty acids in the blood, usually as a result of starvation; gluconeogenesis is the making of sugar from non-sugar chemicals, such as amino acids. "The penguin can tell us a great deal about how our own bodies react to fasting conditions," M. Le Maho said.

He will return to Antarctica, M. Le Maho said, with the French government-sponsored *Expéditions Polaires Françaises* next December. There he will study the growth of the penguin chick, both inside the egg and after birth; will continue to study their mating, and to examine the penguin's blood sugar during fasting.

During the question-and-answer period following his talk, M. Le Maho was asked what the female penguin looks for in a mate. Responding, M. Le Maho drew himself up to his full five-foot-nine and said, *"La grandeur."*

QUESTIONS

1. Outline the essay, and then describe the organization.
2. Pick out three or four sentences that strike you as especially interesting, not just because they contain odd facts but because of the ways the sentences are written.

Can People Be Judged by Their Appearance?

Eric Berne

Everyone knows that a human being, like a chicken, comes from an egg. At a very early stage, the human embryo forms a three-layered tube, the inside layer of which grows into the stomach and lungs, the middle layer into bones, muscles, joints, and blood vessels, and the outside layer into the skin and nervous system.

Usually these three grow about equally, so that the average human being is a fair mixture of brains, muscles, and inward organs. In some eggs, however, one layer grows more than the others, and when the angels have finished putting the child together, he may have more gut than brain, or more brain than muscle. When this happens, the individual's activities will often be mostly with the overgrown layer.

We can thus say that while the average human being is a mixture, some people are mainly "digestion-minded," some "muscle-minded," and some "brain-minded," and correspondingly digestion-bodied, muscle-bodied, or brain-bodied. The digestion-bodied people look thick; the muscle-bodied people look wide; and the brain-bodied people look long. This does not mean the taller a man is the brainier he will be. It means that if a man, even a short man, looks long rather than wide or thick, he will often be more concerned about what goes on in his mind than about what he does or what he eats; but the key factor is slenderness and not height. On the other hand, a man who gives the impression of being thick rather than long or wide will usually be more interested in a good steak than in a good idea or a good long walk.

Medical men use Greek words to describe these types of body-build. For the man whose body shape mostly depends on the inside layer of the egg, they use the word *endomorph*. If it depends mostly upon the middle layer, they call him a *mesomorph*. If it depends upon the outside layer, they call him an *ectomorph*. We can see the same roots in our English words "enter," "medium," and "exit," which might just as easily have been spelled "ender," "mesium," and "ectit."

Since the inside skin of the human egg, or endoderm, forms the inner organs of the belly, the viscera, the endomorph is usually belly-minded; since the middle skin forms the body tissues, or soma, the mesomorph is usually muscle-minded; and since the outside skin forms the brain, or cerebrum, the ectomorph is usually brain-minded. Translating this into Greek, we have the viscerotonic endomorph, the somatotonic mesomorph, and the cerebrotonic ectomorph.

Words are beautiful things to a cerebrotonic, but a viscerotonic knows you cannot eat a menu no matter what language it is printed in, and a somatotonic knows you cannot increase your chest expansion by reading a dictionary. So it is advisable to leave these words and see what kinds of people they actually apply to, remembering again that most individuals are fairly equal mixtures and that what we have to say concerns only the extremes. Up to the present, these types have been thoroughly studied only in the male sex.

Viscerotonic endomorph. If a man is definitely a thick type rather than a broad or long type, he is likely to be round and soft, with a big chest but a bigger belly. He would rather eat than breathe comfortably. He is likely to have a wide face, short, thick neck, big thighs and upper arms, and small hands and feet. He has overdeveloped breasts and looks as though he were blown up a little like a balloon. His skin is soft and smooth, and when he gets bald, as he does usually quite early, he loses the hair in the middle of his head first.

The short, jolly, thickset, red-faced politician with a cigar in his mouth, who always looks as though he were about to have a stroke, is the best example of this type. The reason he often makes a good politician is that he likes people, banquets, baths, and sleep; he is easygoing, soothing, and his feelings are easy to understand.

His abdomen is big because he has lots of intestines. He likes to take in things. He likes to take in food, and affection and approval as well. Going to a banquet with people who like him is his idea of a fine time. It is important for a psychiatrist to understand the natures of such men when they come to him for advice.

Somatotonic mesomorph. If a man is definitely a broad type rather than a thick or long type, he is likely to be rugged and have lots of muscle. He is apt to have big forearms and legs, and his chest and belly are well formed and firm, with the chest bigger than the belly. He would rather breathe than eat. He has a bony head, big shoulders, and a square jaw. His skin is thick, coarse, and elastic, and tans easily. If he gets bald, it usually starts on the front of the head.

Dick Tracy, Li'l Abner, and other men of action belong to this type. Such people make good lifeguards and construction workers.

They like to put out energy. They have lots of muscles and they like to use them. They go in for adventure, exercise, fighting, and getting the upper hand. They are bold and unrestrained, and love to master the people and things around them. If the psychiatrist knows the things which give such people satisfaction, he is able to understand why they may be unhappy in certain situations.

Cerebrotonic ectomorph. The man who is definitely a long type is likely to have thin bones and muscles. His shoulders are apt to sag and he has a flat belly with a dropped stomach, and long, weak legs. His neck and fingers are long, and his face is shaped like a long egg. His skin is thin, dry, and pale, and he rarely gets bald. He looks like an absent-minded professor and often is one.

Though such people are jumpy, they like to keep their energy and don't fancy moving around much. They would rather sit quietly by themselves and keep out of difficulties. Trouble upsets them, and they run away from it. Their friends don't understand them very well. They move jerkily and feel jerkily. The psychiatrist who understands how easily they become anxious is often able to help them get along better in the sociable and aggressive world of endomorphs and mesomorphs.

In the special cases where people definitely belong to one type or another, then, one can tell a good deal about their personalities from their appearance. When the human mind is engaged in one of its struggles with itself or with the world outside, the individual's way of handling the struggle will be partly determined by his type. If he is a viscerotonic he will often want to go to a party where he can eat and drink and be in good company at a time when he might be better off attending to business; the somatotonic will want to go out and do something about it, master the situation, even if what he does is foolish and not properly figured out, while the cerebrotonic will go off by himself and think it over, when perhaps he would be better off doing something about it or seeking good company to try to forget it.

Since these personality characteristics depend on the growth of the layers of the little egg from which the person developed, they are very difficult to change. Nevertheless, it is important for the individual to know about these types, so that he can have at least an inkling of what to expect from those around him, and can make allowances for the different kinds of human nature, and so that he can become aware of and learn to control his own natural tendencies, which may sometimes guide him into making the same mistakes over and over again in handling his difficulties.

QUESTIONS

1. If you found this essay interesting, jot down a few reasons why. If you did not find it interesting, jot down a few reasons and go on to indicate how it might have been improved.
2. Jot down some traits that you guess the late Dr. Berne may have had, judging from the voice you hear in this essay. On the basis of your list, does he seem to fit into any of his three categories?
3. For each of Berne's three categories write the name of a famous person who seems to fit. Then describe all three and explain how they fit, devoting a paragraph to each.

Imagination in Orbit

Isaac Asimov

Science-fiction, as who would have suspected twenty years ago, when I started writing it, is becoming a household word. The atom bomb started it on the road to prominence and the coming of Sputnik put science-fiction into orbit along with itself. Now, with the space age upon us, you find it in movies and on television, in novels (both hard cover and soft), in the slicks and semi-slicks and, of course, in the pulp magazines where it got its start — *Fantasy and Science Fiction, Analog Science Fact and Fiction, Galaxy, Amazing,* and so on. And it is these last-named magazines that are still the training ground and recruitment center of new writers in the field.

Has it occurred to you to try to enter this broadened and peculiarly modern field? Would you like to hoist a rocket and climb the mountains of the Moon by way of your typewriter? I guarantee you a fun and freedom you'll find in no other branch of popular literature.

But do you know anything about science-fiction to begin with? (And let us make an agreement to call it s-f henceforward.) If your only knowledge has been derived from Jules Verne and H. G. Wells, you are hopelessly behind the times. If it is derived from the comic strips or, worse still, from Hollywood, you are wretchedly deceived. If you have no other source of information, we must start at the beginning, and where can one begin best but at a definition.

True s-f is not to be confused with weird stories or horror

stories or tales of the supernatural. It is not the sheer catalog of destruction, designed in Hollywood to appease the rebellious appetites of the teen-ager and to display the tricks and special effects of the camera. The best definition of s-f that I know of is, indeed, almost sociological in its gravity. It goes as follows: *Science-fiction is that branch of literature which is concerned with the impact of scientific and technological advance upon human beings.*

The most important implication of the definition is that s-f deals first and foremost with human beings. This is a point never to be forgotten. It is true, it is possible to write good s-f about a worm-like creature on Mars or about a mechanical man of metal and electricity. Human beings, as such, need not figure in the story in any way. Nevertheless, the story is successful only insofar as the non-human protagonist possesses traits which are recognizably human to the reader. The human body, in other words, may be missing, but the human soul must always be present.

The second implication of the definition is that the humanity with which the story concerns itself is subjected to an alien environment, but one, please note, which could conceivably result from scientific advance. The environment must be alien but not impossible. Neither elves nor anti-gravity exist, and neither may ever exist, but anti-gravity is at least conceivable within the framework of science as we know it, while elves are not.

There is, of course, no set rule as to the degree by which the environment of the story must differ from that of real life. In many cases, the difference is only an apparent one, not to be taken seriously. Science-fiction stories by the thousands have been written which differ from Westerns only by the fact that the prairies become the Martian deserts, the trusty six-shooter becomes a disintegrator gun, and the faithful cayuse a battered spaceship. S-f of that sort is confined largely to the comic strips and to some of the less advanced pulp magazines. They serve a purpose in that they introduce younger readers to the field by easy stages. Good s-f is, of course, much more than such Westerns-with-a-difference.

Now the best way, and, perhaps, the only way, to get into the real spirit of s-f is to look for no further capsule outlines but to tackle the field itself. Fortunately, it will not be necessary for you to limit yourself to the rate at which new issues of s-f magazines appear. Since World War II, about a hundred s-f anthologies have been published. These contain a good portion of the best the field has to offer and a number of them can be found in any public library. The beginner should read as many of these anthologies as he can obtain before setting finger to typewriter.

It may occur to you as you read your way through these anthologies that a scientific background is required to write good s-f. If you think so, you are right! However, the scientific background necessary can be acquired in other ways than studying for an advanced degree, so relax.

Consider that few mystery writers are real detectives and that even fewer western story writers are real cowboys. They may never even have seen a gun or a horse, respectively. What they must know, however, is the lingo of their field; enough of the specialized tricks of the trade to carry conviction to the reader. The same is true of s-f.

Remember this, therefore: *the jargon of the s-f story is science.* It is not a made-up language, but a real one. The average s-f writer talks easily and plainly of light-years and parsecs. He knows the names of the planets and their satellites, their relative sizes and distances from the sun. He has an idea of the distances between stars; the speed of light; the nature of an extra-galactic nebula. He knows the new lore of blast-off, orbits, space-stations and moon-probes. He knows what is mechanically possible in space-travel and what is not. For instance, can a spaceship go two hundred thousand miles a second? Once in outer space, can it shut off its motors and coast to a halt? The answer is that it can do neither. The first statement violates Einstein's theory of relativity, and the second violates Newton's first law of motion.

But all this does not mean, necessarily, a college education and advanced degrees, I repeat. The knowledge required is, after all, at a rather superficial level. Many science-fiction writers, to be sure, have degrees up to, and including, the Ph.D., but others, equally able, stopped after high school. Actually, you will probably learn a great part of what you must know of science merely by reading science-fiction itself. You can pick up what else you must know by reading some of the many books of popularized science that flood the presses. George Gamow, Fred Hoyle and other scientists who write for the layman can teach you more than many college courses can. And you can keep up with modern scientific advances by reading some of the periodicals devoted to explaining science to the general public, notably *Scientific American* and *Science Digest*.

Actually, what you will need even more than a knowledge of science is a really galloping imagination. By imagination, I don't mean merely the ability to dream up plot complications but one which will tell you what characters in the future will wear (what replaces buttons and zippers?), what language they will speak, what family life would be like, exactly how their buildings are built, or, for that matter, what kind of a social system worm-like creatures on

Mars would have. (If you can find some of the novels of Robert A. Heinlein, read them in this connection. He is the perfect example of how a future or alien culture can be completely visualized.)

Granted that you have such an imagination (and you either have it or you don't — it is not something that can be taught), that you have read science-fiction, that you know sufficient science, what next? What about writing a story? What's the formula? . . . Well, there is none that I know of; not for good s-f. That's the beauty and fascination of the field. Nowhere else is the unorthodox and the unexpected demanded of you quite so much.

And yet . . . there are some things you can avoid, and I present them not as unalterable laws but as rule-of-thumb experience. Let me list a few that spring to mind:

1. *Don't waste your time waiting for a completely original idea.* As a corollary, don't be foolish enough to think that any idea you have is completely original. I have heard innumerable ideas from kind-hearted friends who are convinced that I must be forever at a loss for my next story. I have never heard one that hadn't been done innumerable times. They say that H. G. Wells anticipated all the basic plots in science-fiction and I believe it.

Instead, strive for fresh treatments that will make even the most moth-eaten ideas palatable. The invading monsters from Mars, for instance, are just about deadwood as a story base; yet suppose they were harmless and lovable missionaries come to Earth to persuade us to abandon violence and avoid atomic destruction. What would happen to them? My guess is that they would be shot down in cold blood before they as much as began to put their message across. Do you have a different idea as to what might happen? Good. It may make a story.

2. *Don't make your story an essay.* It is tempting for a beginner, fascinated by his own idea, to ignore the story itself for the sake of having one of his characters talk interminable pseudo-science. This is not only bad s-f, but bad writing. By stopping the action, you bore the reader, who is only interested in science as it affects the story, and *no more.* Ideally, the necessary scientific background should be brought to the reader's attention gradually, through normal conversation on the part of the characters, who must be pictured as understanding their own culture. It sounds fishy indeed to have one character explain the ordinary facets of the society of the time to another for the benefit of the reader. Would you explain to your neighbor that to drive a car you must put gasoline in the gas tank?

As a corollary, avoid trying to reproduce in too detailed a

fashion the atmosphere of research science, unless you are a scientist in your own right and know what the atmosphere consists of. You can get away with the barest suggestions of it and be thoroughly convincing. Try to go further and you will frequently become ridiculous. Unfortunately, you see, the laymen's notion of research is rather distorted. Chemical laboratories of any value are far too complicated and expensive these days to be found in private basements. And it is only in patent medicine advertisements that chemists make discoveries by gazing earnestly at test tubes.

3. *Don't be unfair to your reader.* You have a tremendous latitude in s-f. There are virtually no bars to your imagination. How tempting it must be then to get your hero out of a fix by suddenly bringing forth a piece of background you have hitherto kept hidden. Yet you mustn't! For instance, if your hero is being pursued by Martian monsters, you can't have him suddenly remember that carbon dioxide is virulently poisonous to them so that all he need do is breathe in their faces. Any such little trick must be well prepared for in advance. This is among the very elements of good writing, and s-f, however alien and outré, is bound by the laws of good writing just as firmly as is the most prosaic essay. In fact, to avoid the *deus ex machina,* it is wise to accept the general rule, that the alien quality of an s-f environment must always be at the minimum required to support the story and make it plausible, and that all pertinent facets of the alien culture be made clear to the reader as early as possible in the story.

4. *Don't be inconsistent.* This is perhaps the most difficult task of all. It is easy enough to envisage a world in which space-travel by means of anti-gravity motors is common. But in such a world, office elevators would also be run by anti-gravity, or should, unless you have a plausible reason for the contrary. Styles of architecture would change since weaker materials could be used for building. Airplanes with many trailers might replace freight trains.

This does not mean that you must mention all these subsidiary consequences of your major premise. You can ignore them if they play no part in your story. In fact, it is just to avoid these inconsistencies that it is wise to keep the alien qualities of the environment at the bare minimum as stated in the previous rule. Where subsidiary consequences do play an unavoidable role, however, you should make every effort to keep them consistent.

5. *Don't contradict a known scientific fact.* The experienced s-f writer can do so, often, by advancing plausible reasons therefor, but that takes a certain sophistication in the field. For the beginner

there is enough latitude in the unknown. Don't crowd the known. For instance, you can imagine life similar to that of Earth to be existing on the moon — but not on its visible surface. The surface of the moon is known to be airless and waterless and hence incapable of supporting our kind of life. You can have life on the surface of the other side of the moon, if you can think of some plausible reason for air existing in that hemisphere; but now that Lunik III has photographed some of the hidden side, you must not contradict anything revealed in its photographs.

This may surprise you. In writing an s-f story, it may seem to you that a fact or two amiss should be overlooked. You should be informed, therefore, that a very vocal minority of s-f readers look for these scientific errors and write letters to editors about them.

6. *Avoid clichés*. In its short history, s-f has developed quite a few tiresome chestnuts and if your story contains any of them, only the most heroic efforts in the way of writing can make them salable to an s-f market. Forget your mad scientists, especially if they have beautiful daughters. (In any case, since Sputnik, it would be impolitic to suggest that scientists are anything but admirable.) Avoid heroes who single-handedly conquer hordes and hordes of alien monsters. Abandon thought of other-world horrors lusting after beautiful Earth-women (remember that to a hippopotamus, only another hippopotamus is lustworthy). Eschew robots who turn on their creators or the severely moralistic treatment of the dangers of science.

7. *Don't have your story too topical*. It may seem to you simply perfect to have your story take place on Cape Canaveral, with generals, countdowns and Russian spies. The trouble is that the newspapers and general magazines are full of the reality and the reader is saturated with it. If you're going to assault the reader with such chewed-out material, you'll have to be exceptionally good. Why not step a bit farther out into the realm of imagination and avoid the competition of the headlines?

Now, one last word. None of these little hints is law. With experience, you will be able, eventually, to break every one of these rules.

QUESTIONS

1. What criticism does Asimov make of Hollywood s-f? How might you argue that this criticism is, or is not, justified? In your argument would you accept his definition of s-f (paragraphs 4,

5, 6), or would you want to modify that definition? What examples of s-f films would you use in your argument?

2. Assuming that you are not planning a career as an s-f writer (and also assuming that you enjoyed reading "Imagination in Orbit"), explain why you found the essay interesting. What are Asimov's strengths as a writer of expository prose?

7

Persuasion

To persuade is to win over, or to convince. These two are not the same thing; if we win people over by, say, an appeal to their emotions, we have not convinced them, only conquered them. To convince them we must persuade them by presenting evidence and reasonable arguments for our opinions. But first we must present ourselves as writers worth reading.

In any kind of persuasive writing, whether it is emotional or logical or both, you must gain and then keep the audience's confidence. Unfortunately, confidence is easily lost: for instance, a reader is not likely to trust (and therefore not likely to accept the argument of) a writer who spells the word "arguement." The writer's arguments may be sound, but the reader — reluctant to change his views in any case, and certainly unwilling to ally himself with someone who can't even spell — seizes on this irrelevant error and smugly puts the essay aside, confident that he has nothing to learn. Convey your competence and your respect for your reader by getting the right word, defining crucial terms, and providing interesting examples. No writing can persuade if it is imprecise and dull.

PRESENTING EVIDENCE

A good essay not only presents a thesis but also supports it with evidence, just as a paragraph supports with evidence its topic sentence or idea. The evidence may be a series of reasons or, especially in essays on literature, of facts, details, examples, references to the text. The critic William Gass, for example, in a paragraph about William Faulkner, offers two generalizations in the first sentence — the second generalization being the reason ("because") for the first. The rest of the paragraph then offers supporting details.

> Nothing was too mean for his imagination because he did not believe there was any insignificance on earth. A dirt road was worthy of the most elevated consciousness. An old woman or an old mule: he found in them the forms and forces of History itself. To build a house, found a family, lay rails across a state: these were acts an Alexander might have engaged in. The Civil War was War, high water along the river was The Flood, the death of a dog was Sorrow. He managed to give even the mute heart speech, and invest a humble, private, oft-times red-necked life with those epic rhythms and rich sounds which were formerly the hired pomp and commissioned music of emperors and kings.

The details that follow Gass's first sentence are, in effect, pieces of evidence offered to help the reader to accept Gass's point of view.

WIT

One also shows respect for one's reader first by assuming the reader's intelligence and then by challenging it. Let's look briefly at the first pages of Thoreau's *Walden,* to see how wit (especially intelligent use of understatement, overstatement, metaphor, and allusion) can challenge the reader while still engaging the reader's sympathies.

> When I wrote the following pages, or rather the bulk of them, I lived alone, in the woods, a mile from any neighbor, in a house which I had built myself, on the shore of Walden Pond, in Concord, Massachusetts, and earned my living by the labor of my hands only. I lived there two years and two months. At present I am a sojourner in civilized life again.
> I should not obtrude my affairs so much on the notice of my readers if very particular inquiries had not been made by my townsmen concerning my mode of life, which some would call

impertinent, though they do not appear to me at all impertinent, but, considering the circumstances, very natural and pertinent. Some have asked what I got to eat; if I did not feel lonesome; if I was not afraid; and the like. Others have been curious to learn what portion of my income I devoted to charitable purposes; and some, who have large families, how many poor children I maintained. I will therefore ask those of my readers who feel no particular interest in me to pardon me if I undertake to answer some of these questions in this book. In most books, the *I,* or first person, is omitted; in this it will be retained; that, in respect to egotism, is the main difference. We commonly do not remember that it is, after all, always the first person that is speaking. I should not talk so much about myself if there were anybody else whom I knew as well. Unfortunately, I am confined to this theme by the narrowness of my experience. Moreover, I, on my side, require of every writer, first or last, a simple and sincere account of his own life, and not merely what he has heard of other men's lives; some such account as he would send to his kindred from a distant land; for if he has lived sincerely, it must have been in a distant land to me. Perhaps these pages are more particularly addressed to poor students. As for the rest of my readers, they will accept such portions as apply to them. I trust that none will stretch the seams in putting on the coat, for it may do good service to him whom it fits.

I would fain say something, not so much concerning the Chinese and Sandwich Islanders as you who read these pages, who are said to live in New England; something about your condition, especially your outward condition or circumstances in this world, in this town, what it is, whether it is necessary that it be as bad as it is, whether it cannot be improved as well as not. I have traveled a good deal in Concord; and everywhere, in shops, and offices, and fields, the inhabitants have appeared to me to be doing penance in a thousand remarkable ways. What I have heard of Bramins sitting exposed to four fires and looking in the face of the sun; or hanging suspended, with their heads downward, over flames; or looking at the heavens over their shoulders "until it becomes impossible for them to resume their natural position, while from the twist of the neck nothing but liquids can pass into the stomach"; or dwelling, chained for life, at the foot of a tree; or measuring with their bodies, like caterpillars, the breadth of vast empires; or standing on one leg on the tops of pillars — even these forms of conscious penance are hardly more incredible and astonishing than the scenes which I daily witness. The twelve labors of Hercules were trifling in comparison with those which my neighbors have undertaken; for they were only twelve, and had an end; but I could never see that these men slew or captured any monster or finished any labor. They have no friend Iolaus to burn with a hot iron the root of the hydra's head, but as soon as one head is crushed, two spring up.

I see young men, my townsmen, whose misfortune it is to have inherited farms, houses, barns, cattle, and farming tools; for these are more easily acquired than got rid of. Better if they had been born in the open pasture and suckled by a wolf, that they might have seen with clearer eyes what field they were called to labor in. Who made them serfs of the soil? Why should they eat their sixty acres, when man is condemned to eat only his peck of dirt? Why should they begin digging their graves as soon as they are born? They have got to live a man's life, pushing all these things before them, and get on as well as they can. How many a poor immortal soul have I met well nigh crushed and smothered under its load, creeping down the road of life, pushing before it a barn seventy-five feet by forty, its Augean stables never cleansed, and one hundred acres of land, tillage, mowing, pasture, and wood-lot! The portionless, who struggle with no such unnecessary inherited encumbrances, find it labor enough to subdue and cultivate a few cubic feet of flesh.

Now try to answer these questions.

1. In the first paragraph, how does Thoreau gain our respect?
2. In the middle of the second paragraph, Thoreau says "I should not talk so much about myself if there were anybody else whom I knew as well. Unfortunately, I am confined to this theme by the narrowness of my experience." If "unfortunately" were changed to "but," what would be lost? What would be lost if the last sentence of this paragraph were omitted?
3. Why doesn't Thoreau omit the first two paragraphs and simply begin with the first sentence of the third? And in the third paragraph, why does he refer to Bramins and to the twelve labors of Hercules, instead of simply talking about the people he sees in New England?
4. In the fourth paragraph, what is gained by adding, within commas that serve as parentheses, "my townsmen"? What does Thoreau mean when he says some men "eat their sixty acres," and what does he mean when he says "man is condemned to eat only his peck of dirt"? Explain his statement that some men on the road of life push a barn and one hundred acres of land. In fact, why does he at this point not speak merely of a man but of an "immortal soul . . . pushing before it a barn seventy-five feet by forty"? Why the statistics?

Your answers to some of these questions will help you to see how persuasive wit can be. Thoreau offers scarcely anything that in the strict sense can be called an argument, yet attracted by his shrewdness we feel compelled to share his opinions.

Finally, then, almost every sentence in every piece of good writing in one way or another persuades, either by offering evidence or by keeping the reader's sympathy and attention so that the reader will stay with the writer until the end. The whole of this book, even the comments on spelling and punctuation, seeks to help you to write so that your readers are persuaded it is worth their time to listen to you.

AVOIDING SARCASM

Because a writer must, among other things, persuade readers that he is humane, sarcasm has little place in persuasive writing. Although desk dictionaries usually define sarcasm as "bitter, caustic irony" or "a kind of satiric wit," if you think of a sarcastic comment that you have heard you will probably agree that "a crude, sneering remark" is a better definition. Lacking the ingenuity or wit of good satire and the wryness or carefully controlled mockery of irony, sarcasm usually relies on gross overstatement and intends simply to humiliate. *Sarcasm* is derived from a Greek word meaning "to tear flesh" or "to bite the lips in rage," altogether an unattractive business. Sarcasm is unfair, for it dismisses an opponent's arguments with ridicule rather than with reason; it is also unwise, for it turns the reader against you. Readers hesitate to ally themselves with a writer who apparently enjoys humiliating the opposition. A sarcastic remark can turn the hearers against the speaker and arouse sympathy for the victim. In short, sarcasm usually doesn't work.

ARGUMENT

The special kind of persuasive writing that relies chiefly on reasoning, rather than on wit or appeals to the emotions (though it may include both) is usually called *argument*. An argument here is not a wrangle but a reasoned analysis. What separates argument from exposition is this: whereas both consist of statements, in argument some statements are offered as *reasons* for other statements. Another way of characterizing the difference is to say that exposition assumes there is no substantial disagreement between informed persons, and argument assumes there is or may be substantial disagreement. To overcome this disagreement, the writer tries to offer reasons that convince by their logic. Let's briefly examine the reasoning process by considering some obvious errors in reasoning; in logic they are called *fallacies* (from a Latin verb meaning "to deceive"). As Tweedledee says in *Through the Looking-Glass,* "if it were so, it would be; but as it isn't, it ain't. That's logic." You cannot persuade readers unless they think you are reliable; if your argument includes fallacies, thoughtful readers will not take you seriously.

Avoiding Fallacies

1. *False authority.* Don't try to borrow the prestige of authorities who are not authorities on the topic in question — for example, a heart surgeon speaking on politics. You will only discredit yourself if you think that a surgeon's opinions on redistricting or a politician's opinions on whaling have any special weight. Similarly, some former authorities are no longer authorities, because the problems have changed or because later knowledge has superseded their views. Adam Smith, Jefferson, and Einstein remain men of genius, but an attempt to use their opinions when you are examining modern issues — even in their fields — may be questioned. In short, before you rely on an authority, ask yourself if the person in question *is* an authority on the topic. And don't let stereotypes influence your idea of who is an authority. Don't assume that every black is an authority on ghetto life; many have never been in a ghetto. Remember the Yiddish proverb: "A goat has a beard, but that doesn't make him a rabbi."

2. *False quotation.* If you do quote from an authority, don't misquote. One can argue that the Bible itself says "commit adultery" — the words do occur in it — but of course the quotation is taken out of context — the Bible says "Thou shalt not commit adultery." Few writers would misquote so outrageously, but it is easy to slip into taking from an authority the passages that suit us

and neglecting the rest. For example, you may find someone who grants that "there are strong arguments in favor of abolishing the death penalty"; but if he goes on to argue that, on balance, the arguments in favor of retaining it seem stronger to him, it is dishonest to quote his words so as to imply that he favors abolishing it.

3. *Suppression of evidence.* Don't neglect evidence that is contrary to your own argument. To neglect evidence is unfair — and disastrous. You will be found out and your argument will be dismissed, even if it has some merit. You owe it to yourself and your reader to present all the relevant evidence. Be especially careful not to assume that every question is simply a matter of *either/or.* There may be some truth on both sides. Take the following thesis: "Grades encourage unwholesome competition, and should therefore be abolished." Even if the statement about the evil effect of grading is true, it may not be the whole truth, and therefore it may not follow that grades should be abolished. One might point out that grades do other things too: they may stimulate learning, and they may assist students by telling them how far they have progressed. One might nevertheless conclude, on balance, that the fault outweighs the benefits, but one can scarcely hope to be taken seriously if one does not recognize all the facts, or all the supposed facts. Concede to the opposition what is due it, and then outscore the opposition. Any failure to confront the opposing evidence will be noticed; your readers will keep wondering how you can be so foolish as not to see this or that, and soon they will dismiss your argument. Moreover, if you confront the opposition you will almost surely strengthen your own argument. As Edmund Burke said two hundred years ago, "He that wrestles with us strengthens our nerves, and sharpens our skill. Our antagonist is our helper."

4. *Generalization from insufficient evidence.* The process of generalizing (inferring a general principle from particular facts) is called *induction;* we study particular cases and then form a generalization. But the accuracy of the generalization may vary with the size and representativeness of the sampled particulars. If, for example, my first two meals in Tucson are delicious, I may find myself talking about the excellent food there, and I may even slip into saying that all of the restaurants in Tucson serve great food — but if I do say such things I am offering a generalization based on in-

sufficient evidence. This is a gross example, to be sure, but the error can be insidious. Take, for instance, an assertion about student opinion on intercollegiate athletics, based on a careful survey of the opinions of students living in the fraternity houses and dormitories. Such a survey leaves out those students who commute, a group that may be different (economically, religiously, and socially) from the surveyed group. Because the surveyed sample is not fully representative of student opinion, the generalizations drawn from the data may be false. The generalizations may, of course, happen to be true; they may indeed correspond to the views of the commuting students also. But that would be only a lucky accident. In short, when you offer a generalization based on induction, stand back, take another look at your evidence, and decide whether the generalization can be presented as a fact; maybe it's only a probability — or maybe only an opinion.

5. *The genetic fallacy.* Don't assume that something can necessarily be explained in terms of its birth or origin. "He wrote the novel to make money, so it can't be any good" is palpable nonsense. The value of the novel need not depend on the initial pressure that motivated the author. If you think the novel is bad, you'll have to offer better evidence. Another example: "Capital punishment arose in days when men sought revenge, so now it ought to be abolished." Again an unconvincing argument: capital punishment may have some current value; for example, it may serve as a deterrent to crime. But that's another argument, and it needs evidence if it is to be believed. Be on guard, too, against the thoughtless tendency to judge people by their origins: Mr. X has a foreign accent, so he is probably untrustworthy or stupid or industrious.

6. *Begging the question* and *circular reasoning.* Don't assume the truth of the point that you should prove. The term "begging the question" is a trifle odd. It means, in effect, "You, like a beggar, are asking me to grant you something at the outset." Examples: "The barbaric death penalty should be abolished" (you should prove, not assert, that it is barbaric); "This senseless language requirement should be dropped," or "The foreign language requirement, a valuable thing, should be retained" (both of these opposed views assume what they should prove).

Circular reasoning is usually an extended form of begging the question. What ought to be proved is covertly assumed. Example:

"T. S. Eliot is the best twentieth-century poet, because the best critics say so." Who are the best critics? Those who recognize Eliot's supremacy. Circular reasoning, then, normally includes intermediate steps absent from begging the question, but the two fallacies are so closely related that they can be considered one. Another example: "I feel sympathy for him because I identify with him." Despite the "because," no reason is really offered. What follows "because" is merely a restatement, in slightly different words, of what precedes; the shift of words, from "feel sympathy" to "identify with" has misled the writer into thinking he is giving a reason. Other examples: "Students are interested in courses when the subject matter and the method of presentation are interesting"; "There cannot be peace in the Middle East because the Jews and the Arabs will always fight." In each case, an assertion that ought to be proved is reasserted as a reason in support of the assertion.

7. *Post hoc ergo propter hoc.* Latin: "after this, therefore because of this." Don't assume that because X precedes Y, X must cause Y. Example: "He went to college and came back a pothead; college corrupted him." He might have taken up pot even if he had not gone to college. (The error, like the generalizations from insufficient evidence discussed on pages 174–75, is an error in induction.) Another example: "Since they abolished capital punishment, the crime rate in X has increased." But the implication that the crime rate has increased *because* capital punishment was abolished is not proved; it may have increased for other reasons. One more example: "The riots of the sixties were caused by the permissive childrearing of the forties and fifties." Maybe, but you'll have to demonstrate a causal connection.

8. *Argumentum ad hominem.* Here the argument is directed "toward the man," rather than toward the issue. Don't shift from your topic to your opponent. A speaker argues against legalizing abortions and his opponent, instead of facing the merits of the argument, attacks the character or the associations of the opponent: "You're a Catholic, aren't you?"

9. *Argument from analogy.* Don't confuse an analogy with proof. An analogy is an extended comparison between two things; it can be useful in exposition, for it explains the unfamiliar by means of the familiar: "A government is like a ship, and just as a ship has a captain and a crew, so a government has . . ."; "Writing

an essay is like building a house; just as an architect must begin with a plan, so the writer must. . . ." Such comparisons can be useful, helping to clarify what otherwise might be obscure, but their usefulness goes only so far. Everything is what it is, and not another thing. A government is not a ship, and what is true of a captain's power need not be true of a president's power; and a writer is not an architect. Some of what is true about ships may be (roughly) true of governments, and some of what is true about architects may be (again, roughly) true of writers, but there are differences too. Consider the following analogy between a lighthouse and the death penalty:

> The death penalty is a warning, just like a lighthouse throwing its beams out to sea. We hear about shipwrecks, but we do not hear about the ships the lighthouse guides safely on their way. We do not have proof of the number of ships it saves, but we do not tear the lighthouse down.
>
> — J. Edgar Hoover

How convincing is it as an argument, that is, as a reason for retaining the death penalty?

10. *False assumption.* Consider the Scot who argued that Shakespeare must have been a Scot. Asked for his evidence, he replied, "The ability of the man warrants the assumption." Or take such a statement as "She goes to Yale, so she must be rich." Possibly the statement is based on faulty induction (the writer knows four Yale students, and all four are rich) but more likely he is just passing on a cliché. The Yale student in question may be on a scholarship, may be struggling to earn the money, or may be backed by parents of modest means who for eighteen years have saved money for her college education. Other examples: "I haven't heard him complain about French 10, so he must be satisfied"; "She's a writer, so she must be well read." A little thought will show how weak such assertions are; they *may* be true, but they may not.

The errors we have discussed are common, and are unforgivable if they are consciously used. You have a point to make, and you should make it fairly. If it can only be made unfairly, you do an injustice not only to your reader but to yourself; you should try to change your view of the topic. Alas, as George Santayana said,

"Nothing requires a rarer intellectual heroism than willingness to see one's equation written out." Difficult, yes; still, you don't want to be like the politician whose speech had a marginal reminder: "Argument weak; shout here."

Making Reasonable Assumptions

Probably the chief faults in most persuasive writing are not so much faults of reasoning as they are faults of initial assumptions. We may argue with faultless logic from faulty premises which are rooted in our tendency to be intolerant of views and prejudices other than our own. We begin with certain cherished ideas, and then we argue from them, seeing only part of a problem or seeing a generality where there is really only an instance. Take, for example, a passage on page 63 in Caroline Bird's *The Case Against College* (New York: David McKay, 1975). Ms. Bird argues that "in strictly financial terms, college is the dumbest investment a young man can make." She supports her claim thus: a high school graduate of 1972

"Spain — overrated. France — overrated. Switzerland! Germany! Belgium! England! Italy! All overrated!"

Drawing by Koren; © 1978 The New Yorker Magazine, Inc.

will find that it costs about $34,181 to go to Princeton for four years (total costs and "foregone income"); the high school graduate who invests this amount in a savings bank at 7.5 percent interest will, despite the greater earning power of the college graduate, at age 64 be richer than the one who spends the money to go to college. But Ms. Bird overlooks the fact that few people (including those who go to Princeton) have $34,181 to invest at the time they graduate from high school; and so for most people the argument is irrelevant. Like Ms. Bird, we all sometimes reason in a vacuum. We reason — we have a maddening habit of saying "it stands to reason" — but we won't listen to reason. When it comes to listening, we are like the character in Elizabeth Gaskell's *Cranford* who said, "I'll not listen to reason. Reason always means what someone else has got to say."

Deduction

Deduction is the process of reasoning from assumptions (called premises) to a logical conclusion. Here is the classic example:

> *All men are mortal* (the major premise)
> *Socrates is a man* (the minor premise)
> *therefore Socrates is mortal* (the conclusion)

Such an argument, which takes two truths and joins them to produce a third truth, is called a *syllogism* (from Greek for "a reckoning together"). Deduction (from Latin "lead down from") moves from a general statement to a specific application; it is, therefore, the opposite of induction, which moves from specific instances to a general conclusion. *In*duction would note, for example, that Socrates was mortal and that all other observed people were also mortal, and it would thus arrive at the generalization that all people are mortal.

Deduction does not inevitably lead to truth. If a premise of a syllogism is not true, one can reason logically but come to a false conclusion. Example: "All teachers are members of a union"; "Jones is a teacher"; "therefore Jones is a member of a union." Although the process of reasoning is correct, the major premise is false and so the conclusion is worthless — Jones may or may not be a member of a union. Another trap to avoid is an argument that appears logical but is not. Let's take this attempt at a syllogism: "All teachers of Spanish know that in Spanish *hoy* means *today*" (major premise); "John knows that in Spanish *hoy* means *today*" (minor premise); "therefore John is a teacher of Spanish" (conclusion). Both premises are correct, but the conclusion does not follow. What's wrong? For a deduction to be valid, the subject or condition of the major premise (in this case, teachers of Spanish) must appear also in the minor premise, but here it does not. The minor premise should be "John is a teacher of Spanish"; then the conclusion, that "therefore John knows that *hoy* means *today*," would be valid.

One other point. On most questions, say on the value of bilingual education or on the need for rehabilitation programs in prisons, it's not possible to make a strictly logical case, in the sense of an absolutely airtight proof. Don't assume that it is your job to make an absolute proof. What you are expected to do is to offer a reasonable argument.

Organizing an Argument

The word *logic* is from *logos,* Greek for "pattern" or "plan"; and though today logic means the science of correct reasoning, one cannot neglect the pattern or plan. As a rough principle, begin with the simplest argument and work up to the most complex. Such an arrangement will keep your reader with you, step by step.

A second method of organization, which with luck may coincide with the one just suggested, is to arrange arguments in order of increasing strength. Now, the danger in following this plan is that you may lose the reader from the start, because you begin with a weak argument. Avoid the danger by telling your reader that indeed the first argument is relatively weak (if it is terribly weak, it isn't an argument at all, so scrap it), but that you offer it for the sake of completeness or because it is often given, and that you will soon give the reader far stronger arguments. Face the opposition to this initial argument, grant that opposition as much as it deserves, and salvage what is left of the argument. Then proceed to the increasingly strong arguments, devoting at least one paragraph to each. As you treat each argument, it is usually advisable to introduce it with an appropriate transition ("another reason," "even more important," "most convincing of all"), to state it briefly, to summarize the opposing view, and then to demolish this opposition. With this organization, your discussion of each of your own arguments ends affirmatively.

A third method of organizing an argument is, after stating what you wish to prove in an introductory paragraph, to mass all the opposing arguments, and then to demolish them one by one.

In short, remember that when you have done your thinking and your rethinking, you are not done. You still must turn your thinking into writing — courteous, clear, and concrete. Find the right order, get the right words and provide the right transitions, avoid sarcasm and logical fallacies, and enrich your argument with specific examples and perhaps even some narrative — an appropriate anecdote, for instance, or a bit of history. Guide your readers through your analysis of the opposition and bring them to your position.

EXERCISES

1. Read the following passage (by Susan Brownmiller, reviewing a book called *With the Weathermen*) and then try to answer the questions.

Once upon a time, six years ago, a fistful of the most impatient members of this country's white student left broke away from their contemporaries and issued a call to revolutionary arms. Enraged beyond endurance by the peace movement's inability to put a dent in America's war machine and end the madness in Vietnam, they took the madness upon themselves. Unable to erase their upper-middle-class white-skin privilege, they proposed to follow to the death the "vanguard" actions of their Black Panther "brothers." They would be Viet-cong cadre in the United States, exemplary terrorist urban guerrillas, street-fighting men and women. They would smash the state with their iron pipes and homemade bombs, fight the racism they saw all around them by building a new collective life-style based on a celebration of youth, rock 'n' roll, dope, acid and sex. The vision of the role they had ordained themselves to play was not humble. They were The Way, they announced. Those among their friends who refused to follow their leadership were wimpy Running-Dog pigs, among other descriptive phrases.

A summary of this paragraph — the gist of the explicit idea — might go thus: "Six years ago some of the most radical students, exasperated by the failure of the peace movement, arrogantly called for violence and a new life-style, and denounced all who did not follow them."

    a. What is the effect of "Once upon a time, six years ago"? Of "a fistful"? (Why not "a small number" instead of "a fistful"?)

    b. What is the effect of the repetition in "They would be" and "They would smash"?

    c. What is the effect of capitalizing "The Way"?

    d. At the end of the passage, "among other descriptive phrases" is vague and might be considered anticlimactic. How can it be justified?

    e. What is the difference between the summary of the paragraph and the paragraph? Which is more persuasive, and why?

2. Analyze and evaluate each of the following arguments. If any of the arguments contain fallacies, name the fallacies.

    a. To the Editor:
    The recent senseless murder of a 15-year-old seminary student again emphasizes the insanity of our gun laws. No matter how guilty the 13-year-old boy who shot into the head of the victim, it seems that our Congressmen are even more guilty by not enacting stricter gun-control laws. They are supposedly sane, rational men; and the kindest thing that can be said about them is that they are merely motivated by greed.

    b. To the Editor:
    Your editorial last Wednesday arguing against censorship as an infringement on freedom is full of clever arguments but it overlooks an obvious fact. We have Pure Food and Drug laws to protect us against poison, and no one believes that such laws interfere with the freedom of those who produce food and drugs. The public is entitled, then, to laws that will similarly protect us from the poison that some movie-makers produce.

    c. To the Editor:
    On Dec. 5 *The Times* published a story saying that Harvard has come under pressure to improve the "quality of its teaching." Unfortunately nobody knows what good teaching is, let alone how to evaluate it.

Unlike scholarship, which has a visible product, namely published reports, the results of teaching are locked in the heads of students and are usually not apparent, even to the students themselves, for a very long period.

One device which is frequently used is a poll of students, the so-called "student evaluation of teachers." This type of measurement has been studied by Rodin & Rodin, who correlated it with how much the students learned, as demonstrated on tests. The correlation was highly negative ($-.75$). As the Rodins put it, "Students rate most highly instructors from whom they learn least."

What invariably happens is that attempts to reward "good teaching" turn out to reward good public relations.

d. [Written shortly after the United States entered the Second World War] The Pacific Coast is in imminent danger of a combined attack from within and from without. . . . It is [true] . . . that since the outbreak of the Japanese war there has been no important sabotage on the Pacific Coast. From what we know about the fifth column in Europe, this is not, as some have liked to think, a sign that there is nothing to be feared. It is a sign that the blow is well-organized and that it is held back until it can be struck with maximum effect. . . . I am sure I understand fully and appreciate thoroughly the unwillingness of Washington to adopt a policy of mass evacuation and internment of all those who are technically enemy aliens. But I submit that Washington is not defining the problem on the coast correctly. . . . The Pacific Coast is officially a combat zone: some part of it may at any moment be a battlefield. Nobody's constitutional rights include the right to reside and do business on a battlefield. And nobody ought to be on a battlefield who has no good reason for being there.

— Walter Lippmann

3. In the following poem, "The Flea," by John Donne (1572–1631), a man is urging a woman to go to bed with him. Between the second and the third stanzas (that is, between lines 18 and 19) the woman kills the flea. Summarize the man's argument, step by step, and evaluate it as a piece of persuasion.

Mark but this flea, and mark in this
How little that which thou deny'st me is;
It sucked me first, and now sucks thee,
And in this flea our two bloods mingled be;
Thou know'st that this cannot be said   5

A sin, nor shame, nor loss of maidenhead;
   Yet this enjoys before it woo,
   And pampered swells with one blood made of two,
   And this, alas, is more than we would do.

Oh stay, three lives in one flea spare,   10
Where we almost, yea, more than married are.
This flea is you and I, and this
Our marriage bed and marriage temple is;
Though parents grudge, and you, we are met
And cloistered in these living walls of jet.   15
   Though use[1] make you apt to kill me,
   Let not to that, self-murder added be,
   And sacrilege, three sins in killing three.

Cruel and sudden, hast thou since
Purpled thy nail in blood of innocence?   20
Wherein could this flea guilty be,
Except in that drop which it sucked from thee?
Yet thou triumph'st and say'st that thou
Find'st not thyself, nor me the weaker now.
   'Tis true. Then learn how false fears be:
   Just so much honor, when thou yield'st to me,   25
   Will waste, as this flea's death took life from thee.

PERSUASION AT WORK

*Putting the Outside
Inside the Fence of Law*

Christopher D. Stone

    The notion of extending legal rights to environmental objects —
oceans, rivers, forests — sounds absurd and unthinkable when first
encountered. But viewed historically, it is not so. The entire history
of the law has been an ever-widening extension in those "things"
accorded legal rights, and thus constituted "persons" within the law.
In Roman law the father had *jus vitae necisque* — the power of life and

---

[1] custom.

death — over his children. In thirteenth-century England, Jews were treated as men *ferae naturae,* protected by a quasi-forest-law, like the roe and the deer. Women, particularly married women, only recently were recognized as persons fully capable of holding legal rights. So, too, it is only through begrudged evolution — that is still in progress — that rights have been accorded the insane, blacks, aliens, fetuses and Indians.

Nor has human form been a prerequisite to holding rights. Ships, still referred to in the feminine gender by courts, have long had an independent legal life, often with striking implications. The world of the lawyer is "peopled" by such inanimate entities as trusts, corporations, joint ventures, municipalities and nation-states.

It is important to remember, too, that throughout legal history each successive extension of rights to some new entity has at first sounded odd or frightening, or laughable. For until the rightless thing receives its rights, we cannot see it as anything but a *thing* for our use; witness how the slave South, its consciousness dulled and reinforced by slave-property law, looked upon the black.

Now, to say that the natural environment should have rights is not to say anything so silly as that no one should ever be allowed to cut down a tree. Human beings have rights, but there are circumstances under which they may suffer the death penalty. Corporations have rights, but they cannot plead the Fifth Amendment. By the same token, to say that the environment should have rights is not to say that it should have every right we can imagine, or even the same rights human beings have.

In general, to recognize the legal rights of the environment would involve allowing nature three distinct benefits it is denied under common law. The first is standing — the right to have legal actions instituted on its behalf. It is no answer to say that streams and forests cannot speak. Corporations and states cannot speak either. Lawyers speak for them, as they customarily do for ordinary citizens with legal problems. We could treat natural objects as we do legal incompetents, human beings who have become vegetables. A court simply designates someone the incompetent's guardian with the authority to represent him and manage his affairs. By analogy, when a friend (presumably one of the established environmental groups) of a natural object perceives it to be endangered, the friend should be able to apply to a court to establish a guardianship. The guardian would thereafter be the legal voice for the voiceless object, instituting actions in its name and appearing before appropriate agencies on its behalf.

Second, when courts make balances of competing interests, as in deciding whether a company that is polluting a stream should have to shut down, it is the competing human interests that they consider exclusively. What does not, but should, weigh in the balance is the damage to the stream itself, to the fish and turtles and "lower" life.

Third, where relief is granted in an environmental case, there is no reason why damages should not go to the benefit of the environment. The natural object's portion would be put into a trust fund to be administered by the object's guardian, to defray the costs of aerating a polluted stream, stocking it with fish and algae, and so on.

It makes more sense than what we are doing now.

QUESTIONS

1. Explain Stone's strategy in the first sentence of "Putting the Outside Inside the Fence of Law." Given the next few sentences, does the strategy work?
2. In the fifth paragraph, Stone introduces an analogy. Is the analogy useful? Does Stone fallaciously imply that it proves his point?
3. If Stone's last sentence is not offensively aggressive, what keeps it from being so?

Four Letter Words Can Hurt You

Barbara Lawrence

===

Why should any words be called obscene? Don't they all describe natural human functions? Am I trying to tell them, my students demand, that the "strong, earthy, gut-honest" — or, if they are fans of Norman Mailer, the "rich, liberating, existential" — language they use to describe sexual activity isn't preferable to "phony-sounding, middle-class words like 'intercourse' and 'copulate'?" "Cop You Late!" they say with fancy inflections and gagging grimaces. "Now, what is *that* supposed to mean?"

Well, what is it supposed to mean? And why indeed should one group of words describing human functions and human organs be acceptable in ordinary conversation and another, describing presumably the same organs and functions, be tabooed — so much so, in fact, that some of these words still cannot appear in print in many parts of the English-speaking world?

The argument that these taboos exist only because of "sexual hangups" (middle-class, middle-age, feminist), or even that they are a result of class oppression (the contempt of the Norman conquerors for the language of their Anglo-Saxon serfs), ignores a much more likely explanation, it seems to me, and that is the sources and functions of the words themselves.

The best known of the tabooed sexual verbs, for example, comes from the German *ficken,* meaning "to strike"; combined, according to Partridge's etymological dictionary *Origins,* with the Latin sexual verb *futuere;* associated in turn with the Latin *fustis,* "a staff or cudgel"; the Celtic *buc,* "a point, hence to pierce"; the Irish *bot,* "the male member"; the Latin *battuere,* "to beat"; the Gaelic *batair,* "a cudgeller"; the Early Irish *bualaim,* "I strike"; and so forth. It is one of what etymologists sometimes call "the sadistic group of words for the man's part in copulation."

The brutality of this word, then, and its equivalents ("screw," "bang," etc.), is not an illusion of the middle class or a crotchet of Women's Liberation. In their origins and imagery these words carry undeniably painful, if not sadistic, implications, the object of which is almost always female. Consider, for example, what a "screw" actually does to the wood it penetrates; what a painful, even mutilating, activity this kind of analogy suggests. "Screw" is particularly interesting in this context, since the noun, according to Partridge, comes from words meaning "groove," "nut," "ditch," "breeding sow," "scrofula" and "swelling," while the verb, besides its explicit imagery, has antecedent associations to "write on," "scratch," "scarify," and so forth — a revealing fusion of a mechanical or painful action with an obviously denigrated object.

Not all obscene words, of course, are as implicitly sadistic or denigrating to women as these, but all that I know seem to serve a similar purpose: to reduce the human organism (especially the female organism) and human functions (especially sexual and procreative) to their least organic, most mechanical dimension; to substitute a trivializing or deforming resemblance for the complex human reality of what is being described.

Tabooed male descriptives, when they are not openly denigrating to women, often serve to divorce a male organ or function from any significant interaction with the female. Take the word "testes," for example, suggesting "witnesses" (from the Latin *testis*) to the sexual and procreative strengths of the male organ; and the obscene counterpart of this word, which suggests little more than a mechanical shape. Or compare almost any of the "rich," "liberating" sexual verbs, so fashionable today among male writers, with that much-derided Latin word "copulate" ("to bind or join together") or even that Anglo-Saxon phrase (which seems to have had no trouble surviving the Norman Conquest) "make love."

How arrogantly self-involved the tabooed words seem in comparison to either of the other terms, and how contemptuous of the female partner. Understandably so, of course, if she is only a "skirt," a "broad," a "chick," a "pussycat" or a "piece." If she is, in other words, no more than her skirt, or what her skirt conceals; no more than a breeder, or the broadest part of her; no more than a piece of a human being or a "piece of tail."

The most severely tabooed of all the female descriptives, incidentally, are those like a "piece of tail," which suggest (either explicitly or through antecedents) that there is no significant difference between the female channel through which we are all conceived and born and the anal outlet common to both sexes — a distinction that pornographers have always enjoyed obscuring.

This effort to deny women their biological identity, their individuality, their humanness, is such an important aspect of obscene language that one can only marvel at how seldom, in an era preoccupied with definitions of obscenity, this fact is brought to our attention. One problem, of course, is that many of the people in the best position to do this (critics, teachers, writers) are so reluctant today to admit that they are angered or shocked by obscenity. Bored, maybe, unimpressed, aesthetically displeased, but — no matter how brutal or denigrating the material — never angered, never shocked.

And yet how eloquently angered, how piously shocked many of these same people become if denigrating language is used about any minority group other than women; if the obscenities are racial or ethnic, that is, rather than sexual. Words like "coon," "kike," "spic," "wop," after all, deform identity, deny individuality and humanness in almost exactly the same way that sexual vulgarisms and obscenities do.

No one that I know, least of all my students, would fail to question the values of a society whose literature and entertainment rested heavily on racial or ethnic pejoratives. Are the values of a society whose literature and entertainment rest as heavily as ours on sexual pejoratives any less questionable?

QUESTION

In addition to giving evidence to support her view, what persuasive devices (for example, irony, analogy) does Lawrence use?

Love Is a Fallacy

Max Shulman

Cool was I and logical. Keen, calculating, perspicacious, acute and astute — I was all of these. My brain was as powerful as a dynamo, as precise as a chemist's scales, as penetrating as a scalpel. And — think of it! — I was only eighteen.

It is not often that one so young has such a giant intellect. Take, for example, Petey Burch, my roommate at the University of Minnesota. Same age, same background, but dumb as an ox. A nice enough fellow, you understand, but nothing upstairs. Emotional type. Unstable. Impressionable. Worst of all, a faddist. Fads, I submit, are the very negation of reason. To be swept up in every new craze that comes along, to surrender yourself to idiocy just because everybody else is doing it — this, to me, is the acme of mindlessness. Not, however, to Petey.

One afternoon I found Petey lying on his bed with an expression of such distress on his face that I immediately diagnosed appendicitis. "Don't move," I said. "Don't take a laxative. I'll get a doctor."

"Raccoon," he mumbled thickly.

"Raccoon?" I said, pausing in my flight.

"I want a raccoon coat," he wailed.

I perceived that his trouble was not physical, but mental. "Why do you want a raccoon coat?"

"I should have known it," he cried, pounding his temples. "I should have known they'd come back when the Charleston came back. Like a fool I spent all my money for textbooks, and now I can't get a raccoon coat."

"Can you mean," I said incredulously, "that people are actually wearing raccoon coats again?"

"All the Big Men on Campus are wearing them. Where've you been?"

"In the library," I said, naming a place not frequented by Big Men on Campus.

He leaped from the bed and paced the room. "I've got to have a raccoon coat," he said passionately. "I've got to!"

"Petey, why? Look at it rationally. Raccoon coats are unsanitary. They shed. They smell bad. They weigh too much. They're unsightly. They —"

"You don't understand," he interrupted impatiently. "It's the thing to do. Don't you want to be in the swim?"

"No," I said truthfully.

"Well, I do," he declared. "I'd give anything for a raccoon coat. Anything!"

My brain, that precision instrument, slipped into high gear. "Anything?" I asked, looking at him narrowly.

"Anything," he affirmed in ringing tones.

I stroked my chin thoughtfully. It so happened that I knew where to get my hands on a raccoon coat. My father had had one in his undergraduate days; it lay now in a trunk in the attic back home. It also happened that Petey had something I wanted. He didn't *have* it exactly, but at least he had first rights on it. I refer to his girl, Polly Espy.

I had long coveted Polly Espy. Let me emphasize that my desire for this young woman was not emotional in nature. She was, to be sure, a girl who excited the emotions, but I was not one to let my heart rule my head. I wanted Polly for a shrewdly calculated, entirely cerebral reason.

I was a freshman in law school. In a few years I would be out in practice. I was well aware of the importance of the right kind of wife in furthering a lawyer's career. The successful lawyers I had observed were, almost without exception, married to beautiful, gracious, intelligent women. With one omission, Polly fitted these specifications perfectly.

Beautiful she was. She was not yet of pin-up proportions, but I felt sure that time would supply the lack. She already had the makings.

Gracious she was. By gracious I mean full of graces. She had an erectness of carriage, an ease of bearing, a poise that clearly indicated the best of breeding. At table her manners were exquisite. I had seen her at the Kozy Kampus Korner eating the specialty of the house — a sandwich that contained scraps of pot roast, gravy, chopped nuts, and a dipper of sauerkraut — without even getting her fingers moist.

Intelligent she was not. In fact, she veered in the opposite direction. But I believed that under my guidance she would smarten up. At any rate, it was worth a try. It is, after all, easier to make a beautiful dumb girl smart than to make an ugly smart girl beautiful.

"Petey," I said, "are you in love with Polly Espy?"

"I think she's a keen kid," he replied, "but I don't know if you'd call it love. Why?"

"Do you," I asked, "have any kind of formal arrangement with her? I mean are you going steady or anything like that?"

"No. We see each other quite a bit, but we both have other dates. Why?"

"Is there," I asked, "any other man for whom she has a particular fondness?"

"Not that I know of. Why?"

I nodded with satisfaction. "In other words, if you were out of the picture, the field would be open. Is that right?"

"I guess so. What are you getting at?"

"Nothing, nothing," I said innocently, and took my suitcase out of the closet.

"Where are you going?" asked Petey.

"Home for the weekend." I threw a few things into the bag.

"Listen," he said, clutching my arm eagerly, "while you're home, you couldn't get some money from your old man, could you, and lend it to me so I can buy a raccoon coat?"

"I may do better than that," I said with a mysterious wink and closed my bag and left.

"Look," I said to Petey when I got back Monday morning. I threw open the suitcase and revealed the huge, hairy, gamy object that my father had worn in his Stutz Bearcat in 1925.

"Holy Toledo!" said Petey reverently. He plunged his hands into the raccoon coat and then his face. "Holy Toledo!" he repeated fifteen or twenty times.

"Would you like it?" I asked.

"Oh yes!" he cried, clutching the greasy pelt to him. Then a canny look came into his eyes. "What do you want for it?"

"Your girl," I said, mincing no words.

"Polly?" he said in a horrified whisper. "You want Polly?"

"That's right."

He flung the coat from him. "Never," he said stoutly.

I shrugged. "Okay. If you don't want to be in the swim, I guess it's your business."

I sat down in a chair and pretended to read a book, but out of the corner of my eye I kept watching Petey. He was a torn man. First he looked at the coat with the expression of a waif at a bakery window. Then he turned away and set his jaw resolutely. Then he looked back at the coat, with even more longing in his face. Then he turned away, but with not so much resolution this time. Back and forth his head swiveled, desire waxing, resolution waning. Finally he didn't turn away at all; he just stood and stared with mad lust at the coat.

"It isn't as though I was in love with Polly," he said thickly. "Or going steady or anything like that."

"That's right," I murmured.

"What's Polly to me, or me to Polly?"

"Not a thing," said I.

"It's just been a casual kick — just a few laughs, that's all."

"Try on the coat," said I.

He complied. The coat bunched high over his ears and dropped all the way down to his shoe tops. He looked like a mound of dead raccoons. "Fits fine," he said happily.

I rose from my chair. "Is it a deal?" I asked, extending my hand.

He swallowed. "It's a deal," he said and shook my hand.

I had my first date with Polly the following evening. This was in the nature of a survey; I wanted to find out just how much work I had to do to get her mind up to the standard I required. I took her first to dinner. "Gee, that was a delish dinner," she said as we left the restaurant. Then I took her to a movie. "Gee, that was a marvy movie," she said as we left the theater. And then I took her home. "Gee, I had a sensaysh time," she said as she bade me good night.

I went back to my room with a heavy heart. I had gravely underestimated the size of my task. This girl's lack of information was terrifying. Nor would it be enough merely to supply her with information. First she had to be taught to *think*. This loomed as a project of no small dimensions, and at first I was tempted to give her back to Petey. But then I got to thinking about her abundant physical charms and about the way she entered a room and the way she handled a knife and fork, and I decided to make an effort.

I went about it, as in all things, systematically. I gave her a course in logic. It happened that I, as a law student, was taking a course in logic myself, so I had all the facts at my finger tips. "Polly," I said to her when I picked her up on our next date, "tonight we are going over to the Knoll and talk."

"Oo, terrif," she replied. One thing I will say for this girl: you would go far to find another so agreeable.

We went to the Knoll, the campus trysting place, and we sat

down under an old oak, and she looked at me expectantly. "What are we going to talk about?" she asked.

"Logic."

She thought this over for a minute and decided she liked it. "Magnif," she said.

"Logic," I said, clearing my throat, "is the science of thinking. Before we can think correctly, we must first learn to recognize the common fallacies of logic. These we will take up tonight."

"Wow-dow!" she cried, clapping her hands delightedly.

I winced, but went bravely on. "First let us examine the fallacy called Dicto Simpliciter."

"By all means," she urged, batting her lashes eagerly.

"Dicto Simpliciter means an argument based on an unqualified generalization. For example: Exercise is good. Therefore everybody should exercise."

"I agree," said Polly earnestly. "I mean exercise is wonderful. I mean it builds the body and everything."

"Polly," I said gently, "the argument is a fallacy. *Exercise is good* is an unqualified generalization. For instance, if you have heart disease, exercise is bad, not good. Many people are ordered by their doctors *not* to exercise. You must *qualify* the generalization. You must say exercise is *usually* good, or exercise is good *for most people.* Otherwise you have committed a Dicto Simpliciter. Do you see?"

"No," she confessed. "But this is marvy. Do more! Do more!"

"It will be better if you stop tugging at my sleeve," I told her, and when she desisted, I continued. "Next we take up a fallacy called Hasty Generalization. Listen carefully: You can't speak French. I can't speak French. Petey Burch can't speak French. I must therefore conclude that nobody at the University of Minnesota can speak French."

"Really?" said Polly, amazed. *"Nobody?"*

I hid my exasperation. "Polly, it's a fallacy. The generalization is reached too hastily. There are too few instances to support such a conclusion."

"Know any more fallacies?" she asked breathlessly. "This is more fun than dancing even."

I fought off a wave of despair. I was getting nowhere with this girl, absolutely nowhere. Still, I am nothing if not persistent. I continued. "Next comes Post Hoc. Listen to this: Let's not take Bill on our picnic. Every time we take him out with us, it rains."

"I know somebody just like that," she exclaimed. "A girl back home — Eula Becker, her name is. It never fails. Every single time we take her on a picnic —"

"Polly," I said sharply, "it's a fallacy. Eula Becker doesn't *cause* the rain. She has no connection with the rain. You are guilty of Post Hoc if you blame Eula Becker."

"I'll never do it again," she promised contritely. "Are you mad at me?"

I sighed deeply. "No, Polly, I'm not mad."

"Then tell me some more fallacies."

"All right. Let's try Contradictory Premises."

"Yes, let's," she chirped, blinking her eyes happily.

I frowned, but plunged ahead. "Here's an example of Contradictory Premises: If God can do anything, can He make a stone so heavy that He won't be able to lift it?"

"Of course," she replied promptly.

"But if He can do anything, He can lift the stone," I pointed out.

"Yeah," she said thoughtfully. "Well, then I guess He can't make the stone."

"But He can do anything," I reminded her.

She scratched her pretty, empty head. "I'm all confused," she admitted.

"Of course you are. Because when the premises of an argument contradict each other, there can be no argument. If there is an irresistible force, there can be no immovable object. If there is an immovable object, there can be no irresistible force. Get it?"

"Tell me some more of this keen stuff," she said eagerly.

I consulted my watch. "I think we'd better call it a night. I'll take you home now, and you go over all the things you've learned. We'll have another session tomorrow night."

I deposited her at the girls' dormitory, where she assured me that she had had a perfectly terrif evening, and I went glumly home to my room. Petey lay snoring in his bed, the raccoon coat huddled like a great hairy beast at his feet. For a moment I considered waking him and telling him that he could have his girl back. It seemed clear that my project was doomed to failure. The girl simply had a logic-proof head.

But then I reconsidered. I had wasted one evening; I might as well waste another. Who knew? Maybe somewhere in the extinct crater of her mind, a few embers still smoldered. Maybe somehow I could fan them into flame. Admittedly it was not a prospect fraught with hope, but I decided to give it one more try.

Seated under the oak the next evening I said, "Our first fallacy tonight is called Ad Misericordiam."

She quivered with delight.

"Listen closely," I said. "A man applies for a job. When the boss asks him what his qualifications are, he replies that he has a wife and six children at home, the wife is a helpless cripple, the children have nothing to eat, no clothes to wear, no shoes on their feet, there are no beds in the house, no coal in the cellar, and winter is coming."

A tear rolled down each of Polly's pink cheeks. "Oh, this is awful, awful," she sobbed.

"Yes, it's awful," I agreed, "but it's no argument. The man never answered the boss's question about his qualifications. Instead he appealed to the boss's sympathy. He committed the fallacy of Ad Misericordiam. Do you understand?"

"Have you got a handkerchief?" she blubbered.

I handed her a handkerchief and tried to keep from screaming while she wiped her eyes. "Next," I said in a carefully controlled tone, "we will discuss False Analogy. Here is an example: Students should be allowed to look at their textbooks during examinations. After all, surgeons have X-rays to guide them during an operation, lawyers have briefs to guide them during a trial, carpenters have blueprints to guide them when they are building a house. Why, then, shouldn't students be allowed to look at their textbooks during an examination?"

"There now," she said enthusiastically, "is the most marvy idea I've heard in years."

"Polly," I said testily, "the argument is all wrong. Doctors, lawyers, and carpenters aren't taking a test to see how much they have learned, but students are. The situations are altogether different, and you can't make an analogy between them."

"I still think it's a good idea," said Polly.

"Nuts," I muttered. Doggedly I pressed on. "Next we'll try Hypothesis Contrary to Fact."

"Sounds yummy," was Polly's reaction.

"Listen: If Madame Curie had not happened to leave a photographic plate in a drawer with a chunk of pitchblende, the world today would not know about radium."

"True, true," said Polly, nodding her head. "Did you see the movie? Oh, it just knocked me out. That Walter Pidgeon is so dreamy. I mean he fractures me."

"If you can forget Mr. Pidgeon for a moment," I said coldly, "I would like to point out that the statement is a fallacy. Maybe

Madame Curie would have discovered radium at some later date. Maybe somebody else would have discovered it. Maybe any number of things would have happened. You can't start with a hypothesis that is not true and then draw any supportable conclusions from it."

"They ought to put Walter Pidgeon in more pictures," said Polly. "I hardly ever see him any more."

One more chance, I decided. But just one more. There is a limit to what flesh and blood can bear. "The next fallacy is called Poisoning the Well."

"How cute!" she gurgled.

"Two men are having a debate. The first one gets up and says, 'My opponent is a notorious liar. You can't believe a word that he is going to say.' . . . Now, Polly, think. Think hard. What's wrong?"

I watched her closely as she knit her creamy brow in concentration. Suddenly a glimmer of intelligence — the first I had seen — came into her eyes. "It's not fair," she said with indignation. "It's not a bit fair. What chance has the second man got if the first man calls him a liar before he even begins talking?"

"Right!" I cried exultantly. "One hundred percent right. It's not fair. The first man has *poisoned the well* before anybody could drink from it. He has hamstrung his opponent before he could even start. . . . Polly, I'm proud of you."

"Pshaw," she murmured, blushing with pleasure.

"You see, my dear, these things aren't so hard. All you have to do is concentrate. Think — examine — evaluate. Come now, let's review everything we have learned."

"Fire away," she said with an airy wave of her hand.

Heartened by the knowledge that Polly was not altogether a cretin, I began a long, patient review of all I had told her. Over and over and over again I cited instances, pointed out flaws, kept hammering away without let up. It was like digging a tunnel. At first everything was work, sweat, and darkness. I had no idea when I would reach the light, or even *if* I would. But I persisted. I pounded and clawed and scraped, and finally I was rewarded. I saw a chink of light. And then the chink got bigger and the sun came pouring in and all was bright.

Five grueling nights this took, but it was worth it. I had made a logician out of Polly; I had taught her to think. My job was done. She was worthy of me at last. She was a fit wife for me, a proper hostess for my many mansions, a suitable mother for my well-heeled children.

It must not be thought that I was without love for this girl. Quite the contrary. Just as Pygmalion loved the perfect woman he had fashioned, so I loved mine. I determined to acquaint her with my feelings at our very next meeting. The time had come to change our relationship from academic to romantic.

"Polly," I said when next we sat beneath our oak, "tonight we will not discuss fallacies."

"Aw, gee," she said, disappointed.

"My dear," I said, favoring her with a smile, "we have now spent five evenings together. We have gotten along splendidly. It is clear that we are well matched."

"Hasty Generalization," said Polly brightly.

"I beg your pardon," said I.

"Hasty Generalization," she repeated. "How can you say that we are well matched on the basis of only five dates?"

I chuckled with amusement. The dear child had learned her lessons well. "My dear," I said, patting her hand in a tolerant manner, "five dates is plenty. After all, you don't have to eat a whole cake to know that it's good."

"False Analogy," said Polly promptly. "I'm not a cake. I'm a girl."

I chuckled with somewhat less amusement. The dear child had learned her lessons perhaps too well. I decided to change tactics. Obviously the best approach was a simple, strong, direct declaration of love. I paused for a moment while my massive brain chose the proper words. Then I began:

"Polly, I love you. You are the whole world to me, and the moon and the stars and the constellations of outer space. Please, my darling, say that you will go steady with me, for if you will not, life will be meaningless. I will languish. I will refuse my meals. I will wander the face of the earth, a shambling, hollow-eyed hulk."

There, I thought, folding my arms, that ought to do it.

"Ad Misericordiam," said Polly.

I ground my teeth. I was not Pygmalion; I was Frankenstein, and my monster had me by the throat. Frantically I fought back the tide of panic surging through me. At all costs I had to keep cool.

"Well, Polly," I said, forcing a smile, "you certainly have learned your fallacies."

"You're darn right," she said with a vigorous nod.

"And who taught them to you, Polly?"

"You did."

"That's right. So you do owe me something, don't you, my dear? If I hadn't come along you never would have learned about fallacies."

"Hypothesis Contrary to Fact," she said instantly.

I dashed perspiration from my brow. "Polly," I croaked, "you mustn't take all these things so literally. I mean this is just classroom stuff. You know that the things you learn in school don't have anything to do with life."

"Dicto Simpliciter," she said, wagging her finger at me playfully.

That did it. I leaped to my feet, bellowing like a bull. "Will you or will you not go steady with me?"

"I will not," she replied.

"Why not?" I demanded.

"Because this afternoon I promised Petey Burch that I would go steady with him."

I reeled back, overcome with the infamy of it. After he promised, after he made a deal, after he shook my hand! "The rat!" I shrieked, kicking up great chunks of turf. "You can't go with him, Polly. He's a liar. He's a cheat. He's a rat."

"Poisoning the Well," said Polly, "and stop shouting. I think shouting must be a fallacy too."

With an immense effort of will, I modulated my voice. "All right," I said. "You're a logician. Let's look at this thing logically. How could you choose Petey Burch over me? Look at me — a brilliant student, a tremendous intellectual, a man with an assured future. Look at Petey — a knothead, a jitterbug, a guy who'll never know where his next meal is coming from. Can you give me one logical reason why you should go steady with Petey Burch?"

"I certainly can," declared Polly. "He's got a raccoon coat."

QUESTIONS

1. What is unusual about the first sentence? What expectation about the direction of the story does this first sentence create?
2. What other conspicuous features of the narrator's style do you find in the first paragraph? How do they help to characterize him? (How has Shulman "poisoned the well"?)

Confessions of an Erstwhile Child

Anonymous

Some years ago I attempted to introduce a class of Upward Bound students to political theory via More's *Utopia*. It was a mistake; I taught precious little theory and earned More a class full of undying enemies on account of two of his ideas. The first, that all members of a Utopian family were subject to the lifelong authority of its eldest male. The second, the Utopian provision that should a child wish to follow a profession different from that of his family, he could be transferred by adoption to a family that practiced the desired trade. My students were not impressed with my claim that the one provision softened the other and made for a fair compromise — for what causes most of our quarrels with our parents but our choice of life-patterns, of occupation? In objecting to the first provision my students were picturing themselves as children, subject to an unyielding authority. But on the second provision they surprised me by taking the parents' role and arguing that this form of *ad lib* adoption denied them a fundamental right of ownership over their children. It occurred to me that these reactions were two parts of the same pathology: having suffered the discipline of unreasonable parents, one has earned the right to be unreasonable in turn to one's children. The phenomenon has well known parallels, such as frantic martinets who have risen from the ranks. Having served time as property, my Upward Bound students wanted theirs back as proprietors.

I shuddered. It hardly takes an advanced course in Freudian psychology to realize that the perpetuation, generation after generation, of psychic lesions must go right to this source, the philosophically dubious notion that children are the property of their biological parents, compounded with the unphilosophic certitude so many parents harbor, that their children must serve an apprenticeship as like their own as they can manage.

The idea of the child as property has always bothered me, for personal reasons I shall outline. I lack the feeling that I own my children and I have always scoffed at the idea that what they are and do is a continuation or a rejection of my being. I like them, I sympathize with them, I acknowledge the obligation to support them for a term of years — but I am not so fond or foolish as to regard a biological tie as a lien on their loyalty or respect, nor to imagine that I am equipped with preternatural powers of guidance as to their success and happiness. Beyond inculcating some of the obvious social protocols required in civilized life, who am I to pronounce on what makes for a happy or successful life? How many of us can say that we have successfully managed our own lives? Can we do better with our children? I am unimpressed, to say no more, with parents who have no great track record, presuming to oracular powers in regard to their children's lives.

The current debate over the Equal Rights Amendment frequently turns to custody questions. Opponents of ERA have made the horrifying discovery that ERA will spell the end of the mother's presumed rights of custody in divorce or separation cases, and that fathers may begin getting custody rights. Indeed a few odd cases have been so settled recently in anticipation of the ratification of ERA. If ratified, ERA would be an extremely blunt instrument for calling the whole idea of custody into question, but I for one will applaud anything that serves to begin debate. As important as equal rights between adults may be, I think that the rights of children are a far more serious and unattended need. To me, custody by natural parents, far from being a presumed right only re-examined in case of collapsing marriages, should be viewed as a privilege.

At this point I have to explain why I can so calmly contemplate the denial of so-called parental rights.

I am the only child of two harsh and combative personalities who married, seemingly, in order to have a sparring partner always at hand. My parents have had no other consistent or lasting aim in life but to win out over each other in a contest of wills. They still live, vigorous and angry septuagenarians, their ferocity little blunted by age or human respect. My earliest memories — almost my sole memories — are of unending combat, in which I was sometimes an appalled spectator, more often a hopeless negotiator in a war of no quarter, and most often a bystander accused of covert belligerency on behalf of one side or the other, and frequently of both! I grew up with two supposed adults who were absorbed in their hatreds and recriminations to the exclusion of almost all other reality. Not only did I pass by almost unnoticed in their struggle, the Depression and World War II passed them by equally unnoticed. I figured mainly as a practice target for sarcasm and invective, and occasionally as the ultimate culprit responsible for their unhappiness ("If it weren't for you," my mother would sometimes say, "I could leave that SOB," a remark belied by her refusal to leave the SOB during these 20 long years since I left their "shelter.")

The reader may ask, "How did you survive if your parents'

house was all that bad?'' I have three answers. First, I survived by the moral equivalent of running away to sea or the circus, *i.e.,* by burying myself in books and study, especially in the history of faraway and (I thought) more idealistic times than our own, and by consciously shaping my life and tastes to be as different as possible from those of my parents (this was a reproach to them, they knew, and it formed the basis of a whole secondary area of conflict and misunderstanding). Second, I survived because statistically most people "survive" horrible families, but survival can be a qualified term, as it is in my case by a permanently impaired digestive system and an unnatural sensitivity to raised voices. And third, though I found solace in schooling and the rationality, cooperation and basic fairness in teachers that I missed in my parents, I must now question whether it is healthy for a child to count so heavily on schooling for the love and approval that he deserves from his home and family. Even if schooling can do this well, in later life it means that one is loyal and affectionate toward schooling, not toward parents, who may in some sense need affection even if they don't "deserve" it. I am not unaware that however fair and rational I may be in reaction to my parents' counterexamples, I am a very cold-hearted man. I might have done better transferred to a new family, not just by receiving love, but through learning to give it — a lack I mourn as much or more than my failure to receive it.

It is little wonder then that I have an acquired immunity to the notion that parental custody is by and large a preferable thing. In my case, almost anything else would have been preferable, including even a rather callously run orphanage — anything for a little peace and quiet. Some people are simply unfit, under any conditions, to be parents, even if, indeed especially if, they maintain the charade of a viable marriage. My parents had no moral right to custody of children, and I cannot believe that my experience is unique or particularly isolated. There are all too many such marriages, in which some form of horror, congenial enough to adults too sick or crazed to recognize it, works its daily ruination on children. Surely thousands of children conclude at age 10 or 11, as I did, that marriage is simply an institution in which people are free to be as beastly as they have a mind to, which may lead either to a rejection of marriage or to a decision to reduplicate a sick marriage a second time, with another generation of victims. It is time to consider the rights of the victims.

How to implement a nascent theory of justice for children is difficult to say. One cannot imagine taking the word of a five-year-old against his parents, but what about a 10- or 12-year-old? At *some* point, children should have the right to escape the dominance of impossible parents. The matter used to be easier than it has been since World War I. The time-honored solution — for boys — of running away from home has been made infeasible by economic conditions, fingerprints, social security and minimum wage laws. No apprenticeship system exists any more, much less its upperclass medieval version — which required exchange of boys at puberty among noble families to serve as pages and so forth. The adoption system contemplated in More's *Utopia* is a half-remembered echo of medieval life, in which society, wiser than its theory, decreed a general exchange of children at or just before puberty, whether through apprenticeship or page-service, or more informal arrangements, like going to a university at 14 or running away with troubadors or gypsies.

Exchanging children is a wisely conceived safety valve against a too traumatic involvement between the biological parent and the child. Children need an alternative to living all their formative life in the same biological unit. They should have the right to petition for release from some sorts of families, to join other families, or to engage in other sorts of relationships that may provide equivalent service but may not be organized as a family. The nuclear family, after all, is not such an old or proven vehicle. Phillippe Aries' book, *Centuries of Childhood,* made the important point that the idea of helpless childhood is itself a notion of recent origin, that grew up simultaneously in the 16th and 17th centuries with the small and tight-knit nuclear family, sealed off from the world by another recent invention, "privacy." The older *extended* family (which is the kind More knew about) was probably more authoritarian on paper but much less productive of dependency in actual operation. There ought to be more than one way a youngster can enter adult society with more than half of his sanity left. At least no one should be forced to remain in a no-win game against a couple of crazy parents for 15–18 years. At 10 or 12, children in really messy situations should have the legal right to petition for removal from impossible families, and those rights should be reasonably easy to exercise. (This goes on *de facto* among the poor, of course, but it is not legal, and usually carries both stigma and danger.) The minimum wage laws should be modified to exempt such persons, especially if they wish to continue their education, working perhaps for public agencies, if they have no other means of support. If their parents can support them, then the equivalent of child-support should be charged them to maintain their children, not in luxury, but

adequately. Adoption of older children should be facilitated by eas-
ing of legal procedures (designed mainly to govern the adoption of
infants) plus tax advantages for those willing to adopt older children
on grounds of good will. Indeed children wishing to escape impossible family situations should be allowed a fair degree of initiative in
finding and negotiating with possible future families.

Obviously the risk of rackets would be very high unless the
exact terms of such provisions were framed very carefully, but the
possibility of rackets is less frightening to anyone who thinks about
it for long than the dangers of the present situation, which are
evident and unrelieved by any signs of improvement. In barely a
century this country has changed from a relatively loose society in
which Huckleberry Finns were not uncommon, to a society of tense,
airless nuclear families in which unhealthy and neurotic tendencies,
once spawned in a family, tend to repeat themselves at a magnifying
and accelerating rate. We may soon gain the distinction of being the
only nation on earth to need not just medicare but "psychicare." We
have invested far too heavily in the unproved "equity" called the
nuclear family; that stock is about to crash and we ought to begin
finding escape options. In colonial days many New England colonies
passed laws imposing fines or extra taxes on parents who kept their
children under their own roofs after age 15 or 16, on the sensible
notion that a person of that age ought to be out and doing on his
own, whether going to Yale or apprenticing in a foundry. Even
without the benefit of Freud, the colonial fathers had a good sense of
what was wrong with a closely bound and centripetal family structure — it concentrates craziness like compound interest, and so they
hit it with monetary penalties, a proper Protestant response, intolerant at once of both mystery and excuses. But this was the last gasp of
a medieval and fundamentally Catholic idea that children, God help
them, while they may be the children of *these* particular parents
biologically, spiritually are the children of God, and more appositely
are the children of the entire community, for which the entire
community takes responsibility. The unguessed secret of the middle
ages was not that monasteries relieved parents of unwanted children;
more frequently, they relieved children of unwanted parents.

QUESTIONS

1. What is the author's thesis? (Quote the thesis sentence.) Apart
   from his own experience, what evidence or other means does he
   offer to persuade you to accept it? Was he successful?

2. What part does the *tone* of his article play in persuading you to agree with him, or in alienating you? Does his tone strike you, for example, as vigorous or belligerent, as ironic or bitter, as reasonable or hysterical?
3. The author admits (on page 201) that he is "a very cold-hearted man." Do you remember your initial reaction to reading that sentence? What was it? Overall, does the author strengthen or jeopardize his argument by this admission? Explain.
4. If you did not find the article persuasive, did you find it nevertheless interesting? Can you explain why?
5. What, in your opinion, are the three most important sources of quarrels between parents and children? What one reason does the author cite as the most frequent source? Does the article as a whole support his assertion? Do you find in the article evidence to support any of the reasons you listed?

A New Solution for the CIA
I. F. Stone

Stalin did establish one useful precedent. He made it a practice to bump off whoever served as head of his secret police. He never let anybody stay in the job too long. As a successful dictator, Stalin seems to have felt that anybody who had collected so many secrets would be a No. 1 menace to security if he ever went sour. Stalin thought it safer not to wait.

I think we ought to take Stalin's example one step further. I think we ought to get rid of the CIA altogether, lock, stock, and burglar's kit.

We know from recent revelations how J. Edgar Hoover in his lifetime tenure as FBI chief collected dossiers on the sexual and drinking habits of congressmen and high officials. The mere rumor that such secrets were in his files made Hoover the most feared man in the capital, the untouchable of US politics. A similar character could build up a similar empire of fear in and through the CIA.

Those who think it enough to establish new oversight committees should remember that there have been CIA committees in Congress since the agency's formation and they have invariably overlooked the abuses they were supposed to oversee. As for forbidding the agency to engage in "dirty tricks," how enforce such a restriction against an agency so secretive, so far-flung, and so habituated to doing-in political leaders of whom it disapproves? It is hard enough to keep a tight rein on public agencies right here in Washington. How to control, sometimes 10,000 miles away, the kind of adventurers, screwballs, and intriguers an agency like the CIA naturally attracts?

The US government is inundated daily by tidal waves of intelligence. We have a mysterious electronic NSA which taps and tapes all the communications systems of the world; its huge "ears" in Pakistan and Turkey record the slightest Kremlin sneeze. Even in remotest Siberia, no *babushka* can milk her cow without being caught on candid camera from US satellites on eternal patrol.

In the Pentagon are separate intelligence branches of the army, air force, and navy, each with its own military attachés abroad, and over all of them is a defense intelligence agency, a *DIA*. The State Department has its own intelligence and research division; the Foreign Service is its eyes and ears abroad. The departments of Commerce, Labor, and Agriculture have attachés of their own in many US embassies. Businessmen and Washington correspondents who use their publicly available studies on countries and commodities know how much more reliable they are than the spooks.

The Treasury has its narcotics and other agents. Internal Revenue, Customs, and the Post Office have their own gumshoe men. There is the FBI and there is the Secret Service. Nobody seems to know how much all this costs or how many are employed. Congress does know that CIA expenditures hidden in certain crevices of the budget add up to several billions of dollars. The exact amount is unknown.

Originally we were told when the CIA was established by Truman in 1947 that it was necessary — as its name implied — to "centralize" all these intelligence activities and summarize for the White House the information flowing in from them. We were not told, and perhaps Truman never intended, that the CIA would soon be engaged in James Bond melodrama around the world, making and unmaking governments not to our liking, and in the process sentencing other nations' leaders like Mossaddeq of Iran and Allende of Chile to death. Watergate has already shown us that to practice such crime-as-politics abroad is to invite its application sooner or later to politics at home.

As an intelligence service the CIA has been a bust. The Bay of Pigs and the Vietnam war are only the most dramatic demonstrations that public officials would have been better informed — and adopted wiser policies — if they had simply read the newspapers and put all that "classified" information in the wastebasket. The CIA has made the US look like the world's biggest Mafia while helping to trap it into one serious mistake after another. Never have so many billions been squandered on so much misinformation. In its twenty-seven years of existence — even at $2 billion a year — this giddy operation must have cost upward of $50 billion. Why not get rid of it before it can do more damage?

Even when, occasionally, the CIA analyses were accurate they have gone into the bureaucratic wastebaskets because they conflicted with what officials higher up wanted to hear. One example is the sour reports about the Vietnam war which turned up in the Pentagon Papers. Another example (see the exclusive in *The Christian Science Monitor,* January 23, 1975) was the studies showing there was "no evidence to suggest" that the anti-Vietnam war movement was instigated from abroad. The Nixon White House nonetheless ordered the agency to go ahead and compile a list of 10,000 — no less — peaceniks suspected of being foreign agents.

A government, like an individual, hates to hear what it doesn't want to believe. This is why no intelligence agency in any society ever really understands — or can afford to let itself understand — what is going on. The bigger the intelligence agency the more powerfully its sheer inertial weight reinforces the misconceptions of the ruling class it serves. Hence the paradox: the more "intelligence" a government buys the less intelligently it operates. The CIA will go down in the books as a vain attempt to change history by institutionalizing assassination. It deserves a dose of its own favorite medicine.

QUESTIONS

1. In his first paragraph Stone uses Stalin as an authority. How does he indicate that he is not asking us to accept a dictator as a guide?

2. Is the comparison with J. Edgar Hoover, in the third paragraph, reasonable?

3. On page 205 Stone casually refers to the "adventurers, screwballs, and intriguers an agency like the CIA naturally attracts." Is this assertion acceptable? Explain.

4. Suppose someone says to you that Stone says we should abandon all spying. Would you find this an adequate summary of the essay? If not, how would you argue against it?

5. List Stone's arguments for abolishing the CIA. Can you offer replies to some or all?
6. Cite instances of Stone's irony (wry understatement or over-statement) and evaluate their persuasiveness.

Operation Illiteracy

Jonathan Kozol

Twenty percent of adult men and women in this nation cannot read enough to understand a want-ad or write enough to fill in a job application. The term for this condition, which is crippling to any dream of leading a productive or rewarding life, is "functional illiteracy." The figure is higher for blacks (44 percent), even higher for those of Spanish surname (56 percent). The total is 23 million at the lowest — more likely 30 million. The cost to the nation (including welfare and lowered productivity) is $6 billion a year.

The Elementary and Secondary Education Act of 1965 (Title I), the last great hope for an injection of adrenalin into public schools' reading programs, is of no use to adults. Nor is it of much use to those still in classrooms. Title I students receive less time in reading than those not in Title I. The program appears to hinder more children than it helps.

The answer is not another research project.

Rather, it is to turn our backs on this — and on all other standard substitutes for action — and to launch an all-out national attack on adult illiteracy, giving it the same priority as plague, pestilence or war. If we wished to learn from experience, we would start this battle in a non-school setting. We would also insist on a maximum teacher-learner ratio of one-to-five.

Our first need, therefore, is to sign up and prepare five million literacy teachers to go into the homes of 23 million to 30 million illiterate adults. We cannot find this many people in the ranks of classroom teachers. The sole solution is to free from class individuals who have the energy and competence to do the job, and to do it virtually for free: university and high school pupils who can read and write with more than marginal success.

Volunteers might be as young as 15, others might be over 25. They would receive a 10-day crash course in the basics of a strong phonetic method, heightened by addition of specific, charged words, proved in a number of pilot projects to bear the greatest power of provocation. The words (not "Dick" and "Jane," but "grief" and "pain" and "lease" and "license," "power," "protest," "police") are those that set the heart and mind alive with possibilities of making something different of the world.

Volunteers would live in the neighborhoods in which they teach. They would teach (at least two hours with each pupil, every day, five days a week) either in their pupils' homes or in a house especially renovated for this purpose, a "literacy center" large enough to offer the facilities for all their living needs and teaching goals.

If volunteers began their work at school semester's end in June, Christmas might be a logical target date for victory. Other nations (Brazil, Cuba, Israel) have succeeded at the same task in periods that range from 60 days to seven months. If there were to be a follow-up, as literacy experts in most nations recommend, this might take place in a two-month "crash" course running for two years in a row during each of the two subsequent summers.

Volunteers might properly receive course credit from their colleges and high schools for the time devoted to this endeavor. Instead of having spent one full semester studying "Problems of Democracy," they would have done their best to *solve* one such problem.

The volunteers would operate in "teams" — groups of black, white and Hispanic kids selected to provide the class and ethnic mix that has a chance to overcome the usual problems of top-down benevolence.

Volunteers should receive their living-stipend from the Federal Government — $20 a week perhaps, but very little more — and personal back-up, friendship and specific pedagogic counsel from an older man or woman, a "team leader." The leader might be a teacher in the public school or college that the volunteers would attend if they were not in this campaign. When this was the case, the teacher ought to get a normal salary from the local school board, university or college. (In cases where teachers do not wish to leave classrooms, or where school boards won't agree, leaders might easily be found among those several hundred thousand certified teachers who are out of work.)

A question about this proposal is asked repeatedly: "How can we expect so many youngsters to give up a full half-year out of their adolescent lives to join a pedagogic and historic struggle of this kind?" I have just returned from a tour of 30 colleges in 20 states. The myth of student lethargy is just that — a myth — but it is not even working as a self-fulfilling prophecy. The kids I met remain alive and ethical in their convictions. The students are less rhetorical, more realistic; they are determined to take a role in shaping history rather than to watch it on television. One thing they have greatly missed since 1972 has been a single concrete focus for their energies and ideals. This project offers that focus for the first time in seven years.

QUESTIONS

1. Kozol characterizes adult illiteracy as comparable to "plague, pestilence or war" (fourth paragraph). How has he prepared us to accept this characterization?
2. In the third paragraph from the end, Kozol refers to "the usual problems of top-down benevolence." Explain what you think these problems might be, and evaluate Kozol's proposal to overcome them.
3. Convert Kozol's final paragraph into a syllogism.

8

Description

DESCRIPTION AS PERSUASION

Description represents in words our sensory impressions caught in a moment of time. In much descriptive writing visual imagery dominates. Look at the following example, part of a letter Vincent Van Gogh wrote to his brother, Theo.

> Twilight is falling, and the view of the yard from my window is simply wonderful, with that little avenue of poplars — their slender forms and thin branches stand out so delicately against the gray evening sky; and then the old arsenal building in the water — quiet as the "waters of the old pool" in the book of Isaiah — down by the waterside the walls of that arsenal are quite green and weather-beaten. Farther down is the little garden and the fence around it with the rosebushes, and everywhere in the yard the black figures of the workmen, and also the little dog. Just now Uncle Jan with his long black hair is probably making his rounds. In the distance the masts of the ships in the dock can be seen, in front the Atjeh, quite black, and the gray and red monitors — and just now here and there the lamps are being lit. At this moment the bell is ringing and the whole stream of workmen is pouring towards the gate; at the same time the lamplighter is coming to light the lamp in the yard behind the house.

First, notice that Van Gogh does not attempt to describe the view from the window at all times of day, but only now, when "twilight is falling." Thus, the figures of the workmen, the little dog, the masts in the distance, appear black; the evening sky is

gray, and "just now here and there the lamps are being lit."
Second, notice that Vincent tells Theo that he sees not "a row of
trees" but a "little avenue of poplars — their slender forms and thin
branches stand out so delicately against the gray evening sky."
These details, the result of close observation, help the reader to see
what Van Gogh saw, and to feel as he felt. Third, notice that while
Van Gogh describes primarily what he *sees* (not surprising in a
painter) he also notices and tells Theo what he *hears*: "At this
moment the bell is ringing." And through every detail he communicates what he feels about the scene he describes: "the view of
the yard from my window is simply wonderful."

Description is often a kind of persuasion. The writer wishes
to persuade us to share his judgment that what he describes is
beautiful or ugly, noble or ignoble, valuable or worthless. If we are
persuaded, it is as a result less of the writer's telling us what to feel
(often the judgment is not stated, but implied) than of his skill in
representing to us what he sees, or experiences through other
senses.

ORGANIZING A DESCRIPTION

Patient observation of details, and finding exactly the right
words with which to communicate our impressions, are both part
of the secret of good descriptive writing, but another part is organization, the translation of our disorderly, even chaotic, impressions
into orderly structures. Limiting the description to what is sensed at
a particular moment in time in itself imposes some order. But in
addition, our descriptions must have some discernible pattern, such
as from left to right, from bottom to top, from general to particular, or, as in Van Gogh's description, from near to far. Notice this
structure, from near to far, as Walt Whitman uses it in his poem, "A
Farm Picture."

> Through the ample open door of the peaceful country barn,
> A sunlit pasture field with cattle and horses feeding,
> And haze and vista, and the far horizon fading away.

Although the poem is only three lines long, the view is leisurely,
beginning where the observer stands, inside the "ample open

door," and then stretching slowly out to the "sunlit pasture field," still distinct, because still close up, then to the slightly more general "cattle and horses," and last to the indistinct "far horizon fading away." The leisurely pace persuades us that the scene is indeed "peaceful"; the orderly structure of the poem allows us to feel that it is.

Now look, by contrast, at a description not of a place, but of a phenomenon, a phenomenon not seen but felt, not peaceful, but "uneasy."

> There is something uneasy in the Los Angeles air this afternoon, some unnatural stillness, some tension. What it means is that tonight a Santa Ana will begin to blow, a hot wind from the northeast whining down through the Cajon and San Gorgonio Passes, blowing up sandstorms out along Route 66, drying the hills and the nerves to the flash point. For a few days now we will see smoke back in the canyons, and hear sirens in the night. I have neither heard nor read that a Santa Ana is due, but I know it, and almost everyone I have seen today knows it too. We know it because we feel it. The baby frets. The maid sulks. I rekindle a waning argument with the telephone company, then cut my losses and lie down, given over to whatever it is in the air. To live with the Santa Ana is to accept, consciously or unconsciously, a deeply mechanistic view of human behavior.
>
> — Joan Didion

Here the governing pattern of the description is more complex — from the general to the specific, and back to the general. Didion begins with the relatively general statement "There is something uneasy in the Los Angeles air this afternoon," and then moves to the specific details that support the generalization: the visible effects of the unseen wind first on the landscape and then on people (the baby, the maid, Didion herself). In the final sentence, again a relatively general one, she summarizes a further effect of what it is "to live with the Santa Ana." The organization is complex, but the passage is not disorderly. Or, we might say, it is just disorderly enough to make us feel, with the writer, "something uneasy in the Los Angeles air."

Specific details and concrete language help us to imagine what the writer has observed; a suitable organization further assists us in following the writer's representation of impressions and feelings.

ESTABLISHING A POINT OF VIEW

In addition to observing closely, finding the right word, and organizing the material, there is yet another technique that helps persuade the reader to accept the writer's observations as true, and his judgment as sound. This technique can be discovered by comparing two descriptions of a building on fire. The first is by a student, trying her hand at description in a composition class.

> The thick, heavy smoke, that could be seen for miles, filled the blue July sky. Firemen frantically battled the blaze that engulfed Hempstead High School, while a crowd of people sadly looked on. Eyes slowly filled up with tears as the reality of having no school to go to started to sink in. Students that had once downed everything that the high school stood for and did, began to realize how much they cared for their school. But it was too late, it was going up in smoke.

The second is by a professional writer, a practiced hand.

> We were on the porch only a short time when I heard a lot of hollering coming from toward the field. The hollering and crying got louder and louder. I could hear Mama's voice over all the rest. It seemed like all the people in the field were running to our house. I ran to the edge of the porch to watch them top the hill. Daddy was leading the running crowd and Mama was right behind him.
>
> "Lord have mercy, my children is in that house!" Mama was screaming. "Hurry, Diddly!" she cried to Daddy. I turned around and saw big clouds of smoke booming out of the front door and shooting out of cracks everywhere. "There, Essie Mae is on the porch," Mama said. "Hurry, Diddly! Get Adline outta that house!" I looked back at Adline. I couldn't hardly see her for the smoke.
>
> George Lee was standing in the yard like he didn't know what to do. As Mama got closer, he ran into the house. My first thought was that he would be burned up. I'd often hoped he would get killed, but I guess I didn't really want him to die after all. I ran inside after him but he came running out again, knocking me down as he passed and leaving me lying face down in the burning room. I jumped up quickly and scrambled out after him. He had the water bucket in his hands. I thought he was going to try to put out the fire. Instead he placed the bucket on the edge of the porch and picked up Adline in his arms.

Moments later Daddy was on the porch. He ran straight into the burning house with three other men right behind him. They opened the large wooden windows to let some of the smoke out and began ripping the paper from the walls before the wood caught on fire. Mama and two other women raked it into the fireplace with sticks, broom handles, and anything else available. Everyone was coughing because of all the smoke.

— Anne Moody

What can we learn from the professional writer? First notice her patience with detail, the concreteness of the passage. Where the student is content with "Firemen frantically battled the blaze that engulfed Hempstead High School," Anne Moody shows us individuals and exactly what each does. Where the student generalizes the reaction of the observers — "Eyes slowly filled up with tears" and "Students . . . began to realize how much they cared for their school" — in Moody's passage Mama screams, "Lord have mercy, my children is in that house!"

But equally important, the professional writer captures the reader's attention, and secures the reader's identification with the observer or narrator, by establishing the observer's physical position. At the beginning she is on the porch, looking toward the field. It is only when she hears her mother scream that she turns around and sees the smoke. And notice that she *does have to turn,* and the writer has the patience to tell us "I turned around and saw. . . ." We could, if we wished to, place the position of the observer, exactly, throughout the action, as if we were blocking a scene in a play. By contrast, notice that there is no real observer in the student's description. If there were, she would first have to be miles away from the scene and looking up into the sky to see the smoke. Then, in the second sentence she would be across the street, watching the firemen. By the third sentence she'd be closer still — not close to the fire, but close to the other observers. In fact, she'd have to be inside their heads to know what they were thinking. As readers we sense this lack of focus; we have no one to identify with. Though we may find the passage moderately interesting, it will not engage us and we will soon forget it.

In addition to the observer's physical location, a good description also provides a consistent psychological position, or *point of view,* with which we can identify ourselves. In the following passage from *Black Elk Speaks,* Black Elk, an Oglala Sioux holy man, is describing the Battle of Little Bighorn (1876).

> The valley went darker with dust and smoke, and there were only shadows and a big noise of many cries and hoofs and guns. On the left of where I was I could hear the shod hoofs of the soldiers' horses going back into the brush and there was shooting everywhere. Then the hoofs came out of the brush, and I came out and was in among men and horses weaving in and out and going upstream, and everybody was yelling, "Hurry! Hurry!" The soldiers were running upstream and we were all mixed there in the twilight and the great noise. I did not see much; but once I saw a Lakota charge at a soldier who stayed behind and fought and was a very brave man. The Lakota took the soldier's horse by the bridle, but the soldier killed him with a six-shooter. I was small and could not crowd in to where the soldiers were, so I did not kill anybody. There were so many ahead of me, and it was all dark and mixed up.

Black Elk was an old man when he told this story. How old would you guess he was at the time it happened? How do you know?

DESCRIPTION AND NARRATION

At the beginning of this chapter we defined description as a representation, in words, of sensory impressions caught in a moment of time. Strictly speaking, description is static. The passage from Van Gogh's letter, and Whitman's poem, most nearly conform to this definition: they each describe a scene caught in a single moment, like a snapshot. Didion's paragraph about the Santa Ana is less static; it implies the passage of time. That time passes is, however, somewhat masked because Didion represents almost everything as happening simultaneously: "The baby frets. The maid sulks. I rekindle a waning argument with the telephone company." By contrast, in Moody's description of a house on fire, we not only hear (with Essie Mae) "a lot of hollering," and see "big clouds of smoke booming out of the front door and shooting out of cracks everywhere," we also know that moments have passed between the first sensory impression and the second, and that several more have passed before the passage ends with all the adults raking the burning wallpaper into the fireplace. The description is thoroughly interwoven with narration. Black Elk's account of the Battle of Little Bighorn is similarly a blend of description and narration.

Pure descriptive writing is relatively rare; long passages of pure description are even more rare. The reason is simple. A description of a place will be much more interesting if the writer shows us something happening there. Similarly descriptions of people are seldom, except briefly, static. In real life we seldom observe people at dead rest; we see them in action; we form our impressions of them from how they move, what they do. Good descriptions, then, frequently show us a person performing some action, a particularly revealing action, or a characteristic one. If, for example, you want to suggest a person's height and weight, it's much more interesting to show him maneuvering through a subway turnstile, perhaps laden with packages, than to say, "He was only five feet four but weighed 185 pounds" or "he was short and stocky." Here is Maya Angelou describing Mr. Freeman, a man who lived for a while with her mother.

> Mr. Freeman moved gracefully, like a big brown bear, and seldom spoke to us. He simply waited for Mother and put his whole self into the waiting. He never read the paper or patted his foot to the radio. He waited. That was all.
>
> If she came home before we went to bed, we saw the man come alive. He would start out of the big chair, like a man coming out of sleep, smiling. I would remember then that a few seconds before, I had heard a car door slam; then Mother's footsteps would signal from the concrete walk. When her key rattled the door, Mr. Freeman would have already asked his habitual question, "Hey, Bibbi, have a good time?"
>
> His query would hang in the air while she sprang over to peck him on the lips. Then she turned to Bailey and me with the lipstick kisses. "Haven't you finished your homework?" If we had and were just reading — "O.K., say your prayers and go to bed." If we hadn't — "Then go to your room and finish . . . then say your prayers and go to bed."
>
> Mr. Freeman's smile never grew, it stayed at the same intensity. Sometimes Mother would go over and sit on his lap and the grin on his face looked as if it would stay there forever.

Notice how animated this description is, how filled not only with Mr. Freeman's physical presence but also with his mysterious inner life. We have a portrait of Mother, too, reflected in Mr. Freeman's waiting, his concentration on the slam of her car door, her footsteps, her key rattling, and, most of all, in his smile. More subtly and more pervasively, the description is animated by our identification with the observer, the small child watching the man who waits so intently for the woman who is her mother.

EXERCISES

1. In one paragraph, describe what you see from your window. Choose a particular time of day and describe only what you see (or might see) or otherwise sense within a moment or two.
2. In one paragraph, describe something that cannot be seen, or cannot be seen except by the effects it creates. (Something hot, or smelly, or loud?)
3. In one paragraph, describe something from the point of view of a child, or an old person, or someone of the opposite sex. (Note *person*. The point of view of a dog, or stone, or carrot is *out*.)
4. In one paragraph, describe a room by showing something happening in it. Your description should reveal (without explicitly stating) your attitude toward it. The reader should be able to sense that the room is, for example, comfortable or sterile or pretentious or cozy or menacing, though no such words are used in the description.
5. First read the following two paragraphs from Saul Bellow's novel *The Victim*. Then answer the questions that follow the paragraphs.

> Leventhal's apartment was spacious. In a better neighborhood, or three stories lower, it would have rented for twice the amount he paid. But the staircase was narrow and stifling and full of turns. Though he went up slowly, he was out of breath when he reached the fourth floor, and his heart beat thickly. He rested before unlocking the door. Entering, he threw down his raincoat and flung himself on the tapestry-covered low bed in the front room. Mary had moved some of the chairs into the corners and covered them with sheets. She could not depend on him to keep the windows shut and the shades and curtains drawn during the day. This afternoon the cleaning woman had been in and there was a pervasive odor of soap powder. He got up and opened a window. The curtains waved once and then were as

motionless as before. There was a movie house strung with lights across the street; on its roof a water tank sat heavily uneven on its timbers; the cowls of the chimneys, which rattled in the slightest stir of air, were still.

The motor of the refrigerator began to run. The ice trays were empty and rattled. Wilma, the cleaning woman, had defrosted the machine and forgotten to refill them. He looked for a bottle of beer he had noticed yesterday; it was gone. There was nothing inside except a few lemons and some milk. He drank a glass of milk and it refreshed him. He had already taken off his shirt and was sitting on the bed unlacing his shoes when there was a short ring of the bell. Eagerly he pulled open the door and shouted, "Who is it?" The flat was unbearably empty. He hoped someone had remembered that Mary was away and had come to keep him company. There was no response below. He called out again, impatiently. It was very probable that someone had pushed the wrong button, but he heard no other doors opening. Could it be a prank? This was not the season for it. Nothing moved in the stair well, and it only added to his depression to discover how he longed for a visitor. He stretched out on the bed, pulling a pillow from beneath the spread and doubling it up. He thought he would doze off. But a little later he found himself standing at the window, holding the curtains with both hands. He was under the impression that he had slept. It was only eight-thirty by the whirring electric clock on the night table, however. Only five minutes had passed.

Questions: How old, approximately, is Leventhal? Of what social or economic class is he? Who is Mary? What do you know of her relationship to Leventhal? What is the weather like? What is Leventhal's mood? How did you know all these things?

6. In one or two paragraphs, describe a person by showing him or her performing some action that takes less than five minutes. From the description we should be able to infer some of the following: the time of day; the weather; and the person's height, weight, age, sex, occupation, economic or educational background, and mood.

7. Study an advertisement and describe it accurately in about 500 words. To do this, you will need a thesis, such as "This advertisement appeals to male chauvinism," or "This advertisement plays on our fear that we may lack sex appeal." Include a copy of the advertisement with your essay.

8. Choose a current or recent political cartoon to describe and analyze. In your first paragraph, describe the drawing (including any words in it) thoroughly enough so that someone who has not seen it can visualize or even draw it fairly accurately. In a second paragraph explain the political message. Don't inject your own opinion; present the cartoonist's point objectively. Submit a copy of the cartoon with your essay. Be sure to choose a cartoon of sufficient complexity to make the analysis worthwhile.

DESCRIPTION AT WORK

The Use of Sidewalks

Jane Jacobs

Under the seeming disorder of the old city, wherever the old city is working successfully, is a marvelous order for maintaining the safety of the streets and the freedom of the city. It is a complex order. Its essence is intricacy of sidewalk use, bringing with it a constant succession of eyes. This order is all composed of movement and change, and although it is life, not art, we may fancifully call it the art form of the city and liken it to the dance — not to a simple-minded precision dance with everyone kicking up at the same time, twirling in unison and bowing off en masse, but to an intricate ballet in which the individual dancers and ensembles all have distinctive parts which miraculously reinforce each other and compose an orderly whole. The ballet of the good city sidewalk never repeats itself from place to place, and in any one place is always replete with new improvisations.

The stretch of Hudson Street where I live is each day the scene of an intricate sidewalk ballet. I make my own first entrance into it a little after eight when I put out the garbage can, surely a prosaic occupation, but I enjoy my part, my little clang, as the droves of junior high school students walk by the center of the stage dropping candy wrappers. (How do they eat so much candy so early in the morning?)

While I sweep up the wrappers I watch the other rituals of morning: Mr. Halpert unlocking the laundry's handcart from its mooring to a cellar door, Joe Cornacchia's son-in-law stacking out the empty crates from the delicatessen, the barber bringing out his sidewalk folding chair, Mr. Goldstein arranging the coils of wire which proclaim the hardware store is open, the wife of the tenement's superintendent depositing her chunky three-year-old with a toy mandolin on the stoop, the vantage point from which he is learning the English his mother cannot speak. Now the primary children, heading for St. Luke's, dribble through to the south; the children for St. Veronica's cross, heading to the west, and the children for P.S. 41, heading toward the east. Two new entrances are being made from the wings: well-dressed and even elegant women and men with brief cases emerge from doorways and side streets. Most of these are heading for the bus and subways, but some hover on the curbs, stopping taxis which have miraculously appeared at the right moment, for the taxis are part of a wider morning ritual: having dropped passengers from midtown in the downtown financial district, they are now bringing downtowners up to midtown. Simultaneously, numbers of women in housedresses have emerged and as they crisscross with one another they pause for quick conversations that sound with either laughter or joint indignation, never, it seems, anything between. It is time for me to hurry to work too, and I exchange my ritual farewell with Mr. Lofaro, the short, thick-bodied, white-aproned fruit man who stands outside his doorway a little up the street, his arms folded, his feet planted, looking solid as earth itself. We nod; we each glance quickly up and down the street, then look back to each other and smile. We have done this many a morning for more than ten years, and we both know what it means: All is well.

The heart-of-the-day ballet I seldom see, because part of the nature of it is that working people who live there, like me, are mostly gone, filling the roles of strangers on other sidewalks. But from days off, I know enough of it to know that it becomes more and more intricate. Longshoremen who are not working that day gather at the White Horse or the Ideal or the International for beer and conversation. The executives and business lunchers from the industries just to the west throng the Dorgene restaurant and the Lion's Head coffee house; meat-market workers and communications scientists fill the bakery lunchroom. Character dancers come on, a strange old man with strings of old shoes over his shoulders, motor-scooter riders with big beards and girl friends who bounce on the back of the scooters and wear their hair long in front of their faces as well as behind, drunks who follow the advice of the Hat Council and are always turned out in hats, but not hats the Council would approve. Mr. Lacey, the locksmith, shuts up his shop for a while and goes to exchange the time of day with Mr. Slube at the cigar store.

Mr. Koochagian, the tailor, waters the luxuriant jungle of plants in his window, gives them a critical look from the outside, accepts a compliment on them from two passers-by, fingers the leaves on the plane tree in front of our house with a thoughtful gardener's appraisal, and crosses the street for a bite at the Ideal where he can keep an eye on customers and wigwag across the message that he is coming. The baby carriages come out, and clusters of everyone from toddlers with dolls to teen-agers with homework gather at the stoops.

When I get home after work, the ballet is reaching its crescendo. This is the time of roller skates and stilts and tricycles, and games in the lee of the stoop with bottletops and plastic cowboys; this is the time of bundles and packages, zigzagging from the drug store to the fruit stand and back over to the butcher's; this is the time when teen-agers, all dressed up, are pausing to ask if their slips show or their collars look right; this is the time when beautiful girls get out of MG's; this is the time when the fire engines go through; this is the time when anybody you know around Hudson Street will go by.

As darkness thickens and Mr. Halpert moors the laundry cart to the cellar door again, the ballet goes on under lights, eddying back and forth but intensifying at the bright spotlight pools of Joe's sidewalk pizza dispensary, the bars, the delicatessen, the restaurant and the drug store. The night workers stop now at the delicatessen, to pick up salami and a container of milk. Things have settled down for the evening but the street and its ballet have not come to a stop.

I know the deep night ballet and its seasons best from waking long after midnight to tend a baby and, sitting in the dark, seeing the shadows and hearing the sounds of the sidewalk. Mostly it is a sound like infinitely pattering snatches of party conversation and, about three in the morning, singing, very good singing. Sometimes there is sharpness and anger or sad, sad weeping, or a flurry of search for a string of beads broken. One night a young man came roaring along, bellowing terrible language at two girls whom he had apparently picked up and who were disappointing him. Doors opened, a wary semicircle formed around him, not too close, until the police came. Out came the heads, too, along Hudson Street, offering opinion, "Drunk . . . Crazy . . . A wild kid from the suburbs."[1]

Deep in the night, I am almost unaware how many people are on the street unless something calls them together, like the bagpipe.

[1] He turned out to be a wild kid from the suburbs. Sometimes, on Hudson Street, we are tempted to believe the suburbs must be a difficult place to bring up children.

Who the piper was and why he favored our street I have no idea. The bagpipe just skirled out in the February night, and as if it were a signal the random, dwindled movements of the sidewalk took on direction. Swiftly, quietly, almost magically a little crowd was there, a crowd that evolved into a circle with a Highland fling inside it. The crowd could be seen on the shadowy sidewalk, the dancers could be seen, but the bagpiper himself was almost invisible because his bravura was all in his music. He was a very little man in a plain brown overcoat. When he finished and vanished, the dancers and watchers applauded, and applause came from the galleries too, half a dozen of the hundred windows on Hudson Street. Then the windows closed, and the little crowd dissolved into the random movements of the night street.

The strangers on Hudson Street, the allies whose eyes help us natives keep the peace of the street, are so many that they always seem to be different people from one day to the next. That does not matter. Whether they are so many always-different people as they seem to be, I do not know. Likely they are. When Jimmy Rogan fell through a plate-glass window (he was separating some scuffling friends) and almost lost his arm, a stranger in an old T shirt emerged from the Ideal bar, swiftly applied an expert tourniquet and, according to the hospital's emergency staff, saved Jimmy's life. Nobody remembered seeing the man before and no one has seen him since. The hospital was called in this way: a woman sitting on the steps next to the accident ran over to the bus stop, wordlessly snatched the dime from the hand of a stranger who was waiting with his fifteen-cent fare ready, and raced into the Ideal's phone booth. The stranger raced after her to offer the nickel too. Nobody remembered seeing him before, and no one has seen him since. When you see the same stranger three or four times on Hudson Street, you begin to nod. This is almost getting to be an acquaintance, a public acquaintance, of course.

I have made the daily ballet of Hudson Street sound more frenetic than it is, because writing it telescopes it. In real life, it is not that way. In real life, to be sure, something is always going on, the ballet is never at a halt, but the general effect is peaceful and the general tenor even leisurely. People who know well such animated city streets will know how it is. I am afraid people who do not will always have it a little wrong in their heads — like the old prints of rhinoceroses made from travelers' descriptions of rhinoceroses.

On Hudson Street, the same as in the North End of Boston or in any other animated neighborhoods of great cities, we are not innately more competent at keeping the sidewalks safe than are the people who try to live off the hostile truce of Turf in a blind-eyed city. We are the lucky possessors of a city order that makes it relatively simple to keep the peace because there are plenty of eyes on the street. But there is nothing simple about that order itself, or the bewildering number of components that go into it. Most of those components are specialized in one way or another. They unite in their joint effect upon the sidewalk which is not specialized in the least. That is its strength.

QUESTIONS

1. Evaluate the effectiveness of the extended metaphor Jacobs uses. Did the comparison of the activity on her street with a ballet help you to share her point of view, or did you find it obtrusive and distracting? If you found the device useful or pleasing, explain why ballet is a better metaphor than say, concert or circus. Or, can you think of a metaphor that is better than ballet?
2. What is Jacobs's thesis? Locate the thesis sentence, or summarize the thesis in your own words.
3. Would you agree that the inherent superiority of cities over suburbs is a secondary argument or theme of the essay? If so, try to locate the passages in which this argument is stated or implied.
4. In her next-to-last paragraph, Jacobs briefly apologizes for the inadequacy of her description of life on the sidewalk. Does your experience allow you to detect inadequacies in her description? If so, what are they?
5. Explain Jacobs's next-to-last sentence.

Adman's Atlanta[2]

Lynda Martin

===

Centered in the top third of the page is a three-line, deep black headline: "Atlanta's suburban style of urban living." The first A is the only capital letter, there is a period after living, and the letters are the Roman script of a regular typewriter. A round picture in black

---

[2] This essay was written by a freshman in response to an assignment requiring students to describe and analyze an advertisement.

and white with a diameter the size of half the page is separated from the heading by three blocks of copy and a very small black and white rectangular picture. Each photo has a caption under it. In the round picture a beautifully gnarled tree casts its shadow over the driveway and cobblestone sidewalks that front two clean-lined, white apartment buildings at right angles to each other. In the break between the buildings a lamp of five white globes contrasts with dark trees behind it. A well-dressed businessman and businesswoman walk in the sun in front of the building on the left; at the entrance of the other building another suited man climbs into a new-looking compact car. In the other photo Atlanta's skyline glows pale in a flawless afternoon sky behind a mass of trees that covers the bottom two-thirds of the shot. The copy tells of the joys of living in Atlanta, explaining that life there combines the best of the city with the best of the suburb.

In attempting to persuade the reader that "Atlanta's style of living" is worth finding out about (by writing to the Atlanta Chamber of Commerce), the creators of the ad have used several techniques to associate living in Atlanta with business and with luxury; in short, with the common idea of success.

First to catch the reader's eye is the dark solid heading. The forceful deep black print is softened by its curved, but simple, design. Compact but not crowded, these words add up to a plain positive statement with a modestly assertive period at the end.

This business-like handling shows also in the picture centered below. It depicts clean white modern buildings lived in by purposeful people who are apparently going about a normal day in their successful lives. The dominance of the foreground tree and other trees in the background complement the buildings, preventing any appearance of harshness. A sense of gentleness and luxury is augmented by the blurred round border that makes the picture seem to be surrounded by sunlight. The sun is important in this picture, and also in the rectangular picture to the left. In both, the sun heightens the contrast between the clean brightness of the buildings and the luxurious darkness of the trees, producing an atmosphere of happy leisure.

Lest leisure seem to be merely idleness, any emptiness created by the word "suburban" is immediately filled by the word "urban." The copy emphasizes both the convenience of living "close in" — that is, being near "necessities and pleasures: schools, shopping, churches, cultural activities . . ." — and the flexibility of being able to live in the city "in almost any manner you choose," be it some kind of urban apartment or a home of your own. Life in Atlanta is

Atlanta's suburban style of urban living.

In Atlanta you can live close in and still be close to wooded green. This blending of the urban and suburban makes Atlanta one of the most attractive and convenient big cities you'll find. And you can live here in almost any manner you choose. Up in a high-rise. In a formal town house. In a garden apartment with pool and tennis courts. Or amidst a rolling lawn and garden of your own. And no matter which you choose, you're never far from the necessities and pleasures: schools, shopping, churches, cultural activities, entertainment, and of course your office. Find out about Atlanta's style of living. Contact: Paul Miller, Atlanta Chamber of Commerce, 1314 Commerce Building, Atlanta, Ga. 30303. 404—521-0845.

TREES IN ATLANTA REACH INTO THE HEART OF DOWNTOWN.

TREES SURROUND LUXURY APARTMENTS ON PEACHTREE ROAD, 10 MINUTES FROM DOWNTOWN.

urban but "close to the wooded green." This idea is not only brought out in the copy, but is also emphasized in the pictures by beginning both captions with the word "trees."

This advertisement creates a favorable impression of city living, counteracting many readers' associations of a city with dirt, smog, and crowds. It indirectly advertises the "good life" of a prosperous businessman, be it in "a formal town house" or with "a rolling lawn and garden of your own." It also advertises middle-class values, beginning with religion and ending with business: "churches, cultural activities, entertainment, and of course your office."

Los Angeles Notebook
Joan Didion

There is something uneasy in the Los Angeles air this afternoon, some unnatural stillness, some tension. What it means is that tonight a Santa Ana will begin to blow, a hot wind from the northeast whining down through the Cajon and San Gorgonio Passes, blowing up sandstorms out along Route 66, drying the hills and the nerves to the flash point. For a few days now we will see smoke back in the canyons, and hear sirens in the night. I have neither heard nor read that a Santa Ana is due, but I know it, and almost everyone I have seen today knows it too. We know it because we feel it. The baby frets. The maid sulks. I rekindle a waning argument with the telephone company, then cut my losses and lie down, given over to whatever it is in the air. To live with the Santa Ana is to accept, consciously or unconsciously, a deeply mechanistic view of human behavior.

I recall being told, when I first moved to Los Angeles and was living on an isolated beach, that the Indians would throw themselves into the sea when the bad wind blew. I could see why. The Pacific turned ominously glossy during a Santa Ana period, and one woke in the night troubled not only by the peacocks screaming in the olive trees but by the eerie absence of surf. The heat was surreal. The sky had a yellow cast, the kind of light sometimes called "earthquake weather." My only neighbor would not come out of her house for days, and there were no lights at night, and her husband roamed the place with a machete. One day he would tell me that he had heard a trespasser, the next a rattlesnake.

"On nights like that," Raymond Chandler once wrote about the Santa Ana, "every booze party ends in a fight. Meek little wives feel the edge of the carving knife and study their husbands' necks. Anything can happen." That was the kind of wind it was. I did not know then that there was any basis for the effect it had on all of us, but it turns out to be another of those cases in which science bears out folk wisdom. The Santa Ana, which is named for one of the canyons it rushes through, is a *foehn* wind, like the *foehn* of Austria and Switzerland and the *hamsin* of Israel. There are a number of persistent malevolent winds, perhaps the best known of which are the mistral of France and the Mediterranean sirocco, but a *foehn* wind has distinct characteristics: it occurs on the leeward slope of a mountain range and, although the air begins as a cold mass, it is warmed as it comes down the mountain and appears finally as a hot dry wind. Whenever and wherever a *foehn* blows, doctors hear about headaches and nausea and allergies, about "nervousness," about "depression." In Los Angeles some teachers do not attempt to conduct formal classes during a Santa Ana, because the children become unmanageable. In Switzerland the suicide rate goes up during the *foehn,* and in the courts of some Swiss cantons the wind is considered a mitigating circumstance for crime. Surgeons are said to watch the wind, because blood does not clot normally during a *foehn.* A few years ago an Israeli physicist discovered that not only during such winds, but for the ten or twelve hours which precede them, the air carries an unusually high ratio of positive to negative ions. No one seems to know exactly why that should be; some talk about friction and others suggest solar disturbances. In any case the positive ions are there, and what an excess of positive ions does, in the simplest terms, is make people unhappy. One cannot get much more mechanistic than that.

Easterners commonly complain that there is no "weather" at all in Southern California, that the days and the seasons slip by relentlessly, numbingly bland. That is quite misleading. In fact the climate is characterized by infrequent but violent extremes: two periods of torrential subtropical rains which continue for weeks and wash out the hills and send subdivisions sliding toward the sea; about twenty scattered days a year of the Santa Ana, which, with its incendiary dryness, invariably means fire. At the first prediction of a Santa Ana, the Forest Service flies men and equipment from northern California into the southern forests, and the Los Angeles Fire Department cancels its ordinary non-firefighting routines. The Santa Ana caused Malibu to burn the way it did in 1956, and Bel Air in 1961, and Santa Barbara in 1964. In the winter of 1966–67 eleven men were killed fighting a Santa Ana fire that spread through the San Gabriel Mountains.

Just to watch the front-page news out of Los Angeles during a Santa Ana is to get very close to what it is about the place. The longest single Santa Ana period in recent years was in 1957, and it lasted not the usual three or four days but fourteen days, from November 21 until December 4. On the first day 25,000 acres of the San Gabriel Mountains were burning, with gusts reaching 100 miles an hour. In town, the wind reached Force 12, or hurricane force, on the Beaufort Scale; oil derricks were toppled and people ordered off the downtown streets to avoid injury from flying objects. On November 22 the fire in the San Gabriels was out of control. On November 24 six people were killed in automobile accidents, and by the end of the week the Los Angeles *Times* was keeping a box score of traffic deaths. On November 26 a prominent Pasadena attorney, depressed about money, shot and killed his wife, their two sons, and himself. On November 27 a South Gate divorcée, twenty-two, was murdered and thrown from a moving car. On November 30 the San Gabriel fire was still out of control, and the wind in town was blowing eighty miles an hour. On the first day of December four people died violently, and on the third the wind began to break.

It is hard for people who have not lived in Los Angeles to realize how radically the Santa Ana figures in the local imagination. The city burning is Los Angeles's deepest image of itself: Nathanael West perceived that, in *The Day of the Locust*; and at the time of the 1965 Watts riots what struck the imagination most indelibly were the fires. For days one could drive the Harbor Freeway and see the city on fire, just as we had always known it would be in the end. Los Angeles weather is the weather of catastrophe, of apocalypse, and, just as the reliably long and bitter winters of New England determine the way life is lived there, so the violence and the unpredictability of the Santa Ana affect the entire quality of life in Los Angeles, accentuate its impermanence, its unreliability. The wind shows us how close to the edge we are.

QUESTIONS

1. Paraphrase or explain the last sentence of the first paragraph. What passages in the essay offer the most persuasive evidence supporting the point?
2. Beginning with the third paragraph, Didion defines the Santa Ana. Would the essay have been clearer or more effective if the definition had introduced the essay? Explain.
3. Explain the last sentence, and evaluate it as a conclusion.

The Rayburn Building

Ada Louise Huxtable

It is moving time on Capitol Hill for 169 Congressmen eligible for space in the new Rayburn House Office Building. The structure's three-room suites complete with refrigerators and safes are being raffled off to applicants who may have a view of the Capitol dome or an interior court, depending on seniority. Even seniority, however, does not give any legislator a door leading from his office, or his aide's office, to his working staff without passage through a waiting room full of constituents and special pleaders. To correct this small planning error would add $200,000 to costs already estimated at anywhere from $86 million to $122 million for the expensive and controversial building.

Some Congressmen are moving in reluctantly. Representative Thomas L. Ashley, Democrat of Ohio, for one, rejected his office on sight. But he is making the move anyway this week because his present quarters are too small. "This layout could paralyze us," he said during his inspection tour. "It's an ugly building." Mr. Ashley is not alone. The professional architectural press has been bitterly critical as construction progressed. (The building has taken seven years and $22 million more to complete than originally estimated largely as the result of expensive miscalculations; change orders have reached 300 per cent over Government average; bid estimates on contracts have been as much as $45 million off.) There have been accusations of secret planning, pork barrel commissions and possible misuse of public funds. The fact that the general contractor was Matthew J. McCloskey, Democratic party stalwart of Philadelphia, has not escaped notice. But the storm swirls uselessly around a behemoth that is obviously here to stay. Architecturally, the Rayburn Building is a national disaster. Its defects range from profligate mishandling of 50 acres of space to elephantine esthetic banality at record costs. The costs are now being investigated by the General Accounting Office.

Equal to the question of costs, however, is the question of what Congress and the capital have received for the investment. It is quite possible that this is the worst building for the most money in the history of the construction art. It stuns by sheer mass and boring bulk. Only 15 per cent of its space is devoted to the offices and hearing rooms for which it was erected. Forty-two per cent of the floor area is used for parking. Endless corridors have been likened to *Last Year at Marienbad*. Stylistically, it is the apotheosis of humdrum.

It is hard to label the building, but it might be called Corrupt Classic. Its empty aridity and degraded classical details are vulgarization without drama, and to be both dull and vulgar may be an achievement of sorts.

The structure's chief "design features" are hollow exercises in sham grandeur. A supercolossal exterior expanse of stolid, Mussolini-style pomp is embellished with sculpture that would be the apogee of art in the Soviet Union, where overscaled muscles and expressions of empty solemnity are still admired. A monumental entrance at second floor level is reached by pretentious steps that will never be used. The real entrance, on the ground floor just below, abandons false dignity for no dignity at all. The formal marble front with its blank, machine-stamped look sits on a gargantuan base of informal, random-cut granite of obviously miscalculated proportions, an effect comparable to combining a top hat with blue jeans. Groups of columns meant to dress up the drab, flat façade not only fail to suggest that columns are traditionally supporting members, but they also terminate incongruously on balconies that appear to support the columns — a neat combination of structural illogic and stylistic flimflam.

Inside, a pedestrian statue of Sam Rayburn presents the seat of its pants to entering visitors.[3] It faces a huge landscaped central court that is an artless cliché. Embracing Mr. Sam is another cliché, a two-story curved double stair fated to be not only useless but graceless. In the hearing rooms, coarse, lifeless classical cornices and moldings are joined to stock modern acoustic ceilings and panel lighting for a state of esthetic warfare tempered only by their matching mediocrity. This model comes in red, green, gold and blue. Behind the scenes, the classic false front is abandoned and working subcommittee rooms use ordinary partitions and fittings of the lowest commercial common denominator. Throughout the building, the design level is consistent: whatever is not hack is heavy-handed.

For $100 million, give or take a few million (the cost of New York's mammoth Pan Am Building) the gentlemen of the House have got a sterile, stock plan of singularly insensitive design and detailing that was moribund more than half a century ago. Even the basic functional requirements have been insufficiently studied. The making of useful and beautiful public spaces with the power to inspire and symbolize as well as to serve — the timeless aim of

[3] Turned around after this article appeared — the rewards of architectural criticism.

architecture and one that is mandatory for Washington — is conspicuously absent.

The Rayburn Building is the third solid gold turkey in a row to come out of the office of the Architect of the Capitol, J. George Stewart, who is not an architect, but who picks them for Congress. For this one he selected Harbeson, Hough, Livingston & Larson of Philadelphia. He is also responsible for the ill-advised remodeling of the Capitol's East Front and the construction of the new Senate Office Building. There are no controls or reviews for Mr. Stewart's work, and none for the House committee that authorized the Rayburn Building's construction and appropriations, generally behind closed doors.

An old architectural saying has it that there's no point in crying over spilled marble. Seven million pounds of it have been poured onto Capitol Hill in this latest Congressional building venture, and there is nothing quite as invulnerable as a really monumental mistake. The Rayburn Building's ultimate claim to fame may well be that it is the biggest star-spangled architectural blunder of our time.

QUESTIONS

1. What is Huxtable's thesis?
2. Does the description adequately support the thesis? Support your answer by referring to a few passages.

9

Narration

THE USES OF NARRATIVE

Usually we think of narrative writing as the art of the novelist or short story writer, but narratives need not be fictional. Biography and autobiography, history and books of travel are all largely narrative. And of course narrative passages may appear in writings that as a whole are not themselves narratives. For instance, expository and persuasive essays may include narratives — perhaps anecdotes, or brief sketches of historical occurrences or of personal experiences — that serve to clarify the essayist's point. Suppose, for example, that you are writing a paper for a course in ethics, arguing that it is immoral for physicians to withhold the truth (supposedly for the patients' own good) from terminally ill patients. You might include a brief narrative recounting how such a patient, when told the truth, responded not by withdrawing, but by increasing her useful activities — which included helping the members of her family to adjust to her imminent death. In writing any essay you may find that a paragraph or two of narrative helps you first to engage your readers' attention and then to make an abstract point concretely and persuasively.

In the following passage, addressed to English teachers, Paul B. Diederich, a specialist in the teaching of writing, explains mostly through narrative the "effects of excessive correction" on students in writing classes.

I can judge one of the main effects of . . . grading by the attitudes of students who land in my remedial course in college. They hate and fear writing more than anything else they have had to do in school. If they see a blank sheet of paper on which they are expected to write something, they look as though they want to scream. Apparently they have never written anything that anyone thought was good. At least, no one ever *told* them that anything in their writing was good. All their teachers looked for were mistakes, and there are so many kinds of mistakes in writing that their students despair of ever learning to avoid them.

The attitude toward writing that these students have developed is well illustrated by a story told by the Russian writer Chekhov about a kitten that was given to his uncle. The uncle wanted to make the kitten a champion killer of mice, so while it was still very young, he showed it a live mouse in a cage. Since the kitten's hunting instinct had not yet developed, it examined the mouse curiously but without any hostility. The uncle wanted to teach it that such fraternizing with the enemy was wrong, so he slapped the kitten, scolded it, and sent it away in disgrace. The next day the same mouse was shown to the kitten again. This time the kitten regarded it rather fearfully but without any aggressive intent. Again the uncle slapped it, scolded it, and sent it away. This treatment went on day after day. After some time, as soon as the kitten saw or smelled that mouse, it screamed and tried to climb up the walls. At that point the uncle lost patience and gave the kitten away, saying that it was stupid and would never learn. Of course the kitten had learned perfectly, and had learned exactly what it had been taught, but unfortunately not what the uncle intended to teach. "I can sympathize with that kitten," says Chekhov, "because that same uncle tried to teach me Latin."

If everything written by our less gifted writers gets slapped down for its mistakes, and if this treatment continues year after year, can we expect that their attitude toward writing will differ from the attitude of the kitten toward that mouse? I saw the result year after year in my remedial classes. If I asked them to write anything, they reacted as though I had asked them to walk a tightrope sixty feet above the ground with no net to catch them if they fell. It took some time to build up their confidence, to convince them that writing is as simple and natural as talking, and that no reader would mind a few mistakes if he got interested in what was being written about. For some time I never commented adversely on anything they wrote but expressed appreciation of anything I found interesting, no matter how badly it was expressed. After students gained confidence I continued to express appreciation but offered one suggestion for improvement at the end of each paper. If poor writers learn one thing about writing per paper, that is far above the average.

Notice that in the brief passage, three paragraphs in all, there are two narratives. The first, a retelling of Chekhov's anecdote about a kitten, memorably illustrates Diederich's point that students subjected to excessive correction are not taught to write but taught to fear writing. The third paragraph, while mainly expository, recounts Diederich's own experiences — year after year — of restoring confidence in students in his remedial classes.

Often a short narrative provides an arresting opening to an essay. You may have noticed how often speakers rely on this device; writers, too, find it effective. Flannery O'Connor begins "The King of the Birds" (an essay on her passion for collecting and raising peacocks) with the following story:

> When I was five, I had an experience that marked me for life. Pathé News sent a photographer from New York to Savannah to take a picture of a chicken of mine. This chicken, a buff Cochin Bantam, had the distinction of being able to walk either forward or backward. Her fame had spread through the press, and by the time she reached the attention of Pathé News, I suppose there was nowhere left for her to go — forward or backward. Shortly after that she died, as now seems fitting.

What makes this anecdote arresting? First of all, we can hardly read that an experience marked a person for life without wanting to know what the experience was. We expect to learn something sensational; perhaps, human nature being what it is, we hope to learn something horrifying. But O'Connor cannily does not gratify our wish. Instead she treats us to something like a joke. The chicken, whose fame had "spread through the press," has her picture taken by Pathé News (one of the companies that made the newsreels shown regularly in movie theaters before television became popular) and then dies. If the joke is in part on us, O'Connor takes the sting out of it by turning it around on herself. In her second paragraph she explains:

> If I put this information in the beginning of an article on peacocks, it is because I am always being asked why I raise them, and I have no short or reasonable answer.

But of course her answer, contained in the first paragraph, *is* short, and about as reasonable an explanation as any of us can offer about our passion for collecting anything. If these opening paragraphs persuade us to keep reading, it is not because they deliver the melodrama they at first hinted at, but because O'Connor's irony persuades us that she is entertaining, and that she is honest about her experience. We want to learn more about her, and we may thereby be seduced into learning what she wants to teach us about peacocks. Moreover, O'Connor's explanation that she tells the story because "I have no short or reasonable answer," reveals a profound truth about the impulse to tell stories. When a writer, even the writer of an expository essay, tells a story, it is because that story happens to be the best way to make the particular point he or she wants to make.

NARRATIVE PACE

A narrative is concerned with action, and the pace is normally swift. The narrator tries to communicate the concreteness of the events as they occurred, or as they registered on him, at the speed at which they occurred, or seemed to occur. The good storyteller cuts any details or incidents that clog the action or blur the point of the story. The kitten in Chekhov's narrative is shown a live mouse "while [the kitten] was still very young," and again "the next day." Since the kitten's behavior doesn't change (nor, more significantly, does the uncle's) Chekhov swiftly summarizes what happened next: "This treatment went on day after day." We are then given only one sentence of description, directly relevant to the narrative, before we are told that the uncle lost patience and gave the kitten away. It is not important to Chekhov's point, or to Diederich's, whether the kitten was gray or calico, long haired or short, cuddly or scrawny, but only that it "screamed and tried to climb up the walls" when it saw or smelled the mouse. *These* details are the relevant ones, and so Chekhov gives them to us. Similarly, O'Connor describes her chicken only enough to convince us of its reality — it was a "buff Cochin Bantam." The point of the anecdote lies not in the unremarkable chicken (who achieves her fame and dies in three sentences) but in the effect on the writer of a brief moment of celebrity. On a deeper level, the point of the anecdote is the writer's wish to secure our attention and goodwill.

ORGANIZING A NARRATIVE

The organization of a narrative is normally chronological, though purposeful variations are welcome. For example, fairly often narratives begin at the end, for a dramatic opening, and then present the earlier parts of the story in chronological order. Such a structure deliberately dispels surprise about the outcome, but gains suspense; the reader enjoys the pleasure of anticipating how events will move toward the known ending. In the following essay (two paragraphs in all) you'll find the end of the story foreshadowed in the word "amiable" in the first sentence.

> Out in Akron, Ohio, there is an underground church called Alice's Restaurant, which figures in the most amiable story of the season just past. This group, led by unfrocked priests and unchurched ministers, was doing a deal of earnest good work in a quiet way, all to dramatize and protest the commercialization of Christmas. At shopping centers, for instance, they passed out leaflets calling upon shoppers to limit individual gifts to two-fifty and to devote the overplus to the poor. Then it occurred to one underground churchman, David Bullock by name, to demonstrate the fate that would inevitably befall the Holy Family in a society of heartless abundance. "Joseph and Mary were poor people," Mr. Bullock observed, and he proceeded to devise a scheme that would reveal "what would happen when a poor young couple dressed like Joseph and Mary tried to get a room nearly two thousand years after the birth of Christ." And so it came to pass in those days that Mr. Bullock, in beard and robe, walked out of the cold and darkness of Akron into the lobby of the Downtown Holiday Inn, accompanied

by a young woman and a donkey. "I need a room for the night," he told the manager. "My wife is heavy with child." He then filled out the registration form, identifying himself as Joseph of Nazareth, travelling with his wife from Judea. Then he waited. The night manager, Mr. Robert Nagel, affably observed that they had come a long way and handed over the key to Room 101.

We picture Mr. Bullock with the key in his hand, his rented donkey lurking behind him, and his faith in human nature crumbling to the ground. To crown his discomfiture, Mr. Nagel offered the wayfarers a free meal. But, alas, in an era of affluence, satiety, like the indiscriminate rain, is apt to descend upon the just and unjust alike. "We weren't very hungry," Mr. Bullock said later, "so I asked him if we could have some drinks." Then he added, "And you know what? He sent them around." For his own part, Mr. Nagel was under no illusions about the financial standing of his new guests. "I knew they couldn't pay," he said. "I mean, a donkey is not a normal form of transportation." One would like to shake him by the hand. We thank Mr. Nagel for adding immeasurably to the merriment of our Christmas, and for his exhibition of that unpredictable, shrewd, and sometimes highly inconvenient human generosity that makes sweeping moral judgments so risky — even for the most earnest of moralists — and makes life so richly interesting for the rest of us.

Notice that although the narrative within the essay is organized chronologically, it is framed — at the beginning by some background information, and at the end by the writer's response to the incident, his reason for sharing it. Note also that the writer interrupts the narrative briefly at the beginning of the second paragraph to speculate how Mr. Bullock looked and, more important, how he felt. Although the writer makes the point unobtrusively, it is clear that he was not an eyewitness to the story or an actor in it, but pieced it together from two interviews with the participants and perhaps from some additional research. Finally, notice that if you skim the essay you can easily spot the narrative portion by observing the appearance of verbs in the past tense ("walked," "told," "filled out," "waited," "observed," "handed") and by the frequency of the word "then." Narratives, however they are organized, are almost always told in the past tense; and good story-tellers help us to follow the succession of events, the passage of time, by using such transitional words as *first, then, next, at last,* and *finally*.

Finally, we reprint a letter to the editor in which a college student, an assault victim, tells her experience. You may observe here too that the organization is for the most part chronological, made clear by transitions, and framed by the writer's analysis of her experience and of her reasons for revealing it. As readers, we may or may not notice these points; gripped by the story being told, we are largely unaware of the techniques of successful writers. As students of writing, however, we study these techniques.

To the Editor:

I write this letter out of concern for women of the college community. I am one of the two students who were assaulted during the winter recess. I do not feel any shame or embarrassment over what happened. Instead, I want to share some of my experience because in doing so I may help other women to think about rape and rape prevention.

First I think it is important for the community to understand what happened to me. At my request, during the vacation a well-intentioned employee let me into my residence hall to collect some things from my room. It was after dark. I was alone in my room when a man appeared at the door with a stocking over his head and a knife in his hand. He said he was going to rape me. I had no intention of submitting, and I struggled with him for about five minutes. One of the reasons why I chose not to submit but to resist was that as a virgin I did not want my first sexual experience to be the horror of rape. While struggling I tried to get him to talk to me, saying such things as "Why do you want to rape me? Don't you understand I want no part of this? I am a woman, not an object. In God's name, please don't rape me." He finally overpowered me and attempted to rape me, but stopped when he realized I had a tampax in. Then at knife point he asked me a number of questions. He ended by threatening that if I reported and identified him he would kill me. As he was leaving he made me lie on my bed and count to five hundred, which I started to do. Then as I reached one hundred he returned and told me to start over. Thus it was good I did not get up right after he left.

It is impossible to say what should be done in all instances of assault. Each incident is different and requires a different response. I think what helped me most was my ability to remain calm, assess the situation, and then act firmly. I did struggle, I did talk, but I also did act in such a way as to ensure my own safety at knife point.

I believe there are some reasons why I was able to cope with the situation. One is that I had talked with other women about rape and self-defense. As a result I was more aware of the possibility of rape and had thought some about what I might do if confronted with an attacker. Also my active involvement in the women's movement has helped me develop confidence in myself, especially in my strength, both emotional and physical. I believe such confidence helped me not to panic. Another reason why I was able to cope was that I prayed.

I think it is important also to share with you the aftermath of the attack. The first thing I did after leaving my room was to report the incident to security and to the campus police. I did not hesitate to report the attack since I realized that reporting it was vital to protect the safety of the college community. The police were efficient and helpful in taking the report and starting search procedures. (The police also told me they did not think I was in further danger, despite the threats on my life. There seemed to be little reason for him to come back.) Also, two female members of the student services staff stayed with me most of the evening. Their presence and support were very helpful to me, especially while I talked to the police. Since the incident, I have also found support from professional staff and from friends. The residence office, the medical and psychiatric staff, the dean's office, and the chaplaincy staff have all been very helpful. All have protected my confidentiality.

At first I did not realize that I would want or need to seek out people's help, but now I am glad I did. The rape experience goes beyond the assault itself. I have come to understand the importance of dealing with the complex emotions that follow. Also I now know that there is no reason for women to feel ashamed, embarrassed, or scared about seeking help.

I hope you now have a greater concern for your own safety after reading about what happened to me. I think this is the most important point of my writing. It never occurred to me that entering an unoccupied residence hall was dangerous. We all have been too accustomed to doing things on and off this campus without considering our own safety or vulnerability to attacks. But we ourselves are our own best security, so please protect yourselves and each other.

I am aware I will be working through this experience for a long time to come. I am thankful that there are people in this community to help me do that. I in turn want to be helpful in any way I can. So I invite women who are genuinely concerned about rape and assault to join me in sharing experiences and thoughts next Tuesday, February 18 at 7 P.M. in the Women's Center.

Name withheld upon request.

EXERCISES

1. In one or two paragraphs tell a story that illustrates an abstraction, such as courage, endurance, a misunderstanding, a put-down, pride, the generation gap, embarrassment, loneliness. For an example, see "Conceit" (pages 379–80) and the brief discussion following it.

2. In 750–1000 words survey your development as a writer and explain your current attitude toward writing. Focus your essay on one narrative or on two contrasting narratives to exemplify what you have learned and how you learned it. Whether your thesis is stated or implied, be sure that your essay makes a clear point. Your point might be, for example, that you learned more about writing from working on your school newspaper or from studying geometry than from most of your English classes, or that the different approaches of two teachers reinforced each other, or left you hopelessly confused about writing.

3. For an essay on any topic you choose, write an opening paragraph that includes an anecdote. Don't write the essay, but indicate from the anecdote and, if you wish, an additional sentence or two, the topic of your essay.

4. In 500–1000 words narrate an experience in such a way that you communicate not only the experience but the significance of it. For example, you might tell of an interview for a job which gave you some awareness of the attitude of people with jobs toward those without jobs. Or you might narrate an experience at school that seems to you to illuminate the virtues or defects or assumptions of the school. A variation: John Keats in a letter says, "Nothing ever becomes real till it is experienced — Even a proverb is no proverb to you till your life has illustrated it." Recount an experience that has made you feel the truth of a proverb.

NARRATION AT WORK

Shooting an Elephant

George Orwell

In Moulmein, in Lower Burma, I was hated by large numbers of people — the only time in my life that I have been important enough for this to happen to me. I was sub-divisional police officer of the town, and in an aimless, petty kind of way anti-European feeling was very bitter. No one had the guts to raise a riot, but if a European woman went through the bazaars alone somebody would probably spit betel juice over her dress. As a police officer I was an obvious target and was baited whenever it seemed safe to do so. When a nimble Burman tripped me up on the football field and the referee (another Burman) looked the other way, the crowd yelled with hideous laughter. This happened more than once. In the end the sneering yellow faces of young men that met me everywhere, the insults hooted after me when I was at a safe distance, got badly on my nerves. The young Buddhist priests were the worst of all. There were several thousands of them in the town and none of them seemed to have anything to do except stand on street corners and jeer at Europeans.

All this was perplexing and upsetting. For at that time I had already made up my mind that imperialism was an evil thing and the sooner I chucked up my job and got out of it the better. Theoretically — and secretly, of course — I was all for the Burmese and all against their oppressors, the British. As for the job I was doing, I hated it more bitterly than I can perhaps make clear. In a job like that you see the dirty work of Empire at close quarters. The wretched prisoners huddling in the stinking cages of the lock-ups, the grey, cowed faces of the long-term convicts, the scarred buttocks of the men who had been flogged with bamboos — all these oppressed me with an intolerable sense of guilt. But I could get nothing into perspective. I was young and ill-educated and I had had to think out my problems in the utter silence that is imposed on every Englishman in the East. I did not even know that the British Empire is dying, still less did I know that it is a great deal better than the younger empires that are going to supplant it. All I knew was that I was stuck between my hatred of the empire I served and my rage against the evil-spirited little beasts who tried to make my job impossible. With one part of my mind I thought of the British Raj as an unbreakable tyranny, as something clamped down, in *saecula saeculorum,*[1] upon the will of prostrate peoples; with another part I thought that the greatest joy in the world would be to drive a bayonet into a Buddhist priest's guts. Feelings like these are the normal by-products of imperialism; ask any Anglo-Indian official, if you can catch him off duty.

One day something happened which in a roundabout way was enlightening. It was a tiny incident in itself, but it gave me a better glimpse than I had had before of the real nature of imperialism — the real motives for which despotic governments act. Early one morning the sub-inspector at a police station the other end of the town rang me up on the 'phone and said that an elephant was ravaging the bazaar. Would I please come and do something about it? I did not know what I could do, but I wanted to see what was happening and I got on to a pony and started out. I took my rifle, an old .44 Winchester and much too small to kill an elephant, but I thought the noise might be useful *in terrorem.*[2] Various Burmans stopped me on the way and told me about the elephant's doings. It was not, of course, a wild elephant, but a tame one which had gone "must." It had been chained up, as tame elephants always are when their attack of "must" is due, but on the previous night it had broken its chain and escaped. Its mahout, the only person who could manage it when it was in that state, had set out in pursuit, but had taken the wrong direction and was now twelve hours' journey away, and in the morning the elephant had suddenly reappeared in the town. The Burmese population had no weapons and were quite helpless against it. It had already destroyed somebody's bamboo hut, killed a cow and raided some fruit-stalls and devoured the stock; also it had met the municipal rubbish van and, when the driver jumped out and took to his heels, had turned the van over and inflicted violences upon it.

The Burmese sub-inspector and some Indian constables were waiting for me in the quarter where the elephant had been seen. It was a very poor quarter, a labyrinth of squalid bamboo huts, thatched with palmleaf, winding all over a steep hillside. I remember that it was a cloudy, stuffy morning at the beginning of the rains. We began questioning the people as to where the elephant had gone and, as usual, failed to get any definite information. That is invariably the case in the East; a story always sounds clear enough at a distance, but

[1] For world without end.
[2] As a warning.

the nearer you get to the scene of events the vaguer it becomes. Some of the people said that the elephant had gone in one direction, some said that he had gone in another, some professed not even to have heard of any elephant. I had almost made up my mind that the whole story was a pack of lies, when we heard yells a little distance away. There was a loud, scandalized cry of "Go away, child! Go away this instant!" and an old woman with a switch in her hand came round the corner of a hut, violently shooing away a crowd of naked children. Some more women followed, clicking their tongues and exclaiming; evidently there was something that the children ought not to have seen. I rounded the hut and saw a man's dead body sprawling in the mud. He was an Indian, a black Dravidian coolie, almost naked, and he could not have been dead many minutes. The people said that the elephant had come suddenly upon him round the corner of the hut, caught him with its trunk, put its foot on his back and ground him into the earth. This was the rainy season and the ground was soft, and his face had scored a trench a foot deep and a couple of yards long. He was lying on his belly with arms crucified and head sharply twisted to one side. His face was coated with mud, the eyes wide open, the teeth bared and grinning with an expression of unendurable agony. (Never tell me, by the way, that the dead look peaceful. Most of the corpses I have seen look devilish.) The friction of the great beast's foot had stripped the skin from his back as neatly as one skins a rabbit. As soon as I saw the dead man I sent an orderly to a friend's house nearby to borrow an elephant rifle. I had already sent back the pony, not wanting it to go mad with fright and throw me if it smelt the elephant.

The orderly came back in a few minutes with a rifle and five cartridges, and meanwhile some Burmans had arrived and told us that the elephant was in the paddy fields below, only a few hundred yards away. As I started forward practically the whole population of the quarter flocked out of the houses and followed me. They had seen the rifle and were all shouting excitedly that I was going to shoot the elephant. They had not shown much interest in the elephant when he was merely ravaging their homes, but it was different now that he was going to be shot. It was a bit of fun to them, as it would be to an English crowd; besides they wanted the meat. It made me vaguely uneasy. I had no intention of shooting the elephant — I had merely sent for the rifle to defend myself if necessary — and it is always unnerving to have a crowd following you. I marched down the hill, looking and feeling a fool, with the rifle over my shoulder and an ever-growing army of people jostling at my heels. At the bottom, when you got away from the huts, there was a metalled road and beyond that a miry waste of paddy fields a thousand yards across, not yet ploughed but soggy from the first rains and dotted with coarse grass. The elephant was standing eight yards from the road, his left side towards us. He took not the slightest notice of the crowd's approach. He was tearing up bunches of grass, beating them against his knees to clean them and stuffing them into his mouth.

I had halted on the road. As soon as I saw the elephant I knew with perfect certainty that I ought not to shoot him. It is a serious matter to shoot a working elephant — it is comparable to destroying a huge and costly piece of machinery — and obviously one ought not to do it if it can possibly be avoided. And at that distance, peacefully eating, the elephant looked no more dangerous than a cow. I thought then and I think now that his attack of "must" was already passing off; in which case he would merely wander harmlessly about until the mahout came back and caught him. Moreover, I did not in the least want to shoot him. I decided that I would watch him for a little while to make sure that he did not turn savage again, and then go home.

But at that moment I glanced round at the crowd that had followed me. It was an immense crowd, two thousand at the least and growing every minute. It blocked the road for a long distance on either side. I looked at the sea of yellow faces above the garish clothes — faces all happy and excited over this bit of fun, all certain that the elephant was going to be shot. They were watching me as they would watch a conjurer about to perform a trick. They did not like me, but with the magical rifle in my hands I was momentarily worth watching. And suddenly I realized that I should have to shoot the elephant after all. The people expected it of me and I had got to do it; I could feel their two thousand wills pressing me forward, irresistibly. And it was at this moment, as I stood there with the rifle in my hands, that I first grasped the hollowness, the futility of the white man's dominion in the East. Here was I, the white man with his gun, standing in front of the unarmed native crowd — seemingly the leading actor of the piece; but in reality I was only an absurd puppet pushed to and fro by the will of those yellow faces behind. I perceived in this moment that when the white man turns tyrant it is his own freedom that he destroys. He becomes a sort of hollow, posing dummy, the conventionalized figure of a sahib. For it is the condition of his rule that he shall spend his life in trying to impress the "natives," and so in every crisis he has got to do what the "natives" expect of him. He wears a mask, and his face grows to fit it. I had got to shoot the elephant. I had committed myself to doing it when I sent for the rifle. A sahib has got to act like a sahib; he has got to appear resolute, to know his own mind and do definite things. To come all that way, rifle in hand, with two thousand people marching at my heels, and then to trail feebly away, having done nothing — no, that was impossible. The crowd would laugh at me. And my whole life, every white man's life in the East, was one long struggle not to be laughed at.

But I did not want to shoot the elephant. I watched him beating his bunch of grass against his knees, with that preoccupied grandmotherly air that elephants have. It seemed to me that it would be murder to shoot him. At that age I was not squeamish about killing animals, but I had never shot an elephant and never wanted to. (Somehow it always seems worse to kill a *large* animal.) Besides, there was the beast's owner to be considered. Alive, the elephant was worth at least a hundred pounds; dead, he would only be worth the value of his tusks, five pounds, possibly. But I had got to act quickly. I turned to some experienced-looking Burmans who had been there when we arrived, and asked them how the elephant had been behaving. They all said the same thing: he took no notice of you if you left him alone, but he might charge if you went too close to him.

It was perfectly clear to me what I ought to do. I ought to walk up to within, say, twenty-five yards of the elephant and test his behavior. If he charged, I could shoot; if he took no notice of me, it would be safe to leave him until the mahout came back. But also I knew that I was going to do no such thing. I was a poor shot with a rifle and the ground was soft mud into which one would sink at every step. If the elephant charged and I missed him, I should have about as much chance as a toad under a steam-roller. But even then I was not thinking particularly of my own skin, only of the watchful yellow faces behind. For at that moment, with the crowd watching me, I was not afraid in the ordinary sense, as I would have been if I had been alone. A white man mustn't be frightened in front of "natives"; and so, in general, he isn't frightened. The sole thought in my mind was that if anything went wrong those two thousand Burmans would see me pursued, caught, trampled on and reduced to a grinning corpse like that Indian up the hill. And if that happened it was quite probable that some of them would laugh. That would never do. There was only one alternative. I shoved the cartridges into the magazine and lay down on the road to get a better aim.

The crowd grew very still, and a deep, low, happy sigh, as of people who see the theatre curtain go up at last, breathed from innumerable throats. They were going to have their bit of fun after all. The rifle was a beautiful German thing with cross-hair sights. I did not then know that in shooting an elephant one would shoot to cut an imaginary bar running from ear-hole to ear-hole. I ought, therefore, as the elephant was sideways on, to have aimed straight at his ear-hole; actually I aimed several inches in front of this, thinking the brain would be further forward.

When I pulled the trigger I did not hear the bang or feel the kick — one never does when a shot goes home — but I heard the devilish roar of glee that went up from the crowd. In that instant, in too short a time, one would have thought, even for the bullet to get there, a mysterious, terrible change had come over the elephant. He neither stirred nor fell, but every line of his body had altered. He looked suddenly stricken, shrunken, immensely old, as though the frightful impact of the bullet had paralysed him without knocking him down. At last, after what seemed a long time — it might have been five seconds, I dare say — he sagged flabbily to his knees. His mouth slobbered. An enormous senility seemed to have settled upon him. One could have imagined him thousands of years old. I fired again into the same spot. At the second shot he did not collapse but climbed with desperate slowness to his feet and stood weakly upright, with legs sagging and head drooping. I fired a third time. That was the shot that did for him. You could see the agony of it jolt his whole body and knock the last remnant of strength from his legs. But in falling he seemed for a moment to rise, for as his hind legs collapsed beneath him he seemed to tower upward like a huge rock toppling, his trunk reaching skywards like a tree. He trumpeted, for the first and only time. And then down he came, his belly towards me, with a crash that seemed to shake the ground even where I lay.

I got up. The Burmans were already racing past me across the mud. It was obvious that the elephant would never rise again, but he was not dead. He was breathing very rhythmically with long rattling gasps, his great mound of a side painfully rising and falling. His mouth was wide open. I could see far down into caverns of pale pink throat. I waited a long time for him to die, but his breathing did not weaken. Finally I fired my two remaining shots into the spot where I thought his heart must be. The thick blood welled out of him like red velvet, but still he did not die. His body did not even jerk when the shots hit him, the tortured breathing continued without a pause.

He was dying, very slowly and in great agony, but in some world remote from me where not even a bullet could damage him further. I felt I had got to put an end to that dreadful noise. It seemed dreadful to see the great beast lying there, powerless to move and yet powerless to die, and not even to be able to finish him. I sent back for my small rifle and poured shot after shot into his heart and down his throat. They seemed to make no impression. The tortured gasps continued as steadily as the ticking of a clock.

In the end I could not stand it any longer and went away. I heard later that it took him half an hour to die. Burmans were bringing dahs and baskets even before I left, and I was told they had stripped his body almost to the bones by the afternoon.

Afterwards, of course, there were endless discussions about the shooting of the elephant. The owner was furious, but he was only an Indian and could do nothing. Besides, legally I had done the right thing, for a mad elephant has to be killed, like a mad dog, if its owner fails to control it. Among the Europeans opinion was divided. The older men said I was right, the younger men said it was a damn shame to shoot an elephant for killing a coolie, because an elephant was worth more than any damn Coringhee coolie. And afterwards I was very glad that the coolie had been killed; it put me legally in the right and it gave me a sufficient pretext for shooting the elephant. I often wondered whether any of the others grasped that I had done it solely to avoid looking a fool.

QUESTIONS

1. How does Orwell characterize himself at the time of the events he describes? What evidence in the essay suggests that he wrote it some years later?
2. Orwell says the incident was "enlightening." What does he mean? Picking up this clue, state in a sentence or two the thesis or main point of the essay.
3. Compare Orwell's description of the dead coolie (in the fourth paragraph) with his description of the elephant's death (in the eleventh and twelfth paragraphs). Why does Orwell devote more space to the death of the elephant?
4. How would you describe the tone of the last paragraph, particularly of the last two sentences? Do you find the paragraph an effective conclusion to the essay? Explain.

Rejected[3]

Malcolm X

In those days only three things in the world scared me: jail, a job, and the Army. I had about ten days before I was to show up at the induction center. I went right to work. The Army Intelligence soldiers, those black spies in civilian clothes, hung around in Harlem with their ears open for the white man downtown. I knew exactly where to start dropping the word. I started noising around that I was frantic to join . . . the Japanese Army.

When I sensed that I had the ears of the spies, I would talk and act high and crazy. A lot of Harlem hustlers actually had reached that state — as I would later. It was inevitable when one had gone long enough on heavier and heavier narcotics, and under the steadily tightening vise of the hustling life. I'd snatch out and read my Greetings aloud, to make certain they heard who I was, and when I'd report downtown. (This was probably the only time my real name was ever heard in Harlem in those days.)

The day I went down there, I costumed like an actor. With my wild zoot suit I wore the yellow knob-toe shoes, and I frizzled my hair up into a reddish bush of conk.

I went in, skipping and tipping, and I thrust my tattered Greetings at that reception desk's white soldier — "Crazy-o, daddy-o, get me moving. I can't wait to get in that brown — ," very likely that soldier hasn't recovered from me yet.

They had their wire on me from uptown, all right. But they still put me through the line. In that big starting room were forty or fifty other prospective inductees. The room had fallen vacuum-quiet, with me running my mouth a mile a minute, talking nothing but slang. I was going to fight on all fronts: I was going to be a general, man, before I got done — such talk as that.

Most of them were white, of course. The tender-looking ones appeared ready to run from me. Some others had that vinegary "worst kind of nigger" look. And a few were amused, seeing me as the "Harlem jigaboo" archetype.

[3] Editors' title. Two terms in the essay may need explanation. 4-F was the classification draft boards gave to persons thought to be unsuited for military service; "Greetings" was the opening word in the notice from the draft board, telling the recipient to report for a mental and physical examination.

Also amused were some of the room's ten or twelve Negroes. But the stony-faced rest of them looked as if they were ready to sign up to go off killing somebody — they would have liked to start with me.

The line moved along. Pretty soon, stripped to my shorts, I was making my eager-to-join comments in the medical examination rooms — and everybody in the white coats that I saw had 4-F in his eyes.

I stayed in the line longer than I expected, before they siphoned me off. One of the white coats accompanied me around a turning hallway: I knew we were on the way to a headshrinker — the Army psychiatrist.

The receptionist there was a Negro nurse. I remember she was in her early twenties, and not bad to look at. She was one of those Negro "firsts."

Negroes know what I'm talking about. Back then, the white man during the war was so pressed for personnel that he began letting some Negroes put down their buckets and mops and dust rags and use a pencil, or sit at some desk, or hold some twenty-five-cent title. You couldn't read the Negro press for the big pictures of smug black "firsts."

Somebody was inside with the psychiatrist. I didn't even have to put on any act for this black girl; she was already sick of me.

When, finally, a buzz came at her desk, she didn't send me, *she* went in. I knew what she was doing, she was going to make clear, in advance, what she thought of me. This is still one of the black man's big troubles today. So many of those so-called "upper class" Negroes are so busy trying to impress on the white man that they are "different from those others" that they can't see they are only helping the white man to keep his low opinion of *all* Negroes.

And then, with her prestige in the clear, she came out and nodded to me to go in.

I must say this for that psychiatrist. He tried to be objective and professional in his manner. He sat there and doodled with his blue pencil on a tablet, listening to me spiel to him for three or four minutes before he got a word in.

His tack was quiet questions, to get at why I was so anxious. I didn't rush him; I circled and hedged, watching him closely, to let him think he was pulling what he wanted out of me. I kept jerking around, backward, as though somebody might be listening. I knew I was going to send him back to the books to figure what kind of a case I was.

Suddenly, I sprang up and peeped under both doors, the one I'd entered and another that probably was a closet. And then I bent and whispered fast in his ear. "Daddy-o, now you and me, we're from up North here, so don't you tell nobody. . . . I want to get sent down South. Organize them nigger soldiers, you dig? Steal us some guns, and kill up crackers!"

That psychiatrist's blue pencil dropped, and his professional manner fell off in all directions. He stared at me as if I were a snake's egg hatching, fumbling for his red pencil. I knew I had him. I was going back out past Miss First when he said, "That will be all."

A 4-F card came to me in the mail, and I never heard from the Army any more, and never bothered to ask why I was rejected.

QUESTION

The passage not only tells a story, or a history, but includes social comment. Would it be equally interesting if the social comment were omitted? Explain.

Graduation

Maya Angelou

The children in Stamps trembled visibly with anticipation. Some adults were excited too, but to be certain the whole young population had come down with graduation epidemic. Large classes were graduating from both the grammar school and the high school. Even those who were years removed from their own day of glorious release were anxious to help with preparations as a kind of dry run. The junior students who were moving into the vacating classes' chairs were tradition-bound to show their talents for leadership and management. They strutted through the school and around the campus exerting pressure on the lower grades. Their authority was so new that occasionally if they pressed a little too hard it had to be overlooked. After all, next term was coming, and it never hurt a sixth grader to have a play sister in the eighth grade, or a tenth-year student to be able to call a twelfth grader Bubba. So all was endured in a spirit of shared understanding. But the graduating classes themselves were the nobility. Like travelers with exotic destinations on their minds, the graduates were remarkably forgetful. They came to school without their books, or tablets or even pencils. Volunteers fell over themselves to secure replacements for the missing equipment. When accepted, the willing workers might or might not be thanked, and it was of no importance to the pregraduation rites. Even teachers were respectful of the now quiet and aging seniors, and tended to speak to them, if not as equals, as beings only slightly lower than themselves. After tests were returned and grades given, the student body, which acted like an extended family, knew who did well, who excelled, and what piteous ones had failed.

Unlike the white high school, Lafayette County Training School distinguished itself by having neither lawn, nor hedges, nor tennis court, nor climbing ivy. Its two buildings (main classrooms, the grade school and home economics) were set on a dirt hill with no fence to limit either its boundaries or those of bordering farms. There was a large expanse to the left of the school which was used alternately as a baseball diamond or a basketball court. Rusty hoops on the swaying poles represented the permanent recreational equipment, although bats and balls could be borrowed from the P. E. teacher if the borrower was qualified and if the diamond wasn't occupied.

Over this rocky area relieved by a few shady tall persimmon trees the graduating class walked. The girls often held hands and no longer bothered to speak to the lower students. There was a sadness about them, as if this old world was not their home and they were bound for higher ground. The boys, on the other hand, had become more friendly, more outgoing. A decided change from the closed attitude they projected while studying for finals. Now they seemed not ready to give up the old school, the familiar paths and classrooms. Only a small percentage would be continuing on to college — one of the South's A & M (agricultural and mechanical) schools, which trained Negro youths to be carpenters, farmers, handymen, masons, maids, cooks and baby nurses. Their future rode heavily on their shoulders, and blinded them to the collective joy that had pervaded the lives of the boys and girls in the grammar school graduating class.

Parents who could afford it had ordered new shoes and ready-made clothes for themselves from Sears and Roebuck or Montgomery Ward. They also engaged the best seamstresses to make the floating graduating dresses and to cut down secondhand pants which would be pressed to a military slickness for the important event.

Oh, it was important, all right. Whitefolks would attend the ceremony, and two or three would speak of God and home, and the

Southern way of life, and Mrs. Parsons, the principal's wife, would play the graduation march while the lower-grade graduates paraded down the aisles and took their seats below the platform. The high school seniors would wait in empty classrooms to make their dramatic entrance.

In the Store I was the person of the moment. The birthday girl. The center. Bailey had graduated the year before, although to do so he had had to forfeit all pleasures to make up for his time lost in Baton Rouge.

My class was wearing butter-yellow piqué dresses, and Momma launched out on mine. She smocked the yoke into tiny crisscrossing puckers, then shirred the rest of the bodice. Her dark fingers ducked in and out of the lemony cloth as she embroidered raised daisies around the hem. Before she considered herself finished she had added a crocheted cuff on the puff sleeves, and a pointy crocheted collar.

I was going to be lovely. A walking model of all the various styles of fine hand sewing and it didn't worry me that I was only twelve years old and merely graduating from the eighth grade. Besides, many teachers in Arkansas Negro schools had only that diploma and were licensed to impart wisdom.

The days had become longer and more noticeable. The faded beige of former times had been replaced with strong and sure colors. I began to see my classmates' clothes, their skin tones, and the dust that waved off pussy willows. Clouds that lazed across the sky were objects of great concern to me. Their shiftier shapes might have held a message that in my new happiness and with a little bit of time I'd soon decipher. During that period I looked at the arch of heaven so religiously my neck kept a steady ache. I had taken to smiling more often, and my jaws hurt from the unaccustomed activity. Between the two physical sore spots, I suppose I could have been uncomfortable, but that was not the case. As a member of the winning team (the graduating class of 1940) I had outdistanced unpleasant sensations by miles. I was headed for the freedom of open fields.

Youth and social approval allied themselves with me and we trammeled memories of slights and insults. The wind of our swift passage remodeled my features. Lost tears were pounded to mud and then to dust. Years of withdrawal were brushed aside and left behind, as hanging ropes of parasitic moss.

My work alone had awarded me a top place and I was going to be one of the first called in the graduating ceremonies. On the classroom blackboard, as well as on the bulletin board in the auditorium, there were blue stars and white stars and red stars. No absences, no tardinesses, and my academic work was among the best of the year. I could say the preamble to the Constitution even faster than Bailey. We timed ourselves often: "WethepeopleoftheUnitedStates inordertoformamoreperfectunion . . ." I had memorized the Presidents of the United States from Washington to Roosevelt in chronological as well as alphabetical order.

My hair pleased me too. Gradually the black mass had lengthened and thickened, so that it kept at last to its braided pattern, and I didn't have to yank my scalp off when I tried to comb it.

Louise and I had rehearsed the exercises until we tired out ourselves. Henry Reed was class valedictorian. He was a small, very black boy with hooded eyes, a long, broad nose and an oddly shaped head. I had admired him for years because each term he and I vied for the best grades in our class. Most often he bested me, but instead of being disappointed I was pleased that we shared top places between us. Like many Southern black children, he lived with his grandmother, who was as strict as Momma and as kind as she knew how to be. He was courteous, respectful and soft-spoken to elders, but on the playground he chose to play the roughest games. I admired him. Anyone, I reckoned, sufficiently afraid or sufficiently dull could be polite. But to be able to operate at a top level with both adults and children was admirable.

His valedictory speech was entitled "To Be or Not to Be." The rigid tenth-grade teacher had helped him write it. He'd been working on the dramatic stresses for months.

The weeks until graduation were filled with heady activities. A group of small children were to be presented in a play about buttercups and daisies and bunny rabbits. They could be heard throughout the building practicing their hops and their little songs that sounded like silver bells. The older girls (non-graduates, of course) were assigned the task of making refreshments for the night's festivities. A tangy scent of ginger, cinnamon, nutmeg and chocolate wafted around the home economics building as the budding cooks made samples for themselves and their teachers.

In every corner of the workshop, axes and saws split fresh timber as the woodshop boys made sets and stage scenery. Only the graduates were left out of the general bustle. We were free to sit in the library at the back of the building or look in quite detachedly, naturally, on the measures being taken for our event.

Even the minister preached on graduation the Sunday before. His subject was, "Let your light so shine that men will see your good works and praise your Father, Who is in Heaven." Although the sermon was purported to be addressed to us, he used the occasion to speak to backsliders, gamblers and general ne'er-do-wells. But since he had called our names at the beginning of the service we were mollified.

Among Negroes the tradition was to give presents to children going only from one grade to another. How much more important this was when the person was graduating at the top of the class. Uncle Willie and Momma had sent away for a Mickey Mouse watch like Bailey's. Louise gave me four embroidered handkerchiefs. (I gave her three crocheted doilies.) Mrs. Sneed, the minister's wife, made me an underskirt to wear for graduation, and nearly every customer gave me a nickel or maybe even a dime with the instruction "Keep on moving to higher ground," or some such encouragement.

Amazingly the great day finally dawned and I was out of bed before I knew it. I threw open the back door to see it more clearly, but Momma said, "Sister, come away from that door and put your robe on."

I hoped the memory of that morning would never leave me. Sunlight was itself still young, and the day had none of the insistence maturity would bring it in a few hours. In my robe and barefoot in the backyard, under cover of going to see about my new beans, I gave myself up to the gentle warmth and thanked God that no matter what evil I had done in my life He had allowed me to live to see this day. Somewhere in my fatalism I had expected to die, accidentally, and never have the chance to walk up the stairs in the auditorium and gracefully receive my hard-earned diploma. Out of God's merciful bosom I had won reprieve.

Bailey came out in his robe and gave me a box wrapped in Christmas paper. He said he had saved his money for months to pay for it. It felt like a box of chocolates, but I knew Bailey wouldn't save money to buy candy when we had all we could want under out noses.

He was as proud of the gift as I. It was a soft-leather-bound copy of a collection of poems by Edgar Allan Poe, or, as Bailey and I called him, "Eap." I turned to "Annabel Lee" and we walked up and down the garden rows, the cool dirt between our toes, reciting the beautifully sad lines.

Momma made a Sunday breakfast although it was only Friday. After we finished the blessing, I opened my eyes to find the watch on my plate. It was a dream of a day. Everything went smoothly and to my credit. I didn't have to be reminded or scolded for anything. Near evening I was too jittery to attend to chores, so Bailey volunteered to do all before his bath.

Days before, we had made a sign for the Store, and as we turned out the lights Momma hung the cardboard over the doorknob. It read clearly: CLOSED. GRADUATION.

My dress fitted perfectly and everyone said that I looked like a sunbeam in it. On the hill, going toward the school, Bailey walked behind with Uncle Willie, who muttered, "Go on, Ju." He wanted him to walk ahead with us because it embarrassed him to have to walk so slowly. Bailey said he'd let the ladies walk together, and the men would bring up the rear. We all laughed, nicely.

Little children dashed by out of the dark like fireflies. Their crepe-paper dresses and butterfly wings were not made for running and we heard more than one rip, dryly, and the regretful "uh uh" that followed.

The school blazed without gaiety. The windows seemed cold and unfriendly from the lower hill. A sense of ill-fated timing crept over me, and if Momma hadn't reached for my hand I would have drifted back to Bailey and Uncle Willie, and possibly beyond. She made a few slow jokes about my feet getting cold, and tugged me along to the now-strange building.

Around the front steps, assurance came back. There were my fellow "greats," the graduating class. Hair brushed back, legs oiled, new dresses and pressed pleats, fresh pocket handkerchiefs and little handbags, all homesewn. Oh, we were up to snuff, all right. I joined my comrades and didn't even see my family go in to find seats in the crowded auditorium.

The school band struck up a march and all classes filed in as had been rehearsed. We stood in front of our seats, as assigned, and on a signal from the choir director, we sat. No sooner had this been accomplished than the band started to play the national anthem. We rose again and sang the song, after which we recited the pledge of allegiance. We remained standing for a brief minute before the choir director and the principal signaled to us, rather desperately I thought, to take our seats. The command was so unusual that our carefully rehearsed and smooth-running machine was thrown off. For a full minute we fumbled for our chairs and bumped into each other awkwardly. Habits change or solidify under pressure, so in our state of nervous tension we had been ready to follow our usual assembly pattern: the American national anthem, then the pledge of allegiance, then the song every Black person I knew called the Negro

National Anthem. All done in the same key, with the same passion and most often standing on the same foot.

Finding my seat at last, I was overcome with a presentiment of worse things to come. Something unrehearsed, unplanned, was going to happen, and we were going to be made to look bad. I distinctly remember being explicit in the choice of pronoun. It was "we," the graduating class, the unit, that concerned me then.

The principal welcomed "parents and friends" and asked the Baptist minister to lead us in prayer. His invocation was brief and punchy, and for a second I thought we were getting back on the high road to right action. When the principal came back to the dais, however, his voice had changed. Sounds always affected me profoundly and the principal's voice was one of my favorites. During assembly it melted and lowed weakly into the audience. It had not been in my plan to listen to him, but my curiosity was piqued and I straightened up to give him my attention.

He was talking about Booker T. Washington, our "late great leader," who said we can be as close as the fingers on the hand, etc. . . . Then he said a few vague things about friendship and the friendship of kindly people to those less fortunate than themselves. With that his voice nearly faded, thin, away. Like a river diminishing to a stream and then to a trickle. But he cleared his throat and said, "Our speaker tonight, who is also our friend, came from Texarkana to deliver the commencement address, but due to the irregularity of the train schedule, he's going to, as they say, 'speak and run.' " He said that we understood and wanted the man to know that we were most grateful for the time he was able to give us and then something about how we were willing always to adjust to another's program, and without more ado — "I give you Mr. Edward Donleavy."

Not one but two white men came through the door offstage. The shorter one walked to the speaker's platform, and the tall one moved over to the center seat and sat down. But that was our principal's seat, and already occupied. The dislodged gentleman bounced around for a long breath or two before the Baptist minister gave him his chair, then with more dignity than the situation deserved, the minister walked off the stage.

Donleavy looked at the audience once (on reflection, I'm sure that he wanted only to reassure himself that we were really there), adjusted his glasses and began to read from a sheaf of papers.

He was glad "to be here and to see the work going on just as it was in the other schools."

At the first "Amen" from the audience I willed the offender to immediate death by choking on the word. But Amens and Yes, sir's began to fall around the room like rain through a ragged umbrella.

He told us of the wonderful changes we children in Stamps had in store. The Central School (naturally, the white school was Central) had already been granted improvements that would be in use in the fall. A well-known artist was coming from Little Rock to teach art to them. They were going to have the newest microscopes and chemistry equipment for their laboratory. Mr. Donleavy didn't leave us long in the dark over who made these improvements available to Central High. Nor were we to be ignored in the general betterment scheme he had in mind.

He said that he had pointed out to people at a very high level that one of the first-line football tacklers at Arkansas Agricultural and Mechanical College had graduated from good old Lafayette County Training School. Here fewer Amen's were heard. Those few that did break through lay dully in the air with the heaviness of habit.

He went on to praise us. He went on to say how he had bragged that "one of the best basketball players at Fisk sank his first ball right here at Lafayette County Training School."

The white kids were going to have a chance to become Galileos and Madame Curies and Edisons and Gauguins, and our boys (the girls weren't even in on it) would try to be Jesse Owenses and Joe Louises.

Owens and the Brown Bomber were great heroes in our world, but what school official in the white-goddom of Little Rock had the right to decide that those two men must be our only heroes? Who decided that for Henry Reed to become a scientist he had to work like George Washington Carver, as a bootblack, to buy a lousy microscope? Bailey was obviously always going to be too small to be an athlete, so which concrete angel glued to what country seat had decided that if my brother wanted to become a lawyer he had to first pay penance for his skin by picking cotton and hoeing corn and studying correspondence books at night for twenty years?

The man's dead words fell like bricks around the auditorium and too many settled in my belly. Constrained by hard-learned manners I couldn't look behind me, but to my left and right the proud graduating class of 1940 had dropped their heads. Every girl in my row had found something new to do with her handkerchief. Some folded the tiny squares into love knots, some into triangles, but most were wadding them, then pressing them flat on their yellow laps.

On the dais, the ancient tragedy was being replayed. Professor Parsons sat, a sculptor's reject, rigid. His large, heavy body seemed devoid of will or willingness, and his eyes said he was no longer with us. The other teachers examined the flag (which was draped stage right) or their notes, or the windows which opened on our now-famous playing diamond.

Graduation, the hush-hush magic time of frills and gifts and congratulations and diplomas, was finished for me before my name was called. The accomplishment was nothing. The meticulous maps, drawn in three colors of ink, learning and spelling decasyllabic words, memorizing the whole of *The Rape of Lucrece* — it was for nothing. Donleavy had exposed us.

We were maids and farmers, handymen and washerwomen, and anything higher that we aspired to was farcical and presumptuous.

Then I wished that Gabriel Prosser and Nat Turner had killed all whitefolks in their beds and that Abraham Lincoln had been assassinated before the signing of the Emancipation Proclamation, and that Harriet Tubman had been killed by that blow on her head and Christopher Columbus had drowned in the *Santa María*.

It was awful to be Negro and have no control over my life. It was brutal to be young and already trained to sit quietly and listen to charges brought against my color with no chance of defense. We should all be dead. I thought I should like to see us all dead, one on top of the other. A pyramid of flesh with the whitefolks on the bottom, as the broad base, then the Indians with their silly tomahawks and tepees and wigwams and treaties, the Negroes with their mops and recipes and cotton sacks and spirituals sticking out of their mouths. The Dutch children should all stumble in their wooden shoes and break their necks. The French should choke to death on the Louisiana Purchase (1803) while silkworms ate all the Chinese with their stupid pigtails. As a species, we were an abomination. All of us.

Donleavy was running for election, and assured our parents that if he won we could count on having the only colored paved playing field in that part of Arkansas. Also — he never looked up to acknowledge the grunts of acceptance — also, we were bound to get some new equipment for the home economics building and the workshop.

He finished, and since there was no need to give any more than the most perfunctory thank-you's, he nodded to the men on the stage, and the tall white man who was never introduced joined him at the door. They left with the attitude that now they were off to something really important. (The graduation ceremonies at Lafayette County Training School had been a mere preliminary.)

The ugliness they left was palpable. An uninvited guest who wouldn't leave. The choir was summoned and sang a modern arrangement of "Onward, Christian Soldiers," with new words pertaining to graduates seeking their place in the world. But it didn't work. Elouise, the daughter of the Baptist minister, recited "Invictus," and I could have cried at the impertinence of "I am the master of my fate, I am the captain of my soul."

My name had lost its ring of familiarity and I had to be nudged to go and receive my diploma. All my preparations had fled. I neither marched up to the stage like a conquering Amazon, nor did I look in the audience for Bailey's nod of approval. Marguerite Johnson, I heard the name again, my honors were read, there were noises in the audience of appreciation, and I took my place on the stage as rehearsed.

I thought about colors I hated: ecru, puce, lavender, beige and black.

There was shuffling and rustling around me, then Henry Reed was giving his valedictory address, "To Be or Not to Be." Hadn't he heard the whitefolks? We couldn't *be,* so the question was a waste of time. Henry's voice came out clear and strong. I feared to look at him. Hadn't he got the message? There was no "nobler in the mind" for Negroes because the world didn't think we had minds, and they let us know it. "Outrageous fortune"? Now, that was a joke. When the ceremony was over I had to tell Henry Reed some things. That is, if I still cared. Not "rub," Henry, "erase." "Ah, there's the erase." Us.

Henry had been a good student in elocution. His voice rose on tides of promise and fell on waves of warnings. The English teacher had helped him to create a sermon winging through Hamlet's soliloquy. To be a man, a doer, a builder, a leader, or to be a tool, an unfunny joke, a crusher of funky toadstools. I marveled that Henry could go through with the speech as if we had a choice.

I had been listening and silently rebutting each sentence with my eyes closed; then there was a hush, which in an audience warns that something unplanned is happening. I looked up and saw Henry Reed, the conservative, the proper, the A student, turn his back to the audience and turn to us (the proud graduating class of 1940) and sing, nearly speaking,

> Lift ev'ry voice and sing
> Till earth and heaven ring
> Ring with the harmonies of Liberty . . .[4]

It was the poem written by James Weldon Johnson. It was the music composed by J. Rosamond Johnson. It was the Negro national anthem. Out of habit we were singing it.

Our mothers and fathers stood in the dark hall and joined the hymn of encouragement. A kindergarten teacher led the small children onto the stage and the buttercups and daisies and bunny rabbits marked time and tried to follow:

> Stony the road we trod
> Bitter the chastening rod
> Felt in the days when hope, unborn, had died.
> Yet with a steady beat
> Have not our weary feet
> Come to the place for which our fathers sighed?

Every child I knew had learned that song with his ABC's and along with "Jesus Loves Me This I Know." But I personally had never heard it before. Never heard the words, despite the thousands of times I had sung them. Never thought they had anything to do with me.

On the other hand, the words of Patrick Henry had made such an impression on me that I had been able to stretch myself tall and trembling and say, "I know not what course others may take, but as for me, give me liberty or give me death."

And now I heard, really for the first time:

> We have come over a way that with tears has been watered,
> We have come, treading our path through the blood of the slaughtered.

While echoes of the song shivered in the air, Henry Reed bowed his head, said "Thank you," and returned to his place in the line. The tears that slipped down many faces were not wiped away in shame.

We were on top again. As always, again. We survived. The depths had been icy and dark, but now a bright sun spoke to our souls. I was no longer simply a member of the proud graduating class of 1940; I was a proud member of the wonderful beautiful Negro race.

[4] "Lift Ev'ry Voice and Sing" — words by James Weldon Johnson and music by J. Rosamond Johnson. Copyright by Edward B. Marks Music Corporation. Used by permission.

Oh, Black known and unknown poets, how often have your auctioned pains sustained us? Who will compute the lonely nights made less lonely by your songs, or by the empty pots made less tragic by your tales?

If we were a people much given to revealing secrets, we might raise monuments and sacrifice to the memories of our poets, but slavery cured us of that weakness. It may be enough, however, to have it said that we survive in exact relationship to the dedication of our poets (include preachers, musicians and blues singers).

QUESTIONS

1. In the first paragraph, notice such overstatements as "glorious release," "the graduating classes themselves were the nobility," and "exotic destinations." Find some additional examples of similar statements in the next few pages. Why did Angelou use such words?

2. Characterize the writer as you perceive her at the end of the first section (page 254). Support your characterization with references to specific passages. Next, characterize her in the paragraph beginning "It was awful to be Negro" (page 258). Next, characterize her on the basis of the entire essay. Finally, in a sentence, try to describe the change, indicating the chief attitudes or moods that she goes through.

3. How would you define "poets," as Angelou uses the word in the last sentence?

High Horse's Courting
Black Elk

You know, in the old days, it was not so very easy to get a girl when you wanted to be married. Sometimes it was hard work for a young man and he had to stand a great deal. Say I am a young man and I have seen a young girl who looks so beautiful to me that I feel all sick when I think about her. I can not just go and tell her about it and then get married if she is willing. I have to be a very sneaky fellow to talk to her at all, and after I have managed to talk to her, that is only the beginning.

Probably for a long time I have been feeling sick about a certain girl because I love her so much, but she will not even look at me, and her parents keep a good watch over her. But I keep feeling worse and worse all the time; so maybe I sneak up to her tepee in the dark and wait until she comes out. Maybe I just wait there all night and don't get any sleep at all and she does not come out. Then I feel sicker than ever about her.

Maybe I hide in the brush by a spring where she sometimes goes to get water, and when she comes by, if nobody is looking, then I jump out and hold her and just make her listen to me. If she likes me too, I can tell that from the way she acts, for she is very bashful and maybe will not say a word or even look at me the first time. So I let her go, and then maybe I sneak around until I can see her father alone, and I tell him how many horses I can give him for his beautiful girl, and by now I am feeling so sick that maybe I would give him all the horses in the world if I had them.

Well, this young man I am telling about was called High Horse, and there was a girl in the village who looked so beautiful to him that he was just sick all over from thinking about her so much and he was getting sicker all the time. The girl was very shy, and her parents thought a great deal of her because they were not young any more and this was the only child they had. So they watched her all day long, and they fixed it so that she would be safe at night too when they were asleep. They thought so much of her that they had made a rawhide bed for her to sleep in, and after they knew that High Horse was sneaking around after her, they took rawhide thongs and tied the girl in bed at night so that nobody could steal her when they were asleep, for they were not sure but that their girl might really want to be stolen.

Well, after High Horse had been sneaking around a good while and hiding and waiting for the girl and getting sicker all the time, he finally caught her alone and made her talk to him. Then he found out that she liked him maybe a little. Of course this did not make him feel well. It made him sicker than ever, but now he felt as brave as a bison bull, and so he went right to her father and said he loved the girl so much that he would give two good horses for her — one of them young and the other one not so very old.

But the old man just waved his hand, meaning for High Horse to go away and quit talking foolishness like that.

High Horse was feeling sicker than ever about it; but there was another young fellow who said he would loan High Horse two ponies and when he got some more horses, why, he could just give them back for the ones he had borrowed.

Then High Horse went back to the old man and said he would give four horses for the girl — two of them young and the other two not hardly old at all. But the old man just waved his hand and would not say anything.

So High Horse sneaked around until he could talk to the girl again, and he asked her to run away with him. He told her he thought he would just fall over and die if she did not. But she said she would not do that; she wanted to be bought like a fine woman. You see she thought a great deal of herself too.

That made High Horse feel so very sick that he could not eat a bite, and he went around with his head hanging down as though he might just fall down and die any time.

Red Deer was another young fellow, and he and High Horse were great comrades, always doing things together. Red Deer saw how High Horse was acting, and he said: "Cousin, what is the matter? Are you sick in the belly? You look as though you were going to die."

Then High Horse told Red Deer how it was, and said he thought he could not stay alive much longer if he could not marry the girl pretty quick.

Red Deer thought awhile about it, and then he said: "Cousin, I have a plan, and if you are man enough to do as I tell you, then everything will be all right. She will not run away with you; her old man will not take four horses; and four horses are all you can get. You must steal her and run away with her. Then afterwhile you can come back and the old man cannot do anything because she will be your woman. Probably she wants you to steal her anyway."

So they planned what High Horse had to do, and he said he loved the girl so much that he was man enough to do anything Red Deer or anybody else could think up.

So this is what they did.

That night late they sneaked up to the girl's tepee and waited until it sounded inside as though the old man and the old woman and the girl were sound asleep. Then High Horse crawled under the tepee with a knife. He had to cut the rawhide thongs first, and then Red Deer, who was pulling up the stakes around that side of the tepee, was going to help drag the girl outside and gag her. After that, High Horse could put her across his pony in front of him and hurry out of there and be happy all the rest of his life.

When High Horse had crawled inside, he felt so nervous that he could hear his heart drumming, and it seemed so loud he felt sure it would 'waken the old folks. But it did not, and afterwhile he began cutting the thongs. Every time he cut one it made a pop and nearly scared him to death. But he was getting along all right and all the thongs were cut down as far as the girl's thighs, when he became so nervous that his knife slipped and stuck the girl. She gave a big, loud yell. Then the old folks jumped up and yelled too. By this time High Horse was outside, and he and Red Deer were running away like antelope. The old man and some other people chased the young men but they got away in the dark and nobody knew who it was.

Well, if you ever wanted a beautiful girl you will know how sick High Horse was now. It was very bad the way he felt, and it looked as though he would starve even if he did not drop over dead sometime.

Red Deer kept thinking about this, and after a few days he went to High Horse and said: "Cousin, take courage! I have another plan, and I am sure, if you are man enough, we can steal her this time." And High Horse said: "I am man enough to do anything anybody can think up, if I can only get that girl."

So this is what they did.

They went away from the village alone, and Red Deer made High Horse strip naked. Then he painted High Horse solid white all over, and after that he painted black stripes all over the white and put black rings around High Horse's eyes. High Horse looked terrible. He looked so terrible that when Red Deer was through painting and took a good look at what he had done, he said it scared even him a little.

"Now," Red Deer said, "if you get caught again, everybody will be so scared they will think you are a bad spirit and will be afraid to chase you."

So when the night was getting old and everybody was sound asleep, they sneaked back to the girl's tepee. High Horse crawled in with his knife, as before, and Red Deer waited outside, ready to drag the girl out and gag her when High Horse had all the thongs cut.

High Horse crept up by the girl's bed and began cutting at the thongs. But he kept thinking, "If they see me they will shoot me because I look so terrible." The girl was restless and kept squirming around in bed, and when a thong was cut, it popped. So High Horse worked very slowly and carefully.

But he must have made some noise, for suddenly the old

woman awoke and said to her old man: "Old Man, wake up! There is somebody in this tepee!" But the old man was sleepy and didn't want to be bothered. He said: "Of course there is somebody in this tepee. Go to sleep and don't bother me." Then he snored some more.

But High Horse was so scared by now that he lay very still and as flat to the ground as he could. Now, you see, he had not been sleeping very well for a long time because he was so sick about the girl. And while he was lying there waiting for the old woman to snore, he just forgot everything, even how beautiful the girl was. Red Deer who was lying outside ready to do his part, wondered and wondered what had happened in there, but he did not dare call out to High Horse.

Afterwhile the day began to break and Red Deer had to leave with the two ponies he had staked there for his comrade and girl, or somebody would see him.

So he left.

Now when it was getting light in the tepee, the girl awoke and the first thing she saw was a terrible animal, all white with black stripes on it, lying asleep beside her bed. So she screamed, and then the old woman screamed and the old man yelled. High Horse jumped up, scared almost to death, and he nearly knocked the tepee down getting out of there.

People were coming running from all over the village with guns and bows and axes, and everybody was yelling.

By now High Horse was running so fast that he hardly touched the ground at all, and he looked so terrible that the people fled from him and let him run. Some braves wanted to shoot at him, but the others said he might be some sacred being and it would bring bad trouble to kill him.

High Horse made for the river that was near, and in among the brush he found a hollow tree and dived into it. Afterwhile some braves came there and he could hear them saying that it was some bad spirit that had come out of the water and gone back in again.

That morning the people were ordered to break camp and move away from there. So they did, while High Horse was hiding in his hollow tree.

Now Red Deer had been watching all this from his own tepee and trying to look as though he were as much surprised and scared as all the others. So when the camp moved, he sneaked back to where he had seen his comrade disappear. When he was down there in the brush, he called, and High Horse answered, because he knew his friend's voice. They washed off the paint from High Horse and sat down on the river bank to talk about their troubles.

High Horse said he never would go back to the village as long as he lived and he did not care what happened to him now. He said he was going to go on the war-path all by himself. Red Deer said: "No, cousin, you are not going on the war-path alone, because I am going with you."

So Red Deer got everything ready, and at night they started out on the war-path all alone. After several days they came to a Crow camp just about sundown, and when it was dark they sneaked up to where the Crow horses were grazing, killed the horse guard, who was not thinking about enemies because he thought all the Lakotas were far away, and drove off about a hundred horses.

They got a big start because all the Crow horses stampeded and it was probably morning before the Crow warriors could catch any horses to ride. Red Deer and High Horse fled with their herd three days and nights before they reached the village of their people. Then they drove the whole herd right into the village and up in front of the girl's tepee. The old man was there, and High Horse called out to him and asked if he thought maybe that would be enough horses for his girl. The old man did not wave him away that time. It was not the horses that he wanted. What he wanted was a son who was a real man and good for something.

So High Horse got his girl after all, and I think he deserved her.

QUESTIONS

1. The story "High Horse's Courting" is told by Black Elk, an Oglala Sioux holy man. Though High Horse's behavior is amusing and at times ridiculous, how does Black Elk make it clear that he is not ridiculing the young man, but is instead sympathetic with him? Consider the following questions:
   a. What is the effect of the first three paragraphs? Consider the first two sentences, and then the passage beginning "Say I am a young man . . ." and ending ". . . I would give him all the horses in the world if I had them."
   b. Describe the behavior of the young girl, and of her father and mother. How do they contribute to the comedy? How does their behavior affect your understanding of Black Elk's attitude toward High Horse?
   c. What is the function of Red Deer?

d. The narrative consists of several episodes. List them in the order in which they occur, and then describe the narrative's structure. How does the structure of the narrative affect the tone?

e. What is the effect of the last two sentences?

2. What similarities, if any, are there between the courting customs and attitudes toward courting that Black Elk describes and those you are familiar with. Consider the behavior and attitudes not only of High Horse, the girl, her parents, and his friend, but also of the old man who tells the story.

10

The Research Paper

WHAT RESEARCH IS

Because a research paper requires its writer to collect the available evidence — usually including the opinions of earlier investigators — one sometimes hears that a research paper, unlike a critical essay, is not the expression of personal opinion. But such a view is unjust both to criticism and to research. A critical essay is not a mere expression of personal opinion; to be any good it must offer evidence that supports the opinions, thus persuading the reader of their objective rightness. And a research paper is largely personal, because the author continuously uses his own judgment to evaluate the evidence, deciding what is relevant and convincing. A research paper is not merely an elaborately footnoted presentation of what a dozen scholars have already said about a topic; it is a thoughtful evaluation of the available evidence, and so it is, finally, an expression of what the author thinks the evidence adds up to.[1]

Before we talk at some length about research papers, we should mention that you may want to do some research even for a paper that is primarily critical. Consider the difference between a

---

[1] Because footnotes may be useful or necessary in a piece of writing that is *not* a research paper (such as this chapter), and because we wish to emphasize the fact that a thoughtful research paper requires more than footnotes, we have put our discussion of footnotes in another chapter, on pages 549–59.

paper on Bob Dylan's emergence as a popular singer, and a paper on Bob Dylan's songs of social protest. The first of these, necessarily a research paper, will require you to dig into magazines and newspapers to find out about his reception in clubs in New York; but even if you are writing an analysis of his songs of social protest you may want to do a little research into Dylan's indebtedness to Woody Guthrie. You may, for example, study Dylan's record jackets and read some interviews in magazines and newspapers to find out if he has anything to say about his relation to Guthrie. Our point is that writers must learn to use source material thoughtfully, whether they expect to work with few sources or with many.

Research involving many sources can be a tedious and frustrating business; there are hours spent reading books and articles that prove to be irrelevant, there are contradictory pieces of evidence, and there is never enough time. Research, in short, is not a procedure that is attractive to everyone. The poet William Butler Yeats, though an indefatigable worker on projects that interested him, engagingly expressed an indifference to the obligation that confronts every researcher: to look carefully at all of the available evidence. Running over the possible reasons why Jonathan Swift did not marry (that he had syphilis, for instance, or that he feared he would transmit a hereditary madness), Yeats says, "Mr. Shane Leslie thinks that Swift's relation to Vanessa was not platonic, and that whenever his letters speak of a cup of coffee they mean the sexual act; whether the letters seem to bear him out I do not know, for those letters bore me."

Though research sometimes requires one to read boring works, those who engage in it feel, at least at times, an exhilaration, a sense of triumph at having studied a problem thoroughly and at having arrived at conclusions that at least for the moment seem objective and irrefutable. Later perhaps new evidence will turn up that will require a new conclusion, but until that time, one may reasonably feel that one knows *something*.

PRIMARY AND SECONDARY MATERIALS

The materials of most research can be conveniently divided into two sorts, primary and secondary. The primary materials or sources are the real subject of study, the secondary materials are critical and historical accounts already written about these primary materials. For example, if you want to know whether Shakespeare's attitude toward Julius Caesar was highly traditional or highly original, or a little of each, you would read *Julius Caesar,* other Elizabethan writings about Caesar, and Roman writings known to the Elizabethans; and in addition to these primary materials you would also read secondary material such as modern books on Shakespeare and on Elizabethan attitudes toward Rome and toward monarchs.

The line between these two kinds of sources, of course, is not always clear. For example, if you are concerned with the degree to which Joyce's *Portrait of the Artist as a Young Man* is autobiographical, primary materials include not only *A Portrait* and Joyce's letters, but perhaps also his brother Stanislaus' diary and autobiography. Although the diary and autobiography might be considered secondary sources — certainly a scholarly biography about Joyce or his brother would be a secondary source — because Stanislaus' books are more or less contemporary with your subject they can reasonably be called primary sources.

FROM SUBJECT TO THESIS

First, a subject. No subject is unsuited. Perhaps sports, war, art, dreams, food. As G. K. Chesterton said, "There is no such thing on earth as an uninteresting subject; the only thing that can exist is an uninterested person." Research can be done on almost anything that interests you, though you should keep in mind two limitations. First, materials on current events may be extremely difficult to get hold of, since crucial documents may not yet be in print and you may not have access to the people involved. And, second, materials on some subjects may be unavailable to you because they are in languages you can't read or in publications that your library doesn't have. So you probably won't try to work on the stuff of today's headlines, and (because almost nothing in English has been written on it) you won't try to work on Japanese attitudes toward the hunting of whales. But no subject is too trivial for study: Newton, according to legend, wondered why an apple fell to the ground.

You cannot, however, write a research paper on subjects as

broad as sports, war, art, dreams, or food. You have to focus on a much smaller area within such a subject. Let's talk about food. You might want to study the dietary laws of the Jews, the food of American Indians before the white man came, the consumption of whale meat, subsidies to hog farmers, or legislation governing the purity of food. Your own interests will guide you to the topic — the part of the broad subject — that you wish to explore.

But of course, though you have an interest in one of these narrower topics, you don't know a great deal about it; that's one of the reasons you are going to do research on it. Let's say that you happened to read or hear about Ralph Nader's stomach-turning essay on frankfurters (*New Republic,* 18 March 1972, pages 12–13), in which Nader reports that although today's frankfurters contain only 11.7 percent protein (the rest is water, salt, spices, and preservatives), they contain a substantial dose of sodium nitrate to inhibit the growth of bacteria and to keep the meat from turning gray.

Assuming that your appetite for research on food continues, you decide that you want to know something more about additives, that is, substances (such as sodium nitrate) added to preserve desirable properties — color, flavor, freshness — or to suppress undesirable properties. You want to do some reading, and you must now find the articles and books. Of course, as you do the reading, your focus may shift a little; you may stay with frankfurters, you may shift to the potentially dangerous effects, in various foods, of sodium nitrate, or to the controversy over the effects of saccharin (an artificial sweetener), or you may concentrate on so-called enriched bread, which is first robbed of many nutrients by refining and bleaching the flour and is then enriched by the addition of some of the nutrients in synthetic form. Exactly what you will focus on, and exactly what your *thesis* or point of view will be, you may not know until you do some more reading. But how do you find the relevant material?

FINDING THE MATERIAL

You may happen already to know of some relevant material that you have been intending to read, but if you are at a loss where to begin, consult the card catalog of your library and consult the appropriate guides to articles in journals.

The Card Catalog

The card catalog has cards arranged alphabetically not only by author and by title but also by subject. It probably won't have a subject heading for "frankfurter," but it will have one for "food," followed by cards listing books on this topic. And on the "food" card will be a note telling you of relevant subjects to consult. In

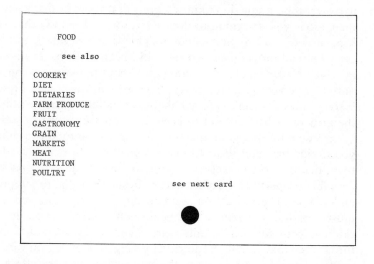

```
        FOOD

           see also

     COOKERY
     DIET
     DIETARIES
     FARM PRODUCE
     FRUIT
     GASTRONOMY
     GRAIN
     MARKETS
     MEAT
     NUTRITION
     POULTRY
                        see next card
```

fact, even before you look at the catalog you can know what subject headings it contains by checking one of two books: *Sears List of Subject Headings* (for libraries that use the Dewey decimal system of arranging books) and *Subject Headings Used in the Dictionary Catalogs of the Library of Congress,* 7th edition. (Because most academic libraries use the Library of Congress system, the second of these is probably the book you'll use.) If you look for "food" in *Subject Headings,* you will find two pages of listings, including cross references such as "*sa* [= see also] Animal Food." Among the subject headings that sound relevant are Bacteriology, Food Contamination, and Preservation. Notice also the abbreviation "xx," referring to broader headings you may want to look at. If you make use of some of these subject headings you will probably find that the library has a fair amount of material on your topic.

Whether you went to *Subject Headings* or to the "food" card, you have now gathered a number of subject headings that seem relevant. With this information you can locate useful books — even though you began without knowing the author or title of even one book — simply by turning to the subject heading in the card file, and writing down the information on the books filed under that subject. For example, if you look up "Diet" or "Nutrition" or "Proteins in Human Nutrition" you will find cards for the books on each topic. Here is an example of a *subject card*. Notice the following about the subject card:

1. The subject is given at the top of the card.
2. The classification number at the left enables you to find the book in the library.
3. The card gives the author's name, title, and other information, such as the fact that this book includes a bibliography.
4. Near the bottom there is a list of other subject headings under which this card is filed. By checking these other subject headings (called *tracings* by librarians), you will be able to find additional books that probably are relevant to your research.

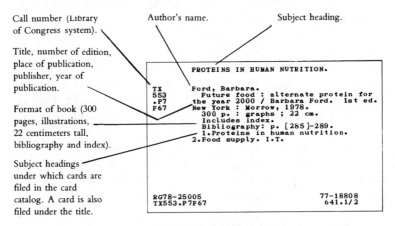

An *author card,* that is, a card filed alphabetically under the author's last name, is identical with a subject card except that the subject is not given at the top of the card. If you know the author's name, just look for it in the catalog.

Finally, a *title card* is identical with an author card, except that the title is added to the top of the card and the card is indexed under the first word of the title, or the second word if the first is *A, An,* or *The,* or a foreign equivalent.

Three Notes on the Alphabetic Arrangement of the Card Catalog

1. The catalog is arranged alphabetically from A to Z, of course, but the arrangement is word by word, not letter by letter. This means, for example, that "ion implantation" *precedes* "ionic crystals," because "i-o-n" precedes "i-o-n-i-c." (If the catalog were letter by letter of course "i-o-n-i-c" would precede "i-o-n-i-m. . . .") Similarly, in the card catalog "folk tales" precedes "folklorists." Here is a short list of cards in the order they are in the catalog:

> Good, Emanuel
> *Good Men and True*
> *Good Old Days*
> Goodall, Ann
> Goodman, Paul

2. Under the author's name, books are usually arranged alphabetically by title, but for highly prolific authors the cards listing the collected works may be grouped before those listing individual works. Cards for books *about* the author follow cards for books *by* the author. Note that authors whose surnames begin *Mc* or *Mac* are all listed — in most libraries — as though spelled *Mac;* authors whose surnames begin with a prefix (for example, *De, Le, Van*) are listed as though the prefixes and surname formed a single word: De Lisle would come after Delano and before Delos.

3. Under the title, remember that books are alphabetized under the *second* word if the first word is *A, An,* or *The,* or a foreign equivalent. Note, too, that words normally abbreviated are spelled out in the catalog: *Doctor Zhivago, Mister Roberts, Saint Joan.*

Scanning Books, Book Reviews, and Encyclopedias

Having checked the card catalog and written down the relevant data (author, title, call number), you can begin to scan the books, or you can postpone looking at the books until you have found some relevant articles in periodicals. For the moment, let's postpone the periodicals.

Put a bunch of books in front of you, and choose one as an introduction. How do you choose one from half a dozen? Partly by its size — choose a thin one — and partly by its quality. Roughly speaking, it should be among the more recent publications, and it should strike you as fair. A pamphlet published by a meat-packers association is desirably thin but you have a hunch that it may be biased. Roger John Williams' *Nutrition in a Nutshell* is published by a well-known commercial press (Doubleday), and it is only 171 pages, but because it was published in 1962 it may not reflect current food chemistry. Though it is rather big (260 pages), Michael Jacobson's *Eater's Digest: The Consumer's Factbook of Food Additives* (New York: Doubleday, 1972) probably is about right.

When you have found the book that you think may serve as your introductory study, read the preface in order to get an idea of the author's purpose and outlook, scan the table of contents in order to get an idea of the organization and the coverage, and scan the final chapter or the last few pages, where you may be lucky enough to find a summary. The index, too, may let you know if the book will suit your purpose, by showing you what topics are covered and how much coverage they get. If the book still seems suitable, scan it.

At this stage it is acceptable to trust one's hunches — you are only going to scan the book, not buy it or even read it — but you may want to look up some book reviews to assure yourself that the book has merit. There are five especially useful indexes to book reviews:

> *Book Review Digest* (published from 1905 onward)
> *Book Review Index* (1965–)
> *Index to Book Reviews in the Humanities* (1960–)
> *Humanities Index* (1974–)
> *Social Sciences Index* (1974–)

The last two publications are chiefly indexes to articles, but at the rear of each issue you'll find indexes to book reviews, arranged alphabetically under the name of the author of the book.

Most reviews of books will come out in the same year as the book, or within the next two years, so if, for example, a book was published in 1976, look in the 1976 volume of the appropriate index and see what is there. If you want some more reviews, look in 1977 and 1978. Begin with *Book Review Digest,* because it includes excerpts from and synopses of the reviews; if it has your book, the excerpts and synopses may be enough, and you won't have to dig out the reviews themselves. But *Book Review Digest* does not have as broad coverage as the other indexes, and you may have to turn to them for citations, and then to the journals to which they refer you. Read the synopses in *Book Review Digest,* or some reviews in journals, and draw some conclusions about the merit of the book in question. Of course you cannot assume that every review is fair, but a book that on the whole gets good reviews is probably at least good enough for a start.

By quickly reading such a book (take few or no notes at this stage) you will probably get an overview of your topic, and you will see exactly what part of the topic you wish to pursue.

We should also mention that often you can get a quick general view of a subject from an encyclopedia. The chief encyclopedias are

> *Chambers's Encyclopaedia* (1973)
>
> *Collier's Encyclopedia* (1972; and the annual *Collier's Encyclopedia Year Book*)
>
> *Encyclopedia Americana* (1974; and the annual yearbook, *The Americana Annual*)
>
> *Encyclopaedia Britannica* (1974; and the annual *Encyclopaedia Britannica: Book of the Year*)

The first three of these encyclopedias simply use an alphabetic arrangement: *aardvark* is in the first volume, *zoo* in the last. But the organization of the *Encyclopaedia Britannica* is somewhat different and so we will briefly explain it here.

The fifteenth edition of the *Britannica* (1974) comprises thirty volumes. These are divided into three parts. (1) *Propaedia: Outline of Knowledge and Guide to the Britannica.* This is one volume. It divides all knowledge into ten categories, with many subdivisions. It is an outline or a table of contents to the remaining volumes. (2) *Micro-paedia: Ready Reference and Index.* This is ten volumes, containing 102,214 short entries arranged alphabetically. No entry is longer than 750 words, which means that only the most essential points get mentioned. (3) *Macropaedia: Knowledge in Depth.* Nineteen volumes containing 4,207 articles averaging five pages each. All of the subjects treated in the *Macropaedia* were also treated, more briefly, in the *Micropaedia.*

Indexes to Periodicals

An enormous amount is published in magazines and scholarly journals; you cannot start thumbing through them at random, but fortunately there are indexes to them. Among the most widely used indexes are

Readers' Guide to Periodical Literature (1900–)
Humanities Index (1974–)
Social Sciences Index (1974–)
Social Sciences and Humanities Index (1965–74)
International Index (1907–64)

Readers' Guide indexes more than one hundred of the more familiar magazines — such as *Atlantic, Ebony, Nation, Scientific American, Sports Illustrated, Time.* The other indexes are guides to many of the less popular, more scholarly journals, for example journals published by learned societies. Notice that *Humanities Index* and *Social Sciences Index* are fairly new; for indexes to older articles in these two fields, look in *Social Sciences and Humanities Index* (1965–74), and for still older ones look in *International Index.*

The names of the periodicals indexed in these volumes are printed at the front of the volumes. All of these invaluable indexes include subject headings as well as entries alphabetically by author. If you know that you are looking for a piece by Ralph Nader, look it up under Nader. But if you don't know the author, look under the subject. For example, if you look up "additives" in the *Readers' Guide* you will find: "Additives. *See* Food additives," and so you next turn to "Food additives," where you will find a listing (by title) of the relevant articles. You will also find, under "Food,"

FOOD additives
  Food additives. G. O. Kermode. il Sci Am
    226:15-21 bibliog(p 126) Mr '72
  Food flavoring additives, how safe? B. T.
    Hunter. Consumer Bull 55:14-15 O '72
  Hysteria about food additives. T. Alexander.
    il Fortune 85:62-5+ Mr '72
  Regular family meal: aargh! C. McCarthy.
    Sat R 55:5-6+ S 2 '72
  Royal crown battles the additive bans. il
    Bus W p60+ Mr 25 '72
  Will added nutrients really help? D. Callo-
    way. il McCalls 99:36 F '72
    See also
  Carrageenan
  Diethyl pyrocarbonate
  Monosodium glutamate
  Sodium nitrite

a note referring you to other subject headings that may be relevant, for example "Food, Organic," and "Food adulteration."

This material is not attractive reading, but it is useful. From the front of the *Readers' Guide* you will learn what the abbreviations mean. The first item here, for example, is an essay called "Culture, Values, and Food Safety," by S. E. Stumpf, published (with a bibliography, here indicated by the abbreviation "bibl") in a journal called *BioScience,* volume 28, pages 186–90, which is the March 1978 issue.

Another index that you are likely to use is *The New York Times Index* (covering from 1851 to the present). This index, enabling you to locate articles that were published in *The Times* newspaper, is especially useful if you are working on a recent public event.

The indexes just mentioned (along with the indexes to book reviews mentioned on page 275) are the ones you are most likely to use, but here are some others that may be valuable, depending on what your topic is:

Applied Science and Technology Index (1958–); formerly *Industrial Arts Index* (1913–57)

Art Index (1929–)

Biological and Agricultural Index (1964–); before 1964 it was known as *Agricultural Index* (1942–64)

Biography Index (1947–)

Business Periodicals Index (1958–)

Dramatic Index (1909–49)

Education Index (1929–)

International Index to Film Periodicals (1972–)

MLA International Bibliography (1921–); an annual listing of books and scholarly articles on linguistics and on literature in modern languages

Monthly Catalog of United States Government Publications (1895–)

Music Index (1949–)

Poole's Index for Periodical Literature (1802–1907)

Public Affairs Information Service Bulletin (1915–)

United Nations Documents Index (1950–)

Whichever indexes you use, begin with the most recent years and work your way back. If you collect the titles of articles published in the last five years you will probably have as much as you can read. These articles will probably incorporate the significant points of earlier writings. But of course it depends on the topic; you may have to — and want to — go back fifty or more years before you find a useful body of material.

Caution: Indexes drastically abbreviate the titles of periodicals. Before you put the indexes back on the shelf, be sure to check the key to the abbreviations, so that you know the full titles of the periodicals you are looking for.

Other Guides to Published Material

There are a great many reference books — not only general dictionaries and encyclopedias but dictionaries of technical words, and encyclopedias of special fields. For example, Leslie Halliwell, *The Filmgoer's Companion,* 6th edition (1977), has thousands of brief entries, listing films, directors, motifs, and so forth. Some of these entries conclude with references to books for further reading. There are also books chiefly devoted to telling you where to find material in special fields. Examples: Helen J. Poulton, *The Historian's Handbook: A Descriptive Guide to Reference Works* (1972); Elizabeth Miller and Mary Fisher, eds., *The Negro in America: A Bibliography,* revised edition (1970); Bernard Klein and Daniel Icolari, eds., *Reference Encyclopedia of the American Indian,* 2nd edition (1971); James Monaco, *Film: How and Where to Find Out What You Want to Know* (1976). The best guide to such guides — a book telling you about such books — is Constance M. Winchell, *Guide to Reference Books,* 9th edition (1976). There are also guides to all of these guides: reference librarians. If you don't know where to turn to find something, turn to the librarian.

TAKING BIBLIOGRAPHIC NOTES

Practice and theory differ. In theory, one should write down each citation (whether a book or an article) on a separate three-by-five index card, giving complete information. Our own practice at the start of any research is more shoddy. Instead of carefully recording all of this information from the card catalog (for a book that may be lost) or from an index to periodicals (for a periodical that may not be in the library) we usually jot down the citations of books on one sheet of paper, and of articles on another sheet. Then we see how much of this material is available. When we actually get hold of the material, we make out a card, as illustrated. True, we sometimes regret our attempted shortcut if we later find that on the sheet we forgot to write the year of the periodical and we must now hunt through indexes again to locate it. We recall the wisdom of the Chinese proverb, "It is foolish to go to bed early to save the candle if the result is twins," but we have never been able to resist economizing at the start.

Caution: Because it is easy to misspell names, turning unfamiliar forms into familiar ones (Barnet into Barnett, Stubbs into Stubbes, and even Christensen into Christianson), it is advisable to *print* the name in block letters, and, having done so, to check your version against the original.

READING AND TAKING NOTES

As you read, you will of course find references to other publications and you will jot these down so that you can look at them later. It may turn out, for example, that a major article was published twenty years ago, and that most commentary is a series of footnotes to this piece. You will have to look at it, of course, even though common sense had initially suggested (incorrectly, it seems) that the article would be out of date.

Our own practice in reading an article or a chapter of a book is to read it through, *not* taking notes. By the time you reach the end, you may find it isn't noteworthy. Or you may find a useful summary near the end that will contain most of what you can get from the piece. Or you will find that, having a sense of the whole, you can now quickly reread the piece and take notes on the chief points.

When you take notes use four-by-six-inch cards, and write on one side only; material on the back of a card is usually neglected when you come to write the paper. Use four-by-six cards because

TX
553. 83
J23

Jacobson, Michael F.
~~Eater's Digest~~ New York: Doubleday 1972

Bibliographic card for a book

Zwerdling, Daniel. "Death for
Dinner," *The New York Review,*
21, No. 1 (21 Feb. 1974), 22-24.

Bibliographic card for an article in a periodical

the smaller cards, suitable for bibliographic notes, do not provide enough space for your summaries of useful material. Here is a guide to note taking:

1. We suggest summaries rather than paraphrases (that is, abridgments rather than restatements which in fact may be as long as or longer than the original) because there is rarely any point to paraphrasing; generally speaking, either quote exactly (and put the passage in quotation marks, with a notation of the source, including the page number or numbers) or summarize, reducing a page or even an entire article or chapter of a book to a single four-by-six card. Even when you summarize, indicate your source (including the page numbers) on the card, so that you can give appropriate credit in your paper.

2. Of course in your summary you will sometimes quote a phrase or a sentence — putting it in quotation marks — but quote sparingly. You are not doing stenography; rather you are assimilating knowledge and you are thinking, and so for the most part your source should be digested rather than engorged whole. Thinking now, while taking notes, will also help you later to avoid plagiarism. If, on the other hand, when you take notes you mindlessly copy material at length, later when you are writing the paper you may be tempted to copy it yet again, perhaps without giving credit. But a terse, thoughtful summary on a note card will give you the point and will also force you to find your own words for it. Most of the direct quotations you copy should be effectively stated passages or crucial passages or both. In your finished paper these quotations will provide authority and emphasis.

3. If you quote but omit some material within the quotation, be sure to indicate the omission by three spaced periods, as explained on page 544.

4. *Never* copy a passage by changing an occasional word, under the impression that you are thereby putting it into your own words. Notes of this sort may find their way into your paper, your reader will sense a style other than your own, and suspicions of plagiarism may follow. (For a detailed discussion of plagiarism, see pages 546–48.)

5. Feel free to jot down your own responses to the note. For example, you may want to say "Gold seems to be generalizing from insufficient evidence," or "Corsa made the same point five years earlier"; but make certain that later you will be able to distinguish between these comments and the notes summarizing or quoting your source. A suggestion: surround all comments recording your responses with double parentheses, thus: ((. . .))

6. In the upper corner of each note card, write a brief key — for example "effect on infants' blood" — so that later you can tell at a glance what is on the card. The sample card shown here summarizes a few pages; notice that it includes a short quotation and records the source. The source is not given in full bibliographic form because the full form is recorded on a bibliography card.

As you work, especially if you are working on a literary or historical topic, you'll of course find yourself returning again and again to the primary materials — and you'll probably find to your surprise that a good deal of the secondary material is unconvincing or even wrong, despite the fact that it is printed in a handsome book. One of the things we learn from research is that not everything in print is true; one of the pleasures we get from research results from this discovery.

WRITING THE PAPER

There remains the difficult job of writing up your findings, usually in 2000–3000 words (eight to twelve double-spaced typed pages). Beyond referring you to the rest of this book, we can offer only seven pieces of advice.

1. Begin by rereading your note cards, sorting them into packets by topic. Put together what belongs together. After sorting and resorting, you will have a kind of first draft without writing a draft.

2. From your packets of cards you can make a first outline. (In arranging the packets into a sequence, and then in sketching an outline, of course you will be guided by your *thesis*. Without a thesis you will have only a lot of note cards, not an essay.) This outline will be a formal outline, indicating not only the major parts of the essay but also the subdivisions within these parts. (The formal outline is discussed on pages 80–81, and an example of an outline preceding a research paper is given on pages 288–89.) Do not, however, confuse this outline with a paragraph outline; when you come to write your essay, a single heading may require two or three or even more paragraphs.

3. When you write your first draft, leave lots of space at the top and bottom of each page so that you can add material, which will be circled and connected by arrows to the proper place. For example, as you are drafting page 6, from perhaps your tenth packet, you may find a note card that now seems more appropriate to a point you made back on page 2. Write it on page 2, and put the card in the appropriate earlier packet so that if for some reason you later have to check your notes you can find it easily.

4. Write or type your quotations, even in the first draft, exactly as you want them to appear in the final version. Short quotations (fewer than three lines of poetry or fewer than five lines of prose) are enclosed within quotation marks but are not otherwise set off; longer quotations, however, are set off (triple space before them and after them), slightly indented, and are *not* enclosed in quotation marks.

5. Include, right in the body of the draft, all of the relevant citations (later these will become footnotes), so that when you come to revise you don't have to start hunting through your notes to find who said what, and where. You can, for the moment, enclose these citations within diagonal lines, or within double parentheses — anything at all to remind you that they will be your footnotes.

6. Beware of the compulsion to include every note card in

your essay. You have taken all these notes, and there is a strong temptation to use them all. But, truth to tell, in hindsight many are useless. Conversely, you will probably find, as you write your draft, that here and there you need to do more research, to check a quotation or to collect additional examples. Probably it is best to continue writing your draft if possible, but remember to insert the necessary material after you get it.

7. As you revise your draft, make sure that you do not merely tell the reader "A says . . . B says . . . C says. . . ." When you write a research paper, you are not merely setting the table with other people's dinnerware; you are cooking the meal. You must have a point, an opinion, a thesis; you are working toward a conclusion, and your readers should always feel they are moving toward that conclusion (by means of your thoughtful evaluation of the evidence) rather than reading an anthology of commentary on the topic.

While you were doing your research you may have noticed that the more interesting writers persuade the reader of the validity of their opinions by (1) letting the reader see that they know what of significance has been written on the topic; (2) letting the reader hear the best representatives of the chief current opinions, whom they correct or confirm; and (3) advancing their opinions, by offering generalizations supported by concrete details. Adopt these techniques in your own writing. Thus, because you have a focus, we should get things like: "There are three common views on. . . . The first two are represented by A and B; the third, and by far the most reasonable, is C's view that . . ." or "A argues . . . but . . ." or "Although the third view, C's, is not conclusive, still . . ." or "Moreover, C's point can be strengthened when we consider a piece of evidence that he does not make use of." We have already mentioned that you cannot merely say "A says . . . , B says . . . , C says . . . ," because your job is not to report what everyone says but to establish the truth of a thesis. When you introduce a quotation, then, try to let the reader see the use to which you are putting it. "A says" is of little help; giving the quotation and then following it with "thus says A" is even worse. You need a lead-in such as "A concisely states the common view,"

"B shrewdly calls attention to a fatal weakness," "Without offering any proof, C claims that. . . ." In short, it is usually advisable to let the reader know why you are quoting, or, to put it a little differently, how the quotation fits into your organization.

Your overall argument, then, is fleshed out with careful summaries and with effective quotations and with judicious analyses of your own, so that by the end of the paper the readers not only have read a neatly typed paper, but they also are persuaded that under your guidance they have seen the evidence, heard the arguments justly summarized, and reached a sound conclusion. They may not become better persons but they are better informed.

When you have finished your paper prepare a final copy that will be easy to read. Type the paper (see pages 539–40), putting the footnotes into the forms given on pages 549–59.

A bibliography or list of works consulted (see pages 559–62) is usually appended to the research paper, so that the reader may easily look further into the primary and secondary material if she wishes. But if you have done your job well, the reader will be content to leave things where you left them, grateful that you have set things straight.

SAMPLE RESEARCH PAPER

Here is a sample research paper. This essay is preceded by a thesis statement and an outline, helpful but not obligatory additions.

Nitrites: Cancer for Many, Money for Few

by

Jacob Alexander

English 1B

Mr. Cavitch

May 10, 1979

Thesis

Sodium nitrite and sodium nitrate, added to cured meats and smoked
fish as a color fixative, combine in meat and in the stomach to form a
powerful carcinogen (cancer-producing substance). This fact puts the
profit motive of the food industry and the health of the American public
squarely into opposition, and thus far the government regulatory agencies
are supporting the food industry.

Outline

    I. Sodium nitrite and nitrate can be poison.

       A. Nitrites combine with blood to form a pink pigment which does not
         carry oxygen.

       B. They have a number of other ominous side-effects.

   II. Nitrites combine with amines to form nitrosamines, among the most
      potent carcinogens known.

       A. Nitrites are likely to combine with amines in the human stomach
         to form nitrosamines.

       B. Animals of all kinds, fed nitrites and amines, develop cancer
         in various parts of their bodies.

       C. Nitrosamines are sometimes present in nitrited food even before
         we ingest it.

 III. Why are nitrites used in food?

       A. Nitrites are traditionally used as color fixers.

       B. Producers argue that they are also preservatives.

  IV. Why does the government allow nitrites?

       A. Nitrites and nitrates have a very long history of use.

       B. Government regulatory mechanisms are full of loopholes.

         1. Delaney Clause in Food Additive Amendment (1958) does not
           apply.

         2. FDA controls fish; USDA controls meats.

         3. Both depend on industry-oriented NAS.

C. The agencies defend themselves.

    1. They find fault with the experiments.

    2. They claim nitrites prevent botulism.

    3. They claim that there is a "no-effect" level of use for carcinogens, though doctors disagree.

V. American government is serving the food industry rather than the people.

    A. Food industry's enormous profits enable them to bring pressure to bear on regulatory agencies.

    B. Hazy patriotic optimism contributes to inaction.

VI. Stop eating nitrated fish and meat.

Americans eat between three thousand and ten thousand additives in their food today, most of them untested[1] and many of them known to be dangerous. Of these, nitrites are among the most hazardous of all. In this country, ham, bacon, corned beef, salami, bologna, lox, and other cold cuts and smoked fish almost invariably contain sodium nitrite (or sodium nitrate, which readily converts to nitrite in the human body). In fact, one-third of the federally inspected meat and fish we consume--more than seven billion pounds of it every year--contains this chemical.[2]

To begin with, nitrite is just plain poison in amounts only slightly greater than those allowed in cured meats. Jacqueline Verrett, who worked for the Food and Drug Administration (FDA) for fifteen years, and Jean Carper list in their book, Eating May Be Hazardous to Your Health, recent instances of people poisoned by accidental overdoses.

> In Buffalo, New York, six persons were hospitalized with "cardiovascular collapse" after they ate blood sausage which contained excessive amounts of nitrites. . . . In New Jersey, two persons died and many others were critically poisoned after eating fish illegally loaded with nitrites. In New Orleans, ten youngsters between the ages of one and a half and five became seriously ill . . . after eating wieners or bologna overnitrited by a local meat-processing firm; one wiener that was obtained later from the plant was found to contain a whopping 6,570 parts per million of nitrate, whereas the federal limitation is 200 parts per million. In Florida, a three-year-old boy died after eating hot dogs with three times greater nitrite concentration than the government allows.[3]

The chemical has the unusual and difficult-to-replace quality of keeping meat a fresh-looking pink throughout the cooking, curing, and

[1] Daniel Zwerdling, "Food Pollution," Ramparts, 9, No. 11 (June 1971), 34.

[2] Michael F. Jacobson, Eater's Digest (New York: Doubleday, 1972), p. 169.

[3] Eating May Be Hazardous to Your Health (New York: Simon and Schuster, 1974), pp. 138-39.

storage process. The nitrous acid from the nitrite combines with the hemoglobin in the blood of the meat, fixing its red color so that the meat does not turn the tired brown or gray natural to cured meats.

Unfortunately, it does much the same thing in humans. Although most of the nitrite passes through the body unchanged, a small amount is released into the bloodstream. This combines with the hemoglobin in the blood to form a pigment called methomoglobin, which cannot carry oxygen. If enough oxygen is incapacitated, a person dies. The allowable amount of nitrite in a quarter pound of meat can incapacitate between 1.4 and 5.7 percent of the hemoglobin in an average-sized adult.[4] When 10 to 20 percent is incapacitated, a victim discolors and has difficulty breathing.[5] One of the problems with nitrite poisoning is that infants under a year, because of the quantity and makeup of their blood, are especially suscep-tible to it.

If the consumer of nitrite is not acutely poisoned, his blood soon returns to normal and this particular danger passes; the chemical, however, has long-term effects. Nitrite can cause headaches in people who are especially sensitive to it, an upsetting symptom in light of the fact that in rats who ate it regularly for a period of time it has produced lasting "epileptic-like" changes in the brain--abnormalities which showed up when the rats were fed only a little more than an American fond of cured meats might eat.[6] Experiments with chickens, cattle, sheep, and rats have shown that nitrite, when administered for several days, inhibits the ability of the liver to store vitamin A and carotene.[7] And, finally,

[4] Verrett and Carper, pp. 138-39.

[5] Jacobson, p. 166.

[6] Harrison Wellford, Sowing the Wind (New York: Bantam, 1973), p. 173.

[7] Beatrice Trum Hunter, Fact/Book on Food Additives and Your Health (New Canaan, Conn.: Keats, 1972), p. 90.

3

Nobel laureate Joshua Lederberg points out that, in microorganisms, nitrite enters the DNA. "If it does the same thing in humans," he says, "it will cause mutant genes." Geneticist Bruce Ames adds, "If out of one million people, one person's genes are mutant, that's a serious problem. . . . If we're filling ourselves now with mutant genes, they're going to be around for generations."[8]

By far the most alarming characteristic of nitrite, however, is that in test tubes, in meats themselves, in animal stomachs, and in human stomachs--wherever a mildly acidic solution is present--it can and does combine with amines to form nitrosamines. And nitrosamines are carcinogens. They cause cancer. Even the food industry and the agencies responsible for allowing the use of nitrite in foods admit that nitrosamines cause cancer. Those people who have studied them feel, in fact, that they are among the surest and most deadly of all the carcinogens currently recognized.

Now it is important to note that nitrite alone, when fed to rats on an otherwise controlled diet, does not induce cancer. It must first combine with amines to form nitrosamines. Considering, however, that the human stomach has the kind of acidic solution in which amines and nitrites readily combine, and considering as well that amines are present in beer, wine, cereals, tea, fish, cigarette smoke, and a long list of drugs including antihistamines, tranquilizers, and even oral contraceptives, it is hardly surprising to find that nitrosamines have been found in human stomachs.

When animals are fed amines in combination with nitrite, they develop cancer with a statistical consistency that is frightening, even to scientists. Verrett and Carper report that William Lijinsky, a scientist at Oak Ridge National Laboratory who has been studying the effects of nitrite

[8] Zwerdling, pp. 34-35.

in food since 1961, after feeding animals 250 parts per million (ppm) of

nitrites and amines--an amount comparable to what some Americans are tak-

ing in today--

> found malignant tumors in 100 percent of the test animals within
> six months, and he thinks they all will be dead in the next three
> months. "Unheard of," he says. . . . "You'd usually expect to
> find 50 percent at the most. And the cancers are all over the
> place--in the brain, lung, pancreas, stomach, liver, adrenals,
> intestines. We open up the animals and they are a bloody mess."[9]
>
> [He] believes that nitrosamines, because of their incredible
> versatility in inciting cancer, may be the key to an explanation
> of the mass production of cancer in seemingly dissimilar popu-
> lations. In other words, nitrosamines may be a common factor
> in cancer that has been haunting us all these years.[10]

Lijinsky also claims that nitrites "seem to be most effective in eliciting

tumors when they are applied in small doses over a long period, rather

than as large single doses."[11]

Verrett and Carper list still more damning evidence. Nitrosamines

have caused cancer in rats, hamsters, mice, guinea pigs, dogs, and

monkeys. It has been proven that nitrosamines of over a hundred kinds

cause cancer. Nitrosamines have been shown to pass through the placenta

from the mother to cause cancer in the offspring. Even the lowest levels

of nitrosamines ever tested have produced cancer in animals. When animals

are fed nitrite and amines separately over a period of time, they develop

cancers of the same kind and at the same frequency as animals fed the

corresponding nitrosamines already formed. In a part of South Africa

where the people drink a locally distilled liquor containing a high concen-

tration of nitrosamines, there is an "extraordinarily high incidence

[9] P. 136.

[10] P. 142.

[11] Statement of Dr. William Lijinsky, Eppely Institute, Univ. of
Nebraska, before the Intergovernmental Relations Subcommittee of the
Committee on Government Operations, U.S. House of Representatives,
16 March 1971, quoted in Wellford, p. 172.

of human esophageal cancer." Finally, Verrett and Carper quote Lijinsky

again:

> We have evidence that while the amount of carcinogen might not
> build up, the effect in the animal body does build up. In
> other words, the more carcinogen you are exposed to, the more
> cells are damaged and the more likely you are to develop a
> tumor within your lifetime. So I feel no amount of a nitrosamine
> can be ignored.[12]

Nitrosamines even form _in_ food, before it reaches the table. Accord-

ing to Verrett and Carper,

> In February 1972 the Agriculture Department and the FDA detected
> nitrosamines in eight samples of processed meat taken from
> packing plants and retail stores. Nitrosamines at levels of
> eleven to forty-eight parts per billion were found in dried beef
> and cured pork, at five parts per billion in ham, and at eighty
> parts per billion in hot dogs. More alarmingly, four bacon
> samples--all different brands--that when raw yielded no nitro-
> samines revealed up to 106 parts per billion of nitrosamines after
> cooking. In November 1972 the FDA revealed that further experi-
> ments had found high levels of a cancer-causing nitrosamine--up
> to 108 parts per billion--in four other brands of bacon that had
> been pan-fried, proving that nitrosamines are widespread in cooked
> bacon. . . . The FDA also found nitrosamines in smoked chub and
> salmon at levels up to twenty-six parts per billion.[13]

As if this were not enough, Beatrice Trum Hunter claims that "some nitro-

samines, in Cantonese dried fish, were capable of inducing cancer by a

single dose."[14]

The question, then, is why nitrite continues to be used in a third

of the meat Americans consume. Although nitrite adds a small amount to

flavor, it is used primarily for cosmetic purposes, and is, in fact,

legally sanctioned _only_ as a color fixative. United States meat proces-

sors, however, are allowed to use up to twenty times as much nitrite as

is needed to fix color.

[12] Pp. 143-46.

[13] Pp. 146-47.

[14] P. 93.

Recently, as controversy over nitrite has accelerated, food producers are arguing that nitrite also prevents the growth of <u>botulinum</u>, an argument to which the public is particularly susceptible because of a number of recent botulism scares. Michael Jacobson explains the preservative action of nitrite:

> Nitrite makes <u>botulinum</u> spores sensitive to heat. When foods are treated with nitrite and then heated, any <u>botulinum</u> spores that may be present are killed. In the absence of nitrite, spores can be inactivated only at temperatures that ruin the meat products. . . . Nitrite's preservative action is particularly important in foods that are not cooked after they leave the factory, such as ham, because these offer an oxygen-free environment, the kind in which <u>botulinum</u> can grow. The toxin does not pose a danger in foods that are always well cooked, such as bacon, because the toxin would be destroyed in cooking. Laboratory studies demonstrate clearly that nitrite <u>can</u> kill <u>botulinum</u>, but whether it actually does in commercially processed meat is now being questioned. Frequently, the levels used may be too low to do anything but contribute to the color.[15]

It seems unlikely that sodium nitrite is really necessary as a preservative. After extensive hearings in 1971, a congressional subcommittee concluded it was not, except possibly in a few cases like that of canned ham.[16] Bratwurst and breakfast sausage are manufactured now without nitrite because they don't need to be colored pink; bacon is always cooked thoroughly enough to kill off any <u>botulinum</u> spores present; and the Maple Crest Sausage Company has been distributing frozen nitrite-free hot dogs, salami, and bologna to health food stores since 1966 without poisoning anyone. Certainly there are other ways of dealing with botulism. High or low temperature prevents botulism. What nitrite undoubtedly does lower, however, is the level of care and sanitation necessary in handling meat.

The use of nitrite in smoked fish is particularly frivolous. If the

[15] P. 165.

[16] Verrett and Carper, p. 138.

fish is heated to 180° for thirty minutes, as it is supposed to be by law, and then distributed with adequate refrigeration, there should be no need for nitrite. The fish industry has appealed to the government with the argument that it should be allowed to use nitrite in more products precisely because some plants do not possess the facilities to process fish at properly high temperatures. Furthermore, the government exercises little control over nitrite in fish. In 1969, three out of six food packaging firms surveyed were putting dangerously high levels of nitrite into their fish, yet only in the most extreme case did the FDA confiscate the fish.[17]

Clearly, the use of nitrite adds immeasurably to the profit-making potential of the meat industry, but why does the federal government allow this health hazard in our food--that same government which stands firmly behind the message that "Americans . . . are blessed with better food at lower costs than anyone in any other country," a message William Robbins calls the "big lie"?[18]

In the first place, nitrite and nitrate have been used for so long that it is hard for lawmakers to get past their instinctive reaction, "But that's the way we've always done it." Indeed, the Romans used saltpeter, a nitrate, to keep meat and, as early as 1899, scientists discovered that the nitrate breaks down into nitrite and that it is the nitrite which actually preserves the red color in meats.[19] Thus, by the time the U.S. Department of Agriculture and the Food and Drug Administration got into the business of regulating food, they tended to accept nitrite and nitrate as givens. For example, the tolerance level of

[17] Verrett and Carper, pp. 149-50.

[18] William Robbins, The American Food Scandal (New York: Morrow, 1974), p. 2.

[19] Jacobson, pp. 164-65.

nitrite set by these agencies is based, not on experiment, but on the level found, in 1925, to be the maximum level usually found in cured ham. Following this government standard, a representative of the fish industry, petitioning to use nitrite, claimed that "no extensive reports of investigations to establish safety are required in view of the long history in common use and the previously accepted safety of these curing agents in the production of meat and fish products within the already established tolerances."[20]

A second reason for the inadequacy of regulation is that government mechanisms for protecting the consumer are full of curious loopholes. In 1958 Congress passed the Food Additive Amendment, including the Delaney Clause which clearly states that additives should be banned if they induce cancer in laboratory animals. Unfortunately, however, the amendment does not apply to additives that were in use before it was passed, so, since nitrite and nitrate had already been in use for a long time, they were automatically included on the list of chemicals "Generally Recognized as Safe." To complicate matters further, nitrite in meat is regulated by the USDA, while nitrite in fish is under the jurisdiction of the FDA. And these agencies generally leave it to industry--the profit-maker--to determine whether or not an additive is safe. The final irony in this long list of governmental errors is that the FDA depends heavily, for "independent" research and advice, on the food committees of the National Academy of Sciences, which Daniel Zwerdling claims are "like a Who's Who of the food and chemical industry."[21]

Nevertheless, as they have come under fire in recent years on the subject of nitrite and nitrate, the FDA and the USDA have found it necessary to give reasons for their continued sanction of these chemicals.

[20] Verrett and Carper, p. 148.

[21] P. 34.

First, they find fault with the experiments done to date. According to the USDA, for example,

> The Department was aware that under certain conditions, nitrites do interact with secondary amines to form nitrosamines and that some nitrosamines are carcinogenic. However, knowledge in this area was limited and analytical methods available to study the possibility of nitrosamine formation in meat food products containing the permissible amounts of sodium nitrate lacked the necessary accuracy and reliability to give conclusive results.[22]

Despite the Delaney Clause, moreover, the FDA points out, "Man is the most important experimental animal and nitrites have not been linked to cancer in all the years that man has been eating the chemical."[23] This is an almost foolproof argument, since cancer usually shows up only after its inception, and it is extremely difficult to trace it to any source. And certainly it is unlikely that any sizeable group will offer to serve as guinea pigs for nitrite experiments. In evaluating this argument, it is significant that humans are generally more susceptible to chemical damage than animals--ten times more so than rats, for example.[24] Following through on its own logic, however, since nitrite has indeed been proven to cause cancer in dogs, the FDA has dutifully and responsibly banned its use in dog food.

The industry's second argument is that nitrite prevents botulism. However, the USDA regulations approve the use of nitrate and nitrite only as color fixers. If they are being used as preservatives, this is a new use and comes squarely under the auspices of the Delaney Clause, which would have them banned outright because they cause cancer in animals.

[22] Verrett and Carper, p. 152.

[23] Regulation of Food Additives and Medicated Animal Feeds, Hearings, Intergovernmental Relations Subcommittee, Committee on Government Operations, U.S. House of Representatives (March 1971), pp. 215 ff., quoted in Wellford, p. 179.

[24] Verrett and Carper, p. 59.

The last argument is that small enough doses of carcinogens are not dangerous. Dr. Leo Friedman, director of the FDA's Division of Toxicology, puts it this way:

> . . . there is always a threshold level below which the substance does not exert any physiologically significant effect. . . . The design of a safety evaluation study is to determine a level at which there is no demonstrable effect. This level, when divided by a suitable safety factor, is then considered to be a safe level, in that there is a practical certainty that no harm will result from the use of the substance at that level.[25]

The medical community does not agree. The Surgeon General's committee stated in 1970, "The principle of a zero tolerance for carcinogenic exposures should be retained in all areas of legislation presently covered by it and should be extended to cover other exposures as well."[26] Hughes Ryser stated in the New England Journal of Medicine: ". . . weak carcinogenic exposures have irreversible and additive effects and cannot be dismissed lightly as standing 'below a threshold of action.' " He also commented that, until the carcinogens are removed from the environment, "efforts must continue to educate populations and government about their presence."[27] Even with this, the FDA Commissioner, Charles Edwards, strenuously disagrees: "We can't deluge the public with scare items based on our suspicions. . . . The pendulum swings too far in most cases, and consumers tend to boycott a product . . . even though we might feel that continued use within certain limits is entirely justified."[28]

Something has gone wrong. The issue is one of what we eat. It makes no sense at all to eat a substance until it is proven to be poison. Even

[25] Memorandum from Dr. Leo Friedman to Dr. Virgil Wodicka, 17 Dec. 1971, quoted in Wellford, p. 180.

[26] Wellford, p. 181.

[27] "Chemical Carcinogenesis," 285, No. 13 (23 Sept. 1971), 721-34, quoted in Wellford, p. 181.

[28] Wellford, p. 18.

a starving man is reluctant to eat mushrooms unless he knows what he's doing. Nitrite is banned altogether in Norway, and forbidden in fish in Canada. European allowances are generally lower than ours, and even the Germans make their "wursts" without nitrite.

One is forced to a radical conclusion. The American government is, in this instance, clearly serving the interests of the industry rather than the people. The fact is that the food industry is willing to spend millions every year to make sure the regulatory agencies act in ways that please them. Each time an additive is banned, the food industry finds itself in the spotlight. It feels an implicit threat to all its other additives, and ultimately to the immense profits Daniel Zwerdling describes:

> This marvelous chemical additive technology has earned $500 million a year for the drug companies . . . and it has given the food manufacturers enormous control over the mass market. Additives like preservatives enable food that might normally spoil in a few days or a week to endure unchanged for weeks, months, or even years. A few central manufacturers can saturate supermarket shelves across the country with their products because there's no chance the food will spoil. Companies can buy raw ingredients when they're cheap, produce and stockpile vast quantities of the processed result, then withhold the products from the market for months, hoping to manipulate prices upward and make a windfall.[29]

Under pressure from the food industry, and probably influenced as well by a sincere, if hazy, patriotic optimism, the FDA issued a fact sheet in May 1967, stating unequivocally that our soil is not being poisoned by fertilizers, that pesticide residues are entirely safe, that our soil is the "envy of every nation," and that food processing is a "modern marvel because the natural value of the food is not lost in the process." It concludes, "Today's scientific knowledge, working through good laws to protect consumers, assures the safety and wholesomeness of every component

[29] "Death for Dinner," The New York Review, 21, No. 1 (21 Feb. 1974), 22.

of our food supply."[30] The FDA's continuing support for nitrite allowances, despite increasing evidence that nitrite is lethal, indicates that
the FDA has not removed its rose-colored glasses.

Until the FDA and other regulatory agencies begin to see clearly, the
American consumer has little choice other than to give up eating the
nitrited cured meats and smoked fish on the market today. If we do so, we
will be following the practice of Dr. William Lijinsky, a biologist who
has studied the problem for fifteen years: "I don't touch any of that stuff
when I know nitrite has been added."[31]

[30] Regulation of Food Additives, pp. 215 ff., quoted in Wellford,
p. 179.

[31] Quoted by Mimi Sheraton, in the New York Times, 9 January 1976,
p. 18.

Works Cited

Hunter, Beatrice Trum. Fact/Book on Food Additives and Your Health.
    New Canaan, Conn.: Keats, 1972.

Jacobson, Michael F. Eater's Digest. New York: Doubleday, 1972.

Robbins, William. The American Food Scandal. New York: Morrow, 1974.

Sheraton, Mimi. "Take Away the Preservatives, and How Do Meats Taste?"
    New York Times, 9 January 1976, p. 18.

Verrett, Jacqueline, and Jean Carper. Eating May Be Hazardous to Your
    Health. New York: Simon and Schuster, 1974.

Wellford, Harrison. Sowing the Wind. New York: Bantam, 1973.

Zwerdling, Daniel. "Death for Dinner." The New York Review, 21, No. 1
    (21 Feb. 1974), 22-24.

_____. "Food Pollution." Ramparts, 9, No. 11 (June 1971), 31-37, 53-54.

EXERCISES (Surviving in the Library)

If you have trouble finding material in the library, don't hesitate to ask a librarian for assistance. But you will soon learn to solve many of the commonest problems yourself. Here are a few.

1. You want to do some research for a paper on Mexican immigrants in the United States. You look in the card catalog and find only one card, reprinted below. How can you find other books on the subject?

```
              The Mexican immigrant.

  JV        Gamio, Manuel, 1883-1960, comp.
  6798          The Mexican immigrant.  New York,
  .M6       Arno Press, 1969.
  G28           xiii, 288 p. map. 22 cm.  (The
  1969      American immigration collection)
                Reprint of the 1931 ed.
                1.United States--Emigration and
            immigration. 2.Mexico--Emigration and
            immigration. 3.Mexicans in the United
            States. I.T.




  RG77-115225  r                    69-18778
  JV6798.M6G28  1969                 301.453/72/
```

2. You want to do a paper on Richard Wright's short stories, and the catalog lists several relevant books, but when you check the stacks you find none of these books is on the shelf. What do you do, short of abandoning the topic or going to another library?

3. You are looking for a book by David McCord, called *Far and Few*. You look under the author's name, but find that a card for "Mbunda (Bantu tribe)" is followed not by a card for McCord but by a card for "Mchedishvili, Georgii." You next look for the book by its title; you find a card for an author named "Faral," and you assume that *Far and Few* should be the next card or so, but in fact the next card is for an author named "Fararo, T. J." Yet you know that the library has McCord's *Far and Few*. Where did you go wrong?

4. You need reviews of a film released a few months ago. There are no books on this film, and the *Readers' Guide* lists nothing under the film's title. What do you do?

5. You find references to *CQ Weekly Report,* the *Department of State Bulletin,* and the *Journal of the American Oriental Society,* but these journals don't seem to be listed alphabetically in the periodical file. Still, you have heard that the library does have them. How can that be?

6. You are looking for an issue of a journal published a few months ago. It is not on the shelf with the current issues, and it is not on the shelf with the bound volumes. Where is it?

7. You want to write a paper on bilingual education, or, more exactly, on bilingual education of Mexican Americans. What do you look for in the card catalog? And what periodical indexes do you consult?

8. You want to know if juvenile delinquency in the Soviet Union increased during the 1970's, but you can't find anything on the topic. What do you do?

A NOTE ON THE USE OF COMPUTERS IN RESEARCH AND WRITING

We've all become familiar in recent years with computers and their seemingly limitless uses: from guiding space vehicles to computing a day's business receipts. When you make an airline reservation, cash a check at a bank, or register as a student in college, the chances are that a computer has assisted (or impeded) you in reserving your air space, checking your balance, or electing your courses. Computers are also being used increasingly in research and writing.

Computers are used in research in at least two ways. First, computer services available at some libraries help scholars to generate bibliographies and refine research problems. If you are interested in food additives, for example, and your library subscribes to *Medline* (a computer-based system operated by the National Library of Medicine), a specially trained librarian can help you to retrieve a printed list of relevant articles published in some 1200 journals of biology, medicine, and related sciences within the last three years. If, after querying the computer and learning that there are some 1500 references, you decide your topic is too broad, you can, again with the assistance of the specialist and the computer, progressively narrow your search to a more compassable topic, perhaps the carcinogenic effects of nitrites in cured meat and fish. In about an hour and a half then — an hour with the computer specialist learning to translate your research problem into the language of the system, and half an hour at the terminal in conversation with the computer — you will not only have retrieved a comprehensive and up-to-date list of articles, you will have retrieved it far more quickly and with less tedium than you could have done by using catalogs, bound indexes, and note cards.

Second, computers are frequently used where research projects require statistical analyses, mathematical computations, or simulated experiments. With access to a computer and knowledge of its language you might, for example, use, modify, or devise a computer program to analyze election data, calculate the weight of a star, or simulate the air flow over an airplane wing.

When you come to write a report, a computer with a text-editing program can further assist you. You will again have to invest some time learning to use it, but if you are doing a substantial piece of work — a thesis, for example — you might find your time well spent. With a text-editing program — which functions something like a smart typewriter with a faultless memory — you can compose, revise, and edit your writing and then make copies of the finished essay, all on the same machine. You can, for example, start by typing a rough draft, then delete whole paragraphs or sections, and continue by adding new material. When you want to check your revisions, you can request a clean copy of any part of your text. If you discover that you have misspelled a word a dozen times, you can, with one command to the computer, correct the error every place it appears. When you have the final version of your essay stored in the computer's memory, you can request as many copies as you want; and, with a sophisticated program, your computer will present them to you correctly paged, footnotes in place, left and right margins adjusted, and all neatly typed.

Computer facilities vary greatly from place to place; those we describe here — automated bibliographic searches and mathematical, scientific, and text-editing programs — are only examples of some of the current uses of computers in research and writing. It's unlikely therefore that all of these particular facilities are available to you now. Even if they all are available, they may not prove useful for any work you are now doing, and even if they're useful, the chances are they'll cost more than you want to spend. (That hour and a half with *Medline* and the specialist, for example, would currently cost about $17.00.) Nevertheless, computers and their applications are proliferating, as computers become not only more powerful and more versatile, but also smaller and cheaper; and we expect them to be more commonly available within the next few years. If any facilities are available to you now, then, we suggest you find out about them and acquire some computer literacy, even if you must take a course, invent a project, or apply for a grant to do it. Look in your college catalog to see what opportunities exist, and ask your instructors and the reference librarian. Sometimes even where computer facilities exist, it takes some persistence to find out about them.

11

Special
Assignments

WRITING AN EXPLICATION

An explication (literally, unfolding or spreading out) is a commentary, usually line by line, on what is going on in a poem or in a short passage of prose. An explication is not concerned with the writer's life or times, nor is it a paraphrase, a rewording — though it may include paraphrase; it is a commentary revealing your sense of the meaning of the work. To this end it calls attention, as it proceeds, to the implications of words, the function of rhymes, the shifts in point of view, the development of contrasts, and any other contributions to the meaning.

Take, for example, the short poem by William Butler Yeats that opens this book, "The Balloon of the Mind":

> Hands, do what you're bid:
> Bring the balloon of the mind
> That bellies and drags in the wind
> Into its narrow shed.

Now, if we have done research on the work of Yeats we may remember that in an autobiography, *Reveries over Childhood and Youth,* Yeats already had used the figure of a balloon (dirigible) to represent mental activity: "My thoughts were a great excitement, but when I tried to do anything with them, it was like trying to pack a balloon into a shed in a high wind." But because explication usually confronts the work itself, without relating it to biography, we can pass over this interesting anticipation and confine ourselves to the poem's four lines. Here is the final version of an explication that went through several drafts after many readings (some aloud) of the poem. After reading this explication do not chastise yourself for not seeing all the subtleties when you read the poem. The writer herself did not see them all during the first, or even the fifth, reading. Notice that among the topics discussed are the tone (of the first line), the lengths of the lines, and the effect of patterns of sound, including rhythm, rhyme, and alliteration.

Yeats's "Balloon of the Mind" is about poetry, specifically about the difficulty of getting one's floating thoughts down into lines on the page. The first line, a short, stern, heavily stressed command to the speaker's hands, implies by its impatient tone that these hands will be disobedient or inept or careless if not watched closely: the poor bumbling body so often fails to achieve the goals of the mind. The bluntness of the command in the first line ("Hands, do what you're bid") is emphasized by the fact that it has fewer syllables than each of the subsequent lines. Furthermore, the first line is a grammatically complete sentence, whereas the thought of line 2 spills over into the subsequent lines, implying the difficulty of fitting ideas into confining spaces. Lines 2 and 3 amplify the metaphor already stated in the title (a thought is an airy but unwieldy balloon) and they also contain a second command, "Bring." Alliteration ties this command, "*B*ring," to the earlier "*b*id"; it also ties both of these verbs to their object, "*b*alloon," and to the verb that most effectively describes the balloon, "*b*ellies." In comparison with the peremptory first line of the poem, lines 2 and 3 themselves seem almost swollen, bellying and dragging, an effect aided by using adjacent unstressed syllables ("of the," "[bell]ies and," "in the") and by using an eye rhyme ("mind" and "wind") rather than an exact rhyme. And then comes the short last line: almost before we could expect it, the cumbersome balloon — here, the idea that is to be packed into the stanza — is successfully lodged in its "narrow shed." Aside from the relatively colorless "into," the only words of more than one syllable in the poem are "narrow," "balloon," and "bellies," and all three of them emphasize the difficulty of the task. But after "narrow" (the word itself almost looks long and narrow, in this context like a hangar) we get the simplicity of the monosyllable "shed," and the difficult job is done, the thought is safely packed away, the poem is completed — but again with an off rhyme ("bid" and "shed"), for neatness can go only so far when hands and the mind and a balloon are involved.

Because the language of a literary work is denser (richer in associations or connotations) than the language of discursive prose, such as this paragraph, explication is concerned with bringing to the surface the meanings that are in the words but may not be immediately apparent. Explication, in short, seeks to make explicit the implicit.

The reader of an explication needs to see the text. Since the explicated text is usually short, it is advisable to quote the entire text. You can quote it, complete, at the outset, or you can quote the first unit (for example, a stanza) and then explicate the unit, and then quote the next unit and explicate it, and so on. If the poem or passage of prose is longer than, say, six lines, it is advisable to number each line at the right for easy reference.

WRITING A BOOK REVIEW

Because a book review in a newspaper or magazine is usually about a newly published work, the reviewer normally assumes that his readers will be unfamiliar with the book. The reviewer takes it as his job to acquaint readers with the book, its contents and its value, and to help them decide whether or not they wish to read it. Since most reviews are brief (500–1500 words) they cannot, like explications, comment on everything. On the other hand they cannot, like analyses, focus on one aspect of the writing; they attempt in some way to cover the book. Reviews, then, usually contain more summary and more evaluation than explications or analyses. Nevertheless the reviewer must approach the task analytically if he is to accomplish it in the relatively small space allotted. And he must, to be convincing, support his opinions by quotations (usually indispensable), examples, and specific references to the text so that readers may think and feel the way the reviewer thinks and feels.

A review commonly has a structure something like this:

1. an opening paragraph that names the author and the title, gives the reader some idea of the nature and scope of the work (perhaps by briefly setting it in a context of related works), and establishes the tone of the review (more about tone in a moment)

2. a paragraph or two of plot summary if the book is a novel; some summary of the contents if it is not
3. a paragraph on the theme, purpose, idea, or vision embodied in the book, again perhaps within a context of related works
4. A paragraph or two on the strengths, if any
5. a paragraph or two on the weaknesses, if any
6. a concluding paragraph in which the reviewer delivers the point he has to make — but the point in some degree has probably been implied from the beginning, because the concluding paragraph is a culmination rather than a surprise

Tone, as we suggest elsewhere in this book (see pages 392–94) usually refers to the writer's attitude toward his subject, his readers, and himself. The tone of a review is therefore somewhat dependent on the publication in which it will appear. A review in *Scientific American* will have a different tone from one in *Ms.* Since you have not been commissioned to write your review and are essentially playing a game, you must *imagine* your reader. It's a reasonable idea to imagine that your classmates are your readers, forgetting of course that they may be reviewing the same book you are. (It's a very bad idea to imagine that your teacher is your reader.) And it's always productive to treat both your reader and your subject with respect. This does not mean you need to be solemn or boring; on the contrary, the best way to show your respect for your reader is to write something you would be interested in reading yourself.

Here is a published book review. Although some reviews are untitled, this one has a title; unless your instructor tells you otherwise, give your review a title. (Finding your title will help you, in revising your review, to see if you have focused your essay.)

Family Man (Wampeters, Foma, & Granfalloons: Opinions by Kurt Vonnegut, Jr.)

W. T. Lhamon, Jr.

Readers of Vonnegut's novels will like these essays, speeches, reviews and an interview. But those who think his fiction thin, unformed and full of cheap tickles will find these essays just that.

Vonnegut seems an honest man, which is admirable enough

these days. Yet honesty leaves him confessing many sad things. When he was confronted with a list of his publications, for instance, he "felt like a person who was creepily alive, still, and justly accused of petty crime." He says he has tried to "tell the truth plonkingly." That is, the writing trades "allow mediocre people who are patient and industrious to revise their stupidity, to edit themselves into something like intelligence." He goes on: "my career astonishes me. How could anybody have come this far with so little information, with such garbled ideas of what other writers have said?" He was the 98-pound weakling to whom a high school coach once awarded a Charles Atlas course. He remembers his family's maid reading to him from a book called *More Heart Throbs* — and he thinks that she contributed to the "almost intolerable sentimentality about everything" he's written.

There have of course been other contributions to that sentimentality. His mother committed suicide. As a POW he survived the fire-bombing of Dresden. The University of Chicago gave him his happiest day when they accepted him as a graduate student in anthropology — but then they rejected his thesis. To his own three children, his sister's early death from cancer added three more lives for him to father. And so he had a large family there on Cape Cod in his struggling days of what he calls "sleazo" paperbacks and short stories, when no one was reviewing him and, it seemed, not very many were reading him either.

Now, when people are reading him by the millions, he still has a feel for families, and especially for the fathering of families. He admires the Biafran extended families who obviated government welfare programs during much of that land's short life. And he yearns for a return to the 19th-century family structure as a sort of not-so-voluntary group. His next novel will even propose assigned families: the government will provide the same middle name — Chromium or Daffodil — to random groups of 20,000 persons, and these people will all rely on each other, just like cousins supposedly used to do. If he's thinking a lot about families these days, the father-family axis is still all the more telling as the sustenance of his style. Which is to say that his writing has a modern paternalism to it — that of a father who would like also to be a buddy. Or, of a buddy who would also like to be a father.

That is, Vonnegut is a sneaky moralist. He admires the simplicity and untextured responses of the young, just as they admire his reductiveness and his untextured precepts. He speaks to an audience which has not been compromised by the corruptions and conventions of getting on. And he hankers for an age that has not suffered the same fate. His analogies, therefore, are to the 19th century. Since the 19th century will not return, his plots are into the vague future. And so on.

The phrases *and so on* and *so it goes* are so essential to Vonnegut that even though his critics have complained that such expressions are irking, he's not about to excise them. He can't. The world is full of binary and-so-ons for him: people whose lives are compromised and those whose lives are not; bad officers and nice enlisted men; innocent scientists who cause harm, and cynical scientists who hate the destruction to which they inevitably contribute; smart people and dumb people; happy people and lonely people; and so it goes. People who are caught in this world, and those with the liberated perspective of having lived in space, and so on. People who are substantial and those who are not: the somebodies and the nothings; those who are the "merest wisp of an implication" and those who slip back into Nothing, and so it goes. He's not trying to be vague. Rather he's emphasizing how eternally the world is a simple place which we overcome or in which we are overcome. And so on.

The world is not that sort of place: not so clean nor well-lighted. It is messy, in fact, and most of us keep on going during and after being overcome by the dirt and the dark. Vonnegut knows that, and his life shows it if his writing does not. His taste shows it too. That he admires George Orwell and raves over Hunter Thompson tells us much about his own work. Orwell punctured duplicity with angry clarity and had the presence to keep it up all alone. Thompson overwhelms duplicity with manic rage. But Vonnegut has neither the clarity nor the rage of the authors he respects. Instead he has the professional's ability to send back a cable. He says, "I come to work every morning and I see what words come out of the typewriter. I feel like a copyboy whose job is to tear off stories from the teletype machine and deliver them to an editor." Creepily, plonkingly, he's still alive. This is the feeling of an honest man who is hoping at best for the merest wisp of an implication, for a whisper rebuking his silence and the silence around him: Billy Pilgrim wandering in snowdrifts, muttering. Still it would surely be great fun to drive across country with him, or share a bottle with him, or have him for a father. And, because he believes in all the right things even if loosely and only tepidly, he already is a brother.

QUESTIONS

1. Characterize or describe the tone of Lhamon's review.
2. Write a one-sentence summary of each paragraph. Your list of sentences should resemble an outline. (See the paragraph outline on page 79.)
3. How well does your outline correspond with the structure we say reviews commonly have? (See pages 309–10.)
4. If there are discrepancies between what we have said about reviews and the review by Lhamon, can you offer a reasonable explanation for these discrepancies? Or would you argue that we revise our discussion, or that we choose a different review as an example?
5. Write a brief argument (two or three paragraphs) defending your answer to question 4.

TAKING ESSAY EXAMINATIONS

What Examinations Are

An examination not only measures learning and thinking but stimulates them. Even so humble an examination as a short-answer quiz — chiefly a device to coerce the student to do the assigned reading — is a sort of push designed to move the student forward. Of course internal motivation is far superior to external, but even such crude external motivation as a quiz can have a beneficial effect. Students know this; indeed they often seek external compulsion, choosing a course "because I want to know something about it, and I know that I won't do the reading on my own." (Teachers often teach a new course for the same reason; we want to become knowledgeable about, say, the theater of the absurd, and we know that despite our lofty intentions we may not seriously confront the subject unless we are under the pressure of facing a class.) In short, however ignoble it sounds, examinations force the student to acquire learning and then to convert learning into thinking.

Sometimes it is not until preparing for the final examination that the student — rereading the chief texts and classroom notes — sees what the course was really about; until this late stage, the trees obscured the forest, but now, as the student reviews and sorts things out, a pattern emerges. The experience of reviewing and then of writing an examination, though fretful, can be highly exciting as connections are made and ideas take on life. Such discoveries about the whole subject matter of a course can almost never be made by writing critical essays on topics of one's own construction, for such topics rarely require a view of the whole. Furthermore, most of us are more likely to make imaginative leaps when trying to answer questions that other people pose to us, than when we are trying to answer questions we pose to ourselves. And although questions posed by others cause anxiety, when they have been confronted and responded to on an examination students often make yet another discovery — a self-discovery, a sudden and satisfying awareness of powers they didn't know they had.

Writing Essay Answers

We assume that before the examination you have read the assigned material, made notes in the margins of your books, made summaries of the reading and of the classroom comments, reviewed all of this material, and had a decent night's sleep. Now you are facing the examination sheet.

Here are eight obvious but important practical suggestions.

1. Take a moment to jot down, as a kind of outline or source of further inspiration, a few ideas that strike you after you have thought a little about the question. You may at the outset realize there are three points you want to make: unless you jot these down — three key words will do — you may spend all the allotted time on only one.

2. Don't bother to copy the question in the examination booklet, but if you have been given a choice of questions do indicate the question number, or write a word or two that will serve as a cue to the reader.

3. Answer the question. Consider this question: "Fromm and Lorenz try to explain aggression. Compare their theories, and discuss the extent to which they assist us in understanding the Arab-Israeli conflict." Notice that you must compare — not just summarize — two theories, and that you must also evaluate their relevance to a particular conflict. In short, take seriously such

words as *compare, define, evaluate,* and *summarize.* And don't waste time generalizing about aggression; again, answer the question.

4. You can often get a good start merely by turning the question into an affirmation, for example by turning "In what ways is the poetry of Ginsberg influenced by Whitman?" into "The poetry of Ginsberg is influenced by Whitman in at least . . . ways."

5. Don't waste time summarizing at length what you have read, unless asked to do so — but of course occasionally you may have to give a brief summary in order to support a point. The instructor wants to see that you can *use* your reading, not merely that you have done the reading.

6. Budget your time. Do not spend more time on a question than the allotted time.

7. Be concrete. Illustrate your arguments with facts — names, dates, and quotations if possible.

8. Leave space for last minute additions. Either skip a page between essays, or write only on the right-hand pages so that on rereading you can add material at the appropriate place on the left-hand pages.

Beyond these general suggestions, we can best talk about essay examinations by looking at specific types of questions.

Questions on Literature

The five most common sorts of questions encountered in literature examinations are:

1. a passage to explicate
2. a historical question, such as "Trace T. S. Eliot's religious development," "Trace the development of Shakespeare's conception of the tragic hero," or "How is Frost's nature poetry indebted to Emerson's thinking?"
3. a critical quotation to be evaluated
4. a comparison, such as "Compare the dramatic monologues of Browning with those of T. S. Eliot"
5. a wild question, such as "What would Dickens think of Vonnegut's *Cat's Cradle*?" or "What would Macbeth do if he were in Hamlet's position?"

A few remarks on each of these types may be helpful:

1. For a discussion of how to write an explication, see pages 307–09. As a short rule, look carefully at the tone (speaker's attitude toward self, subject, and audience) and at the implications of the words (the connotations or associations), and see if there is a pattern of imagery. For example, religious language ("adore," "saint") in a secular love poem may define the nature of the lover and of the beloved. Remember, *an explication is not a paraphrase* (a putting into other words) but an attempt to show the relations of the parts, especially by calling attention to implications. Organization of such an essay is rarely a problem, since most explications begin with the first line and go on to the last.

2. A good essay on a historical question will offer a nice combination of argument and evidence; the thesis will be supported by concrete details (names, dates, perhaps even brief quotations). A discussion of Eliot's movement toward the Church of England cannot be convincing if it does not specify certain works as representative of Eliot in certain years. If you are asked to relate a writer or a body of work to an earlier writer or period, list the chief characteristics of the earlier writer or the period and then show *specifically* how the material you are discussing is related to these characteristics. And if you can quote some relevant lines from the works, your reader will feel that you know not only titles and stock phrases but also the works themselves.

3. If you are asked to evaluate a critical quotation, read it carefully and in your answer take account of *all* of the quotation. If the critic has said, "Eliot in his plays always . . . but in his poems rarely . . ." you will have to write about both the plays and the poems; it will not be enough to talk only about the plays (unless, of course, the instructions on the examination ask you to take only as much of the quotation as you wish). Watch especially for words like "always," "for the most part," "never"; although the passage may on the whole approach the truth, you may feel that some important qualifications are needed. This is not being picky; true thinking involves making subtle distinctions, yielding assent only so far and no further. And, again, be sure to give concrete details, supporting your argument with evidence.

4. Comparisons are discussed on pages 38–44. Because

comparisons are especially difficult to write, be sure to take a few moments to jot down a sort of outline so that you can know where you will be going. A comparison of Browning's and Eliot's monologues might treat three poems by each, devoting alternate paragraphs to one author; or it might first treat one author's poems and then turn to the other. But if it adopts this second strategy, the essay may break into two parts. You can guard against this weakness by announcing at the outset that you will treat the authors separately, then by reminding your reader during your treatment of the first author that certain points will be picked up when you get to the second author, and again by briefly reminding your reader during the second part of the essay of certain points already made.

5. Curiously, a wild question such as "What would Dickens think of *Cat's Cradle?*" or "What would Macbeth do in Hamlet's position?" usually produces tame answers: a half dozen ideas about Dickens or Macbeth are neatly applied to Vonnegut or Hamlet, and the gross incompatibilities are thus revealed. But, as the previous paragraph suggests, it may be necessary to do more than to set up bold and obvious oppositions. The interest in such a question and in the answer to it may largely be in the degree to which superficially different figures *resemble* each other in some important ways. And remember that the wildness of the question does not mean that all answers are equally acceptable; as usual, a good answer will be supported by concrete details.

Questions on the Social Sciences

The techniques students develop in answering questions on literature may be transferred to examinations in the social sciences. A political science student, for example, can describe through explication the implicit tone or attitude in some of the landmark decisions of the Supreme Court. Similarly, the student of history who has learned to write an essay with a good combination of argument and evidence will not simply offer generalizations or present a list of facts unconnected by some central thesis, but will use relevant facts to support a thesis. The student who is able to evaluate a critical quotation or to compare literary works can also evaluate and compare documents in all the social sciences. Answers to wild questions can be as effective or as trite in the social sciences as in literature. "You are the British ambassador in Petrograd in November 1918. Write a report to your government about the Bolshevik revolution of that month" is to some instructors and students an absurd question but to others it is an interesting and effective way of ascertaining whether a student has not only absorbed the facts of an event but has also learned how to interpret them.

Questions on the Physical Sciences and Mathematics

Although the answer to an examination question in the physical sciences usually requires a mathematical computation, a few sentences may be useful in explaining the general plan of the computation, the assumptions involved, and sometimes the results.

It is particularly valuable to set down at the outset in a brief statement, probably a single sentence, your plan for solving the problem posed by the examination question. The statement is equivalent to the topic sentence of a paragraph. For instance, if the examination question is "What is the time required for an object to fall from the orbit of the moon to the earth?" the statement of your plan might be: "The time required for an object to fall from the orbit of the moon to the earth can be obtained by integration from Newton's law of motion, taking account of the increasing gravitational force as the object approaches the earth." Explicitly setting down your plan in words is useful first in clarifying your thought: is the plan a complete one leading to the desired answer? Do I know what I need to know to implement the plan? If your plan doesn't make sense you can junk it right away before wasting more time on it.

The statement of plan is useful also in communicating with the instructor. Your plan of solution, although valid, may be a surprise to the instructor. (She may have expected a solution to the problem posed above starting from Kepler's laws without any integration.) When this is so, the instructor will need your explanation to become oriented to your plan, and to properly assess its merits. Then if you botch the subsequent computation or can't remember how the gravitational force varies with the distance you will still have demonstrated that you have some comprehension of the problem. If on the other hand you present an erroneous computation without any explanation, the instructor will see nothing but chaos in your effort.

Further opportunities to use words will occur when you make assumptions or simplifications: "I assume the body is released with zero velocity and accordingly set b = 0," or "The third term is negligible and I drop it."

Finally, the results of your computation should be summarized or interpreted in words to answer the question asked. "The object will fall to the earth in five days." (The correct answer, for those who are curious.) Or, if you arrive at the end of your computation and of the examination hour and find you have a preposterous result, you can still exit gracefully (and increase your partial credit) with an explanation: "The answer of 53 days is clearly erroneous since the fall time of an object from the moon's orbit must be less than the 7 days required for the moon to travel a quarter orbit."

PART TWO
Revising

The friends that have it I do wrong
When ever I remake a song,
Should know what issue is at stake:
It is myself that I remake.
　　　— WILLIAM BUTLER YEATS

12

Revising for Conciseness

Excess is the common substitute for energy.
— MARIANNE MOORE

All writers who want to keep the attention and confidence of their readers revise for conciseness. The general rule is to say everything relevant in as few words as possible. The conclusion of the Supreme Court's decision in *Brown* v. *The Board of Education of Topeka,* for example — "Separate educational facilities are inherently unequal" — says it all in six words.

The writers of the following sentences talk too much; they bore us because they don't make every word count.

> There are two pine trees which grow behind this house.
>
> On his left shoulder is a small figure standing. He is about the size of the doctor's head.
>
> The judge is seated behind the bench and he is wearing a judicial robe.

Compare those three sentences with these revisions:

> Two pine trees grow behind this house.
>
> On his left shoulder stands a small figure, about the size of the doctor's head.
>
> The judge, wearing a robe, sits behind the bench.

We will soon discuss in some detail the chief patterns of wordiness, but here it is enough to say that if you prefer the revisions you already have a commendable taste for conciseness. What does your taste tell you to do with the following sentence?

> A black streak covers the bottom half. It appears to have been painted with a single stroke of a large brush.

The time to begin revising for conciseness is when you have an acceptable first draft in hand — something that pretty much covers your topic and comes reasonably close to saying what you believe about it. As you go over it, study each sentence to see what, without loss of meaning or emphasis, can be deleted. (Delete by crossing out, not erasing; this saves time, and keeps a record of something you may want to reintroduce.) Read each paragraph, preferably aloud, to see if each sentence supports the topic sentence or idea and clarifies the point you are making. Leave in the concrete and specific details and examples that support your ideas (you may in fact be adding more) but cut out all the deadwood that chokes them: extra words, empty or pretentious phrases, weak qualifiers, redundancies, negative constructions, wordy uses of the verb *to be,* and other extra verbs and verb phrases. We'll discuss these problems in the next pages, but first we offer some examples of sentences that cannot be improved upon; they're so awful there's nothing to do but cross them out and start over. Zonker, in Garry Trudeau's cartoon, is a master of what we call Instant Prose (stuff that sounds like the real thing, but isn't).

INSTANT PROSE
(ZONKERS)

Here are some examples of Instant Prose from students' essays:

> Frequently a chapter title in a book reveals to the reader the main point that the author desires to bring out during the course of the chapter.

DOONESBURY

by Garry Trudeau

We could try revising this, cutting the twenty-seven words down to seven:

A chapter's title often reveals its thesis.

But why bother? Unless the title is an exception, is the point worth making?

> The two poems are basically similar in many ways, yet they have their significant differences.

True; all poems are both similar to and different from other poems. Start over with your next sentence, perhaps something like: "The two poems, superficially similar in rough paraphrase, are strikingly different in diction and theme."

> Although the essay is simple in plot, the theme encompasses many vital concepts of emotional makeup.

> Following a transcendental vein, the nostalgia in the poem takes on a spiritual quality.

> Cassell only presents a particular situation concerning the issue, and with clear descriptions and a certain style sets up an interesting article.

Pure zonkers. Not even the writers of these sentences now know what they mean.

Writing Instant Prose is an acquired habit, like smoking cigarettes or watching soap operas; fortunately it's easier to kick. It often begins in high school, sometimes earlier, when the victim is assigned a ten-page paper, or is told that a paragraph *must* contain at least three sentences, or that a thesis is stated in the introduction to an essay, elaborated in the body, and repeated in the conclusion. If the instructions appear arbitrary, and the student is bored or intimidated by them, his response is likely to be, like Zonker's, meaningless and mechanical. He forgets, or never learns, the true purpose of writing — the discovery and communication of ideas, attitudes, and judgments — and concentrates instead on the word count: stuffing sentences, padding paragraphs, stretching and repeating points, and adding flourishes. Rewarded by a satisfactory grade, he repeats the performance, and in time, through practice, develops some fluency in spilling out words without thought or commitment, and almost without effort. Such a student enters, as Zonker would say, the college of his choice, feeling somehow inauthentic, perhaps even aware that he doesn't really mean what he writes: symptoms of habitual use of, or addiction to, Instant Prose.

How to Avoid Instant Prose

1. Trust yourself. Writing Instant Prose is not only a habit; it's a form of alienation. If you habitually write zonkers you probably don't think of what you write as your own but as something you produce on demand for someone else. (Clearly Zonker is writing for that unreasonable authority, the teacher, whose mysterious whims and insatiable appetite for words he must somehow satisfy.) Breaking the habit begins with recognizing it, and then acknowledging the possibility that you can take yourself and your work seriously. It means learning to respect your ideas and experiences (unlearning the passive habits that got you through childhood) and determining that when you write you'll write what you mean — nothing more, nothing less. This involves taking some risks, of course; habits offer some security or they would have no grip on us. Moreover, we all have moments when we doubt that our ideas are worth taking seriously. Keep writing honestly anyway. The self-doubts will pass; accomplishing something — writing one clear sentence — can help make them pass.

2. Distrust your first draft. Learn to recognize Instant Prose Additives when they crop up in your writing, and in what you read. And you *will* find them in what you read — in textbooks and in academic journals, notoriously.

Here's an example from a recent book on contemporary theater:

> One of the principal and most persistent sources of error that tends to bedevil a considerable proportion of contemporary literary analysis is the assumption that the writer's creative process is a wholly conscious and purposive type of activity.

Notice all the extra stuff in the sentence: "principal and most persistent," "tends to bedevil," "considerable proportion," "type of activity." Cleared of deadwood the sentence might read: "The assumption that the writer's creative process is wholly conscious bedevils much contemporary criticism."

3. Acquire two things: a new habit, Revising for Conciseness; and what Isaac Singer calls "the writer's best friend," a wastebasket.

REVISING FOR CONCISENESS

Extra Words and Empty Words

Extra words should, by definition, be eliminated; vague, empty, or pretentious words and phrases may be replaced by specific and direct language.

Wordy

However, it must be remembered that Ruth's marriage could have positive effects on Naomi's situation.

Concise

Ruth's marriage, however, will also provide security for Naomi.

In the second version, the unnecessary "it must be remembered that" has been eliminated; for the vague "positive effects" and "situation," specific words communicating a precise point have been substituted. The revision, though briefer, says more.

Wordy

In high school, where I had the opportunity for three years of working with the student government, I realized how significantly a person's enthusiasm could be destroyed merely by the attitudes of his superiors.

Concise

In high school, during three years on the student council, I saw students' enthusiasm destroyed by insecure teachers and cynical administrators.

Again, the revised sentence gives more information in fewer words. How?

Wordy

The economic situation of Miss Moody was also a crucial factor in the formation of her character.

Concise

Anne Moody's poverty also helped to form her character.

"Economic situation" is evasive for poverty; "crucial factor" is pretentious. Both are Instant Prose.

Wordy

It creates a better motivation of learning when students can design their own programs involving education. This way students' interests can be focused on.

Concise

Motivation improves when students design their own programs, focused on their own interests.

Now revise the following wordy sentences:

1. Perhaps they basically distrusted our capacity to judge correctly.
2. The use of setting is also a major factor in conveying a terrifying type atmosphere.

Notice how, in the examples provided, the following words crop up: "basically," "significant," "situation," "factor," "involving," "effect," "type." These words have legitimate uses, but are often no more than Instant Prose Additives. Cross them out whenever you can. Similar words to watch out for: *aspect, facet, fundamental, manner, nature, ultimate, utilization, viable, virtually, vital.* If they make your writing sound good don't hesitate — cross them out at once.

Weak Intensifiers and Qualifiers

Words like *very, quite, rather, completely, definitely,* and *so* can usually be struck from a sentence without loss. Paradoxically, sentences are often more emphatic without intensifiers. Try reading the following sentences both with and without the bracketed words:

At that time I was [very] idealistic.
We found the proposal [quite] feasible.
The remark, though unkind, was [entirely] accurate.
It was a [rather] fatuous statement.
The scene was [extremely] typical.
Both films deal with disasters [virtually] beyond our control.
The death scene is [truly] grotesque.
What she did next was [completely] inexcusable.
The first line [definitely] establishes that the father had been drinking.

Always avoid using intensifiers with *unique.* Either something is unique — the only one of its kind — or it is not. It can't be very, quite, so, pretty, or fairly unique.

Circumlocutions

Roundabout ways of saying things enervate your prose and tire your reader. Notice how each circumlocution in the first column is matched by a concise expression in the second.

I came to the realization that	I realized that
She is of the opinion that	She thinks that
The quotation is supportive of	The quotation supports
Concerning the matter of	About
During the course of	During
For the period of a week	For a week
In the event that	If
In the process of	During, while
Regardless of the fact that	Although
Due to the fact that	Because
For the simple reason that	Because
The fact that	That
Inasmuch as	Since
If the case was such that	If
It is often the case that	Often
In all cases	Always
I made contact with	I called, saw, phoned, wrote
At that point in time	Then
At this point in time	Now

Now revise this sentence:

> These movies have a large degree of popularity for the simple reason that they give the viewers insight in many cases.

Wordy Beginnings

Vague, empty words and phrases clog the beginnings of some sentences. They're like elaborate windups before the pitch.

1. *Wordy*

By analyzing carefully the last lines in this stanza, you find the connections between the loose ends of the poem.

Concise

The last lines of the stanza connect the loose ends of the poem.

2. *Wordy*

What the cartoonist is illustrating and trying to get across is the greed of the oil producers.

Concise

The cartoon illustrates the greed of the oil producers.

3. *Wordy*

Dealing with the crucial issue of the year, the editorial is expressing ironical disbelief in any possible solution to the Middle East crisis.

Concise

The editorial ironically expresses disbelief in the proposed solutions to the Middle East crisis.

4. *Wordy*

In the last stanza is the conclusion (as usual) and it tells of the termination of the dance.

Concise

The last stanza concludes with the end of the dance.

5. *Wordy*

In opposition to the situation of the younger son is that of the elder who remained in his father's house, working hard and handling his inheritance wisely.

Concise

The elder son, by contrast, remained in his father's house, worked hard, and handled his inheritance wisely.

Notice in the above examples that when the deadwood is cleared from the beginning of the sentence, the subject appears early, and the main verb appears close to it:

1. The last lines . . . connect . . .
2. The cartoon illustrates . . .
3. The editorial . . . expresses . . .
4. The last stanza concludes . . .
5. The elder son . . . remained . . .

Locating the right noun for the subject, and the right verb for the predicate, is the key to revising sentences with wordy beginnings. Try revising the following sentences:

1. The way that Mabel reacts toward her brother is a fine representation of her nature.
2. In Langston Hughes's case he was "saved from sin" when he was going on thirteen.

Empty Conclusions

Often a sentence that begins well has an empty conclusion. The words go on but the sentence seems to stand still; if it's not revised, it requires another sentence to explain it. A short sentence is not necessarily concise.

1. *Empty*

"Those Winter Sundays" is composed so that a reader can feel what the poet was saying. (How is it composed? What is he saying?)

Concise

"Those Winter Sundays" describes the speaker's anger as a child, and his remorse as an adult.

2. *Empty*

In both Orwell's and Baldwin's essays the feeling of white supremacy is very important. (Why is white supremacy important?)

Concise

Both Orwell and Baldwin trace the insidious consequences of white supremacy.

3. *Empty*

Being the only white girl among about ten black girls was quite a learning experience. (What did she learn?)

Concise

As the only white girl among about ten black girls, I began to understand the experiences of isolation, helplessness, and rage regularly reported by minority students.

Wordy Uses of the Verbs "To Be," "To Have," and "To Make"

Notice that in the preceding unrevised sentences a form of the verb *to be* introduces the empty conclusion: "*was* saying," "*is* very important," "*was* quite a learning experience." In each revision, the right verb added and generated substance. In the following sentences, substitutions for the verb *to be* both invigorate and shorten otherwise substantial sentences.

1. *Wordy*

The scene is taking place at night, in front of the capitol building.

Concise

The scene takes place at night, in front of the capitol building.

2. *Wordy*

In this shoeshining and early rising there are indications of church attendance.

Concise

The early rising and shoeshining indicate church attendance.

3. *Wordy*

The words "flashing," "rushing," "plunging," and "tossing" are suggestive of excitement.

Concise

The words "flashing," "rushing," "plunging," and "tossing" suggest excitement.

The rule is, whenever you can, replace a form of the verb *to be* with a stronger verb.

To Be	*Strong Verb*
1. and a participle ("is taking")	1. takes
2. and a noun ("are indications")	2. indicate
3. and an adjective ("are suggestive")	3. suggest

Try revising the following sentence:

The rising price of sugar is representative of the spiraling cost of all goods.

Sentences with the verbs *to have* and *to make* can similarly be reduced:

1. *Wordy*

The Friar has knowledge that Juliet is alive.

Concise

The Friar knows that Juliet is alive.

2. *Wordy*

The stanzas make a vivid contrast between Heaven and Hell.

Concise

The stanzas vividly contrast Heaven and Hell.

Like all rules, this one has exceptions. We don't list them here; you'll discover them by listening to your sentences.

Redundancy

This term, derived from a Latin word meaning "overflowing, overlapping," refers to unnecessary repetition in the expression of ideas. Unlike repetition, which often provides emphasis or coherence (for example, "government of the people, by the people, for the people") redundancy can always be eliminated.

1. *Redundant*

Any student could randomly sit anywhere. (If the students could sit anywhere, the seating was random.)

Concise

Students could sit anywhere.
Students chose their seats at random.

2. *Redundant*

I have no justification with which to excuse myself.

Concise

I have no justification for my action.
I can't justify my action.
I have no excuse for my action.
I can't excuse my action.

3. *Redundant*

In the orthodox Cuban culture, the surface of the female role seemed degrading. (Perhaps this sentence means what it says. More probably "surface" and "seemed" are redundant.)

Concise

In the orthodox Cuban culture, the female role seemed degrading.
In the orthodox Cuban culture, the female role was superficially degrading.

4. *Redundant*

In "Araby" the boy feels alienated emotionally from his family.

Concise

In "Araby" the boy feels alienated from his fanily.

Try eliminating redundancy from the following sentences:

1. The reason why she hesitates is because she is afraid.
2. Marriage in some form has long existed since prehistoric times.

What words can be crossed out of the following phrases?

1. throughout the entire article
2. her attitude of indifference
3. a conservative type suit
4. all the different tasks besides teaching
5. his own personal opinion
6. elements common to both of them
7. emotions and feelings
8. shared together
9. falsely padded expense accounts
10. alleged suspect

Many phrases in common use are redundant. Watch for phrases like these when you revise:

round in shape	resulting effect
purple in color	close proximity
poetic in nature	connected together
tall in stature	prove conclusively
autobiography of her life	must necessarily
basic fundamentals	very unique
true fact	very universal
free gift	the reason why is because

Negative Constructions

Negative constructions are often wordy and sometimes pretentious.

1. *Wordy*

Housing for married students is not unworthy of consideration.

Concise

Housing for married students is worthy of consideration.

Better

The trustees should earmark funds for married students' housing. (Probably what the author meant)

2. *Wordy*

After reading the second paragraph you aren't left with an immediate reaction as to how the story will end.

Concise

The first two paragraphs create suspense.

The following example from a syndicated column is not untypical:

> Although it is not reasonably to be expected that someone who fought his way up to the Presidency is less than a largely political animal and sometimes a beast, it is better not to know — really — exactly what his private conversations were composed of.

The Golden Rule of writing is "Write for others as you would have them write for you," not "Write for others in a manner not unrea-

"See what I mean? You're never sure just where you stand with them."
Drawing by Ross; © 1971 The New Yorker Magazine, Inc.

sonably dissimilar to the manner in which you would have them write for you." (But see the discussion of *not . . . un-* on page 610 for effective use of the negative.)

Extra Sentences, Extra Clauses: Subordination

Sentences are sometimes wordy because ideas are given more elaborate grammatical constructions than they need. In revising, these constructions can be grammatically subordinated, or reduced. Two sentences, for example, may be reduced to one, or a clause may be reduced to a phrase.

1. *Wordy*

The Book of Ruth was probably written in the fifth century B.C. It was a time when women were considered the property of men.

Concise

The book of Ruth was probably written in the fifth century B.C., when women were considered the property of men.

2. *Wordy*

The first group was the largest. This group was seated in the center of the dining hall.

Concise

The first group, the largest, was seated in the center of the dining hall.

3. *Wordy*

The colonists were upset over the tax on tea and they took action against it.

Concise

The colonists, upset over the tax on tea, took action against it.

Watch particularly for clauses beginning with *who, which,* and *that.* Often they can be shortened.

1. *Wordy*

George Orwell is the pen name of Eric Blair who was an English writer.

Concise

George Orwell is the pen name of Eric Blair, an English writer.

2. *Wordy*

They are seated at a table which is covered with a patched and tattered cloth.

Concise

They are seated at a table covered with a patched and tattered cloth.

3. *Wordy*

There is one feature that is grossly out of proportion.

Concise

One feature is grossly out of proportion.

Also watch for sentences and clauses beginning with *it is, this is, there are.* (Again, wordy uses of the verb *to be.*) These expressions often lead to a *which,* but even when they don't they may be wordy.

1. *Wordy*

This is a quotation from Black Elk's autobiography which discloses his prophetic powers.

Concise

This quotation from Black Elk's autobiography discloses his prophetic powers.

2. *Wordy*

It is frequently considered that *Hamlet* is Shakespeare's most puzzling play.

Concise

Hamlet is frequently considered Shakespeare's most puzzling play.

3. *Wordy*

In Notman's photograph of Buffalo Bill and Sitting Bull there are definite contrasts between the two figures.

Concise

Notman's photograph of Buffalo Bill and Sitting Bull contrasts the two figures.

Try revising the following sentences:

1. There are many writers who believe that writing can't be taught.
2. This is an indication that the child has a relationship with his teacher which is very respectful.

(For further discussion of subordination see pages 384–86. On *which* clauses, see also page 617.)

SOME CONCLUDING REMARKS

We spoke earlier about how students learn to write Instant Prose and acquire other wordy habits — by writing what they think the teacher has asked for. We haven't forgotten that teachers assign papers of a certain length in college too. But the length given is not an arbitrary limit that must be reached — the teacher who asks for a five-page or twenty-page paper is probably trying to tell you the degree of elaboration expected on the assignment. Such, apparently, was the intention of William Randolph Hearst, the newspaper publisher, who cabled an astronomer, "Is there life on Mars? Cable reply 1000 words." The astronomer's reply was, "Nobody knows," repeated five hundred times.

What do you do when you've been asked to produce a ten-page paper and after diligent writing and revising you find you've said everything relevant to your topic in seven and a half pages? Our advice is, hand it in. We can't remember ever counting the words or pages of a substantial, interesting essay; we assume that our colleagues elsewhere are equally reasonable and equally over-worked. If we're wrong, tell us about it — in writing, and in the fewest possible words.

EXERCISE

First identify the fault or faults that make the following sentences wordy, and then revise them for conciseness.

1. There were quite a number of contrasts that White made between the city school and the country school which was of a casual nature all throughout.
2. The study of political topics involves a careful researching of the many components of the particular field.
3. Virtually the most significant feature of any field involving science is the vital nature of the technical facilities, the fundamental factor of all research.

4. Like a large majority of American people, I, too, have seen the popular disaster films.

5. Something which makes this type of film popular (disaster) is the kind of subconscious aspect of "Can man overcome this problem?" Horror films, on the other hand, produce the aspects of whether or not man can make amends for his mistakes.

6. The average American becomes disappointed and downtrodden due to the fact that he can't help himself and is at the mercy of inflation and unemployment.

7. Some relationships have split up because of the simple fear of having an abnormal child, while perhaps there might have been other alternatives for these couples.

8. Reading has always been a fascinating and exciting pastime for me for as long as I can remember.

9. This cartoon appeared in the 17 September 1979 issue of *Newsweek*. This political cartoon was originally taken from the *Tulsa Tribune*. The cartoonist is Simpson.

10. Only once in the first two sentences does the author make reference to the first person.

11. The length of the sentences are similar in moderation and in structural clarity.

12. The magnitude of student satisfaction with the program ranged from total hatred to enthusiastic approval.

13. Taking a look at the facial expressions of the man and the woman in both pictures one can see a difference in mood.

14. One drawing is done in watercolor and the other is done in chalk which is a revision of the watercolor.

15. The dialogue places the role of the two gods on a believable basis.

16. Senseless crimes such as murder and muggings are committed on a daily basis.

17. One must specify that the current disco craze which is so very popular today is not considered to be black music.

18. The two major aspects behind the development of a performer are technique and musicianship.

19. I remember my first desire to smoke cigarettes as I watched my father smoke. My father often sat in his favorite easy chair idly smoking cigarettes.

20. Christopher Stone's article "Putting the Outside Inside the Fence of Law" is concerning the legal rights of the environment. He comments on the legal rights of other inanimate entities which seem to be acceptable. Just as these entities are represented, so should the environment be represented.

13
Revising for Clarity

CLARITY

We have seen new realities created by the advance of physics. But this chain of creation can be traced back far beyond the starting point of physics. One of the most primitive concepts is that of an object. The concepts of a tree, a horse, any material body, are creations gained on the basis of experience, though the impressions from which they arise are primitive in comparison with the world of physical phenomena. A cat teasing a mouse also creates, by thought, its own primitive reality. The fact that the cat reacts in a similar way toward any mouse it meets shows that it forms concepts and theories which are its guide through its own world of sense impressions.

— Albert Einstein and Leopold Infeld

Skills constitute the manipulative techniques of human goal attainment and control in relation to the physical world, so far as artifacts or machines especially designed as tools do not yet supplement them. Truly human skills are guided by organized and codified *knowledge* of both the things to be manipulated and the human capacities that are used to manipulate them. Such knowledge is an aspect of cultural-level symbolic processes, and, like other aspects to be discussed presently, requires the capacities of the human central nervous system, particularly the brain. This organic system is clearly essential to all of the symbolic processes; as we well know, the human brain is far superior to the brain of any other species.

— Talcott Parsons

Why is the first passage easier to understand than the second?

Both passages discuss the relationship between the brain and the physical world it attempts to understand. The first passage, by Einstein and Infeld is, if anything, more complex both in what it asserts and in what it suggests than the second, by Parsons. Both passages explain that the brain organizes sense impressions. But Einstein and Infeld further explain that the history of physics can be understood as an extension of the simplest sort of organization, such as we all make in distinguishing a tree from a horse, or such as even a cat makes in teasing a mouse. Parsons only promises that "other aspects" will "be discussed presently." How many of us are eager for those next pages?

Good writing is clear, not because it presents simple ideas, but because it presents ideas in the simplest form the subject permits. A clear analysis doesn't reduce a complex problem to a simple one; it breaks it down into its simple, comprehensible parts and discusses them, one by one, in a logical order. A clear paragraph explains one of these parts coherently, thoroughly, and in language as simple and as particular as the reader's understanding requires and the context allows. Where Parsons writes of "organized and codified *knowledge* of . . . the things to be manipulated," Einstein and Infeld write simply of the concept of an object. And even "object," a simple but general word, is further clarified by the specific, familiar examples, "tree" and "horse." Parsons writes of "the manipulative techniques of . . . goal attainment and control in relation to the physical world, so far as artifacts or machines especially designed as tools do not yet supplement them." Einstein and Infeld show us a cat teasing a mouse.

Notice also the clear organization of Einstein and Infeld's paragraph. The first sentence, clearly transitional, refers to the advance of physics traced in the preceding pages. The next sentence, introduced by "But," reverses our direction: we are now going to look not at an advance, but at primitive beginnings. And the following sentences, to the end of the paragraph, fulfill that promise. We move back to primitive human concepts, clarified by examples, and finally to the still more primitive example of the cat. Parsons' paragraph is also organized, but the route is much more difficult to follow.

Why do people write obscurely? Walter Kaufmann, in an

introduction to Martin Buber's *I and Thou,* says "Men love jargon. It is so palpable, tangible, visible, audible; it makes so obvious what one has learned; it satisfies the craving for results. It is impressive for the uninitiated. It makes one feel that one belongs. Jargon divides men into Us and Them."

Maybe. (For our definition of jargon, see pages 350–51.) Surely some students learn to write obscurely by trying to imitate the style of their teachers or textbooks. The imitation may spring from genuine admiration for these authorities, mixed perhaps with an understandable wish to be one of Us (the authorities) not one of Them (the dolts). Or students may feel that a string of technical-sounding words is what the teacher expects. If this thought has crossed your mind, we can't say you're entirely wrong. Learning a new discipline often involves acquiring a specialized vocabulary. But we add the following cautions:

1. What teachers expect is that your writing show thought and make sense. They are likely to be puzzled by the question, "Do you want me to use technical terms in this paper?"
2. If you try to use technical terms appropriate to one field when you write about another, you are likely to write nonsense. Don't write "the machine was viable" if you mean only that it worked.
3. When you do write for specialists in a particular field use technical terms precisely. Don't write in an art history paper, "This print of Van Gogh's *Sunflowers*" if you mean "This reproduction of Van Gogh's *Sunflowers.*"
4. No matter what you are writing, don't become so enamored of technical words that you can't write a sentence without peppering it with *input, interface, death-symbol, parameter, feedback,* and so on.

But to return to the question, "Why do people write obscurely?" — we'd like to offer a second answer to Kaufmann's "Men love jargon." It's difficult to write clearly.[1] Authorities may be unintelligible not because they want to tax you with unnecessary difficulties, but because they don't know how to avoid them. In our era, when we sometimes seem to be drowning in a flood of print, few persons who write know how to write well. If you have ever tried to assemble a mechanical toy or to thread an unfamiliar

[1] Our first draft of this sentence read "Writing clearly is difficult." Can you see why we changed it?

sewing machine by following the "easy instructions," you know that the simplest kind of expository writing, giving instructions, can foil the writers most eager for your good will (that is, those who want you to use their products). Few instructions, unfortunately, are as unambiguous as "Go to jail. Go directly to jail. Do not pass Go. Do not collect $200."

You can, though, learn to write clearly, by learning to recognize common sources of obscurity in writing and by consciously revising your own work. We offer, to begin with, three general rules:

1. Use the simplest, most exact, most specific language your subject allows.
2. Put together what belongs together, in the essay, in the paragraph, and in the sentence.
3. Keep your reader in mind, particularly when you revise.

Now for more specific advice, and examples — the cats and mice of revising for clarity.

CLARITY AND EXACTNESS: USING THE RIGHT WORD

Denotation

Be sure the word you choose has the right *denotation* (explicit meaning). Did you mean sarcastic or ironic? Fatalistic or pessimistic? Disinterested or uninterested? Biannual or semiannual? Enforce or reinforce? Use or usage? If you're not sure, check the dictionary. You'll find some of the most commonly misused words discussed in Chapter 21. Here are examples of a few others.

1. Daru faces a dilemma between his humane feelings and his conceptions of justice. (Strictly speaking, a dilemma requires a choice between two equally unattractive alternatives. "Conflict" would be a better word here.)
2. However, as time dragged on, exercising seemed to lose its charisma. (What is charisma? Why is it inexact here?)
3. Ms. Wu's research contains many symptoms of depression which became evident during the reading period. (Was Ms. Wu depressed by her research? We hope not. Probably she described or listed the symptoms.)

4. When I run I don't allow myself to stop until I have reached my destiny. (Which word is inexact?)

Connotation

Be sure the word you choose has the right *connotation* (association, implication). As Mark Twain said, the difference between the right word and the almost right word is the difference between lightning and the lightning bug.

1. Boston politics has always upheld the reputation of being especially crooked. ("Upheld" inappropriately suggests that Boston has proudly maintained its reputation. "Has always had" would be appropriate here, but pale. "Deserved" would, in this context, be ironic, implying — accurately — the writer's scorn.)
2. This book, unlike many other novels, lacks tedious descriptive passages. ("Lacks" implies a deficiency. How would you revise the sentence?)
3. New Orleans, notorious for its good jazz and good food. . . . (Is "notorious" the word here? or "famous"?)
4. Sunday, Feb. 9. Another lingering day at Wellesley. (In this entry from a student's journal, "lingering" strikes us as right. What does "lingering" imply about Sundays at Wellesley that "long" would not?)

Because words have connotations, most writing — even when it pretends to be objective — conveys attitudes as well as facts. Consider, for example, this passage by Jessica Mitford, describing part of the procedure used today for embalming:

A long, hollow needle attached to a tube . . . is jabbed into the abdomen, poked around the entrails and chest cavity, the contents of which are pumped out. . . .

In a way this passage accurately describes part of the procedure, but it also, of course, records Mitford's contempt for the procedure. Suppose she wanted to be more respectful — suppose, for example, she were an undertaker writing an explanatory pamphlet. Instead of the needle being "jabbed" it would be "inserted," and instead of being "poked around the entrails" it would be "guided around the viscera," and the contents would not be "pumped out" but would be "drained." Mitford's words would be the wrong words for an undertaker explaining embalming to apprentices or to the general public, but, given her purpose, they are exactly the right ones because they convey her attitude with great clarity.

Note too that many words have social, political, or sexist overtones. We read for example of the *children* of the rich, but the *offspring* of the poor. What is implied by the distinction? Consider the differences in connotation in each of the following series:

1. friend, boyfriend, young man, lover (What age is the speaker?)
2. dine, eat (What was on the menu? Who set the table?)
3. spinster, bachelor (Which term is likely to be considered an insult?)
4. underdeveloped nations, developing nations, emerging nations
5. preference, bias, prejudice
6. upbringing, conditioning, brainwashing
7. message from our sponsor, commercial, ad, plug
8. intelligence gathering, espionage, spying
9. emigrate, defect, seek asylum
10. anti-abortion, pro-life; pro-abortion, pro-choice

Quotation Marks as Apologies

When you have used words with exact meanings (denotations) and appropriate associations (connotations) for your purpose, don't apologize for them by putting quotation marks around them. If the words *copped a plea, ripped off,* or *kids* suit you better than *plea-bargained, stolen,* or *children,* use them. If they are inappropriate, don't put them in quotation marks; find the right words.

Being Specific

In writing descriptions, catch the richness, complexity, and uniqueness of things. Suppose, for example, you are describing a scene from your childhood, a setting you loved. There was, in particular, a certain tree . . . and you write: "Near the water there was a big tree that was rather impressive." Most of us would produce something like that sentence. Here is the sentence Ernesto Galarza wrote in *Barrio Boy:*

> On the edge of the pond, at the far side, there was an enormous walnut tree, standing like an open umbrella whose ribs extended halfway across the still water of the pool.

We probably could not have come up with the metaphor of the umbrella because we wouldn't have seen the similarity. (As Aristotle observed, the gift for making metaphors distinguishes the poet from the rest of us.) But we can all train ourselves to be accurate observers and reporters. For "the water" (general) we can *specify* "pond"; for "near" we can say how near, "on the edge of the pond," and add the specific location, "at the far side"; for "tree" we can give the *species,* "walnut tree"; and for "big" we can provide a picture, its branches "extended halfway across" the pond: it was, in fact, "enormous."

Galarza does not need to add limply, as we did, that the tree "was rather impressive." The tree he describes *is* impressive. That he accurately remembered it persuades us that he was impressed, without his having to tell us he was. For writing descriptions, a good general rule is: show, don't tell.

Be as specific as you can be in all forms of exposition too. Take the time, when you revise, to find the exact word to replace vague, woolly phrases or clichés. (In the following examples we have had to guess or invent what the writer meant.)

1. *Vague*

The clown's part in *Othello* is very small.

Specific

The clown appears in only two scenes in *Othello*.
The clown in *Othello* speaks only thirty lines.
(Notice the substitution of the verb "appears" or "speaks" for the frequently debilitating "is." And in place of the weak intensifier "very" we have specific details to tell us how small the role is.)

2. *Vague*

He feels uncomfortable at the whole situation. (Many feelings are uncomfortable. Which one does he feel? What's the situation?)

Specific

He feels guilty for having distrusted his father.

3. *Vague*

The passage reveals a somewhat calculating aspect behind Antigone's noble motives. ("A somewhat calculating aspect" is vague — and wordy — for "calculation." Or did the writer mean "shrewdness"? What differences in connotation are there between "shrewd" and "calculating"?)

4. *Vague*

She uses simplicity in her style of writing. (Do we know, exactly, what simplicity in style means?)

Specific

She uses familiar words, normal word order, and conversational phrasing.

5. *Vague Cliché*

Then she criticized students for living in an ivory tower. (Did she criticize them for being detached or secluded? For social irresponsibility or studiousness?)

Specific

Then she criticized students for being socially irresponsible.

Using Examples

In addition to exact words and specific details, illustrative examples make for clear writing. Einstein and Infeld, in the passage quoted on page 341, use as an example of a primitive concept a cat teasing not only its first mouse, but "any mouse it meets." Here are two paragraphs which clarify their topic sentences through examples; the first is again from *Barrio Boy*.

> In Jalco people spoke in two languages — Spanish and with gestures. These signs were made with the face or hands or a combination of both. If you bent one arm and tapped the elbow with the other hand, it meant "He is stingy." When you sawed one arm across the other you were saying that someone you knew played the fiddle terribly. To say that a man was a tippler you made a set of cow's horns with the little finger and the thumb of one hand, bending the three middle fingers to the palm and pointing the thumb at your mouth. And if you wanted to indicate, without saying so for the sake of politeness, that a mutual acquaintance was daffy, you tapped three times on your forehead with your middle finger.
>
> — Ernesto Galarza

In the next paragraph, Northrop Frye, writing about the perception of rhythm, illustrates his point:

> Ideally, our literary education should begin, not with prose, but with such things as "this little pig went to market" — with verse

> rhythm reinforced by physical assault. The infant who gets bounced on somebody's knee to the rhythm of "Ride a cock horse" does not need a footnote telling him that Banbury Cross is twenty miles northeast of Oxford. He does not need the information that "cross" and "horse" make (at least in the pronunciation he is most likely to hear) not a rhyme but an assonance. . . . All he needs is to get bounced.

Frye does not say our literary education should begin with "simple rhymes" or with "verse popular with children." He says "with such things as 'this little pig went to market,'" and then he goes on to add "Ride a cock horse." We know exactly what he means. Notice, too, that we do not need a third example. Be detailed, but know when to stop.

Your reader is likely to be brighter and more demanding than Lady Pliant, who in a seventeenth-century play says to a would-be seducer, "You are very alluring — and say so many fine Things, and nothing is so moving to me as a fine Thing." "Fine Things," of course, are what is wanted, but only exact words and apt illustrations will convince intelligent readers that they are hearing fine things.

Now look at a paragraph from a student's essay whose thesis is that rage can be a useful mechanism for effecting change. Then compare the left hand paragraph with the same paragraph, revised, at the right. Note the specific ways, sentence by sentence, the student revised for clarity.

In my high school we had little say in the learning processes that were used. The subjects that we were required to take were irrelevant. One had to take them to earn enough points to graduate. Some of the teachers were sympathetic to our problem. They would tell us about when they were young, how they tried to oppose their school system. But when they were young it was a long time ago, for most of them. The principal would call assemblies to speak on the subject.	In my high school we had little say about our curriculum. We were required, for example, to choose either American or European History to earn enough points for graduation. We wanted, but were at first refused, the option of Black History. Some of our teachers were sympathetic with us; one told me about her fight opposing the penmanship course required in her school. Nor was the principal totally indifferent — he called assemblies. I remember one talk he

They were entitled, "The Value of an Education" or "Get a Good Education to Have a Bright Future." The titles were not inviting. They had nothing to do with our plight. Most students never came to any agreements with the principal because most of his thoughts and views seemed old and outdated.

gave called "The Value of an Education in Today's World," and another, "Get a Good Education to Have a Bright Future." I don't recall hearing about a Black History course in either talk. Once, he invited a group of us to meet with him in his office, but we didn't reach any agreement. He solemnly showed us an American History text (not the one we used) that had a whole chapter devoted to Black History.

Jargon and Technical Language

Jargon is the unnecessary, inappropriate, or inexact use of technical or specialized language. Look at this passage:

*Dodgers Keep Perfect Record
in Knocking Out Southpaws*

NEW YORK (AP) — The Brooklyn Dodgers didn't win the first World Series game yesterday, but they got a measure of comfort in that they maintained one of their season records.

No left-hander went the distance in beating them the past season. Six lefties got the decision but none was around at the end.

New York hurler Whitey Ford made No. 7, but he, too, went the way of the other southpaws . . . empty consolation, to be sure, in view of the Yanks' 6–5 victory in the World Series opener.

Consider the diction of this sports story: "went the distance," "lefties," "got the decision," "around at the end," "hurler," "southpaws," "opener," "made No. 7." Do you understand the individual words? Most of them, probably. Do you know what the item is about? Some of us do, some don't. Is it written in technical language, or jargon?

The answer depends, as we define jargon, on where the story appeared, and for whom it was intended. Because it appeared on the sports page of a newspaper, we would classify the diction as technical language, not jargon. Properly used, technical language communicates information concisely and clearly, and can, as it does here, create a comfortable bond between reader and writer. Both are having fun. If the same story appeared on the front page of the newspaper, we would classify the language as jargon because it would baffle the general reader.

"With you, I think I've found a maximization of experience."
Drawing by Donald Reilly; © 1978 The New Yorker Magazine, Inc.

If the baseball story makes perfect sense to you, as an exercise, try to explain it in nontechnical language to someone who does not understand it. And while you're at it, can you explain why baseball fans are particularly interested in left-handed pitchers — in other words, what makes the statistic here a statistic? Why are baseball fans so interested in statistics anyway — more interested, say, than football or hockey fans? Is it because baseball is intrinsically boring?

Let's move quickly to another example:

> For many years Boston parents have tried to improve the public schools. But any input the parents might have desired has been stifled by the Boston School Committee.

What does "input" mean in this sentence? Is the term used as technical language here, or jargon? (And by the way, how would you go about stifling an input?)

A student wrote the passage just quoted. But recently in Dallas, parents of children in kindergarten through third grade received a twenty-eight page manual written by a professional educator to help them decipher their children's report cards. The title of the manual: *Terminal Behavioral Objectives for Continuous Progression Modules in Early Childhood Education.* Terminal objectives, it seems, means goals. What does the rest mean? If you were one of the parents, would you expect much help from the manual?

Here's a film critic discussing the movie *Last Tango in Paris:*

> The failure of the relationship between Paul and Jeanne is a function of the demands placed on the psyche by bourgeois society, and it is the family as mediator of psychological and social repression which provides the dialectic of Bertolucci's film.

Perhaps some film criticism should be x-rated?

And finally, a deliberate parody. A. P. Herbert in his book *What a Word!* tells us how a social scientist might write a familiar Biblical command:

> In connection with my co-citizens, a general standard of mutual good will and reciprocal non-aggression is obviously incumbent upon me.

What is the command? (See Leviticus xix. 18.)

In general, when you write for nonspecialists, avoid technical terms; if you must use them, define them. If you use a technical term when writing for specialists, be sure you know its precise meaning. But whenever you can, even among specialists, use plain English.

Clichés

Clichés (literally, in French, molds from which type is cast) are trite expressions, mechanically — that is, mindlessly — produced. Since they are available without thought they are great Instant Prose Additives (see pages 324–26). Writers who use them are usually surprised to be criticized: they find the phrases attractive, and may even think them exact. (Phrases become clichés precisely because they have wide appeal and therefore wide use.) But clichés, by their very nature, cannot communicate the uniqueness of your thoughts. Furthermore, because they come instantly to mind, they tend to block the specific detail or exact expression that will let the reader know what precisely is in your mind. When, in

*"You're right as rain. It's the dawn of history,
and there are no clichés as yet. I'll drink to that!"*

Drawing by Handelsman; © 1972 The New Yorker Magazine, Inc.

revising, you strike out a cliché, you force yourself to do the work of writing clearly. The following examples are full of clichés:

> Finally, the long awaited day arrived. Up bright and early. . . .
>
> She peered at me with suspicion; then a faint smile crossed her face.

Other examples:

first and foremost	time honored
the acid test	bustled to and fro
fatal flaw	short but sweet
budding genius	few and far between
slowly but surely	D-day arrived
little did I know	sigh of relief
the big moment	last but not least

In attempting to avoid clichés, however, don't go to the other extreme of wildly original, super-vivid writing — "'well then, say something to her,' he roared, his whole countenance gnarled in rage." It's often better to simply say, "he said." (Anyone who intends to write dialogue should memorize Ring Lardner's intentionally funny line, "'Shut up!' he explained.") Note also that such common expressions as "How are you?" "Please pass the salt," and "So long" are not clichés; they make no claim to be colorful.

Mixed Metaphors

Ordinary speech abounds with metaphors (implied comparisons). We speak or write of the foot of a mountain, the germ (seed) of an idea, the root of a problem. Metaphors so deeply embedded in the language that they no longer evoke pictures in our minds are called *dead metaphors*. Ordinarily, they offer us, as writers, no problems: we need neither seek them nor avoid them; they are simply there. (Notice, for example, "embedded" two sentences back.) Such metaphors become problems, however, when we unwittingly call them back to life. Howard Nemerov observes: "That these metaphors may be not dead but only sleeping, or that they may arise from the grave and walk in our sentences, is something that has troubled everyone who has ever tried to write plain expository prose. . . ."

Dead metaphors are most likely to haunt us when they are embodied in clichés. Since we use clichés without attention to what they literally say or point to, we are unlikely to be aware of the dead metaphors buried in them. But when we attach one cliché to another, we may raise the metaphors from the grave. The result is likely to be a mixed metaphor; the effect is almost always absurd.

> Water seeks its own level whichever way you want to slice it.
>
> Traditional liberal education has run out of gas and educational soup kitchens are moving into the vacuum.
>
> The low ebb has been reached and hopefully it's turned the corner.
>
> Her energy, drained through a stream of red tape, led only to closed doors.
>
> We no longer ask for whom the bell tolls but simply chalk it up as one less mouth to feed.

As Joe E. Lewis observed, "Show me a man who builds castles in the air and I'll show you a crazy architect." Unless you're sure that you've hit on an original and accurate comparison leave metaphor making to poets and comedians.

Euphemisms

Euphemisms are words substituted for other words thought to be offensive. In deodorant advertisements there are no armpits, only *underarms,* which may *perspire*, but not sweat, and even then they don't smell. A parent reading a report card is likely to learn not that his child got an F in conduct, but that she "experiences difficulty exercising self-control: (a) verbally (b) physically." And where do old people go? To Sun City, "a retirement community for senior citizens."

Euphemisms are used for two reasons: to avoid giving offense, and, sometimes unconsciously, to disguise fear and animosity. We do not advise you to write or speak discourteously; we do advise you, though, to use euphemisms consciously and sparingly, when tact recommends them. It's customary in a condolence letter to avoid the word *"death*," and, depending both on your own feelings and those of the bereaved, you may wish to follow that custom. But there's no reason on earth to write "Hamlet passes on." You should be aware, moreover, that some people find euphemisms themselves offensive. There may be more comfort for your friend in "I'm sorry about his death" or even in "too bad about your old lady," than in "I regret to hear of your loss." And speaking of old ladies, there is one in Philadelphia, Margaret Kuhn, who would probably prefer to be called a woman than a lady, and certainly prefers "old" to "senior" — because "Old," she says, "is the right word. . . . I think we should wear our gray hair, wrinkles, and crumbling joints as badges of distinction. After all, we worked damn hard to get them." She has organized a militant group called the Gray Panthers to fight agism.

In revising, replace needless euphemisms with plain words. Your writing will be sharper, and you might, in examining and confronting them, free yourself of a mindless habit, an unconscious prejudice, or an irrational fear.

A Digression on Public Lying

Mr. Wilson: How do you know that, Mr. Chairman?
Senator Ervin: Because I can understand the English language. It is my mother tongue.

— From the Senate hearings on Watergate

There is a kind of lying which, in the words of Walker Gibson, we may call *public lying*. Its rules are to avoid substance, direct answers, and plain words. Its tendency is to subvert the English language. It employs and invents euphemisms, but the public liar intends to protect not his listeners, but himself and his friends, and he misleads and deceives consciously. Public lying was not invented during the Vietnam War or the Watergate hearings. (In 1946 George Orwell had already written the definitive essay on it, "Politics and the English Language.") Nor did it cease with the return of American prisoners, or with the resignation of our thirty-seventh president. But the war and the hearings produced some classic examples, from which we select a few.

The war, of course, was not a war, but a "conflict" or an "era." "Our side" never attacked "the other side," we made "protective reaction raids"; we didn't invade, we "incursed." We didn't bomb villages, we "pacified" them; peasants were not herded into concentration camps, but "relocated." We didn't spray the countryside with poisons, destroying forests, endangering or killing plant, animal, and human life, we "practiced vegetation control."

"In the interests of national security," some buildings and rooms ("the White House," "the Oval Office") hired not burglars but "electronic surveillance experts" who didn't bug, spy, break and enter, or steal, but "performed intelligence-gathering operations" — all of this according to "a game plan" designed to ensure "deniability."

More recently, it was disclosed that the CIA experimented with brainwashing under cover of "The Society for Investigation of Human Ecology." The Pentagon now refers to the neutron bomb (which kills all living creatures but leaves valuable buildings intact) as a "radiation enhancement weapon." And when approximately a million people in four counties surrounding the Three Mile Island nuclear power plant in Pennsylvania were threatened with "radiation enhancement" following a series of accidents, an officer of the Nuclear Regulatory Commission arrived to "dispel some of the multi-directional reports or facts." When asked by a reporter whether a menacing hydrogen bubble that had formed in the reactor could be removed, another official explained: "We are in a situation not comparable to previous conditions."

There is a Gresham's law in rhetoric as there is in economics: bad language drives out good. Bad language is contagious; learn to detect the symptoms: use of vague words for clear words; use of sentences or phrases where words suffice; evasive use of the passive voice; and outright lying.

Feiffer

© 1978 Jules Feiffer

Passive or Active Voice?

1. I baked the bread. (Active voice)
2. The bread was baked by me. (Passive voice)
3. The bread will be baked. (Passive voice)

Although it is the verb that is in the active or the passive voice, notice that the words *active* and *passive* describe the subjects of the sentences. That is, in the first sentence the verb "baked" is in the active voice; the subject "I" acts. In the second and third sentences the verbs "was baked" and "will be baked" are in the passive voice; the subject "bread" is acted upon. Notice also the following points:

1. The *voice* of the verb is distinct from its *tense.* Don't confuse the passive voice with the past tense. (Sentence 2 happens to be in the past tense, but 3 is not; both 2 and 3 are in the passive voice.)
2. The passive voice uses more words than the active voice. (Compare sentences 1 and 2.)
3. A sentence with a verb in the passive voice may leave the doer of the action unidentified. (See sentence 3.)
4. Finally, notice that in each of the three sentences the emphasis is different.

In revising, take a good look at each sentence in which you have used the passive voice. If the passive clarifies your meaning, retain it; if it obscures your meaning, change it. More often than not, the passive voice obscures meaning.

1. *Obscure*

The revolver given Daru by the gendarme is left in the desk drawer. (Left by whom? The passive voice here obscures the point.)

Clear

Daru leaves the gendarme's revolver in the desk drawer.

2. *Obscure*

Daru serves tea and the Arab is offered some. (Confusing shift from the active voice "serves" to the passive voice "is offered.")

Clear

Daru serves tea and offers the Arab some.

3. *Appropriate*

For over fifty years *Moby-Dick* was neglected. ("Was neglected" suggests that the novel was neglected by almost everyone. The passive voice catches the passivity of the response. Changing the sentence to "For over fifty years few readers read *Moby-Dick*" would make "readers" the subject of the sentence, but the true subject is — as in the original — *Moby-Dick*.)

Finally, avoid what has been called the Academic Passive: "In this essay it has been shown that. . . ." This cumbersome form used to be common in academic writing (to convey scientific objectivity) but *I* is usually preferable to such stuffiness.

The Writer's "I"

It is seldom necessary in writing an essay (even on a personal experience) to repeat "I think that" or "in my opinion." Your reader knows that what you write is your opinion. Nor is it necessary, if you've done your job well, to apologize. "After reading the story over several times I'm not really sure what it is about, but. . . ." Write about something you are reasonably sure of. Occasionally, though, when there is a real problem in the text, for example the probable date of the Book of Ruth, it is not only permissible to disclose doubts and to reveal tentative conclusions; it may be necessary to do so.

Note also that there is no reason to avoid the pronoun *I* when you are in fact writing about yourself. Attempts to avoid *I* ("this writer," "we," expressions in the passive voice such as "it has been said above" and "it was seen") are noticeably awkward and distracting. And sometimes you may want to focus on your subjective response to a topic in order to clarify a point. The following opening paragraph of a movie review provides an example:

> I take the chance of writing about Bergman's *Persona* so long after its showing because this seems to me a movie there's no hurry about. It will be with us a long time, just as it has been on my mind for a long time. Right now, when I am perhaps still under its spell, it seems to me Bergman's masterpiece, but I can't imagine ever thinking it less than one of the great movies. This of course is opinion; what I know for certain is that *Persona* is also one of the most difficult

movies I will ever see; and I am afraid that in this case there is a direct connection between difficulty and value. It isn't only that *Persona* is no harder than it has to be; its peculiar haunting power, its spell, and its value come directly from the fact that it's so hard to get a firm grasp on.

— Robert Garis

Students who have been taught not to begin sentences with *I* often produce sentences that are eerily passive even when the verbs are in the active voice. For example:

1. Two reasons are important to my active participation in dance.
2. The name of the program that I was in is the Health Careers Summer Program.
3. An eager curiosity overcame my previous feeling of fear to make me feel better.

But doesn't it make more sense to say:

1. I dance for two reasons.
2. I was enrolled in the Health Careers Summer Program.
3. My curiosity aroused, I was no longer afraid.

A good rule: make the agent of the action the subject of the sentence. A practical suggestion: to avoid a boring series of sentences all beginning with *I*, subordinate for conciseness and emphasis. (See pages 336–38 and 384–86.)

CLARITY AND COHERENCE

Writing a coherent essay is hard work; it requires mastery of a subject and skill in presenting it; it always takes a lot of time. Writing a coherent paragraph often takes more fussing and patching than you expect, but once you have the hang of it, it's relatively easy and pleasant. Writing a coherent sentence requires only that you stay awake until you get to the end of it. We all do nod sometimes, even over our own prose. But if you make it a practice to read your work over several times, at least once aloud, you give yourself a chance to spot the incoherent sentence before your reader does, and to revise it. Once you see that a sentence is incoherent, it's usually easy to recast it.

Cats Are Dogs

In some sentences a form of the verb *to be* asserts that one thing is in a class with another. Passover is a Jewish holiday. Dartmouth is a college. But would anyone not talking in his sleep say "Dartmouth is a Jewish holiday"? Are cats dogs? Students did write the following sentences:

1. *Incoherent*

X. J. Kennedy's poem "Nothing in Heaven Functions as It Ought" is a contrast between Heaven and Hell. (As soon as you ask yourself the question "Is a poem a contrast?" you have, by bringing the two words close together, isolated the problem. A poem may be a sonnet, an epic, an ode — but not a contrast. The writer was trying to say what the poem does, not what it is.)

Coherent

X. J. Kennedy's poem "Nothing in Heaven Functions as It Ought" contrasts Heaven and Hell.

2. *Incoherent*

Besides, he tells himself, a matchmaker is an old Jewish custom. (Is a matchmaker a custom?)

Coherent

Besides, he tells himself, consulting a matchmaker is an old Jewish custom.

Try revising the following:

The essay is also an insight into imperialism.

In a related problem, one part of the sentence doesn't know what the other is doing:

1. *Incoherent*

Ruth's devotion to Naomi is rewarded by marrying Boaz. (Does devotion marry Boaz?)

Coherent

Ruth's marriage to Boaz rewards her devotion to Naomi.

2. *Incoherent*

He demonstrates many human frailties, such as the influence of others' opinions upon one's actions. (Is influence a frailty? How might this sentence be revised?)

False Series

If you were given a shopping list that mentioned apples, fruit, and pears, you would be puzzled and possibly irritated by the inclusion of "fruit." Don't puzzle or irritate your reader. Analyze sentences containing items in a series to be sure that the items are of the same order of generality. For example:

False Series

His job exposed him to the "dirty work" of the British and to the evils of imperialism. ("The 'dirty work' of the British" is a *specific* example of the more *general* "evils of imperialism." The false series makes the sentence incoherent.)

Revised

His job, by exposing him to the "dirty work" of the British, brought him to understand the evils of imperialism.

In the following sentence, which item in the series makes the sentence incoherent?

Why should one man, no matter how important, be exempt from investigation, arrest, trial, and law enforcing tactics?

Modifiers

A modifier should appear close to the word it modifies (that is, describes or qualifies). Three kinds of faulty modifiers are common.

1. If the modifier seems to modify the wrong word, it is called *misplaced*. Misplaced modifiers are often unintentionally funny. The judo parlor that advertised "For $20 learn basic methods of protecting yourself from an experienced instructor" probably attracted more amused readers than paying customers.
2. If the modifier is ambiguous, that is, if it can be applied equally to more than one term, it is sometimes called a *squinting modifier*.
3. If the term it should modify appears nowhere in the sentence, the modifier is called *dangling*.

MISPLACED MODIFIERS

1. *Misplaced*

Orwell shot the elephant under pressured circumstances. (Orwell was under pressure, not the elephant. Put the modifier near what it modifies.)

Revised

Orwell, under pressure, shot the elephant.

2. *Misplaced*

Orwell lost his individual right to protect the elephant as part of the imperialistic system. (The elephant was not part of the system; Orwell was.)

Revised

As part of the imperialistic system, Orwell lost his right to protect the elephant.

3. *Misplaced*

Amos Wilder has been called back to teach at Harvard Divinity School after ten years retirement due to a colleague's illness. (Did Wilder retire for ten years because a colleague was ill? Revise the sentence.)

Revise the following:

1. Sitting Bull and William Cody stand side by side, each supporting a rifle placed between them with one hand.
2. Complete with footnotes the author has provided her readers with some background information.

Sometimes other parts of sentences are misplaced:

1. *Misplaced*

We learn from the examples of our parents who we are. (The sentence appears to say we are our parents.)

Revised

We learn who we are from the examples of our parents.

2. *Misplaced*

It is up to the students to revise the scheme, not the administrators. (We all know you can't revise administrators. Revise the sentence.)

SQUINTING MODIFIERS

1. *Squinting*

Being with Jennifer more and more enrages me. (Is the writer spending more time with Jennifer, or is he more enraged? Probably more enraged.)

Revised

Being with Jennifer enrages me more and more.

2. *Squinting*

Writing clearly is difficult. (The sentence may be talking about writing — it's clearly difficult to write — or about writing clearly — it's difficult to write clearly.)

3. *Squinting*

Students only may use this elevator. (Does "only" modify students? If so, no one else may use the elevator. Or does it modify elevator? If so, students may use no other elevator.)

Revised

Only students may use this elevator.
Students may use only this elevator.

Note: the word *only* often squints. In general, put *only* immediately before the word or phrase it modifies. Often it appears too early in the sentence. (See page 611.)

DANGLING MODIFIERS

1. *Dangling*

Being small, his ear scraped against the belt when his father stumbled. (The writer meant that the boy was small, not the ear. But the boy is not in the sentence.)

Revised

Because the boy was small his ear scraped against the belt when his father stumbled.
Being small, the boy scraped his ear against the belt when his father stumbled.

2. *Dangling*

A meticulously organized person, his suitcase could be tucked under an airplane seat. (How would you revise the sentence?)

The general rule: *when you revise sentences, put together what belongs together.*

Reference of Pronouns

A pronoun is used in place of a noun. Because the noun usually precedes the pronoun, the noun to which the pronoun refers is called the antecedent (Latin: "going before"). For example: in "When Sheriff Johnson was on a horse, he was a big man" the noun, "Sheriff Johnson," precedes the pronoun, "he." But the noun can also follow the pronoun, as in "When he was on a horse, Sheriff Johnson was a big man."

Be sure that whenever possible a pronoun has a clear reference. Sometimes it isn't possible: *it* is commonly used with an unspecified reference, as in "It's hot today," and "Hurry up please, it's time"; and there can be no reference for interrogative pronouns: "What's bothering you?" and "Who's on first?" But otherwise always be sure that you've made clear what noun the pronoun is standing for.

VAGUE REFERENCES

1. *Vague*

Apparently, they fight physically and it can become rather brutal. ("It" doubtless refers to "fight," but "fight" in this sentence is the verb, not an antecedent noun.)

Clear

Their fights are apparently physical, and sometimes brutal.

2. *Vague*

I was born in Colon, the second largest city in the Republic of Panama. Despite this, Colon is still an undeveloped town. ("This" has no specific antecedent. It appears to refer to the writer's having been born in Colon.)

Clear

Although Colon, where I was born, is the second largest city in Panama, it remains undeveloped.

(On *this,* see also page 615.)

Revise the following sentence:

> They're applying to medical school because it's a well-paid profession.

SHIFT IN PRONOUNS

This common error is easily corrected.

1. In many instances the child was expected to follow the profession of your father. (Expected to follow the profession of whose father, "yours" or "his"?)
2. Having a tutor, you can get constant personal encouragement and advice that will help me budget my time. (If "you" have a tutor will that help "me"?)
3. If one smokes, you should at least ask permission before you light up. (If "one" smokes, why should "you" ask permission? But here the change to "If one smokes, one should at least ask permission before one lights up," though correct, sounds inappropriately formal. Omit a "one": "If one smokes, one should at least ask permission before lighting up." Or forget about "one" and use "you" throughout the sentence.)

Revise the following sentences:

1. Schools bring people of the same age together and teach you how to get along with each other.
2. If asked why you went to a mixer, one might say they were simply curious.

AMBIGUOUS REFERENCE OF PRONOUNS

A pronoun normally refers to the first appropriate noun or pronoun preceding it. Same-sex pronouns and nouns, like dogs, often get into scraps.

1. *Ambiguous*

Her mother died when she was eighteen. (Who was eighteen, the mother or the daughter?)

Clear

Her mother died when Mabel was eighteen.
Her mother died at the age of eighteen. (Note the absence of ambiguity in "His mother died when he was eighteen.")

2. *Ambiguous*

Daru learns that he must take an Arab to jail against his will. (Both Daru and the Arab are male. The writer of the sentence meant that Daru learns he must act against his will.)

Clear

Daru learns that he must, against his will, take an Arab to jail.

The general rule: *put together what belongs together.*

Agreement

NOUN AND PRONOUN

Everyone knows that a singular noun requires a singular pronoun, and a plural noun requires a plural pronoun, but writers sometimes slip.

1. *Faulty*

A dog can easily tell if people are afraid of them.

Correct

A dog can easily tell if people are afraid of it.

2. *Faulty*

Every student feels that Wellesley expects them to do their best.

Correct

Every student feels that Wellesley expects her to do her best.

Each, everybody, nobody, no one, and *none* are especially troublesome. See the entries on these words in the chapter on usage.

SUBJECT AND VERB

A singular subject requires a singular verb, a plural subject a plural verb.

Faulty

Horror films bring to light a subconscious fear and shows a character who succeeds in coping with it.

Correct

Horror films bring to light a subconscious fear and show a character who succeeds in coping with it.

The student who wrote "shows" instead of "show" thought that the subject of the verb was "fear," but the subject really is "Horror films," a plural.

Faulty

The manager, as well as the pitcher and the catcher, were fined.

Correct

The manager, as well as the pitcher and the catcher, was fined.

If the sentence had been "The manager and the pitcher . . . ," the subject would have been plural and the required verb would be "were," but in the sentence as it is given, "as well as" (like *in addition to, with,* and *together with*) does *not* add a subject to a subject and thereby make a plural subject. "As well as" merely indicates that what is said about the manager applies to the pitcher and the catcher.

Revise the following:

About mid-morning during Spanish class the sound of jeeps were heard.

Sometimes a sentence that is grammatically correct may nevertheless sound awkward:

One of its most noticeable features is the lounges.

Because the subject is "one," the verb must be singular, "is," but "is" sounds odd when it precedes the plural "lounges." The solution: revise the sentence.

Among the most noticeable features are the lounges.

Repetition and Variation

1. Don't be afraid to repeat a word if it is the best word. The following paragraph repeats "interesting," "paradox," "Salinger," "What makes," and "book"; notice also "feel" and "feeling." Repetition, a device necessary for continuity and clarity, holds the paragraph together.

The reception given to *Franny and Zooey* in America has illustrated again the interesting paradox of Salinger's reputation there; great public enthusiasm, of the *Time* magazine and Best Seller List kind, accompanied by a repressive coolness in the critical journals. What makes this a paradox is that the book's themes are among the most ambitiously highbrow, and its craftsmanship most uncompromisingly virtuoso. What makes it an interesting one is that those who are most patronising about the book are those who most resemble its characters; people whose ideas and language in their best moments resemble Zooey's. But they feel they ought not to enjoy the book. There is a very strong feeling in American literary circles that Salinger and love of Salinger must be discouraged.

— Martin Green

2. Use pronouns, when their reference is clear, as substitutes for nouns. Notice Green's use of pronouns; notice also his substitution of "the book," for *"Franny and Zooey,"* and then "its" for "the book's." Substitutions that neither confuse nor distract keep a paragraph from sounding like a broken phonograph record.

3. Do not, however, confuse the substitutions we have just spoken of with the fault called Elegant Variation. A groundless fear of repetition sometimes leads students to write first, for example, of "Salinger," then of "the writer," then of "our author." Such variations strike the reader as silly. They can, moreover, be confusing. Does "the writer" mean "Salinger," or the person writing about him? Substitute "he" for "Salinger" if "he" is clear and sounds better. Otherwise, repeat "Salinger."

4. But don't repeat a word if it is being used in two different senses.

1. *Confusing*

Green's theme focuses on the theme of the book. (The first "theme" means "essay"; the second means "underlying idea" or "motif.")

Clear

Green's essay focuses on the theme of the book.

2. *Confusing*

Caesar's character is complex. The comic characters, however, are simple. (The first "character" means "personality"; the second means "persons" or "figures in the play.")

Clear

Caesar is complex; the comic characters, however, are simple.

5. Finally, eliminate words repeated unnecessarily. Use of

words like *surely, in all probability, it is noteworthy* may become habitual. If they don't help your reader to follow your thoughts, they are Instant Prose Additives. Cross them out.

In general, when you revise, decide if a word should be repeated, varied, or eliminated, by testing sentences and paragraphs for both sound and sense.

Euphony

The word is from the Greek, "sweet voice," and though you need not aim at sweetness, try to avoid cacophony, or "harsh voice." Avoid distracting repetitions of sound, as in "The story is marked by a remarkable mystery," and "This is seen in the scene in which. . . ." Such echoes call attention to themselves, getting in the way of the points you are making. When you revise, tune out irrelevant sound effects.

Not all sound effects are irrelevant; some contribute meaning. James Baldwin, in his essay "Stranger in the Village," argues that the American racial experience has permanently altered black and white relationships throughout the world. His concluding sentence is, "This world is white no longer, and it will never be white again." As the sentence opens, the repetition of sounds in "*w*orld is *w*hite," binds the two words together, but the idea that they are permanently bound is swiftly denied by the more emphatic repetition of sounds in "*no,*" "*never,*" "*again,*" as the sentence closes. Or take another example: America, Love It or Leave It. If it read America, Love It or Emigrate, would the bumper sticker still imply, as clearly and menacingly, that there are only two choices, and for the patriot only one?

Transitions

Repetition holds a paragraph together by providing continuity and clarity. Transitions such as *next, on the other hand,* and *therefore* also provide continuity and clarity. Because we discuss transitions at length on pages 95–97, in our chapter on paragraphs, we here only remind you to make certain that the relation between one sentence and the next, and one paragraph and the next, is clear. Often it will be clear without an explicit transition:

"She was desperately unhappy. She quit school." But do not take too much for granted; relationships between sentences may not be as clear to your readers as they are to you. You know what you are talking about; they don't. After reading the passage readers may see, in retrospect, that you have just given an example, or a piece of contrary evidence, or an amplification, but readers like to know in advance where they are going; brief transitions such as *for example, but, finally* (readers are keenly interested in knowing when they are getting near the end) are enormously helpful.

CLARITY AND SENTENCE STRUCTURE: PARALLELISM

Make the structure of your sentence reflect the structure of your thought. This is not as formidable as it sounds. If you keep your reader in mind, remembering that you are explaining something to someone who understands it less well than you, you will almost automatically not only say what you think but show how you think.

Almost automatically. In revising, read your work as if you were not the writer of it, but your intended reader. If you reach a bump or snag, where the shape of your thought, or the direction of it, isn't clear, revise your sentence structure. Three general rules help:

1. Put main ideas in main (independent) clauses.
2. Subordinate the less important elements in the sentence to the more important.
3. Put parallel ideas and details in parallel constructions.

The time to consult these rules consciously is not while you write, but while you revise. (The first two rules are amplified in the next chapter, "Revising for Emphasis." Clarity and emphasis are closely related, as the following discussion of parallel construction makes evident.)

Consider the following sentence and the revision:

Awkward
He liked eating and to sleep.

Parallel

He liked to eat and to sleep.

In the first version, "eating" and "to sleep" are not grammatically parallel; the difference in grammatical form blurs the writer's point that there is a similarity. Use parallel constructions to clarify relationships — for instance to emphasize similarities or to define differences.

> I divorce myself from my feelings and immerse myself in my obligations.
>
> — From a student journal

> She drew a line between respect, which we were expected to show, and fear, which we were not.
>
> — Ernesto Galarza

> I will not accept if nominated and will not serve if elected.
>
> — William Tecumseh Sherman

> Fascist art glorifies surrender; it exalts mindlessness; it glamorizes death.
>
> — Susan Sontag

In the following examples, the parallel construction is printed in italic type.

1. *Awkward*

The dormitory rules needed revision, a smoking area was a necessity, and a generally more active role for the school in social affairs were all significant to her.

Parallel

She recommended that the school *revise* its dormitory rules, *provide* a smoking area, and *organize* more social activities.

2. *Awkward*

Most Chinese parents disapprove of interracial dating or they just do not permit it.

Parallel

Most Chinese parents *disapprove* of interracial dating, and many *forbid* it.

Revise the following sentence:

The rogallo glider is recommended for beginners because it is easy to assemble, to maintain, and it is portable.

In parallel constructions, be sure to check the consistency of articles, prepositions, and conjunctions. For example, "He wrote papers on a play by Shakespeare, a novel by Dickens, and a story by Oates," *not* "He wrote papers on a play by Shakespeare, a novel of Dickens, and a story by Oates." The shift from "by" to "of" and back to "by" serves no purpose and is merely distracting.

Let's study this matter a little more, using a short poem as our text.

Love Poem
Robert Bly

When we are in love, we love the grass,
And the barns, and the lightpoles,
And the small mainstreets abandoned all night.

Suppose we change "Love Poem" by omitting a conjunction or an article here and there:

When we are in love, we love the grass,
Barns, and lightpoles,
And the small mainstreets abandoned all night.

We've changed the rhythm, of course, but we still get the point: the lover loves all the world. In the original poem, however, the syntax of the sentence, the consistent repetition of "and the . . ." "and the . . ." makes us feel, without our thinking about it, that when we are in love we love the world, everything in it, equally. The list could extend infinitely, and everything in it would give us identical pleasure. In our altered version, we sacrifice this unspoken assurance. We bump a little, and stumble. As readers, without consciously being aware of it, we wonder if there's some distinction being made, some qualification we've missed. We still get the point of the poem, but we don't feel it the same way.

To sum up:

A pupil once asked Arthur Schnabel [the noted pianist] whether

it was better to play in time or to play as one feels; his characteristic
mordant reply was another question: "Why not feel in time?"

— David Hamilton

EXERCISES

1. Identify the specific faults that make the following sentences
   unclear, then revise each sentence for clarity. (Note that you
   will often have to invent what the writer thought he or she had
   said.)

   a. Actually, she was aging, and quite average in other respects.
   b. If technology cannot sort out its plusses and minuses, and work to
      improve them, man must.
   c. Brooks stresses the farm workers' strenuous way of life and the fact
      that they have the bare necessities of life.
   d. Instead of movable furniture, built-in ledges extend into the center
      of the room to be used as tables or to sit on.
   e. The issue has been saved for my final argument because it is
      controversial.
   f. I am neither indifferent nor fond of children.
   g. When the students heard that their proposal was rejected a meet-
      ing was called.
   h. A viable library is the cornerstone of any college campus.
   i. Her main fault was that she was somewhat lacking in decision-
      making capabilities.
   j. After industrialization a swarm of immigrants came bantering to
      our shores.
   k. Each group felt there was very personal rapport and thus very
      candid feedback resulted.
   l. He can tolerate crowding and pollution and seems disinterested or
      ignorant of these dangers.
   m. The wooden door occupies the majority of the stone wall.
   n. In *A History of the English Church and People* Bede uses examples
      from the past to enforce his own position.
   o. One must strive hard to reach their goal.
   p. Yale students frequently write to Ann Landers telling her fictional
      stories of their so-called troubles as a childish prank.
   q. At my grandmother's house vegetables were only served because
      meat was forbidden.
   r. My firm stand seemed to melt a little.
   s. The conclusion leaves the conflict neatly tied in smooth knots.
   t. The paragraph reeks of blandness.

2. The following sentences, published in *AIDE,* a magazine put out by an insurance company, were written to the company by various policyholders. The trouble is that the writers mean one thing but their sentences say another. Make each sentence clearly say what the writer means.

    a. The other car collided with mine without giving warning of its intentions.
    b. I collided with a stationary truck coming the other way.
    c. The guy was all over the road; I had to swerve a number of times before I hit him.
    d. I pulled away from the side of the road, glanced at my mother-in-law, and headed over the embankment.
    e. In my attempt to kill a fly, I drove into a telephone pole.
    f. I had been driving for forty years when I fell asleep at the wheel and had the accident.
    g. To avoid hitting the bumper of the car in front, I struck the pedestrian.
    h. The pedestrian had no idea which direction to run, so I ran over him.
    i. The indirect cause of this accident was a little guy in a small car with a big mouth.

14
Revising for Emphasis

In revising for conciseness and clarity we begin to discover what we may have been largely unaware of in the early stages of writing: what in our topic most concerns us and precisely why it interests us. That moment of discovery (or those several discrete moments) yields more pleasure than any other in writing. From there on we work, sometimes as if inspired, to make our special angle of vision seem as inevitable to our readers as it is to us. Now as we tighten sentences or expand them, as we shift the position of a word or a paragraph, or as we subordinate a less important idea to a more important one, we are assigning relative value and weight to each of our statements. The expression of value and weight is what is meant by emphasis.

Inexperienced writers may *try* to achieve emphasis as Queen Victoria did, by a style consisting *almost entirely* of italics and exclamation marks!!! Or they may spice their prose with clichés ("little did I realize," "believe it or not") or with a liberal sprinkling of intensifiers ("really beautiful," "definitely significant," and so on). But experienced writers abandon these unconvincing devices. Emphasis is more securely achieved by exploiting the possibilities of position, of brevity and length, of repetition, and of subordination.

EMPHASIS BY POSITION

First, let's see how a word or phrase may be emphasized. If it appears in an unusual position it gains emphasis, as in "This course he liked." Because in English the object of the verb usually comes after the verb (as in "He liked this course"), the object is emphasized if it appears first. But this device is tricky; words in an unusual position often seem ludicrous, the writer fatuous: "A mounted Indian toward the forest raced."

Let's now consider a less strained sort of emphasis by position. The beginning and the end of a sentence or a paragraph are emphatic positions; of these two positions, the end is usually the more emphatic. What comes last is what stays most in the mind. Compare these two sentences:

> The essay is brief but informative.
> The essay is informative but brief.

The first sentence leaves the reader with the impression that the essay, despite its brevity, is worth looking at. The second, however, ends more negatively, leaving the reader with the impression that the essay is so brief that its value is fairly slight. Because the emphasis in each sentence is different, the two sentences say different things.

It usually makes sense, then, to put the important point near the end, lest the sentence become anticlimactic. Here is a sentence that properly moves to an emphatic end:

> Although I could not read its six hundred pages in one sitting, I never willingly put it down.

If the halves are reversed the sentence trails off:

> I never willingly put it down, although I could not read its six hundred pages in one sitting.

This second version straggles away from the real point — that the book was interesting.

Anticlimactic

Besides not owning themselves women also could not own property.

Emphatic

Women could not own property; in fact, they did not own themselves.

The commonest anticlimaxes are caused by weak qualifiers (*in my opinion, it seems to me, in general, etc.*) tacked on to interesting statements. Weak qualifiers usually can be omitted. Even useful ones rarely deserve an emphatic position.

Anticlimactic

Poodles are smart but they are no smarter than pigs, I have read.

Emphatic

Poodles are smart, but I have read that they are no smarter than pigs.

The rule: try to bury dull but necessary qualifiers in the middle of the sentence.

EMPHASIS BY BREVITY AND LENGTH: SHORT AND LONG SENTENCES

How long should a sentence be? One recalls Lincoln's remark to a heckler who asked him how long a man's legs should be: "Long enough to reach the ground." No rules about length can be given, but be careful not to bore your reader with a succession of short sentences (say, under ten words) and be careful not to tax your reader with a monstrously long sentence. Victor Hugo's sentence in *Les Misérables* containing 823 words punctuated by ninety-three commas, fifty-one semicolons, and four dashes, is not a good model for beginners.

Consider this succession of short sentences:

The purpose of the refrain is twofold. First, it divides the song into stanzas. Second, it reinforces the theme of the song.

These sentences are clear, but since the points are simple the reader feels he is addressed as though he were a kindergarten child. There is too much emphasis (too many heavy pauses) on too little. The reader can take all three sentences at once:

The purpose of the refrain is twofold: it divides the song into stanzas and it reinforces the theme.

The three simple sentences have been turned into one compound sentence, allowing the reader to keep going for a while.

Now compare another group of sentences with a revision.

> Hockey is by far the fastest moving team sport in America. The skaters are constantly on the go. They move at high speeds. The action rarely stops.

These four sentences, instead of suggesting motion, needlessly stop us. Here is a revision:

> Hockey is by far the fastest moving team sport in America. The skaters, constantly on the go, move at high speeds, and the action rarely stops.

By combining the second, third, and fourth sentences, the reader, like the players, is kept on the go.

Next, a longer example that would be thoroughly delightful if parts of it were less choppy.

Conceit

At my high school graduation we had two speakers. One was a member of our class, and the other was a faculty member. The student speaker's name was Alva Reed. The faculty speaker's name was Mr. Williams. The following conversation took place after the graduation ceremony. Parents, relatives, faculty, and friends were all outside the gymnasium congratulating the class of 1979. Alva was surrounded by her friends, her parents, and some faculty members who were congratulating her on her speech. Not standing far from her was Mr. Williams with somewhat the same crowd.

"Alva dear, you were wonderful!"

"Thanks Mom. I sure was scared though; I'm glad it's over."

At that moment, walking towards Alva were her grandparents. They both were wearing big smiles on their faces. Her grandfather said rather loudly, "That was a good speech dear. Nicely done, nicely done." Walking past them at that moment was Mr. Williams. He stuck his head into their circle and replied, "Thank you," and walked away.

The first four sentences seem to be written in spurts. They can easily be combined and improved thus:

> At my high school graduation we had two speakers. One was a member of our class, Alva Reed, and the other was a faculty member, Mr. Williams.

If we think that even this version, two sentences instead of four, is a little choppy, we can rewrite it into a single sentence:

> At my high school graduation we had two speakers, Alva Reed, a member of our class, and Mr. Williams, a faculty member.

Or:

> The two speakers at my high school graduation were Alva Reed, a member of our class, and Mr. Williams, a faculty member.

The rest of the piece is less choppy, but reread it and see if you don't discover some other sentences that should be combined. Revise them.

Sometimes, however, the choppiness of a succession of short sentences is effective. Look at this description of the methods by which George Jackson, in prison, resisted efforts to destroy his spirit:

> He trains himself to sleep only three hours a night. He studies Swahili, Chinese, Arabic and Spanish. He does pushups to control his sexual urge and to train his body. Sometimes he does a thousand a day. He eats only one meal a day. And, always, he is reading and thinking.
>
> — Julius Lester

That the author is capable of writing longer, more complicated sentences is evident in the next paragraph:

> Yet, when his contact with the outside world is extended beyond his family to include Angela Davis, Joan, a woman who works with the Soledad defense committee, and his attorney, he is able to find within himself feelings of love and tenderness.

Can we account for the success of the passage describing Jackson's prison routine? First, the short sentences, with their repeated commonplace form (subject, verb, object) in some degree imitate Jackson's experience: they are almost monotonously disciplined, almost as regular as the pushups the confined Jackson does. Later, when Jackson makes contact with Angela Davis and others, the long sentence helps to suggest the expansion of his world. Second, the brevity of the sentences suggests their enormous importance, certainly to Jackson and to Julius Lester and, Lester hopes, to the reader.

Keep in mind this principle: *any one sentence in your essay is roughly equal to any other sentence.* If a sentence is short, it must be relatively weighty. A lot is packed into a little. Less is more. (The chief exceptions are transitional sentences such as, "Now for the second point.") Consider the following passage:

> It happened that in September of 1933 Lord Rutherford, at the British Association meeting, made some remark about atomic energy never becoming real. Leo Szilard was the kind of scientist, perhaps just the kind of good-humored, cranky man, who disliked any statement that contained the word "never," particularly when made by a distinguished colleague. So he set his mind to think about the problem.
>
> — Jacob Bronowski

The first two sentences are relatively long (twenty-three words and thirty-one words); the third is relatively short (ten words), and its brevity — its weight or density — emphasizes Szilard's no-nonsense attitude.

EMPHASIS BY REPETITION

Don't be afraid to repeat a word if it is important. The repetition will add emphasis. Notice in these lucid sentences by Helen Gardner the effective repetition of "end" and "beginning."

> *Othello* has this in common with the tragedy of fortune, that the end in no way blots out from the imagination the glory of the beginning. But the end here does not merely by its darkness throw up into relief the brightness that was. On the contrary, beginning and end chime against each other. In both the value of life and love is affirmed.

The substitution of "conclusion" or "last scene" for the second "end" would be worse than pointless; it would destroy Miss Gardner's point that there is *identity* or correspondence between beginning and end.

EMPHASIS BY SUBORDINATION

Five Kinds of Sentences

Before we can discuss the use of subordination for emphasis, we must first talk about what a sentence is, and about five kinds of sentences.

If there is an adequate definition of a sentence, we haven't found it. Perhaps the best definition is not the old one, "a complete thought," but "a word or group of words that the reader takes to be complete." This definition includes such utterances as "Who?" and "Help!" and "Never!" and "Maybe." Now, in speaking, "While he was walking down the street" may be taken as a complete thought, if it answers the question "When did the car hit him?" In writing, however, it would be a sentence fragment that probably should be altered to, say, "While he was walking down the street he was hit by a car." We will discuss intentional fragments on pages 383–84 and ways to correct unintentional fragments on pages 565–66. But first we should take a closer look at complete sentences.

Usually a sentence names someone or something (this is the subject) and it tells us something about the subject (this is the predicate); that is, it "predicates" something about the subject. Let us look at five kinds of sentences: simple, compound, complex, compound-complex, and sentence fragments.

1. A *simple sentence* has one predicate, here italicized:

Shakespeare *died*.
Shakespeare and Jonson *were contemporaries*.

The subject can be elaborated ("Shakespeare and Jonson, England's chief Renaissance dramatists, were contemporaries"), or the predicate can be elaborated ("Shakespeare and Jonson were contemporaries in the Renaissance England of Queen Elizabeth"); but the sentence remains technically a simple sentence, consisting of only one main (independent) clause with no dependent (subordinate) clause.

2. A *compound sentence* has two or more main clauses, each containing a subject and a predicate. It is, then, two or more simple sentences connected by a coordinating conjunction (*and, but, for,*

nor, or, yet) or by *not only . . . but also,* or by a semicolon or colon or, rarely, by a comma.

> Shakespeare died in 1616, and Jonson died in 1637.
> Shakespeare not only wrote plays, but he also acted in them.
> Shakespeare died in 1616; Jonson died twenty-one years later.

3. A *complex sentence* has one main (independent) clause and one or more subordinate (dependent) clauses. Here the main clause is italicized.

> Although Shakespeare died, *England survived.*
>
> *Jonson did not write a commemorative poem* when Shakespeare died.

The parts not italicized are subordinate or dependent because they cannot stand as sentences by themselves.

4. A *compound-complex sentence* has two or more main clauses (here italicized) and one or more subordinate clauses.

> *In 1616 Shakespeare died* and *his wife inherited the second-best bed* because he willed it to her.

Each of the two italicized passages could stand by itself as a sentence, but "because he willed it to her" could not (except as the answer to a question). Each italicized passage, then, is a main (independent) clause, and "because he willed it to her" is a subordinate (dependent) clause.

We will return to subordination, but let us first look at the fifth kind of sentence, the sentence fragment.

5. A *sentence fragment* does not fit the usual definition of a sentence, but when the fragment is intended the thought is often clear and complete enough. Intentional fragments are common in advertisements:

> Made of imported walnut. For your pleasure. At finer stores.
>
> More native than the Limbo. More exciting than the beat of a steel drum. Tia Maria. Jamaica's haunting liqueur.

And yet another example, this one not from an advertisement but from an essay on firewood:

> Piles of it. Right off the sidewalk. Split from small logs of oak or ash or maple. Split. Split again.
>   — John McPhee

All these examples strike us as pretentious in their obviously studied efforts at understatement. Words are hoarded, as though there is much in little, and as though to talk more fully would demean the speaker and would desecrate the subject. A few words, and then a profound silence. Here less is not more; it is too much. The trouble with these fragmentary sentences is not that they don't convey complete thoughts but that they attract too much attention to themselves; they turn our minds too emphatically to their writers, and conjure up images of unpleasantly self-satisfied oracles.

Here, however, is a passage from a student's essay, where the fragmentary sentences seem satisfactory to us. The passage begins with a simple sentence, and then gives three fragmentary sentences.

> The film has been playing to sellout audiences. Even though the acting is inept. Even though the sound is poorly synchronized. Even though the plot is incoherent.

If this passage is successful, it is because the emphasis is controlled. The author is dissatisfied, and by means of parallel fragments (each beginning with the same words) she conveys a moderately engaging weariness and a gentle exasperation.

Then, too, we see that if the first three periods were changed to commas we would have an orthodox complex sentence. In short, because the fragments are effective we find them acceptable.

For ways to correct ineffective or unacceptable fragments, see pages 565–66.

Subordination

Having surveyed the kinds of sentences, we can at last talk about using subordination to give appropriate emphasis.

Make sure that the less important element is subordinate to the more important. In the following example the first clause, summarizing the writer's previous sentences, is a subordinate or dependent clause; the new material is made emphatic by being put into two independent clauses, italicized here:

> As soon as the Irish Literary Theatre was assured of a nationalist backing, *it started to dissociate itself from any political aim,* and *the long struggle with the public began.*

The second and third clauses in this sentence, linked by "and," are coordinate — that is, of equal importance.

Probably most of the sentences that you read and write are complex sentences: an independent clause and one or more subordinate clauses. Whatever is outside of the independent clause is subordinate, less important. Consider this sentence:

> Aided by Miss Horniman's money, Yeats dreamed of a poetic drama.

The writer puts Yeats's dream in the independent clause, subordinating the relatively unimportant Miss Horniman. Miss Horniman and her money are of some importance, of course, or they would not have been mentioned, but they are *less* important than Yeats's dream. (Notice, by the way, that emphasis by subordination often works along with emphasis by position. Here the independent clause comes *after* the subordinate clause; the writer appropriately put the more important material in the more emphatic position.) Had the writer wished to give Miss Horniman more prominence, the passage might have run:

> Yeats dreamed of a poetic drama, and Miss Horniman subsidized that dream.

Here Miss Horniman at least stands in an independent clause, linked to the previous independent clause by "and." The two clauses, and the two people, are now of approximately equal importance. If the writer had wanted to emphasize Miss Horniman and to deemphasize Yeats, she might have written:

> While Yeats dreamed of a poetic drama, Miss Horniman provided the money.

Here Yeats is reduced to the subordinate clause, and Miss Horniman is given the dignity of the only independent clause. (And again notice that the important point is also in the emphatic position, near the end of the sentence. A sentence is likely to sprawl if an independent clause comes first, followed by a long subordinate clause of lesser importance, such as the sentence you are now reading. See the discussion of emphasis by position on pages 377–81.)

In short, though simple sentences and compound sentences have their place, they make everything of equal importance. Since everything is not of equal importance, you must often write complex and compound-complex sentences, subordinating some things to other things. Look again at the first four sentences of "Conceit" (page 379), and at the suggested revisions.

Having made the point that subordination reduces monotony and conveys appropriate emphasis, we must again say that there are times when a succession of simple or compound sentences is effective, as in the passage on page 380 describing George Jackson. As a rough rule, however, don't write more than two consecutive simple sentences unless you know what you are doing.

EXERCISES

1. Here is one way to test your grasp of the relationship of independent and subordinate elements in a sentence. This *haiku* (a Japanese poetic form) consists of one sentence which can be written as prose: "After weeks of watching the roof leak, I fixed it tonight by moving a single board."

   Hitch Haiku
   Gary Snyder

   After weeks of watching the roof leak
   　I fixed it tonight
   by moving a single board.

   ---

   a. Identify the independent clause and the subordinate elements in the poem.
   b. The "I" in the poem's sentence does or has done three things. Write three simple sentences, each expressing one of the actions.
   c. Write one sentence in which all three of the poem's actions are expressed, but put in the independent clause one of the two actions that appear in a subordinate element in the poem.
   d. Compare your sentence with the poem's. Both sentences should be clear. How do they vary in emphasis?

e. Optional: Compare the original sentence written as poetry and written as prose.

2. First identify the fault or faults that make the following sentences unemphatic, and then revise them for emphasis.

a. He lists some of the rights given to humans and things and both admits and accounts for the oddity of his proposal well by citing examples.

b. Rights for women, blacks and the insane were granted though many couldn't see the value in it and so now our environment should be granted rights even though it takes some getting used to the idea.

c. Thus Creon's pride forces Antigone's death which drives his son to suicide and then his wife.

d. Stock breeding will give the same result as population evolution, defenders of positive eugenics claim.

e. The family today lacks the close relationship it had before the industrial age, for example.

f. The woman's face is distraught, her hair is unkempt, and her dress is rumpled.

g. There is probably no human being who would enjoy being eaten by a shark.

PART THREE
Acquiring Style and Fluency

Two monks were arguing about a flag. One said: "The flag is moving."

The other said: "The wind is moving."

The sixth patriarch happened to be passing by. He told them: "Not the wind, not the flag: mind is moving."

— ZEN ANECDOTE

15
Defining Style

STYLE

The style is the man.
— BUFFON
(or the woman)
— BARNET AND STUBBS

Style is not simply a flower here and some gilding there; it pervades the whole work. Van Gogh's style, or Walt Disney's, let us say, consists in part of features recurring throughout a single work and from one work to the next: angular or curved lines, hard or soft edges, strong or gentle contrasts, and so on. Pictures of a seated woman by each of the two artists are utterly different, and if we have seen a few works by each, we can readily identify who did which one. Artists leave their fingerprints, so to speak, all over their work; writers leave their voiceprints.

The word *style* comes from the Latin *stilus,* a Roman writing instrument. Even in Roman times *stilus* had acquired a figurative sense, referring not only to the instrument but also to the writer's choice of words and arrangement of words into sentences. But is it simply the choice and arrangement of words we comment on when we speak of a writer's style, or are we also commenting on the writer himself? Don't we feel that a piece of writing, whether it's on Civil War photographs or on genetics and intelligence, is also about the writer? His writing, after all, sets forth his views of his topic, his perceptions and responses to something he has thought about, his evidence and his conclusions; he has, from the start, from his choice of a topic, revealed that he found it worth thinking about. His essay, in attempting to persuade us to think as he does, reveals not only how and what he thinks, but what he values.

When we write about things "out there," our writing always reveals the form and likeness of our minds, just as every work of art reveals the creator as well as the ostensible subject. A portrait painting, for example, is not only about the sitter; it is about the artist's perceptions of the sitter, hence the saying that every portrait is a self-portrait. Even photographs are as much about the photographer as they are about the subject. Richard Avedon said of his portraits of famous people, "They are all pictures of me, of the way I feel about the people I photograph." A student's essay similarly, if it is truly written, is not exclusively about "*La Causa* and the New Chicana"; it is also about June Ojeda's perceptions and responses to both racism and sexism.

STYLE AND TONE

The style is the man. Rather say the
style is the way the man takes himself.
— ROBERT FROST

Suppose we take a page of handwriting, or even a signature. We need not believe that graphology is an exact science to believe that the shape of the ink-lines on paper (apart from the meaning of the words) often tells us something about the writer. We look at a large, ornate signature, and we sense that the writer is confident; we look at a tiny signature written with the finest of pens, and we wonder why anyone is so self-effacing.

More surely than handwriting, the writer's style reveals, among other things, his attitude toward himself (as Frost's addition to Buffon's epigram suggests), toward his reader, and toward his subject. The writer's attitudes are reflected in what is usually called *tone*. It is difficult to distinguish between style and tone, but we can try. Most discussions of style concentrate on what might be thought of as ornament: figurative language ("a sea of troubles"), inversion ("A leader he is not"), repetition and parallelism ("government of the people, by the people, for the people"), balance and antithesis ("It was the best of times, it was the worst of times"). Indeed, for centuries style has been called "the dress of thought," implying that the thought is something separate from the expression; the thought, in this view, is dressed up in stylistic devices. But in most of the writing that we read with interest and pleasure the stylistic devices are not ornamental and occasional but integral and pervasive. When we talk about wit, sincerity, tentativeness, self-assurance, aggressiveness, objectivity, and so forth, we can say we are talking about style, but we should recognize that style now is not a matter of ornamental devices that dress up some idea, but part of the idea itself. And "the idea itself" includes the writer's unified yet appropriately varied tone of voice. To take a brief example: the famous English translation of Caesar's report of a victory, "I came, I saw, I conquered," might be paraphrased thus: "After getting to the scene of the battle I studied the situation. Then I devised a strategy that won the battle." But this paraphrase loses much of Caesar's message; the brevity and the parallelism of the famous version, as well as the alliteration (*c*ame, *c*onquered) convey tight-lipped self-assurance — convey, that is, the tone that reveals Caesar to us. And this tone is a large part of Caesar's message. Caesar is really telling us not only about what he did, but about what sort of person he is. (The Latin original is even more tight-lipped and more alliterative: *veni, vidi, vici.*)

Here is a short paragraph from John Szarkowski's *Looking at Photographs.* Szarkowski is writing about one of Alexander Gardner's photographs of a dead Confederate sharpshooter.

> Among the pictures that Gardner made himself is the one reproduced here. Like many Civil War photographs, it showed that the dead of both sides looked very much the same. The pictures of earlier wars had not made this clear.

Try, in a word or two, to characterize the tone (the attitude, as we sense it in the inflection of the voice) of the first sentence. Next, the tone of the second, and then of the third. Suppose the second and third sentences had been written thus:

> It showed that the dead of both sides looked very much the same. This is made clear in Civil War photographs, but not in pictures of earlier wars.

How has the tone changed? What word can you find to characterize the tone of the whole, as Szarkowski wrote it?

Now another passage from Szarkowski's book:

> Jacob A. Riis was a newspaper reporter by occupation and a social reformer by inclination. He was a photographer rather briefly and apparently rather casually; it seems beyond doubt that he considered photography a useful but subservient tool for his work as reporter and reformer. It is clear that he had no interest in "artistic" photography, and equally clear that the artistic photographers of his time had no interest in him.

Do you find traces of Szarkowski's voiceprint here?

Finally, a longer passage by the same writer. After you read it, try to verbalize the resemblances between this and the other passages — the qualities that allow us to speak of the writer's tone.

> There are several possible explanations for the fact that women have been more important to photography than their numbers alone would warrant. One explanation might be the fact that photography has never had licensing laws or trade unions, by means of which women might have been effectively discriminated against. A second reason might be the fact that the specialized technical preparation for photography need not be enormously demanding, so that the medium has been open to those unable to spend long years in formal study.
>
> A third possible reason could be that women have a greater natural talent for photography than men do. Discretion (or cowardice) suggests that this hypothesis is best not pursued, since a freely speculative exploration of it might take unpredictable and indefensible lines. One might for example consider the idea that the art of photography is in its nature receptive, or passive, thus suggesting that women are also.

STYLE AND LEVELS OF USAGE

Although the dividing lines between levels of usage cannot always be drawn easily, tradition recognizes three: formal, informal, and popular or vulgar. Sometimes *popular* is used to designate a level between informal and vulgar. (*Vulgar* here doesn't mean dirty words; rather, it refers to the speech characteristic of uneducated people, speech that uses such expressions as *ain't, nohow,* and *he don't.*) In textbooks, the most obvious purpose of discussions of these levels has been to dislodge older, more rigid ideas about "good" and "bad" or "correct" and "incorrect" English, and to replace them with the more flexible and more accurate standard of appropriateness. The labels formal and informal (we can for the moment drop vulgar, since few essays are written in it) attempt to describe the choices a writer makes under particular circumstances, rather than to prescribe those he ought to make under all circumstances. The choices, often unconscious, include those of vocabulary, sentence structure, and tone.

Formal writing, found mostly in scholarly articles, textbooks, ceremonial speeches, and scientific reports, assumes an audience, not only generally well educated but also with special knowledge of or interest in the writer's subject. The writer can therefore use a wide vocabulary (including words and references that in another context would be pretentious or obscure) and sentence patterns that demand close attention. A noted figure, say a respected literary critic, examining an influential book and addressing the world of thoughtful readers, may use a formal style, as Lionel Trilling does here in a criticism of V. L. Parrington's *Main Currents in American Literature.* Trilling assumes an attentive reader, capable of holding in mind a long sentence.

> To throw out Poe because he cannot be conveniently fitted into a theory of American culture, to speak of him as a biological sport and as a mind apart from the main current, to find his gloom to be merely personal and eccentric, "only the atrabilious wretchedness of a dipsomaniac," as Hawthorne's was "no more than the skeptical questioning of life by a nature that knew no fierce storms," to judge Melville's response to American life to be less noble than that of Bryant or of Greeley, to speak of Henry James as an escapist, as an artist similar to Whistler, a man characteristically afraid of stress — this is not merely to be mistaken in aesthetic judgment; rather it is to examine without attention and from the point of view of a limited and essentially arrogant conception of reality the documents which are in some respects the most suggestive testimony to what America was and is, and of course to get no answer from them.
> — Lionel Trilling

Now, although "to throw out" is fairly informal, as opposed to, say, "to dismiss," the sentence as a whole is formal. Notice the structure: "To throw . . . to speak . . . to find . . . to judge . . . to speak," and we still do not have an independent clause. Two-thirds of the way through, with "this is not merely to be mistaken," the previous words come into focus, but the meaning is still incomplete. To do such-and-such "is not merely to be mistaken," but what *is* it to be? At last we are told: "it is to examine without attention . . . and . . . to get no answer. . . ."

A formal sentence need not be long. Here is a fairly short formal sentence by W. H. Auden:

> Owing to its superior power as a mnemonic, verse is superior to prose as a medium for didactic instruction.

In another frame of mind Auden might have written something less formal, along these lines:

> Because it stays more easily in the memory, verse is better than prose for teaching.

This revision of Auden's sentence can be called informal, but it is high on the scale, the language of an educated man writing courteously to an audience he conceives of as his peers. It is the level of almost all serious writing about literature. A low informal version might be:

> Poetry sticks in the mind better than prose; so if you want to teach something, poetry is better.

This is the language any of us might use in conversation; it is almost never the language used in writing to our peers.

Finding the Appropriate Level

What is appropriate in writing, as in dress, is subject to change, and the change recently has been to greater informality in both. Students who attend classes, concerts, and even their own weddings in blue jeans might experiment with similar freedom in writing college essays, and work toward a style that feels comfortable and natural to them. Developing a natural style, writing at an appropriate level, does take work. Consider, for example, the following opening paragraph from a student's theme:

> The college experience is traumatic, often because one must adjust not only to new academic horizons and new friends but also to the new physical environment constituted by the college and by the community surrounding it. One might think that, coming from a

"Robert? Oh, he's out somewhere chasing a buck."

Drawing by Whitney Darrow, Jr.; © 1978 The New Yorker Magazine, Inc.

city only sixty miles from Wellesley, I would be exempt from this aspect of adaptation. However, this assumption has proven to be false.

"Traumatic"? "Academic horizons"? "Constituted"? "Exempt from this aspect of adaptation"? "Assumption . . . proven to be false"? There's nothing wrong with the language here, that is, nothing ungrammatical. But the paragraph has a hollow ring, a tone of insincerity, because the diction and syntax — the writer's level of usage — so ill suit the theme: a personal and spirited defense of the writer's lower-middle-class industrial home town, whose liveliness, friendliness, and above all, informality, she emphatically prefers to the aloofness of suburban Wellesley.

By contrast, in a review of *Soledad Brother — The Prison Letters of George Jackson,* another student described Jackson's style as "clear, simple, expressive, and together." The word "together," though technically incorrect (an adverb, here used as an adjective) strikes us, in context, as exactly right. And, when later in the essay we read "Surviving on glasses of water, crumbs of bread, deep concentration, daily push-ups, and cigarettes, Jackson shouts to the black world to wake up: get off your knees and start kicking asses," we feel that the deliberately inconsistent use of the formal series of parallels with the colloquial or vulgar "kicking asses" exactly expresses both Jackson's discipline and rage, and the writer's empathy with them.

In most of your college writing you are addressing people like yourself; use a language that you would like to read, neither stuffy nor aggressively colloquial. Probably it will stand somewhere in between the levels of "aspects of adaptation" and "kicking asses."

Tone: Four Examples

The first two excerpts are the opening paragraphs of two speeches. The third, though not an opening paragraph, is also from a speech. The fourth, by Pauline Kael, is the beginning of an essay on the tedium of most modern films.

1. It is indeed both an honor and a challenge to be invited to participate in this most significant occasion, the observance of the one hundredth anniversary of the birth of Max Weber. It is

also a great pleasure to revisit the University of Heidelberg, though not quite for the first time, just short of forty years after my enrollment here as a student in 1925. This was too late to know Max Weber in person, but of course his intellectual influence was all-pervasive in the Heidelberg of that time, constituting the one primary point of reference about which all theoretical and much empirical discussion in the social and cultural fields revolved. I was also privileged to know his gracious and highly intelligent widow, Marianne Weber, in particular to attend a number of her famous "sociological teas" on Sunday afternoons. It was an extraordinarily stimulating intellectual environment, participation in which was one of the most important factors in determining my whole intellectual and professional career.

— Talcott Parsons

2. It has been suggested that I discuss what it is like to be a poet these days (the only days in which my opinion could possibly be useful), or, if that is immodest, what it is like to write poetry, what one thinks about the art, what its relation is to the life we supposedly live these days, and so on. This is a fascinatingly large range in which to wander, and I shall be interested to find out what I do think. I hope you will be interested, too. But I must advise you that this will not be a coherently organized essay running in a smooth and logical progression from question to conclusion. Nor will the views expressed necessarily be consistent. I have consulted with my selves, and come up, as usual, with a number of fragmentary notions, many of them aphoristic in expression, and I believe I will do best simply to put these before you without much in the way of explanation or connective tissue.

— Howard Nemerov

3. Style, in its finest sense, is the last acquirement of the educated mind; it is also the most useful. It pervades the whole being. The administrator with a sense for style hates waste; the engineer with a sense for style economizes his material; the artisan with a sense for style prefers good work. Style is the ultimate morality of mind. . . . With style the end is attained without side issues, without raising undesirable inflammations. With style you attain your end and nothing but your end. With style the effect of your activity is calculable, and foresight is the last gift of gods to men. With style your power is increased, for your mind is not distracted with irrelevancies, and you are more likely to attain your object.

— Alfred North Whitehead

4. Early this year, the most successful of the large-circulation magazines for teen-age girls took a two-page spread in the *Times* for an "interview" with its editor-in-chief, and after the now ritual bulling (Question: "You work with young people — what is your view of today's generation?" Answer: "My faith in them is enormous. They make a sincere attempt at being totally honest, at sharing. They're happily frank about their experiences. They're the most idealistic generation in history. . . . When you consider the vast problems confronting us, their optimism and activism is truly inspirational"), and after the obeisance to the new myths ("They are the best-educated and most aware generation in history"), the ad finally got to the come-on. Question: "Is it true that your readers don't differentiate between your ads and your editorials?" Answer: "Yes, that's true. Our readers are very impressionable, not yet cynical about advertising . . . eager to learn . . . to believe." The frightening thing is, it probably is true that the teen-agers don't differentiate between the ads and the editorials, and true in a much more complex sense than the delicately calculated Madison Avenue-ese of the editor's pitch to advertisers indicates. Television is blurring the distinction for all of us; we don't know what we're reacting to anymore, and, beyond that, it's becoming just about impossible to sort out the con from the truth because a successful con makes its lies come true.

— Pauline Kael

EXERCISES

1. What is Parsons's attitude toward himself? Exactly how do you know?
2. What is Nemerov's attitude toward himself, and how do you know?
3. Suppose that the first sentence of Whitehead's passage began thus: "I want to point out to you today that style may be regarded not only as the last acquirement of what I consider the mind that has been well educated, but it is also the most useful, I definitely believe." What is lost?
4. Do you think that Pauline Kael knows what she is talking about? Why?

A RANGE OF STYLES

The Boiler Room and the Computer

Tom Wolfe

Such heaving!
Such groaning!
Such peeling squealing
Biting sticking
Ramming jamming
Gobble licking
Nuzzling guzzling
Coconut ilia
Rut-boar grunting
Skotophilia
Lapping gashing
Crinkly chasms
Prescribed therapeutic spasms —
— and if there is any justice up in heaven, Dr. Freud has been assigned a corner apartment with one of those little concrete balconies or "terraces," of the Collins Avenue condominium-tower variety, rigged out with a telescope and an infrared X-ray attachment that enables him to look down through every roof and every ceiling in the United States . . . day or night, into overstore massage parlors on lower State Street as easily as the flimsiest cinder-block motel room, even into the utter darkness of the Lido East movie theater . . . so that he may enjoy every last jerk, shudder, and gush that his remarkable brain — clinically dead since 1939 — continues to trigger in our time . . . I doubt that there is another man in history whose ideas, unaided by any political apparatus, have directly influenced the behavior of so many people in the generations immediately following his death. Darwin and Marx are in the running perhaps; perhaps Zoroaster, if what little has been recorded of his history is to be believed; possibly Rousseau, although it is difficult to say that his influence was direct. No, on second thought the good doctor stands alone . . . on his condominium terrace, I like to think . . . clapping his hands together like a child with mittens, as he so often did when he was praised during his lifetime.

Now, the complex and subtle parts of Freud's theory, featuring elaborate literary conceits and marvelous leaps of analogy, have scarcely made a dent on posterity. What has sunk in so deeply has been a single, simple notion of his concerning sexuality. This notion bears none of the elegant nomenclature which he loved so much, nothing on the order of *the Oedipus complex* (he adored italics), *libido,* or *Ego&Id&Superego.* In fact, he gave it no name at all, since it grew out of a mere habit of thought whose importance he never recognized.

During Freud's university years (the late 1870's and early 1880's) young enthusiasts in the fuzzier disciplines, such as psychology, liked to borrow terminology from the more rigorous and established field of mechanical physics. The borrowed terms became, in fact, metaphor; and metaphor, like a shrewd servant, has a way of ruling its master. Thus Freud wound up with the idea that libido or sexual "energy," as he called it, is a pressure that builds up within a closed system to the point where it demands release, as in a steam engine. "It seems that an accumulation of narcissistic libido over and above a certain level becomes intolerable," he would say. "It depends on the *amount* of undischarged libido that a person can hold freely suspended . . ." "The next disturbance of the shifting forces will cause symptoms to develop, unless he can yet find other outlets for his pent-up libido . . ." In short, a head of steam. When it builds up high enough, the foreman (the ego) either opens up some workable valve and lets it out — or it's hamburger heaven for one and all in the boiler room! (in the form of obsessional neurosis, hysteria, or much worse).

Such, in brief, is the history of the piece of conventional wisdom that today animates what is known as the "sexual revolution": namely, the belief that regular release of the steam, in the form of guilt-free orgasm, is essential to a healthy psyche and a healthy society.

Over the past four years women's-liberation theorists have criticized Freud as a man who put forth ideas as if they applied equally to men and women but who actually thought like a man. And they are quite correct. Yet in the same breath they (along with sexologists such as the Drs. Reuben, Comfort, and Brothers, the spouses O'Neill, and Madame Hollander & Co.) proceed to press Freud's Boiler Room Axiom on their sisters. Stand up like a man! Go forth! Get it on! Take the sexual initiative! Be free! Let the steam out! Get well soon!

Meanwhile, on other fronts it is much the same. The pornographers argue (with many intellectuals in accord) that their product is society's "safety valve"; the potential rapist or other twisted sex geek discharges his steam manually in the gloaming of the peep-show booth or at home with the aid of a stroke magazine (the cathartic theory) . . . Or, on a more sophisticated level, that the stroke magazine or "erotic art" — to use the term they prefer — creates a liberating atmosphere in which the individual is encouraged to clean out his (and, presumably, her) valves and pipes without the hazards of guilt and repression (the therapeutic theory). Likewise, the massage parlor, as one learns regularly in magazine and television interviews, "helps save marriages, because a man can come here and get what he needs when he can't get it at home. Anyway, it beats masturbation." Swinging, or group sex, becomes the answer to the problem of "different and ever-changing sexual urges. To think that the traditional marriage partnership can take care of them is unrealistic. Isn't it healthier for couples to join groups where variety is the norm and you can shed your inhibitions and let your sexual energy flow freely?"

Lovely . . . Freud's Boiler Room Axiom — on all fronts! You can't make the pressure go away, friends — so make the most of it! Tune up the machine! Oil the works! Go with the flow!

In the midst of all the solemn and dedicated groin spasms that have ensued . . . arrives one as yet tiny but disturbing note. It is this: over the past twenty years, thanks to the refinement of techniques such as the stereotaxic needle implant, neurophysiologists have begun to study the actual workings of the brain and central nervous system. These investigators find no buildups of "pressure" or "energy," sexual or otherwise, for the simple reason that the central nervous system is not analogous to an engine. They regard it as more like an electronic circuit, such as a computer or a telephone system. Millions of neurons fire continually, and the electrical energy within the system remains constant. Behavior is determined, instead, by which lines are open and what messages get through. According to this model, what is the effect of pornography — or group sex — or "massages" — or orgasmic regularity? Far from being a safety valve releasing energy that has built up inside the system, any such pastime is more like an input that starts turning on the YES gates . . . to the point where its message (*Sex!*) closes out all others and takes over the entire circuit . . .

In one way, of course, the neurophysiologists are doing exactly what Freud did a century ago: they are adopting the most fashionable machine metaphor of their own day — namely, computer terminology. And perhaps they, as well, stand to delude themselves. But they also have one advantage. Freud began and ended with a hypothesis; with the techniques available in his time he could go no further. The neurophysiologists are at least able to proceed down the chain of hypothesis, deduction, observation, and verification. And so far they have found nothing to indicate that the entire body of psychoanalysis has any more to offer on the subject of sexuality than the Lights Out league manual for boys concerning what to do with your hands when the Cosmic Itch gets aggravated (Answer: Sit on them).

Freud's biographers tell us that his preoccupation with sex began in earnest when he psychoanalyzed himself and discovered that throughout his boyhood he had lusted for his mother. *Sex!* How irresistible it is to speculate that if the lad had but run around the block a few times in a spirited fashion whenever the evil impulse seized him and taken cold showers regularly, each afternoon, for a few weeks, as it suggests in the manual, the tenor of life today in the United States, and throughout the West, might be radically different. Cooler and less humid, in any event; so much less heaving groaning peeling squealing biting sticking ramming jamming gobble licking nuzzling guzzling und so weiter, mein Freunde.[1]

QUESTIONS

1. Characterize Wolfe's style. What do you like about it? What do you dislike about it?
2. On page 402, in the paragraph beginning "During Freud's university years," Wolfe attempts to summarize and to clarify Freud's remarks on the function of the ego. Write a paragraph in which you summarize the point, using a style that you would expect to find in a psychology textbook. (You may want to do a little research, in an encyclopedia or at least a dictionary. See pages 546–49 on acknowledging sources.)
3. What is Wolfe's attitude toward Freud? How do you know? To what extent does Wolfe's style convey his attitude?
4. Take a proverbial expression or idea, for example "A rolling stone gathers no moss," and pretend that it is an axiom derived from the writings of an important thinker. Then write, in a parody of Wolfe's style, an exposition and a criticism of the idea.

---

[1] Editors' note: German for "and so forth, my friend."

Professions for Women
Virginia Woolf[2]

When your secretary invited me to come here, she told me that your Society is concerned with the employment of women and she suggested that I might tell you something about my own professional experiences. It is true I am a woman; it is true I am employed; but what professional experiences have I had? It is difficult to say. My profession is literature; and in that profession there are fewer experiences for women than in any other, with the exception of the stage — fewer, I mean, that are peculiar to women. For the road was cut many years ago — by Fanny Burney, by Aphra Behn, by Harriet Martineau, by Jane Austen, by George Eliot — many famous women, and many more unknown and forgotten, have been before me, making the path smooth, and regulating my steps. Thus, when I came to write, there were very few material obstacles in my way. Writing was a reputable and harmless occupation. The family peace was not broken by the scratching of a pen. No demand was made upon the family purse. For ten and sixpence one can buy paper enough to write all the plays of Shakespeare — if one has a mind that way. Pianos and models, Paris, Vienna and Berlin, masters and mistresses, are not needed by a writer. The cheapness of writing paper is, of course, the reason why women have succeeded as writers before they have succeeded in the other professions.

But to tell you my story — it is a simple one. You have only got to figure to yourselves a girl in a bedroom with a pen in her hand. She had only to move that pen from left to right — from ten o'clock to one. Then it occurred to her to do what is simple and cheap enough after all — to slip a few of those pages into an envelope, fix a penny stamp in the corner, and drop the envelope into the red box at the corner. It was thus that I became a journalist; and my effort was rewarded on the first day of the following month — a very glorious day it was for me — by a letter from an editor containing a check for one pound ten shillings and sixpence. But to show you how little I deserve to be called a professional woman, how little I know of the struggles and difficulties of such lives, I have to admit that instead of spending that sum upon bread and butter, rent, shoes and stockings, or butcher's bills, I went out and bought a cat — a beautiful cat, a

---

[2] This essay was originally a talk delivered in 1931 to the Women's Service League.

Persian cat, which very soon involved me in bitter disputes with my neighbors.

What could be easier than to write articles and to buy Persian cats with the profits? But wait a moment. Articles have to be about something. Mine, I seem to remember, was about a novel by a famous man. And while I was writing this review, I discovered that if I were going to review books I should need to do battle with a certain phantom. And the phantom was a woman, and when I came to know her better I called her after the heroine of a famous poem, The Angel in the House. It was she who used to come between me and my paper when I was writing reviews. It was she who bothered me and wasted my time and so tormented me that at last I killed her. You who come of a younger and happier generation may not have heard of her — you may not know what I mean by the Angel in the House. I will describe her as shortly as I can. She was intensely sympathetic. She was immensely charming. She was utterly un-selfish. She excelled in the difficult arts of family life. She sacrificed herself daily. If there was chicken, she took the leg; if there was a draught she sat in it — in short she was so constituted that she never had a mind or a wish of her own, but preferred to sympathize always with the minds and wishes of others. Above all — I need not say it — she was pure. Her purity was supposed to be her chief beauty — her blushes, her great grace. In those days — the last of Queen Victoria — every house had its Angel. And when I came to write I encoun-tered her with the very first words. The shadow of her wings fell on my page; I heard the rustling of her skirts in the room. Directly, that is to say, I took my pen in hand to review that novel by a famous man, she slipped behind me and whispered: "My dear, you are a young woman. You are writing about a book that has been written by a man. Be sympathetic; be tender; flatter; deceive; use all the arts and wiles of our sex. Never let anybody guess that you have a mind of your own. Above all, be pure." And she made as if to guide my pen. I now record the one act for which I take some credit to myself, though the credit rightly belongs to some excellent ancestors of mine who left me a certain sum of money — shall we say five hundred pounds a year? — so that it was not necessary for me to depend solely on charm for my living. I turned upon her and caught her by the throat. I did my best to kill her. My excuse, if I were to be had up in a court of law, would be that I acted in self-defense. Had I not killed her she would have killed me. She would have plucked the heart out of my writing. For, as I found, directly I put pen to paper, you cannot review even a novel without having a mind of your own, without expressing what you think to be the truth about human relations, morality, sex. And all these questions, according to the Angel in the House, cannot be dealt with freely and openly by women; they must charm, they must conciliate, they must — to put it bluntly — tell lies if they are to succeed. Thus, whenever I felt the shadow of her wing or the radiance of her halo upon my page, I took up the inkpot and flung it at her. She died hard. Her fictitious nature was of great assistance to her. It is far harder to kill a phantom than a reality. She was always creeping back when I thought I had despatched her. Though I flatter myself that I killed her in the end, the struggle was severe; it took much time that had better have been spent upon learning Greek grammar; or in roaming the world in search of adventures. But it was a real experience; it was an experience that was bound to befall all women writers at that time. Killing the Angel in the House was part of the occupation of a woman writer.

But to continue my story. The Angel was dead; what then remained? You may say that what remained was a simple and common object — a young woman in a bedroom with an inkpot. In other words, now that she had rid herself of falsehood, that young woman had only to be herself. Ah, but what is "herself"? I mean, what is a woman? I assure you, I do not know. I do not believe that you know. I do not believe that anybody can know until she has expressed herself in all the arts and professions open to human skill. That indeed is one of the reasons why I have come here — out of respect for you, who are in process of showing us by your experiments what a woman is, who are in process of providing us, by your failures and successes, with that extremely important piece of information.

But to continue the story of my professional experiences. I made one pound ten and six by my first review; and I bought a Persian cat with the proceeds. Then I grew ambitious. A Persian cat is all very well, I said; but a Persian cat is not enough. I must have a motor car. And it was thus that I became a novelist — for it is a very strange thing that people will give you a motor car if you will tell them a story. It is a still stranger thing that there is nothing so delightful in the world as telling stories. It is far pleasanter than writing reviews of famous novels. And yet, if I am to obey your secretary and tell you my professional experiences as a novelist, I must tell you about a very strange experience that befell me as a novelist. And to understand it you must try first to imagine a novelist's state of mind. I hope I am not giving away professional secrets if I say that a novelist's chief desire is to be as unconscious as possible. He has to induce in himself a state of perpetual lethargy. He

wants life to proceed with the utmost quiet and regularity. He wants
to see the same faces, to read the same books, to do the same things
day after day, month after month, while he is writing, so that
nothing may break the illusion in which he is living — so that
nothing may disturb or disquiet the mysterious nosings about, feelings round, darts, dashes and sudden discoveries of that very shy and
illusive spirit, the imagination. I suspect that this state is the same
both for men and women. Be that as it may, I want you to imagine
me writing a novel in a state of trance. I want you to figure to
yourselves a girl sitting with a pen in her hand, which for minutes,
and indeed for hours, she never dips into the inkpot. The image that
comes to my mind when I think of this girl is the image of a
fisherman lying sunk in dreams on the verge of a deep lake with a
rod held out over the water. She was letting her imagination sweep
unchecked round every rock and cranny of the world that lies
submerged in the depths of our unconscious being. Now came the
experience, the experience that I believe to be far commoner with
women writers than with men. The line raced through the girl's
fingers. Her imagination had rushed away. It had sought the pools,
the depths, the dark places where the largest fish slumber. And then
there was a smash. There was an explosion. There was foam and
confusion. The imagination had dashed itself against something
hard. The girl was roused from her dream. She was indeed in a state
of the most acute and difficult distress. To speak without figure she
had thought of something, something about the body, about the
passions which it was unfitting for her as a woman to say. Men, her
reason told her, would be shocked. The consciousness of what men
will say of a woman who speaks the truth about her passions had
roused her from her artist's state of unconsciousness. She could write
no more. The trance was over. Her imagination could work no
longer. This I believe to be a very common experience with women
writers — they are impeded by the extreme conventionality of the
other sex. For though men sensibly allow themselves great freedom
in these respects, I doubt that they realize or can control the extreme
severity with which they condemn such freedom in women.

These then were two very genuine experiences of my own.
These were two of the adventures of my professional life. The first
— killing the Angel in the House — I think I solved. She died. But
the second, telling the truth about my own experiences as a body, I
do not think I solved. I doubt that any woman has solved it yet. The
obstacles against her are still immensely powerful — and yet they are
very difficult to define. Outwardly, what is simpler than to write
books? Outwardly, what obstacles are there for a woman rather than

for a man? Inwardly, I think, the case is very different; she has still many ghosts to fight, many prejudices to overcome. Indeed it will be a long time still, I think, before a woman can sit down to write a book without finding a phantom to be slain, a rock to be dashed against. And if this is so in literature, the freest of all professions for women, how is it in the new professions which you are now for the first time entering?

Those are the questions that I should like, had I time, to ask you. And indeed, if I have laid stress upon these professional experiences of mine, it is because I believe that they are, though in different forms, yours also. Even when the path is nominally open — when there is nothing to prevent a woman from being a doctor, a lawyer, a civil servant — there are many phantoms and obstacles, as I believe, looming in her way. To discuss and define them is I think of great value and importance; for thus only can the labor be shared, the difficulties be solved. But besides this, it is necessary also to discuss the ends and the aims for which we are fighting, for which we are doing battle with these formidable obstacles. Those aims cannot be taken for granted; they must be perpetually questioned and examined. The whole position, as I see it — here in this hall surrounded by women practising for the first time in history I know not how many different professions — is one of extraordinary interest and importance. You have won rooms of your own in the house hitherto exclusively owned by men. You are able, though not without great labor and effort, to pay the rent. You are earning your five hundred pounds a year. But this freedom is only a beginning; the room is your own, but it is still bare. It has to be furnished; it has to be decorated; it has to be shared. How are you going to furnish it, how are you going to decorate it? With whom are you going to share it, and upon what terms? These, I think, are questions of the utmost importance and interest. For the first time in history you are able to ask them; for the first time you are able to decide for yourselves what the answers should be. Willingly would I stay and discuss those questions and answers — but not tonight. My time is up; and I must cease.

QUESTIONS

1. Try to characterize Woolf's tone, especially her attitude toward her subject and herself, in the first paragraph.
2. What do you think Woolf means when she says (page 407), "It is far harder to kill a phantom than a reality"?

3. Woolf conjectures (page 418) that she has not solved the problem of "telling the truth about my own experiences as a body." Is there any reason to believe that today a woman has more difficulty than a man in telling the truth about the experiences of the body?

4. In her final paragraph, Woolf suggests that phantoms as well as obstacles impede women from becoming doctors and lawyers. What might some of these phantoms be?

5. This essay is highly metaphoric. Speaking roughly (or, rather, as precisely as possible) what is the meaning of the metaphor of "rooms" in the final paragraph? What does Woolf mean when she says, "The room is your own, but it is still bare. . . . With whom are you going to share it, and upon what terms?"

6. Evaluate the last two sentences. Are they too abrupt and mechanical? Or do they provide a fitting conclusion to the speech?

Beer Can

John Updike

This seems to be an era of gratuitous inventions and negative improvements. Consider the beer can. It was beautiful — as beautiful as the clothespin, as inevitable as the wine bottle, as dignified and reassuring as the fire hydrant. A tranquil cylinder of delightfully resonant metal, it could be opened in an instant, requiring only the application of a handy gadget freely dispensed by every grocer. Who can forget the small, symmetrical thrill of those two triangular punctures, the dainty *pffff*, the little crest of suds that foamed eagerly in the exultation of release? Now we are given, instead, a top beetling with an ugly, shmoo-shaped "tab," which, after fiercely resisting the tugging, bleeding fingers of the thirsty man, threatens his lips with a dangerous and hideous hole. However, we have discovered a way to thwart Progress, usually so unthwartable. *Turn the beer can upside down and open the bottom.* The bottom is still the way the top used to be. True, this operation gives the beer an unsettling jolt, and the sight of a consistently inverted beer can might make people edgy, not to say queasy. But the latter difficulty could be eliminated if manufacturers would design cans that looked the same whichever end was up, like playing cards. What we need is Progress with an escape hatch.

QUESTIONS

1. What is the tone of the first sentence? What effect is gained by following this relatively long sentence with a short one? What would be lost or gained if Updike had written, instead of "Consider the beer can," "Think of a beer can"?
2. Do you intend to use a can opener on the bottom of a beer can?

The Iks

Lewis Thomas

The small tribe of Iks, formerly nomadic hunters and gatherers in the mountain valleys of northern Uganda, have become celebrities, literary symbols for the ultimate fate of disheartened, heartless mankind at large. Two disastrously conclusive things happened to them: the government decided to have a national park, so they were compelled by law to give up hunting in the valleys and become farmers on poor hillside soil, and then they were visited for two years by an anthropologist who detested them and wrote a book about them.

The message of the book is that the Iks have transformed themselves into an irreversibly disagreeable collection of unattached, brutish creatures, totally selfish and loveless, in response to the dismantling of their traditional culture. Moreover, this is what the rest of us are like in our inner selves, and we will all turn into Iks when the structure of our society comes all unhinged.

The argument rests, of course, on certain assumptions about the core of human beings, and is necessarily speculative. You have to agree in advance that man is fundamentally a bad lot, out for himself alone, displaying such graces as affection and compassion only as learned habits. If you take this view, the story of the Iks can be used to confirm it. These people seem to be living together, clustered in small, dense villages, but they are really solitary, unrelated individuals with no evident use for each other. They talk, but only to make ill-tempered demands and cold refusals. They share nothing. They never sing. They turn the children out to forage as soon as they can walk, and desert the elders to starve whenever they can, and the foraging children snatch food from the mouths of the helpless elders. It is a mean society.

They breed without love or even casual regard. They defecate on each other's doorsteps. They watch their neighbors for signs of misfortune, and only then do they laugh. In the book they do a lot of laughing, having so much bad luck. Several times they even laughed at the anthropologist, who found this especially repellent (one senses, between the lines, that the scholar is not himself the world's luckiest man). Worse, they took him into the family, snatched his food, defecated on his doorstep, and hooted dislike at him. They gave him two bad years.

It is a depressing book. If, as he suggests, there is only Ikness at the center of each of us, our sole hope for hanging on to the name of humanity will be in endlessly mending the structure of our society, and it is changing so quickly and completely that we may never find the threads in time. Meanwhile, left to ourselves alone, solitary, we will become the same joyless, zestless, untouching lone animals.

But this may be too narrow a view. For one thing, the Iks are extraordinary. They are absolutely astonishing, in fact. The anthropologist has never seen people like them anywhere, nor have I. You'd think, if they were simply examples of the common essence of mankind, they'd seem more recognizable. Instead, they are bizarre, anomalous. I have known my share of peculiar, difficult, nervous, grabby people, but I've never encountered any genuinely, consistently detestable human beings in all my life. The Iks sound more like abnormalities, maladies.

I cannot accept it. I do not believe that the Iks are representative of isolated, revealed man, unobscured by social habits. I believe their behavior is something extra, something laid on. This unremitting, compulsive repellence is a kind of complicated ritual. They must have learned to act this way; they copied it, somehow.

I have a theory, then. The Iks have gone crazy.

The solitary Ik, isolated in the ruins of an exploded culture, has built a new defense for himself. If you live in an unworkable society you can make up one of your own, and this is what the Iks have done. Each Ik has become a group, a one-man tribe on its own, a constituency.

Now everything falls into place. This is why they do seem, after all, vaguely familiar to all of us. We've seen them before. This is precisely the way groups of one size or another, ranging from committees to nations, behave. It is, of course, this aspect of humanity that has lagged behind the rest of evolution, and this is why the Ik seems so primitive. In his absolute selfishness, his incapacity to give anything away, no matter what, he is a successful committee. When he stands at the door of his hut, shouting insults at his neighbors in a loud harangue, he is city addressing another city.

Cities have all the Ik characteristics. They defecate on doorsteps, in rivers and lakes, their own or anyone else's. They leave rubbish. They detest all neighboring cities, give nothing away. They even build institutions for deserting elders out of sight.

Nations are the most Iklike of all. No wonder the Iks seem familiar. For total greed, rapacity, heartlessness, and irresponsibility there is nothing to match a nation. Nations, by law, are solitary, self-centered, withdrawn into themselves. There is no such thing as affection between nations, and certainly no nation ever loved another. They bawl insults from their doorsteps, defecate into whole oceans, snatch all the food, survive by detestation, take joy in the bad luck of others, celebrate the death of others, live for the death of others.

That's it, and I shall stop worrying about the book. It does not signify that man is a sparse, inhuman thing at his center. He's all right. It only says what we've always known and never had enough time to worry about, that we haven't yet learned how to stay human when assembled in masses. The Ik, in his despair, is acting out this failure, and perhaps we should pay closer attention. Nations have themselves become too frightening to think about, but we might learn some things by watching these people.

QUESTIONS

1. Find the grim joke in the first paragraph.
2. Suppose that "of course" were omitted from the first sentence of the third paragraph. Would anything significant be lost? Suppose in the second sentence of the third paragraph, instead of "You have to agree," Thomas had written "One has to agree." What would be gained or lost?
3. In the third and fourth paragraphs, what is the effect of repeating the structure of subject and verb: "They talk . . . ," "They share . . . ," "They never sing," "They turn . . . ," "They breed . . . ," and so on?
4. Point to a few colloquial expressions, and to a few notably informal sentences. Do you find them inappropriate to a discussion of a serious topic?
5. What is Thomas's attitude toward the anthropologist and his book? Cite some passages that convey his attitude, and explain how they convey it, or how they attempt to persuade us to share it.

16

Acquiring Style

Draw lines, young man,
draw many lines
— OLD INGRES TO
THE YOUNG DEGAS

In the preceding pages on style we said that your writing reveals not only where you stand (your topic) and how you think (the structure of your argument), but also who you are and how you take yourself (your tone). To follow our argument to its limit, we might say that everything in this book — including rules on the comma (where you breathe) — is about style. We do. What more is there to say?

CLARITY AND TEXTURE

First, a distinction Aristotle makes between two parts of style: that which gives *clarity,* and that which gives *texture*. Exact words, concrete illustrations of abstractions, conventional punctuation, and so forth — matters we treat in some detail in the sections on revising and editing — make for clarity. On the whole, this part of style is inconspicuous when present; when absent the effect ranges from mildly distracting to ruinous. Clarity is the foundation of style. It can be achieved by anyone willing to make the effort.

Among the things that give texture, or individuality, are effective repetition, variety in sentence structure, wordplay, and so forth. This second group of devices, on the whole more noticeable, makes the reader aware of the writer's particular voice. These devices can be learned too, but seldom by effort alone. In fact playfulness helps here more than doggedness. Students who work at this part of style usually enjoy hanging around words. At the same time, they're likely to feel that when they put words on paper, even in a casual letter to a friend, they're putting themselves on the line. Serious, as most people are about games they really care about, but not solemn, they'll come to recognize the rules of play in John Holmes's advice to young poets: "You must believe that your feelings and your words for your feelings are important. . . . That they are unique is a fact; that you believe they are unique is necessary."

A REPERTORY OF STYLES

We make a second distinction: between style as the reader perceives it from the written word, and style as the writer experiences it. The first is static: it's fixed in writing or print; we can point to it, discuss it, analyze it. The second, the writer's experience of his own style, changes as the writer changes. In his essay "Why I Write" George Orwell said, "I find that by the time you have perfected any style of writing, you have always outgrown it." An exaggeration that deposits a truth. The essay concludes, however, "Looking back through my work, I see that it is invariably where I lacked a *political* purpose that I wrote lifeless books and was betrayed into purple passages, sentences without meaning, decorative adjectives and humbug generally." A suggestion surely, that through trial and error, and with maturity, a writer comes to a sense of self, a true style, not static and not constantly changing, but achieved.

Undergraduates seldom know what purpose, in Orwell's sense, they will have. You may be inclined toward some subjects and against others, you may have decided on a career — many times. But if your education is worth anything like the money and time invested in it, your ideas and feelings will change more rapidly in the next few years than ever before in your memory, and perhaps more than they ever will again. Make use of the confusion you're in. Reach out for new experiences to assimilate; make whatever connections you can from your reading to your inner life, reaching back into your past and forward into your future. And keep writing: "Draw lines . . . draw many lines."

To keep pace with your changing ideas — and here is our main point — you'll need to acquire not one style, but a repertory of styles, a store of writing habits on which you can draw as the need arises.

ORIGINALITY AND IMITATION

Finally, a paradox: one starts to acquire an individual style by studying and imitating the style of others. The paradox isn't limited to writing. Stylists in all fields begin as apprentices. The young ball player imitates the movements of Reggie Jackson, the potter joins a workshop in California to study under Marguerite Wildenhain, the chess player hangs around the park or club watching the old pros, then finds a book that probably recommends beginning with Ruy Lopez' opening. When Michelangelo was an apprentice he copied works by his predecessors; when Millet was young he copied works by Michelangelo; when Van Gogh was young he copied works by Millet. The would-be writer may be lucky enough to have a teacher, one he can imitate; more likely he will, in W. H. Auden's words, "serve his apprenticeship in the library."

PRACTICE IN ACQUIRING STYLE

Benjamin Franklin's Exercise

Benjamin Franklin says in his *Autobiography*, "Prose writing has been of great use to me in the course of my life, and was a principal means of my advancement," and he reveals how he acquired his ability in it. (He had just abandoned, at about the age of eleven, his ambition to be a great poet — after his father told him that "verse-makers were generally beggars.")

> About this time I met with an odd volume of the *Spectator*. It was the third. I had never before seen any of them. I bought it, read it over and over, and was much delighted with it. I thought the writing excellent, and wished, if possible, to imitate it. With that view I took some of the papers, and making short hints of the sentiment in each sentence, laid them by a few days, and then, without looking at the book, tried to complete the papers again by expressing each sentiment at length, and as fully as it had been expressed before, in any suitable words that should come to hand. Then I compared my *Spectator* with the original, discovered some of my faults, and corrected them.

A few pages later Franklin confides, with characteristic under-statement (which he learned, he thought, by imitating Socrates), "I sometimes had the pleasure of fancying that in certain particulars of small import I had been lucky enough to improve the method or the language."

EXERCISES

1. Outline, in a list of brief notes, Franklin's exercise.
2. Choose a passage of current prose writing whose style you admire and follow Franklin's method. (Don't forget the last step: where you've improved on your model, congratulate yourself with becoming modesty.)

Paraphrasing

Do not confuse a paraphrase with a summary.

A summary is always much shorter than the original; a para-phrase is often a bit longer. To paraphrase a sentence, replace each word or phrase in it with one of your own. (Articles, pronouns, and conjunctions need not be replaced.) Your sentence should say substantially what the original says, but in your own words, and in a fluent, natural style. Consider the following sentence by W. H. Auden, and the paraphrase that follows it:

> Owing to its superior power as a mnemonic, verse is superior to prose as a medium for didactic instruction.
> — W. H. Auden

> Because it is more easily memorized and can be retained in the mind for a longer time, poetry is better than prose for teaching moral lessons.

Paraphrasing is useful for several reasons. First, paraphrasing helps you to increase your vocabulary. (Many students say that a limited vocabulary is their chief source of difficulty in writing.) You may know, for example, that "didactic" means "intended for instruction, or instructive." But why then does Auden say "didactic instruction"? Are the words redundant, or is Auden stipulating a kind of instruction? Your dictionary, which may list "tending to teach a moral lesson" as one of three or four meanings of didactic, will help you understand Auden's sentence. But notice, first, that you'll have to choose the appropriate definition, and second, that you won't be able to insert that definition as is into your sentence. To paraphrase "didactic instruction" you'll have to put "didactic" in your own words. (If you look up "mnemonic" you'll find an even more complex puzzle resolved in our paraphrase.) Paraphrasing, then, expands your vocabulary because to paraphrase accurately and gracefully you must actively understand the use of an unfamiliar word, not simply memorize a synonym for it.

Paraphrasing also helps you to focus your attention on what you read. If you want, for example, to become a better reader of poetry, the best way is to *pay attention,* and the best way of paying attention is to try paraphrasing a line whose meaning escapes you. So too with understanding art history or economics or any specialized study. If you come across a difficult passage, don't just stare at it, paraphrase it. (If you don't have time to stop and puzzle through a sentence that is not entirely clear to you, you can always make time to jot it down on a three-by-five card. As Stanislav Andreski says, "Paper is patient.")

Finally, in paraphrasing, you are observing closely and actively the way another mind works. You are, in effect, serving as an apprentice stylist. (Some masters, of course, are not worth serving or emulating. Be discriminating.)

EXERCISE

Try paraphrasing the following sentences:

Generally speaking and to a varying extent, scientists follow their temperaments in their choice of problems.
— Charles Hermite

To commit violent and unjust acts, it is not enough for a government to have the will or even the power; the habits, ideas, and passions of the time must lend themselves to their committal.
— Alexis de Tocqueville

The most intolerable people are provincial celebrities.
— Anton Chekhov

A distinction must be made between my uncle's capricious brutality and my aunt's punishments and repressions, which seem to have been dictated to her by her conscience.
— Mary McCarthy

Consciousness reigns but doesn't govern.
— Paul Valéry

The more extensive your acquaintance is with the works of those who have excelled, the more extensive will be your powers of invention, and what may appear still more like a paradox, the more original will be your composition.
— Sir Joshua Reynolds

The fashion wears out more apparel than the man.
— William Shakespeare

What is expressed is impressed.
— Aristotle

All the road to heaven is heaven.
— Saint Teresa of Avila

Imitating the Cumulative Sentence

When you write, you make a point, not by subtracting as though you sharpened a pencil, but by adding. When you put one word after another, your statement should be more precise the more you add. If the result is otherwise, you have added the wrong thing, or you have added more than was needed.
— John Erskine

In *Notes Toward a New Rhetoric* Francis Christensen cites "Erskine's principle" and argues that "the cumulative sentence" best fulfills it. The cumulative sentence makes a statement in the main clause; the rest of the sentence consists of modifiers *added* to make the meaning of the statement more precise. The cumulative sentence adds *texture* to writing because as the writer adds modifiers he is examining his impressions, summarized in the main clause. At the same time he reveals to the reader how those impressions impinged on his mind. Here are some of Christensen's examples:

> He dipped his hands in the bichloride solution and shook them, a quick shake, fingers down, like the fingers of a pianist above the keys.
> — Sinclair Lewis

> The jockeys sat bowed and relaxed, moving a little at the waist with the movement of their horses.
> — Katherine Anne Porter

> The Texan turned to the nearest gatepost and climbed to the top of it, his alternate thighs thick and bulging in the tight trousers, the butt of the pistol catching and losing the sun in pearly gleams.
> — William Faulkner

> George was coming down in the telemark position, kneeling, one leg forward and bent, the other trailing, his sticks hanging like some insect's thin legs, kicking up puffs of snow, and finally the whole kneeling, trailing figure coming around in a beautiful right curve like points of light, all in a wild cloud of snow.
> — Ernest Hemingway

EXERCISE

Try writing a cumulative sentence. First, reread Christensen's sample sentences out loud. Then, during a second reading, try to sense the similarities in structure. For the next few days train yourself to observe people closely, the way they walk, move, gesture, smile, speak. Take notes when you can. Then, after reading the sentences again, try writing one. Either imitate one of the sentences closely, word by word (substituting your own words) or start with your subject, imitating the structure you have detected or have simply absorbed.

Transformations

If you take a proverb, an epigram, or any interesting, suggestive sentence and change it enough to make it say something else, something on *your* mind, you have a transformation. To cite a famous example, G. K. Chesterton transformed

> If a thing is worth doing it is worth doing well

to

> If a thing is worth doing it is worth doing badly.

Professor Marion Levy transformed Leo Durocher's

> Nice guys finish last

to

> Last guys don't finish nice.

A student transformed Marianne Moore's

> We must be as clear as our natural reticence allows us to be

to

> We must be as outspoken as our adversaries would forbid us to be.

EXERCISE

How can you transform one or more of the following?

When a poor man eats a chicken, one of them is sick.
— Yiddish proverb

The Battle of Waterloo was won on the playing fields of Eton.
— Attributed to the Duke of Wellington

You can't step into the same river twice.
— Heraclitus

Mañana es otro día.
— Proverb

Finding Poems

Finding poems is a variation of the language game called acquiring style. It amuses the student who enjoys hanging around words but who is tired of writing, tired of pulling words out of his mind and making them shape up — weary too, very weary, of reading "fine things." Still, he hungers for print, consuming the words on the cereal box along with the cereal, reading last week's classified ads when he has nothing to sell, no money to buy. What can be made of such an affliction? A poem.

Here are X. J. Kennedy's directions for finding a poem.

> In a newspaper, magazine, catalogue, textbook, or advertising throwaway, find a sentence or passage that (with a little artistic manipulation on your part) shows promise of becoming a poem. Copy it into lines like poetry, being careful to place what seem to be the most interesting words at the ends of lines to give them greatest emphasis. According to the rules of found poetry you may excerpt, delete, repeat, and rearrange elements but not add anything.

Here are some examples of "found poems." The first, "And All Those Others," was found by Jack S. Margolis in the Watergate transcripts; he published it in *The Poetry of Richard Milhous Nixon*.

> I'm the President
> Of the country —
> And I'm going
> To get on with it
> > And meet
> > Italians
> > and
> > Germans,
> And all those others.

Here is a passage from a textbook, followed by the poem, "Symbolism," a student found in it:

> A symbol, then, is an image so loaded with significance that it is not simply literal, and it does not simply stand for something else; it is both itself *and* something else that it richly suggests, a kind of manifestation of something too complex or too elusive to be otherwise revealed.

> An image
> so loaded with
> > significance
> that it is not
> > simply literal,
> and it does not
> > simply stand
> for
> > something else;

> it is both
>   itself
> and
>   something else
> that it
>   richly suggests,
> a kind of
>   manifestation
> of
>   something
>   too complex
> or
>   too elusive
> to be
>   otherwise revealed,
> is a
>   *symbol.*

Finally, a poem found by a student in an advertisement in *Newsweek:*

> Winchester model 101
> made for hands
> that know the difference
> There's more
> than meets the eye
> to any fine
> shotgun

EXERCISES

1. Find a poem.
2. Explain in one sentence (a) how finding poems might help you acquire style or (b) why such an exercise is a waste of time.

17

Acquiring Fluency

Nulla dies sine linea.
No day without a line.

KEEPING A JOURNAL

Sometimes our efforts to improve our writing make us too conscious of what we say, or too self-critical to say anything. To guard against hyperconsciousness, or as an antidote to it, practice writing daily: keep a journal. The word *journal* derives from the Latin *dies* ("day") and *diurnalis* ("daily"), which became *journal* ("daily") in medieval French. Keep a journal: *nulla dies sine linea.*

Writing in a journal keeps your writing loose, fluent. It helps you to overcome the fear of writing most people have, and it gives you a chance to practice skills you are acquiring. As we said at the start, writing is a physical act, and to keep in trim, you should practice daily. (Or, to be honest, as close to daily as you can manage.) Keeping a journal then is practical; for many students it is, from the start, enjoyable.

If keeping a journal is an assignment in your composition course, your instructor may ask you to write in a loose–leaf notebook — so that pages may be turned in occasionally, and the instructor won't have to stagger home with twenty or thirty notebooks. If you're keeping a journal strictly for your own use, write with, and on, whatever materials feel comfortable: pen, pencil, typewriter; loose sheets, bound notebook, or whatever. (Dr. William Carlos Williams often wrote poems on prescription blanks.)

When to write? Any time; ten to fifteen minutes a day. Some people find it helpful to establish a regular time of day for writing, just before they go to sleep, for example. Habits can be helpful; but not all of us can or should lead well-regulated lives. Suit yourself.

How long is an entry? An entry may be a few words, a line or two, a few pages. There's no special length, but keep writing for at least the minimum recommended time.

Write freely. Don't correct or revise, don't worry about spelling, vocabulary, punctuation. Use whatever language, idiom, voice you wish. If you have a "home language" — black or Puerto Rican, for example — write entries in it. It's a good way to keep in touch with yourself, and the friends and family you've temporarily left. You *can* go home again; you can, that is, if you don't leave college an educated zombie.

As for content, write about anything that comes to mind. But don't confuse a journal with a diary. A diary mentions things that have happened ("Concert at 8, with J. and R."); a journal reflects on the happenings. A diary lists appointments; a journal records events, but gives some sense of why they were meaningful. Think of your journal as a record of your life now, which you might read with pleasure some years from now when many of the rich details of your daily experience would otherwise be buried in your memory. Still, it's probably better to write "Had a peanut butter sandwich for lunch" than to write nothing.

Write down your thoughts, feelings, impressions, responses, dreams, memories. May Sarton once said, "The senses are the keys to the past." If you have a strong sensory memory of something — the mixed smell of saltwater, sand, and machinery oil, for example — try to describe it in words, and then to track it down. You may find a buried scene from your childhood that you can rescue from your memory by a train of associations. If you keep tracking, and writing, you may discover why that scene is important to you still.

But don't be afraid to embroider the truth a little, or to understate it. As Santayana observed, "Sometimes we have to change the truth in order to remember it."

Jot down reactions, ideas, feelings about something you are reading, something you may want to use later, in an essay. Did you stop reading and start daydreaming? What is the link between the text and your daydream? If you write it down, you may be able to cut down on the daydreaming, or, better still, make something out of it.

Practice writing descriptions; short, medium, long; of persons, places, things; literal, figurative, or impressionistic. Try cross-cutting from one description of a scene or an experience to another which might illuminate it. (When writing about real people observe one caution: use fictitious names.)

When you have nothing to say, write anyway. Practice writing paraphrases and transformations (see pages 417–19 and 420–21). Or copy out a passage of someone else's writing. If you can, explain why you find it attractive, why you want to remember it.

If you're too preoccupied to write because there's a decision you must make, and can't make, start writing. List all the reasons for following a course of action; then all the reasons against it.

Here, to prime the pump, are some examples of journal entries. Some are by professional writers, others by students. You'll find nothing remarkable in many of these entries (except honesty) and perhaps you'll discover in yourself the assurance that you can do as well or better.

SOME JOURNAL ENTRIES
BY PUBLISHED WRITERS

You hear a lot of jazz about Soul Food. Take chitterlings: the ghetto blacks eat them from necessity while the black bourgeoisie has turned it into a mocking slogan. Eating chitterlings is like going slumming to them. Now that they have the price of a steak here they come prattling about Soul Food. The people in the ghetto want steaks. *Beef Steaks.* I wish I had the power to see to it that the bourgeoisie really *did* have to make it on Soul Food.

— Eldridge Cleaver

August A sudden idea of the relationship between "lovers." We are neither male nor female. We are a compound of both. I choose the male who will develop and expand the male in me; he chooses me to expand the female in him. Being made whole. . . . And why I choose *one* man for this rather than many is for safety. We bind ourselves within a ring and that ring is as it were a wall against the outside world. It is our refuge, our shelter. Here the tricks of life will not be played. Here is *safety* for us to *grow. Why, I talk like a child.*

— Katherine Mansfield

Wanted: a dog that neither barks nor bites, eats broken glass and shits diamonds.

— Goethe

The difficulty about all this dying is that you can't tell a fellow anything about it, so where does the fun come in?

— Alice James

With Brett to a nearby "movie," perhaps a little worse than the usual average of mediocrity. Yet why is it that I can be emotionally moved at the most vapid climax, the while I intellectually deride the whole false and mushy mess? It is of course but the awakening of memories by some act or gesture related to the past, — some unrealized hope is returned, a lost thread is for the moment woven into reality. However, the absurdity of my Jekyll and Hyde situation, with my mouth in a grin and my throat choked, and this from viewing some quite preposterous melodrama, ridiculously conceived, acted by imbeciles, presented for bovine clodhoppers, brings the question am I infantile? senile? maudlin? or also beef-witted? With a superlative stretch of the neck I answer these questions, "No!" — yet feeling uneasy over the sureness of my self-estimation. Better to wink at my weakness than to discover it a truth!

I have my horoscope at last. Mrs. Severy, after making many charts, decided on Gemini as my rising sign: and, I have a bad year ahead! Which does not worry me for time passes. Too, the human element enters in. She may be wrong, not having my hour. Eight charts were made before Gemini was decided upon. I am not a skeptic, I am always inclined toward unorthodox viewpoints, I see no reason to doubt that the stars have a definite effect upon the human race, but I wonder whether anyone can interpret them. An orthodox belief is merely a prevailing one, popular at the moment: astrology was no doubt once quite orthodox, just as vaccination is now. And someday vaccination will be generally regarded as a superstition comparable to witchcraft.

— Edward Weston

The man who would be stupid enough to defend the present economic order would be ass enough to do nothing for it.

Disorderly thinking should be as unwelcome in polite society as disorderly conduct. In fact, it *is* disorderly conduct.

On the sands of Ogunquit I saw a sandpiper, one of whose legs was lamed, rest on its wings as a man would on a pair of crutches.

— Lewis Mumford

It is so many years before one can believe enough in what one feels even to know what the feeling is.

For some months now I have lived with my own youth and childhood, not always writing indeed but thinking of it almost every day, and I am sorrowful and disturbed. It is not that I have accomplished too few of my plans, for I am not ambitious; but when I think of all the books I have read, and of the wise words I have heard spoken, and of the anxiety I have given to parents and grandparents, and of the hopes that I have had, all life weighed in the scales of my own life seems to me a preparation for something that never happens.

— William Butler Yeats

From *Blue-Collar Journal*

John R. Coleman[1]

Monday, March 26

Cold rain after the warmth of Sunday. Spring has pulled back to wait for a while. Few people seemed to want to eat, even Oyster House food. Not many customers, not much excitement, not much work.

This was a half day for me. Because I'd be getting my own dinner on the hot plate back in my room, I slipped over to the Faneuil Hall markets about 2:00 to get a piece of meat and some vegetables. My uniform worked wonders this time. At the three counters where I stopped, I got warm greetings and questions about

---

[1] In 1973, during a leave of absence from his job as president of Haverford College, John Coleman held a series of blue-collar jobs. He worked on sewers in Georgia, in kitchens in Boston, and on a garbage truck in Maryland. He wrote entries in a journal every night, and then expanded the entries for publication. A few selections are included.

how business was at the Oyster House. Had I been in my Haverford clothes, I'd have received the polite "May-I-help-you" treatment that I get at the Wayne Farmers' Market near home every Saturday morning at 7:00. But today the butcher and the vegetable men gave me the "Here's-one-of-us" treatment. It felt good.

I didn't pay any less for what I bought. But I did get told at one counter, "No, you don't want that one," and had a better squash placed in my hand. That's almost the same as paying less.

Tuesday, March 27

One of the waitresses I find hard to take asked me at one point today, "Are you the boy who cuts the lemons?"

"I'm the man who does," I replied.

"Well, there are none cut." There wasn't a hint that she heard my point.

Dana, who has cooked here for twelve years or so, heard that exchange.

"It's no use, Jack," he said when she was gone. "If she doesn't know now, she never will." There was a trace of a smile on his face, but it was a sad look all the same.

In that moment, I learned the full thrust of those billboard ads of a few years ago that said, "BOY. Drop out of school and that's what they'll call you the rest of your life." I had read those ads before with a certain feeling of pride; education matters, they said, and that gave a lift to my field. Today I saw them saying something else. They were untrue in part; it turns out that you'll get called "boy" if you do work that others don't respect even if you have a Ph.D. It isn't education that counts, but the job in which you land. And the ads spoke too of a sad resignation about the world. They assumed that some people just won't learn respect for others, so you should adapt yourself to them. Don't try to change them. Get the right job and they won't call *you* boy any more. They'll save it for the next man.

It isn't just people like this one waitress who learn slowly, if at all. Haverford College has prided itself on being a caring, considerate community in the Quaker tradition for many long years. Yet when I came there I soon learned that the cleaning women in the dormitories were called "wombats" by all the students. No one seemed to know where the name came from or what connection, if any, it had with the dictionary definition. *The American College Dictionary* says a wombat is "any of three species of burrowing marsupials of Australia . . . somewhat resembling ground hogs." The name was just one of Haverford's unexamined ways of doing things.

It didn't take much persuasion to get the name dropped. Today there are few students who remember it at all. But I imagine the cleaning women remember it well.

Certainly I won't forget being called a boy today.

Wednesday, March 28

A day off once again.

I went into a restaurant downtown, the first time since I started work as a sandwich man. My curiosity won out. I ordered a club sandwich just to see how well it held together. It was noon, and I knew the man or woman in the kitchen must be having a rough time at that hour, but I ordered it just the same.

The sandwich looked fine, and its ingredients were fresh. I sent my compliments to the sandwich man, but I think the waitress thought I was nuts.

The place where I really wanted to eat was the Oyster House. I wanted to sit down at one of the tables and have someone — one of the many waitresses I like — bring me the menu. I wanted to order that stuffed fillet of sole, after some oysters at the bar. And I wanted the salad on the side, complete with cherry tomato and cucumber slice, and blue cheese dressing on top. I know some of the inside secrets of the place. I know, for example, that yesterday a customer got a thumbtack in his corn chowder (he was very nice about it). But I know too that the sanitation is generally good and that the people who work here care. I just wanted to see the whole meal come together as a production, fashioned by people whom I knew.

I'll eat there someday as a customer. And nothing that happens will escape my eye.

Sunday, April 1

It was hard, steady work all day long.

The rhythm of each day and even of each week is familiar enough that it should be getting boring by now. It doesn't seem that way yet. There is enough variety in the flow of orders and of people too that I seldom feel I have been through all this before. Cleaning up the aluminum trays, where my supplies are kept, at the end of each day is dull; I'd happily skip that if I could. But even in that there is a small element of suspense: the question each time is how far I can get with closing up for the night before the last waitress comes in with an order that requires getting the supplies out again.

I wonder how many loaves of bread and heads of lettuce I'd go through if I stuck at this job until retirement age.

Friday, April 6

We made the first stop. I had thought to bring gloves along with the work clothes in my gear, and I had them with me now. I was the only one who pulled gloves on. Each of us took a very large green or orange plastic barrel out of the back of the truck. Each barrel had a hole near the top to hold it by.

Steve took me into the first yard with him. "This is the way it's done," he said as he dumped the contents from three containers at the back door into his tub. Then in a flash he jumped into the barrel and trampled down what was there. "This way we can get more houses in one trip," he said as he jumped. In another flash he was out of the barrel, the load was on his back, and he was off for the house next door.

That was the training course.

He told me which houses to "pull." With three of us on the crew and only two sides to the street, Steve had some maneuvers to work out as to who pulled where. For the most part, he left Kenny on one side and me on the other, while he crossed back and forth to get the trash a few doors ahead of where we were. He also moved the truck.

I don't know just what I expected to find in the first house-holder's can on my route, but I know I took the lid off gingerly. It was full of garbage. Right on, I thought.

I couldn't quite bring myself to jump in and out of the barrel the way Steve had done. Instead, I pushed down hard with my gloved hand to make room for the next set of cans. With two houses pulled, the barrel was full. I lifted it up to my shoulder with a grunt (that seemed easier than swinging it around and onto my back) and headed for the truck. All kids — and many grown men — have an urge to throw at least one load of garbage into the waiting jaws of a sanitation truck and to pull the lever that sets the compacting unit to work. I threw my first load in with a feeling of fulfillment.

One thing about being a trashman is that, after your first load, you pretty well know the job. The only progress from then on comes in learning your route, developing your muscles, and picking up speed. I could never have imagined how heavy some of those barrels could be. Most times I got three households' worth of trash into one load, since that was the best way to save time on the route. But sometimes the resulting weight was more than I could lift even to my waist, let alone shoulder high. I had to drag some of those loads down the driveway or across the lawn to the truck. The noise of the barrel being dragged on the road gave me away, of course. Steve smiled patiently at that, and Kenny pretended not to see. It sobered me too to note that, while they never once dragged a load, they both cursed the weight on their backs a couple of times. I knew then that there's no such thing as getting used to what we had to heave.

This work was a far cry from what I had watched the Haverford Township sanitation men do back home. They work hard and fast, and they probably pull a longer route than we do. But their work consists of lifting the householders' cartons or cans from the curb to the truck. They miss the extra miles of walking through yards, the hoisting of loads to the shoulder or back, and the extra physical contact with the trash as it goes from the cans into the barrel. The driver there stays in the truck; perhaps he is someone who has done his share of years on the dirty end of the truck. Here he pulls trash with his crew. Still, I now feel an affinity with the Haverford Township men that I hadn't quite felt before.

Steve was in charge at all times. He directed us where to go, kept tabs on us, and kept the truck moving ahead so that we never had far to walk once we got our loads from the backyards to the street. This has been his route for well over a year and he knows every house on the route well. (We are the only crew working this part of town. The other trucks from Liberty Refuse go to other towns in this county, and the part of Dryden lying across the county line is serviced by some other firm.) He had scared me with that talk early in the morning about keeping up with him. A look at his muscles and the way he moved told me I was in for a test. But, as the day went by, I saw I didn't have to be afraid of him. I was not as fast as he or Kenny, but he never once got on my back. He set an example instead.

Two mysteries about the job were cleared up for me on this first day. One was where we could have lunch. The answer to that one was that we didn't have any. We worked straight through until the route was done. Then we drove back to the yard, punched the clock, and went home to eat as we chose. I was glad my breakfast was big.

The other mystery was about taking care of bodily functions at work. Dryden is strictly residential. There are no gas stations on our route and no cafés. There are woods at the end of a few streets but they're spaced far apart. There didn't seem to be householders who were about to invite us into their homes. But happily we carried our own facilities with us. Next time I see a trashman jump into the open space where the garbage goes at the back of the truck and seem to stare at the curved metal wall in front of him, I'll know he's not looking for flaws. He's taking a leak.

The Pillow Book
of Sei Shōnagon[2]

Hateful Things

One is in a hurry to leave, but one's visitor keeps chattering away. If it is someone of no importance, one can get rid of him by saying, "You must tell me all about it next time"; but, should it be the sort of visitor whose presence commands one's best behavior, the situation is hateful indeed.

One finds that a hair has got caught in the stone on which one is rubbing one's inkstick, or again that gravel is lodged in the inkstick, making a nasty, grating sound.

One is just about to be told some interesting piece of news when a baby starts crying.

A flight of crows circle about with loud caws.

An admirer has come on a clandestine visit, but a dog catches sight of him and starts barking. One feels like killing the beast.

One has gone to bed and is about to doze off when a mosquito appears, announcing himself in a reedy voice. One can actually feel the wind made by his wings and, slight though it is, one finds it hateful in the extreme.

One is telling a story about old times when someone breaks in with a little detail that he happens to know, implying that one's own version is inaccurate — disgusting behavior!

Very hateful is a mouse that scurries all over the place.

Some children have called at one's house. One makes a great fuss of them and gives them toys to play with. The children become accustomed to this treatment and start to come regularly, forcing their way into one's inner rooms and scattering one's furnishings and possessions. Hateful!

A man with whom one is having an affair keeps singing the praises of some woman he used to know. Even if it is a thing of the past, this can be very annoying. How much more so if he is still seeing the woman! (Yet sometimes I find that it is not as unpleasant as all that.)

---

[2] Perhaps the most marvelous of all journals is the one kept about a thousand years ago by Sei Shōnagon, a Japanese woman who served for some ten years as lady-in-waiting to an empress. Presumably she wrote most of these entries before going to bed, hence the title: *The Pillow Book of Sei Shōnagon*. We give a few selections, translated by Ivan Morris.

A lover who is leaving at dawn announces that he has to find his fan and his paper. "I know I put them somewhere last night," he says. Since it is pitch dark, he gropes about the room, bumping into the furniture and muttering, "Strange! Where on earth can they be?" Finally he discovers the objects. He thrusts the paper into the breast of his robe with a great rustling sound; then he snaps open his fan and busily fans away with it. Only now is he ready to take his leave. What charmless behavior! "Hateful" is an understatement.

Equally disagreeable is the man who, when leaving in the middle of the night, takes care to fasten the cord of his headdress. This is quite unnecessary; he could perfectly well put it gently on his head without tying the cord. And why must he spend time adjusting his cloak or hunting costume? Does he really think someone may see him at this time of night and criticize him for not being impeccably dressed?

A good lover will behave as elegantly at dawn as at any other time. He drags himself out of bed with a look of dismay on his face. The lady urges him on: "Come, my friend, it's getting light. You don't want anyone to find you here." He gives a deep sigh, as if to say that the night has not been nearly long enough and that it is agony to leave. Once up, he does not instantly pull on his trousers. Instead he comes close to the lady and whispers whatever was left unsaid during the night. Even when he is dressed, he still lingers, vaguely pretending to be fastening his sash.

Presently he raises the lattice, and the two lovers stand together by the side door while he tells her how he dreads the coming day, which will keep them apart; then he slips away. The lady watches him go, and this moment of parting will remain among her most charming memories.

Indeed, one's attachment to a man depends largely on the elegance of his leave-taking. When he jumps out of bed, scurries about the room, tightly fastens his trouser-sash, rolls up the sleeves of his Court cloak, overrobe, or hunting costume, stuffs his belongings into the breast of his robe and then briskly secures the outer sash — one really begins to hate him.

Rare Things

People who live together and still manage to behave with reserve towards each other. However much these people may try to hide their weaknesses, they usually fail.

To avoid getting ink stains on the notebook into which one is copying stories, poems, or the like. If it is a very fine notebook, one takes the greatest care not to make a blot; yet somehow one never seems to succeed.

One has given some silk to the fuller and, when he sends it back, it is so beautiful that one cries out in admiration.

Enviable People

One has been learning a sacred text by heart; but, though one has gone over the same passage again and again, one still recites it haltingly and keeps on forgetting words. Meanwhile one hears other people, not only clerics (for whom it is natural) but ordinary men and women, reciting such passages without the slightest effort, and one wonders when one will ever be able to come up to their standard.

When one is ill in bed and hears people walking about, laughing loudly and chatting away as if they did not have a care in the world, how enviable they seem!

SOME JOURNAL ENTRIES
BY STUDENTS

Helpless! I remember when I used to stand on a kitchen chair with both my arms raised in the air so that my grandmother could dress me for school. I was so spoiled that the only muscles I moved were in my mouth. Those were the days when breakfast tasted good.

The Rat: "You gap-legged, sky-scraping, knock-kneed, pot-bellied, flat-chested, slack-behind, wooly-headed hollow sculpture of a man!" . . . I died laughing!

I divorce myself from my feelings and immerse myself in my obligations.

It is difficult to believe that not understanding a physics problem isn't the worst problem in the world.

The rain can be heard on the roof and I feel a steady sprinkling through the open window. Trucks are loading and unloading down in the courtyard. Cars beeping as they turn the blind corner. Distraction . . .

The trees swish outside, the curtains inside. . . .

Anticipating something is like falling off a cliff and never reaching the bottom.

63rd Street Rap: What's happening? Ain't nothing to it. What's going on at the Woods? Everything is Everything. Been to any sets lately? Yeah it was on 64th street last night. We partied back. Wish I could have made it. Well times will get better they can't get no worse. Right On! Right On!

Translation: Hello. How are you. I am fine. What activities are taking place at your high school named Englewood? There are many exciting activities taking place at my high school. Have you attended any parties recently? Yes I attended a party on 64th street last night. We had a very nice time. I wish I could have attended the party also. Well you will probably be fortunate enough to attend the next party, there is no logical reason for you not to. That is correct, that is correct.

School begins at 8:40 and ends at 2:00 the next morning. What did you say about revising for conciseness?

It seems that much of my daily writing consists of unresolved questions to which I am still seeking answers. Every answer that I do find serves to ask more questions. Finding answers to my questions creates such a feeling of accomplishment within me that I feel as though I could burst with happiness. However questions that remain unresolved for any length of time begin to puzzle me more and more. I find myself thinking about them at the oddest and most inconvenient times . . . sitting in French class. . . .

PART FOUR

Additional
Readings

Stranger in the Village

James Baldwin

From all available evidence no black man had ever set foot in this tiny Swiss village before I came. I was told before arriving that I would probably be a "sight" for the village; I took this to mean that people of my complexion were rarely seen in Switzerland, and also that city people are always something of a "sight" outside of the city. It did not occur to me — possibly because I am an American — that there could be people anywhere who had never seen a Negro.

It is a fact that cannot be explained on the basis of the inaccessibility of the village. The village is very high, but it is only four hours from Milan and three hours from Lausanne. It is true that it is virtually unknown. Few people making plans for a holiday would elect to come here. On the other hand, the villagers are able, presumably, to come and go as they please — which they do: to another town at the foot of the mountain, with a population of approximately five thousand, the nearest place to see a movie or go to the bank. In the village there is no movie house, no bank, no library, no theater; very few radios, one jeep, one station wagon; and at the moment, one typewriter, mine, an invention which the woman next door to me here had never seen. There are about six hundred people living here, all Catholic — I conclude this from the fact that the Catholic church is open all year round, whereas the Protestant chapel, set off on a hill a little removed from the village, is open only in the summertime when the tourists arrive. There are four or five hotels, all closed now, and four or five *bistros*,[3] of which, however, only two do any business during the winter. These two do not do a great deal, for life in the village seems to end around nine or ten o'clock. There are a few stores, butcher, baker, *épicerie*,[4] a hardware store, and a money-changer — who cannot change travelers' checks, but must send them down to the bank, an operation which takes two or three days. There is something called the *Ballet Haus*, closed in the winter and used for God knows what, certainly not ballet, during the summer. There seems to be only one schoolhouse in the village, and this for the quite young children; I suppose this to mean that their older brothers and sisters at some

[3] Editors' note: French for "taverns" or "bars."

[4] Editors' note: French for "grocery," but more properly translated as "grocer" in this context.

point descend from these mountains in order to complete their education — possibly, again, to the town just below. The landscape is absolutely forbidding, mountains towering on all four sides, ice and snow as far as the eye can reach. In this white wilderness, men and women and children move all day, carrying washing, wood, buckets of milk or water, sometimes skiing on Sunday afternoons. All week long boys and young men are to be seen shoveling snow off the rooftops, or dragging wood down from the forest in sleds.

The village's only real attraction, which explains the tourist season, is the hot spring water. A disquietingly high proportion of these tourists are cripples, or semi-cripples, who come year after year — from other parts of Switzerland, usually — to take the waters. This lends the village, at the height of the season, a rather terrifying air of sanctity, as though it were a lesser Lourdes. There is often something beautiful, there is always something awful, in the spectacle of a person who has lost one of his faculties, a faculty he never questioned until it was gone, and who struggles to recover it. Yet people remain people, on crutches or indeed on deathbeds; and wherever I passed, the first summer I was here, among the native villagers or among the lame, a wind passed with me — of astonishment, curiosity, amusement, and outrage. That first summer I stayed two weeks and never intended to return. But I did return in the winter, to work; the village offers, obviously, no distractions whatever and has the further advantage of being extremely cheap. Now it is winter again, a year later, and I am here again. Everyone in the village knows my name, though they scarcely ever use it, knows that I come from America — though, this, apparently, they will never really believe: black men come from Africa — and everyone knows that I am the friend of the son of a woman who was born here, and that I am staying in their chalet. But I remain as much a stranger today as I was the first day I arrived, and the children shout *Neger! Neger!* as I walk along the streets.

It must be admitted that in the beginning I was far too shocked to have any real reaction. In so far as I reacted at all, I reacted by trying to be pleasant — it being a great part of the American Negro's education (long before he goes to school) that he must make people "like" him. This smile-and-the-world-smiles-with-you routine worked about as well in this situation as it had in the situation for which it was designed, which is to say that it did not work at all. No one, after all, can be liked whose human weight and complexity cannot be, or has not been, admitted. My smile was simply another unheard-of phenomenon which allowed them to see my teeth —

they did not, really, see my smile and I began to think that, should I take to snarling, no one would notice any difference. All of the physical characteristics of the Negro which had caused me, in America, a very different and almost forgotten pain were nothing less than miraculous — or infernal — in the eyes of the village people. Some thought my hair was the color of tar, that it had the texture of wire, or the texture of cotton. It was jocularly suggested that I might let it all grow long and make myself a winter coat. If I sat in the sun for more than five minutes some daring creature was certain to come along and gingerly put his fingers on my hair, as though he were afraid of an electric shock, or put his hand on my hand, astonished that the color did not rub off. In all of this, in which it must be conceded there was the charm of genuine wonder and in which there were certainly no element of intentional unkindness, there was yet no suggestion that I was human: I was simply a living wonder.

I knew that they did not mean to be unkind, and I know it now; it is necessary, nevertheless, for me to repeat this to myself each time that I walk out of the chalet. The children who shout *Neger!* have no way of knowing the echoes this sound raises in me. They are brimming with good humor and the more daring swell with pride when I stop to speak with them. Just the same, there are days when I cannot pause and smile, when I have no heart to play with them; when, indeed, I mutter sourly to myself, exactly as I muttered on the streets of a city these children have never seen, when I was no bigger than these children are now: *Your* mother *was a nigger*. Joyce is right about history being a nightmare — but it may be the nightmare from which no one *can* awaken. People are trapped in history and history is trapped in them.

There is a custom in the village — I am told it is repeated in many villages — of "buying" African natives for the purpose of converting them to Christianity. There stands in the church all year round a small box with a slot for money, decorated with a black figurine, and into this box the villagers drop their francs. During the *carnaval* which precedes Lent, two village children have their faces blackened — out of which bloodless darkness their blue eyes shine like ice — and fantastic horsehair wigs are placed on their blond heads; thus disguised, they solicit among the villagers for money for the missionaries in Africa. Between the box in the church and the blackened children, the village "bought" last year six or eight African natives. This was reported to me with pride by the wife of one of the *bistro* owners and I was careful to express astonishment and pleasure at the solicitude shown by the village for the souls of black folks. The *bistro* owner's wife beamed with a pleasure far more genuine than my own and seemed to feel that I might now breathe more easily concerning the souls of at least six of my kinsmen.

I tried not to think of these so lately baptized kinsmen, of the price paid for them, or the peculiar price they themselves would pay, and said nothing about my father, who having taken his own conversion too literally never, at bottom, forgave the white world (which he described as heathen) for having saddled him with a Christ in whom, to judge at least from their treatment of him, they themselves no longer believed. I thought of white men arriving for the first time in an African village, strangers there, as I am a stranger here, and tried to imagine the astounded populace touching their hair and marveling at the color of their skin. But there is a great difference between being the first white man to be seen by Africans and being the first black man to be seen by whites. The white man takes the astonishment as tribute, for he arrives to conquer and to convert the natives, whose inferiority in relation to himself is not even to be questioned; whereas I, without a thought of conquest, find myself among a people whose culture controls me, has even, in a sense, created me, people who have cost me more in anguish and rage than they will ever know, who yet do not even know of my existence. The astonishment with which I might have greeted them, should they have stumbled into my African village a few hundred years ago, might have rejoiced their hearts. But the astonishment with which they greet me today can only poison mine.

And this is so despite everything I may do to feel differently, despite my friendly conversations with the *bistro* owner's wife, despite their three-year-old son who has at last become my friend, despite the *saluts* and *bonsoirs* which I exchange with people as I walk, despite the fact that I know that no individual can be taken to task for what history is doing, or has done. I say that the culture of these people controls me — but they can scarcely be held responsible for European culture. America comes out of Europe, but these people have never seen America, nor have most of them seen more of Europe than the hamlet at the foot of their mountain. Yet they move with an authority which I shall never have; and they regard me, quite rightly, not only as a stranger in their village but as a suspect latecomer, bearing no credentials, to everything they have — however unconsciously — inherited.

For this village, even were it incomparably more remote and incredibly more primitive, is the West, the West onto which I have been so strangely grafted. These people cannot be, from the point of view of power, strangers anywhere in the world; they have made the modern world, in effect, even if they do not know it. The most illiterate among them is related, in a way that I am not, to Dante, Shakespeare, Michelangelo, Aeschylus, Da Vinci, Rembrandt, and Racine; the cathedral at Chartres says something to them which it cannot say to me, as indeed would New York's Empire State Building, should anyone here ever see it. Out of their hymns and dances come Beethoven and Bach. Go back a few centuries and they are in their full glory — but I am in Africa, watching the conquerors arrive.

The rage of the disesteemed is personally fruitless, but it is also absolutely inevitable; this rage, so generally discounted, so little understood even among the people whose daily bread it is, is one of the things that makes history. Rage can only with difficulty, and never entirely, be brought under the domination of the intelligence and is therefore not susceptible to any arguments whatever. This is a fact which ordinary representatives of the *Herrenvolk,*[5] having never felt this rage and being unable to imagine, quite fail to understand. Also, rage cannot be hidden, it can only be dissembled. This dissembling deludes the thoughtless, and strengthens rage and adds, to rage, contempt. There are, no doubt, as many ways of coping with the resulting complex of tensions as there are black men in the world, but no black man can hope ever to be entirely liberated from this internal warfare — rage, dissembling, and contempt having inevitably accompanied his first realization of the power of white men. What is crucial here is that, since white men represent in the black man's world so heavy a weight, white men have for black men a reality which is reciprocal; and hence all black men have toward all white men an attitude which is designed, really, either to rob the white man of the jewel of his naiveté, or else to make it cost him dear.

The black man insists, by whatever means he finds at his disposal, that the white man cease to regard him as an exotic rarity and recognize him as a human being. This is a very charged and difficult moment, for there is a great deal of will power involved in the white man's naïveté. Most people are not naturally reflective any more than they are naturally malicious, and the white man prefers to keep the black man at a certain human remove because it is easier for him thus to preserve his simplicity and avoid being called to account for crimes committed by his forefathers, or his neighbors. He is inescap-

---

[5] Editors' note: German for "master race."

ably aware, nevertheless, that he is in a better position in the world than black men are, nor can he quite put to death the suspicion that he is hated by black men therefore. He does not wish to be hated, neither does he wish to change places, and at this point in his uneasiness he can scarcely avoid having recourse to those legends which white men have created about black men, the most usual effect of which is that the white man finds himself enmeshed, so to speak, in his own language which describes hell, as well as the attributes which lead one to hell, as being as black as night.

Every legend, moreover, contains its residuum of truth, and the root function of language is to control the universe by describing it. It is of quite considerable significance that black men remain, in the imagination, and in overwhelming numbers in fact, beyond the disciplines of salvation; and this despite the fact that the West has been "buying" African natives for centuries. There is, I should hazard, an instantaneous necessity to be divorced from this so visibly unsaved stranger, in whose heart, moreover, one cannot guess what dreams of vengeance are being nourished; and, at the same time, there are few things on earth more attractive than the idea of the unspeakable liberty which is allowed the unredeemed. When, beneath the black mask, a human being begins to make himself felt one cannot escape a certain awful wonder as to what kind of human being it is. What one's imagination makes of other people is dictated, of course, by the laws of one's own personality and it is one of the ironies of black-white relations that, by means of what the white man imagines the black man to be, the black man is enabled to know who the white man is.

I have said, for example, that I am as much a stranger in this village today as I was the first summer I arrived, but this is not quite true. The villagers wonder less about the texture of my hair than they did then, and wonder rather more about me. And the fact that their wonder now exists on another level is reflected in their attitudes and in their eyes. There are the children who make those delightful, hilarious, sometimes astonishingly grave overtures of friendship in the unpredictable fashion of children; other children, having been taught that the devil is a black man, scream in genuine anguish as I approach. Some of the older women never pass without a friendly greeting, never pass, indeed, if it seems that they will be able to engage me in conversation; other women look down or look away or rather contemptuously smirk. Some of the men drink with me and suggest that I learn how to ski — partly, I gather, because they cannot imagine what I would look like on skis — and want to know if I am married, and ask questions about my *métier*. [6] But some of the men have accused *le sale negre* [7] — behind my back — of stealing wood and there is already in the eyes of some of them that peculiar, intent paranoiac malevolence which one sometimes surprises in the eyes of American white men when, out walking with their Sunday girl, they see a Negro male approach.

There is a dreadful abyss between the streets of this village and the streets of the city in which I was born, between the children who shout *Neger!* today and those who shouted *Nigger!* yesterday — the abyss is experience, the American experience. The syllable hurled behind me today expresses, above all, wonder: I am a stranger here. But I am not a stranger in America and the same syllable riding on the American air expresses the war my presence has occasioned in the American soul.

For this village brings home to me this fact: that there was a day, and not really a very distant day, when Americans were scarcely Americans at all but discontented Europeans, facing a great uncon-quered continent and strolling, say, into a marketplace and seeing black men for the first time. The shock this spectacle afforded is suggested, surely, by the promptness with which they decided that these black men were not really men but cattle. It is true that the necessity on the part of the settlers of the New World of reconciling their moral assumptions with the fact — and the necessity — of slavery enhanced immensely the charm of this idea, and it is also true that this idea expresses, with a truly American bluntness, the attitude which to varying extents all masters have had toward all slaves.

But between all former slaves and slave-owners and the drama which begins for Americans over three hundred years ago at James-town, there are at least two differences to be observed. The Ameri-can Negro slave could not suppose, for one thing, as slaves in past epochs had supposed and often done, that he would ever be able to wrest the power from his master's hands. This was a supposition which the modern era, which was to bring about such vast changes in the aims and dimensions of power, put to death; it only begins, in unprecedented fashion, and with dreadful implications, to be resur-rected today. But even had this supposition persisted with undi-minished force, the American Negro slave could not have used it to lend his condition dignity, for the reason that this supposition rests on another: that the slave in exile yet remains related to his past, has

[6] Editors' note: French for "profession."
[7] Editors' note: French for "the dirty black man."

some means — if only in memory — of revering and sustaining the forms of his former life, is able, in short, to maintain his identity.

This was not the case with the American Negro slave. He is unique among the black men of the world in that his past was taken from him, almost literally, at one blow. One wonders what on earth the first slave found to say to the first dark child he bore. I am told that there are Haitians able to trace their ancestry back to African kings, but any American Negro wishing to go back so far will find his journey through time abruptly arrested by the signature on the bill of sale which served as the entrance paper for his ancestor. At the time — to say nothing of the circumstances — of the enslavement of the captive black man who was to become the American Negro, there was not the remotest possibility that he would ever take power from his master's hands. There was no reason to suppose that his situation would ever change, nor was there, shortly, anything to indicate that his situation had ever been different. It was his necessity, in the words of E. Franklin Frazier, to find a "motive for living under American culture or die." The identity of the American Negro comes out of this extreme situation, and the evolution of this identity was a source of the most intolerable anxiety in the minds and the lives of his masters.

For the history of the American Negro is unique also in this: that the question of his humanity, and of his rights therefore as a human being, became a burning one for several generations of Americans, so burning a question that it ultimately became one of those used to divide the nation. It is out of this argument that the venom of the epithet *Nigger!* is derived. It is an argument which Europe has never had, and hence Europe quite sincerely fails to understand how or why the argument arose in the first place, why its effects are frequently disastrous and always so unpredictable, why it refuses until today to be entirely settled. Europe's black possessions remained — and do remain — in Europe's colonies, at which remove they represented no threat whatever to European identity. If they posed any problem at all for the European conscience, it was a problem which remained comfortingly abstract: in effect, the black man, as a *man*, did not exist for Europe. But in America, even as a slave, he was an inescapable part of the general social fabric and no American could escape having an attitude toward him. Americans attempt until today to make an abstraction of the Negro, but the very nature of these abstractions reveals the tremendous effects the presence of the Negro has had on the American character.

When one considers the history of the Negro in America it is of the greatest importance to recognize that the moral beliefs of a person, or a people, are never really as tenuous as life — which is not moral — very often causes them to appear; these create for them a frame of reference and a necessary hope, the hope being that when life has done its worst they will be enabled to rise above themselves and to triumph over life. Life would scarcely be bearable if this hope did not exist. Again, even when the worst has been said, to betray a belief is not by any means to have put oneself beyond its power; the betrayal of a belief is not the same thing as ceasing to believe. If this were not so there would be no moral standards in the world at all. Yet one must also recognize that morality is based on ideas and that all ideas are dangerous — dangerous because ideas can only lead to action and where the action leads no man can say. And dangerous in this respect: that confronted with the impossibility of remaining faithful to one's beliefs, and the equal impossibility of becoming free of them, one can be driven to the most inhuman excesses. The ideas on which American beliefs are based are not, though Americans often seem to think so, ideas which originated in America. They came out of Europe. And the establishment of democracy on the American continent was scarcely as radical a break with the past as was the necessity, which Americans faced, of broadening this concept to include black men.

This was, literally, a hard necessity. It was impossible, for one thing, for Americans to abandon their beliefs, not only because these beliefs alone seemed able to justify the sacrifices they had endured and the blood that they had spilled, but also because these beliefs afforded them their only bulwark against a moral chaos as absolute as the physical chaos of the continent it was their destiny to conquer. But in the situation in which Americans found themselves, these beliefs threatened an idea, which, whether or not one likes to think so, is the very warp and woof of the heritage of the West, the idea of white supremacy.

Americans have made themselves notorious by the shrillness and the brutality with which they have insisted on this idea, but they did not invent it; and it has escaped the world's notice that those very excesses of which Americans have been guilty imply a certain, unprecedented uneasiness over the idea's life and power, if not, indeed, the idea's validity. The idea of white supremacy rests simply on the fact that white men are the creators of civilization (the present civilization, which is the only one that matters; all previous civilizations are simply "contributions" to our own) and are therefore civilization's guardians and defenders. Thus it was impossible for

Americans to accept the black man as one of themselves, for to do so was to jeopardize their status as white men. But not so to accept him was to deny his human reality, his human weight and complexity, and the strain of denying the overwhelmingly undeniable forced Americans into rationalizations so fantastic that they approached the pathological.

At the root of the American Negro problem is the necessity of the American white man to find a way of living with the Negro in order to be able to live with himself. And the history of this problem can be reduced to the means used by Americans — lynch law and law, segregation and legal acceptance, terrorization and concession — either to come to terms with this necessity, or to find a way around it, or (most usually) to find a way of doing both these things at once. The resulting spectacle, at once foolish and dreadful, led someone to make the quite accurate observation that "the Negro-in-America is a form of insanity which overtakes white men."

In this long battle, a battle by no means finished, the unforeseeable effects of which will be felt by many future generations, the white man's motive was the protection of his identity; the black man was motivated by the need to establish an identity. And despite the terrorization which the Negro in America endured and endures sporadically until today, despite the cruel and totally inescapable ambivalence of his status in his country, the battle for his identity has long ago been won. He is not a visitor to the West, but a citizen there, an American; as American as the Americans who despise him, the Americans who fear him, the Americans who love him — the Americans who became less than themselves, or rose to be greater than themselves by virtue of the fact that the challenge he represented was inescapable. He is perhaps the only black man in the world whose relationship to white men is more terrible, more subtle, and more meaningful than the relationship of bitter possessed to uncertain possessors. His survival depended, and his development depends, on his ability to turn his peculiar status in the Western world to his own advantage and, it may be, to the very great advantage of that world. It remains for him to fashion out of his experience that which will give him sustenance, and a voice.

The cathedral at Chartres, I have said, says something to the people of this village which it cannot say to me; but it is important to understand that this cathedral says something to me which it cannot say to them. Perhaps they are struck by the power of the spires, the glory of the windows; but they have known God, after all, longer than I have known him, and in a different way, and I am terrified by the slippery bottomless well to be found in the crypt, down which heretics were hurled to death, and by the obscene, inescapable gargoyles jutting out of the stone and seeming to say that God and the devil can never be divorced. I doubt that the villagers think of the devil when they face a cathedral because they have never been identified with the devil. But I must accept the status which myth, if nothing else, gives me in the West before I can hope to change the myth.

Yet, if the American Negro has arrived at his identity by virtue of the absoluteness of his estrangement from his past, American white men still nourish the illusion that there is some means of recovering the European innocence, of returning to a state in which black men do not exist. This is one of the greatest errors Americans can make. The identity they fought so hard to protect has, by virtue of that battle, undergone a change: Americans are as unlike any other white people in the world as it is possible to be. I do not think, for example, that it is too much to suggest that the American vision of the world — which allows so little reality, generally speaking, for any of the darker forces in human life, which tends until today to paint moral issues in glaring black and white — owes a great deal to the battle waged by Americans to maintain between themselves and black men a human separation which could not be bridged. It is only now beginning to be borne in on us — very faintly, it must be admitted, very slowly, and very much against our will — that this vision of the world is dangerously inaccurate, and perfectly useless. For it protects our moral high-mindedness at the terrible expense of weakening our grasp of reality. People who shut their eyes to reality simply invite their own destruction, and anyone who insists on remaining in a state of innocence long after that innocence is dead turns himself into a monster.

The time has come to realize that the interracial drama acted out on the American continent has not only created a new black man, it has created a new white man, too. No road whatever will lead Americans back to the simplicity of this European village where white men still have the luxury of looking on me as a stranger. I am not, really, a stranger any longer for any American alive. One of the things that distinguishes Americans from other people is that no other people has ever been so deeply involved in the lives of black men, and vice versa. This fact, faced, with all its implications, it can be seen that the history of the American Negro problem is not merely shameful, it is also something of an achievement. For even when the worst has been said, it must also be added that the perpetual challenge posed by this problem was always, somehow, perpetually met. It is precisely this black-white experience which may prove of indispensable value to us in the world we face today. This world is white no longer, and it will never be white again.

QUESTIONS

1. Why does Baldwin establish at the beginning of the essay, and at some length, the Swiss village's isolation?

2. Explain in your own words the chief differences, according to Baldwin, between the experience of a white man arriving as a stranger in an African village, and a black man arriving as a stranger in a white village.

3. Baldwin's densely packed, highly allusive sentences often require close study. Try to paraphrase (that is, rewrite in your words) or to explain the meaning of the following sentences (pages 442–43):

   a. "For this village, even were it incomparably more remote and incredibly more primitive, is the West, the West onto which I have been so strangely grafted."

   b. "The rage of the disesteemed is personally fruitless, but it is also absolutely inevitable; this rage, so generally discounted, so little understood even among the people whose daily bread it is, is one of the things that makes history."

4. Why, according to Baldwin, have whites created legends about blacks? What legends does Baldwin refer to in this essay?

5. On page 451 Baldwin refers to American beliefs that were threatened by the idea of white supremacy. What were those beliefs?

6. Baldwin wrote "Stranger in the Village" in the early 1950s. Does his conclusion still ring true? Explain.

Mayhem in the Industrial Paradise

Wendell Berry

> . . . they have made my pleasant field a
> desolate wilderness. . . .
>
> — JEREMIAH 12:10

I have just spent two days flying over the coal fields of both eastern and western Kentucky, looking at the works of the strip miners. Several times before, I had driven and walked to look at strip mines, mainly in the eastern part of the state, but those earlier, ground-level experiences did not prepare me at all for what I saw from the air. In scale and desolation — and, I am afraid, in duration — this industrial vandalism can be compared only with the desert badlands of the West. The damage has no human scale. It is a geologic upheaval. In some eastern Kentucky counties, for mile after mile after mile, the land has been literally hacked to pieces. Whole mountain tops have been torn off and cast into the valleys. And the ruin of human life and possibility is commensurate with the ruin of the land. It is a scene from the Book of Revelation. It is a domestic Vietnam.

So far as I know, there are only two philosophies of land use. One holds that the earth is the Lord's, or it holds that the earth belongs to those yet to be born as well as to those now living. The present owners, according to this view, only have the land in trust, both for all the living who are dependent on it now, and for the unborn who will be dependent on it in time to come. The model of this sort of use is a good farm — a farm that, by the return of wastes and by other safeguards, preserves the land in production without diminishing its ability to produce. The standard of this sort of land use is fertility, which preserves the interest of the future.

The other philosophy is that of exploitation, which holds that the interest of the present owner is the only interest to be considered. The standard, according to this view, is profit, and it is assumed that whatever is profitable is good. The most fanatical believers in the rule of profit are the strip miners. The earth, these people would have us believe, is not the Lord's, nor do the unborn have any share in it. It belongs, instead, to rich organizations with names like Peabody, Kentucky River Coal, Elkhorn Coal, National Steel, Bethlehem Steel, Occidental Petroleum, The Berwind Corporation, Tennessee Valley Authority, Chesapeake & Ohio, Ford Motor Company, and many others. And the earth, they would say, is theirs not just for a time, but forever, and in proof of their claim they do not hesitate to destroy it forever — that is, if it is profitable to do so, and earth-destruction has so far been exceedingly profitable to these organizations.

The gospel of the strip miners is the "broad form deed," under which vast acreages of coal rights were bought up for as little as twenty-five and fifty cents an acre before modern strip-mine technology ever had been conceived. The broad form deed holds that the coal may be taken out "in any and every manner that may be deemed necessary or convenient for mining. . . ." Kentucky is one of the few coal states that still honor the broad form deed. In Kentucky, under the sanction of this deed, the strip miners continue to ravage other people's private property. They have overturned or covered up thousands of acres of farm and forest land; they have destroyed the homes and the burial grounds of the people; they have polluted thousands of miles of streams with silt and mine acid; they have cast the overburden of the mines into the water courses and into the public roads. Their limits are technological, not moral. They have made it plain that they will stop at nothing to secure the profit, which is their only motive. And in Kentucky they have been aided and abetted at every turn by lawmakers, judges, and other public officials who are too cowardly or too greedy to act in the interest of those they are sworn to protect. Though the violations of the inadequate strip-mine regulations passed by the legislature have been numerous and well publicized, the regulations have been weakly enforced.

If the model of good land use is to be found in a good farm, then it is a strange sort of farming indeed that is practiced by these strip miners, whose herds are not cattle eating grass, but machines devouring the earth. That sounds fantastical, but then strip mining is an industry *based* upon fantasy. It proceeds upon the assumption that there is no law of gravity, that no heavy rains will fall, that water and mud and rock will not move downhill, that money is as fertile as topsoil, that the wealthy do not ultimately share the same dependences and the same fate as the poor, that the oppressed do not turn against their oppressors — that, in other words, there are no natural or moral or social consequences. Such are the luxuries that our society affords to the warlords of the exploitive industries.

People who live nearer to the results of strip mining know better. Those whose homes and belongings have been destroyed, or who live beneath the spoil banks, or who inhabit the flood plains of mutilated streams and rivers, or who have been driven into ruin and exile — and there are now many thousands of them — they know that the costs are inconceivably greater than any shown on coal-company ledgers, and they are keeping their own accounts. They know that the figment of legality that sanctions strip mining is contrary to the laws of nature and of morality and of history. And they know that in such a contradiction is the seed of social catastrophe.

The most vicious fantasy of all is the endlessly publicized notion that the net profit of the coal companies somehow represents the net profit of the whole society. Historically, however, the enrichment of

the coal interests in Kentucky has always involved the impoverish-
ment of the people of the mining regions. And of all methods of
mining, strip mining is the most enriching to the rich and the most
impoverishing to the poor; it has fewer employees and more victims.
The net profit is net only to the coal companies, only on the basis of
an annual accounting. The corporate profit is reckoned on so short a
term. But the public expenditure that supports this private profit is
long-term; the end of it is not now foreseeable. By the time all the
reclaimable mined lands are reclaimed, and all the social and environmental damages accounted for, strip mining will be found to
have been the most extravagantly subsidized adventure ever undertaken.

An estimate of the public meaning of strip-mine profits may be
made from the following sentences by James Branscome in the New
York *Times* of December 12, 1971: "The Corps of Engineers has
estimated . . . that it would cost the public $26-million to restore
the extensively strip-mined Coal River watershed in West Virginia.
This is an amount approximately equal to the private profit taken by
the mining companies from the watershed." But even this may be
too limited an accounting. It does not consider the environmental
damage, or the property damage, that may have occurred outside the
boundaries of the immediate watershed between the opening of the
coal seam and the completion of reclamation. It does not attempt to
compute the cost of what may have been the permanent degradation
of the appearance and the fertility of the land. Nor does it consider
the economic consequences of the social upheaval that must always
accompany an upheaval of the environment. There is, then, every
reason to believe that the large net profit of a strip-mine company
will prove to be a large net loss to society.

This, as all Kentuckians should be aware, is largely the responsibility of absentee owners. Of the thirty-three largest owners of
mineral rights in the Kentucky coal fields, as recently listed by the
Courier-Journal, only two are based in the state. But even those
owners who live in the state are absentee owners in the strict sense of
the term: they do not live with the consequences of what they do. As
exploitive industrialists have done from the beginning, they live
apart, in enclaves of the well-to-do, where they are neither offended
nor immediately threatened by the ugliness and the dangers that they
so willingly impose upon others. It is safe, I think, to say that not
many coal-company executives and stockholders are living on the
slopes beneath the spoil banks of their mines; not many of them have
had their timber uprooted and their farms buried by avalanches of

overburden; not many of them have had their water supply polluted by mine acid, or had their houses torn from the foundations by man-made landslides; not many of them see from their doorsteps the death of the land of their forefathers and the wreckage of their own birthright; not many of them see in the faces of their wives and children the want and the grief and the despair with which the local people subsidize the profits of strip mining. On the contrary, the worries of the coal companies are limited strictly to coal. When the coal is gone they do not care what is left. The inescapable conclusion is that Kentucky has been made a colony of the coal companies, who practice here a mercantilism as heartless and greedy as any in history.

In this new year[8] the state's lawmakers have once again assembled in Frankfort. Again they have the opportunity to put a stop to this awful destruction, and to assure to the state the benefits of its own wealth, and to give to the people of the coal fields the same protections of the law that are enjoyed by people everywhere else. If the men in power will do these things that are so clearly right and just, they will earn the gratitude of the living and of the unborn. If they will not do them, they will be infamous, and will be unworthy of the respect of any honest citizen.[9]

Remembering the new deserts of this once bountiful and beautiful land, my mind has gone back repeatedly to those Bible passages that are haunted by the memory of good land laid waste, and by fear of the human suffering that such destruction has always caused. Our own time has come to be haunted by the same thoughts, the same sense of a fertile homeland held in the contempt of greed, sold out, and destroyed. Jeremiah would find this evil of ours bitterly familiar:

> I brought you into a fruitful land
> > to enjoy its fruit and the goodness of it;
> > but when you entered upon it you defiled it
> > and made the home I gave you loathsome.

The damages of strip mining are justified in the name of electrical power. We need electrical power, the argument goes, to run our factories, to heat and light and air-condition our homes, to run our household appliances, our TV sets, our children's toys, and our mechanical toothbrushes. And we must have more and more electricity because we are going to have more and more gadgets that will make us more and more comfortable. This, of course, is the reason-

---

[8] 1972 [Berry's note].

[9] They did not do them, and they are as unworthy of respect as I said they would be [Berry's note].

ing of a man eating himself to death. We have to begin to distinguish
between the uses that are necessary and those that are frivolous.
Though it is the last remedy that would occur to a glutton or a
coal company, we must cut down on our consumption — that is,
our destruction — of the essential energies of our planet. We must
use these energies less and with much greater care. We must see the
difference between the necessity of warmth in winter and the luxury
of air conditioning in the summer, between light to read or work by
and those "security lights" with which we are attempting to light the
whole outdoors, between an electric sewing machine and an electric
toothbrush. Immediate comfort, we must say to the glutton, is no
guarantee of a long life; too much now is, rather, a guarantee of too
little later on. Our comfort will be paid for by someone else's
distress. "We dig coal to light your tree," said a recent advertisement
of the coal industry. That, we must realize, is not a Christmas
greeting, but a warning of our implication in an immitigable evil.

In the name of Paradise, Kentucky, and in its desecrations by the
strip miners, there is no shallow irony. It was named Paradise
because, like all of Kentucky in the early days, it was recognized as a
garden, fertile and abounding and lovely; some pioneer saw that it
was good. ("Heaven," said one of the frontier preachers, "is a
Kentucky of a place.") But the strip miners have harrowed Paradise,
as they would harrow heaven itself were they to find coal there.
Where the little town once stood in the shade of its trees by the
riverbank, there is now a blackened desert. We have despised our
greatest gift, the inheritance of a fruitful land. And for such despite
— for the destruction of Paradise — there will be hell to pay.

QUESTIONS

1. Analyze Berry's use of sentences of varying length in his first
   paragraph. Why are some sentences shorter than others?
2. In his first two sentences Berry uses "I" three times, and "me"
   once. Do you feel that he is talking too much about himself?
3. Analyze the development of the first paragraph. Notice, for
   example, that in the middle of the paragraph Berry says, "It is a
   geologic upheaval," and at the end of the paragraph he says "It is
   a domestic Vietnam." (The essay was published in 1972.) Do
   you think that if he were writing the paragraph today he might
   put his sentences into a different order?
4. What persuasive devices does Berry use throughout the essay?

Joey: A "Mechanical Boy"
Bruno Bettelheim

Joey, when we began our work with him, was a mechanical boy. He functioned as if by remote control, run by machines of his own powerfully creative fantasy. Not only did he himself believe that he was a machine but, more remarkably, he created this impression in others. Even while he performed actions that are intrinsically human, they never appeared to be other than machine-started and executed. On the other hand, when the machine was not working we had to concentrate on recollecting his presence, for he seemed not to exist. A human body that functions as if it were a machine and a machine that duplicates human functions are equally fascinating and frightening. Perhaps they are so uncanny because they remind us that the human body can operate without a human spirit, that body can exist without soul. And Joey was a child who had been robbed of his humanity.

Not every child who possesses a fantasy world is possessed by it. Normal children may retreat into realms of imaginary glory or magic powers, but they are easily recalled from these excursions. Disturbed children are not always able to make the return trip; they remain withdrawn, prisoners of the inner world of delusion and fantasy. In many ways Joey presented a classic example of this state of infantile autism.

At the Sonia Shankman Orthogenic School of the University of Chicago it is our function to provide a therapeutic environment in which such children may start life over again. I have previously described the rehabilitation of another of our patients ("Schizophrenic Art: A Case Study"; *Scientific American,* April 1952). This time I shall concentrate upon the illness, rather than the treatment. In any age, when the individual has escaped into a delusional world, he has usually fashioned it from bits and pieces of the world at hand. Joey, in his time and world, chose the machine and froze himself in its image. His story has a general relevance to the understanding of emotional development in a machine age.

Joey's delusion is not uncommon among schizophrenic children today. He wanted to be rid of his unbearable humanity, to become completely automatic. He so nearly succeeded in attaining this goal that he could almost convince others, as well as himself, of his mechanical character. The descriptions of autistic children in the literature take for their point of departure and comparison the normal or abnormal human being. To do justice to Joey I would have to compare him simultaneously to a most inept infant and a highly complex piece of machinery. Often we had to force ourselves by a conscious act of will to realize that Joey was a child. Again and again his acting-out of his delusions froze our own ability to respond as human beings.

During Joey's first weeks with us we would watch absorbedly as this at once fragile-looking and imperious nine-year-old went about his mechanical existence. Entering the dining room, for example, he would string an imaginary wire from his "energy source" — an imaginary electric outlet — to the table. There he "insulated" himself with paper napkins and finally plugged himself in. Only then could Joey eat, for he firmly believed that the "current" ran his ingestive apparatus. So skillful was the pantomime that one had to look twice to be sure there was neither wire not outlet nor plug. Children and members of our staff spontaneously avoided stepping on the "wires" for fear of interrupting what seemed the source of his very life.

For long periods of time, when his "machinery" was idle, he would sit so quietly that he would disappear from the focus of the most conscientious observation. Yet in the next moment he might be "working" and the center of our captivated attention. Many times a day he would turn himself on and shift noisily through a sequence of higher and higher gears until he "exploded," screaming "Crash, crash!" and hurling items from his ever-present apparatus — radio tubes, light bulbs, even motors or, lacking these, any handy breakable object. (Joey had an astonishing knack for snatching bulbs and tubes unobserved.) As soon as the object thrown had shattered, he would cease his screaming and wild jumping and retire to mute, motionless nonexistence.

Our maids, inured to difficult children, were exceptionally attentive to Joey; they were apparently moved by his extreme infantile fragility, so strangely coupled with megalomaniacal superiority. Occasionally some of the apparatus he fixed to his bed to "live him" during his sleep would fall down in disarray. This machinery he contrived from masking tape, cardboard, wire and other paraphernalia. Usually the maids would pick up such things and leave them on a table for the children to find, or disregard them entirely. But Joey's machine they carefully restored: "Joey must have the carburetor so he can breathe." Similarly they were on the alert to pick up and preserve the motors that ran him during the day and the exhaust pipes through which he exhaled.

How had Joey become a human machine? From intensive interviews with his parents we learned that the process had begun even before birth. Schizophrenia often results from parental rejection, sometimes combined ambivalently with love. Joey, on the other hand, had been completely ignored.

"I never knew I was pregnant," his mother said, meaning that she had already excluded Joey from her consciousness. His birth, she said, "did not make any difference." Joey's father, a rootless draftee in the wartime civilian army, was equally unready for parenthood. So, of course, are many young couples. Fortunately most such parents lose their indifference upon the baby's birth. But not Joey's parents. "I did not want to see or nurse him," his mother declared. "I had no feeling of actual dislike — I simply didn't want to take care of him." For the first three months of his life Joey "cried most of the time." A colicky baby, he was kept on a rigid four-hour feeding schedule, was not touched unless necessary and was never cuddled or played with. The mother, preoccupied with herself, usually left Joey alone in the crib or playpen during the day. The father discharged his frustrations by punishing Joey when the child cried at night.

Soon the father left for overseas duty, and the mother took Joey, now a year and a half old, to live with her at her parents' home. On his arrival the grandparents noticed that ominous changes had occurred in the child. Strong and healthy at birth, he had become frail and irritable; a responsive baby, he had become remote and inaccessible. When he began to master speech, he talked only to himself. At an early date he became preoccupied with machinery, including an old electric fan which he could take apart and put together again with surprising deftness.

Joey's mother impressed us with a fey quality that expressed her insecurity, her detachment from the world and her low physical vitality. We were struck especially by her total indifference as she talked about Joey. This seemed much more remarkable than the actual mistakes she made in handling him. Certainly he was left to cry for hours when hungry, because she fed him on a rigid schedule; he was toilet-trained with great rigidity so that he would give no trouble. These things happen to many children. But Joey's existence never registered with his mother. In her recollections he was fused at one moment with one event or person; at another, with something or somebody else. When she told us about his birth and infancy, it was as if she were talking about some vague acquaintance, and soon her thoughts would wander off to another person or to herself.

When Joey was not yet four, his nursery school suggested that he enter a special school for disturbed children. At the new school his autism was immediately recognized. During his three years there he experienced a slow improvement. Unfortunately a subsequent two years in a parochial school destroyed this progress. He began to develop compulsive defenses, which he called his "preventions." He could not drink, for example, except through elaborate piping systems built of straws. Liquids had to be "pumped" into him, in his fantasy, or he could not suck. Eventually his behavior became so upsetting that he could not be kept in the parochial school. At home things did not improve. Three months before entering the Orthogenic School he made a serious attempt at suicide.

To us Joey's pathological behavior seemed the external expression of an overwhelming effort to remain almost nonexistent as a person. For weeks Joey's only reply when addressed was "Bam." Unless he thus neutralized whatever we said, there would be an explosion, for Joey plainly wished to close off every form of contact not mediated by machinery. Even when he was bathed he rocked back and forth with mute, engine-like regularity, flooding the bathroom. If he stopped rocking, he did this like a machine too; suddenly he went completely rigid. Only once, after months of being lifted from his bath and carried to bed, did a small expression of puzzled pleasure appear on his face as he said very softly: "They even carry you to your bed here."

For a long time after he began to talk he would never refer to anyone by name, but only as "that person" or "the little person" or "the big person." He was unable to designate by its true name anything to which he attached feelings. Nor could he name his anxieties except through neologisms or word contaminations. For a long time he spoke about "master paintings" and "a master painting room" (i.e., masturbating and masturbating room). One of his machines, the "criticizer," prevented him from "saying words which have unpleasant feelings." Yet he gave personal names to the tubes and motors in his collection of machinery. Moreover, these dead things had feelings; the tubes bled when hurt and sometimes got sick. He consistently maintained this reversal between animate and inanimate objects.

In Joey's machine world everything, on pain of instant destruction, obeyed inhibitory laws much more stringent than those of physics. When we came to know him better, it was plain that in his moments of silent withdrawal, with his machine switched off, Joey was absorbed in pondering the compulsive laws of his private universe. His preoccupation with machinery made it difficult to establish even practical contacts with him. If he wanted to do something with a counselor, such as play with a toy that had caught his vague attention, he could not do so: "I'd like this very much, but first I have to turn off the machine." But by the time he had fulfilled all the requirements of his preventions, he had lost interest. When a toy was offered to him, he could not touch it because his motors and his tubes did not leave him a hand free. Even certain colors were dangerous and had to be strictly avoided in toys and clothing, because "some colors turn off the current, and I can't touch them because I can't live without the current."

Joey was convinced that machines were better than people. Once when he bumped into one of the pipes on our jungle gym he kicked it so violently that his teacher had to restrain him to keep him from injuring himself. When she explained that the pipe was much harder than his foot, Joey replied: "That proves it. Machines are better than the body. They don't break; they're much harder and stronger." If he lost or forgot something, it merely proved that his brain ought to be thrown away and replaced by machinery. If he spilled something, his arm should be broken and twisted off because it did not work properly. When his head or arm failed to work as it should, he tried to punish it by hitting it. Even Joey's feelings were mechanical. Much later in his therapy, when he had formed a timid attachment to another child and had been rebuffed, Joey cried: "He broke my feelings."

Gradually we began to understand what had seemed to be contradictory in Joey's behavior — why he held onto the motors and tubes, then suddenly destroyed them in a fury, then set out immediately and urgently to equip himself with new and larger tubes. Joey had created these machines to run his body and mind because it was too painful to be human. But again and again he became dissatisfied with their failure to meet his need and rebellious at the way they frustrated his will. In a recurrent frenzy he "exploded" his light bulbs and tubes, and for a moment became a human being — for one crowning instant he came alive. But as soon as he had asserted his dominance through the self-created explosion, he felt his life ebbing away. To keep on existing he had immediately to restore his machines and replenish the electricity that supplied his life energy.

What deep-seated fears and needs underlay Joey's delusional system? We were long in finding out, for Joey's preventions effectively concealed the secret of his autistic behavior. In the meantime we dealt with his peripheral problems one by one.

During his first year with us Joey's most trying problem was toilet behavior. This surprised us, for Joey's personality was not "anal" in the Freudian sense; his original personality damage had antedated the period of his toilet-training. Rigid and early toilet-training, however, had certainly contributed to his anxieties. It was our effort to help Joey with this problem that led to his first recognition of us as human beings.

Going to the toilet, like everything else in Joey's life, was surrounded by elaborate preventions. We had to accompany him; he had to take off all his clothes; he could only squat, not sit, on the toilet seat; he had to touch the wall with one hand, in which he also clutched frantically the vacuum tubes that powered his elimination. He was terrified lest his whole body be sucked down.

To counteract this fear we gave him a metal wastebasket in lieu of a toilet. Eventually, when eliminating into the wastebasket, he no longer needed to take off all his clothes, nor to hold on to the wall. He still needed the tubes and motors which, he believed, moved his bowels for him. But here again the all-important machinery was itself a source of new terrors. In Joey's world the gadgets had to move their bowels, too. He was terribly concerned that they should, but since they were so much more powerful than men, he was also terrified that if his tubes moved their bowels, their feces would fill all of space and leave him no room to live. He was thus always caught in some fearful contradiction.

Our readiness to accept his toilet habits, which obviously entailed some hardship for his counselors, gave Joey the confidence to express his obsessions in drawings. Drawing these fantasies was a first step toward letting us in, however distantly, to what concerned him most deeply. It was the first step in a year-long process of externalizing his anal preoccupations. As a result he began seeing feces everywhere; the whole world became to him a mire of excrement. At the same time he began to eliminate freely wherever he happened to be. But with this release from his infantile imprisonment in compulsive rules, the toilet and the whole process of elimination became less dangerous. Thus far it had been beyond Joey's comprehension that anybody could possibly move his bowels without mechanical aid. Now Joey took a further step forward; defecation became the first physiological process he could perform without the help of vacuum tubes. It must not be thought that he was proud of this ability. Taking pride in an achievement presupposes that one accomplishes it of one's own free will. He still did not feel himself an autonomous person who could do things on his own. To Joey defecation still seemed enslaved to some incomprehensible but utterly binding cosmic law, perhaps the law his parents had imposed on him when he was being toilet-trained.

It was not simply that his parents had subjected him to rigid, early training. Many children are so trained. But in most cases the parents have a deep emotional investment in the child's performance. The child's response in turn makes training an occasion for interaction between them and for the building of genuine relationships. Joey's parents had no emotional investment in him. His obedience gave them no satisfaction and won him no affection or approval. As a toilet-trained child he saved his mother labor, just as household machines saved her labor. As a machine he was not loved for his performance, nor could he love himself.

So it had been with all other aspects of Joey's existence with his parents. Their reactions to his eating or noneating, sleeping or wakening, urinating or defecating, being dressed or undressed, washed or bathed did not flow from any unitary interest in him, deeply embedded in their personalities. By treating him mechanically his parents made him a machine. The various functions of life — even the parts of his body — bore no integrating relationship to one another or to any sense of self that was acknowledged and confirmed by others. Though he had acquired mastery over some functions, such as toilet-training and speech, he had acquired them separately and kept them isolated from each other. Toilet-training had thus not gained him a pleasant feeling of body mastery; speech had not led to communication of thought or feeling. On the contrary, each achievement only steered him away from self-mastery and integration. Toilet-training had enslaved him. Speech left him talking in neologisms that obstructed his and our ability to relate to each other. In Joey's development the normal process of growth had been made to run backward. Whatever he had learned put him not at the end of his infantile development toward integration but, on the contrary, farther behind than he was at its very beginning. Had we understood this sooner, his first years with us would have been less baffling.

It is unlikely that Joey's calamity could befall a child in any time and culture but our own. He suffered no physical deprivation; he starved for human contact. Just to be taken care of is not enough for relating. It is a necessary but not a sufficient condition. At the extreme where utter scarcity reigns, the forming of relationships is certainly hampered. But our society of mechanized plenty often makes for equal difficulties in a child's learning to relate. Where parents can provide the simple creature-comforts for their children only at the cost of significant effort, it is likely that they will feel pleasure in being able to provide for them; it is this, the parents' pleasure, that gives children a sense of personal worth and sets the process of relating in motion. But if comfort is so readily available that the parents feel no particular pleasure in winning it for their children, then the children cannot develop the feeling of being worthwhile around the satisfaction of their basic needs. Of course parents and children can and do develop relationships around other situations. But matters are then no longer so simple and direct. The child must be on the receiving end of care and concern given with pleasure and without the exaction of return if he is to feel loved and worthy of respect and consideration. This feeling gives him the ability to trust; he can entrust his well-being to persons to whom he is so important. Out of such trust the child learns to form close and stable relationships.

For Joey relationship with his parents was empty of pleasure in comfort-giving as in all other situations. His was an extreme instance of a plight that sends many schizophrenic children to our clinics and hospitals. Many months passed before he could relate to us; his despair that anybody could like him made contact impossible.

When Joey could finally trust us enough to let himself become more infantile, he began to play at being a papoose. There was a corresponding change in his fantasies. He drew endless pictures of himself as an electrical papoose. Totally enclosed, suspended in empty space, he is run by unknown, unseen powers through wireless electricity.

As we eventually came to understand, the heart of Joey's delusional system was the artificial, mechanical womb he had created and into which he had locked himself. In his papoose fantasies lay the wish to be entirely reborn in a womb. His new experiences in the school suggested that life, after all, might be worth living. Now he was searching for a way to be reborn in a better way. Since machines were better than men, what was more natural than to try rebirth through them? This was the deeper meaning of his electrical papoose.

As Joey made progress, his pictures of himself became more dominant in his drawings. Though still machine-operated, he has grown in self-importance. Now he has acquired hands that do something, and he has had the courage to make a picture of the machine that runs him. Later still the papoose became a person, rather than a robot encased in glass.

Eventually Joey began to create an imaginary family at the school: the "Carr" family. Why the Carr family? In the car he was enclosed as he had been in his papoose, but at least the car was not stationary; it could move. More important, in a car one was not only driven but also could drive. The Carr family was Joey's way of exploring the possibility of leaving the school, of living with a good family in a safe, protecting car.

Joey at last broke through his prison. In this brief account it has not been possible to trace the painfully slow process of his first true relations with other human beings. Suffice it to say that he ceased to be a mechanical boy and became a human child. This newborn child was, however, nearly 12 years old. To recover the lost time is a tremendous task. That work has occupied Joey and us ever since. Sometimes he sets to it with a will; at other times the difficulty of real life makes him regret that he ever came out of his shell. But he has never wanted to return to his mechanical life.

One last detail and this fragment of Joey's story has been told. When Joey was 12, he made a float for our Memorial Day parade. It carried the slogan: "Feelings are more important than anything under the sun." Feelings, Joey had learned, are what make for humanity; their absence, for a mechanical existence. With this knowledge Joey entered the human condition.

QUESTIONS

1. Write a paragraph outline (see page 79) of Bettelheim's essay, and compare it to another possible structure for the same material.
2. Bettelheim suggests that the parents' behavior was mainly responsible for Joey's condition, but he also suggests that our "time and culture," "our society of . . . plenty," is partly responsible. Explain how he tries to link these two. How adequate is the entire explanation when applied to Joey?

To Lie or Not To Lie? — The Doctor's Dilemma

Sissela Bok

Should doctors ever lie to benefit their patients — to speed recovery or to conceal the approach of death? In medicine as in law, government, and other lines of work, the requirements of honesty often seem dwarfed by greater needs: the need to shelter from brutal news or to uphold a promise of secrecy; to expose corruption or to promote the public interest.

What should doctors say, for example, to a 46-year-old man coming in for a routine physical checkup just before going on vacation with his family who, though he feels in perfect health, is found to have a form of cancer that will cause him to die within six months? Is it best to tell him the truth? If he asks, should the doctors deny that he is ill, or minimize the gravity of the prognosis? Should they at least conceal the truth until after the family vacation?

Doctors confront such choices often and urgently. At times, they see important reasons to lie for the patient's own sake; in their eyes, such lies differ sharply from self-serving ones.

Studies show that most doctors sincerely believe that the seriously ill do not want to know the truth about their condition, and that informing them risks destroying their hope, so that they may recover more slowly, or deteriorate faster, perhaps even commit suicide. As one physician wrote: "Ours is a profession which traditionally has been guided by a precept that transcends the virtue of uttering the truth for truth's sake, and that is 'as far as possible do no harm.'"

Armed with such a precept, a number of doctors may slip into deceptive practices that they assume will "do no harm" and may well help their patients. They may prescribe innumerable placebos, sound more encouraging than the facts warrant, and distort grave news, especially to the incurably ill and the dying.

But the illusory nature of the benefits such deception is meant to bestow is now coming to be documented. Studies show that, contrary to the belief of many physicians, an overwhelming majority of patients do want to be told the truth, even about grave illness, and feel betrayed when they learn that they have been misled. We are also learning that truthful information, humanely conveyed, helps patients cope with illness: helps them tolerate pain better, need less medication, and even recover faster after surgery.

Not only do lies not provide the "help" hoped for by advocates of benevolent deception; they invade the autonomy of patients and render them unable to make informed choices concerning their own health, including the choice of whether to *be* a patient in the first place. We are becoming increasingly aware of all that can befall patients in the course of their illness when information is denied or distorted.

Dying patients especially — who are easiest to mislead and most often kept in the dark — can then not make decisions about the end of life: about whether or not to enter a hospital, or to have surgery; about where and with whom to spend their remaining time; about how to bring their affairs to a close and take leave.

Lies also do harm to those who tell them: harm to their integrity and, in the long run, to their credibility. Lies hurt their colleagues as well. The suspicion of deceit undercuts the work of the many doctors who are scrupulously honest with their patients; it contributes to the spiral of litigation and of "defensive medicine," and thus it injures, in turn, the entire medical profession.

Sharp conflicts are now arising. Patients are learning to press for answers. Patients' bills of rights require that they be informed about their condition and about alternatives for treatment. Many doctors go to great lengths to provide such information. Yet even in hospitals with the most eloquent bill of rights, believers in benevolent deception continue their age-old practices. Colleagues may disapprove but refrain from remonstrating. Nurses may bitterly resent having to take part, day after day, in deceiving patients, but feel powerless to take a stand.

There is urgent need to debate this issue openly. Not only in medicine, but in other professions as well, practitioners may find themselves repeatedly in straits where serious consequences seem avoidable only through deception. Yet the public has every reason to be wary of professional deception, for such practices are peculiarly likely to become ingrained, to spread, and to erode trust. Neither in medicine, nor in law, government, or the social sciences can there be comfort in the old saw, "What you don't know can't hurt you."

QUESTIONS

1. Is there anything in Bok's opening paragraph that prepares the reader for Bok's own position on whether or not lying is ever justifiable?

2. List the reasons Bok offers on behalf of telling the truth to patients. Are some of these reasons presented more convincingly than others? If any are unconvincing, rewrite them to make them more convincing.

3. Suppose Bok's last sentence was revised to read thus: "In medicine, law, government, and the social sciences, what you don't know *can* hurt you." Which version do you prefer, and why?

4. "What you don't know can't hurt you." Weigh the truth of this assertion in your own life. Were there instances of a truth being withheld from you that did hurt you? Were there occasions when

you were told a truth that you now judge would have been better withheld? On the whole, do you come out in favor of the assertion, against it, or somewhere in between?

5. How much should adopted children be told about their biological parents? Consider reasons both for and against telling all. Use not only your own experiences and opinions but those of others, such as friends and classmates. If you read some relevant books or articles, see pages 546–49 on acknowledging sources.

Every Species Has Its Niche
Paul Colinvaux

Every species has its niche, its place in the grand scheme of things.

Consider a wolf-spider as it hunts through the litter of leaves on the woodland floor. It must be a splendid hunter; that goes without saying for otherwise its line would long since have died out. But it must be proficient at other things too. Even as it hunts, it must keep some of its eight eyes on the look-out for the things that hunt it; and when it sees an enemy it must do the right thing to save itself. It must know what to do when it rains. It must have a life style that enables it to survive the winter. It must rest safely when the time is not apt for hunting. And there comes a season of the year when the spiders, as it were, feel the sap rising in their eight legs. The male must respond by going to look for a female spider, and when he finds her, he must convince her that he is not merely something to eat — yet. And she, in the fullness of time, must carry an egg-sack as she goes about her hunting, and later must let the babies ride on her back. They, in turn, must learn the various forms of fending for themselves as they go through the different moults of the spider's life until they, too, are swift-running, pouncing hunters of the woodland floor.

Wolf-spidering is a complex job, not something to be undertaken by an amateur. We might say that there is a profession of wolf-spidering. It is necessary to be good at all its manifold tasks to survive at it. What is more, the profession is possible only in very restricted circumstances. A woodland floor is necessary, for instance, and the right climate with a winter roughly like that your ancestors were used to; and enough of the right sorts of things to hunt; and the right shelter when you need it; and the numbers of natural enemies must be kept within reasonable bounds. For success, individual spiders must be superlatively good at their jobs and the right circumstances must prevail. Unless both the skills of spidering and the opportunity are present, there will not be any wolf-spiders. The "niche" of wolf-spidering will not be filled.

"Niche" is a word ecologists have borrowed from church architecture. In a church, of course, "niche" means a recess in the wall in which a figurine may be placed; it is an address, a location, a physical place. But the ecologist's "niche" is more than just a physical place: it is a place in the grand scheme of things. The niche is an animal's (or a plant's) profession. The niche of the wolf-spider is everything it does to get its food and raise its babies. To be able to do these things it must relate properly to the place where it lives and to the other inhabitants of that place. Everything the species does to survive and stay "fit" in the Darwinian sense is its niche.

The physical living place in an ecologist's jargon is called the *habitat*. The habitat is the "address" or location in which individuals of a species live. The woodland floor hunted by the wolf-spiders is the habitat, but wolf-spidering is their niche. It is the niche of wolf-spidering that has been fashioned by natural selection.

The idea of "niche" at once gives us a handle to one of those general questions that ecologists want to answer — the question of the constancy of numbers. The common stay common, and the rare stay rare, because the opportunities for each niche, or profession, are set by circumstance. Wolf-spidering needs the right sort of neighbors living in the right sort of wood, and the number of times that this combination comes up in any country is limited. So the number of wolf-spiders is limited also; the number was fixed when the niche was adopted. This number is likely to stay constant until something drastic happens to change the face of the country.

Likening an animal's niche to a human profession makes this idea of limits to number very clear. Let us take the profession of professing. There can only be as many professors in any city as there are teaching and scholarship jobs for professors to do. If the local university turns out more research scholars than there are professing jobs, then some of these hopeful young people will not be able to accept the scholar's tenure, however *cum laude* their degrees. They will have to emigrate, or take to honest work to make a living.

Likewise there cannot be more wolf-spiders than there are wolf-spider jobs, antelopes than there are antelope jobs, crab grass than there are crab grass jobs. Every species has its niche. And once its niche is fixed by natural selection, so also are its numbers fixed.

This idea of niche gets at the numbers problem without any discussion of breeding effort. Indeed, it shows that the way an animal breeds has very little to do with how many of it there are. This is a very strange idea to someone new to it, and it needs to be thought about carefully. *The reproductive effort makes no difference to the eventual size of the population.* Numerous eggs may increase numbers in the short term, following some disaster, but only for a while. The numbers that may live are set by the number of niche-spaces (jobs) in the environment, and these are quite independent of how fast a species makes babies.

But all the same each individual must try to breed as fast as it can. It is in a race with its neighbors of the same kind, a race that will decide whose babies will fill the niche-space jobs of the next generation. The actual number of those who will be able to live in that next generation has been fixed by the environment; we may say that the population will be a function of the *carrying capacity* of the land for animals of this kind in that time and place. But the issue of whose babies will take up those limited places is absolutely open. It is here that natural selection operates. A "fit" individual is, by definition, one that successfully takes up one of the niche-spaces from the limited pool, and the fitness of a parent is measured by how many future niche-spaces her or his offspring take up. "Survival of the fittest" means survival of those who leave the most living descendants. A massive breeding effort makes no difference to the future population, but it is vital for the hereditary future of one's own line. This is why everything that lives has the capacity for large families.

Yet there are degrees of largeness in wild families, and these degrees of largeness make sense when looked at with an ecologist's eye. The intuitively obvious consequence of a law that says "Have the largest possible family or face hereditary oblivion," is the family based on thousands of tiny eggs or seeds. This seems to be the commonest breeding strategy. Houseflies, mosquitoes, salmon, and dandelions all do it. I call it "the small-egg gambit." It has very obvious advantages, but there are also costs, which the clever ones with big babies avoid.

For users of the small-egg gambit, natural selection starts doing the obvious sums. If an egg is made just a little bit smaller, the parent might be able to make an extra egg for the same amount of food eaten, and this will give it a slight edge in the evolutionary race. It is enough. Natural selection will therefore choose families that make more and more of smaller and smaller eggs until a point of optimum smallness is reached. If the eggs are any smaller than this, the young may all die; if they are any larger, one's neighbor will swamp one's posterity with her mass-production. The largest number of the smallest possible eggs makes simple Darwinian sense.

But the costs of the small-egg gambit are grim. An inevitable consequence is that babies are thrown out into the world naked and tiny. Most of them as a result die, and early death is the common lot of baby salmon, dandelions, and the rest. In the days before Darwin, people used to say that the vast families of salmon, dandelions, and insects were compensations for the slaughter of the young. So terrible was the life of a baby fish that Providence provided a salmon with thousands of eggs to give it a chance that one or two might get through. It seems a natural assumption, and one that still confuses even some biologists. But the argument is the wrong way round. A high death rate for the tiny, helpless young is a consequence of the thousands of tiny eggs, not a cause. A selfish race of neighbor against neighbor leads to those thousands of tiny eggs, and the early deaths of the babies are the cost of this selfishness.

There is this to be said for the small-egg gambit, though; once you have been forced into it, there are the gambler's compensations. Many young scattered far and wide mean an intensive search for opportunity, and this may pay off when opportunity is thinly scattered in space. Weed and plague species win this advantage, as when the parachute seed of a dandelion is wafted between the trunks of the trees of a forest to alight on the fresh-turned earth of a rabbit burrow. The small-egg gambits of weeds may be likened to the tactics of a gambler at a casino who covers every number with a low-value chip. If he has enough chips, he is bound to win, particularly if big payoffs are possible. He does have to have very many chips to waste, though. This is why economists do not approve of gamblers.

To the person with an economic turn of mind, the small-egg gambit, for all its crazy logic, does not seem a proper way to manage affairs. The adherents of this gambit spend all their lives at their professions, winning as many resources as possible from their living places, and then they invest these resources in tiny babies, most of whom are going to die. What a ridiculously low return on capital. What economic folly. Any economist could tell these animals and plants that the real way to win in the hereditary stakes is to put all your capital into a lesser number of big strong babies, all of which are going to survive. A number of animals in fact do this. I call it "the large-young gambit."

In the large-young gambit one either makes a few huge eggs out of the food available, or the babies actually grow inside their mother, where they are safe. Either way, each baby has a very good chance of living to grow up. It is big to start with and it is fed or defended by parents until it can look after itself. Most of the food the parents collect goes into babies who live. There is little waste. Natural selection approves of this as much as do economists. Big babies who have a very good chance of long life mean more surviving offspring for the amount of food-investment in the end. This prudent outlay of resources is arranged by birds, viviparous snakes, great white sharks, goats, tigers, and people.

Having a few, large young, and then nursing them until they are big and strong, is the surest existing method of populating the future. Yet the success of this gambit assumes one essential condition. You must start with just the right number of young. If you lay too many monster hen's eggs or drop too many bawling brats, you may not be able to supply them with enough food, and some or all will die. You have then committed the economic wastefulness of those of the tiny eggs. So you must not be too ambitious in your breeding. But the abstemious will also lose out, because its neighbor may raise one more baby, may populate the future just that little bit better, and start your line on a one-way ride to hereditary oblivion. You must get it just right; not too many young, and not too few. Natural selection will preserve those family strains which are programmed to "choose" the best or optimum size of family.

Many ecologists have studied birds with these ideas in mind, and they have found that there is often a very good correlation between the number of eggs in a clutch and the food supply. In a year when food is plentiful a bird may lay, on the average, one or two eggs more than in a lean season. The trend may be slight but sometimes is quite obvious. Snowy owls, which are big white birds of the arctic tundra, build vast nests on the ground. They feed their chicks on lemmings, the small brown arctic mice. When lemmings are scarce, there may be only one or two eggs in each owl's nest, but when the tundra is crawling with lemmings, the nests may well have ten eggs each. The owls are evidently clever at assessing how many chicks they can afford each year.

But people are cleverer than snowy owls and have brought the large-young gambit to its perfection. They can read the environment, guess the future, and plan their families according to what their intelligence tells them they can afford. Even the infanticide practiced by various peoples at various times serves the cause of Darwinian fitness, rather than acting as a curb on population. There is no point in keeping alive babies who could not be supported for long. Killing babies who could not be safely reared gives a better chance of survival to those who are left, and infanticide in hard times can mean that more children grow up in the end.

Thus, every species has its niche, its place in the grand scheme of things; and every species has a breeding strategy refined by natural selection to leave the largest possible number of surviving offspring. The requirement for a definite niche implies a limit to the size of the population because the numbers of the animal or plant are set by the opportunities for carrying on life in that niche. The kind of breeding strategy, on the other hand, has no effect on the size of the usual population, and the drive to breed is a struggle to decide which family strains have the privilege of taking up the limited numbers of opportunities for life. Every family tries to outbreed every other, though the total numbers of their kind remain the same. These are the principles on which an ecologist can base his efforts to answer the major questions of his discipline.

QUESTIONS

1. In the second paragraph Colinvaux uses "it must" seven times. What is the purpose of this repetition? Judging from this paragraph alone, what is Colinvaux's attitude toward the wolf-spider?
2. A writer is a teacher. Drawing on the first eight paragraphs, list some of the devices that Colinvaux uses in an effort to teach effectively.

My Wood

E. M. Forster

A few years ago I wrote a book which dealt in part with the difficulties of the English in India. Feeling that they would have had no difficulties in India themselves, the Americans read the book freely. The more they read it the better it made them feel, and a cheque to the author was the result. I bought a wood with the cheque. It is not a large wood — it contains scarcely any trees, and it is intersected, blast it, by a public footpath. Still, it is the first property that I have owned, so it is right that other people should participate in my shame, and should ask themselves, in accents that will vary in horror, this very important question: What is the effect of property upon the character? Don't let's touch economics; the effect of private ownership upon the community as a whole is another question — a more important question, perhaps, but another one. Let's keep to psychology. If you own things, what's their effect on you? What's the effect on me of my wood?

In the first place, it makes me feel heavy. Property does have this effect. Property produces men of weight, and it was a man of weight who failed to get into the Kingdom of Heaven. He was not wicked, that unfortunate millionaire in the parable, he was only stout; he stuck out in front, not to mention behind, and as he wedged himself this way and that in the crystalline entrance and bruised his well-fed flanks, he saw beneath him a comparatively slim camel passing through the eye of a needle and being woven into the robe of God. The Gospels all through couple stoutness and slowness. They point out what is perfectly obvious, yet seldom realized: that if you have a lot of things you cannot move about a lot, that furniture requires dusting, dusters require servants, servants require insurance stamps, and the whole tangle of them makes you think twice before you accept an invitation to dinner or go for a bathe in the Jordan. Sometimes the Gospels proceed further and say with Tolstoy that property is sinful; they approach the difficult ground of asceticism here, where I cannot follow them. But as to the immediate effects of property on people, they just show straightforward logic. It produces men of weight. Men of weight cannot, by definition, move like the lightning from the East unto the West, and the ascent of a fourteen-stone bishop into a pulpit is thus the exact antithesis of the coming of the Son of Man. My wood makes me feel heavy.

In the second place, it makes me feel it ought to be larger.

The other day I heard a twig snap in it. I was annoyed at first, for I thought that someone was blackberrying, and depreciating the value of the undergrowth. On coming nearer, I saw it was not a man who had trodden on the twig and snapped it, but a bird, and I felt pleased. My bird. The bird was not equally pleased. Ignoring the relation between us, it took fright as soon as it saw the shape of my face, and flew straight over the boundary hedge into a field, the property of Mrs. Henessy, where it sat down with a loud squawk. It had become Mrs. Henessy's bird. Something seemed grossly amiss here, something that would not have occurred had the wood been larger. I could not afford to buy Mrs. Henessy out, I dared not murder her, and limitations of this sort beset me on every side. Ahab did not want that vineyard — he only needed it to round off his property, preparatory to plotting a new curve — and all the land around my wood has become necessary to me in order to round off the wood. A boundary protects. But — poor little thing — the boundary ought in its turn to be protected. Noises on the edge of it. Children throw stones. A little more, and then a little more, until we reach the sea. Happy Canute! Happier Alexander! And after all, why should even the world be the limit of possession? A rocket containing a Union Jack, will, it is hoped, be shortly fired at the moon. Mars. Sirius. Beyond which . . . But these immensities ended by saddening me. I could not suppose that my wood was the destined nucleus of universal dominion — it is so very small and contains no mineral wealth beyond the blackberries. Nor was I comforted when Mrs. Henessy's bird took alarm for the second time and flew clean away from us all, under the belief that it belonged to itself.

In the third place, property makes its owner feel that he ought to do something to it. Yet he isn't sure what. A restlessness comes over him, a vague sense that he has a personality to express — the same sense which, without any vagueness, leads the artist to an act of creation. Sometimes I think I will cut down such trees as remain in the wood, at other times I want to fill up the gaps between them with new trees. Both impulses are pretentious and empty. They are not honest movements towards money-making or beauty. They spring from a foolish desire to express myself and from an inability to enjoy what I have got. Creation, property, enjoyment form a sinister trinity in the human mind. Creation and enjoyment are both very very good, yet they are often unattainable without a material basis, and at such moments property pushes itself in as a substitute, saying, "Accept me instead — I'm good enough for all three." It is not enough. It is, as Shakespeare said of lust, "The expense of spirit in a waste of shame": it is "Before, a joy proposed; behind, a dream." Yet we don't know how to shun it. It is forced on us by our economic system as the alternative to starvation. It is also forced on us by an internal defect in the soul, by the feeling that in property may lie the germs of self-development and of exquisite or heroic deeds. Our life on earth is, and ought to be, material and carnal. But we have not yet learned to manage our materialism and carnality properly; they are still entangled with the desire for ownership, where (in the words of Dante) "Possession is one with loss."

And this brings us to our fourth and final point: the blackberries.

Blackberries are not plentiful in this meagre grove, but they are easily seen from the public footpath which traverses it, and all too easily gathered. Foxgloves, too — people will pull up the foxgloves, and ladies of an educational tendency even grub for toadstools to show them on the Monday in class. Other ladies, less educated, roll down the bracken in the arms of their gentlemen friends. There is paper, there are tins. Pray, does my wood belong to me or doesn't it? And, if it does, should I not own it best by allowing no one else to walk there? There is a wood near Lyme Regis, also cursed by a public footpath, where the owner has not hesitated on this point. He has built high stone walls each side of the path, and has spanned it by bridges, so that the public circulate like termites while he gorges on the blackberries unseen. He really does own his wood, this able chap. Dives in Hell did pretty well, but the gulf dividing him from Lazarus could be traversed by vision, and nothing traverses it here.[10] And perhaps I shall come to this in time. I shall wall in and fence out until I really taste the sweets of property. Enormously stout, endlessly avaricious, pseudo-creative, intensely selfish, I shall weave upon my forehead the quadruple crown of possession until those nasty Bolshies come and take it off again and thrust me aside into the outer darkness.

QUESTION

Much of the strength of the essay is in its concrete presentation of generalities. Note, for example, that the essay is called "My Wood," but we might say that the general idea of the essay is "The Effect of Property on Owners." Forster gives four effects, chiefly through concrete statements. What are they? Put these four effects in four general statements.

A Proposal to Abolish Grading
Paul Goodman

Let half a dozen of the prestigious Universities — Chicago, Stanford, the Ivy League — abolish grading, and use testing only and entirely for pedagogic purposes as teachers see fit.

Anyone who knows the frantic temper of the present schools will understand the transvaluation of values that would be effected by this modest innovation. For most of the students, the competitive grade has come to be the essence. The naïve teacher points to the

[10] Editors' note: According to Christ's parable in Luke xvi. 19–26, the rich man (unnamed, but traditionally known as Dives), at whose gate the poor man Lazarus had begged, was sent to hell, from where he could see Lazarus in heaven.

beauty of the subject and the ingenuity of the research; the shrewd student asks if he is responsible for that on the final exam.

Let me at once dispose of an objection whose unanimity is quite fascinating. I think that the great majority of professors agree that grading hinders teaching and creates a bad spirit, going as far as cheating and plagiarizing. I have before me the collection of essays, *Examining in Harvard College*, and this is the consensus. It is uniformly asserted, however, that the grading is inevitable; for how else will the graduate schools, the foundations, the corporations *know* whom to accept, reward, hire? How will the talent scouts know whom to tap?

By testing the applicants, of course, according to the specific task-requirements of the inducting institution, just as applicants for the Civil Service or for licenses in medicine, law, and architecture are tested. Why should Harvard professors do the testing *for* corporations and graduate-schools?

The objection is ludicrous. Dean Whitla, of the Harvard Office of Tests, points out that the scholastic-aptitude and achievement tests used for *admission* to Harvard are a super-excellent index for all-around Harvard performance, better than high-school grades or particular Harvard course-grades. Presumably, these college-entrance tests are tailored for what Harvard and similar institutions want. By the same logic, would not an employer do far better to apply his own job-aptitude test rather than to rely on the vagaries of Harvard section-men. Indeed, I doubt that many employers bother to look at such grades; they are more likely to be interested merely in the fact of a Harvard diploma, whatever that connotes to them. The grades have most of their weight with the graduate schools — here, as elsewhere, the system runs mainly for its own sake.

It is really necessary to remind our academics of the ancient history of Examination. In the medieval university, the whole point of the gruelling trial of the candidate was whether or not to accept him as a peer. His disputation and lecture for the Master's was just that, a master-piece to enter the guild. It was not to make comparative evaluations. It was not to weed out and select for an extra-mural licensor or employer. It was certainly not to pit one young fellow against another in an ugly competition. My philosophic impression is that the medievals thought they knew what a good job of work was and that we are competitive because we do not know. But the more status is achieved by largely irrelevant competitive evaluation, the less will we ever know.

(Of course, our American examinations never did have this purely guild orientation, just as our faculties have rarely had absolute autonomy; the examining was to satisfy Overseers, Elders, distant Regents — and they as paternal superiors have always doted on giving grades, rather than accepting peers. But I submit that this set-up itself makes it impossible for the student to *become* a master, to *have* grown up, and to commence on his own. He will always be making A or B for some overseer. And in the present atmosphere, he will always be climbing on his friend's neck.)

Perhaps the chief objectors to abolishing grading would be the students and their parents. The parents should be simply disregarded; their anxiety has done enough damage already. For the students, it seems to me that a primary duty of the university is to deprive them of their props, their dependence on extrinsic valuation and motivation, and to force them to confront the difficult enterprise itself and finally lose themselves in it.

A miserable effect of grading is to nullify the various uses of testing. Testing, for both student and teacher, is a means of structuring, and also of finding out what is blank or wrong and what has been assimilated and can be taken for granted. Review — including high-pressure review — is a means of bringing together the fragments, so that there are flashes of synoptic insight.

There are several good reasons for testing, and kinds of test. But if the aim is to discover weakness, what is the point of down-grading and punishing it, and thereby inviting the student to conceal his weakness, by faking and bulling, if not cheating? The natural conclusion of synthesis is the insight itself, not a grade for having had it. For the important purpose of placement, if one can establish in the student the belief that one is testing *not* to grade and make invidious comparisons but for his own advantage, the student should normally seek his own level, where he is challenged and yet capable, rather than trying to get by. If the student dares to accept himself as he is, a teacher's grade is a crude instrument compared with a student's self-awareness. But it is rare in our universities that students are encouraged to notice objectively their vast confusion. Unlike Socrates, our teachers rely on power-drives rather than shame and ingenuous idealism.

Many students are lazy, so teachers try to goad or threaten them by grading. In the long run this must do more harm than good. Laziness is a character-defense. It may be a way of avoiding learning, in order to protect the conceit that one is already perfect (deeper, the despair that one *never* can). It may be a way of avoiding just the risk of failing and being down-graded. Sometimes it is a way of politely saying, "I won't." But since it is the authoritarian grown-up demands that have created such attitudes in the first place, why repeat the trauma? There comes a time when we must treat people as adult, laziness and all. It is one thing courageously to fire a do-nothing out of your class; it is quite another thing to evaluate him with a lordly F.

Most important of all, it is often obvious that balking in doing the work, especially among bright young people who get to great universities, means exactly what it says: The work does not suit me, not this subject, or not at this time, or not in this school, or not in school altogether. The student might not be bookish; he might be school-tired; perhaps his development ought now to take another direction. Yet unfortunately, if such a student is intelligent and is not sure of himself, he *can* be bullied into passing, and this obscures everything. My hunch is that I am describing a common situation. What a grim waste of young life and teacherly effort! Such a student will retain nothing of what he has "passed" in. Sometimes he must get mononucleosis to tell his story and be believed.

And ironically, the converse is also probably commonly true. A student flunks and is mechanically weeded out, who is really ready and eager to learn in a scholastic setting, but he has not quite caught on. A good teacher can recognize the situation, but the computer wreaks its will.

QUESTIONS

1. In his opening paragraph Goodman limits his suggestion about grading and testing to "half a dozen of the prestigious Universities." Does he offer any reason for this limitation? Can you?
2. In the third paragraph Goodman says that "the great majority of professors agree that grading hinders teaching." What evidence does he offer to support this claim? What arguments might be offered that grading assists teaching? Should Goodman have offered them?
3. Have grades helped you to learn or hindered you? Explain.

Clothes Make the Man — Uneasy
Anne Hollander

The last decade has made a large number of men more uneasy about what to wear than they might ever have believed possible. The idea that one might agonize over whether to grow sideburns

(sideburns!) or wear trousers of a radically different shape had never occurred to whole generations. Before the mid-'60s whether to wear a tie was about the most dramatic sartorial problem: everything else was a subtle matter of surface variation. Women have been so accustomed to dealing with extreme fashion for so long that they automatically brace themselves for whatever is coming next, including their own willingness to resist or conform and all the probable masculine responses. Men in modern times have only lately felt any pressure to pay that kind of attention. All the delicate shades of significance expressed by the small range of possible alternatives used to be absorbing enough: Double- or single-breasted cut? Sports jacket and slacks or a suit? Shoes with plain or wing tip? The choices men had had to make never looked very numerous to a feminine eye accustomed to a huge range of personally acceptable possibilities, but they always had an absolute and enormous meaning in the world of men, an identifying stamp usually incomprehensible to female judgment. A hat with a tiny bit of nearly invisible feather was separated as by an ocean from a hat with none, and white-on-white shirts, almost imperceptibly complex in weave, were totally shunned by those men who favored white oxford-cloth shirts. Women might remain mystified by the ferocity with which men felt and supported these tiny differences, and perhaps they might pity such narrow sartorial vision attaching so much importance to half an inch of padding in the shoulders or an inch of trouser cuff.

But men knew how lucky they were. It was never very hard to dress the part of oneself. Even imaginative wives and mothers could eventually be trained to reject all seductive but incorrect choices with respect to tie fabric and collar shape that might connote the wrong flavor of spiritual outlook, the wrong level of education or the wrong sort of male bonding. It was a well ordered world, the double standard flourished without hindrance, and no man who stuck to the rules ever needed to suspect that he might look ridiculous.

Into this stable system the width-of-tie question erupted in the early '60s. Suddenly, and for the first time in centuries, the rate of change in masculine fashion accelerated with disconcerting violence, throwing a new light on all the steady old arrangements. Women looked on with secret satisfaction, as it became obvious that during the next few years men might think they could resist the changes, but they would find it impossible to ignore them. In fact to the discomfiture of many, the very look of having ignored the changes suddenly became a distinct and highly conspicuous way of dressing, and everyone ran for cover. Paying no attention whatever to nipped-in waistlines, vivid turtlenecks, long hair with sideburns and bell-bottom trousers could not guarantee any comfy anonymity, but rather stamped one as a convinced follower of the old order — thus adding three or four dangerous new meanings to all the formerly reliable signals. A look in the mirror suddenly revealed man to himself wearing his obvious chains and shackles, hopelessly unliberated.

Now that fashion is loose upon the whole male sex, many men are having to discard an old look for a new, if only to maintain the desired distance from the avant-garde, as women have always known how to do. Just after the first few spurts of creative masculine dress in the mid-'60s, like the Beatle haircut and the wide ties, daring young women began to appear in the miniskirt, and men were temporarily safe from scrutiny as those thousands of thighs came into view. The other truly momentous fashion phenomenon to arise at the same moment, the counterculture costume, established itself absolutely but almost unnoticeably among both sexes while all eyes were glued to those rising hems. In fact miniskirts were the last spectacular and successful sexist thunderbolt to be hurled by modern women, before the liberation movement began to conspire with the nature movement to prevent semi-nudity from being erotic (hot pants, rightly short lived, were too much like science fiction). Men who might have longed in adolescence for the sight of unconfined breasts were perhaps slightly disconcerted when breasts at last appeared, bouncing and swaying on the public streets in the late '60s, since they were often quite repellently presented to the accompaniment of costumes and facial expressions somehow calculated to quell the merest stirring of a lustful thought. But that was only at the beginning, of course. Since then the visible nipple has become delightfully effective under proper management.

Following bare legs, free breasts and the perverse affectation of poverty, dress suddenly became a hilarious parlor game, and men were playing too. Chains, zippers, nailheads and shiny leather were available in any sort of combination. Extremely limp, tired and stained old clothes could also be tastefully festooned on anybody who preferred those. Universal ethnic and gypsy effects, featuring extraordinary fringes and jewelry worn in unusual places, vied with general romantic and menace effects, featuring dark glasses, sinister hats and occasional black capes. In addition all the parts were interchangeable. Both sexes participated, but then finally many people got tired and felt foolish and gave it up. Men, however, had had a taste of what it could be like, and all the extreme possibilities still echoed long after the extreme practices had subsided, even in the consciousness of those who had observed and never tried to join.

During the whole trend men floundered, and still do, longing for the familiar feel of solid ground. Hoping to appease the unleashed tide with one decisive gesture, many men bought a turtleneck dress shirt and wore it uncomfortably but hopefully with a medallion on a chain, only to discover within three months that it would not do. Many a conservative minded but imaginative fellow, eager to avoid new possibilities for feeling foolish and to look at least attuned to the modern world, had expensive tailoring done in a bold and becoming new shape, hoping to stay exactly like that for the rest of his life, or at least for a few more years. He then discovered himself still handsome but hopelessly dated in a season or two. Mustaches sprouted and hastily vanished again, sideburns were cultivated and sometimes proved to grow in upsettingly silver gray. Hair, once carefully prevented from exhibiting wayward traits, was given its head. Men balding on top could daringly relish luxuriant growth around the sides, and the Allen Ginsberg phenomenon frequently occurred: a man once clean-shaven and well furred on top would compensate for a thinning poll by growing a lengthy fringe around its edges and often adding an enormous beard. The result was a sort of curious air of premature wisdom, evoking mental images of the young Walt Whitman spiced with swami. Other, more demanding solutions to the problem of thinning hair among those wishing to join the thick thatch with sideburns group required an elaborate styling of the remaining sparse growth, complete with teasing and spray and a consequent new dependence, quite equal to anything women submit to, upon the hairdressing skill of the professional, the family or the self.

Early in the game, of course, long hair for men had just been another badge. Most men had felt quite safe from any temptation to resemble those youthful and troublesome citizens who were always getting into the newspapers and the jails. Some young people, eager to maintain a low profile, had also found the hairy and ragged look an excellent disguise for masking a serious interest in studying the violin or any similar sort of heterodox concern. During all this time no one ever bothered girls about the length of *their* hair, or found any opportunity to throw them out of school for wearing crew cuts for instance. Even if half-inch fuzz had been the revolutionary mode for girls, they would have undoubtedly been exempt from official hassling, except possibly by their mothers. But, as it happened, the gradually evolved migrant worker, bowery bum costume worn by the armies of the young required long hair for both sexes. The very similarity of coiffure helped, paradoxically, to emphasize the difference of sex. After a while the potent influence of this important subfashion that was at first so easy to ridicule came steadily to bear on the general public's clothes-consciousness. The hairy heads and worn-blue denim legs all got easier to take, and indeed they looked rather attractive on many of them. People became quite accustomed to having their children look as if they belonged to a foreign tribe, possibly hostile; after all under the hair it was still Tom and Kathy.

In general, men of all ages turn out not to want to give up the habit of fixing on a suitable self-image and then carefully tending it, instead of taking up all the new options. It seems too much of a strain to dress for all that complex multiple role-playing, like women. The creative use of male plumage for sexual display, after all, has had a very thin time for centuries: the whole habit became the special prerogative of certain clearly defined groups, ever since the overriding purpose of male dress had been established as that of precise identification. No stepping over the boundaries was thinkable — ruffled evening shirts were for them, not me; and the fear of the wrong associations was the strongest male emotion about clothes, not the smallest part being fear of association with the wrong sex.

The difference between men's and women's clothes used to be an easy matter from every point of view, all the more so when the same tailors made both. When long ago all elegant people wore brightly colored satin, lace and curls, nobody had any trouble sorting out the sexes or worrying whether certain small elements were sexually appropriate. So universal was the skirted female shape and the bifurcated male one that a woman in men's clothes was completely disguised (see the history of English drama), and long hair or gaudy trimmings were never the issue. It was the 19th century, which produced the look of the different sexes coming from different planets, that lasted such a very long time. It also gave men official exemption from fashion risk, and official sanction to laugh at women for perpetually incurrring it.

Women apparently love the risk of course, and ignore the laughter. Men secretly hate it and dread the very possibility of a smile. Most of them find it impossible to leap backward across the traditional centuries into a comfortable renaissance zest for these dangers, since life is hard enough now anyway. Moreover along with fashion came the pitiless exposure of masculine narcissism and vanity, so long submerged and undiscussed. Men had lost the habit of having their concern with personal appearance show as blatantly as women's — the great dandies provided no continuing tradition, except perhaps among urban blacks. Men formerly free from doubt wore their new finery with colossal self-consciousness, staring covertly at everyone else to find out what the score really was about all this stuff. Soon enough the identifying compartments regrouped themselves to include the new material. High heels and platform soles, once worn by the Sun King and other cultivated gentlemen of the past, have been appropriated only by those willing to change not only their heights but their way of walking. They have been ruled out, along with the waist-length shirt opening that exposes trinkets nestling against the chest hair, by men who nevertheless find themselves willing to wear long hair and fur coats and carry handbags. Skirts, I need not add, never caught on.

What of women during the rest of this revolutionary decade? The furor over the miniskirt now seems quaint, like all furors about fashion, and the usual modifications have occurred in everybody's eyesight to make them seem quite ordinary. Trousers have a longer and more interesting history. Women only very recently learned that pants are sexy when fitted tightly over the female pelvis. When trousers were first worn by women, they were supposed to be another disturbingly attractive masculine affectation, perfectly exemplified by Marlene Dietrich doing her white tie and tails number in *Morocco*. They were also supposed to be suitable for very slim, rangy outdoor types low on sex appeal. Jokes used to fly about huge female behinds looking dreadful in pants, and those who habitually wore them had to speak loudly about their comfort and practicality. Gradually, however, it became obvious that pants look sensational, not in the least masculine, and the tighter the better. Long trousers, along with lots of hair, breasts and bareness, became sexy in their own right. Everybody promptly forgot all about how comfortable and practical they were supposed to be, since who cared when they obviously simply looked marvelous. They are in fact a great bore on slushy pavements and very hot in summer but nobody minds. Nevertheless the extremely ancient prejudice against women in trousers lingered for a very long time. Many schools forbade pants for girls even though they might wear their hair as they liked, and the same restaurants that required the male necktie prohibited the female trouser. Even in quite recent times pants still seemed to connote either excessively crude informality or slightly perverted, raunchy sex. The last decade has seen the end of all this, since those sleek housewives in TV ads who used to wear shirtdresses all wear pants now, and dignified elderly ladies at all economic levels wear them too, with crystal earrings and nice, neat handbags. After all these anxious and newsworthy borrowings, all the classes and sexes remain as distinguishable as ever.

QUESTIONS

1. How would you describe the tone of this essay? Point to three or four sentences that seem to you to be especially clear illustrations of the dominant tone.
2. What does Hollander mean (in the fourth paragraph) when she says hot pants "were too much like science fiction" and (in the fifth paragraph) when she speaks of the "perverse affectation of poverty"? Or, choose two other succinct observations you would enjoy thinking more about, and elaborate on them.
3. A comparison of men's and women's attitudes toward clothes and fashion runs throughout the essay. Summarize the main points of the comparison.
4. From your own observation of the clothing of men and women, rich and poor, do you agree with Hollander's assertion in the last paragraph that "all the classes and the sexes remain as distinguishable as ever"?

Who Killed King Kong?

X. J. Kennedy

===

The ordeal and spectacular death of King Kong, the giant ape, undoubtedly have been witnessed by more Americans than have ever seen a performance of *Hamlet, Iphigenia at Aulis*, or even *Tobacco Road*. Since RKO-Radio Pictures first released *King Kong*, a quarter-century has gone by; yet year after year, from prints that grow more rain-beaten, from sound tracks that grow more tinny, ticket-buyers by thousands still pursue Kong's luckless fight against the forces of technology, tabloid journalism, and the DAR. They see him chloroformed to sleep, see him whisked from his jungle isle to New York and placed on show, see him burst his chains to roam the city (lugging a frightened blonde), at last to plunge from the spire of the Empire State Building, machine-gunned by model airplanes.

Though Kong may die, one begins to think his legend unkillable. No clearer proof of his hold upon the popular imagination may be seen than what emerged one catastrophic week in March 1955, when New York WOR-TV programmed *Kong* for seven evenings in a row (a total of sixteen showings). Many a rival network vice-president must have scowled when surveys showed that *Kong* — the 1933 B-picture — had lured away fat segments of the viewing populace from such powerful competitors as Ed Sullivan, Groucho Marx and Bishop Sheen.

But even television has failed to run *King Kong* into oblivion. Coffee-in-the-lobby cinemas still show the old hunk of hokum, with the apology that in its use of composite shorts and animated models the film remains technically interesting. And no other monster in movie history has won so devoted a popular audience. None of the plodding mummies, the stultified draculas, the white-coated Lugosis with their shiny pinball-machine laboratories, none of the invisible stranglers, berserk robots, or menaces from Mars has ever enjoyed so many resurrections.

Why does the American public refuse to let King Kong rest in peace? It is true, I'll admit, that *Kong* outdid every monster movie before or since in sheer carnage. Producers Cooper and Schoedsack crammed into it dinosaurs, headhunters, riots, aerial battles, bullets, bombs, bloodletting. Heroine Fay Wray, whose function is mainly to scream, shuts her mouth for hardly one uninterrupted minute from first reel to last. It is also true that *Kong* is larded with good healthy sadism, for those whose joy it is to see the frantic girl dangled from cliffs and harried by pterodactyls. But it seems to me that the abiding appeal of the giant ape rests on other foundations.

Kong has, first of all, the attraction of being manlike. His simian nature gives him one huge advantage over giant ants and walking vegetables in that an audience may conceivably identify with him. Kong's appeal has the quality that established the Tarzan series as American myth — for what man doesn't secretly image himself a huge hairy howler against whom no other monster has a chance? If Tarzan recalls the ape in us, then Kong may well appeal to that great-granddaddy primordial brute from whose tribe we have all deteriorated.

Intentionally or not, the producers of *King Kong* encourage this identification by etching the character of Kong with keen sympathy. For the ape is a figure in a tradition familiar to moviegoers: the tradition of the pitiable monster. We think of Lon Chaney in the role of Quasimodo, of Karloff in the original *Frankenstein*. As we watch the Frankenstein monster's fumbling and disastrous attempts to be-friend a flower-picking child, our sympathies are enlisted with the monster in his impenetrable loneliness. And so with Kong. As he roars in his chains, while barkers sell tickets to boobs who gape at him, we perhaps feel something more deep than pathos. We begin to sense something of the problem that engaged Eugene O'Neill in *The Hairy Ape:* the dilemma of a displaced animal spirit forced to live in a jungle built by machines.

King Kong, it is true, had special relevance in 1933. Landscapes of the depression are glimpsed early in the film when an impresario, seeking some desperate pretty girl to play the lead in a jungle movie, visits souplines and a Woman's Home Mission. In Fay Wray — who's been caught snitching an apple from a fruitstand — his search is ended. When he gives her a big feed and a movie contract, the girl is magic-carpeted out of the world of the National Recovery Act. And when, in the film's climax, Kong smashes that very Third Avenue landscape in which Fay had wandered hungry, audiences of 1933 may well have felt a personal satisfaction.

What is curious is that audiences of 1960 remain hooked. For in the heart of urban man, one suspects, lurks the impulse to fling a bomb. Though machines speed him to the scene of his daily grind, though IBM comptometers ("freeing the human mind from drudgery") enable him to drudge more efficiently once he arrives, there comes a moment when he wishes to turn upon his machines and kick hell out of them. He wants to hurl his combination radio-alarmclock out the bedroom window and listen to its smash. What subway commuter wouldn't love — just for once — to see the downtown express smack head-on into the uptown local? Such a wish is gratified in that memorable scene in *Kong* that opens with a wide-angle shot: interior of a railway car on the Third Avenue El. Strap-hangers are nodding, the literate refold their newspapers. Unknown to them, Kong has torn away a section of trestle toward which the train now speeds. The motorman spies Kong up ahead, jams on the brakes. Passengers hurtle together like so many peas in a pail. In a window of the car appear Kong's bloodshot eyes. Women shriek. Kong picks up the railway car as if it were a rat, flips it to the street and ties knots in it, or something. To any commuter the scene must appear one of the most satisfactory pieces of celluloid ever exposed.

Yet however violent his acts, Kong remains a gentleman. Remarkable is his sense of chivalry. Whenever a fresh boa constrictor threatens Fay, Kong first sees that the lady is safely parked, then manfully thrashes her attacker. (And she, the ingrate, runs away every time his back is turned.) Atop the Empire State Building, ignoring his pursuers, Kong places Fay on a ledge as tenderly as if she were a dozen eggs. He fondles her, then turns to face the Army Air Force. And Kong is perhaps the most disinterested lover since Cyrano: his attentions to the lady are utterly without hope of reward. After all, between a five-foot blonde and a fifty-foot ape, love can hardly be more than an intellectual flirtation. In his simian way King Kong is the hopelessly yearning lover of Petrarchan convention. His forced exit from his jungle, in chains, results directly from his single-minded pursuit of Fay. He smashes a Broadway theater when the notion enters his dull brain that the flashbulbs of photographers somehow endanger the lady. His perilous shinnying up a skyscraper to pluck Fay from her boudoir is an act of the kindliest of hearts. He's impossible to discourage even though the love of his life can't lay eyes on him without shrieking murder.

The tragedy of King Kong then, is to be the beast who at the end of the fable fails to turn into the handsome prince. This is the conviction that the scriptwriters would leave with us in the film's closing line. As Kong's corpse lies blocking traffic in the street, the entrepreneur who brought Kong to New York turns to the assembled reporters and proclaims: "That's your story, boys — it was Beauty killed the Beast!" But greater forces than those of the screaming Lady have combined to lay Kong low, if you ask me. Kong lives for a time as one of those persecuted near-animal souls bewildered in the middle of an industrial order, whose simple desires are thwarted at every turn. He climbs the Empire State Building because in all New York it's the closest thing he can find to the clifftop of his jungle isle. He dies, a pitiful dolt, and the army brass and publicity-men cackle over him. His death is the only possible outcome to as neat a tragic dilemma as you can ask for. The machine-guns do him in, while the manicured human hero (a nice clean Dartmouth boy) carries away Kong's sweetheart to the altar. O, the misery of it all. There's far more truth about upper-middle-class American life in *King Kong* than in the last seven dozen novels of John P. Marquand.

A Negro friend from Atlanta tells me that in movie houses in colored neighborhoods throughout the South, *Kong* does a constant business. They show the thing in Atlanta at least every year, presumably to the same audiences. Perhaps this popularity may simply be due to the fact that Kong is one of the most watchable movies ever constructed, but I wonder whether Negro audiences may not find some archetypical appeal in this serio-comic tale of a huge black powerful free spirit whom all the hardworking white policemen are out to kill.

Every day in the week on a screen somewhere in the world, King Kong relives his agony. Again and again he expires on the Empire State Building, as audiences of the devout assist his sacrifice. We watch him die, and by extension kill the ape within our bones, but these little deaths of ours occur in prosaic surroundings. We do not die on a tower, New York before our feet, nor do we give our lives to smash a few flying machines. It is not for us to bring to a momentary standstill the civilization in which we move. King Kong does this for us. And so we kill him again and again, in much-spliced celluloid, while the ape in us expires from day to day, obscure, in desperation.

QUESTIONS

1. What is your response to Kennedy's colloquial expressions, such as "lugging a frightened blonde," "hunk of hokum," "snitching an apple"? Are they used for a purpose?
2. In the third paragraph Kennedy calls *King Kong* "the old hunk of hokum." Does he consistently maintain the attitude implied here?
3. How persuasive do you find Kennedy's analysis? Is any of it useful in explaining the appeal of other films you have seen?
4. Kennedy refers to *King Kong* as a "monster movie." Can you think of other films you would place in that category? How would you define "horror movie" or "disaster film" or "science fiction film"? Are these, and "monster movie," distinct or overlapping categories?

Vivisection

C. S. Lewis

It is the rarest thing in the world to hear a rational discussion of vivisection. Those who disapprove of it are commonly accused of "sentimentality," and very often their arguments justify the accusation. They paint pictures of pretty little dogs on dissecting tables. But the other side lie open to exactly the same charge. They also often defend the practice by drawing pictures of suffering women and children whose pain can be relieved (we are assured) only by the fruits of vivisection. The one appeal, quite as clearly as the other, is addressed to emotion, to the particular emotion we call pity. And neither appeal proves anything. If the thing is right — and if right at all, it is a duty — then pity for the animal is one of the temptations we must resist in order to perform that duty. If the thing is wrong, then pity for human suffering is precisely the temptation which will most probably lure us into doing that wrong thing. But the real question — *whether* it is right or wrong — remains meanwhile just where it was.

A rational discussion of this subject begins by inquiring whether pain is, or is not, an evil. If it is not, then the case against vivisection falls. But then so does the case for vivisection. If it is not defended on the ground that it reduces human suffering, on what ground can it be defended? And if pain is not an evil, why should human suffering be reduced? We must therefore assume as a basis for the whole discussion that pain is an evil, otherwise there is nothing to be discussed.

Now if pain is an evil then the infliction of pain, considered in itself, must clearly be an evil act. But there are such things as necessary evils. Some acts which would be bad, simply in themselves, may be excusable and even laudable when they are necessary means to a greater good. In saying that the infliction of pain, simply in itself, is bad, we are not saying that pain ought never to be inflicted. Most of us think that it can rightly be inflicted for a good purpose — as in dentistry or just and reformatory punishment. The point is that it always requires justification. On the man whom we find inflicting pain rests the burden of showing why an act which in itself would be simply bad is, in those particular circumstances, good. If we find a man giving pleasure it is for us to prove (if we criticize him) that his action is wrong. But if we find a man inflicting pain it is for him to prove that his action is right. If he cannot, he is a wicked man.

Now vivisection can only be defended by showing it to be right that one species should suffer in order that another species should be happier. And here we come to the parting of the ways. The Christian defender and the ordinary "scientific" (i.e., naturalistic) defender of vivisection, have to take quite different lines.

The Christian defender, especially in the Latin countries, is very apt to say that we are entitled to do anything we please to animals because they "have no souls." But what does this mean? If it means that animals have no consciousness, then how is this known? They certainly behave as if they had, or at least the higher animals do. I myself am inclined to think that far fewer animals than is supposed have what we should recognize as consciousness. But that is only an opinion. Unless we know on other grounds that vivisection is right we must not take the moral risk of tormenting them on a mere opinion. On the other hand, the statement that they "have no souls" may mean that they have no moral responsibilities and are not immortal. But the absence of "soul" in that sense makes the infliction of pain upon them not easier but harder to justify. For it means that animals cannot deserve pain, nor profit morally by the discipline of pain, nor be recompensed by happiness in another life for suffering in this. Thus all the factors which render pain more tolerable or make it less totally evil in the case of human beings will be lacking in the beasts. "Soullessness," in so far as it is relevant to the question at all, is an argument against vivisection.

The only rational line for the Christian vivisectionist to take is to say that the superiority of man over beast is a real objective fact, guaranteed by Revelation, and that the propriety of sacrificing beast to man is a logical consequence. We are "worth more than many sparrows," [11] and in saying this we are not merely expressing a natural preference for our own species simply because it is our own but conforming to a hierarchical order created by God and really present in the universe whether any one acknowledges it or not. The position may not be satisfactory. We may fail to see how a benevolent Deity could wish us to draw such conclusions from the hierarchical order He has created. We may find it difficult to formulate a human right of tormenting beasts in terms which would not equally imply an angelic right of tormenting men. And we may feel that though objective superiority is rightly claimed for men, yet that very superiority ought partly to *consist in* not behaving like a vivisector: that we ought to prove ourselves better than the beasts precisely by the fact of acknowledging duties to them which they do not acknowledge to us. But on all these questions different opinions can be honestly held. If on grounds of our real, divinely ordained, superiority a Christian pathologist thinks it right to vivisect, and does so with scrupulous care to avoid the least dram or scruple of unnecessary pain, in a trembling awe at the responsibility which he assumes, and with a vivid sense of the high mode in which human life must be lived if it is to justify the sacrifices made for it, then (whether we agree with him or not) we can respect his point of view.

But of course the vast majority of vivisectors have no such theological background. They are most of them naturalistic and Darwinian. Now here, surely, we come up against a very alarming

[11] Matthew x. 31.

fact. The very same people who will most contemptuously brush aside any consideration of animal suffering if it stands in the way of "research" will also, on another context, most vehemently deny that there is any radical difference between man and the other animals. On the naturalistic view the beasts are at bottom just the same *sort* of thing as ourselves. Man is simply the cleverest of the anthropoids. All the grounds on which a Christian might defend vivisection are thus cut from under our feet. We sacrifice other species to our own not because our own has any objective metaphysical privilege over others, but simply because it is ours. It may be very natural to have this loyalty to our own species, but let us hear no more from the naturalists about the "sentimentality" of anti-vivisectionists. If loyalty to our own species, preference for man simply because we are men, is not a sentiment, then what is? It may be a good sentiment or a bad one. But a sentiment it certainly is. Try to base it on logic and see what happens!

But the most sinister thing about modern vivisection is this. If a mere sentiment justifies cruelty, why stop at a sentiment for the whole human race? There is also a sentiment for the white man against the black, for a *Herrenvolk*[12] against the non-Aryans, for "civilized" or "progressive" peoples against "savages" or "backward" peoples. Finally, for our own country, party or class against others. Once the old Christian idea of a total difference in kind between man and beast has been abandoned, then no argument for experiments on animals can be found which is not also an argument for experiments on inferior men. If we cut up beasts simply because they cannot prevent us and because we are backing our own side in the struggle for existence, it is only logical to cut up imbeciles, criminals, enemies or capitalists for the same reasons. Indeed, experiments on men have already begun. We all hear that Nazi scientists have done them. We all suspect that our own scientists may begin to do so, in secret, at any moment.

The alarming thing is that the vivisectors have won the first round. In the nineteenth and eighteenth centuries a man was not stamped as a "crank" for protesting against vivisection. Lewis Carroll protested, if I remember his famous letter correctly, on the very same ground which I have just used.[13] Dr. Johnson — a man whose

[12] Editors' note: German for "master race."

[13] "Vivisection as a Sign of the Times," *The Works of Lewis Carroll,* ed. Roger Lancelyn Green (London, 1965), pp. 1089–92. See also "Some Popular Fallacies about Vivisection," ibid., pp. 1092–1100.

mind had as much *iron* in it as any man's — protested in a note on *Cymbeline* which is worth quoting in full. In Act I, scene v, the Queen explains to the Doctor that she wants poisons to experiment on "such creatures as We count not worth the hanging, — but none human." [14] The Doctor replies:

> Your Highness
> Shall from this practice but make hard your heart. [15]

Johnson comments: "The thought would probably have been more amplified, had our author lived to be shocked with such experiments as have been published in later times, by a race of men that have practised tortures without pity, and related them without shame, and are yet suffered to erect their heads among human beings." [16]

The words are his, not mine, and in truth we hardly dare in these days to use such calmly stern language. The reason why we do not dare is that the other side has in fact won. And though cruelty even to beasts is an important matter, their victory is symptomatic of matters more important still. The victory of vivisection marks a great advance in the triumph of ruthless, non-moral utilitarianism over the old world of ethical law; a triumph in which we, as well as animals, are already the victims, and of which Dachau and Hiroshima mark the more recent achievements. In justifying cruelty to animals we put ourselves also on the animal level. We choose the jungle and must abide by our choice.

You will notice I have spent no time in discussing what actually goes on in the laboratories. We shall be told, of course, that there is surprisingly little cruelty. That is a question with which, at present, I have nothing to do. We must first decide what should be allowed: after that it is for the police to discover what is already being done.

QUESTIONS

1. What purpose does Lewis's first paragraph serve? Is his implied definition of sentimentality adequate for his purpose?
2. By the end of the second paragraph are you willing to agree, at least for the sake of argument, that pain is an evil?
3. In the third paragraph Lewis gives two examples (dentistry and reformatory punishment) to prove that the infliction of pain

[14] Shakespeare, *Cymbeline,* I, v, 19–20.
[15] Ibid., 23.
[16] *Johnson on Shakespeare: Essays and Notes Selected and Set Forth with an Introduction* by Sir Walter Raleigh (London, 1908), p. 181.

"always requires justification." Are these two examples adequate and effective?

4. By the end of the fifth paragraph (the paragraph beginning "The Christian defender") are we more or less convinced that Lewis is fully aware of both sides of the argument? Do we feel he is fairly presenting both sides?

5. Characterize the tone (Lewis's attitude) implied in "The position may not be satisfactory" (page 490). Notice also the effect of the repetition (in the same paragraph) of "We may fail to see," "We may find it difficult," "And we may feel. . . ." How tentative do you think Lewis really is?

6. The eighth paragraph begins, "But the most sinister thing about modern vivisection is this." How surprising is the word "sinister"? And why does Lewis bring in (drag in?) racist and religious persecution?

7. Late in his essay (pages 491–92) Lewis quotes Lewis Carroll, Shakespeare, and Dr. Johnson. Except for a phrase from the Bible, these are the first quotations he uses. Should he have introduced these quotations, or others, earlier?

8. Analyze the final paragraph. Is Lewis correct in dismissing the question of how much cruelty there is in laboratories? Characterize the tone of the last sentence.

New Superstitions for Old

Margaret Mead

Once in a while there is a day when everything seems to run smoothly and even the riskiest venture comes out exactly right. You exclaim, "This is my lucky day!" Then as an afterthought you say, "Knock on wood!" Of course, you do not really believe that knocking on wood will ward off danger. Still, boasting about your own good luck gives you a slightly uneasy feeling — and you carry out the little protective ritual. If someone challenged you at that moment, you would probably say, "Oh, that's nothing. Just an old superstition."

But when you come to think about it, what is a superstition?

In the contemporary world most people treat old folk beliefs as superstitions — the belief, for instance, that there are lucky and unlucky days or numbers, that future events can be read from omens, that there are protective charms or that what happens can be influenced by casting spells. We have excluded magic from our current world view, for we know that natural events have natural causes.

In a religious context, where truths cannot be demonstrated, we accept them as a matter of faith. Superstitions, however, belong to the category of beliefs, practices and ways of thinking that have been discarded because they are inconsistent with scientific knowledge. It is easy to say that other people are superstitious because they believe what we regard to be untrue. "Superstition" used in that sense is a derogatory term for the beliefs of other people that we do not share. But there is more to it than that. For superstitions lead a kind of half life in a twilight world where, sometimes, we partly suspend our disbelief and act as if magic worked.

Actually, almost every day, even in the most sophisticated home, something is likely to happen that evokes the memory of some old folk belief. The salt spills. A knife falls to the floor. Your nose tickles. Then perhaps, with a slightly embarrassed smile, the person who spilled the salt tosses a pinch over his left shoulder. Or someone recites the old rhyme, "Knife falls, gentleman calls." Or as you rub your nose you think, That means a letter. I wonder who's writing? No one takes these small responses very seriously or gives them more than a passing thought. Sometimes people will preface one of these ritual acts — walking around instead of under a ladder or hastily closing an umbrella that has been opened inside a house — with such a remark as "I remember my great-aunt used to . . ." or "Germans used to say you ought not . . ." And then, having placed the belief at some distance away in time or space, they carry out the ritual.

Everyone also remembers a few of the observances of childhood — wishing on the first star; looking at the new moon over the right shoulder; avoiding the cracks in the sidewalk on the way to school while chanting, "Step on a crack, break your mother's back"; wishing on white horses, on loads of hay, on covered bridges, on red cars; saying quickly, "Bread-and-butter" when a post or a tree separated you from the friend you were walking with. The adult may not actually recite the formula "Star light, star bright . . ." and may not quite turn to look at the new moon, but his mood is tempered by a little of the old thrill that came when the observance was still freighted with magic.

Superstition can also be used with another meaning. When I discuss the religious beliefs of other peoples, especially primitive peoples, I am often asked, "Do they really have a religion, or is it all just superstition?" The point of contrast here is not between a scientific and a magical view of the world but between the clear, theologically defensible religious beliefs of members of civilized societies and what we regard as the false and childish views of the heathen who "bow down to wood and stone." Within the civilized religions, however, where membership includes believers who are educated and urbane and others who are ignorant and simple, one always finds traditions and practices that the more sophisticated will dismiss offhand as "just superstition" but that guide the steps of those who live by older ways. Mostly these are very ancient beliefs, some handed on from one religion to another and carried from country to country around the world.

Very commonly, people associate superstition with the past, with very old ways of thinking that have been supplanted by modern knowledge. But new superstitions are continually coming into being and flourishing in our society. Listening to mothers in the park in the 1930's, one heard them say, "Now, don't you run out into the sun, or Polio will get you." In the 1940's elderly people explained to one another in tones of resignation, "It was the Virus that got him down." And every year the cosmetics industry offers us new magic — cures for baldness, lotions that will give every woman radiant skin, hair coloring that will restore to the middle-aged the charm and romance of youth — results that are promised if we will just follow the simple directions. Families and individuals also have their cherished, private superstitions. You must leave by the back door when you are going on a journey, or you must wear a green dress when you are taking an examination. It is a kind of joke, of course, but it makes you feel safe.

These old half-beliefs and new half-beliefs reflect the keenness of our wish to have something come true or to prevent something bad from happening. We do not always recognize new superstitions for what they are, and we still follow the old ones because someone's faith long ago matches our contemporary hopes and fears. In the past people "knew" that a black cat crossing one's path was a bad omen, and they turned back home. Today we are fearful of taking a journey and would give anything to turn back — and then we notice a black cat running across the road in front of us.

Child psychologists recognize the value of the toy a child holds in his hand at bedtime. It is different from his thumb, with which he can close himself in from the rest of the world, and it is different from the real world, to which he is learning to relate himself.

Psychologists call these toys — these furry animals and old, cozy baby blankets — "transitional objects"; that is, objects that help the child move back and forth between the exactions of everyday life and the world of wish and dream.

Superstitions have some of the qualities of these transitional objects. They help people pass between the areas of life where what happens has to be accepted without proof and the areas where sequences of events are explicable in terms of cause and effect, based on knowledge. Bacteria and viruses that cause sickness have been identified; the cause of symptoms can be diagnosed and a rational course of treatment prescribed. Magical charms no longer are needed to treat the sick; modern medicine has brought the whole sequence of events into the secular world. But people often act as if this change had not taken place. Laymen still treat germs as if they were invisible, malign spirits, and physicians sometimes prescribe antibiotics as if they were magic substances.

Over time, more and more of life has become subject to the controls of knowledge. However, this is never a one-way process. Scientific investigation is continually increasing our knowledge. But if we are to make good use of this knowledge, we must not only rid our minds of old, superseded beliefs and fragments of magical practice, but also recognize new superstitions for what they are. Both are generated by our wishes, our fears and our feeling of helplessness in difficult situations.

Civilized peoples are not alone in having grasped the idea of superstitions — beliefs and practices that are superseded but that still may evoke compliance. The idea is one that is familiar to every people, however primitive, that I have ever known. Every society has a core of transcendent beliefs — beliefs about the nature of the universe, the world and man — that no one doubts or questions. Every society also has a fund of knowledge related to practical life — about the succession of day and night and of the seasons; about correct ways of planting seeds so that they will germinate and grow; about the processes involved in making dyes or the steps necessary to remove the deadly poison from manioc roots so they become edible. Island peoples know how the winds shift and they know the star toward which they must point the prow of the canoe exactly so that as the sun rises they will see the first fringing palms on the shore toward which they are sailing.

This knowledge, based on repeated observations of reliable sequences, leads to ideas and hypotheses of the kind that underlie scientific thinking. And gradually as scientific knowledge, once developed without conscious plan, has become a great self-corrective system and the foundation for rational planning and action, old magical beliefs and observances have had to be discarded.

But it takes time for new ways of thinking to take hold, and often the transition is only partial. Older, more direct beliefs live on in the hearts and minds of elderly people. And they are learned by children who, generation after generation, start out life as hopefully and fearfully as their forebears did. Taking their first steps away from home, children use the old rituals and invent new ones to protect themselves against the strangeness of the world into which they are venturing.

So whatever has been rejected as no longer true, as limited, provincial and idolatrous, still leads a half life. People may say, "It's just a superstition," but they continue to invoke the ritual's protection or potency. In this transitional, twilight state such beliefs come to resemble dreaming. In the dream world a thing can be either good or bad; a cause can be an effect and an effect can be a cause. Do warts come from touching toads, or does touching a toad cure the wart? Is sneezing a good omen or a bad omen? You can have it either way — or both ways at once. In the same sense, the half-acceptance and half-denial accorded superstitions give us the best of both worlds.

Superstitions are sometimes smiled at and sometimes frowned upon as observances characteristic of the old-fashioned, the unenlightened, children, peasants, servants, immigrants, foreigners or backwoods people. Nevertheless, they give all of us ways of moving back and forth among the different worlds in which we live — the sacred, the secular and the scientific. They allow us to keep a private world also, where, smiling a little, we can banish danger with a gesture and summon luck with a rhyme, make the sun shine in spite of storm clouds, force the stranger to do our bidding, keep an enemy at bay and straighten the paths of those we love.

QUESTIONS

1. What definition of superstition is implied in the third paragraph? Does the definition shift in the fourth paragraph, or is it amplified?
2. What relationship does Mead imply between superstition and magic? To what extent do you agree with her assertion in the third paragraph that "We have excluded magic from our current world view"?

3. Is Mead's distinction between superstition and religion clear? Can you give an example of a matter of religious faith and an example of superstition, consistent with Mead's definitions, and explain what distinguishes them?

4. According to Mead, what value do superstitions have? On page 496 she says "we must not only rid our minds of old, superseded beliefs and fragments of magical practice, but also recognize new superstitions for what they are." How can this statement be reconciled with her explanation of the value of superstition?

Total Effect and the Eighth Grade

Flannery O'Connor

In two recent instances in Georgia, parents have objected to their eighth- and ninth-grade children's reading assignments in modern fiction. This seems to happen with some regularity in cases throughout the country. The unwitting parent picks up his child's book, glances through it, comes upon passages of erotic detail or profanity, and takes off at once to complain to the school board. Sometimes, as in one of the Georgia cases, the teacher is dismissed and hackles rise in liberal circles everywhere.

The two cases in Georgia, which involved Steinbeck's *East of Eden* and John Hersey's *A Bell for Adano,* provoked considerable newspaper comment. One columnist, in commending the enterprise of the teachers, announced that students do not like to read the fusty works of the nineteenth century, that their attention can best be held by novels dealing with the realities of our own time, and that the Bible, too, is full of racy stories.

Mr. Hersey himself addressed a letter to the State School Superintendent in behalf of the teacher who had been dismissed. He pointed out that his book is not scandalous, that it attempts to convey an earnest message about the nature of democracy, and that it falls well within the limits of the principle of "total effect," that principle followed in legal cases by which a book is judged not for isolated parts but by the final effect of the whole book upon the general reader.

I do not want to comment on the merits of these particular

cases. What concerns me is what novels ought to be assigned in the eighth and ninth grades as a matter of course, for if these cases indicate anything, they indicate the haphazard way in which fiction is approached in our high schools. Presumably there is a state reading list which contains "safe" books for teachers to assign; after that it is up to the teacher.

English teachers come in Good, Bad, and Indifferent, but too frequently in high schools anyone who can speak English is allowed to teach it. Since several novels can't easily be gathered into one textbook, the fiction that students are assigned depends upon their teacher's knowledge, ability, and taste: variable factors at best. More often than not, the teacher assigns what he thinks will hold the attention and interest of the students. Modern fiction will certainly hold it.

Ours is the first age in history which has asked the child what he would tolerate learning, but that is a part of the problem with which I am not equipped to deal. The devil of Educationism that possesses us is the kind that can be "cast out only by prayer and fasting." No one has yet come along strong enough to do it. In other ages the attention of children was held by Homer and Virgil, among others, but, by the reverse evolutionary process, that is no longer possible; our children are too stupid now to enter the past imaginatively. No one asks the student if algebra pleases him or if he finds it satisfactory that some French verbs are irregular, but if he prefers Hersey to Hawthorne, his taste must prevail.

I would like to put forward the proposition, repugnant to most English teachers, that fiction, if it is going to be taught in the high schools, should be taught as a subject and as a subject with a history. The total effect of a novel depends not only on its innate impact, but upon the experience, literary and otherwise, with which it is approached. No child needs to be assigned Hersey or Steinbeck until he is familiar with a certain amount of the best work of Cooper, Hawthorne, Melville, the early James, and Crane, and he does not need to be assigned these until he has been introduced to some of the better English novelists of the eighteenth and nineteenth centuries.

The fact that these works do not present him with the realities of his own time is all to the good. He is surrounded by the realities of his own time, and he has no perspective whatever from which to view them. Like the college student who wrote in her paper on Lincoln that he went to the movies and got shot, many students go to college unaware that the world was not made yesterday; their studies began with the present and dipped backward occasionally when it seemed necessary or unavoidable.

There is much to be enjoyed in the great British novels of the nineteenth century, much that a good teacher can open up in them for the young student. There is no reason why these novels should be either too simple or too difficult for the eighth grade. For the simple, they offer simple pleasures; for the more precocious, they can be made to yield subtler ones if the teacher is up to it. Let the student discover, after reading the nineteenth-century British novel, that the nineteenth-century American novel is quite different as to its literary characteristics, and he will thereby learn something not only about these individual works but about the sea-change which a new historical situation can effect in a literary form. Let him come to modern fiction with this experience behind him, and he will be better able to see and to deal with the more complicated demands of the best twentieth-century fiction.

Modern fiction often looks simpler than the fiction that preceded it, but in reality it is more complex. A natural evolution has taken place. The author has for the most part absented himself from direct participation in the work and has left the reader to make his own way amid experiences dramatically rendered and symbolically ordered. The modern novelist merges the reader in the experience; he tends to raise the passions he touches upon. If he is a good novelist, he raises them to effect by their order and clarity a new experience — the total effect — which is not in itself sensuous or simply of the moment. Unless the child has had some literary experience before, he is not going to be able to resolve the immediate passions the book arouses into any true, total picture.

It is here the moral problem will arise. It is one thing for a child to read about adultery in the Bible or in *Anna Karenina,* and quite another for him to read about it in most modern fiction. This is not only because in both the former instances adultery is considered a sin, and in the latter, at most, an inconvenience, but because modern writing involves the reader in the action with a new degree of intensity, and literary mores now permit him to be involved in any action a human being can perform.

In our fractured culture, we cannot agree on morals; we cannot even agree that moral matters should come before literary ones when there is a conflict between them. All this is another reason why the high schools would do well to return to their proper business of preparing foundations. Whether in the senior year students should be assigned modern novelists should depend both on their parents' consent and on what they have already read and understood.

The high-school English teacher will be fulfilling his responsibility if he furnishes the student a guided opportunity, through the best writing of the past, to come, in time, to an understanding of the best writing of the present. He will teach literature, not social studies or little lessons in democracy or the customs of many lands.

And if the student finds that this is not to his taste? Well, that is regrettable. Most regrettable. His taste should not be consulted; it is being formed.

QUESTIONS

1. What is the function of the first three paragraphs of "Total Effect and the Eighth Grade"? Can you justify O'Connor's abrupt dismissal ("I do not want to comment on the merits of these particular cases") of the opposing argument summarized in the second and third paragraphs? How?
2. "English teachers come in Good, Bad, and Indifferent, but too frequently in high schools anyone who can speak English is allowed to teach it." Can you, from your own experience, support this view?
3. Is the tone of the sixth paragraph, beginning "Ours is the first age," sarcastic? If not, how would you characterize it?
4. Which of O'Connor's arguments might be used to support the rating of movies X, R, PG, and G? Are you for or against these ratings? How would you support your position?

Politics and the English Language
George Orwell

Most people who bother with the matter at all would admit that the English language is in a bad way, but it is generally assumed that we cannot by conscious action do anything about it. Our civilization is decadent and our language — so the argument runs — must inevitably share in the general collapse. It follows that any struggle against the abuse of language is a sentimental archaism, like preferring candles to electric light or hansom cabs to aeroplanes. Underneath this lies the half-conscious belief that language is a natural growth and not an instrument which we shape for our own purposes.

Now, it is clear that the decline of a language must ultimately have political and economic causes: it is not due simply to the bad influence of this or that individual writer. But an effect can become a cause, reinforcing the original cause and producing the same effect in an intensified form, and so on indefinitely. A man may take to drink because he feels himself to be a failure, and then fail all the more completely because he drinks. It is rather the same thing that is happening to the English language. It becomes ugly and inaccurate because our thoughts are foolish, but the slovenliness of our language makes it easier for us to have foolish thoughts. The point is that the process is reversible. Modern English, especially written English, is full of bad habits which spread by imitation and which can be avoided if one is willing to take the necessary trouble. If one gets rid of these habits one can think more clearly, and to think clearly is a necessary first step towards political regeneration: so that the fight against bad English is not frivolous and is not the exclusive concern of professional writers. I will come back to this presently, and I hope that by that time the meaning of what I have said here will have become clearer. Meanwhile, here are five specimens of the English language as it is now habitually written.

These five passages have not been picked out because they are especially bad — I could have quoted far worse if I had chosen — but because they illustrate various of the mental vices from which we now suffer. They are a little below the average, but are fairly representative samples. I number them so that I can refer back to them when necessary:

(1) I am not, indeed, sure whether it is not true to say that the Milton who once seemed not unlike a seventeenth-century Shelley had not become, out of an experience ever more bitter in each year, more alien [*sic*] to the founder of that Jesuit sect which nothing could induce him to tolerate.
— Professor Harold Laski (Essay in *Freedom of Expression*)

(2) Above all, we cannot play ducks and drakes with a native battery of idioms which prescribes such egregious collocations of vocables as the basic *put up with* for *tolerate* or *put at a loss* for *bewilder*.
— Professor Lancelot Hogben (*Interglossa*)

(3) On the one side we have the free personality: by definition it is not neurotic, for it has neither conflict nor dream. Its desires, such as they are, are transparent, for they are just what institutional approval keeps in the forefront of consciousness; another institutional pattern would alter their number and intensity; there is little in them that is natural, irreducible, or culturally dangerous. But *on the other side,* the social bond itself is nothing but the mutual reflection of these self-secure integrities. Recall the definition of love. Is not this the very picture of a small academic? Where is there a place in this hall of mirrors for either personality or fraternity?
— Essay on psychology in *Politics* (New York)

(4) All the "best people" from the gentlemen's clubs, and all the frantic fascist captains, united in common hatred of Socialism and bestial horror of the rising tide of the mass revolutionary movement, have turned to acts of provocation, to foul incendiarism, to medieval legends of poisoned wells, to legalize their own destruction of proletarian organizations, and rouse the agitated petty-bourgeoisie to chauvinistic fervor on behalf of the fight against the revolutionary way out of the crisis.

— Communist Pamphlet

(5) If a new spirit is to be infused into this old country, there is one thorny and contentious reform which must be tackled, and that is the humanization and galvanization of the B.B.C. Timidity here will bespeak canker and atrophy of the soul. The heart of Britain may be sound and of strong beat, for instance, but the British lion's roar at present is like that of Bottom in Shakespeare's *Midsummer Night's Dream* — as gentle as any sucking dove. A virile new Britain cannot continue indefinitely to be traduced in the eyes or rather ears, of the world by the effete languors of Langham Place, brazenly masquerading as "standard English." When the voice of Britain is heard at nine o'clock, better far and infinitely less ludicrous to hear aitches honestly dropped than the present priggish, inflated, inhibited, school-ma'amish arch braying of blameless bashful mewing maidens!

— Letter in *Tribune*

Each of these passages has faults of its own, but, quite apart from avoidable ugliness, two qualities are common to all of them. The first is staleness of imagery; the other is lack of precision. The writer either has a meaning and cannot express it, or he inadvertently says something else, or he is almost indifferent as to whether his words mean anything or not. This mixture of vagueness and sheer incompetence is the most marked characteristic of modern English prose, and especially of any kind of political writing. As soon as certain topics are raised, the concrete melts into the abstract and no one seems able to think of turns of speech that are not hackneyed: prose consists less and less of *words* chosen for the sake of their meaning, and more and more of *phrases* tacked together like the sections of a prefabricated hen-house. I list below, with notes and examples, various of the tricks by means of which the work of prose-construction is habitually dodged:

Dying metaphors. A newly invented metaphor assists thought by evoking a visual image, while on the other hand a metaphor which is technically "dead" (e.g. *iron resolution*) has in effect reverted to being an ordinary word and can generally be used without loss of vividness. But in between these two classes there is a huge dump of worn-out metaphors which have lost all evocative power and are merely used because they save people the trouble of inventing phrases for themselves. Examples are: *Ring the changes on, take up the cudgels for, toe the line, ride roughshod over, stand shoulder to shoulder with, play into the hands of, no axe to grind, grist to the mill, fishing in troubled waters, on the order of the day, Achilles' heel, swan song, hotbed.* Many of these are used without knowledge of their meaning (what is a "rift," for instance?), and incompatible metaphors are frequently mixed, a sure sign that the writer is not interested in what he is saying. Some metaphors now current have been twisted out of their original meaning without those who use them even being aware of the fact. For example, *toe the line* is sometimes written *tow the line.* Another example is the *hammer and the anvil*, now always used with the implication that the anvil gets the worst of it. In real life it is always the anvil that breaks the hammer, never the other way about: a writer who stopped to think what he was saying would be aware of this, and would avoid perverting the original phrase.

Operators or *verbal false limbs.* These save the trouble of picking out appropriate verbs and nouns, and at the same time pad each sentence with extra syllables which give it an appearance of symmetry. Characteristic phrases are *render inoperative, militate against, make contact with, be subjected to, give rise to, give grounds for, have the effect of, plays a leading part (role) in, make itself felt, take effect, exhibit a tendency to, serve the purpose of,* etc., etc. The keynote is the elimination of simple verbs. Instead of being a single word, such as *break, stop, spoil, mend, kill,* a verb becomes a *phrase,* made up of a noun or adjective tacked on to some general-purpose verb such as *prove, serve, form, play, render.* In addition, the passive voice is wherever possible used in preference to the active, and noun constructions are used instead of gerunds (*by examination of* instead of *by examining*). The range of verbs is further cut down by means of the *-ize* and *de-* formations, and the banal statements are given an appearance of profundity by means of the *not un-* formation. Simple conjunctions and prepositions are replaced by such phrases as *with respect to, having regard to, the fact that, by dint of, in view of, in the interests of, on the hypothesis that;* and the ends of sentences are saved from anticlimax by such resounding common-places as *greatly to be desired, cannot be left out of account, a development to be expected in the near future, deserving of serious consideration, brought to a satisfactory conclusion,* and so on and so forth.

Pretentious diction. Words like *phenomenon, element, individual* (as noun), *objective, categorical, effective, virtual, basic, primary, promote, constitute, exhibit, exploit, utilize, eliminate, liquidate,* are used to dress up simple statements and give an air of scientific impartiality to biased judgments. Adjectives like *epoch-making, epic, historic, un-forgettable, triumphant, age-old, inevitable, inexorable, veritable,* are used to dignify the sordid processes of international politics, while writing that aims at glorifying war usually takes on an archaic color, its characteristic words being: *realm, throne, chariot, mailed fist, trident, sword, shield, buckler, banner, jackboot, clarion.* Foreign words and expressions such as *cul de sac, ancien régime, deus ex machina, mutatis mutandis, status quo, gleichschaltung, weltanschauung,* are used to give an air of culture and elegance. Except for the useful abbreviations *i.e., e.g.,* and *etc.,* there is no real need for any of the hundreds of foreign phrases now current in English. Bad writers, and especially scientific, political and sociological writers, are nearly always haunted by the notion that Latin or Greek words are grander than Saxon ones, and unnecessary words like *expedite, ameliorate, predict, extraneous, deracinated, clandestine, subaqueous* and hundreds of others constantly gain ground from their Anglo-Saxon opposite numbers.[17] The jargon peculiar to Marxist writing (*hyena, hangman, cannibal, petty bourgeois, these gentry, lacquey, flunkey, mad dog, White Guard,* etc.) consists largely of words and phrases translated from Russian, German or French; but the normal way of coining a new word is to use a Latin or Greek root with the appropriate affix and, where necessary, the *-ize* formation. It is often easier to make up words of this kind (*deregionalize, impermissible, extramarital, non-fragmentary* and so forth) than to think up the English words that will cover one's meaning. The result, in general, is an increase in slovenliness and vagueness.

Meaningless words. In certain kinds of writing, particularly in art criticism and literary criticism, it *is* normal to come across long passages which are almost completely lacking in meaning.[18] Words

---

[17] An interesting illustration of this is the way in which the English flower names which were in use till very recently are being ousted by Greek ones, *snapdragon* becoming *antirrhinum, forget-me-not* becoming *myosotis,* etc. It is hard to see any practical reason for this change of fashion: it is probably due to an instinctive turning-away from the more homely word and a vague feeling that the Greek word is scientific.

[18] Example: "Comfort's catholicity of perception and image, strangely Whitmanesque in range, almost the exact opposite in aesthetic compulsion, continues to evoke that trembling atmospheric accumulative hinting at a cruel, an inexorably serene timelessness. . . . Wrey Gardiner scores by aiming at simple bull's-eyes with precision. Only they are not so simple, and through this contented sadness runs more than the surface bittersweet of resignation." (*Poetry Quarterly.*)

like *romantic, plastic, values, human, dead, sentimental, natural, vitality,*
as used in art criticism, are strictly meaningless, in the sense that they
not only do not point to any discoverable object, but are hardly ever
expected to do so by the reader. When one critic writes, "The
outstanding feature of Mr. X's work is its living quality," while
another writes, "The immediately striking thing about Mr. X's
work is its peculiar deadness," the reader accepts this as a simple
difference of opinion. If words like *black* and *white* were involved,
instead of the jargon words *dead* and *living,* he would see at once that
language was being used in an improper way. Many political words
are similarly abused. The word *Fascism* has now no meaning except
in so far as it signifies "something not desirable." The words *democ-*
racy, socialism, freedom, patriotic, realistic, justice, have each of them
several different meanings which cannot be reconciled with one
another. In the case of a word like *democracy,* not only is there no
agreed definition, but the attempt to make one is resisted from all
sides. It is almost universally felt that when we call a country
democratic we are praising it: consequently the defenders of every
kind of régime claim that it is a democracy, and fear that they might
have to stop using the word if it were tied down to any one meaning.
Words of this kind are often used in a consciously dishonest way.
That is, the person who uses them has his own private definition, but
allows his hearer to think he means something quite different.
Statements like *Marshal Pétain was a true patriot, The Soviet Press is the*
freest in the world, The Catholic Church is opposed to persecution, are
almost always made with intent to deceive. Other words used in
variable meanings, in most cases more or less dishonestly, are: *class,*
totalitarian, science, progressive, reactionary, bourgeois, equality.

Now that I have made this catalogue of swindles and perver-
sions, let me give another example of the kind of writing that they
lead to. This time it must of its nature be an imaginary one. I am
going to translate a passage of good English into modern English of
the worst sort. Here is a well-known verse from *Ecclesiastes:*

> I returned and saw under the sun, that the race is not to the swift,
> nor the battle to the strong, neither yet bread to the wise, nor yet riches
> to men of understanding, nor yet favor to men of skill; but time and
> chance happeneth to them all.

Here it is in modern English:

> Objective consideration of contemporary phenomena compels the
> conclusion that success or failure in competitive activities exhibits no
> tendency to be commensurate with innate capacity, but that a consider-
> able element of the unpredictable must invariably be taken into account.

This is a parody, but not a very gross one. Exhibit (3), above, for instance, contains several patches of the same kind of English. It will be seen that I have not made a full translation. The beginning and ending of the sentence follow the original meaning fairly closely, but in the middle the concrete illustrations — race, battle, bread — dissolve into the vague phrase "success or failure in competitive activities." This had to be so, because no modern writer of the kind I am discussing — no one capable of using phrases like "objective consideration of contemporary phenomena" — would ever tabulate his thoughts in that precise and detailed way. The whole tendency of modern prose is away from concreteness. Now analyse these two sentences a little more closely. The first contains forty-nine words but only sixty syllables, and all its words are those of everyday life. The second contains thirty-eight words of ninety syllables: eighteen of its words are from Latin roots, and one from Greek. The first sentence contains six vivid images, and only one phrase ("time and chance") that could be called vague. The second contains not a single fresh, arresting phrase, and in spite of its ninety syllables it gives only a shortened version of the meaning contained in the first. Yet without a doubt it is the second kind of sentence that is gaining ground in modern English. I do not want to exaggerate. This kind of writing is not yet universal, and outcrops of simplicity will occur here and there in the worst-written page. Still, if you or I were told to write a few lines on the uncertainty of human fortunes, we should probably come much nearer to my imaginary sentence than to the one from *Ecclesiastes*.

As I have tried to show, modern writing at its worst does not consist in picking out words for the sake of their meaning and inventing images in order to make the meaning clearer. It consists in gumming together long strips of words which have already been set in order by someone else, and making the results presentable by sheer humbug. The attraction of this way of writing is that it is easy. It is easier — even quicker, once you have the habit — to say *In my opinion it is not an unjustifiable assumption that* than to say *I think*. If you use ready-made phrases, you not only don't have to hunt about for words; you also don't have to bother with the rhythms of your sentences, since these phrases are generally so arranged as to be more or less euphonious. When you are composing in a hurry — when you are dictating to a stenographer, for instance, or making a public speech — it is natural to fall into a pretentious, Latinized style. Tags like *a consideration which we should do well to bear in mind* or *a conclusion to which all of us would readily assent* will save many a sentence from coming down with a bump. By using stale metaphors, similes and idioms, you save much mental effort, at the cost of leaving your meaning vague, not only for your reader but for yourself. This is the significance of mixed metaphors. The sole aim of a metaphor is to call up a visual image. When these images clash — as in *The Fascist octopus has sung its swan song, the jackboot is thrown into the melting pot* — it can be taken as certain that the writer is not seeing a mental image of the objects he is naming; in other words he is not really thinking. Look again at the examples I gave at the beginning of this essay. Professor Laski (1) uses five negatives in fifty-three words. One of these is superfluous, making nonsense of the whole passage, and in addition there is the slip *alien* for *akin,* making further nonsense, and several avoidable pieces of clumsiness which increase the general vagueness. Professor Hogben (2) plays ducks and drakes with a battery which is able to write prescriptions, and, while disapproving of the everyday phrase *put up with,* is unwilling to look *egregious* up in the dictionary and see what it means; (3), if one takes an uncharitable attitude towards it, is simply meaningless: probably one could work out its intended meaning by reading the whole of the article in which it occurs. In (4), the writer knows more or less what he wants to say, but an accumulation of stale phrases chokes him like tea leaves blocking a sink. In (5), words and meaning have almost parted company. People who write in this manner usually have a general emotional meaning — they dislike one thing and want to express solidarity with another — but they are not interested in the detail of what they are saying. A scrupulous writer, in every sentence that he writes, will ask himself at least four questions, thus: What am I trying to say? What words will express it? What image or idiom will make it clearer? Is this image fresh enough to have an effect? And he will probably ask himself two more: Could I put it more shortly? Have I said anything that is avoidably ugly? But you are not obliged to go to all this trouble. You can shirk it by simply throwing your mind open and letting the ready-made phrases come crowding in. They will construct your sentences for you — even think your thoughts for you, to a certain extent — and at need they will perform the important service of partially concealing your meaning even from yourself. It is at this point that the special connection between politics and the debasement of language becomes clear.

In our time it is broadly true that political writing is bad writing. Where it is not true it will generally be found that the writer is some kind of rebel, expressing his private opinions and not a "party line." Orthodoxy, of whatever color, seems to demand a lifeless, imitative style. The political dialects to be found in pamphlets, leading articles, manifestos, White Papers and the speeches of under-secretaries do, of course, vary from party to party, but they are all alike in that one almost never finds in them a fresh, vivid, home-made turn of speech. When one watches some tired hack on the platform mechanically repeating the familiar phrases — *bestial atrocities, iron heel, bloodstained tyranny, free peoples of the world, stand shoulder to shoulder* — one often has a curious feeling that one is not watching a live human being but some kind of dummy: a feeling which suddenly becomes stronger at moments when the light catches the speaker's spectacles and turns them into blank discs which seem to have no eyes behind them. And this is not altogether fanciful. A speaker who uses that kind of phraseology has gone some distance towards turning himself into a machine. The appropriate noises are coming out of his larynx but his brain is not involved as it would be if he were choosing his words for himself. If the speech he is making is one that he is accustomed to make over and over again, he may be almost unconscious of what he is saying, as one is when one utters the responses in church. And this reduced state of consciousness, if not indispensable, is at any rate favorable to political conformity.

In our time, political speech and writing are largely the defence of the indefensible. Things like the continuance of British rule in India, the Russian purges and deportations, the dropping of the atom bombs on Japan, can indeed be defended, but only by arguments which are too brutal for most people to face, and which do not square with the professed aims of political parties. Thus political language has to consist largely of euphemism, question-begging and sheer cloudy vagueness. Defenceless villages are bombarded from the air, the inhabitants driven out into the countryside, the cattle machine-gunned, the huts set on fire with incendiary bullets: this is called *pacification*. Millions of peasants are robbed of their farms and sent trudging along the roads with no more than they can carry: this is called *transfer of population* or *rectification of frontiers*. People are imprisoned for years without trial, or shot in the back of the neck or sent to die of scurvy in Arctic lumber camps: this is called *elimination of unreliable elements*. Such phraseology is needed if one wants to name things without calling up mental pictures of them. Consider for instance some comfortable English professor defending Russian totalitarianism. He cannot say outright, "I believe in killing off your opponents when you can get good results by doing do." Probably, therefore, he will say something like this:

> While freely conceding that the Soviet régime exhibits certain features which the humanitarian may be inclined to deplore, we must, I think, agree that a certain curtailment of the right to political opposition

is an unavoidable concomitant of transitional periods, and that the rigors which the Russian people have been called upon to undergo have been amply justified in the sphere of concrete achievement.

The inflated style is itself a kind of euphemism. A mass of Latin words falls upon the facts like soft snow, blurring the outlines and covering up all the details. The great enemy of clear language is insincerity. When there is a gap between one's real and one's declared aims, one turns as it were instinctively to long words and exhausted idioms, like a cuttlefish squirting out ink. In our age there is no such thing as "keeping out of politics." All issues are political issues, and politics itself is a mass of lies, evasions, folly, hatred and schizophrenia. When the general atmosphere is bad, language must suffer. I should expect to find — this is a guess which I have not sufficient knowledge to verify — that the German, Russian and Italian languages have all deteriorated in the last ten to fifteen years, as a result of dictatorship.

But if thought corrupts language, language can also corrupt thought. A bad usage can spread by tradition and imitation, even among people who should and do know better. The debased language that I have been discussing is in some ways very convenient. Phrases like *a not unjustifiable assumption, leaves much to be desired, would serve no good purpose, a consideration which we should do well to bear in mind,* are a continuous temptation, a packet of aspirins always at one's elbow. Look back through this essay, and for certain you will find that I have again and again committed the very faults I am protesting against. By this morning's post I have received a pamphlet dealing with conditions in Germany. The author tells me that he "felt impelled" to write it. I open it at random, and here is almost the first sentence that I see: "[The Allies] have an opportunity not only of achieving a radical transformation of Germany's social and political structure in such a way as to avoid a nationalistic reaction in Germany itself, but at the same time of laying the foundations of a cooperative and unified Europe." You see, he "feels impelled" to write — feels, presumably, that he has something new to say — and yet his words, like cavalry horses answering the bugle, group themselves automatically into the familiar dreary pattern. This invasion of one's mind by ready-made phrases (*lay the foundations, achieve a radical transformation*) can only be prevented if one is constantly on guard against them, and every such phrase anaesthetizes a portion of one's brain.

I said earlier that the decadence of our language is probably curable. Those who deny this would argue, if they produced an

argument at all, that language merely reflects existing social conditions, and that we cannot influence its development by any direct
tinkering with words and constructions. So far as the general tone or
spirit of a language goes, this may be true, but it is not true in detail.
Silly words and expressions have often disappeared, not through any
evolutionary process but owing to the conscious action of a minority. Two recent examples were *explore every avenue* and *leave no stone
unturned,* which were killed by the jeers of a few journalists. There is
a long list of flyblown metaphors which could similarly be got rid of
if enough people would interest themselves in the job; and it should
also be possible to laugh the *not un-* formation out of existence,[19] to
reduce the amount of Latin and Greek in the average sentence, to
drive out foreign phrases and strayed scientific words, and, in general, to make pretentiousness unfashionable. But all these are minor
points. The defence of the English language implies more than this,
and perhaps it is best to start by saying what it does *not* imply.

To begin with it has nothing to do with archaism, with the
salvaging of obsolete words and turns of speech, or with the setting
up of a "standard English" which must never be departed from. On
the contrary, it is especially concerned with the scrapping of every
word or idiom which has outworn its usefulness. It has nothing to
do with correct grammar and syntax, which are of no importance so
long as one makes one's meaning clear, or with the avoidance of
Americanisms, or with having what is called a "good prose style."
On the other hand it is not concerned with fake simplicity and the
attempt to make written English colloquial. Nor does it even imply
in every case preferring the Saxon word to the Latin one, though it
does imply using the fewest and shortest words that will cover one's
meaning. What is above all needed is to let the meaning choose the
word, and not the other way about. In prose, the worst thing one
can do with words is to surrender to them. When you think of a
concrete object, you think wordlessly, and then, if you want to
describe the thing you have been visualizing you probably hunt
about till you find the exact words that seem to fit it. When you
think of something abstract you are more inclined to use words from
the start, and unless you make a conscious effort to prevent it, the
existing dialect will come rushing in and do the job for you, at the
expense of blurring or even changing your meaning. Probably it is
better to put off using words as long as possible and get one's

[19] One can cure oneself of the *not un-* formation by memorizing this
sentence: *A not unblack dog was chasing a not unsmall rabbit across a not ungreen field.*

meaning as clear as one can through pictures or sensations. Afterwards one can choose — not simply *accept* — the phrases that will best cover the meaning, and then switch round and decide what impression one's words are likely to make on another person. This last effort of the mind cuts out all stale or mixed images, all prefabricated phrases, needless repetitions, and humbug and vagueness generally. But one can often be in doubt about the effect of a word or a phrase, and one needs rules that one can rely on when instinct fails. I think the following rules will cover most cases:

(i)   Never use a metaphor, simile or other figure of speech which you are used to seeing in print.
(ii) Never use a long word where a short one will do.
(iii) If it is possible to cut a word out, always cut it out.
(iv) Never use the passive where you can use the active.
(v)   Never use a foreign phrase, a scientific word or a jargon word if you can think of an everyday English equivalent.
(vi) Break any of these rules sooner than say anything outright barbarous.

These rules sound elementary, and so they are, but they demand a deep change of attitude in anyone who has grown used to writing in the style now fashionable. One could keep all of them and still write bad English, but one could not write the kind of stuff that I quoted in those five specimens at the beginning of this article.

I have not here been considering the literary use of language, but merely language as an instrument for expressing and not for concealing or preventing thought. Stuart Chase and others have come near to claiming that all abstract words are meaningless, and have used this as a pretext for advocating a kind of political quietism. Since you don't know what Fascism is, how can you struggle against Fascism? One need not swallow such absurdities as this, but one ought to recognize that the present political chaos is connected with the decay of language, and that one can probably bring about some improvement by starting at the verbal end. If you simplify your English, you are freed from the worst follies of orthodoxy. You cannot speak any of the necessary dialects, and when you make a stupid remark its stupidity will be obvious, even to yourself. Political language — and with variations this is true of all political parties, from Conservatives to Anarchists — is designed to make lies sound truthful and murder respectable, and to give an appearance of solidity to pure wind. One cannot change this all in a moment, but one can at least change one's own habits, and from time to time one can even, if one jeers loudly enough, send some worn-out and useless phrase — some *jackboot*, *Achilles' heel*, *hotbed*, *melting pot*, *acid test*, *veritable inferno* or other lump of verbal refuse — into the dustbin where it belongs.

QUESTIONS

1. Revise one or two of Orwell's examples of bad writing.
2. Examine Orwell's metaphors. Do they fulfill his requirements for good writing?
3. Look again at Orwell's grotesque revision (page 506) of a passage from the Bible. Write a similar version of another passage from the Bible.
4. Examine an editorial on a political issue. Analyze the writing as Orwell might have.

Fathers and Sons
Studs Terkel

Glenn Stribling[20]

A casual encounter on a plane; a casual remark: he and his wife are returning from a summer cruise. It was their first vacation in twenty-five years. He is forty-eight.

He and his son are partners in the business: Glenn & Dave's Complete Auto Repair. They run a Texaco service station in a fairly affluent community some thirty miles outside Cleveland. "There's eight of us on the payroll, counting my son and I. Of course, the wife, she's the bookkeeper." There are three tow trucks.

"Glenn & Dave's is equipped to do all nature of repair work: everything from transmission, air conditioning, valves, all . . . everything. I refer to it as a garage because we do everything garages do.

"We have been here four years." He himself has been at it "steady" for twenty-nine years. "When I was a kid in high school I worked at the Studebaker garage part-time for seven dollars a week. And I paid seven

[20] Terkel's book, *Working*, consists of edited versions of more than a hundred interviews with workers of all sorts. Here we reprint an interview with Glenn Stribling and another with Stribling's son, Dave.

*dollars a week board and room." (Laughs.) "It more or less runs in our
family. My great-grandfather used to make spokes for automobiles back in
Pennsylvania when they used wooden wheels. I have a brother, he's a
mechanic. I have another brother in California, he's in the same business as
I'm in. My dad, he was a steam engine repairman.*

*"Another reason I went into this business: it's Depression-proof. A
good repairman will always have a job. Even though they're making cars so
they don't last so long and people trade 'em in more often, there's still gonna
be people that have to know what they're doing."*

I work eight days a week. (Laughs.) My average weeks usually
run to eighty, ninety hours. We get every other Sunday off, my son
and I. Alternate, you know. Oh, I love it. There's never a day long
enough. We never get through. And that's a good way to have it,
'cause people rely on you and you rely on them, and it's one big
business. Sometimes they're all three trucks goin'. All we sell is
service, and if you can't give service, you might as well give up.

All our business has come to us from mouth to mouth. We've
never run a big ad in the paper. That itself is a good sign that people
are satisfied. Of course, there's some people that nobody could
satisfy. I've learned: Why let one person spoil your whole day?

A new customer comes to town, he would say, "So-and-so, I
met him on the train and he recommended you folks very highly."
Oh, we've had a lot of compliments where people, they say they've
never had anything like that done to a car. They are real happy that
we did point out things and do things. Preventive maintenance I call
it.

A man come in, we'd Xed his tires, sold him a set of shocks,
repacked his wheel bearings, aligned his front, serviced his car — by
service I mean lubricate, change oil, filter . . . But he had only one
tail light working and didn't know it. So we fixed that and he'll be
grateful for it. If it's something big, a matter of a set of tires or if he
needs a valve job, we call the customer and discuss it with him.

Sometimes, but not very often, I've learned to relax. When I
walk out of here I try to leave everything, 'cause we have a loud bell
at home. If I'm out in the yard working, people call. They want to
know about a car, maybe make a date for next week, or maybe
there's a car here that we've had and there's a question on it. The
night man will call me up at home. We have twenty-four-hour
service, too, towing. My son and I, we take turns. So this phone is
hooked up outside so you can hear it. And all the neighbors can hear
it too. (Laughs.)

Turn down calls? No, never. Well, if it's some trucking outfit and they don't have an account with us — they're the worst risk there is. If they don't have a credit card or if the person they're delivering won't vouch for them, there's gotta be some sort of agreement on payment before we go out. Of course, if it's a stranger, if it's broke down, naturally we have the car.

Sometimes if we're busy, bad weather and this and that, why we won't get any lunch, unless the wife runs uptown and grabs a sandwich. I usually go home, it varies anywhere between six thirty, seven, eight. Whatever the public demands. In the wintertime, my God, we don't get out of here till nine. I have worked thirty-seven hours non-stop.

I don't do it for the money. People are in trouble and they call you and you feel obligated enough to go out there and straighten them out as much as you can. My wife tells me I take my business more serious than a doctor. Every now and then a competitor will come down and ask me to diagnose something. And I go ahead and do it. I'll tell anybody anything I know if it'll help him. That's a good way to be. You might want a favor from them sometime. Live and let live.

You get irritated a lot of times, but you keep it within yourself. You can't be too eccentric. You gotta be the same. Customers like people the same all the time. Another thing I noticed: the fact that I got gray hair, that helps in business. Even though my son's in with me and we have capable men working for us, they always want to talk to Glenn. They respect me and what I tell 'em.

If I'm tensed up and there'll be somebody pull in on the drive-way, ring all the bells, park right in front of the door, then go in and use the washroom — those kind of people are the most inconsiderate kind of people there is. If you're out there in the back, say you're repacking wheel bearings. Your hands are full of grease. In order to go out in that drive, you have to clean your hands. And all the customer wanted to know was where the courtroom is. When I travel, if I want information, I'll park out on the apron. Sometimes we have as high as fifty, sixty people a day in here for information. They pull up, ring all the bells . . . You can imagine how much time it takes if you go out fifty, sixty times and you don't pump gas. I call 'em IWW: Information, wind, and water. It's worse the last four years we've been here. People don't care. They don't think of us. All they think of is themself.

Oh, I lose my temper sometimes. You wouldn't be a red-blooded American if you wouldn't, would you? At the same time you're dealing with the public. You have to control yourself. Like I say, people like an even-tempered person. When I do lose my temper, the wife, she can't get over it. She says, "Glenn, I don't know how you can blow your stack at one person and then five minutes later you're tellin' him a joke." I don't hold grudges. Why hold a grudge? Let people know what you think, express your opinion, and then forget it. Of course, you don't forget, you just don't keep harpin' on it.

In the summertime, when I get home I don't even go in the house. I grab a garden tool and go out and work till dark. I have a small garden — lettuce, onions, small vegetables. By the time you're on your feet all day you're ready to relax, watch television, sometimes have a fire in the fireplace. At social gatherings, if somebody's in the same business, we compare notes. If we run into something that's a time saver, we usually exchange. But not too much. Because who likes to talk shop?

There's a few good mechanics left. Most of 'em in this day and age, all they are is parts replacers. This is a new trend. You need an air conditioner, you don't repair 'em any more. You can get exchange units, factory guaranteed and much cheaper, much faster. People don't want to lay up their car long enough to get it fixed. If they can't look out and see their car in the driveway, they feel like they've lost something. They get nervous. It's very seldom people will overhaul a car. They'll trade it in instead.

This is something hard to find any more, a really good, conscientious worker. When the whistle blows, they're all washed up, ready to go before they're punched out. You don't get a guy who'll stay two or three hours later, just to get a job done.

Take my son, Dave. Say a person's car broke down. It's on a Sunday or a Saturday night. Maybe it would take an hour to fix. Why, I'll go ahead and fix it. Dave's the type that'll say, "Leave it sit till Monday." I put myself in the other guy's boots and I'll go ahead and fix his car, because time don't mean that much to me. Consequently we got a lot of good customers. Last winter we had a snowstorm. People wanted some snow tires. I put 'em on. He's a steady customer now. He just sold his house for $265,000.

When we took this last cruise, my customers told me Dave did a terrific job. "Before, we didn't think much of him. But he did a really good job this last time." I guess compared to the average young person Dave is above average as far as being conscientious. Although he does sleep in the morning. Today's Wednesday? Nine o'clock this morning. It was ten o'clock yesterday morning. He's supposed to be here at seven. Rather than argue and fight about it, I just forget it.

Another thing I trained myself: I know the address and phone number of all the places we do business with and a lot of our customers. I never even look in the phone book. (Dave had just made a phone call after leafing through the directory.) If he asked me, I coulda told him.

Dave Stribling

He is twenty-three, married, and has two baby children. He has been working with his father "more or less since I was twelve years old. It's one of those deals where the son does carry on the family tradition.

"I actually worked full-time when I was in junior high school. School was a bore. But when you stop and look back at it you wish to hell you'd done a lot more. I wanted to go get that fast buck. Some people are fortunate to make it overnight. My dad and I had a few quarrels and I quit him. I used to work down at Chrysler while I was in high school. I worked at least eight hours a day. That was great. You don't work Saturdays and you don't work Sundays. Then I came back and worked for my dad."

How would I describe myself? Mixed up really. (Laughs.) I like my work. (Sighs.) But I wish I hadn't started that early. I wish I would have tried another trade, actually. At my age I could quit this. I could always come back. But I'm pretty deep now. If I were to walk out, it would be pretty bad. (Laughs.) I don't think I'll change my occupation, really.

I think I'da tried to be an architect or, hell, maybe even a real top-notch good salesman. Or maybe even a farmer. It's hard to say. The grass is always greener on the other side of the fence. You turn around and there's an attorney. It makes you feel different. You work during the day and you're dirty from this and that. The majority of the people overlook the fact as long as you're established and this and that. They don't really care what your occupation is as long as you're a pretty good citizen.

Where it really gets you down is, you're at some place and you'll meet a person and strike up a conversation with 'em. Naturally, sometime during that conversation he's going to ask about your occupation, what you do for a living. So this guy, he manages this, he manages that, see? When I tell him — and I've seen it happen lots of times — there's a kind of question mark in his head. Just what is this guy? You work. You just sweat. It's not mental. 'Cause a lot of these jobs that you do, you do so many of the same thing, it just becomes automatic. You know what you're doing blindfolded.

It's made me a pretty good livin' so far. But I don't have a lot of time that a lot of these guys do that are in my age and in the same status that I am. I put in every week at least sixty, sixty-five hours. And then at night, you never know. If somebody breaks down, you can't tell 'em no. You gotta go. My friends work forty hours a week and they're done. Five days a week. I work seven, actually. Every other Sunday. I have to come and open up.

I don't really like to talk about my work with my friends. They don't really seem to, either. A lot of times somebody will ask me something about their car. How much will this cost? How much will that cost? I don't really even want to quote my price to them. A couple of 'em work for the state, in an office. A couple of 'em are body men. One's a carpenter, one's a real estate salesman. A few of 'em, they just work.

I come home, I gotta go in the back door, 'cause I've got on greasy boots. (Laughs.) If it does happen to be about six thirty, then I won't get cleaned up before I eat. I'll sit down and eat with the wife and kids. If they've already eaten, I'll take a shower and I'll get cleaned up and I'll come down and eat. If it's a nice night, I might go out and putz around the yard. If it's not nice outside, I'll just sit and watch the TV. I don't really read that much. I probably read as much as the average American. But nothing any more. Sometimes you really put out a lot of work that day — in general, I'm tired. I'm asleep by ten o'clock at night. I come to work, it varies, I might come in between eight and nine, maybe even ten o'clock in the morning. I like my sleep. (Laughs.)

He's the one that opens it up. He believes the early bird gets the worm. But that's not always true either. I might come in late, but actually I do more work than he does here in a day. Most of it probably is as careful as his. I can't understand a lot of the stuff he does. But he can't understand a lot of the stuff I do either. (Laughs.) He's getting better. He's kinda come around. But he still does think old-fashioned.

Like tools. You can buy equipment, it might cost a lot more money but it'll do the job faster and easier. He'll go grab hand tools, that you gotta use your own muscle. He doesn't go in for power tools.

Like judging people. Anybody with long hair is no good to him — even me. If he caught me asleep, he'd probably give me a Yul Brynner. Hair doesn't have anything to do with it. I've met a lot of people with hair really long, just like a female. They're still the same. They still got their ideas and they're not hippies or anything. They go to work every day just like everybody else does. It gets him. Especially if someone will come in and ask him to do something, he'll let them know he doesn't like them. I don't give people that much static.

When somebody comes in and they're in a rage and it's all directed at you, I either go get the hell out of there or my rage is brought up towards them. I've definitely lost customers by tellin' 'em. I don't know how to just slough it off. In the majority of cases you're sorry for it.

I've seen my father flare up a lot of times. Somebody gives him a bad time during the day, he'll take it home. Whereas instead of tellin' 'em right there on the spot, he'll just keep it within himself. Then half-hour later he might be mumblin' somethin'. When I used to live at home, you could tell by thirty seconds after he got in the door that he either didn't feel good or somebody gave him a bad time. He just keeps it going through his mind. He won't forget it. Whereas when I go home to the wife and the two kids, I just like to forget it. I don't want to talk about it at all.

I yell a lot, cuss a lot. I might throw things around down here, take a hammer and hit the bench as hard as it'll go, I'm getting better though, really. I used to throw a lot of stuff. I'd just grab and throw a wrench or something. But I haven't done that in a long time now. When you get older and you start thinking about it, you really have changed a lot in the last few years. (Laughs.) It'll stay inside me. You learn to absorb more of it. More so than when you were a kid. You realize you're not doing any good. Lotta times you might damage something. It's just gonna come out of your pocket.

When I was younger, if there was something I didn't agree upon, I was ready to go right then against it. But now I don't. I kinda step back a half a step and think it out. I've gotten into pretty good arguments with my buddies. It never really comes down to fists, but if you're with somebody long enough, it's bound to happen, you're gonna fight. You had a hard day and somebody gave you a hard time and, say you went out to eat and the waitress, she screwed something up? Yeah, it'll flare up. But not as much as it used to be.

As far as customers goes, there's not too many of 'em I like. A lot of customers, you can joke with, you can kid with. There are a lot of 'em, they don't want to hear any of it. They don't want to discuss anything else but the business while they're here. Older people, yeah, they're pretty hard. Because they've gone through a change from a Model T to what you got nowadays. Nowadays a lot of 'em will put up the hood and they just shake their heads. They just can't figure it out.

Some of 'em, when they get old they get real grumpy. Anything you say, you're just a kid and you don't know what you're doin'. (Laughs.) They don't want to listen to you, they want to talk to somebody else. There's a lot of 'em that'll just talk to him. But there's a lot of 'em that want to talk to me and don't want to talk to him. My-age people. It's a mixed-up generation. (Laughs.)

I have pride in what I do. This day and age, you don't always repair something. You renew. Whereas in his era you could buy a kit to rebuild pretty near anything. Take a water pump. You can buy 'em. You can put on a new one. I wouldn't even bother to repair a water pump. You can buy rebuilts, factory rebuilts. Back in his time you rebuilt water pumps.

His ideas are old, really. You gotta do this a certain way and this a certain way. There's short cuts found that you could just eliminate half the stuff you do. But he won't. A lot of the new stuff that comes out, he won't believe anybody. He won't even believe me. He might call three or four people before he'll believe it. Why he won't believe me I don't know. I guess he must figure I bull him a lot. (Laughs.)

When he was working for a living as a mechanic, his ability was pretty good. Actually, he doesn't do that much work. I mean, he more or less is a front. (Laughs.) Many people come in here that think he does work on their car. But he doesn't. He's mostly the one that meets people. He brings the work in. In his own mind he believes he's putting out the work. But we're the ones that put out the work.

He's kind of funny to figure out. (Laughs.) He has no hobbies, really. When he's out he'll still talk his trade. He just can't forget it, leave it go.

I'd like to go bigger in this business, but father says no for right now. He's too skeptical. We're limited here. He doesn't want to go in debt. But you gotta spend money to make money. He's had to work harder than I have. There's nobody that ever really gave him anything. He's had to work for everything he's got. He's given me a lot. Sometimes he gives too much. His grand-kids, they've got clothes at home still in boxes, brand-new as they got 'em. He just goes overboard. If I need money, he'll loan it to me. He's lent me money that I haven't even paid back, really. (Laughs.)

(Sighs.) I used to play music. I used to play in a rock group. Bass. I didn't know very much on the bass. Everybody that was in the band really didn't know all that much. We more or less progressed together. We played together for a year and a half, then everything just broke up. Oh yeah, we enjoyed it. It was altogether different. I like to play music now but don't have the time . . . I like to play, but you can't do both. This is my living. You have to look at it that way.

QUESTIONS

1. How accurate do you think Glenn Stribling's view of his son is?
2. How accurate do you think Dave Stribling's view of his father is?

Altruism

Lewis Thomas

One of the most astonishing things about human society, from a biologist's point of view, is that it is made up of individual, distinguishable, specifically marked selves, all apparently out on their own. Here we are, now four billion of us, each one labeled as an absolute entity, fundamentally different from all the rest. The labels are not just the visible, behavioral marks — the way a head is turned, the special manner of a smile, the pitch of a voice — these are obvious distinctions; despite superficial resemblances and reminders, no one is precisely a duplicate of anyone else except the occasional pairs of identical twins. Then there are the biochemical marks of self, even more specific and rigid than our behavior, setting us apart. The surfaces of our cells are sufficiently different that immunologists can detect the biochemical difference among all four billion. We probably have different smells as well; a tracking hound can sense the uniqueness of every man's footprint, except for those of twins.

At first glance, you'd think nature had endowed us with everything needed for solitary, independent lives. Much of the time this is how we like to think of ourselves, a world of self-sufficient, free-standing creatures, obsessively individualistic, the brainiest things on earth. Full of ourselves.

The only other social animals we know much about, in any real detail, are the social insects, and they are outlandish forms of life, unearthly and embarrassing. We prefer to think of termites, ants, social bees and wasps as things dropped from another planet, totally without meaning for us. They seem to have evolved by giving up all vestiges of individuality; they live as though all the creatures in the hill or hive had joined together so intimately and interdependently as to be the working parts of a single, huge beast. The isolated ant, out on a trout line of ants, cast from the nest across the path and down into the culvert for the retrieval of a dead moth, doesn't seem to know the difference between himself and any other ant in the line. Ants touch each other ceaselessly, exchanging white bits of information carried in their jaws, spraying tiny droplets of pheromone as they go in order to inform late comers that the moth lies in that direction. The nest, writhing like an enormous ameboid cell, is where the brains are. By itself, the solitary ant has nothing much to think with; a few strings of ganglia connected by nerve fibers, several kinds of pheromone glands for sending messages about safety or danger, or food sources ahead, or orders to aggregate together in platoons for combat. The whole nest thinks, lays plans for the future, figures things out. It is somehow done by pooling all the information, from all the ganglia.

There are no individual creatures in a termite hill. They are a million connected parts, working like the components of a machine. Everything is done automatically. There is something profoundly disturbing about such a way of living. We think of it as repellent, inhuman.

And yet, here we are. For social interdependence, for compulsive collaborative living, for lives driven from beginning to end by connectedness, there is nothing to touch human society. We are, despite all our marks of individuality and our displays of independence, the most biologically social of all the species on earth.

Moreover, we seem to be still in the earliest stages of our evolution. It has only been for 20,000 years or so that we've been leaving evidences of group living, no time at all in the scale of evolution. We must be the youngest form of complex social life on earth, just getting under way.

We can be forgiven blunders, being so juvenile.

One thing we are highly skilled at doing, so universally adept as to suggest that the talent is a genetic endowment: We make language. This is our equivalent of the geometrically flawless wax cells of the hive, or the perfect arches and vaulted, ventilated chambers of the termitarium. We have genes for making words, DNA for syntax, neuronal structures for grammar.

It is our obsession, it is what we do with our lives. Without speech we would not be human beings. We might engage in thought of a kind, but no one can imagine what that thought, wordless and metaphorless, would be like.

It is not just the making of language that sets us apart. Somehow, by some autonomic system over which we have no sort of conscious control, we *build* language. It grows like a living being on its own, changing the sound and meaning of its words, inventing new words and transforming old ones, and all the time none of us realizes that this is happening, nor how. We are no more in charge of the evolution of language than ants control the distribution of twigs of different sizes in the endless construction of their nests. Committees do not make or change, or keep from changing, a language. Governments cannot control the development of speech. It is uncontrollable, ungovernable, unconscious behavior, in which we are all engaged, for all our lives.

It holds us together as a kind of shelter for our minds, and we live inside the structure. In this sense it is our hill, our hive. It provides our music and poetry, our art, and all the fun of our lives. This is the ultimate proof, I think, that nature has endowed us with the means and the urge to live cooperatively as part of a single cell, on the bigger cell, the earth.

Very well. If this is true, we should be looking again, and harder, at the other social species, to learn how they achieved their kind of success and survival, for we are in need of survival as never before in our short history.

How do they do it, the ants and bees and termites? Is there an underlying force that holds them together, drives them along? Are there laws? It will take a lot of study, probably years of time, no doubt endless arrays of computers. Great sums of money. Maybe a National Institute of Sociobiology. Better make it an International Institute, and soon. Now that we are a single community of four billion, scheduled to double again in a few years, so densely packed as to touch hand to hand, almost, all around the earth, it is already late in the day to discover how a social species functions.

One thing we already know, thanks to the biologists. The weirdest aspect of the behavior of social animals, beyond scientific understanding, is their ceaseless giving away of things. They carry food to each other all day long, they shelter and protect each other, and on occasion they drop dead for each other. The trait seems to be genetically determined, and the biologists have already made up a technical term, borrowed from an old word, now part of the professional jargon: *altruism.*

We could begin by examining this behavioral trait in ourselves.

There are signs that it is there, not as spectacularly as in the insects but nonetheless there. We make efforts to suppress it, some of us even write tracts to condemn it as beneath human dignity, a violation of selfness; it is perhaps around this issue that our group consciousness, animated by all our brilliant marks of individual identity, comes into conflict with our collective unconscious, if we have such a thing. Maybe altruism is our most primitive attribute, out of reach, beyond our control. Or perhaps it is immediately at hand, disguised now, in our kind of civilization as affection or friendship or love, maybe as music. I don't see why it should be unreasonable for human beings to have strands of DNA, coiled up in chromosomes, coding out instincts for usefulness and helpfulness. I think it is likely true for all my friends, and I don't see why your family and friends should be any different.

QUESTIONS

1. Writers on technical subjects sometimes adopt a highly colloquial style in order to seem regular guys. The result can be a loathsome locker-room heartiness. Cite some colloquial expressions in Thomas's essay — expressions that perhaps you would hesitate to use in an essay — and then describe Thomas's overall tone.
2. Thomas says, in his last paragraph, that some people believe that altruism is "beneath human dignity, a violation of selfness." Whether or not you believe this position, try to explain it.

Who's Afraid of Math, and Why?
Sheila Tobias

The first thing people remember about failing at math is that it felt like sudden death. Whether the incident occurred while learning "word problems" in sixth grade, coping with equations in high school, or first confronting calculus and statistics in college, failure came suddenly and in a very frightening way. An idea or a new operation was not just difficult, it was impossible! And, instead of asking questions or taking the lesson slowly, most people remember having had the feeling that they would never go any further in mathematics. If we assume that the curriculum was reasonable, and that the new idea was but the next in a series of learnable concepts, the feeling of utter defeat was simply not rational; yet "math anxious" college students and adults have revealed that no matter how much the teacher reassured them, they could not overcome that feeling.

A common myth about the nature of mathematical ability holds that one either has or does not have a mathematical mind. Mathematical imagination and an intuitive grasp of mathematical principles may well be needed to do advanced research, but why should people who can do college-level work in other subjects not be able to do college-level math as well? Rates of learning may vary. Competency under time pressure may differ. Certainly low self-esteem will get in the way. But where is the evidence that a student needs a "mathematical mind" in order to succeed at learning math?

Consider the effects of this mythology. Since only a few people are supposed to have this mathematical mind, part of what makes us so passive in the face of our difficulties in learning mathematics is that we suspect all the while we may not be one of "them," and we spend our time waiting to find out when our nonmathematical minds will be exposed. Since our limit will eventually be reached, we see no point in being methodical or in attending to detail. We are grateful when we survive fractions, word problems, or geometry. If that certain moment of failure hasn't struck yet, it is only temporarily postponed.

Parents, especially parents of girls, often expect their children to be nonmathematical. Parents are either poor at math and had their own sudden-death experiences, or, if math came easily for them, they do not know how it feels to be slow. In either case, they unwittingly foster the idea that a mathematical mind is something one either has or does not have.

Mathematics and Sex

Although fear of math is not a purely female phenomenon, girls tend to drop out of math sooner than boys, and adult women experience an aversion to math and math-related activities that is akin to anxiety. A 1972 survey of the amount of high school mathematics taken by incoming freshmen at Berkeley revealed that while 57 percent of the boys had taken four years of high school math, only 8 percent of the girls had had the same amount of preparation. Without four years of high school math, students at Berkeley, and at most other colleges and universities, are ineligible for the calculus sequence, unlikely to attempt chemistry or physics, and inadequately prepared for statistics and economics.

Unable to elect these entry-level courses, the remaining 92 percent of the girls will be limited, presumably, to the career choices that are considered feminine: the humanities, guidance and counseling, elementary school teaching, foreign languages, and the fine arts.

Boys and girls may be born alike with respect to math, but certain sex differences in performance emerge early according to several respected studies, and these differences remain through adulthood. They are:

1. Girls compute better than boys (elementary school and on).
2. Boys solve word problems better than girls (from age thirteen on).
3. Boys take more math than girls (from age sixteen on).
4. Girls learn to hate math sooner and possibly for different reasons.

Why the differences in performance? One reason is the amount of math learned and used at play. Another may be the difference in male-female maturation. If girls do better than boys at all elementary school tasks, then they may compute better for no other reason than that arithmetic is part of the elementary school curriculum. As boys and girls grow older, girls become, under pressure, academically less competitive. Thus, the falling off of girls' math performance between ages ten and fifteen may be because:

1. Math gets harder in each successive year and requires more work and commitment.
2. Both boys and girls are pressured, beginning at age ten, not to excel in areas designated by society to be outside their sex-role domains.
3. Thus girls have a good excuse to avoid the painful struggle with math; boys don't.

Such a model may explain girls' lower achievement in math overall, but why should girls even younger than ten have difficulty in problem-solving? In her review of the research on sex differences, psychologist Eleanor Maccoby noted that girls are generally more conforming, more suggestible, and more dependent upon the opinion of others than boys (all learned, not innate, behaviors). Being so, they may not be as willing to take risks or to think for themselves, two behaviors that are necessary in solving problems. Indeed, in one test of third-graders, girls were found to be not nearly as willing to estimate, to make judgments about "possible right answers," or to work with systems they had never seen before. Their very success at doing what is expected of them up to that time seems to get in the way of their doing something new.

If readiness to do word problems, to take one example, is as much a function of readiness to take risks as it is of "reasoning ability," then mathematics performance certainly requires more than memory, computation, and reasoning. The differences in math performance between boys and girls — no matter how consistently those differences show up — cannot be attributed simply to differences in innate ability.

Still, if one were to ask the victims themselves, they would probably disagree: they would say their problems with math have to do with the way they are "wired." They feel they are somehow missing something — one ability or several — that other people have. Although women want to believe they are not mentally inferior to men, many fear that, where math is concerned, they really are. Thus, we have to consider seriously whether mathematical ability has a biological basis, not only because a number of researchers believe this to be so, but because a number of victims agree with them.

The Arguments from Biology

The search for some biological basis for math ability or disability is fraught with logical and experimental difficulties. Since not all math underachievers are women, and not all women are mathematics-avoidant, poor performance in math is unlikely to be due to some genetic or hormonal difference between the sexes. Moreover, no amount of research so far has unearthed a "mathematical competency" in some tangible, measurable substance in the body. Since "masculinity" cannot be injected into women to test whether or not it improves their mathematics, the theories that attribute such ability to genes or hormones must depend for their proof on circumstantial evidence. So long as about 7 percent of the Ph.D.'s in mathematics are earned by women, we have to conclude either that these women have genes, hormones, and brain organization different from those of the rest of us, or that certain positive experiences in their lives have largely undone the negative fact that they are female, or both.

Genetically, the only difference between males and females (albeit a significant and pervasive one) is the presence of two chromosomes designated X in every female cell. Normal males exhibit an X-Y combination. Because some kinds of mental retardation are associated with sex-chromosomal anomalies, a number of researchers have sought a converse linkage between specific abilities and the presence or absence of the second X. But the linkage between genetics and mathematics is not supported by conclusive evidence.

Since intensified hormonal activity commences at adolescence, a time during which girls seem to lose interest in mathematics, much more has been made of the unequal amounts in females and males of the sex-linked hormones androgen and estrogen. Biological researchers have linked estrogen — the female hormone — with "simple repetitive tasks," and androgen — the male hormone — with "complex restructuring tasks." The assumption here is not only that such specific talents are biologically based (probably undemonstrable) but also that one cannot be good at *both* repetitive and restructuring kinds of assignments.

Sex Roles and Mathematics Competence

The fact that many girls tend to lose interest in math at the age they reach puberty (junior high school) suggests that puberty might in some sense cause girls to fall behind in math. Several explanations come to mind: the influence of hormones, more intensified sex-role socialization, or some extracurricular learning experience exclusive to boys of that age.

One group of seventh-graders in a private school in New England gave a clue as to what children themselves think about all of this. When asked why girls do as well as boys in math until the sixth grade, while sixth-grade boys do better from that point on, the girls responded: "Oh, that's easy. After sixth grade, we have to do real math." The answer to why "real math" should be considered to be "for boys" and not "for girls" can be found not in the realm of biology but only in the realm of ideology of sex differences.

Parents, peers, and teachers forgive a girl when she does badly in math at school, encouraging her to do well in other subjects instead. " 'There, there,' my mother used to say when I failed at math," one woman says. "But I got a talking-to when I did badly in French." Lynn Fox, who directs a program for mathematically gifted junior high boys and girls on the campus of Johns Hopkins University, has trouble recruiting girls and keeping them in her program. Some parents prevent their daughters from participating altogether for fear that excellence in math will make them too different. The girls themselves are often reluctant to continue with mathematics, Fox reports, because they fear social ostracism.

Where do these associations come from?

The association of masculinity with mathematics sometimes extends from the discipline to those who practice it. Students, asked on a questionnaire what characteristics they associate with a mathematician (as contrasted with a "writer"), selected terms such as rational, cautious, wise, and responsible. The writer, on the other hand, in addition to being seen as individualistic and independent, was also described as warm, interested in people, and altogether more compatible with a feminine ideal.

As a result of this psychological conditioning, a young woman may consider math and math-related fields to be inimical to femininity. In an interesting study of West German teenagers, Erika Schildkamp-Kuendiger found that girls who identified themselves with the feminine ideal underachieved in mathematics, that is, did less well than would have been expected of them based on general intelligence and performance in other subjects.

Street Mathematics:
Things, Motion, Scores

Not all the skills that are necessary for learning mathematics are learned in school. Measuring, computing, and manipulating objects that have dimensions and dynamic properties of their own are part of the everyday life of children. Children who miss out on these experiences may not be well primed for math in school.

Feminists have complained for a long time that playing with dolls is one way of convincing impressionable little girls that they may only be mothers or housewives — or, as in the case of the Barbie doll, "pinup girls" — when they grow up. But doll-playing may have even more serious consequences for little girls than that. Do girls find out about gravity and distance and shapes and sizes playing with dolls? Probably not.

A curious boy, if his parents are tolerant, will have taken apart a number of household and play objects by the time he is ten, and, if his parents are lucky, he may even have put them back together again. In all of this he is learning things that will be useful in physics and math. Taking parts out that have to go back in requires some examination of form. Building something that stays up or at least stays put for some time involves working with structure.

Sports is another source of math-related concepts for children which tends to favor boys. Getting to first base on a not very well hit grounder is a lesson in time, speed, and distance. Intercepting a football thrown through the air requires some rapid intuitive eye calculations based on the ball's direction, speed, and trajectory. Since physics is partly concerned with velocities, trajectories, and collisions of objects, much of the math taught to prepare a student for physics deals with relationships and formulas that can be used to express motion and acceleration.

What, then, can we conclude about mathematics and sex? If math anxiety is in part the result of math avoidance, why not require girls to take as much math as they can possibly master? If being the only girl in "trig" is the reason so many women drop math at the end of high school, why not provide psychological counseling and support for those young women who wish to go on? Since ability in mathematics is considered by many to be unfeminine, perhaps fear of success, more than any bodily or mental dysfunction, may interfere with girls' ability to learn math.

QUESTIONS

1. Would anything be lost if the essay began with what is now the fifth paragraph? Explain.
2. Tobias often uses "may" in this essay, thereby suggesting that the evidence explaining girls' math-fear is inconclusive. How uncertain do you think she is? To what extent is her tentativeness a pose, allowing her to persuade without seeming to be dogmatic?

The Door

E. B. White

Everything (he kept saying) is something it isn't. And everybody is always somewhere else. Maybe it was the city, being in the city, that made him feel how queer everything was and that it was something else. Maybe (he kept thinking) it was the names of the things. The names were tex and frequently koid. Or they were flex and oid or they were duroid (sani) or flexsan (duro), but everything was glass (but not quite glass) and the thing that you touched (the surface, washable, crease-resistant) was rubber, only it wasn't quite rubber and you didn't quite touch it but almost. The wall, which was glass but thrutex, turned out on being approached not to be a wall, it was something else, it was an opening or doorway — and the doorway (through which he saw himself approaching) turned out to be something else, it was a wall. And what he had eaten not having agreed with him.

He was in a washable house, but he wasn't sure. Now about

those rats, he kept saying to himself. He meant the rats that the
Professor had driven crazy by forcing them to deal with problems
which were beyond the scope of rats, the insoluble problems. He
meant the rats that had been trained to jump at the square card with
the circle in the middle, and the card (because it was something it
wasn't) would give way and let the rat into a place where the food
was, but then one day it would be a trick played on the rat, and the
card would be changed, and the rat would jump but the card
wouldn't give way, and it was an impossible situation (for a rat) and
the rat would go insane and into its eyes would come the unspeak-
ably bright imploring look of the frustrated, and after the convulsions
were over and the frantic racing around, then the passive stage would
set in and the willingness to let anything be done to it, even if it was
something else.

He didn't know which door (or wall) or opening in the house to
jump at, to get through, because one was an opening that wasn't a
door (it was a void, or koid) and the other was a wall that wasn't an
opening, it was a sanitary cupboard of the same color. He caught a
glimpse of his eyes staring into his eyes, in the thrutex, and in them
was the expression he had seen in the picture of the rats — weary
after convulsions and the frantic racing around, when they were
willing and did not mind having anything done to them. More and
more (he kept saying) I am confronted by a problem which is
incapable of solution (for this time even if he chose the right door,
there would be no food behind it) and that is what madness is, and
things seeming different from what they are. He heard, in the house
where he was, in the city to which he had gone (as toward a door
which might, or might not, give way), a noise — not a loud noise
but more of a low prefabricated humming. It came from a place in
the base of the wall (or stat) where the flue carrying the filterable air
was, and not far from the Minipiano, which was made of the same
material nailbrushes are made of, and which was under the stairs.
"This, too, has been tested," she said, pointing, but not at it, "and
found viable." It wasn't a loud noise, he kept thinking, sorry that he
had seen his eyes, even though it was through his own eyes that he
had seen them.

First will come the convulsions (he said), then the exhaustion,
then the willingness to let anything be done. "And you better believe
it *will* be."

All his life he had been confronted by situations which were
incapable of being solved, and there was a deliberateness behind all
this, behind this changing of the card (or door), because they would
always wait till you had learned to jump at the certain card (or door)

— the one with the circle — and then they would change it on you. There have been so many doors changed on me, he said, in the last twenty years, but it is now becoming clear that it is an impossible situation, and the question is whether to jump again, even though they ruffle you in the rump with a blast of air — to make you jump. He wished he wasn't standing by the Minipiano. First they would teach you the prayers and the Psalms, and that would be the right door (the one with the circle) and the long sweet words with the holy sound, and that would be the one to jump at to get where the food was. Then one day you jumped and it didn't give way, so that all you got was the bump on the nose, and the first bewilderment, the first young bewilderment.

I don't know whether to tell her about the door they substituted or not, he said, the one with the equation on it and the picture of the amoeba reproducing itself by division. Or the one with the photostatic copy of the check for thirty-two dollars and fifty cents. But the jumping was so long ago, although the bump is . . . how those old wounds hurt! Being crazy this way wouldn't be so bad if only, if only. If only when you put your foot forward to take a step, the ground wouldn't come up to meet your foot the way it does. And the same way in the street (only I never get back to the street unless I jump at the right door), the curb coming up to meet your foot, anticipating ever so delicately the weight of the body, which is somewhere else. "We could take your name," she said, "and send it to you." And it wouldn't be so bad if only you could read a sentence all the way through without jumping (your eye) to something else on the same page; and then (he kept thinking) there was that man out in Jersey, the one who started to chop his trees down, one by one, the man who began talking about how he would take his house to pieces, brick by brick, because he faced a problem incapable of solution, probably, so he began to hack at the trees in the yard, began to pluck with trembling fingers at the bricks in the house. Even if a house is not washable, it is worth taking down. It is not till later that the exhaustion sets in.

But it is inevitable that they will keep changing the doors on you, he said, because that is what they are for; and the thing is to get used to it and not let it unsettle the mind. But that would mean not jumping, and you can't. Nobody can not jump. There will be no not-jumping. Among rats, perhaps, but among people never. Everybody has to keep jumping at a door (the one with the circle on it) because that is the way everybody is, especially some people. You wouldn't want me, standing here, to tell you, would you, about my friend the poet (deceased) who said, "My heart has followed all my days something I cannot name"? (It had the circle on it.) And like many poets, although few so beloved, he is gone. It killed him, the jumping. First, of course, there were the preliminary bouts, the convulsions, and the calm and the willingness.

I remember the door with the picture of the girl on it (only it was spring), her arms outstretched in loveliness, her dress (it was the one with the circle on it) uncaught, beginning the slow, clear, blinding cascade — and I guess we would all like to try that door again, for it seemed like the way and for a while it was the way, the door would open and you would go through winged and exalted (like any rat) and the food would be there, the way the Professor had it arranged, everything O.K., and you had chosen the right door for the world was young. The time they changed that door on me, my nose bled for a hundred hours — how do you like that, Madam? Or would you prefer to show me further through this so strange house, or you could take my name and send it to me, for although my heart has followed all my days something I cannot name, I am tired of the jumping and I do not know which way to go, Madam, and I am not even sure that I am not tried beyond the endurance of man (rat, if you will) and have taken leave of sanity. What are you following these days, old friend, after your recovery from the last bump? What is the name, or is it something you cannot name? The rats have a name for it by this time, perhaps, but I don't know what they call it. I call it plexikoid and it comes in sheets, something like insulating board, unattainable and ugli-proof.

And there was the man out in Jersey, because I keep thinking about his terrible necessity and the passion and trouble he had gone to all those years in the indescribable abundance of a householder's detail, building the estate and the planting of the trees and in spring the lawn-dressing and in fall the bulbs for the spring burgeoning, and the watering of the grass on the long light evenings in summer and the gravel for the driveway (all had to be thought out, planned) and the decorative borders, probably, the perennials and the bug spray, and the building of the house from plans of the architect, first the sills, then the studs, then the full corn in the ear, the floors laid on the floor timbers, smoothed, and then the carpets upon the smooth floors and the curtains and the rods therefor. And then, almost without warning, he would be jumping at the same old door and it wouldn't give: they had changed it on him, making life no longer supportable under the elms in the elm shade, under the maples in the maple shade.

"Here you have the maximum of openness in a small room."

It was impossible to say (maybe it was the city) what made him feel the way he did, and I am not the only one either, he kept thinking — ask any doctor if I am. The doctors, they know how many there are, they even know where the trouble is only they don't like to tell you about the prefrontal lobe because that means making a hole in your skull and removing the work of centuries. It took so long coming, this lobe, so many, many years. (Is it something you read in the paper, perhaps?) And now, the strain being so great, the door having been changed by the Professor once too often . . . but it only means a whiff of ether, a few deft strokes, and the higher animal becomes a little easier in his mind and more like the lower one. From now on, you see, that's the way it will be, the ones with the small prefrontal lobes will win because the other ones are hurt too much by this incessant bumping. They can stand just so much, eh, Doctor? (And what is that, pray, that you have in your hand?) Still, you never can tell, eh, Madam?

He crossed (carefully) the room, the thick carpet under him softly, and went toward the door carefully, which was glass and he could see himself in it, and which, at his approach, opened to allow him to pass through; and beyond he half expected to find one of the old doors that he had known, perhaps the one with the circle, the one with the girl her arms outstretched in loveliness and beauty before him. But he saw instead a moving stairway, and descended in light (he kept thinking) to the street below and to the other people. As he stepped off, the ground came up slightly, to meet his foot.

QUESTIONS

1. What information does the first paragraph give us about the story's setting and about the main character? What is the effect of all the parenthetical interruptions? How can White's use of a fragmentary sentence at the end of the paragraph be defended?

2. In the second paragraph, the man recalls an account of a psychologist's experiment. What was the experiment's purpose? Why does the man recall it?

3. Beginning with the fifth paragraph ("All his life"), the man reflects on the last twenty years of his life and on the "doors" that were constantly changed on him. What do the doors and their constant changing symbolize? He gives four examples. What are they, and what does each represent? Do the examples

suggest that the man's problem is unique, or that it is shared by many of us?

4. What do the "man out in Jersey" and the "poet (deceased)" and the man have in common? How are they dissimilar?

5. In the next-to-last paragraph, the doctor offers the man a solution of a kind. What is it? What does White think of this solution?

6. Does the story have a happy ending? Explain.

PART FIVE
Editing

No iron can stab the heart
with such force as a period
put just at the right place.
— Isaac Babel

18
Manuscript
Form

To edit a manuscript is to refine it for others to read. When your essay at last says what you want to say, you are ready to get it into good physical shape, into an edited manuscript.

BASIC MANUSCRIPT FORM

Much of what follows is nothing more than common sense. Unless your instructor specifies something different, you can adopt these principles as a guide.

1. Use 8½-by-11-inch paper of good weight. Keep as light-weight a carbon copy as you wish, but hand in a sturdy original. Do not use paper torn out of a spiral notebook; the ragged edges are distracting to a reader.

2. Write on one side of the page only. If you typewrite, double-space, typing with a reasonably fresh ribbon. If you submit a handwritten copy, use lined paper and write, in ink, on every other line if the lines are closely spaced.

3. Put your name and class or course number in the upper left-hand corner of the first page. It is a good idea to put your name in the upper left corner of each page, so the instructor can easily reassemble your essay if somehow a page gets detached and mixed with other papers.

4. Center the title of your essay about two inches from the top of the first page. Capitalize the first letter of the first and last words of your title, the first word after a semicolon or colon if you use either one, and the first letter of all the other words except articles, conjunctions, and prepositions, thus:

```
The Diabolic and Celestial Images in The Scarlet Letter
```

Notice that your title is neither underlined nor enclosed in quotation marks (though of course if, as here, it includes material that would normally be italicized or in quotation marks that material continues to be so written).

5. Begin the essay an inch or two below the title. If your instructor prefers a title page, begin the essay on the next page.

6. Leave an adequate margin — an inch or an inch and a half — at top, bottom, and sides.

7. Number the pages consecutively, using arabic numerals in the upper right-hand corner. If you give the title on a separate page, do not number that page; the page that follows it is page 1.

8. Indent the first word of each paragraph five spaces from the left margin.

9. Fasten the pages of your paper with a paper clip in the upper left-hand corner. Stiff binders are unnecessary; indeed, they are a nuisance to the instructor, adding bulk and making it awkward to write annotations.

CORRECTIONS IN THE FINAL COPY

Your extensive revisions should have been made in your drafts, but minor last-minute revisions may be made on the finished copy. Proofreading may catch some typographical errors, and you may notice some small weaknesses. For example, you may notice in the final copy an error in agreement between subject and verb, as in "The insistent demands for drastic reform has disappeared from most of the nation's campuses." The subject is "demands" and so the verb should be plural, "have" rather than "has." You need not retype the page, or even erase. You can make corrections with the following proofreader's symbols.

Changes in wording may be made by crossing through words and rewriting just above them, either on the typewriter or by hand in pen:

```
                                        have
The insistent demands for drastic reform has disappeared from most of

the nation's campuses.
```

Additions should be made above the line, with a caret (∧) below the line at the appropriate place:

```
                                             from
The insistent demands for drastic reform have disappeared∧most of the

nation's campuses.
```

Transpositions of letters may be made thus:

```
The insistent demadns for drastic reform have disappeared from most of

the nation's campuses.
```

Deletions are indicated by a horizontal line through the word or words to be deleted. Delete a single letter by drawing a vertical or diagonal line through it.

```
The insistent demands for drastic reform reform have disappeared from

most of the nation's campuses.
```

Separation of words accidentally run together is indicated by a vertical line, *closure* by a curved line connecting the things to be closed up.

```
The insistent|demands for drastic reform have disappeared f rom most of

the nation's campuses.
```

Paragraphing may be indicated by the symbol ¶ before the word that is to begin the new paragraph.

```
The insistent demands for drastic reform have disappeared from most of

the nation's campuses. ¶Another sign that the country's
```

QUOTATIONS AND
QUOTATION MARKS

Quotations from the material you are writing about are indispensable. They not only let your readers know what you are talking about; they give your readers the material you are responding to, thus letting them share your responses.

Here are some mechanical matters:

1. Distinguish between short and long quotations, and treat each appropriately. Short quotations (usually defined as fewer than three lines of poetry or five lines of prose) are enclosed within quotation marks and run into the text (rather than set off, without quotation marks).

```
LeRoi Jones's "Preface to a Twenty Volume Suicide Note" ends with a

glimpse of the speaker's daughter peeking into her "clasped hands,"

either playfully or madly.


Pope's Essay on Criticism begins informally with a contraction, but the

couplets nevertheless have an authoritative ring: " 'Tis hard to say,

if greater want of skill / Appear in writing or in judging ill."
```

Notice that in the second example a slash (diagonal line, virgule) is used to indicate the end of a line of verse other than the last line quoted. The slash is, of course, not used if the poetry is set off, indented, and printed as verse, thus:

```
Pope's Essay on Criticism begins informally with a contraction, but the

couplets nevertheless have an authoritative ring:


    'Tis hard to say, if greater want of skill
    Appear in writing or in judging ill;
    But of the two less dangerous is the offense
    To tire our patience than mislead our sense.
```

Material that is set off (usually three or more lines of verse, five or more lines of prose) is *not* enclosed within quotation marks. To set it off, triple-space before and after the quotation and single-space the quotation, indenting prose quotations five spaces (ten spaces for the first line, if the quotation begins with the opening of a paragraph) and centering quotations of poetry. (Note: our suggestion that you single-space longer quotations seems reasonable to us but is at odds with various manuals that tell how to prepare a manuscript for publication. Such manuals usually say that material that is set off should be indented and double-spaced. Find out if your instructor has a preference.) Be sparing in your use of long quotations. Use quotations as evidence, not as padding. If the exact wording of the original is crucial, or especially effective, quote it directly, but if it is not, don't bore the reader with material that can be effectively reduced either by summarizing or by cutting. If you cut, indicate ellipses as explained below under point 3.

2. An embedded quotation (that is, a quotation embedded into a sentence of your own) must fit grammatically into the sentence of which it is a part. For example, suppose you want to use Othello's line, "I have done the state some service."

Incorrect

Near the end of the play Othello says that he "have done the state some service."

Correct

Near the end of the play Othello says that he has "done the state some service."

Correct

Near the end of the play, Othello says, "I have done the state some service."

Don't try to introduce a long quotation (say, more than a complete sentence) into the middle of one of your own sentences. It is almost impossible for the reader to come out of the quotation and to pick up the thread of your own sentence. It is better to lead into the long quotation with "Jones says . . ." and then, after the quotation, to begin a new sentence of your own.

3. The quotation must be exact. Any material that you add must be in square brackets (not parentheses), thus:

```
When Pope says that Belinda is "the rival of his [i.e., the sun's]
beams," he uses comic hyperbole.
```

```
Stephen Dedalus sees the ball as a "greasy leather orb [that] flew like
a heavy bird through the grey light."
```

If you wish to omit material from within a quotation, indicate the ellipsis by three spaced periods. If a sentence ends in an omission, add a regular period and then three spaced periods to indicate the omission. The following example is based on a quotation from the sentences immediately above this one:

```
The manual says that "if you . . . omit material from within a
quotation, [you must] indicate the ellipsis. . . . If a sentence ends
in an omission, add a  regular  period and then three spaced
periods. . . ."
```

Notice that if you begin the quotation with the beginning of a sentence (in the example we have just given, "If you" is the beginning of a quoted sentence) you do *not* indicate that material preceded the words you are quoting. Similarly, if you end your quotation with the end of the quoted sentence, you give only a single period, not four periods, although of course the material from which you are quoting may have gone on for many more sentences. But if you begin quoting from the middle of a sentence, or end quoting before you reach the end of a sentence in your source, it is customary to indicate the omissions. But even such omissions need not be indicated when the quoted material is obviously incomplete — when, for instance, it is a word or phrase. (See the first example in this section, which quotes Pope's phrase "the rival of his beams.") Notice, too, that although quotations must be given word for word, the initial capitalization can be adapted, as here where "If" is reduced to "if."

When a line or more of verse is omitted from a passage that is set off, the three spaced periods are printed on a separate line.

4. Identify the speaker or writer of the quotation, so that readers are not left with a sense of uncertainty. Usually this identification precedes the quoted material (e.g., "Smith says . . .") in accordance with the principle of letting readers know where they are going, but occasionally it may follow the quotation, especially if it will provide something of a pleasant surprise. For example, in a discussion of T. S. Eliot's poetry, you might quote a hostile comment on one of the poems and then reveal that Eliot himself was the speaker.

5. Commas and periods go inside the quotation marks; semicolons and colons go outside. Question marks, exclamation points, and dashes go inside if they are part of the quotation, outside if they are your own.

```
Amanda ironically says to her daughter, "How old are you, Laura?" Is

it possible to fail to hear Laura's weariness in her reply, "Mother, you

know my age"?
```

6. Use *single* quotation marks for material contained within a quotation that itself is within quotation marks, thus:

```
T. S. Eliot says, "Mr. Richards observes that 'poetry is capable of

saving us.' "
```

7. Use quotation marks around titles of short works, that is, for titles of chapters in books and for stories, essays, short poems, songs, lectures, and speeches. Titles of unpublished works, even book-length dissertations, are also enclosed in quotation marks. But underline — to indicate *italics* — titles of pamphlets and of books, that is, novels, periodicals, collections of essays, and long poems, such as *The Rime of the Ancient Mariner* and *Paradise Lost.* Underline also titles of films, radio and television programs, ballets and operas, works of art, and the names of planes, ships, and trains.

Exception: titles of sacred works (for example, the Old Testament, the Bible, Genesis, Acts, the Gospels, the Koran) are neither underlined nor enclosed within quotation marks. To cite a book of the Bible with chapter and verse, give the name of the book, then a space, then a small roman numeral for the chapter, a period, and an arabic numeral (*not* preceded by a space) for the

verse, thus: Exodus xx.14–15. Standard abbreviations for the
books of the Bible (for example, Chron.) are permissible in footnotes and in parenthetic citations within the text.

ACKNOWLEDGING SOURCES

Borrowing without Plagiarizing

Honesty requires that you acknowledge your indebtedness
for material when (1) you quote directly from a work, or (2) you
paraphrase or summarize someone's words (the words of your
paraphrase or summary are your own, but the points are not), or
(3) you appropriate an idea that is not common knowledge.

Let's suppose you are going to make use of Ralph Linton's
comment on definitions of primitive art:

> The term "primitive art" has come to be used with at least three
> distinct meanings. First and most legitimate is its use with reference
> to the early stages in the development of a particular art, as when one
> speaks of the Italian primitives. Second is its use to designate works
> of art executed by persons who have not had formal training in our
> own art techniques and aesthetic canons. Third is its application to
> the art works of all but a small group of societies which we have
> chosen to call civilized. The present discussion will deal only with
> the last.
>
> — Ralph Linton, Preface to Eliot Elisofon,
> *The Sculpture of Africa*
> (New York: Frederick A. Praeger, 1958), p. 9.

1. *Acknowledging a direct quotation.* You may want to use some
or all of Linton's words, in which case you will write something
like this:

As Ralph Linton says, "The term 'primitive art' has come to be
used with at least three distinct meanings. First and most legitimate
is its use with reference to the early stages in the development of a
particular art, as when one speaks of the Italian primitives."[1]

Notice that the digit, indicating a footnote, is raised, and that it
follows the period and the quotation marks. (The form of footnotes
is specified on pages 549–59.) And, of course, in a relatively
informal paper it may be enough merely to mention, in the body of

the paper, the author and title, without using a footnote specifying place of publication, publisher, and date. Our point here is not that you must use detailed footnotes, but that you must give credit.

2. *Acknowledging a paraphrase or summary.* We have already suggested (page 282) that summaries (abridgments) are usually superior to paraphrases (rewordings, of approximately the same length as the original) because summaries are briefer; but occasionally you may find that you cannot greatly abridge a passage in your source and yet don't want to quote it word for word — perhaps because it is too technical or poorly written. Even though you are changing some or all of the words, you must give credit to the source because the idea is not yours. Here is an example of a summary:

> Ralph Linton, in his Preface to Eliot Elisofon's The Sculpture of Africa, suggests that there are at least three common but distinct meanings of the term "primitive art": the early stages of a particular art; the art of untrained artists; and the art of societies that we consider uncivilized.

Not to give credit to Linton is to plagiarize, even though the words are yours. And of course if you say something like this, and do not give credit, you are also plagiarizing:

> "Primitive art" is used in three different senses. First and most reasonable is the use of the word to refer to the early years of a certain art....

It is pointless to offer this sort of rewording; if there is a point, it is to conceal the source and to take credit for thinking that is not your own.

3. *Acknowledging an idea.* Let us say that you have read an essay in which Irving Kristol argues that journalists who pride themselves on being tireless critics of national policy are in fact irresponsible critics because they have no policy they prefer. If this strikes you as a new idea and you adopt it in an essay — even though you set it forth entirely in your own words and with examples not offered by Kristol — you should acknowledge your

debt to Kristol. Not to acknowledge such borrowing is plagiarism. Your readers will not think the less of you for naming your source; rather, they will be grateful to you for telling them about an interesting writer.

In short, acknowledge your source (1) if you quote directly, and put the quoted words in quotation marks, (2) if you summarize or paraphrase someone's material, even though not one word of your source is retained, and (3) if you borrow a distinctive idea, even though the words and the concrete application are your own.

Fair Use of Common Knowledge

If in doubt as to whether or not to give credit (either in a footnote or merely in an introductory phrase such as "Ralph Linton says . . ."), give credit. But as you begin to read widely in your field or subject, you will develop a sense of what is considered common knowledge. Unsurprising definitions in a dictionary can be considered common knowledge, and so there is no need to say "According to Webster, a novel is a long narrative in prose." (That's weak in three ways: it's unnecessary, it's uninteresting, and it's unclear, since "Webster" appears in the titles of several dictionaries, some good and some bad.) Similarly, the date of Freud's death can be considered common knowledge. Few can give it when asked, but it can be found out from innumerable sources, and no one need get the credit for providing you with the date. Again, if you simply *know*, from your reading of Freud, that Freud was interested in literature, you need not cite a specific source for an assertion to that effect, but if you know only because some commentator on Freud said so, and you have no idea whether the fact is well known or not, you should give credit to the source that gave you the information. Not to give credit — for ideas as well as for quoted words — is to plagiarize.

"But How Else Can I Put It?"

If you have just learned — say from an encyclopedia — something that you sense is common knowledge, you may wonder, How can I change into my own words the simple, clear words that this source uses in setting forth this simple fact? For example, if before writing about the photograph of Buffalo Bill and Sitting Bull (page 49), you look up these names in the *Encyclopaedia Britannica,* you will find this statement about Buffalo Bill (William F. Cody): "In 1883 Cody organized his first Wild West exhibition." You cannot use this statement as your own, word for word, without feeling uneasy. But to put in quotation marks such a routine statement of what can be considered common knowledge, and to cite a source for it, seems pretentious. After all, the *Encyclopedia Americana* says much the same thing in the same routine way: "In 1883, . . . Cody organized Buffalo Bill's Wild West." It may be that the word "organized" is simply the most obvious and the best word, and perhaps you will end up using it. Certainly to change "Cody organized" into "Cody presided over the organization of" or "Cody assembled" or some such thing, in an effort to avoid plagiarizing, would be to make a change for the worse and still to be guilty of plagiarism. But you won't get yourself into this mess of wondering whether to change clear, simple wording into awkward wording if in the first place, when you take notes, you summarize your sources, thus: "1883: organized Wild West," or "first Wild West: 1883." Later (even if only thirty minutes later), when drafting your paper, if you turn this nugget — probably combined with others — into the best sentence you can, you will not be in danger of plagiarizing, even if the word "organized" turns up in your sentence. Of course you may want to say somewhere that all your facts are drawn from such-and-such a source, but you offer this statement not to avoid charges of plagiarism, but to protect yourself in case your source contains errors of fact.

FOOTNOTES AND ENDNOTES

Kinds of Notes

When we speak of kinds of notes we are not distinguishing between footnotes, which appear at the bottom of the page, and endnotes, which appear at the end of the essay; for simplicity, we will use *footnote* to cover both of these types. Rather, we are distinguishing between notes that (1) give the sources of quotations, facts, and opinions used, and (2) those that give additional comment that would interrupt the flow of the argument in the body of the paper. This second type perhaps requires a comment. A writer may wish to indicate that he is familiar with an opinion contrary to the one he is offering, but he may not wish to digress upon it during the course of his argument. A footnote lets him refer to it and indicate why he is not considering it. Or a footnote may contain full statistical data that support his point but that would seem unnecessarily detailed and even tedious in the body of the paper.

But this kind of footnote, which gives additional commentary, should be used sparingly. There are times when supporting details may be appropriately relegated to a footnote, but if the thing is worth saying, it is usually worth saying in the body of the paper. A writer should not get into the habit of affixing either trivia or miniature essays to the bottom of each page of an essay.

Reducing the Number of Footnotes

Similarly, the number of footnotes citing sources should be reduced — kept down to an honest minimum, partly by including the documentation within the body of the paper where reasonable and partly by not cluttering up the bottoms of the pages with reference to material that is common knowledge. If you give frequent quotations from one book — for example, *Black Elk Speaks* or a play by Shakespeare — you can, in the footnote to the first quotation, specify which edition you are using, and then mention that all subsequent quotations from the work are from that edition. After each subsequent quotation, then, you need only put parentheses including the page number or — a more useful procedure when you are quoting from plays — act, scene, and line numbers (III.ii.178); if you are quoting from various plays, be sure to include the title of the play in the parentheses. If the quotation is run into the text, close the quotation, give the parenthetic material, and then add the final period.

Let's assume that you have already quoted from *Black Elk Speaks,* and have cited the edition. When you next quote from the book you do not need another footnote, for you may cite the page immediately after the quotation marks, thus:

Artists have painted pretty pictures of Custer just before his death, standing gorgeous against the sun, but we have Black Elk's word that "it was all dark and mixed up" (p. 113).

Another example, this time quoting from a play:

The idea that a tragic hero has exhausted all of his life's possibilities is revealed in Macbeth, when Malcolm says, "Macbeth / Is ripe for shaking" (IV.iii.237-38).

If the quotation is set off, end the quotation with a period (unless what follows in your essay is a continuation of a sentence, of which the quotation is a part), and then, after allowing two spaces to follow the period, put the page number within parentheses. This parenthetic identification in the body of the paper does everything that a footnote would do.

Here is part of a student's essay that includes a set-off quotation followed by a page reference:

Huckleberry Finn, whether he consciously knows it or not, identifies his own flight with Nigger Jim's attempt to escape from slavery. When Huck learns that the Duke and the King have sold Jim, Mark Twain gives these words to Huck:

> I went to the raft and set down in the wigwam to think. But I couldn't come to nothing. I thought till I wore my head sore, but I couldn't see no way out of the trouble. After all this long journey, and after all we'd done for them scoundrels, here it was all come to nothing, everything all busted up and ruined, because they could have the heart to serve Jim such a trick as that, and make him a slave again for all his life, and amongst strangers, too, for forty dirty dollars. (P. 105)

Of course Huck does not explicitly equate himself with Jim, but the reader understands that Jim's freedom has become part of Huck's own goal.

Footnote Numbers and Position

Number the notes consecutively throughout the essay or chapter. Although some instructors allow students to group all of the notes at the rear of the essay, most instructors — and surely all readers — believe that the best place for a footnote is at the foot of the appropriate page. If in your draft you type all your footnotes, when typing your final copy you can easily gauge how much space the footnotes for any given page will require. Micrometric carbon paper (carbon paper with a protruding margin which bears the line numbers from 64, at the top, down to 1, at the bottom) is a great help.

Footnote Style

The principles discussed here are commonly observed in writing about the humanities. But some of the sciences and social sciences use different principles; it is therefore advisable to ask your instructors if they have strong ideas about footnote style.

To indicate that there is a footnote, put a raised arabic numeral (without a period and without parentheses) after the final punctuation of the sentence, unless clarity requires it earlier. (In a sentence about Albee, Beckett, and Cocteau you may need a footnote for each and a corresponding numeral after each name instead of one at the end of the sentence, but usually a single reference at the end will do. The single footnote might explain that Albee says such and such in his book entitled ———, Beckett says such and such in his book entitled ———, and Cocteau says such and such in his book entitled ———.) At the bottom of the page triple-space before giving the first footnote. Then indent five spaces, raise the typewriter carriage half a line, and type the arabic numeral (without a period). Lower the carriage to the regular position, skip one space, and type the footnote, single-spacing it. (Some manuals suggest double-spacing footnotes that run more than one line. Ask your instructor if she has a preference.) If the note runs more than one line, the subsequent lines are flush with the left margin, but each new note begins with an indentation of five spaces. Each note begins with an indented, raised numeral, then a capital letter, and ends with a period or other terminal punctuation. Double-space between footnotes.

FIRST REFERENCE TO A BOOK

Here is a typical first reference to a book:

[1] Curtis F. Brown, <u>Ingrid Bergman</u> (New York: Pyramid, 1973), p. 55.

Notice that you give the author's name as it appears on the title page, *first name first.* You need not give the subtitle, but if you do give it, put a colon between the title and the subtitle and underline the subtitle. The name of the city (without the state or country) is usually enough; but if the city is not well known, or may be confused with another city of the same name (Cambridge, England, and Cambridge, Massachusetts), the state or country is added. The name of the publisher (here, Pyramid Publications) may be shortened. The conventional abbreviation for page is "p." and for pages is "pp." (*not* "pg." and "pgs."). If you give the author's name in the body of the page — for example, in such a sentence as "Curtis F. Brown says that Bergman . . ." — do not repeat the name in the footnote. Merely begin with the title.

[1] <u>Ingrid Bergman</u> (New York: Pyramid, 1973), p. 55.

But do not get carried away by the principle of not repeating in the note any material already given in the body of the paper. If the author and the title are given, convention nevertheless requires you to repeat the title — though not the author's name — in the first note citing the source.

For a book in one volume, by one author, revised edition:

[2] X. J. Kennedy, <u>An Introduction to Poetry</u>, 3d ed. (Boston: Little, Brown, 1974), p. 41.

For a book in one volume, by one author, later reprint:

[3] D. H. Lawrence, <u>Studies in Classic American Literature</u> (1923; rpt. Garden City, N.Y.: Doubleday, 1953), pp. 87-88.

For a book in more than one volume (notice that the volume number is given in roman numerals, the page number in arabic numerals, and abbreviations such as "vol." and "p." are *not* used):

[4] Frank Freidel, <u>Franklin D. Roosevelt: Launching the New Deal</u> (Boston: Little, Brown, 1973), IV, 197-201.

For a book by more than one author (if there are more than three authors, give the full name of the first author and add *et al.*, the Latin abbreviation for "and others"):

[5] Carl Bernstein and Bob Woodward, <u>All the President's Men</u> (New York: Simon and Schuster, 1974), pp. 163-72.

For an edited or translated book:

[6] <u>The Letters of John Keats, 1814-1821</u>, ed. Hyder Edward Rollins (Cambridge, Mass.: Harvard Univ. Press, 1958), II, 129.

[7] Paul Ginestier, <u>The Poet and the Machine</u>, trans. Martin B. Friedman (Chapel Hill: Univ. of North Carolina Press, 1961), p. 28.

[8] Albert Gilman and Roger Brown, "Personality and Style in Concord," in <u>Transcendentalism and Its Legacy</u>, ed. Myron Simon and Thornton H. Parsons (Ann Arbor: Univ. of Michigan Press, 1966), pp. 103-104.

As note 8 indicates, when you are quoting from an essay in an edited book, you begin with the essayist(s) and the essay, then go on to give the title of the book and the name of the editor(s).

For an encyclopedia, publisher and place of publication need not be given. If the article is signed, begin with the author's name (first name first); if it is unsigned, simply begin with the title of the article, in quotation marks. The first example is for a signed article on William F. Cody, known as Buffalo Bill:

[9] Don Russell, "Cody, William Frederick," <u>Encyclopedia Americana</u>, 1973, VII, 177.

Some manuals say that references to alphabetically arranged articles (signed or unsigned) need not include the volume and page number, but if you do include them, as we just did, use roman numerals for the volume (but do not write "vol.") and arabic numerals for the page (but do not write "p.").

The most recent edition of the *Encyclopaedia Britannica,* as we explain on page 276, comprises three groups of books, called *Propaedia, Micropaedia,* and *Macropaedia,* so you must specify which of the three you are referring to. The following example cites an unsigned article on Sitting Bull:

[10] "Sitting Bull," <u>Encyclopaedia Britannica</u>: <u>Micropaedia</u>, 1974, IX, 243-44.

FIRST REFERENCE TO A JOURNAL

Footnote 11 is for a journal (here, volume 43) paginated consecutively throughout the year; footnote 12 is for a journal that paginates each issue separately. A journal paginated separately requires you to list the issue number or month or week or day as well as the year because if it is, for example, a monthly, there will be twelve page 10's in any given year. Current practice favors omitting the volume number for popular weeklies (see footnote 13) and for newspapers, in which case the full date is given without parentheses.

[11] John Demos, "The American Family in Past Time," <u>American Scholar</u>, 43 (1974), 423-24.

[12] Hortense J. Spillers, "Martin Luther King and the Style of the Black Sermon," <u>The Black Scholar</u>, 3, No. 1 (1971), 15.

[13] Bernard McCabe, "Taking Dickens Seriously," <u>Commonweal</u>, 14 May 1965, p. 245.

Notice that footnote 11 identifies volume 43 as having been issued in 1974. If a journal begins a new volume with each new calendar year, the season or month need not be specified; but if the volume number straddles two calendar years, say from Summer 1978 through Spring 1979, the season or month is specified inside the parentheses, before the year.

The author's name and the title of the article are given as they appear in the journal (*first name first*), the title of the article in quotation marks and the title of the journal underlined (to indicate italics). Until recently the volume number, before the date, was given with capital roman numerals, the page or pages with arabic numerals, but current practice uses arabic numerals for both the volume and the page or pages. Notice that when a volume number is given, as in notes 11 and 12, the page number is *not* preceded by *p.* or *pp.*

If a book review has a title, the review may be treated as an article. If, however, the title is merely that of the book reviewed, or even if the review has a title but for clarity you wish to indicate that it is a review, the following form is commonly used:

[14] N. R. McWilliams, review of Kate Millett, <u>Sexual</u> <u>Politics</u> (Garden City, N.Y.: Doubleday, 1970), <u>Commonweal</u>, 2 October 1970, p. 25.

FIRST REFERENCE TO A NEWSPAPER

The first example is for a *signed article,* the second is for an *unsigned one.*

[15] Bertha Brody, "Illegal Immigrant Allowed to Stay," <u>New</u> <u>York</u> <u>Times</u>, 8 March 1979, Sec. B, p. 12, col. 2.

[16] "Fossils Stolen Again," <u>Washington</u> <u>Post</u>, 28 February 1979, p. 7, col. 3.

SUBSEQUENT REFERENCES

If you quote a second or third or fourth time from a work and you do not wish to incorporate the reference within your text, use a short form in your footnote. The most versatile short form is simply the author's last name and the page number, thus:

[17] Lawrence, p. 34.

You can even dispense with the author's name if you have mentioned it in the sentence to which the footnote is keyed. That is, if you have said "Lawrence goes on to say . . . ," the footnote need only be:

[18] P. 34.

If, however, you have made reference to more than one work by the author, you must indicate by a short title which work you are referring to, thus:

[19] Lawrence, <u>Studies</u>, p. 34.

Or, if your sentence mentions that you are quoting Lawrence, the footnote may be:

[20] Studies, p. 34.

If you have said something like "Lawrence, in *Studies in Classic American Literature,* argues . . . ," the reference may be merely:

[21] P. 34.

In short, a subsequent reference should be as brief as clarity allows. The form "ibid." (for *ibidem,* in the same place), indicating that the material being footnoted comes from the same place as the material of the previous footnote, is no longer preferred for second references. "Op. cit." (for *opere citato,* in the work cited) and "loc. cit." (for *loco citato,* in the place cited) have almost disappeared. Identification by author, or by author and short title if necessary, is preferable.

A reminder: as pages 550–51 suggest, if you are going to quote frequently from one source, it will be best to say in your first reference to this source that sources of subsequent quotations from this work will be cited in parentheses within the body of the paper.

REFERENCES
TO INTRODUCTIONS AND TO
REPRINTED ESSAYS

You may want to footnote some material that is printed along with a reprint of a work of literature. If, for example, you use Robert B. Heilman's edition of Shakespeare's *The Taming of the Shrew,* and you say "Robert B. Heilman points out . . . ," your footnote will look like this:

[22] Introd. to William Shakespeare, The Taming of the Shrew (New York: New American Library, 1966), p. xxv.

Heilman's edition of the play includes, as a sort of appendix, several previously published commentaries. If you want to quote from one of them, the monstrous, but accurate, footnote to the quotation might run:

[23] Maynard Mack, "Engagement and Detachment in Shakespeare's Plays," in <u>Essays</u> <u>on</u> <u>Shakespeare</u> <u>and</u> <u>Elizabethan</u> <u>Drama</u> <u>in</u> <u>Honor</u> <u>of</u> <u>Hardin</u> <u>Craig,</u> ed. Richard Hosley (Columbia: Univ. of Missouri Press, 1962), rpt. in William Shakespeare, <u>The</u> <u>Taming</u> <u>of</u> <u>the</u> <u>Shrew</u>, ed. Robert B. Heilman (New York: New American Library, 1966), p. 213.

(You learned from Heilman's credit-note the title, editor, etc., of the book in which Mack's essay originally appeared.)

SECONDHAND REFERENCES

If you are quoting, say, Sir Arthur Pickard-Cambridge, but have derived the quotation not from his book, *Dithyramb, Tragedy and Comedy,* but from a book or article that quotes from his book, your footnote should indicate both the place where you found it and (if possible) the place where the original passage appears.

[24] Sir Arthur Pickard-Cambridge, <u>Dithyramb</u>, <u>Tragedy</u> and <u>Comedy</u> (Oxford: 1927), p. 243, quoted in Katherine Lever, <u>The</u> <u>Art</u> <u>of</u> <u>Greek</u> <u>Comedy</u> (London: Methuen, 1956), p. 57.

In this example, Lever's book is what you read. If her book had mentioned the publisher of Pickard-Cambridge's book, you would have included that too. Another example, this one from a journal which quoted from Charles Reich's *The Greening of America:*

[25] Charles A. Reich, <u>The</u> <u>Greening</u> <u>of</u> <u>America</u>, quoted in Carl H. Madden, "The Greening of Economics," <u>Virginia</u> <u>Quarterly</u> <u>Review</u>, 50 (Spring 1974), 161.

In this example, Madden's article is what you read. If Madden had given the place, publisher, date, and page of Reich's book, you would have included all that material in your footnote; but he didn't, so you give only as much as you can. In any case, honesty requires you to cite Madden as well as Reich. And not only honesty, but self-protection: if it turns out that Madden has quoted Reich inaccurately, the blame falls not on you, but on Madden.

FOOTNOTING INTERVIEWS, LECTURES, LETTERS

[26] Interview with Rose Moss, novelist, Wellesley College, Wellesley, Mass., 1 March 1979.

[27] Howard Saretta, "Buying College Athletes," lecture delivered at Atlantic College, Hudson, N.Y., 3 March 1979.

[28] Information in a letter to the author, from William Takayanagi of Atlantic College, Hudson, N.Y., 28 February 1979.

BIBLIOGRAPHY

A bibliography is a list of the works cited in the piece of writing or, less often, a list of all the relevant writing. (There is rarely much point in the second sort; if you haven't made use of a particular book or article, why list it?) Normally a bibliography is given only in a long manuscript such as a research paper or a book, but instructors may require a bibliography even for a short paper if they wish to see at a glance the material that the student has used. In this case, a heading such as "Works Consulted" or "Works Cited" is less pretentious than "Bibliography."

Because a bibliography is arranged alphabetically by author, the author's last name is given first. If a work is by more than one author, it is given under the first author's name; his last name is given first, but the other author's or authors' names follow the normal order of first name first. (See the entry under "Brown," page 560.) Anonymous works are sometimes grouped at the beginning, arranged alphabetically under the first word of the title (or the second word, if the first word is an article, that is, *A, An,* or *The*), but the recent tendency has been to list them at the appropriate alphabetical place, giving the initial article, if any, but alphabetizing under the next word. Thus, an anonymous article entitled "A View of Freud" would retain the "A" but would be alphabetized under V.

In addition to giving the last name first, a bibliographic entry differs from a footnote in several ways. For example, a bibliographic entry does not put parentheses around the place of publication, the publisher, and the date. In typing an entry, begin flush with the left-hand margin; if the entry runs over the line, indent the subsequent lines of the entry five spaces. Double-space between entries. (Some manuals suggest double-spacing throughout.)

A book by one author:

Aries, Philippe. <u>Western Attitudes Toward Death</u>: <u>From the Middle Ages to the Present</u>, trans. Patricia M. Ranum. Baltimore: Johns Hopkins Univ. Press, 1974.

A book by more than one author:

Brown, Roger, and Richard J. Herrnstein. <u>Psychology</u>. Boston: Little, Brown, 1975.

Notice, in this last entry, that the book is alphabetized under the *last name* of the *first* author, but that the name of the second author is given in the ordinary way, first name first.

An essay or other work within an edited volume:

Bush, Douglas. "Wordsworth: A Minority Report," in <u>Wordsworth</u>: <u>Centenary Studies</u>, ed. Gilbert T. Dunklin. Princeton: Princeton Univ. Press, 1951, pp. 3-22.

Two or more works by the same author:

Frye, Northrop. <u>Fables of Identity</u>: <u>Studies in Poetic Mythology</u>. New York: Harcourt, 1963.

————. <u>The Secular Scripture</u>. Cambridge, Mass.: Harvard Univ. Press, 1976.

The horizontal line indicates that the author (in this case Northrop Frye) is the same as in the previous item; multiple titles by one author are arranged alphabetically, as here where *Fables* precedes *Secular*. By the way, the reason that the second of these entries includes "Mass." is to distinguish Cambridge, Massachusetts, from Cambridge, England. Indicate the state only if two cities share a name, or if the name of the city is not likely to be known.

Encyclopedia articles:

"Journalism." <u>Encyclopaedia Britannica</u>: <u>Micropaedia</u>. 1978 ed.

Lang, Andrew. "Ballads." <u>Encyclopaedia Britannica</u>. 11th ed.

The first of these two encyclopedia articles is unsigned, so the article is listed under its title. The second of the articles is signed, so it is listed under its author. Note that an encyclopedia article does not require volume or page, or place or date of publication; the edition, however, must be identified somehow, and usually the date is the best identification.

An introduction to a book by another author:

MacCaffrey, Isabel Gamble.   Introd. to John Milton, <u>Samson</u> <u>Agonistes</u> <u>and</u> <u>the</u> <u>Shorter</u> <u>Poems</u>.   New York: New American Library, 1966.

The last entry suggests that the student made use of the introduction, rather than the main body, of the book; if the body of the book were used, the book would be alphabetized under M for Milton, and the form would resemble that of the next item, with "ed. Isabel Gamble MacCaffrey" following the title.

An edition:

Pope, Alexander.   <u>The</u> <u>Correspondence</u> <u>of</u> <u>Alexander</u> <u>Pope</u>, ed. George Sherburn.   5 vols.   Oxford: Clarendon, 1956.

A periodical:

Reynolds, Lloyd G.   "Making a Living in China," <u>Yale</u> <u>Review</u>, 53 (June 1974), 481-97.

A newspaper:

Romero, Juanita.   "Panda Rejects Spouse." <u>Washington</u> <u>Post</u>, 18 March 1979, p. 6, col. 4.

"Shakespeare Proved Not Bacon." <u>New</u> <u>York</u> <u>Times</u>, 21 January 1979, Sec. D, p. 29, col. 2.

The first of these newspaper articles is signed, so it is listed under the author's last name. The second article is unsigned, so it is listed under the first word of the title.

An anthology:

Valdez, Luis, and Stan Steiner, eds. <u>Aztlan</u>, <u>An</u> <u>Anthology</u> <u>of</u> <u>Mexican</u> <u>American</u> <u>Literature</u>.   New York: Knopf, 1972.

This entry lists the anthology alphabetically under the editor's name, but an anthology may be entered either under the editor's name or under its title. See below, *Victorian Poetry*.

A book review:

Vendler, Helen.   Review of <u>Essays</u> <u>on</u> <u>Style</u>, ed. Roger Fowler.   <u>Essays</u>
<u>in</u> <u>Criticism</u>, 16 (1966), 457-63.

An anthology (this one listed by title rather than by editor):

<u>Victorian</u> <u>Poetry</u> <u>and</u> <u>Poetics</u>, 2nd ed., ed. Walter E. Houghton and
G. Robert Stange.   Boston: Houghton Mifflin, 1968.

19
Punctuation

Speakers can raise or lower the volume or pitch of their voices; they can speak a phrase slowly and distinctly and then (making a parenthetical remark, perhaps) quicken the pace. They can wave their arms, pound a table, or pause meaningfully. But writers, physically isolated from their audience, have only paper and ink to work with. Nevertheless, they can embody some of the tones and gestures of speech — in the patterns of their written sentences, and in the dots, hooks, and dashes of punctuation that clarify those patterns.

Punctuation clarifies, first of all, by removing or reducing ambiguity. Consider the following sentence:

He arrived late for the rehearsal didn't end until midnight.

Almost surely you stumbled in the middle of the sentence, thinking that it was about someone arriving tardily at a rehearsal, and then, since what followed made no sense, you probably went back and mentally added the comma (by pausing) at the necessary place:

He arrived late, for the rehearsal didn't end until midnight.

Punctuation helps to keep the reader on the right path. And the path is your train of thought. If your punctuation is faulty, you unintentionally point the reader off your path and toward dead end streets and quagmires. Let's look at an example.

Once more, with feeling.
Once more with feeling.

Is there a difference between these two sentences or do they have identical meanings? Well, if punctuation is not just ink on paper, the first sentence means something like "Let's do it again, but this time do it with feeling," while the second sentence means "The last performance had feeling, and so let's do it once more, keeping the feeling."

Even when punctuation is not the key to meaning, it usually helps you to get your meaning across neatly. Consider the following sentences:

> There are two kinds of feminism — one is the growing struggle of women to understand and change the shape of their lives and the other is a narrow ideology whose adherents are anxious to clear away whatever does not conform to their view.

This is clear enough, but by changing the punctuation it can be sharpened. Because a dash usually indicates an abrupt interruption — it usually precedes a sort of afterthought — a colon would be better. The colon, usually the signal of an amplification of what precedes it, here would suggest that the two classifications are not impromptu thoughts but carefully considered ones. Second, and more important, in the original version the two classifications are run together without any intervening punctuation, but since the point is that the two are utterly different, it is advisable to separate them by inserting a comma or a semicolon, indicating a pause. A comma before "and the other" would do, but probably a semicolon — without the "and" — is preferable because it is a heavier pause, thereby making the separation clearer. Here is the sentence, revised:

> There are two kinds of feminism: one is the growing struggle of women to understand and change the shape of their lives; the other is a narrow ideology whose adherents are anxious to clear away whatever does not conform to their view.

The right punctuation enables the reader to move easily through the sentence.

Now, although punctuation helps a reader to move through a sentence, it must be admitted that some of the rules of punctuation do not contribute to meaning or greatly facilitate reading. For example, in American usage a period never comes immediately after quotation marks; it precedes quotation marks, thus:

> She said, "Put the period inside the quotation marks."

If you put the period after the closing quotation mark, the meaning remains the same, but you are also informing your reader that you don't know the relevant convention. Since a misspelled word or a misplaced period often gives the impression of laziness, ignorance, or incompetence, why not generate as little friction as possible by learning the chief conventions?

THREE COMMON ERRORS: FRAGMENTS, COMMA SPLICES, AND RUN-ON SENTENCES

Fragments and How to Correct Them

A fragment is a part of a sentence set off as if it were a complete sentence: *Because I didn't care. Being an accident. Later in the week. For several reasons. My oldest sister.* Fragments are common in speech, but they are used sparingly in writing, for particular effects (see pages 383–84). A fragment used carelessly in writing often looks like an afterthought — usually because it *was* an afterthought, that is, an explanation or other addition that really belongs to the previous sentence. With appropriate punctuation (and sometimes with no punctuation at all) a fragment can usually be connected to the previous sentence.

1. *Incorrect*

Many nineteenth-century horror stories have been made into films. Such as *Dracula* and *Frankenstein*.

Correct

Many nineteenth-century horror stories have been made into films, such as *Dracula* and *Frankenstein*.

2. *Incorrect*

Many schools are putting renewed emphasis on writing. Because SAT scores have declined for ten years.

Correct

Many schools are putting renewed emphasis on writing, because SAT scores have declined for ten years.

3. *Incorrect*

He practiced doing card tricks. In order to fool his friends.

Correct

He practiced doing card tricks in order to fool his friends.

4. *Incorrect*

She wore only rope sandals. Being a strict vegetarian.

Correct

Being a strict vegetarian, she wore only rope sandals.
She wore only rope sandals because she was a strict vegetarian.

5. *Incorrect*

A fragment often looks like an afterthought. Perhaps because it *was* an afterthought.

Correct

A fragment often looks like an afterthought — perhaps because it *was* an afterthought.

6. *Incorrect*

He hoped to get credit for two summer school courses. Batik and Hang-Gliding.

Correct

He hoped to get credit for two summer school courses: Batik and Hang-Gliding.

Notice in the examples above that, depending upon the relationship between the two parts, the fragment and the preceding statement can be joined by a comma, a dash, a colon, or by no punctuation at all.

Notice also that unintentional fragments often follow subordinating conjunctions, such as *because* and *although*. Subordinating conjunctions introduce a subordinate (dependent) clause; such a clause cannot stand as a sentence. Here is a list of the commonest subordinating conjunctions.

after	though
although	unless
because	until
before	when
if	where
provided	whereas
since	while

Fragments also commonly occur when the writer, as in the fourth example, mistakenly uses *being* as a main verb.

Comma Splices and Run-on Sentences, and How to Correct Them

An error known as a *comma splice* or *comma fault* results when a comma is mistakenly placed between two independent clauses that are not joined by a coordinating conjunction: *and, or, nor, but, for, yet, so*. If the comma is omitted, the error is called a *run-on sentence*.
Examples of the two errors:

comma splice (or comma fault): In the second picture the man leans on the woman's body, he is obviously in pain.

run-on sentence: In the second picture the man leans on the woman's body he is obviously in pain.

Run-on sentences and comma splices may be corrected in five principal ways.

1. Use a period. Write two sentences.

In the second picture the man leans on the woman's body. He is obviously in pain.

2. Use a semicolon.

In the second picture the man leans on the woman's body; he is obviously in pain.

3. Use a comma and a coordinating conjunction (and, or, nor, but, for, yet, so).

In the second picture the man leans on the woman's body, and he is obviously in pain.

4. Make one of the clauses dependent (subordinate). Use a subordinating conjunction such as *after, although, because, before, if, since, though, unless, until, when, where, while*.

In the second picture the man leans on the woman's body because he is in pain.

5. Reduce one of the independent clauses to a phrase, or even to a single word.

In the second picture the man, obviously in pain, leans on the woman's body.

Run-on sentences and comma splices are especially common in

sentences beginning with transitional words or phrases such as the following:

also	however
besides	indeed
consequently	in fact
for example	nevertheless
furthermore	therefore
hence	

When these words join independent clauses, the clauses cannot be linked by a comma.

> incorrect: She argued from faulty premises, however the conclusions happened to be correct.

Here are five correct revisions, following the five rules we have just given. (In the first two revisions we place "however" after, rather than before, "the conclusions" because we prefer the increase in emphasis, but the grammatical point is the same.)

1. She argued from faulty premises. The conclusions, however, happened to be correct. (Two sentences)
2. She argued from faulty premises; the conclusions, however, happened to be correct. (Semicolon)
3. She argued from faulty premises, but the conclusions happened to be correct. (Coordinating conjunction)
4. Although she argued from faulty premises, the conclusions happened to be correct. (Subordinating conjunction)
5. She argued from faulty premises to correct conclusions. (Reduction of an independent clause to a phrase)

It should now be evident that the following sentence contains a comma splice:

> The husband is not pleased, in fact, he is embarrassed.

And the ways of repairing it are equally evident.

THE PERIOD

1. Periods are used to mark the ends of sentences (or intentional sentence fragments) other than questions and exclamations.

A sentence normally ends with a period.

She said, "I'll pass."

Yes.

Once more, with feeling.

But a sentence within a sentence is punctuated according to the needs of the longer sentence. Notice, in the following example, that periods are *not* used after "pass" or directly after "said."

"I'll pass," she said (she meant she hoped she would).

If a sentence ends with a quotation, the period goes *inside* the quotation marks unless parenthetic material follows the quotation.

Brutus says, "Antony is but a limb of Caesar."

Brutus says, "Antony is but a limb of Caesar" (*Julius Caesar,* II.i.165).

2. Periods are used with abbreviations of titles and terms of reference.

Dr., Mr., Mrs., Ms.

p., pp. (for "page" and "pages"), i.e., e.g., etc.

But when the capitalized initial letters of the words naming an organization are used in place of the full name, the periods are commonly omitted:

CBS, CORE, IBM, NBA, UCLA, UNICEF, USAF

3. Periods are also used to separate chapter from verse in the Bible.

Genesis iii.2, Mark vi.10

For further details on references to the Bible, see page 545.

THE COLON

The colon has three chief uses: to introduce a list or series of examples; to introduce an amplification of what precedes the colon; and to introduce a quotation (though a quotation can be introduced by other means). A fourth, less important, use is in the indication of time.

1. The colon may introduce a list or series.

> He excelled in sports: swimming, tennis, hockey, gymnastics, and wrestling.

Note, however, that a colon is *not* used if the series is introduced by *such as, for example,* or a similar transitional phrase.

2. As a formal introduction to an amplification, the colon is almost equivalent to *namely,* or *that is.* What is on one side of the colon more or less equals what is on the other side. The material on either side of the colon can stand as a separate sentence.

> She explained her fondness for wrestling: she did it to shock her parents.

> The forces which in China created a central government were absent in Japan: farming had to be on a small scale, there was no need for extensive canal works, and a standing army was not required to protect the country from foreign invaders.

> Many of the best of the Civil War photographs must be read as the fossils of earlier events: The caissons with their mud-encrusted wheels, the dead on the field, the empty landscapes, all speak of deeds already past.
>
> — John Szarkowski

Notice in this last example that the writer uses a capital letter after the colon; the usage is acceptable when a complete sentence follows the colon, as long as that style is followed consistently throughout a paper. But most students find it easier to use lowercase letters after colons, the prevalent style in writing today.

3. The colon, like the comma, may be used to introduce a quotation; it is more formal than the comma, setting off the quotation to a greater degree.

> The black sculptor Ed Wilson tells his students: "Malcolm X is my brother, Martin Luther King is my brother, Eldridge Cleaver is my brother! But Michelangelo is my grandfather!"
>
> — Albert E. Elsen

4. A colon is used to separate the hour from the minutes when the time is given in figures.

> 9:15, 12:00

Colons (like semicolons) go outside of closing quotation marks if they are not part of the quotation.

"There is no such thing as a free lunch": the truth of these words is confirmed every day.

THE SEMICOLON

Typographically a semicolon is part comma, part period; and it does indeed function as a strong comma or as a weak period. It can never function as a colon.

1. As a strong comma, the semicolon can be used as follows:

Only in countries touching on the Mediterranean has the nude been at home; and even there its meaning was often forgotten.

In the greatest age of painting, the nude inspired the greatest works; and even when it ceased to be a compulsive subject it held its position as an academic exercise and a demonstration of mastery.

As a strong comma, it can be used to separate a series of phrases or clauses with internal commas.

He had a car, which he hadn't paid for; a wife, whom he didn't love; and a father, who was unemployed.

But:

He had a car, a wife, and a father.

2. As a weak period, the semicolon joins independent statements that the writer wishes to bring together more closely than a period allows.

When a cat washes its face it does not move its paw; it moves its face.

Others merely live; I vegetate.

All the windows seemed to be in the wrong places; it was a house designed to hold the darkness.
— Sharon R. Curtin

The catacombs were not underground churches where Christians secretly worshiped; they were burial chambers connected by long passages, and they were well known to official Rome.

He never complained; he knew it wouldn't do any good.

With short clauses, such as those in the last example, a comma could be used, but some purists would object, saying that joining even short clauses with a comma would produce a run-on sentence of the sort known as a comma splice or a comma fault (see pages 567–68).

Use a semicolon also before a conjunctive adverb (that is, a transitional word such as *also, consequently, furthermore, however, moreover, nevertheless, therefore*) connecting independent clauses, and put a comma after the conjunctive adverb.

Her hair was black and wavy; however, it was false.

Semicolons (like colons) go outside of closing quotation marks if they are not part of the quotation.

He said, "I do"; moreover, he repeated the words.

THE COMMA

A comma (from a Greek word meaning "to cut") indicates a relatively slight pause within a sentence. If after checking the rules you are still uncertain of whether or not to use a comma in a given sentence, read the sentence aloud and see if it sounds better with or without a pause, and then add or omit the comma. In typing, always follow a comma with a space.

Here is a table of contents for these pages on the comma:

1. Independent clauses (unless short) joined by a coordinating

conjunction (*and, or, nor, but, for, yet, so*) take a comma before the conjunction.

> Most students see at least a few football games, and many go to every game of the season.
>
> Most students seem to have an intuitive sense of when to use a comma, but in fact the "intuition" is the result of long training.

If the introductory independent clause is short, the comma is usually omitted:

> She dieted but she continued to gain weight.

2. An introductory subordinate clause or long phrase is usually followed by a comma.

> Having revised his manuscript for the third time, he went to bed.
>
> In order to demonstrate her point, the instructor stood on her head.

If the introductory subordinate clause or phrase is short, say four words or fewer, the comma may be omitted, provided no ambiguity results from the omission.

> Having left he soon forgot.

But compare this last example with the following:

> Having left, the instructor soon forgot.

If the comma is omitted, the sentence is misread. Where are commas needed in the following sentences?

> Instead of discussing the book she wrote a summary.
>
> When Shakespeare wrote comedies were already popular.
>
> While he ate his poodle would sit by the table.
>
> As we age small things become killers.

3. A subordinate clause or long modifying phrase tacked on as an afterthought is usually preceded by a comma.

> I have decided not to be nostalgic about the 1950's, despite the hoopla over Elvis.
>
> Buster Keaton fell down a flight of stairs without busting, thereby gaining his nickname from Harry Houdini.
>
> By the time he retired Hank Aaron had 755 home runs, breaking Babe Ruth's record by 41.

With afterthoughts, the comma may be omitted if there is a clear sequence of cause and effect, signaled by such words as *because, for,* and *so.* Compare the two following examples:

> In 1601 Shakespeare wrote *Hamlet,* probably his best-known play.

> In 1601 Shakespeare wrote *Hamlet* because revenge tragedy was in demand.

4. A pair of commas can serve as a pair of unobtrusive parentheses. Be sure not to omit the second comma.

> Doctors, I think, have an insufficient knowledge of acupuncture.

> The earliest known paintings of Christ, dating from the third century, are found in the catacombs outside of Rome.

> Medicare and Medicaid, the chief sources of federal support for patients in nursing homes, are frequently confused.

Under this heading we can include a conjunctive adverb (a transitional adverb such as *also, besides, consequently, however, likewise, nevertheless, therefore*) inserted within a sentence. These transitional words are set off between a pair of commas.

> Her hair, however, was stringy.

If one of these words begins a sentence, the comma after it is optional. Notice, however, that the presence of such a word as "however" is not always a safeguard against a run-on sentence or comma splice; if the word occurs between two independent clauses and it goes with the second clause, you need a semicolon before it and a comma after it.

> Her hair was black and wavy; however, it was false.

(See the discussion of comma splice on pages 567–68.)

5. Use a comma to set off a nonrestrictive modifier. A nonrestrictive modifier, as the following examples will make clear, is a sort of parenthetical addition; it gives supplementary information about the subject, but it can be omitted without changing the subject. A restrictive modifier, however, is not supplementary but essential; if a restrictive modifier is omitted, the subject becomes more general. In Dorothy Parker's celebrated poem,

Men seldom make passes
At girls who wear glasses,

"who wear glasses" is a restrictive modifier, narrowing or restricting the subject down from "girls" to a particular group of girls, "girls who wear glasses."

Here is a *non*restrictive modifier:

For the majority of immigrants, who have no knowledge of English, language is the chief problem.

Now a restrictive modifier:

For the majority of immigrants who have no knowledge of English, language is the chief problem.

The first version says — in addition to its obvious message that language is the chief problem — that the majority of immigrants have no knowledge of English. The second version makes no such assertion; it talks not about the majority of immigrants but only about a more restricted group — those immigrants who have no knowledge of English.

Other examples:

Shakespeare's shortest tragedy, *Macbeth*, is one of his greatest plays.

In this sentence, "*Macbeth*" is nonrestrictive because the subject is already as restricted as possible; Shakespeare can have written only one "shortest tragedy." That is, "*Macbeth*" is merely an explanatory equivalent of "Shakespeare's shortest tragedy" and it is therefore enclosed in commas. (A noun or noun phrase serving as an explanatory equivalent to another, and in the same syntactical relation to other elements in the sentence, is said to be in apposition.) But compare

Shakespeare's tragedy *Macbeth* is one of his greatest plays.

with the misleadingly punctuated sentence,

Shakespeare's tragedy, *Macbeth*, is one of his greatest plays.

The first of these is restrictive, narrowing or restricting the subject "tragedy" down to one particular tragedy, and so it rightly does not separate the modifier from the subject by a comma. The second, punctuated so that it is nonrestrictive, falsely implies that *Macbeth* is

Shakespeare's only tragedy. Here is an example of a nonrestrictive modifier correctly punctuated:

> Women, who constitute 51.3 percent of the population and 53 percent of the electorate, constitute only 2.5 percent of the House of Representatives and 1 percent of the Senate.

In the next two examples, the first illustrates the correct use of commas after a nonrestrictive appositive, and the second illustrates the correct omission of commas after a restrictive appositive.

> Houdini, the American magician, died in 1926.
>
> The American magician Houdini died in 1926.

6. Words, phrases, and clauses in series take a comma after each item except the last. The comma between the last two items may be omitted if there is no ambiguity.

> Photography is a matter of eyes, intuition, and intellect.
> — John Szarkowski
>
> She wrote plays, poems, and stories.
>
> He wrote plays, sang songs, and danced jigs.
>
> She wrote a wise, witty, humane book.

But adjectives in a series may cause difficulty. The next two examples correctly omit the commas.

> a funny silent film
>
> a famous French professor

In each of these last two examples, the adjective immediately before the noun forms with the noun a compound that is modified by the earlier adjective. That is, the adjectives are not a coordinate series (what is funny is not simply a film but a silent film, what is famous is not simply a professor but a French professor) and so commas are not used. Compare:

> a famous French professor
>
> a famous, arrogant French professor

In the second example, only "famous" and "arrogant" form a coordinate series. If in doubt, see if you can replace the commas with "and"; if you can, the commas are correct. In the example given, you could insert "and" between "famous" and "arrogant," but not between "famous" and "French."

Commas are not needed if all the members of the series are connected by conjunctions.

> He ate steak for breakfast and lunch and supper.

7. Use a comma to set off direct discourse.

> "It's a total failure," she said.
> She said, "It's a total failure."

But do not use a comma for indirect discourse.

> She said that it is a total failure.
> She said it is a total failure.

8. Use a comma to set off "yes" and "no."

> Yes, he could take Freshman English at ten o'clock.

9. Use a comma to set off words of address.

> Look, Bill, take Freshman English at ten o'clock.

10. Use a comma to separate a geographical location within another geographical location.

> She was born in Brooklyn, New York, in 1895.

Another way of putting it is to say that a comma is used after each unit of an address, except that a comma is *not* used between the name of the state and the zip code.

11. Use a comma to set off the year from the month or day.

> He was born on June 10, 1957 (No comma is needed if you use the form "10 June 1957.")

A note on the position of the comma. If a comma is required with parenthetic material, it follows the second parenthesis.

> Because Japan was secure from invasion (even the Mongols were beaten back), her history is unusually self-contained.

The only time a comma may precede a parenthesis is when parentheses surround a digit or letter used to enumerate a series.

Questions usually fall into one of three categories: (1) true-false, (2) multiple choice, (3) essay.

A comma always goes inside closing quotation marks unless the quotation is followed by a parenthesis.

"Sayonara," he said.

"Sayonara" (Japanese for "goodbye"), he said.

THE DASH

A dash — made by typing two hyphens without hitting the space-bar before, between, or after — indicates an abrupt break or pause. Overuse of the dash gives writing an unpleasantly explosive quality.

1. The material within dashes may be, in a sense, parenthetic, though the dashes indicate that it is less dispensable than is parenthetic material.

The bathroom — that private place — has rarely been the subject of scholarly study.

The Great Wall of China forms a continuous line over 1400 miles long — the distance from New York to Kansas City — running from Peking to the edge of the mountains of Central Asia.

The old try to survive by cutting corners — eating less, giving up small pleasures like tobacco and movies, doing without warm clothes — and pay the price of ill-health and a shortened life-span.
— Sharon R. Curtin

Notice that when two dashes are used, if the material within them is deleted the remainder still forms a grammatical sentence.

2. A dash can serve, somewhat like a colon, as a pause before a series. It is more casual than a colon.

The earliest Shinto holy places were natural objects — trees, boulders, mountains, islands.

Each of the brothers had his distinct comic style — Groucho's double-talk, Chico's artfully stupid malapropisms, Harpo's horseplay.
Gerald Mast

Especially in this last example, where the series is elaborated, a colon could have been used, but it would have been more formal; here the dash is more appropriate to the subject.

A dash is never used next to a comma, and it is used before a period only to indicate that the sentence is interrupted. When used with closing quotation marks it goes inside if it is part of the quotation, outside if it is not.

PARENTHESES

First, a caution: avoid using parentheses to explain pronouns: "In his speech he (Hamlet) says . . ." If "he" needs to be explained by "Hamlet," omit the "he" and just say "Hamlet."

1. Parentheses subordinate material; what is in parentheses is almost a casual aside, less essential than similar material set off in commas, less vigorously spoken than similar material set off in dashes.

> While guest curator for the Whitney (he has since returned to the Denver Art Museum), Feder assembled a magnificent collection of masks, totems, paintings, clothing, and beadwork.

Two cautions: avoid an abundance of these interruptions, and avoid a long parenthesis within a sentence (you are now reading a simple example of this annoying but common habit of writers who have trouble sticking to the point) because the reader will lose track of the main sentence.

2. Use parentheses to enclose digits or letters in a list that is given in running text.

> The exhibition included: (1) decorative screens, (2) ceramics, (3) ink paintings, (4) kimonos.

3. Do not confuse parentheses with square brackets, which are used around material you add to a quotation. See page 544.

4. For the use of parentheses in footnotes, see pages 553–56.

A note on the position of other punctuation with a parenthesis. The example under rule number 2, of commas preceding parentheses enclosing digits or letters in a list given in running text, is the rare exception to the rule that within a sentence, punctuation other than quotation marks never immediately precedes an opening parenthesis. Notice that in the example under rule number 1, the comma *follows* the closing parenthesis:

> While guest curator for the Whitney (he has since returned to the Denver Art Museum), Feder assembled a magnificent collection of masks, totems, paintings, clothing, and beadwork.

If an entire sentence is in parentheses, put the final punctuation (period, question mark, or exclamation mark) inside the closing parenthesis.

QUOTATION MARKS

1. Use quotation marks to attribute words to a speaker or writer. (Long quotations that are set off do not take quotation marks. See pages 542–43.) If your quotation includes a passage that was enclosed in quotation marks, alter these inner quotation marks to single quotation marks.

> According to Professor Hugo, "The male dragon in Chinese art has deep-set eyes, the female has bulging eyes, but as one Chinese scholar put it, 'This is a matter of interest only to dragons.'"

British quotation marks are just the reverse: single for ordinary quotations, double for inner quotations. If you are quoting from a passage that includes such quotation marks, change them to the American form.

2. Use quotation marks to indicate the title of unpublished works, like dissertations, and of short works — for example, a lecture, speech, newspaper article, essay, chapter, short story, or song, as well as a poem of less than, say, twenty pages. (But magazines and pamphlets, like books, are underlined.)

3. Use quotation marks to identify a word or term to which you wish to call special attention. (But italics, indicated by underlining, may be used instead of quotation marks.)

By "comedy" I mean not only a funny play, but any play that ends happily.

Do *not* use quotation marks to enclose slang or a term that you fear is low; use the term or don't use it, but don't apologize by putting it in quotation marks, as in these examples.

Incorrect

"Streaking" was first popularized by Lady Godiva.

Incorrect

Because of "red tape" it took three years.

Incorrect

At last I was able to "put in my two cents."

In all three of these sentences the writers are signaling their uneasiness; in neither the first nor the second is there any cause for uneasiness, but probably the third should be rewritten to get rid of the cliché.

Be sparing, too, in using quotation marks to convey sarcasm, as in

These "poets" are mere dispensers of fantasies.

Sarcasm is usually a poor form of argument, best avoided. But of course there are borderline cases when you may want to convey your dissatisfaction with a word used by others.

African sculpture has a long continuous tradition, but this tradition has been jeopardized recently by the introduction of "civilization" to Africa.

Perhaps the quotation marks here are acceptable, because the writer's distaste has not yet become a sneer and because she is, in effect, quoting. But why not change "civilization" to "western culture," omitting the quotation marks?

Commas and periods go inside closing quotation marks except when the quotation marks are followed by parentheses, in which case they follow the closing parenthesis. Colons, semicolons, and footnote numbers go outside closing quotation marks. Question marks and exclamation points go inside if they are part of the quotation, outside if they are not.

While Thelma Todd rows the canoe, Groucho listens to her

chatter, looks at a duck swimming near the canoe, and asks, "Did that come out of you or the duck?"

What is funny about Groucho saying, "Whatever it is, I'm against it"?

ITALICS

Italic type is indicated by *underlining*.

1. Underline the name of a plane, ship, train, movie, radio or television program, record album, musical work, statue, painting, play, pamphlet, and book (except sacred works such as the Bible, the Koran, Acts of the Apostles). Notice that when you write of *The New York Times,* you underline *New York* because it is part of the title, but when you write of the London *Times,* you do not underline "London" because "London" is not part of the title, only information added for clarity. Similarly, when you refer to *Time* magazine do not underline "magazine."

2. As suggested on page 358, use italics only sparingly for emphasis. Sometimes, however, this method of indicating your tone of voice is exactly right.

> In 1911 Jacques Henri Lartigue was not merely as unprejudiced as a child; he *was* a child.
>
> — John Szarkowski

3. Use italics for foreign words that have not become a part of the English language.

> Acupuncture aims to affect the *ch'i,* a sort of vital spirit which circulates through the bodily organs.

But:

> He ate a pizza.
>
> She behaved like a prima donna.
>
> Avoid clichés.

4. You may use italics in place of quotation marks to identify a word or term to which you wish to call special attention.

> Claude Lévi-Strauss tells us that one of the great purposes of art

is that of *miniaturization*. He points out that most works of art are miniatures, being smaller (and therefore more easily understood) than the objects they represent.

CAPITAL LETTERS

Certain obvious conventions — the use of a capital for the first word in a sentence, for names (of days of the week, holidays, months, people, countries), and for words derived from names (such as pro-French) — need not be discussed here.

1. Titles of works in English are usually given according to the following formula. Use a capital for the first letter of the first word, for the first letter of the last word, and for the first letter of all other words that are not articles, conjunctions, or prepositions.

The Merchant of Venice
A Midsummer Night's Dream
Up and Out
"The Short Happy Life of Francis Macomber"
The New York Times

2. Use a capital for a quoted sentence within a sentence, but not for a quoted phrase (unless it is at the beginning of the sentence) and not for indirect discourse.

He said that you can even fool some of the people all of the time.
He said you can fool some people "all of the time."
He said that you can even fool some of the people all of the time.

3. Use a capital for a rank or title preceding a proper name or for a title substituting for a proper name.

She said she was Dr. Perez.
He told President Carter that the Vice President was away.

But:

Why would anyone wish to be president?
Washington was the first president.

4. Use a capital when the noun designating a family relationship is used as a substitute for a proper noun.

If Mother is busy, ask Tim.

But:

Because my mother was busy, I asked Tim.

5. Formal geographical locations (but not mere points on the compass) are capitalized.

North America, Southeast Asia, the Far East

In the Southwest, rain sometimes evaporates before touching the ground.

Is Texas part of the South?

The North has its share of racism.

But:

The wind came from the south.
Czechoslovakia is adjoined on the north by East Germany.

Do *not* capitalize the names of the seasons.

THE HYPHEN

The hyphen has five uses, all drawing on the etymology of the word *hyphen,* which comes from the Greek for "in one," "together."

1. Use a hyphen to attach certain prefixes from root words. *All-, pro-, ex-,* and *self-* are the most common of these ("all-powerful," "ex-wife," "pro-labor," "self-made"), but note that even these prefixes are not always followed by a hyphen. If in doubt, check a dictionary. Prefixes before proper names are always followed by a hyphen:

anti-Semite, pro-Kennedy, un-American

Prefixes ending in *i* are hyphenated before a word beginning with *i:*

anti-intellectual, semi-intelligible

A hyphen is normally used to break up a triple consonant resulting from the addition of a prefix:

ill-lit, all-loving

2. Use a hyphen to tie compound adjectives into a single visual unit:

out-of-date theory, twenty-three books, long-term loan

eighteenth- and nineteenth-century novels

The sea-tossed raft was a common nineteenth-century symbol of man's tragic condition.

But if a compound modifier follows the modified term, it is usually not hyphenated, thus:

The theory was out of date.

3. Use a hyphen to join some compound nouns:

Scholar-teacher, philosopher-poet

4. Use a hyphen to divide a word at the end of a line. Because words may be divided only as indicated by a dictionary, it is easier to end the line with the last complete word you can type than to keep reaching for a dictionary. But here are some principles governing the division of words at the end of a line:

a. Never hyphenate words of one syllable, such as *called, doubt, right, through.*
b. Never hyphenate so that a single letter stands alone: *a-bout, hair-y.*
c. If a word already has a hyphen, divide it at the hyphen: *anti-intellectual, semi-intelligible.*
d. Divide prefixes and suffixes from the root: *mis-spell, pro-vide, drunken-ness, walk-ing.*
e. Divide between syllables. If you aren't sure of the proper syllabification, check a dictionary.

5. Use a hyphen to indicate a span of dates or page numbers:

1957-59, pp. 162-68.

THE APOSTROPHE

Use an apostrophe to indicate the possessive, to indicate a contraction, and for certain unusual plurals.

1. The possessive. The most common way to indicate the possessive of a singular noun is to add an apostrophe and then an *s*.

> A dog's life, a week's work
> a mouse's tail, Keats's poems, Marx's doctrines

But many authorities suggest that for a proper noun of more than one syllable which ends in *s* or another silibant (*-cks, -x, -z*), it is better to add only an apostrophe:

> Jesus' parables, Sophocles' plays, Chavez' ideas

When in doubt, say the name aloud and notice if you are adding an *s*. If you are adding an *s* when you say it, add an apostrophe and an *s* when you write it.

Pronouns do not take an apostrophe.

> his book, its fur ("it's fur" is short for "it is fur")
> The book is hers, not ours.
> The book is theirs.

(Exception: indefinite pronouns take an apostrophe, as in "one's hopes" and "others' opinions.")

For plurals ending in *s*, add only an apostrophe to indicate the possessive:

> the boys' father, the Smiths' house, the Joneses' car

If the plural does not end in *s*, add an apostrophe and an *s*.

> women's clothing, mice's eyes

Don't try to form the possessive of the title of a work (for example, of a play, a book, or a film): Write "the imagery in *The Merchant of Venice*" rather than "*The Merchant of Venice*'s imagery." Using an apostrophe gets you into the problem of whether or not to italicize the *s;* similarly, if you use an apostrophe for a work normally enclosed in quotation marks, you can't put the apostrophe and the *s* after the quotation marks, but you can't put them inside either. And the work really can't possess anything anyway — the imagery, or whatever else, is the author's.

2. Contractions. Use an apostrophe to indicate the omitted letters or numbers in contractions.

She won't.
It's time to go.
the class of '79

3. Unusual plurals. Use an apostrophe to make plurals of words that do not usually have a plural, and (this is optional) to make the plurals of digits and letters.

Her speech was full of if's and and's and but's.
Ph.D.'s don't know everything.
Mind your p's and q's.
I got two A's and two B's.
He makes his 4's in two ways.
the 1920's

But if the number is written out, it does not take an apostrophe:

In the envelope were two tens and two fives.
She is in her twenties.

ABBREVIATIONS

In general, avoid abbreviations except in footnotes and except for certain common ones listed below. And don't use an ampersand (&) unless it appears in material you are quoting, or in a title. Abundant use of abbreviations makes an essay sound like a series of newspaper headlines. Usually *United States* is better than *U.S.* and *the Soviet Union* better than *U.S.S.R.*

1. Abbreviations, with the first letter capitalized, are used before a name.

Dr. Bellini, Ms. Smith, St. Thomas

But:

The doctor took her temperature and ten dollars.

2. Degrees that follow a name are abbreviated:

B.A., D.D.S., M.D., Ph.D.

3. Other acceptable abbreviations include:

A.D., B.C., A.M., P.M., e.g., i.e.

(By the way, *e.g.* means *for example; i.e.* means *that is*. The two ought not to be confused. See pages 604 and 607.)

4. The name of an agency or institution (for instance, the Committee on Racial Equality; International Business Machines; Southern Methodist University) may be abbreviated by using the initial letters, capitalized and usually without periods (e.g., CORE), but it is advisable to give the name in full when first mentioning it (not everyone knows that AARP means American Association of Retired Persons, for instance), and to use the abbreviation in subsequent references.

NUMBERS

1. Write them out if you can do so in fewer than three words; otherwise, use figures.

sixteen, seventy-two, ten thousand, one sixth
10,200; 10,200,000
There are 336 dimples on a golf ball

But always write out round millions and billions, to avoid a string of zeroes.

a hundred and ten million

Some handbooks say that because a figure cannot be capitalized, if a number begins a sentence it should always be written out.

2. Use figures in dates, addresses, decimals, percentages, page numbers, and hours followed by A.M. or P.M.

February 29, 1900; .06 percent; 6 percent; 8:16 A.M.

But hours unmodified by minutes are usually written out, and followed by *o'clock*.

Executions in England regularly took place at eight o'clock.

3. To make the plural of figures (but not of numbers written out) use an apostrophe.

three 6's, two tens

Use an apostrophe to indicate omitted figures.

class of '79

But use a hyphen to indicate a span.

    1975-79, pp. 162-68

EXERCISES

1. In the following sentences, decide what punctuation is needed, and then add it. If the sentence is correctly punctuated, place a check mark to the left of it.

   a. Around his neck is a scarf knotted in front and covering his head is a wide brimmed hat.

   b. Buffalo Bill radiates confidence in his bold stance and looks self assured with his head held high.

   c. The demands that men and women make on marriage will never be fully met they cannot be.

   d. The case for nuclear power has always rested on two claims that reactors were reasonably safe and that they were indispensable as a source of energy.

   e. Boys on the whole do not keep diaries.

   f. Children are unwelcome in most New York restaurants that are not Chinese.

   g. Shlomo a giraffe in the Tel Aviv zoo succumbed to the effects of falling down after efforts to raise him with ropes and pulleys were unsuccessful.

   h. Character like a photograph develops in darkness.

   i. In a grief reaction especially when the person has suffered a loss crying comes easily and produces a healthy release from pent up emotion.

   j. There is no God but Allah and Mohammed is His prophet.

2. We reprint below the fourth paragraph of Jeff Greenfield's essay, "Columbo Knows the Butler Didn't Do It," but without punctuation. Go through the paragraph, adding the punctuation you find necessary. Check your work against the original paragraph on page 54. If you find differences between your punctuation and Greenfield's, try to explain why Greenfield made the choices he did.

   columbos villains are not simply rich they are privileged they live the lives that are for most of us hopeless daydreams houses on top of mountains with pools servants and sliding doors parties with women in slinky dresses and endless food and drink plush enclosed box seats at professional sports events the envy and admiration of the crowd while we choose between johnny carson and *invasion of the body snatchers* they are at screenings of movies the rest of us wait in line for on third avenue three months later

3. Here are the first two paragraphs — but without punctuation — of Raymond A. Sokolov's review of a book by Sarah Stage, *Female Complaints: Lydia Pinkham and the Business of Women's Medicine.* Add the necessary punctuation.

home at the range victorian women in america suffered in shame from all manner of female complaints too intimate to name many of them were the fault of men gonorrhea or men doctors prolapsed uterus and women shrewdly kept shy of the ineffectual and often positively harmful doctors of their day instead they doctored themselves with so called patent medicines the most famous of these was lydia pinkhams vegetable compound mrs pinkham actually existed in lynn mass a center of the progressive spirit hotbed of abolition and feminism

sarah stage who has taught american history at williams college had the acuity to see that lydia pinkham was more than a quaint picture on a label that she was a paradigm of the independent woman of her day building a big business with a home remedy to save her family from bankruptcy caused by a neer do well husband she saw furthermore that many of the important themes and forces of american society before world war I clustered around the medicine itself which was largely alcoholic but respectably bitter

20
Spelling

Life would be easier if a sound were always represented by the same letter. Some modern European languages come close to this principle, but English is not among them. George Bernard Shaw once called attention to some of the oddities of English spelling by saying that *fish* might be spelled *ghoti*. How? *Gh* is *f*, as in *enough; o* is *i*, as in *women; ti* is *sh*, as in *notion*. So, *ghoti* spells *fish*.

This is not the place to explain why English spelling is so erratic, but it may be consoling to know that the trouble goes back at least to the Norman French Conquest of England in 1066; after the Conquest, French scribes spelled English words more or less as though the words were French. Moreover, though pronunciation kept changing, spelling became relatively fixed, so that even in Shakespeare's time spelling often reflected a pronunciation that had long been abandoned. And today the spelling of many words still reflects the long-lost medieval pronunciation. The silent *e* in *life*, and the silent consonants in *knight* and *through*, for example, were pronounced in Chaucer's day.

But medieval pronunciation accounts for only some of our spellings. There are many other reasons for the oddities: the *b* in *debt* is there, for example, because scholars mistakenly thought the word came into English through the Latin *debitum*. Most rules for spelling, then, must immediately be modified with lists of exceptions. Even the most famous,

> *I* before *e* except after *c*
> Or when sounded as *a*
> In *neighbor* and *sleigh,*

No, no it's 🍿 *before* 🌫 *except after* 🍿 *!*

has more exceptions than cheery handbooks admit. Always *ei* after *c*? What about *ancient, efficient,* and *sufficient*? Oh, but in these words the *c* is pronounced *sh,* an easy enough exception to keep in mind. But how can we explain *financier*? And of words where a *c* does not precede the letters in question, does the rule *ie* really govern all those not "sounded as *a* / In *neighbor* and *sleigh*"? How about *counterfeit, deity, either, foreign, forfeit, heifer, height, neither, leisure, protein, seize, their, weird*?

Instead of offering rules with menacing lists of exceptions, we offer a single list of words commonly misspelled in college writing. And here are four suggestions:

1. Read the list, mark any words whose spelling surprises you, and make a conscientious effort to memorize them.

2. Keep a dictionary at hand, and consult it while you are editing your work.

3. Begin keeping a list of words you misspell, and write them over and over until the correct spellings become automatic.

4. For words that you persistently misspell, invent some device to assist your memory. For example, if you erroneously put an *a* in *cemetery* in place of an *e,* say to yourself "people r*e*st in a cemetery." When you next have to write the word *cemetery* you will remember the associative device (r*e*st), and you will spell *cemetery* with an *e.* Another example: if you repeatedly leave out an *l* from *balloon,* say to yourself — really say it — "a ba*ll*oon is a ball." The next time you have to write *balloon* you will remember *ball.* Similarly, tell yourself there's *a rat* in *separate.* A last example, for people who mistakenly put an *n* in *dilemma:* "Emma is in a dilemma." Generally speaking, the sillier the phrase, the more memorable it will be.

abridgment	all right (*not*	beginner
absence	alright)	believe
accessible	a lot (*not* alot)	benefit
accidentally	already (*not* all	bourgeois
accommodate	ready)	bourgeoisie
achievement	alter (to change)	Britain
acknowledgment	altogether	bureau
acquire	analysis	bureaucracy
across	analyze	burglar
actually	apparent	business
address	appearance	calendar
adjacent	appreciate	capital (noun: seat
adolescence	arctic	of government,
adolescent	argument	money; adjective:
advice (noun)	assassin	chief)
advise (verb)	assistance	capitol (building)
aggravate	assistant	category
aggressive	athlete	ceiling
aging	attendance	cemetery
alcohol	balloon	changeable
allege	beggar	chief

choose (present
tense)
chose (past tense)
chosen (participle)
commit
committee
comparative
competent
complement (noun:
that which
completes; verb:
to complete)
compliment (praise)
conferred
congratulate
conscience
conscious
consistent
controlled
controversy
coolly
corollary
counterfeit
criticism
criticize
curiosity
deceive
decision
defendant
definite
deity
dependent
description
desirable
despair
desperate
develop, develops
development
dilemma
disappear
disappoint
disastrous

divide
divine
dormitory
eighth
embarrass
envelop (verb)
envelope (noun)
environment
equipped
equivalent
especially
essence
exaggerate
exceed
excellence
excellent
exhilarate
existence
experience
explanation
familiar
fascinate
fiend
fiery
foreign
foreword (preface)
forty
fourth
friend
gauge
genealogy
goddess
government
grammar
grievance
guarantee
height
heroes
hoping
humorous
hypocrisy
imagery

imagination
immediately
impel
incidentally
incredible
independence
independent
indispensable
insistence
insistent
intelligent
interest
interpretation
interrupt
irrelevant
irresistible
judgment
led (past tense of *to
lead*)
leisure
license
loneliness
loose (adjective)
lose (verb)
losing
maneuver
marriage
mathematics
medicine
mischievous
misspell
naive
necessary
necessity
niece
ninety
noticeable
occasion
occasionally
occur
occurred
omit

omitted
original
parallel
pastime
peaceable
performance
permanent
persistent
playwright
possession
practically
precede
predominant
preferred
prejudice
prevalent
principal (adjective:
   foremost; noun:
   chief)
principle (noun:
   rule)
privilege
probably
procedure
proceed
prominent
prophecy (noun)
prophesy (verb)
pursue
quantity
realize

really
receipt
receiving
recommend
referring
relevance
relevant
relieve
remembrance
repentance
repetition
resistance
rhyme
rhythm
sacrifice
secretary
seize
sense
separate
shining
shriek
siege
significance
similar
solely
specimen
sponsor
stationary (still)
stationery (paper)
strength
subtlety

subtly
succeed
supersede
surprise
syllable
temperament
tendency
theories
therefore
thorough
tragedy
transferred
tried
truly
unnecessary
useful
usually
various
vengeance
villain
weird
wholly
who's (contraction:
   who is)
whose (possessive
   pronoun:
   belonging to
   whom)
withhold
writing

21
Usage

Some things are said or written and some are not. More precisely, anything can be said or written, but only some things are acceptable to the ears and minds of many readers. "I don't know nothing about it" has been said and will be said again, but many readers who encounter this expression might judge the speaker as a person with nothing of interest to say — and immediately tune out.

Although such a double negative today is not acceptable, it used to be: Chaucer's courteous Knight never spoke no baseness, and Shakespeare's courtly Mercutio, in *Romeo and Juliet,* "will not budge for no man." But things have changed; what was acceptable in the Middle Ages and the Renaissance (for example, emptying chamber pots into the gutter) is not always acceptable now. And some of what was once unacceptable has become acceptable. At the beginning of the twentieth century, grammarians suggested that one cannot use *drive* in speaking of a car; one drives (forces into motion) an ox, or even a person ("He drove her to distraction"), but not a machine. Some seventy years of usage, however, have erased all objections.

This chapter presents a list of expressions that, although commonly used, set many teeth on edge. Seventy years from now some of these expressions may be as acceptable as "drive a car"; but we are writing for today, and we might as well try to hold today's readers by following today's taste. If our essays are thoughtful, they will provide enough challenges to the reader; we should not use constructions that will arouse antagonism or that will allow the reader to brush us off as ignoramuses.

You may not be familiar with some of the abuses in the following list; if so, our citing them will not instruct you, but may entertain you.

A NOTE ON IDIOMS

An idiom (from a Greek word meaning "peculiar") is a fixed group of words, peculiar to a given language. Thus, in English we say "I caught a cold" but we do not say "I seized a cold." If someone who is not a native speaker of English tells us that she thought "catch" and "seize" are synonymous, we may sympathize with her problem but we can only insist that in English one cannot seize a cold. Anyone who says or writes, "I seized a cold" is using *un*idiomatic English, just as anyone who says he knows a poem "at heart" instead of "by heart" is using unidiomatic English.

Probably most unidiomatic expressions use the wrong preposition. Examples:

Unidiomatic	Idiomatic
Comply to	Comply with
superior with	superior to

Sometimes while we write, or even while we speak, we are unsure of the idiom and we pause to try an alternative — "parallel with?" "parallel to?" — and we don't know which sounds more natural, more idiomatic. At such moments, more often than not, either is acceptable, but if you are in doubt, check a dictionary when you are editing your work. (*The American Heritage Dictionary* has notes on usage following the definitions of hundreds of its words.)

In any case, if you are a native speaker of English, when you read your draft you will probably detect unidiomatic expressions such as *superior with;* that is, you will hear something that sounds odd, and so you will change it to something that sounds familiar, idiomatic — here, *superior to.* If any unidiomatic expressions remain in your essay, the trouble may be that an effort to write impressively has led you to use unfamiliar language. A reader who sees such unidiomatic language will know that you are trying to gain stature by walking on stilts.

GLOSSARY

a, an Use *a* before words beginning with a consonant ("a book") or with a vowel sounded as a consonant ("a one-way ticket," "a university"). Use *an* before words beginning with a vowel sound, including those beginning with a silent *h* ("an egg," "an hour"). Either *a* or *an* is acceptable before an initial *h* that is pronounced (for example, in "hundred"), but *an* may sound affected, so it is better to use *a*.

above Try to avoid writing *for the above reasons, in view of the above, as above,* etc. These expressions sound unpleasantly legalistic. Substitute *for these reasons,* or *therefore,* or some such expression or word.

academics Only two meanings of this noun are widely accepted: (1) "members of an institution of higher learning," and (2) "persons who are academic in background or outlook." Avoid using it to mean "academic subjects," as in "A student should pay attention not only to academics but also to recreation."

accept, except *Accept* means "to receive with consent." *Except* means "to exclude" or "excluding."

affect, effect *Affect* is usually a verb, meaning (1) "to influence, to produce an effect, to impress," or (2) "to pretend, to put on," as in "He affected an English accent." Psychologists use it as a noun for "feeling," e.g., "The patient experienced no affect." *Effect,* as a verb, means "to bring about" ("The workers effected the rescue in less than an hour"). As a noun, *effect* means "result" ("The effect was negligible").

aggravate "To worsen, to increase for the worse," as in "Smoking aggravated the irritation." Although it is widely used to mean "annoy" ("He aggravated me"), many readers are annoyed by such a use.

all ready, already *All ready* means "everything is ready." *Already* means "by this time."

all right, alright The first of these is the preferable spelling; for some readers it is the only acceptable spelling.

all together, altogether *All together* means that members of a group act or are gathered together ("They voted all together"); *altogether* is an adverb meaning "entirely," "wholly" ("This is altogether unnecessary").

allusion, reference, illusion An *allusion* is an implied or indirect reference. "As Lincoln says" is a *reference* to Lincoln, but "As a great man has said," along with a phrase quoted from the Gettysburg Address, constitutes an *allusion* to Lincoln. The student who, in a demonstration at Berkeley, carried a placard saying "I am a human being — please do not fold, spindle, or mutilate," *referred* to himself and *alluded* to a computer card. *Allusion* has nothing to do with *illusion* (a deception). Note the spelling (especially the second *i*) in "disillusioned" (left without illusions, disenchanted).

a lot Two words (not *alot*).

among, between See *between*.

amount, number *Amount* refers to bulk or quantity: "A small amount of gas was still in the tank." Use *number,* not *amount,* to refer to separate (countable) units: "A large number of people heard the lecture" (not "a large amount of people"). Similarly, "an amount of money," but "a number of dollars."

analyzation Unacceptable; use *analysis*.

and/or Acceptable, but a legalism and unpleasant-sounding. Often *or* by itself will do, as in "students who know Latin or Italian." When *or* is not enough ("The script was written by Groucho and/or Harpo") it is better to recast ("The script was written by Groucho or Harpo, or both").

and etc. Because *etc.* is an abbreviation for *et cetera* ("and others"), the *and* in *and etc.* is redundant. (See also the entry on *et cetera*.)

ante, anti *Ante* means "before" (*antebellum,* "before the Civil War"); *anti* means "against" (*antivivisectionist*). Hyphenate *anti* before capitals (*anti-Semitism*) and before *i* (*anti-intellectual*).

anthology, collection Because an *anthology* is a collection of writings by several authors, one cannot speak of "an anthology of poems by Robert Frost"; one can speak of a "collection of poems by Robert Frost."

anxious Best reserved for uses that suggest anxiety ("He was anxious before the examination"), though some authorities now accept it in the sense of "eager" ("He was anxious to serve the community").

anybody An indefinite pronoun, written as one word; if two words (*any body*), you mean any corpse ("Several people died in the fire, but the police cannot identify any body").

anyone One word, unless you mean "any one thing," as in "Here are three books; you may take any one."

area of Like *field of* and *topic of* ("the field of literature," "the topic of politics"), *area of* can usually be deleted. "The area of literature" equals "literature."

around Avoid using *around* in place of *about:* "He wrote it in about three hours." See also *centers on.*

as, like *As* is a conjunction; use it in forming comparisons, to introduce clauses. (A clause has a subject and a verb.)

> You can learn to write, as you can learn to swim.
> Huck speaks the truth as he sees it.
> He is as tall as I.

In "He is as tall as I," notice that the clause introduced by the second "as" consists of the subject "I" and the implied verb "am."

> He is as tall as I (am).

As can also introduce a clause in which both the subject and the verb are implied:

> Rose distrusts him as much as (she distrusts) me.

But notice that the last sentence means something different from the next:

> Rose distrusts him as much as I (do).

Like is a preposition; use it to introduce prepositional phrases:

> He looks like me.
> Like Hamlet, Laertes has lost a father.
> She thinks like a lawyer.

Writers who are fearful of incorrectly using *like* resort to cumbersome evasions: "He eats in the same manner that a pig eats." But there's nothing wrong with "He eats like a pig."

as of now Best deleted, or replaced by *now.* Not "As of now I don't smoke" but "Now I don't smoke" or "I don't smoke now" or "I don't smoke."

aspect Literally, "a view from a particular point," but it has come to mean *topic,* as in "There are several aspects to be considered."

Try to get a sharper word; for example, "There are several problems to be considered," or "There are several consequences to be considered."

as such Often meaningless, as in "Tragedy as such evokes pity."

as to Usually *about* is preferable. Not "I know nothing as to the charges," but "I know nothing about the charges."

bad, badly *Bad* used to be only an adjective ("a bad movie"), and *badly* was an adverb ("she sings badly"). In "I felt bad," *bad* describes the subject, not the verb. (Compare "I felt happy." After verbs of appearing, such as "feel," "look," "seem," "taste," an adjective, not an adverb, is used.) But today "I feel badly" is acceptable and even preferred by many. Note, however, this distinction: "This meat smells bad" (an adjective describing the meat), and "Because I have a stuffed nose I smell badly" (an adverb describing my ability to smell something).

being Do not use *being* as a main verb, as in "The trouble being that his reflexes were too slow." The result is a sentence fragment. See pages 555–56.

being that, being as A sentence such as "Being that she was a stranger . . ." sounds like an awkward translation from the Latin. Use *because*.

beside, besides *Beside* means "at the side of." Because *besides* can mean either "in addition to" or "other than," it is ambiguous, as in "Something besides TB caused his death." It is best, then, to use *in addition to* or *other than*, depending on what you mean.

between Only English teachers who have had a course in Middle English are likely to know that it comes from *by twain*. And only English teachers and editors are likely to object to its use (and to call for *among*) when more than two are concerned, as in "among the three of us." Note, too, that even conservative usage accepts *between* in reference to more than two when the items are at the moment paired: "Negotiations *between* Israel and Egypt, Syria, and Lebanon seem stalled." *Between*, a preposition, takes an object ("between you and me"); only people who mistakenly think that "me" is vulgar say "between you and I."

biannually, bimonthly, biweekly Every two years, every two months, every two weeks (*not* twice a year, etc.). Twice a year is *semiannually*. Because *biannually, bimonthly,* and *biweekly* are commonly misunderstood, it is best to avoid them and to say "every two . . . ."

Black, black Although one sometimes sees the word capitalized when it refers to race, most publishers use a lowercase letter, making it consistent with _white_, which is never capitalized.

can, may When schoolchildren asked "Can I leave the room," their teachers used to correct them thus: "You _can_ leave the room if you have legs, but you _may not_ leave the room until you receive permission." In short, _can_ indicates physical possibility, _may_ indicates permission. But because "you may not" and "why mayn't I?" sound not merely polite but stiff, _can_ is usually preferred except in formal contexts.

centers on, centers around Use _centers on,_ because _center_ refers to a point, not to a movement around.

collective nouns A collective noun, singular in form, names a collection of individuals. Examples: _audience, band, committee, crowd, jury, majority, minority, team._ When you are thinking chiefly of the whole as a unit, use a singular verb (and a singular pronoun, if any): "The majority rules"; "The jury is announcing its verdict." But when you are thinking of the individuals, use a plural verb (and pronoun, if any): "The majority are lawyers"; "The jury are divided and they probably cannot agree." If the plural sounds odd, you can usually rewrite: "The jurors are divided and they probably cannot agree."

compare, contrast To _compare_ is to note likenesses or differences: "Compare a motorcycle with a bicycle." To _contrast_ is to emphasize differences.

complement, compliment _Complement_ as a noun means "that which completes"; as a verb, "to fill out, to complete." _Compliment_ as a noun is an expression of praise; as a verb it means "to offer praise."

comprise "To include, contain, consist of": "The university comprises two colleges and a medical school" (not "is comprised of"). Conservative authorities hold that "to be comprised of" is always incorrect, and they reject the form one often hears: "Two colleges and a medical school comprise the university." Here the word should be _compose,_ not _comprise._

concept Should often be deleted. For "The concept of the sales tax is regressive" write "The sales tax is regressive."

contact Because it is vague, avoid using *contact* as a verb. *Not* "I contacted him" but "I spoke with him" or "I wrote to him," or whatever.

continual, continuous Conservative authorities hold that *continuous* means "uninterrupted," as in "It rained continuously for six hours"; *continually* means "repeated often, recurring at short intervals," as in "For a year he continually wrote letters to her."

could have, could of See *of.*

criteria Plural of *criterion,* hence it is always incorrect to speak of "a criteria," or to say "The criteria is . . . ."

data Plural of *datum.* Although some social scientists speak of "this data," "these data" is preferable: "These data are puzzling." Because the singular, *datum,* is rare and sounds odd, it is best to substitute *fact* or *figure* for *datum.*

different from Prefer it to *different than,* unless you are convinced that in a specific sentence *different from* sounds terribly wrong, as in "These two books are more different than I had expected." (In this example, "more," not "different," governs "than." But this sentence, though correct, is awkward and therefore it should be revised: "These two books differ more than I had expected.")

dilemma A situation requiring a choice between equally undesirable alternatives; not every difficulty or plight or predicament is a *dilemma.* Not "Her dilemma was that she had nowhere to go," but "Her dilemma was whether to go out or to stay home: one was frightening, the other was embarrassing." And note the spelling (two *m*'s, no *n*).

disinterested Though the word is often used to mean "indifferent," "unconcerned," "uninterested," reserve it to mean "impartial": "A judge should be disinterested."

due to Some people, holding that *due to* cannot modify a verb (as in "He failed due to illness"), tolerate it only when it modifies a noun or pronoun ("His failure was due to illness"). They also insist that it cannot begin a sentence ("Due to illness, he failed"). In fact, however, daily usage accepts both. But because it almost always sounds stiff, try to substitute *because of,* or *through.*

due to the fact that Wordy for *because.*

each Although many authorities hold that *each,* as a subject, is singular, even when followed by "them" ("Each of them is satisfactory"), some authorities accept and even favor the plural ("Each of them are satisfactory"). But it is usually better to avoid the awkwardness by substituting *all* for *each*: "All of them are satisfactory." When *each* is in apposition with a plural subject, the verb must be plural: "They each have a book"; "We each are trying." *Each* cannot be made into a possessive; you cannot say "Each's opinion is acceptable."

effect See *affect*.

e.g. Abbreviation for *exempli gratia,* meaning "for example." It is thus different from *i.e.* (an abbreviation for *id est,* meaning "that is"). E.g. (not italicized) introduces an example; i.e. (also not italicized) introduces a definition. Because these two abbreviations of Latin words are often confused, it may be preferable to avoid them and use their English equivalents.

either . . . or, neither . . . nor If the subjects are singular, use a singular verb: "Either the boy or the girl is lying." If one of the subjects joined by *or* or *nor* is plural, most grammarians say that the verb agrees with the nearer subject, thus: "A tree or two shrubs are enough," or "Two shrubs or a tree is enough." But because the singular verb in the second of these sentences may sound odd, follow the first construction; that is, put the plural subject nearer to the verb and use a plural verb.

enthuse Objectionable to many readers. For "He enthused," say "He was enthusiastic." Use *enthuse* only in the sense of "to be excessively enthusiastic," "to gush."

et cetera, etc. Latin for "and other things"; if you mean "and other people," you need *et al.,* short for *et alii.* Because *etc.* is vague, its use is usually inadvisable. Not "He studied mathematics, etc." but "He studied mathematics, history, economics, and French." Or, if the list is long, cut it by saying something a little more informative than *etc.* — for example, "He studied mathematics, history, and other liberal arts subjects." Even *and so forth* or *and so on* is preferable to *etc.* Confine *etc.* (and most other abbreviations, including *et al.*) to footnotes, and even in footnotes try to avoid it.

everybody, everyone These take a singular verb ("Everybody is here"), and a pronoun referring to them is usually singular ("Everybody thinks his problems are suitable topics of conversation"), but use a plural pronoun if the singular would seem unnatural ("Everybody was there, weren't they?").

except See *accept*.

exists Often unnecessary and a sign of wordiness. Not "The problem that *exists* here is" but "The problem here is."

expound Usually pretentious for *explain* or *say*. To *expound* is to give a methodical explanation, especially of theological or philosophical matters.

facet Literally "little face," especially one of the surfaces of a gem. Don't use it (and don't use *aspect* or *factor* either) to mean "part" or "topic." It is most acceptable when, close to its literal meaning, it suggests a new appearance, as when a gem is turned: "Another *facet* appears when we see this law from the taxpayer's point of view."

the fact that Usually wordy. "Because of the fact that boys played female roles in Elizabethan drama" can be reduced to "Because boys played female roles in Elizabethan drama."

factor Strictly speaking, a *factor* helps to produce a result, but students commonly use it in the sense of "point": "Another factor to be studied is. . . ." Used with the sense of "point" it usually sounds pretentious: "The possibility of plagiarism is a factor that must be considered" simply adds up to "The possibility of plagiarism must be considered." *Factor* is almost never the precise word: "the factors behind Gatsby's actions" are, more precisely, "Gatsby's motives."

farther, further Some purists claim that *farther* always refers to distance and *further* to time ("The gymnasium is farther than the library"; "Let us think further about this"). But many people substitute *further* for *farther:* "I walked further than that."

fatalistic, pessimistic *Fatalistic* means "characterized by the belief that all events are predetermined and therefore inevitable"; *pessimistic,* "characterized by the belief that the world is evil," or, less gloomily, "expecting the worst."

fewer, less See *less*.

field of See *area of*.

firstly, secondly Acceptable, but it is better to use *first, second*.

former, latter These words are acceptable, but they are often annoying because they force the reader to reread earlier material in order to locate what *the former* and *the latter* refer to. The expressions are legitimately used in order to avoid repeating lengthy terms, but if you are talking about an easily repeated subject — say, Lincoln and Grant — don't hesitate to replace *the* *former* and *the latter* with their names. The repetition will clarify rather than bore.

good, well *Good* is an adjective ("a good book"), *well* is usually an adverb ("She writes well"). Standard English does not accept "She writes good." But Standard English requires *good* after verbs of appearing, such as "seems," "looks," "sounds," "tastes": "it looks good," "it sounds good." *Well* can also be an adjective meaning "healthy": "I am well."

graduate, graduate from Use *from* if you name the institution or if you use a substitute word as in "She graduated from high school"; if the institution (or substitute) is not named, *from* is omitted: "She graduated in 1977." The use of the passive ("She was graduated from high school") is acceptable but sounds fussy to many.

he or she, his or her These expressions are awkward, but the implicit male chauvinism in the generic use of the male pronoun ("A citizen should exercise his right to vote") may be more offensive than the awkwardness of *he or she* and *his or her*. Moreover, sometimes the male pronoun, when used for males and females, is ludicrous, as in "The more violence a youngster sees on television, regardless of his age or sex, the more aggressive he is likely to be." Do what you can to avoid the dilemma. Sometimes you can use the plural *their:* "Students are expected to hand in their papers on Monday" (instead of "The student is expected to hand in his or her paper on Monday"). Or eliminate the possessive: "The student must hand in a paper on Monday." See also *man, mankind*.

hopefully Commonly used to mean "I hope" or "It is hoped" ("*Hopefully,* the rain will stop soon"), but it is best to avoid what some consider a dangling modifier. After all, the rain itself is not hopeful. If you mean "I hope the rain will soon stop," say exactly that. Notice, too, that *hopefully* is often evasive; if the president of the college says, "Hopefully tuition will not rise next year," don't think that you have heard a promise to fight against an increase; you only have heard someone evade making a promise. In short, confine *hopefully* to its adverbial use, meaning "in a hopeful manner": "Hopefully he uttered a prayer."

however It is preferable not to begin a sentence with *however* unless it is an adverb meaning "to whatever extent or degree," as in "However hard he studied, he couldn't remember irregular verbs." When *however* is a conjunctive adverb, it usually gains emphasis if you put it later in the sentence, between commas: "He failed the examination, however, and didn't graduate." (Compare, "However, he failed the examination and didn't graduate.") Unless *however* is set off in commas it usually sounds insufficiently emphatic. If you want to begin a sentence with a sharp contrast, use *but* or *nevertheless.* Note too that you cannot link independent clauses with a *however* preceded by a comma; you need a semicolon ("He tried; however, he failed"). Even here, however, *but* is usually preferable, without a semicolon.

the idea that Usually dull and wordy. Not "The idea that we grow old is frightening," but "That we grow old is frightening," or (probably better) "Growing old is frightening."

identify When used in the psychological sense, "to associate oneself closely with a person or an institution," it is preferable to include a reflexive pronoun, thus: "He identified himself with Hamlet," *not* "He identified with Hamlet."

i.e. Latin for *id est,* "that is." The English words are preferable to the Latin abbreviation. On the distinction between *i.e.* and *e.g.,* see *e.g.*

immanent, imminent *Immanent,* "remaining within, intrinsic"; *imminent,* "likely to occur soon, impending."

imply, infer The writer or speaker *implies* (suggests); the perceiver *infers* (draws a conclusion): "Karl Marx implied that . . . but his modern disciples infer from his writings that . . ." Although *infer* is widely used for *imply,* preserve the distinction.

individual Avoid using the word to mean only "person": "He was a generous individual." But it is precise when it implicitly makes a contrast with a group: "In a money-mad society, he was a generous individual"; "Although the faculty did not take a stand on this issue, faculty members as individuals spoke out."

instances Instead of *in many instances* use *often.* Strictly speaking an *instance* is not an object or incident in itself but one offered as an example. Thus "another instance of his failure to do his duty" (not "In three instances he failed to do his duty").

irregardless Unacceptable; use *regardless.*

it is Usually this expression needlessly delays the subject: "It is unlikely that many students will attend the lecture" could just as well be "Few students are likely to attend the lecture."

its, it's The first is a possessive pronoun ("The flock lost its leader"); the second is a contraction of *it is* ("It's a wise father that knows his child.") You'll have no trouble if you remember that the possessive pronoun *its*, like other possessive pronouns such as *our, his, their,* does *not* use an apostrophe.

kind of Singular, as in "That kind of movie bothers me." (*Not:* "Those kind of movies bother me.") If, however, you are really talking about more than one kind, use *kinds* and be sure that the demonstrative pronoun and the verb are plural: "Those kinds of movies bother me."

latter See under *former.*

lay, lie To *lay* means "to put, to set, to cause to rest." It takes an object: "May I lay the coats on the table?" The past tense and the participle are *laid:* "I laid the coats on the table"; "I have laid the coats on the table." To *lie* means "to recline," and it does not take an object: "When I am tired I lie down." The past tense is *lay,* the participle is *lain:* "Yesterday I lay down"; "I have lain down hundreds of times without wishing to get up."

lend, loan The usual verb is *lend:* "Lend me a pen." The past tense and the participle are both *lent. Loan* is a noun: "This isn't a gift, it's a loan." But, curiously, *loan* as a verb is acceptable in past forms: "I loaned him my bicycle." In its present form ("I often loan money") it is used chiefly by bankers.

less, fewer *Less* (as an adjective) refers to bulk amounts (also called mass nouns): less milk, less money, less time. *Fewer* refers to separate (countable) items: fewer glasses of milk, fewer dollars, fewer hours.

lifestyle, life-style, life style All three forms are acceptable, but because many readers regard the expression as imprecise and faddish, try to find a substitute such as *values.*

like, as See under *as.*

literally It means "strictly in accord with the primary meaning; not metaphorically." It is not a mere intensive. "He was literally dead" means that he was a corpse; if he was merely exhausted, *literally* won't do. You cannot be "literally stewed" (except by cannibals), "literally tickled pink," or "literally head over heels in love."

the majority of Usually a wordy way of saying *most*. Of course if you mean "a bare majority," say so; otherwise *most* will usually do. Certainly "The majority of the basement is used for a cafeteria" should be changed to "Most of the basement is used for a cafeteria."

man, mankind Because these words strike many readers as sexist, expressions such as "man's brain" and "the greatness of mankind" should be revised where possible. Consider using such words as *human being, person, humanity, people*.

may, can See under *can*.

me The right word in such expressions as "between you and me" and "They gave it to John and me." It is the object of verbs and of prepositions. In fact, *me* rather than *I* is the usual form after any verb, including the verb *to be*; "It is me" is nothing to be ashamed of.

medium, media *Medium* is singular, *media* is plural: "TV is the medium to which most children are most exposed. Other media include film, radio, and publishing." It follows, then, that *mass media* takes a plural verb: "The mass media exert an enormous influence."

most Although it is acceptable in speech to say "most everyone" and "most anybody," it is preferable in writing to use "almost everyone," "almost anybody." But of course: "Most students passed."

nature You can usually delete *the nature of*, as in "The nature of my contribution is not political but psychological."

needless to say The reader may well wonder why you go on to say it. Of course this expression is used to let readers know that they are probably familiar with what comes next, but usually *of course* will better serve as this sign.

Negro Capitalized, whether a noun or an adjective, though *white* is not. In recent years *Negro* has been replaced by *black*.

neither . . . nor See *either . . . or*, page 604.

nobody, no one, none *Nobody* and *no one* are singular, requiring a singular verb ("Nobody believes this," "No one knows"); but they can be referred to by a plural pronoun: "Nobody believes this, do they?" "No one knows, do they?" *None*, though it comes from *no one*, almost always requires a plural verb when it refers to people ("Of the ten people present, none are freshmen") and a singular verb when it refers to things ("Of the five assigned books, none is worth reading").

not . . . un- Such an expression as "not unfamiliar" is useful only if it conveys something different from the affirmative. Compare the frostiness of "I am not unfamiliar with your methods" with "I am familiar with your methods." If the negative has no evident advantage, use the affirmative. See page 336.

notorious Widely and unfavorably known; not merely famous, but famous for some discreditable trait or deed.

a number of requires a plural verb: "A number of women are presidents of corporations." But when *number* is preceded by *the* it requires a singular verb: "The number of women who are presidents is small." (The plural noun after *number* of course may require a plural verb, as in "women are," but *the number* itself remains singular, hence its verb is singular, as in "is small.")

of Be careful not to use *of* when *have* is required. Not "He might of died in the woods," but "He might have died in the woods." Note that what we often hear as "would've" or "should've" or "must've" or "could've" is "would have" or "should have" or "must have" or "could have," *not* "would of," etc.

off of Use *off* or *from:* "Take it off the table"; "He jumped from the bridge."

often-times Use *often* instead.

old-fashioned, old-fashion Only the first is acceptable.

one British usage accepts the shift from *one* to *he* in "One begins to die the moment he is born," but American usage prefers "One begins to die the moment one is born." A shift from *one* to *you* ("One begins to die the moment you are born") is unacceptable. As a pronoun, *one* can be useful in impersonal statements such as the sentence about dying, at the beginning of this entry, where it means "a person," but don't use it as a disguise for yourself ("One objects to Smith's argument"). Try to avoid *one*; one *one* usually leads to another, resulting in a sentence that, in James Thurber's words, "sounds like a trombone solo" ("If one takes oneself too seriously, one begins to . . .").

one of Takes a plural noun, and if this is followed by a clause, the preferred verb is plural: "one of those students who are," "one of those who feel." Thus, in such a sentence as "One of the coaches who have resigned is now seeking reinstatement," notice that "have" is correct, for it agrees with its subject, "coaches." Coaches have resigned, though "one . . . is seeking reinstatement." But in such an expression as "one out of a hundred," the following verb may be singular or plural ("One out of a hundred is," "One out of a hundred are").

only Be careful where you put it. The classic textbook example points out that in the sentence "I hit him in the eye," *only* can be inserted in seven places (beginning in front of "I" and ending after "eye") with at least six different meanings. Try to put it just before the expression it qualifies. Thus, not "Presidential aides are only responsible to one man," but "Presidential aides are responsible to only one man" (or "to one man only"). See page 364.

other Often necessary in comparisons. "No American president served as many terms as Franklin Roosevelt" falsely implies that Roosevelt was not an American president. The sentence should be revised to "No other American president served as many terms as Franklin Roosevelt."

per Usually it sounds needlessly technical ("twice per hour") or disturbingly impersonal ("as per your request"). Preferable: "twice an hour," "according to your request," or "as you requested."

per cent, percent, percentage The first two of these are interchangeable; both mean "per hundred," "out of a hundred," as in "Ninety per cent (or percent) of the students were white." *Per cent* and *percent* are always accompanied by a number (written out, or in figures). It is usually better to write out *per cent* or *percent* than to use a per cent sign (12%), except in technical or statistical papers. *Percentage* means "a proportion or share in relation to the whole," as in "A very large percentage of the student body is white." Many authorities insist that *percentage* is never preceded by a number. Do not use percentage to mean "a few," as in "Only a percentage of students attended the lecture"; a percentage can be as large as 99.99. It is usually said that with *per cent, percent,* and *percentage,* whether the verb is singular or plural depends on the number of the noun that follows the word, thus: "Ninety percent of his books are paperbacks"; "Fifty percent of his library is worthless"; "A large percentage of his books are worthless." But some readers (including the authors of this book) prefer a singular verb after *percentage* unless the resulting sentence is as grotesque as this one: "A large percentage of the students is unmarried." Still, rather than say a "percentage . . . are," we would recast the sentence: "A large percentage of the student body is unmarried," or "Many (or "Most," or whatever) of the students are unmarried."

per se Latin for "by itself." Usually sounds legalistic or pedantic, as in "Meter per se has an effect."

pessimistic See *fatalistic*.

phenomenon, phenomena The plural is *phenomena;* thus, "these phenomena" but "this phenomenon."

plus Unattractive and imprecise as a noun meaning "asset" or "advantage" ("When he applied for the job, his appearance was a plus"), and equally unattractive as a substitute for *moreover* ("The examination was easy, plus I had studied") or as a substitute for *and* ("I studied the introduction plus the first chapter").

politics Preferably singular ("Ethnic politics has been a strong force for a century") but a plural verb is acceptable.

prejudice, prejudiced *Prejudice* is a noun: "It is impossible to live entirely without prejudice." But use the past participle *prejudiced* as an adjective: "He was prejudiced against me from the start."

preventative, preventive Both are acceptable but the second form is the form now used by writers on medicine ("preventive medicine"); *preventative* therefore has come to seem amateurish.

prior to Pretentious for *before*.

protagonist Literally, the first actor, and, by extension, the chief actor. It is odd, therefore, to speak of "the protagonists" in a single literary work or occurrence. Note also that the prefix is *proto,* "first," not *pro,* "for"; it does *not* mean one who strives for something.

quite Usually a word to delete, along with *definitely, pretty, rather,* and *very*. See page 329. *Quite* used to mean "completely" ("I quite understand") but it has come also to mean "to a considerable degree," and so it is ambiguous as well as vague.

quotation, quote The first is a noun, the second a verb. "I will quote Churchill" is fine, but not "these quotes from Churchill." And remember, you may *quote* one of Hamlet's speeches, but Hamlet does not *quote* them; he says them.

rather Avoid use with strong adjectives. "Rather intelligent" makes sense, but "rather tremendous" does not. "Rather brilliant" probably means "bright"; "rather terrifying" probably means "frightening," "rather unique" probably means "unusual." Get the right adjective, not *rather* and the wrong adjective.

the reason . . . is because Usually *because* is enough (not "The reason they fail is because they don't study," but simply "They fail because they don't study"). Similarly, *the reason why* can usually be reduced to *why*. Notice, too, that because *reason* is a noun, it cannot neatly govern a *because* clause: not "The reason for his absence is because he was sick," but "The reason for his absence was illness."

rebut, refute To rebut is to argue against, but not necessarily successfully. If you mean "to disprove," use *disprove* or *refute*.

in regard to, with regard to Often wordy for *about, concerning,* or *on,* and sometimes even these words are unnecessary. Compare: "He knew a great deal in regard to jazz"; "He knew a great deal about jazz." Compare: "Hemingway's story is often misunderstood with regard to Robert Wilson's treatment of Margot Macomber"; "In Hemingway's story, Robert Wilson's treatment of Margot Macomber is often misunderstood."

relate to Usually a vague expression, best avoided, as in "I can relate to Hedda Gabler." Does it mean "respond favorably to," "identify myself with," "interact with" (and how can a reader "interact with" a character in a play?). Use *relate to* only in the sense of "have connection with" (as in "How does your answer relate to my question?"); even in such a sentence a more exact expression is preferable.

repel, repulse Both verbs mean "to drive back," but only *repel* can mean "to cause distaste," "to disgust," as in "His obscenities repelled the audience."

sarcasm Heavy, malicious sneering ("Oh, you're really a great friend, aren't you?" addressed to someone who won't lend the speaker ten dollars). If the apparent praise, which really communicates dispraise, is at all clever, conveying, say, a delicate mockery or wryness, it is irony, not sarcasm. The passages by Szarkowski on pages 393–94 are ironic, not sarcastic.

seem Properly it suggests a suspicion that appearances may be deceptive: "He seems honest (but . . .)." Don't say "The book seems to lack focus" if you believe it does lack focus.

shall, will, should, would The old principle held that in the first person *shall* is the future indicative of *to be* and *should* the conditional ("I shall go," "We should like to be asked"); and that *will* and *would* are the forms for the second and third persons. When the forms are reversed ("I will go," "Government of the people . . . shall not perish from the earth"), determination is expressed. But today almost nobody adheres to these principles. Indeed, *shall* (except in questions) sounds stilted to many ears.

simplistic Means "falsely simplified by ignoring complications." Do not confuse it with *simplified,* whose meanings include "reduced to essentials" and "clarified."

since Traditional objections to *since,* in the sense of "because," have all but vanished. Note, however, that when *since* is ambiguous and may also refer to time ("Since he joined the navy, she found another boyfriend") it is better to say *because* or *after,* depending on which you mean.

situation Overused, vague, and often unnecessary. "His situation was that he was unemployed," adds up to "He was unemployed. And "an emergency situation" is probably an emergency.

split infinitives The infinitive is the verb form that merely names the action, without indicating when or by whom performed ("walk," rather than "walked" or "I walk"). Grammarians, however, developed the idea that the infinitive was "to walk," and they held that one cannot separate or split the two words: "to quickly walk." But James Thurber says this idea is "of a piece with the sentimental and outworn notion that it is always wrong to strike a lady." Notice, however, that often the inserted word can be deleted ("to really understand" is "to understand"), and that if many words are inserted between *to* and the verb, the reader may get lost ("to quickly and in the remaining few pages before examining the next question conclude").

stanza See under *verse.*

than, then *Than* is used chiefly in making comparisons ("German is harder than French"), but also after "rather," "other," "different," and "else" ("I'd rather take French than German"; "He thinks of nothing other than sex"). *Then* commonly indicates time ("She took German then, but now she takes French"; "Until then, I'll save you a seat"), but it may also mean "in that case" ("It's agreed, then, that we'll all go") or "on the other hand" ("Then again, she may find German easy"). The simplest guide: use *than* after comparisons and after "rather," "other," "different," "else"; otherwise use *then.*

that, which, who Many pages have been written on these words; opinions differ, but you will offend no one if you observe the following principles. (1) Use *that* in restrictive (that is, limiting) clauses: "The rocking chair that creaks is on the porch." (2) Use *which* in nonrestrictive (in effect, parenthetic) clauses: "The rocking chair, which creaks, is on the porch." (See pages 574–76.) The difference between these two sentences is this: in the first, one rocking chair is singled out from several — the one that creaks; in the second, the fact that the rocking chair creaks is simply tossed in, and is not added for the purpose of identifying the one chair out of several. (3) Use *who* for people, in restrictive and in nonrestrictive clauses: "The men who were playing poker ignored the women"; "The men, who were playing poker, ignored the women." But note that often *that, which,* and *who* can be omitted: "The creaky rocking chair is on the porch"; "The men, playing poker, ignored the women." In general, omit these words if the sentence remains clear. See pages 337–38.

their, there, they're The first is a possessive pronoun: "Chaplin and Keaton made their first films before sound tracks were developed." The second, *there,* sometimes refers to a place ("Go there," "Do you live there?"), and sometimes is what is known in grammar as an introductory expletive ("There are no solutions to this problem"). The third, *they're,* is a contraction of "they are" ("They're going to stay for dinner").

this Often refers vaguely to "what I have been saying." Does it refer to the previous sentence, the previous paragraph, the previous page? Try to modify it by being specific: "this last point," "This clue gave the police all they needed."

thusly Unacceptable; *thus* is an adverb and needs no adverbial ending.

till, until Both are acceptable, but *until* is preferable because *till* — though common in speech — looks literary in print. The following are *not* acceptable: *til, 'til, 'till.*

topic of See *area of*.

toward, towards Both are standard English; *toward* is more common in the United States, *towards* in Great Britain.

type Often colloquial (and unacceptable in most writing) for *type of*, as in "this type teacher." But *type of* is not especially pleasing either. Better to write "this kind of teacher." And avoid using *type* as a suffix: "essay-type examinations" are essay examinations; "natural-type ice cream" is natural ice cream. Sneaky manufacturers make "Italian-type cheese," implying that their domestic cheese is imported and at the same time protecting themselves against charges of misrepresentation.

unique The only one of its kind. Someone or something cannot be "rather unique" or "very unique" or "somewhat unique," any more than a woman can be somewhat pregnant. Instead of saying "rather unique," then, say *rare,* or *unusual,* or *extraordinary*, or whatever seems to be the best word.

U.S., United States Generally, *United States* is preferable to *U.S.;* similarly, *the Soviet Union* is preferable to *the U.S.S.R.*

usage Don't use *usage* where *use* will do, as in "Here Vonnegut completes his usage of dark images." *Usage* properly implies a customary practice that has created a standard: "Usage has eroded the difference between 'shall' and 'will.'"

use of The use of *use of* is usually unnecessary. "Through the use of setting he conveys a sense of foreboding" may be reduced to "The setting conveys" or "His setting conveys."

utilize, utilization Often inflated for *use* and *using*, as in "The infirmary has noted that it is freshmen who have most utilized the counseling service."

verbal Often used where *oral* would be more exact. *Verbal* simply means "expressed in words," and thus a *verbal agreement* may be either written or spoken. If you mean spoken, call it an *oral agreement*.

verse, stanza A *verse* is a single line of a poem; a *stanza* is a group of lines, commonly bound by a rhyme scheme. But in speaking or writing about songs, usage sanctions *verse* for *stanza,* as in "Second verse, same as the first."

viable A term from physiology, meaning "capable of living" (for example, referring to a fetus at a stage of its development). Now pretentiously used and overused, especially by politicians and journalists, to mean "workable," as in "a viable presidency." Avoid it.

we If you mean *I*, say *I*. Not "The first fairy tale we heard" but "the first fairy tale I heard." (But of course *we* is appropriate in some statements: "We have all heard fairy tales"; "If we look closely at the evidence, we can agree that. . . .") The rule: don't use *we* as a disguise for *I*. See pages 359–60.

well See *good*.

well known, widely known Athletes, performers, politicians, and such folk are not really *well known* except perhaps by a few of their friends and their relatives; use *widely known* if you mean they are known (however slightly) to many people.

which Often can be deleted. "Students are required to fill out scholarship applications which are lengthy" can be written "Students are required to fill out lengthy scholarship applications." Another example: "*The Tempest,* which is Shakespeare's last play, was written in 1611"; "*The Tempest,* Shakespeare's last play, was written in 1611," or "Shakespeare wrote his last play, *The Tempest,* in 1611." For the distinction between *which* and *that*, see the entry on *that*.

while Best used in a temporal sense, meaning "during the time": "While I was speaking, I suddenly realized that I didn't know what I was talking about." While it is not wrong to use *while* in a nontemporal sense, meaning "although" (as at the beginning of this sentence), it is better to use *although* in order to avoid any ambiguity. Note the ambiguity in: "While he was fond of movies he chiefly saw westerns." Does it mean "Although he was fond of movies," or does it mean "During the time when he was fond of movies"? Another point: do not use *while* if you mean *and*: "Freshmen take English 1–2, while sophomores take English 10–11" (substitute *and* for *while*).

who, whom Strictly speaking, *who* must be used for subjects, even when they look like objects: "He guessed who would be chosen." (Here *who* is the subject of the clause "who would be chosen.") *Whom* must be used for the objects of a verb, verbal (gerund, participle), or preposition: "Whom did he choose?"; "Whom do you want me to choose?"; "To whom did he show it?" We may feel stuffy in writing "Whom did he choose?" or "Whom are you talking about?" but to use *who* is certain to annoy some reader. Often you can avoid the dilemma by rewriting: "Who was chosen?"; "Who is the topic of conversation?" See also the entry on *that*.

whoever, whomever The second of these is the objective form. It is often incorrectly used as the subject of a clause. "Open the class to whomever wants to take it" is incorrect. The object of "to" is not "whomever" but is the entire clause — "whoever wants to take it" — and of course "whoever" is the subject of "wants."

who's, whose The first is a contraction of *who is* ("I'm everybody who's nobody"). The second is a possessive pronoun: "Whose book is it?" "I know whose it is."

would "I would think that" is a wordy version of "I think that."

your, you're The first is a possessive pronoun ("your book"); the second is a contraction of *you are* ("You're mistaken").

LAST WORDS

A rich patron once gave money to the painter Chu Ta, asking him to paint a picture of a fish. Three years later, when he still had not received the painting, the patron went to Chu Ta's house to ask why the picture was not done. Chu Ta did not answer, but dipped a brush in ink and with a few strokes drew a splendid fish. "If it is so easy," asked the patron, "why didn't you give me the picture three years ago?" Again Chu Ta did not answer. Instead, he opened the door of a large cabinet. Thousands of pictures of fish tumbled out.

AUTHOR
BIOGRAPHIES

Maya Angelou was born in St. Louis in 1928. Among her writings are two books of poetry and three autobiographical books. "Graduation" (editors' title) is from the first autobiographical volume, *I Know Why the Caged Bird Sings*.

Isaac Asimov, born in Russia in 1920 and brought to the United States in 1923, became a naturalized citizen in 1928. He holds three degrees from Columbia University and has taught biochemistry at Boston University, but chiefly he is a writer. By the end of 1978 he had published two hundred (yes, two hundred) books.

James Baldwin was born in Harlem in 1924, and graduated from De Witt Clinton High School. For a while he did odd jobs while he wrote, and in 1948 he received a fellowship that enabled him to go to Paris, where he wrote two novels (*Go Tell It on the Mountain* and *Giovanni's Room*), as well as essays published in *Notes of a Native Son*. He returned to the United States in 1955, where he has continued to publish fiction, plays, and essays.

Eric Berne (1910–1970), a New York psychiatrist, achieved national fame with *The Mind in Action, Games People Play,* and *Sex in Human Loving.*

Wendell Berry, poet, novelist, essayist, and educator, was born (in 1934) and educated in Kentucky, and teaches at the University of Kentucky. Most of his writings deal with his native state but their implications make them of interest to all readers.

Bruno Bettelheim was born in Vienna in 1903. He came to the United States in 1939, and became a naturalized citizen in 1944. From 1943 to 1973 he was head of the Sonia Shankman Orthogenic School in Chicago, where he also taught psychology at the University of Chicago. He is now retired, but continues to write on psychology.

Black Elk, a *wichasha wakon* (holy man) of the Oglala Sioux, as a small boy witnessed the Battle of Little Bighorn (1876). He lived to see his people all but annihilated and his hopes for them extinguished. In 1931, toward the end of his life, he told his life story to the poet and scholar John G. Neihardt in order to preserve a sacred vision given him. "High Horse's Courting" provides a comic interlude in a predominantly tragic memoir.

Sissela Bok teaches courses in medical ethics and in decision-making at the Harvard Medical School. She is the author of *Lying,* a book concerned with such problems as whether or not to lie to people for their own good.

J. Bronowski (1908–1974) was born in Poland and was educated in England. Although trained as a mathematician, Bronowski distinguished himself as a writer not only about science but also about literature and psychology.

Leonard Cammer (1914–1978), a specialist in the treatment of severe depression and schizophrenia, taught and practiced psychiatry in New York City.

John R. Coleman, born in Ontario in 1921, did his undergraduate work at the University of Toronto, then came to the United States to do graduate work in economics. He has taught economics in this country, and served as the president of Haverford College in Pennsylvania.

Paul Colinvaux was born in England in 1930. He received his Ph.D. from Duke University, and he now teaches zoology at Ohio State University. The essay that we reprint is a chapter from his fascinating book *Why Big Fierce Animals Are Rare.*

Lewis Coser, born in Berlin, Germany, in 1913, was educated at the Sorbonne in Paris, and at Columbia University, where he received a Ph.D. in sociology in 1954. He now teaches at the State University of New York, Stony Brook, where he holds the title of Distinguished Professor.

Joan Daremo, born in Tulsa in 1950, is largely self-educated. She is a free-lance writer who is especially interested in art and in psychology.

Joan Didion was born in California in 1934 and educated at the University of California, Berkeley. While she was still a senior she wrote a prize-winning essay for a contest sponsored by *Vogue,* and soon she became an associate feature editor for *Vogue.* She has written novels, essays, and screenplays.

Bergen Evans (1904–1978) taught English at Northwestern University for many years, and achieved national prominence as the moderator of several television programs and as the author of *The Natural History of Nonsense* and other books.

E[dward] M[organ] Forster (1879–1970) was born in London and was graduated from King's College, Cambridge. He traveled widely and lived for a while in India, but most of his life was spent back at King's College. His best-known novel is *A Passage to India* (1926).

Paul Goodman (1911–1972) received his bachelor's degree from City College in New York, and his Ph.D. from the University of Chicago. He taught in several colleges and universities, and wrote prolifically on literature, politics, and education.

Jeff Greenfield has written speeches for Robert F. Kennedy and John V. Lindsay, and has exchanged sharp words with William F. Buckley on television. He has published essays on sports and on other popular entertainments.

Anne Hollander was born in Cleveland in 1930, and educated at Barnard College. She has published essays on the history of fashion and a book, *Seeing Through Clothes,* on the clothed figure in art.

Joseph Hudnut (1886–1968) was educated as an architect at the University of Michigan. In addition to practicing architecture, he taught at several universities. Our selection comes from *Architecture and the Spirit of Man;* the title of the selection is the editors'.

Ada Louise Huxtable was born and educated in New York City. From 1946 to 1950 she served as assistant curator of architecture and design at the Museum of Modern Art in New York; since 1963 she has written on architecture for *The New York Times.*

Jane Jacobs was born in Scranton, Pennsylvania, in 1916. From 1952 until 1962 she served as an associate editor of *Architectural Forum.* In addition to writing *The Death and Life of Great American Cities,* from which our selection comes, she has written *The Economy of Cities.*

Jonathan Kozol, born in 1936, has taught in elementary schools in Massachusetts. The author of several books, he is best known for *Death at an Early Age: The Destruction of the Hearts and Minds of Negro Children in the Boston Public Schools.*

Chuck Kraemer was born in 1945 in Marysville, Kansas. He received a bachelor's degree from the University of Kansas and did graduate work in film at Boston University. He has written essays, chiefly on film, for *The New York Times* and for other newspapers.

Barbara Lawrence was born in Hanover, New Hampshire, and was educated at Connecticut College and at New York University. She teaches at the State University of New York, at Old Westbury.

C[live] S[taples] Lewis (1898–1963) taught medieval and Renaissance literature at Oxford and later at Cambridge. In addition to writing about literature, he wrote fiction (including children's books), poetry, and numerous essays and books on moral and religious topics.

W. T. Lhamon was born in Washington, D.C., in 1945. He has published essays on literature in various journals, and he writes a column on rock and jazz for *The New Republic.*

Malcolm X, born Malcolm Little in Nebraska in 1925, was the son of a Baptist minister. He completed the eighth grade but then got into trouble and was sent to a reformatory. After his release he became a thief, dope peddler, and pimp; in 1944 he was sent to jail, where he spent six and a half years. During his years in jail he became a convert to the Black Muslim faith. Paroled in 1950, he served as a minister and founded Muslim temples throughout the United States. In 1964, however, he broke with Elijah Muhammad, leader of the Black Muslims, and formed a new group, the Organization of Afro-American Unity. The next year he was assassinated in New York.

Anne Hebald Mandelbaum was born in New York City in 1944, and was educated at Radcliffe College and Yale University. She is a free-lance writer.

Margaret Mead (1901–1978) was born in Philadelphia and educated at De Pauw University, Barnard College, and Columbia University. She lived in Samoa in 1925 and 1926; in 1928 she published the book that promptly established her reputation, *Coming of Age in Samoa.* Throughout the next fifty years she wrote prolifically and lectured widely on sociological and anthropological subjects.

Stanley Milgram, professor of social psychology at the Graduate Center of the City University of New York, is the author of *Obedience to Authority.*

Flannery O'Connor (1925–1964) was born in Georgia and spent most of her short life there. *The Complete Stories of Flannery O'Connor* received the National Book Award for fiction in 1971; another posthumous volume, *Mystery and Manners,* includes essays on literature and an account of her experiences raising peacocks in Georgia.

Iona and *Peter Opie* (wife and husband) are English writers who specialize in the lore, literature, and activities of children. If they lived in the United States they would probably be called sociologists, but then they would write less well.

George Orwell (1903–1950), an Englishman, adopted this name; he was born Eric Blair, in India. He was educated at Eton, in England, but in 1921 he returned to the East and served for five years as a police officer in Burma. He then returned to Europe, doing odd jobs while writing novels and stories. In 1936 he fought in the Spanish Civil War on the side of the Republicans, an experience reported in *Homage to Catalonia* (1938). His last years were spent writing in England.

Robert M. Pirsig, born in Minneapolis in 1928, has published one book, *Zen and the Art of Motorcycle Maintenance,* a narrative of a motorcycle trip taken by a father and his eleven-year-old, who travel from Minneapolis to the Pacific. As our extract on "Mechanic's Feel" suggests, the book is highly meditative, in large part an account of complex relationships with our environment.

James Harvey Robinson (1863–1936) taught American history at the University of Pennsylvania and later at Columbia University, but in 1919 he resigned from Columbia in protest against the dismissal of some professors who opposed World War I. He then helped to found the New School for Social Research in New York City.

Philip Roth was born in Newark, New Jersey, in 1933. His first book, *Goodbye, Columbus,* won a National Book Award for fiction. Among his other notable books are *Letting Go, Portnoy's Complaint,* and *Reading Myself and Others.*

Sei Shōnagon was born about 965 in Japan; for some ten years she served as lady-in-waiting to the Empress Sadako. The tradition that she died poor and alone may be true, or it may be the moralists' attempt to reply to her sensual life.

Max Shulman, born in St. Paul in 1919, is the author of many humorous books and of the television series *Dobie Gillis.*

Christopher D. Stone was born in 1937 in New York City. He holds a law degree from Yale, and teaches law at the University of Southern California.

I[sidore] F[einstein] Stone, born in Philadelphia in 1907, was educated at the University of Pennsylvania. For some twenty years he worked as a reporter and edited a leftist newsletter, *I. F. Stone's Bi-weekly,* noted for its incisive criticism of American politics. He now occasionally publishes in *The New York Review of Books.*

Studs Terkel was born Louis Terkel in New York City in 1912. He was brought up in Chicago and was graduated from the University of Chicago. Terkel has been an actor, playwright, columnist, and disc jockey, but he is best known as the man who makes books out of tape recordings of people he gets to talk. These oral histories are *Division Street: America* (1966), *Hard Times* (1970), and *Working* (1974). In 1978 Terkel published his memoirs, *Talking to Myself.*

Lewis Thomas was born in 1913. A distinguished medical researcher and administrator, he is president of the Memorial Sloan-Kettering Cancer Center in New York. He is also a writer; he has published *Lives of a Cell,* a collection of twenty-nine short essays, which won a National Book Award in 1974, and *Medusa and the Snail.*

Sheila Tobias, born in New York City in 1935, has taught history at the College of the City of New York, and has served as an administrator at Cornell University and at Wesleyan University. She is now an educational consultant.

John Updike was born in Shillington, Pennsylvania, in 1932. He has published stories, novels, and essays. In 1963, *The Centaur,* a novel, received a National Book Award.

E[lwyn] B[rooks] White was born in 1899. In 1926 he joined *The New Yorker,* and he published essays and stories regularly in it until 1938, when he became a columnist for *Harper's.* He returned to *The New Yorker* in 1945. He is now retired, in Maine, but continues to write.

Tom Wolfe, born in Richmond, Virginia, holds a Ph.D. from Yale. After receiving his degree he worked as a reporter for the Washington *Post* and the New York *Herald Tribune,* but he found journalism too restrictive and so he turned to free-lance writing. His usual subject is contemporary culture.

Virginia Woolf (1882–1941) was born in London into an upper-middle class literary family. In 1912 she married a writer, and with him she founded The Hogarth Press, whose important publications included not only books by T. S. Eliot but her own novels.

(Continued from page iv)

Bruno Bettelheim, "Joey: A Mechanical Boy," *Scientific American*, March 1959. Reprinted with permission; copyright © 1959 by Scientific American, Inc. All rights reserved.

Robert Bly, "Love Poem," *Silence in the Snowy Fields* (Middletown, Conn.: Wesleyan University Press, 1962), p. 41. Copyright © 1962 by Robert Bly. Reprinted by permission of the author.

Sissela Bok, "To Lie or Not to Lie? — The Doctor's Dilemma," *The New York Times* 18 April 1978. © 1978 by The New York Times Company. Reprinted by permission.

Jacob Bronowski, "The Reach of Imagination," *A Sense of the Future* (Cambridge, Mass.: MIT Press, 1977), pp. 22–31. Originally in *Proceedings of the American Academy of Arts and Letters and the National Institute of Arts and Letters* (1967) 2d series, II, and reprinted with their permission.

Susan Brownmiller, "With the Weathermen," *The New York Times*, 15 June 1975. © 1975 by The New York Times Company. Reprinted by permission.

John R. Coleman, journal entries, *Blue-Collar Journal: A College President's Sabbatical* (New York: J. B. Lippincott). Copyright © 1974 by John R. Coleman. Reprinted by permission of Harper & Row, Publishers, Inc.

Paul A. Colinvaux, "Every Species Has Its Niche," *Why Big Fierce Animals Are Rare: An Ecologist's Perspective,* pp. 10–17. Copyright © 1978 by Paul A. Colinvaux. Reprinted by permission of Princeton University Press.

Lewis Coser, "Socialization," Sociology Through Literature: An Introductory Reader, © 1963, pp. 58–59. Reprinted by permission of Prentice-Hall, Inc., Englewood Cliffs, New Jersey.

Joan Didion, from "Los Angeles Notebook," *Slouching Towards Bethlehem*, Copyright © 1967, 1968 by Joan Didion. Reprinted by permission of Farrar, Straus and Giroux, Inc.

Bergen Evans, "Sophistication," *The New York Times Book Review,* 7 September 1961. © 1961 by The New York Times Company. Reprinted by permission.

E. M. Forster, "My Wood," *Abinger Harvest*, copyright 1936, 1964 by E. M. Forster. Reprinted by permission of Harcourt Brace Jovanovich, Inc. and Edward Arnold Publishers Ltd.

Margaret Gooch, "Library Exercises," (after research paper in chapter 10), reprinted by permission of Margaret Gooch, Wessell Library, Tufts University.

Paul Goodman, "A Proposal to Abolish Grading" (editors' title), *Compulsory Miseducation and the Community of Scholars,* pp. 155–159. Copyright 1964, and reprinted by permission of the publisher, Horizon Press, New York.

Jeff Greenfield, "Columbo Knows the Butler Didn't Do It," *The New York Times*, 22 April 1973. © 1973 by The New York Times Comapny. Reprinted by permission.

Anne Hollander, "Clothes Make the Man — Uneasy," *The New Republic*, 7 September 1975. Reprinted by permission of *The New Republic*, © 1975 The New Republic, Inc.

Joseph Hudnut, "A Perfectly Beautiful Laundress" (editors' title), *Architecture and the Spirit of Man* (Cambridge, Mass.: Harvard University Press, 1949), pp. 3–4. © 1949 by the President and Fellows of Harvard College; renewed © 1977 by Elizabeth Deviney.

Ada Louise Huxtable, "The Rayburn Building," *The New York Times*, 30 March 1965, p. 32. © 1965 by The New York Times Company. Reprinted by permission.

"In Search of the Elusive Pingo" (Ideas and Trends), *The New York Times*, 5 May 1974. © 1974 by The New York Times Company. Reprinted by permission.

Jane Jacobs, "The Use of Sidewalks" (orignal title, "The Uses of Sidewalks: Safety"), *The Death and Life of Great American Cities*, pp. 50–54. Copyright © 1961 by Jane Jacobs. Reprinted by permission of Random House, Inc.

James Weldon Johnson, "Lift Ev'ry Voice and Sing," © Copyright: Edward B. Marks Music Corporation. Used by permission.

X. J. Kennedy, "Who Killed King Kong?" *Dissent* Magazine, Spring 1960. Reprinted by permission of the publisher.

Jonathan Kozol, "Operation Illiteracy," *The New York Times*, 5 March 1979. © 1979 by The New York Times Company. Reprinted by permission.

Chuck Kraemer, "Indecent Exposure," *The Real Paper*, 4 June 1975. Reprinted by permission of *The Real Paper*.

Barbara Lawrence, "Four-Letter Words Can Hurt You," (original title, "——— isn't a dirty word") *The New York Times,* 27 October 1973. © 1973 by The New York Times Company. Reprinted by permission.

C. S. Lewis, "Vivisection," *Undeceptions*, edited by Walter Hooper (London: Geoffrey Bles, 1971), pp. 182–186. Reprinted by permission of Wm. Collins Publishers.

"Letter to the Editor" by Leonard S. Charlap, *The New York Times*, 19 December 1977. © 1977 by The New York Times Company. Reprinted by permission.

"Letter to the Editor" by Ruth H. Cohn, *The New York Times,* 20 July 1978. © 1978 by The New York Times Company. Reprinted by permission.

W. T. Lhamon, Jr., "Family Man," *The New Republic*, 1 June 1974, pp. 27–28. Reprinted by permission of *The New Republic*, © 1974 by The New Republic, Inc.

Walter Lippmann, excerpt from column, *The New York Times*, 20 February 1942. © 1942 by The New York Times Company. Reprinted by permission.

Malcolm X with the assistance of Alex Haley, "Rejected" (editors' title), *The Autobiography of Malcolm X*, pp. 105–107. Copyright © 1964 by Alex Haley and Malcolm X. Copyright © 1965 by Alex Haley and Betty Shabazz. Reprinted by permission of Random House, Inc.

Anne Hebald Mandelbaum, "It's the Portly Penguin That Gets the Girl, French Biologist Claims," *Harvard University Gazette*, 30 January 1976, pp. 3, 5. Reprinted by permission of the *Harvard University Gazette*.

Jack Margolis, "And All Those Others," *The Poetry of Richard Milhous Nixon* (Los Angeles: Cliff House Books, 1974). Reprinted by permission.

Gerald Mast, *The Comic Mind*, pp. 281–282, 282–283. Copyright © 1973 by Gerald Mast, reprinted by permission of the publisher, The Bobbs-Merrill Company, Inc.

Margaret Mead and Rhoda Metraux, "New Superstitions for Old," *A Way of Seeing* (1970). Copyright © 1966 by Margaret Mead and Rhoda Metraux. By permission of William Morrow & Company.

Stanley Milgram, "Confessions of a News Addict" (original title, "Reflections on News"), *The Antioch Review*, Vol. 35, nos. 2–3. Copyright © 1977 by The Antioch Review, Inc. Reprinted by the permission of the Editors.

Anne Moody, *Coming of Age in Mississippi*, p. 5. © 1968 by Anne Moody. Used with permission of The Dial Press.

Joseph Morgenstern, "On the Road," *Newsweek*, 21 July 1969, p. 95. Copyright © 1969 by Newsweek, Inc. All rights reserved. Reprinted by permission.

John G. Neihardt, "High Horse's Courting," *Black Elk Speaks* (Lincoln, Neb.: University of Nebraska Press, 1972), pp. 67–76. Copyright 1959, 1961 by John G. Neihardt. Reprinted courtesy John G. Neihardt Trust.

"Notes and Comment," *The New Yorker Magazine*, 10 January 1970. Reprinted by permission; © 1970 The New Yorker Magazine, Inc.

"Notes and Comment," *The New Yorker Magazine*, 22 September 1975. Reprinted by permission; © 1975 The New Yorker Magazine, Inc.

Flannery O'Connor, "Total Effect and the Eighth Grade," *Mystery and Manners*, ed. Sally and Robert Fitzgerald, pp. 135–140. Copyright © 1957, 1961, 1963, 1964, 1966, 1967, 1969 by the Estate of Mary Flannery O'Connor. Copyright © 1962 by Flannery O'Connor. Reprinted by permission of Farrar, Straus and Giroux, Inc.

Iona and Peter Opie, "The Appeal of the Games," *Children's Games in Street and Playground*, pp. 2–4. © Iona and Peter Opie 1969. Reprinted by permission of Oxford University Press.

George Orwell, from "England Your England," *The Collected Essays, Journalism and Letters, Vol. II: My Country Right or Left, 1940–1943*, Angus, Ian, and Sonia Orwell, eds. (New York: Harcourt Brace Jovanovich, Inc., 1968), pp. 61–62.

George Orwell, "Politics and the English Language," *Shooting an Elephant and Other Essays.* Copyright 1950 by Sonia Brownell Orwell; renewed 1978 by Sonia Pitt-Rivers. Reprinted by permission of Harcourt Brace Jovanovich, Inc., Mrs. Sonia Brownell Orwell and Martin Secker & Warburg Ltd.

George Orwell, "Shooting an Elephant," *Shooting an Elephant and Other Essays*, copyright 1945, 1946, 1949, 1950 by Sonia Brownell Orwell; renewed 1973, 1974, 1977 by Sonia Orwell; renewed 1978 by Sonia Pitt-Rivers. Reprinted by permission of Harcourt Brace Jovanovich, Inc., Mrs. Sonia Brownell Orwell and Martin Secker & Warburg Ltd.

Dorothy Parker, "News Item," *The Portable Dorothy Parker*, revised and enlarged edition. Copyright 1936, Copyright © renewed 1964 by Dorothy Parker. Reprinted by permission of Viking Penguin Inc.

Robert M. Pirsig, "Mechanic's Feel," *Zen and the Art of Motorcycle Maintenance*, p. 14, pp. 323–324. Copyright © 1974 by Robert M. Pirsig. By permission of William Morrow & Company.

Charles T. Powers, "Say One Word and I'll Cut Your Throat," *Los Angeles Times*, 13 January 1974. Copyright, 1974, Los Angeles Times. Reprinted by permission.

Paul Reps, No. 29 from "The Gateless Gate," *Zen Flesh, Zen Bones* (Tokyo: Charles E. Tuttle, 1957), p. 114. Reprinted by permission of Charles E. Tuttle Co.

Reuters, "Fish Eat Brazilian Fishermen," *The Boston Globe*, 17 January 1971. Reprinted by permission of Reuters.

James Harvey Robinson, "On Various Kinds of Thinking," *The Mind in the Making*. Copyright 1921 by Harper & Row, Publishers, Inc. Reprinted by permission of Harper & Row, Publishers, Inc.

Philip Roth, "The Newark Public Library" (original title, "Topics: Reflections on the Death of a Library"), *The New York Times*, 1 March 1969. © 1969 by The New York Times Company. Reprinted by permission.

David Royce, "Moby Balloon," *The New York Times Magazine*, 26 May 1974. © 1974 by The New York Times Company. Reprinted by permission.

"Science and the Citizen: Hyperactivity and Drugs," *Scientific American*, July 1974. Reprinted by permission of W. H. Freeman and Company.

Sei Shōnagon, *The Pillow Book of Sei Shōnagon*, translated and edited by Ivan Morris, and published by Oxford University Press (1967). Reprinted by permission of the publisher.

Max Shulman, "Love Is a Fallacy," *The Many Loves of Dobie Gillis* (New York: Doubleday, 1951). Copyright © 1951 by Max Shulman, copyright renewed 1979. Reprinted by permission of the Harold Matson Company, Inc.

Gary Snyder, "Hitch Haiku," *The Back Country*. Copyright © 1968 by Gary Snyder. Reprinted by permission of New Directions Publishing Corporation.

Raymond A. Sokolov, excerpt from book review, *The New York Times*, 22 April 1979. © 1979 by The New York Times Company. Reprinted by permission.

Christopher D. Stone, "Putting the Outside Inside the Fence of the Law," *The New York Times*, 29 August 1974. © 1974 by The New York Times Company. Reprinted by permission.

I. F. Stone, "A New Solution for the CIA," *The New York Review of Books*, 20 February 1975. Reprinted with permission from *The New York Review of Books*. Copyright © 1975 Nyrev, Inc.

Studs Terkel, "Glenn Stribling" and "Dave Stribling," *Working: People Talk about What They Do All Day and How They Feel about What They Do*. Copyright © 1972, 1974 by Studs Terkel. Reprinted by permission of Random House, Inc.

Lewis Thomas, "The Iks," *The Lives of a Cell*. Copyright © 1973 by the Massachusetts Medical Society. Originally appeared in the *New England Journal of Medicine*. Reprinted by permission of Viking Penguin Inc.

Lewis Thomas, "Altruism," *The New York Times*, 4 July 1976. © 1976 by The New York Times Company. Reprinted by permission.

Time, excerpt from "Lord, They've Done It All," 6 May 1974. Reprinted by permission from *Time*, The Weekly Newsmagazine; Copyright Time Inc. 1974.

Sheila Tobias, "Who's Afraid of Math, and Why?" *Overcoming Math Anxiety*. Reprinted by permission of W. W. Norton & Company, Inc. Originally appeared in *The Atlantic Monthly*. Copyright © 1978 by Sheila Tobias.

John Updike, "Beer Can," *Assorted Prose*, p. 115. Copyright © 1965 by John Updike. Reprinted by permission of Random House, Inc.

E. B. White, "Education — March, 1939" (first section), from *One Man's*

Meat. Copyright 1939, 1967 by E. B. White. Reprinted by permission of Harper & Row, Publishers, Inc.

E. B. White, "The Door," *The Second Tree from the Corner*. Copyright 1939, 1967 by E. B. White. Originally appeared in *The New Yorker*. Reprinted by permission of Harper & Row, Publishers, Inc.

Virginia Woolf, "Professions for Women," *The Death of the Moth and Other Essays*, pp. 235–242. Copyright 1942 by Harcourt Brace Jovanovich, Inc.; copyright 1970 by Marjorie T. Powers, executrix. Reprinted by permission of Harcourt Brace Jovanovich, Inc., the Author's Literary Estate and The Hogarth Press Ltd.

Tom Wolfe, "The Boiler Room and the Computer," *Mauve Gloves & Madmen, Clutter & Vine*. Copyright © 1973, 1976 by Tom Wolfe. Reprinted by permission of Farrar, Straus and Giroux, Inc.

William Butler Yeats, "The Balloon of the Mind." Reprinted with permission of Macmillan Publishing Co., Inc. and A. P. Watt Ltd., from *Collected Poems* by William Butler Yeats. Copyright 1919 by Macmillan Publishing Co., Inc., renewed 1947 by Bertha Georgie Yeats.

William Butler Yeats, "The friends that have it I do wrong." Reprinted with permission of Macmillan Publishing Co., Inc. and A. P. Watt Ltd., from *The Variorum Edition of the Poems of W. B. Yeats*, Allt and Alspach, eds. Copyright 1957 by Macmillan Publishing Co., Inc.

Art

Pieter Breughel, "The Painter and the Connoisseur." From the Graphic Collection of the Albertina Museum, Vienna. Reprinted by permission.

Buddha, Courtesy of the Museum of Fine Arts, Boston. Reprinted by permission.

Bodhisattva, Courtesy of the Museum of Fine Arts, Boston. Reprinted by permission.

William Notman, "Buffalo Bill and Sitting Bull." From the Notman Photographic Archives, McCord Museum. Reprinted by permission.

Photographer unknown. "Picasso's Son Paul on a Donkey," c. 1923. Photograph, Collection Pablo Picasso. From Van Deren Coke, *The Painter and the Photographer* (Albuquerque: University of New Mexico Press, 1962).

Pablo Picasso, "Paul, Son of the Artist." 1923. Gouache, 40 × 32 inches. Collection of Pablo Picasso, Grasse, France. Permission © S.P.A.D.E.M., Paris/V.A.G.A., New York.

Francisco Goya, "Woman Holding Up Her Dying Lover." Courtesy of the Museum of Fine Arts, Boston. Reprinted by permission.

Francisco Goya, "El amor y la muerte." Courtesy, Museo del Prado, Madrid.

Leonardo da Vinci, "Mona Lisa." Courtesy, Musée de Louvre, Paris. Reprinted by permission, Scala New York/Florence.

"Spaghetti," reprinted from *Mazes 2* by Vladimir Koziakin. Copyright © 1972 by Vladimir Koziakin. Used by permission of Grosset & Dunlap, Inc.

Index

To the Student

Please help us make *Barnet & Stubbs's Practical Guide to Writing, With Additional Readings,* an even better book. To improve our textbooks, we revise them every few years, taking into account the experiences of both instructors and students with the previous editions. At some time, your instructor will most likely be asked to comment extensively on *Barnet & Stubbs's Practical Guide to Writing, With Additional Readings.* Now we would like to hear from you.

Complete this questionnaire and return it to:

College English Developmental Group
Little, Brown and Company
34 Beacon St.
Boston, MA 02106

School _____

City, State, Zip Code _____

Course title _____

Instructor's full name _____

Other books required _____

_____

1. Did you like the book? _____

2. Was it too easy? _____ Too difficult? _____

   Did you read it all? _____

   Which chapters were most useful? Why? _____

   _____

   _____

   Which chapters were least useful? Why? _____

   _____

   _____

3. Were the exercises useful? _____

4. Did you like the examples? _____

5. Please give us your reactions to the anthologized selections.

	Keep	Drop	Didn't Read
James Baldwin, "Stranger in the Village"	___	___	___
Wendell Berry, "Mayhem in the Industrial Paradise	___	___	___
Bruno Bettelheim, "Joey: A 'Mechanical Boy' "	___	___	___
Sissela Bok, "To Lie or Not to Lie? — The Doctor's Dilemma"	___	___	___
Paul Colinvaux, "Every Species Has Its Niche"	___	___	___
E. M. Forster, "My Wood"	___	___	___
Paul Goodman, "A Proposal to Abolish Grading"	___	___	___
Anne Hollander, "Clothes Make the Man — Uneasy"	___	___	___
X. J. Kennedy, "Who Killed King Kong?"	___	___	___
C. S. Lewis, "Vivisection"	___	___	___
Margaret Mead, "New Superstitions for Old"	___	___	___
Flannery O'Connor, "Total Effect and the Eighth Grade"	___	___	___
George Orwell, "Politics and the English Language"	___	___	___
Studs Terkel, "Fathers and Sons"	___	___	___
Lewis Thomas, "Altruism"	___	___	___
Sheila Tobias, "Who's Afraid of Math, and Why?"	___	___	___
E. B. White, "The Door"	___	___	___

6. Do you feel the professor should continue to assign this book next

year?_____ Did you tell her or him? _____

7. What would you have us change next time? _____

_____

_____

8. May we quote you in our promotion efforts for this book?

_____ Yes _____ No

_____

Date   Signature

_____

Mailing address

SYMBOLS COMMONLY USED IN MARKING PAPERS

All instructors have their own techniques for annotating essays, but many instructors make substantial use of the following symbols.

ab   faulty or undesirable abbreviation (see pages 587–588)

agr   faulty agreement between subject and verb (pages 367–368) or between pronoun and antecedent (page 367)

apos   apostrophe (pages 585–587)

awk (k)   awkward

cap   use a capital letter (pages 583–584)

cf   comma fault (pages 567–568)

choppy   too many short sentences — subordinate (pages 378–381)

cl   cliché (pages 353–354)

coh   paragraph lacks coherence (pages 94–98) ; sentence lacks coherence (pages 360–371)

cs   comma splice (pages 567–568)

dev   paragraph poorly developed (pages 82–88)

dm   dangling modifier (pages 362, 364–365)

emph   emphasis obscured (pages 376–386)

good   a good point; or, well expressed

frag   fragmentary sentence (pages 383–384, 565–566)

id   unidiomatic expression (page 597)

ital   underline to indicate italics (pages 582–583)

k (awk)   awkward